Emil R. Cox

THE AMERICAN IDEA

150 YEARS OF WRITERS AND THINKERS
WHO SHAPED OUR HISTORY

THE AMERICAN IDEA

‖ THE BEST OF **The Atlantic Monthly** ‖

EDITED BY ROBERT VARE
WITH DANIEL B. SMITH

DOUBLEDAY NEW YORK LONDON TORONTO SYDNEY AUCKLAND

PUBLISHED BY DOUBLEDAY

Published in the United States by Doubleday, an imprint of
The Doubleday Broadway Publishing Group, a division
of Random House, Inc., New York.

www.doubleday.com

DOUBLEDAY and the portrayal of an anchor with a dolphin are
registered trademarks of Random House, Inc.

Permission credits appear before the acknowledgments.

LIBRARY OF CONGRESS CATALOGING-IN-PUBLICATION DATA
The American idea : the best of the Atlantic monthly : 150 years
of writers and thinkers who shaped our history / edited by
Robert Vare. — 1st ed.
  p. cm.
  1. United States—Civilization—Miscellanea. 2. United States—
Intellectual life—Miscellanea. 3. National characteristics, American—
Miscellanea. 4. United States—Civilization—Literary collections.
5. National characteristics, American—Literary collections. 6. American
essays. 7. American fiction. 8. American poetry. I. Vare, Robert.
II. Atlantic monthly.
  E169.1.A47216 2007
  973—dc22

                                                      2007015042

ISBN 978-0-385-52108-6

PRINTED IN THE UNITED STATES OF AMERICA

10 9 8 7 6 5 4 3 2 1

FIRST EDITION

To all Atlantic Monthly *staff members and contributors —past, present, and future*

Contents

‖ BLACK AND WHITE

‖ GODS AND MONSTERS

‖ BEHIND THE SCENES

‖ STATES OF WAR

‖ CONTROVERSIES

‖ CAPITALISM AND ITS DISCONTENTS

‖ THE NATURAL WORLD

‖ CROWD PLEASERS

‖ THE AMERICAN IDEA

THE AMERICAN IDEA

Introduction

The Atlantic Monthly celebrates its 150th birthday this fall. In and of itself, this is a remarkable achievement. The failure rate of American magazines is notorious, rivaling big-city restaurants, network television pilots, and Internet startups for claimant to the title of world's riskiest venture. Since the first general interest publication, *The American Magazine*, came into existence in the United States, in 1741, there has been a consistent pattern: few magazines survive their first issues, and, even today, in this cautious, safety-net age of focus groups and other prepublication marketing hedges, the average life expectancy of a new magazine is something closer to 150 *days*—not 150 years.

Exactly how *The Atlantic* managed to avoid the fate of so many other magazines is an open question, but its longevity seems attributable, at least in part, to the circumstances of its creation. While most magazines owe their start to editors, publishers, businesspeople, or investors, *The Atlantic* was founded largely by writers—an illustrious group that included Ralph Waldo Emerson, Oliver Wendell Holmes, Henry Wadsworth Longfellow, and James Russell Lowell—and it has always been, at its core, a writers' magazine. What does it mean to be "a writers' magazine"? For one thing, writers who work for *The Atlantic* know that they have entrée to a highly educated audience that is in the habit of devoting serious blocks of time to reading its articles, essays, columns, and poems. For another, writers who work for *The Atlantic* know that they will be given the time and space to tell their stories dramatically and in depth, and that they will have a forum to develop their arguments in all their nuance and complexity. And finally, writers who work for *The Atlantic* know that their prose will never be subjected to ideological litmus tests or homogenizing, voice-eviscerating editing.

All of which may begin to explain how *The Atlantic* has managed to attract so many of the most revered writers and thinkers of the last century and a half: from novelists (Nathaniel Hawthorne, Edith Wharton, William Faulkner, Saul Bellow, Philip Roth) to scientists (Albert Einstein, J. Robert Oppenheimer, James D. Watson, Stephen Jay Gould, Edward O. Wilson); from economists (John Maynard Keynes, John Kenneth Galbraith, Milton Friedman) to humorists (Mark Twain, H. L. Mencken, Garrison Keillor, Ian Frazier); from muckrakers (Jacob Riis, Lincoln Steffens, Henry Demarest Lloyd) to philosophers (William James, Bertrand Russell, Alfred North

Whitehead); from poets (William Butler Yeats, Wallace Stevens, Robert Lowell, Sylvia Plath, W. H. Auden) to future presidents (Theodore Roosevelt, Woodrow Wilson, John Fitzgerald Kennedy).

The long roll call of marquee names that have appeared between the magazine's covers is, naturally, a source of pride for those who work at *The Atlantic*. But another test of a magazine is its ability to recognize and discover unknown talent, and here *The Atlantic* has posted an impressive track record of finding, recruiting, and mentoring writers whose reputations have not yet taken flight. The magazine provided an early and important publishing home for the work of Henry James, Robert Frost, and Ernest Hemingway, and it published Walt Whitman, Vladimir Nabokov, Dylan Thomas, Eudora Welty, and Joyce Carol Oates when they were all relatively obscure. More recent discoveries have encompassed many of contemporary nonfiction's leading lights, including James Fallows, William Langewiesche, Tracy Kidder, Nicholas Lemann, Eric Schlosser, Robert D. Kaplan, and Samantha Power.

And yet it would be a mistake to think of *The Atlantic* as merely a pantheon, a hilltop Hall of Fame one visits to commune with the august. When I started work on this book, in early 2006, I was keenly aware of the premium that the magazine has always placed on cutting through the tangle of daily headlines and digging down to the larger and longer-lasting stories that lie beneath. What I hadn't expected was that my trip through the magazine's leather-bound and online archives would afford such a splendid view of many of the major events and currents of American history.

For example, *The Atlantic* published some of the landmark documents of the abolitionist movement (Ralph Waldo Emerson's "American Civilization," James Russell Lowell's "The Election in November"); of the progressive movement (Jacob Riis's "The Battle with the Slum," Jane Addams's "The Devil-Baby at Hull House"); of the environmental movement (Henry David Thoreau's "Walking," John Muir's "The American Forests," John Burroughs's "The Divine Soil"); of the nuclear nonproliferation movement (Albert Einstein's "Atomic War and Peace," J. Robert Oppenheimer's "The Open Mind"); of the civil rights movement (W.E.B. Du Bois's "The Souls of Black Folk," Martin Luther King, Jr.'s "Letter from Birmingham Jail"); of the feminist movement (Margaret Deland's "The Change in the Feminine Ideal," Nora Johnson's "The Captivity of Marriage"); of the gay rights movement (Chandler Burr's "Homosexuality and Biology"); of the victims' rights movement (Eric Schlosser's "A Grief Like No Other"); and of the human rights movement (Samantha Power's "Bystanders to Genocide").

If *The Atlantic* has a long history of wading into turbulent waters, it has an equally persistent one of challenging the reigning orthodoxy. At the time of the magazine's birth, slavery was still legal in parts of the United States, and *The Atlantic*'s founders—all ardent abolitionists—made the emancipation cause the fulcrum of their new publication. *The Atlantic* endorsed Abraham Lincoln for president in October 1860, a time when many abolitionists were still wary of him and impatient with his moderate views on ending slavery. The support of an important antislavery periodical just weeks before the election was considered crucial to Lincoln's victory.

The Atlantic was the first American magazine to recognize the importance of Charles Darwin and to champion his theories. Seventy-five years before "diversity" and "multiculturalism" became household words, it was the first magazine to denounce prevailing tendencies to foist Anglo-Saxon culture on America's growing, increasingly heterogeneous immigrant population. In 1890, *The Atlantic* published a seminal essay by the military theorist Alfred Thayer Mahan that called for an end to American isolationism and proclaimed the need for the United States to transform itself into a sea power, particularly in the Pacific. One avid reader of that article was a future *Atlantic* contributor named Theodore Roosevelt, then a member of the U.S. Civil Service Commission. Ten years later, Roosevelt would adapt many of Mahan's key ideas into policy cornerstones of his presidency. Roosevelt also fell under the spell of another frequent contributor, John Muir, whose impassioned essays on the necessity of preserving the American wilderness helped persuade the president to place millions of acres of woodlands under federal protection.

The Atlantic virtually invented a whole new genre—the "big idea" piece that challenges conventional belief about, or awakens public interest in, a significant political or social issue. Emblematic of such pioneering, and often uncannily prophetic, articles was the 1945 essay "As We May Think," by Vannevar Bush, an engineer, military research and development expert, and high-tech visionary. A half century before anybody had heard the term "online," Bush's essay presaged not only the coming of the Internet but also its dominant role in global communications. In 1982, the magazine published what many criminologists contend was one of the twentieth century's most influential articles on law enforcement; that cover story, "Broken Windows," by James Q. Wilson and George L. Kelling, introduced to a national audience the concept of "community policing" and changed the face of police departments around the country. A full two decades before the attacks of 9/11, *The Atlantic* published V. S. Naipaul's excoriating chronicle of the rise of Islamic fundamentalism, "Among the Believers" (the opening chapter from his famously controversial book of the same name), and a decade later followed up with a much-discussed cover story by the Princeton historian Bernard Lewis ("The Roots of Muslim Rage") explaining why the growing radical Muslim movement, fueled by virulent anti-Americanism, was becoming a powerful and dangerous force in the world. And in 2002, when most of the American media seemed to be operating in lockstep with the Bush administration's preparations for invading Iraq, *The Atlantic*'s longtime correspondent James Fallows was one of the few voices to call into question the war's official rationales and long-range planning. Published six months before the war even began, Fallows's cover story "The Fifty-first State" spelled out in elaborate detail nearly every one of the major problems that has bedeviled the occupation over the ensuing years.

All this is not to suggest that there have been no missteps along the way. Indeed, some of the gaffes have bordered on the spectacular. In the nineteenth century, *The Atlantic* repeatedly rejected the submissions of a subscriber and aspiring poet from Amherst, Massachusetts, named Emily Dickinson—a failure of judgment that would not be rectified until five years after her death. And the magazine is still trying to live down its September 1999 cover story, which fearlessly and ditzily forecasted an imminent, astronomical rise in stock prices—"Dow 36,000"—just six months before the dot-com bubble burst and the market began a precipitous descent. But to dwell on the scorecard of highs and lows is to obscure an essential point about *The Atlantic Monthly*: its unusually strong sense of institutional mission. To properly understand this feeling of collective purpose, whose roots trace directly back to the founding of the magazine, requires a brief exercise in time travel.

WHEN *THE ATLANTIC*'S FOUNDING BRAIN TRUST GATHERED at the elegant Parker House Hotel in Boston to hash out final plans for their new magazine, on May 5, 1857, there was no shortage at the table of social connection, cultural cachet, or sheer literary candlepower. Among those in attendance for that now-legendary dinner, in the hotel's main dining room, were four of the leading writers and intellectuals of their day: Ralph Waldo Emerson, the celebrated philosopher whose insistence upon the sanctity of individual conscience had reverberated through the halls of academia and organized religion; Oliver Wendell Holmes, the preternaturally gifted essayist, poet, and Harvard Medical School professor, who seemed to have all of Western literature and scientific knowledge on the tip of his tongue; Henry Wadsworth Longfellow, the inventor of the American epic poem and the most popular poet in the United States; and James Russell Lowell, the next generation's brightest star in the literary firmament. Despite their Brahmin pedigrees and tripartite names, these men did not always see eye to eye on matters of politics and art. What drew them together, aside from a genuine affection for each other's company, was an intellectual intrepidity across a great range of subjects, a deep-seated conviction that the written word had an almost religious duty to instruct and inspire, and a collective ambition to scale the heights of philosophy, political thought, and poetry.

And yet for all their eminence and accomplishments, each of these four men, like the four other planners who would join them for dinner that spring afternoon, was painfully aware—some from firsthand experience—of the difficulties of starting and sustaining a magazine. Emerson, for one, had suffered a serious disappointment in the magazine business with *The Dial*, a spirited monthly publication that he had cofounded in 1840 in order to give voice to the transcendentalist cause. Although *The Dial* had managed to lure some of the best-known writers in Emerson's close-knit Concord circle, the magazine drew criticism for being too narrowly focused and, enfeebled by circulation problems, folded in 1844. Lowell, for his part, had had his own misadventures in the magazine world, incurring substantial personal debts when *The Pioneer*, a brash literary monthly he cofounded in 1843, failed after only three issues—a victim, by common consent, of acute undercapitalization. Indeed, the number of magazine meltdowns in and around Boston at that time had prompted Emerson to question in his journal whether any publication of true quality could make it financially in New England, and, in an 1850 letter to a friend, he compared trying to launch a magazine with "the measles, the influenza, and . . . [other] periodic distempers."

In the months leading up to the Parker House conclave, the magazine bug was going around again. The prime carrier on this occasion was Francis Underwood, whose age (thirty-two) and position (publisher's assistant) made him the youngest and most junior-level participant at the meeting but belied the crucial role that he would play in the magazine's founding. Underwood is the unsung hero of *The Atlantic*'s early years. Overcoming an impoverished upbringing in western Massachusetts and a faltering start at college, he had eventually managed to earn a law degree in Kentucky—where he came to abhor the institution of slavery—and later found work as a law clerk to the Massachusetts state senate. Underwood's heart, however, was not in the legal profession. A passionate reader of poetry, fiction, and essays, he was particularly enamored of the writings of the men who had assembled, at his invitation, at the Parker House to brainstorm a new magazine that would, in Underwood's words, "bring the literary influence of New England letters to the anti-slavery cause."

The men seated around the table tended to view their prospective magazine as part of a revolution that was taking place in American literature. In an explosion of artistic innovation, American writers were breaking free of the old ties that had bound them for decades to Europe and creating works with a distinctly American voice, a distinctly American point of view, and distinctly American themes. Emerson himself had first sounded the call to arms for a liberated, indigenous literature in his celebrated 1837 address "The American Scholar," which Holmes would later call "our intellectual Declaration of Independence." And in the first half of the 1850s, writers in the United States responded with an outpouring of literary brilliance the likes of which the country has seldom seen: Nathaniel Hawthorne's *The Scarlet Letter* (1850), Herman Melville's *Moby-Dick* (1851), Henry David Thoreau's *Walden* (1854), and Walt Whitman's *Leaves of Grass* (1855). The epicenter of this new movement was in New England, particularly in the fertile literary soil in and around Boston. To Underwood and the others gathered around the table, the time seemed finally ripe, both editorially and commercially, for an ambitious national magazine of politics, science, literature, and the arts that would mirror and draw sustenance from the larger literary culture.

The kind of magazine these men wanted to read and to write for was nowhere to be found in America. Of the handful of successful publications, both national and regional, then in operation, most were heavily dependent on reprints (often pirated) from periodicals abroad, particularly in the realm of fiction. *Harper's New Monthly Magazine*, which had been founded in 1850, did publish some original essays by American writers, but Emerson, Holmes, Longfellow, and Lowell regarded its editorial content, at least in the early years, as more than a little shallow and overly beholden to popular taste. (Lowell once referred to *Harper's* owners as "those Scribes and Pharisees.") The four belletrists had been contributing for years to *The North American Review*, a small literary quarterly that had begun publishing out of Boston in 1815, but they had grown frustrated with its tiny readership and commensurately low pay. *The Atlantic*'s founders, it should be said, were motivated by more than moral outrage over slavery or high-minded thoughts of reinventing the American magazine. Like freelancers of any era, they hungered for a dependable and remunerative outlet for their essays, fiction, and poems.

Their best hope for making these dreams reality resided in Underwood, who had risen through the ranks of the prestigious Boston publishing house of Phillips, Sampson & Co., to become chief assistant to the publisher, Moses Phillips. For three years, Underwood had been lobbying his boss to underwrite his magazine project. At first, Phillips was skeptical—he had seen too many publications come to grief. But at the urging of his most popular writer, Harriet Beecher Stowe, whom Underwood had enlisted in his campaign, Phillips slowly began to warm to the idea. He had agreed to host this Parker House dinner, to listen carefully to the arguments, and to render his final decision.

Unfortunately, many of the details of the dinner are lost to history and to us. What we do know is that it lasted well into the evening (for five hours the participants dined on fresh oysters and thick cuts of beef and consumed prodigious quantities of champagne and brandy) and that by the end of the proceedings, Phillips had embraced the concept of the new magazine with a convert's zeal. In a letter to his niece written soon after the event, the publisher made no secret of the exhilaration he felt merely to be in such exalted company. "We sat down at three p.m. and arose at eight," he reported. "The time occupied was longer by about four hours and thirty minutes than I am in the habit of consuming in that kind of occupation, but it was the richest time intellectually by all odds that I have ever had."

The dinner also settled the question of who would be the magazine's first editor-in-chief. Toward the end of the evening, Underwood had placed one name in nomination, which was immediately seconded around the table. The overwhelming consensus was that the man for the job was James Russell Lowell. A popular poet, a respected scholar, an accomplished essayist, a commanding critic, a caustic satirist, and a fierce opponent of slavery, Lowell was already, at thirty-eight, one of the grandees of nineteenth-century American letters. Despite his earlier setback with the short-lived *Pioneer*, the presence of his name atop the magazine's masthead conferred instant credibility and prestige.

In the weeks following the fateful Parker House meeting, the naturally gregarious Lowell went on a charm offensive, capitalizing on his large network of relationships in both the literary and the antislavery communities. He was a man with a Rolodex of golden names in his head, and he was soon generating assignments and reeling in manuscripts not only from Emerson, Holmes, and Longfellow but also from Nathaniel Hawthorne, John Greenleaf Whittier, and Harriet Beecher Stowe (whose novel *Uncle Tom's Cabin* was outselling everything but the Holy Bible). In these recruiting efforts, he was ably assisted by his good friend Underwood, who had assumed the title of "office editor" to serve at Lowell's right hand. In the meantime, Holmes had proposed a name for the magazine—*The Atlantic Monthly*—that struck a euphonious chord with Lowell and the others. By invoking the vast body of water separating them from Europe, the title seemed to contain within itself at once an acknowledgment of their indebtedness to the Old World and an assertion of autonomy from it.

The magazine was an immediate hit with readers. The first-issue print run of twenty thousand sold out within days, and within a couple of years, circulation had climbed above thirty thousand. These numbers are a far cry from the subscription and newsstand totals of today, but the new publication's rapid rise and high visibility were the envy of the mid-nineteenth-century magazine world. *The Atlantic* became a must-read among educated Americans—primarily in New England but also, unexpectedly, in far-flung pockets of the country. On a lecture tour of the hinterlands, one of the magazine's frequent contributors, the literary critic Thomas Wentworth Higginson, reported back to the home office how wonderful it was "to dip down into these little western towns and find an audience . . . of readers of the Atlantic, so glad to see me. . . . One man told me of a village [Casper, Iowa] with fifty houses and a club of twenty-five subscribers to The Atlantic Monthly."

The centrality of Lowell not only to the early success but also to the enduring editorial direction of *The Atlantic* cannot be overstated. His outsized character and passion, as well as his remarkable breadth of interests, left an imprint on the magazine that continues to be felt to this day. Lowell was a scholar—a Harvard professor of Romance languages—but he wore his learning lightly, and his intellectual sights were trained intently on the modern world in all its complexity. He was a Boston Brahmin with strong opinions but without a hint of holier-than-thou, a man of deeply held democratic principles but also one of acerbically irreverent impulses, a genuine moralist who distrusted official pieties. He had pinpoint instincts about the subjects and genres that would appeal to a general audience, but he was not afraid, as Emerson put it, "to defy the public," by which Emerson meant that Lowell would neither lower his standards to enlarge his readership nor hesitate, when the spirit moved him, to storm the battlements of established institutions and received wisdom.

Yet despite the magazine's fast start, most members of the official *Atlantic* family tended to downplay the good news of the moment and to take the long view. One of these was Charles Eliot Norton, an early contributor and eminent Harvard art historian who, in a letter to Lowell, articulated a hope that has only now, a century and a half later, been fulfilled.

"Of course, it will succeed with you as its Editor," Norton wrote. "But such things are never permanent in our country. They burn brightly for a while, and then burn out—and some other light takes their place. It would be a great thing for us if any undertaking of this kind could live long enough to get affections and associations connected with it, whose steady glow should take the place of, and more than supply, the shine of novelty, and the dazzle of the first go-off. I wish we had a Sylvanus Urban,* a hundred and fifty years old. I wish, indeed, we had something so old in America; I would give a thousand of our new lamps for the one old, battered, but true magical light."

MY OWN HOPE is that readers will find the selections in this anthology to be suffused with the "steady glow" of "true magical light" to which Norton gives such eloquent expression. Making the final choices has been no easy task. Although the book is substantial, many worthy candidates have had to be left out, either because of space limitations or because they didn't fit the anthology's thematic structure. I would love to have included such stellar works as Anna Leonowens's "The English Governess at the Siamese Court" (which inspired the musical *The King and I*), Sarah Orne Jewett's "River Driftwood," Felix Frankfurter's "The Case of Sacco and Vanzetti," Edmund Wilson's "The Man Who Shot Snapping Turtles," Rebecca West's "Black Lamb and Grey Falcon," "One Woman's Abortion," by "Mrs. X." (who can now shed her cloak of anonymity and be identified by her real name, Lou Ashworth), Tracy Kidder's "House," Edward O. Wilson's "The Biological Basis of Morality," David Brooks's "The Organization Kid," Benjamin R. Barber's "Jihad vs. McWorld," and Ron Rosenbaum's "Sex Week at Yale."

But in the end, from the more than 150 million words that *The Atlantic* has published over approximately eighteen hundred issues, the selection process has found its way to some seventy-eight articles, essays, short stories, and poems. Each of these offerings has been chosen for its literary or rhetorical merit, of course, but candidates have also been judged on the basis of the reaction they stirred, the long-term impact they had, and the aura of timelessness they continue to project—their inherent appeal to contemporary readers. Like small pieces of a gigantic jigsaw puzzle, each part—whether on-scene report, character study, or lyric poem—is intended to serve the

---

*The pen name of Edward Cave (1691–1754), the editor and publisher of *The Gentleman's Magazine*, which was founded in London in 1731 and is widely considered to be the world's first general interest magazine. Following Cave's death, the pseudonym continued to be used by subsequent editors of the magazine.

whole, to be structurally and thematically in harmony with the other parts, so that a coherent and vivid picture of the last 150 years can emerge.

Three points about editorial format:

First, in order to accommodate the book's large number of selections, it was necessary to make cuts, especially among the lengthier essays, narratives, and firsthand reports. In these cases, I have made every effort to be as true to the original work as possible. Although I recognize that these abridgments may raise hackles in some precincts, I would contend that, taken as a whole, they constitute a compromise worth making—the best way to conjure the magazine's cornucopia of interests and enthusiasms.

Second, in studying previous magazine collections, I was surprised to find that, more often than not, they failed to furnish their entries with introductory setup commentaries, or "headnotes," as they're sometimes called. Anthologies devoid of headnotes strike me as a strange and unnecessary exercise in flying blind, turning all but the most expert readers into first-time pilots trying to locate the landing strip without benefit of runway lights, control towers, or instrumentation. Every offering here is ushered in by a comprehensively researched headnote that tries to tell readers something intriguing about the piece at hand: how, for example, a glowing review of Mark Twain's *The Innocents Abroad* (written by *The Atlantic*'s third editor-in-chief, William Dean Howells) lured the elusive author to the magazine's offices, and eventually into its pages; how Martin Luther King, Jr., writing perfervidly from an Alabama prison cell, succeeded in smuggling out a handwritten draft that would become the classic "Letter from Birmingham Jail"; how the journalist William Langewiesche, in the chaotic days after 9/11, managed to persuade New York City officials to sanction his becoming the only writer with round-the-clock access to the devastated World Trade Center site—a reportorial coup that would help pave the way for "American Ground," his remarkable three-part series about the rescue-and-recovery operation; or how the 1862 submission of a little-known poet named Julia Ward Howe became the ubiquitous anthem "Battle Hymn of the Republic"—in the words of one former *Atlantic* editor, "the best four dollars we ever spent."

Third, I have taken the liberty of setting this anthology free of a strict chronological organization in favor of a structure that is essentially thematic—grouping the material into a series of categories, defined by subjects, genres, and ideas, that have loomed large for the magazine over the past century and a half. By identifying and highlighting *The Atlantic*'s principal and perennial areas of interest, this structure itself becomes a kind of narrative device for telling the story of the magazine and the parallel story of the world it has been covering for fifteen decades. And by enabling readers to immerse themselves in one subject at a time, it encourages them to make their own connections, to compare and contrast what different authors have said in different eras about such topics as corporate chicanery, the challenge of race, and America's proper place in the world.

THE ANTHOLOGY IS DIVIDED INTO TEN SECTIONS:

FIRSTS

The leadoff section highlights *The Atlantic*'s performance history of being ahead of the curve—paying tribute not just to the literary giants whose early reputations were fired in the crucible of the magazine's pages but also to the visionaries of science and technology who were able to direct their gaze beyond the horizon and foresee the immense significance of such developments as evolution, photography, and the Internet (Asa Gray, Oliver Wendell Holmes, Vannevar Bush). This section also pulls together a sampling of the magazine's breakthrough pieces of geopolitical analysis, public affairs commentary, and investigative reporting that helped reconfigure popular perceptions of national and global issues. In addition to a number of articles already cited—Lowell on Lincoln's election, Muir on wilderness conservation, Wilson and Kelling on crime, Lewis on Islam, and Fallows on the Iraq War—"Firsts" showcases Governor Al Smith's historic affirmation of the compatibility of public service and Catholicism; James Mann's eerily prescient speculations about one of American journalism's most enduring mysteries, the identity of "Deep Throat"; and Robert D. Kaplan's dystopian vision of imminent institutional collapse in the Third World.

BLACK AND WHITE

The second section focuses on the fraught problem of race relations in America. *The Atlantic*'s birth as an antislavery publication marked only the beginning of its passionate preoccupation with this subject. More than any other magazine of its kind, *The Atlantic* has provided a stage for the towering figures of African American history—Frederick Douglass, Booker T. Washington, W.E.B. Du Bois, and Martin Luther King are all represented here—and it has indelibly shaped historical debates about racial equality and black identity. This section also features a short story by Flannery O'Connor on the dangers of even talking about race and a groundbreaking article by Nicholas Lemann on the forces behind the making of the black underclass.

GODS AND MONSTERS

The third section presents a portrait gallery of some of the most prominent heroes and villains of the past 150 years. From George Bancroft's elegant encomium to Abraham Lincoln to Mark Bowden's chillingly detailed picture of the workaday life of Saddam Hussein, this section puts on full display the magazine's long commitment to capturing the essential character of history's larger-than-life figures. Starting with Emerson's eulogy for his close friend Thoreau, a prototype of the modern profile in its attention to both defects and virtues, and ending with Walter Kirn's provocative depiction of Warren Buffett as a great communicator in the tradition of Mark Twain and Will Rogers, this section seeks to show how the magazine has turned the crafts of profile writing and essayistic portraiture into high art.

BEHIND THE SCENES

The arrival of Michael Kelly as *The Atlantic*'s twelfth editor-in-chief, in 2000, set in motion an era of unprecedented enthusiasm at the magazine for the genre known as narrative nonfiction. Kelly, himself an outstanding practitioner of the form, dedicated vast tracts of editorial space to articles that combined storytelling and journalism, that harnessed the techniques of fiction to the force of facts. Yet as the anthology's fourth section reveals, narrative-driven journalism of one kind or another has always had a place in the magazine's pages. Bookended by Nathaniel Hawthorne's vibrant dispatches from the Civil War and William Langewiesche's terrifying reenactment of the mysterious crash of an Egyptian passenger jet, this section represents some of *The Atlantic*'s proudest moments in narrative nonfiction writing.

STATES OF WAR

The portents of civil war were already hovering over a deeply divided nation when *The Atlantic* made its debut in late 1857. After extensively covering the bloodiest conflict in American history, the magazine would return to the front lines, over the next century and a half, in seven other major wars and innumerable minor ones. The fifth section recaptures a mythopoetic moment of the Revolutionary War (Longfellow's "Paul Revere's Ride") and offers one U.S. Marine's brutally honest account of fighting the Japanese in World War II (Studs Terkel's "'The Good War'"). But the spirit of this section is less reportorial than it is philosophical. William James,

Albert Einstein, and the journalist Thomas Powers all raise urgent questions about the nature of war—its psychological origins, its capacity for global destruction, and its tendency to persist long after initial causes have either faded from memory or lost credibility.

CONTROVERSIES

The sixth section zeroes in on conflict of a different kind. Early on, Lowell had expressed his determination "to have a *free* magazine in its true sense"—by which he meant that his *Atlantic* would attempt to avoid the political timidity and intellectual faintheartedness he found in other magazines. Although *The Atlantic* has never courted controversy for its own sake, it has made a habit of diving headlong into thorny cultural issues of religion, gender, sexual orientation, the family, abortion, drugs, ethnicity, and color. This section brings together four strikingly disparate writers—Saul Bellow, V. S. Naipaul, Robert Lowell, and the sociologist Barbara Dafoe Whitehead—whose work provoked political firestorms.

CAPITALISM AND ITS DISCONTENTS

Through tumultuous periods of boom and bust, *The Atlantic* has sought to penetrate the fog of confusion that all too often enshrouds the realms of economics and markets. In the depths of the Great Depression, the renowned British economist John Maynard Keynes chose the magazine as his platform to criticize the policies of governments he believed were exacerbating the crisis by keeping a tight rein on spending. Three decades later, at the height of the Cold War, the Harvard economist John Kenneth Galbraith defied deepening mistrust of centralized economies by arguing forcefully in our pages for more governmental oversight of financial markets. But with the selections in this seventh section, I've opted to put the spotlight on three of the most fascinating and rigorously reported examples of corporate investigative journalism the magazine has ever published: the trailblazing muckraker Henry Demarest Lloyd's "Story of a Great Monopoly," Eric Schlosser's "Why McDonald's Fries Taste So Good," and Edward Jay Epstein's "Have You Ever Tried to Sell a Diamond?"

THE NATURAL WORLD

Among a growing number of people in the United States and around the world, there are few issues of greater moment today than that of climate change. Reports of looming planetary peril have brought new questions and fears about the environment to the forefront of public consciousness and regenerated a hunger for writing that explores, in an ambitious and original way, the complex relationship between man and nature. *The Atlantic* pioneered this kind of writing, particularly with the work of Thoreau, who is represented in this section by his canonical essay "Walking," and of John Muir, whose "The American Forests" appears in "Firsts." These writers, as the journalist and environmental activist Bill McKibben has pointed out, "gave rise to movements." The selections of this eighth section show the magazine endeavoring to look beyond the familiar political and social issues of environmentalism to larger questions of beauty, morality, and belief.

CROWD PLEASERS

Mark Twain once said that he relished writing humor for *The Atlantic* because its editors did not ask him to stand on his head to get laughs. From Twain to H. L. Mencken to Ian Frazier, the magazine has a rich, if sometimes underrecognized, tradition of publishing humor that inclines toward the trenchant and the cerebral and shuns the obvious and the broad. At the beginning of this project, I had intended to devote a section exclusively to the magazine's most memorable humor writing. But as the process unfolded—and wonderful suggestions came pouring in from *Atlantic* colleagues—I realized that the original concept of the section needed to evolve and expand. The ninth section of the book is an attempt to gather together in one place an unabashedly eclectic group of pieces that seem on the surface to have little in common other than literary distinction. The decisive quality that runs through all of these selections is that they are, from every indication, truly beloved—not just by people inside the magazine but by readers as well.

THE AMERICAN IDEA

If there is a single section of this anthology that stands above the rest in importance, it is the tenth and final one. From the beginning, *The Atlantic* has reserved a special place for writing that grapples with the larger questions of our national life: What does it mean to be American? What constitutes the national interest? What should be America's role in the world? The answers to these questions vary, of course, according to the time and place in which they are asked, and no matter how much they are discussed, debated, and dilated upon, precise definitions prove frustratingly elusive. Nevertheless, the questions continue to exert a strong magnetic pull on many of our best minds, including the distinguished writers and thinkers represented in this section.

The term "The American Idea" emanates from *The Atlantic*'s inaugural issue. On the back cover of the magazine, the founding editors published an unsigned Declaration of Purpose that described their publication's broad objectives in a few muted sentences. *The Atlantic*, its editors wrote, "will be the organ of no party or clique. . . . It will not rank itself with any sect of antis: but with that body of men which is in favor of Freedom, National Progress, and Honor, whether public or private."

But at the heart of the magazine's mission, according to the Declaration, was an explicit commitment to exploring, monitoring, and promoting what the editors called "the American idea." Exactly what they meant by that three-word phrase they never made clear, either in the Declaration itself or anywhere else in their public statements or private journals. Were they pledging themselves to advancing political democracy? Personal freedom? Social justice? Economic progress? Some ineffable combination of all of the above? It is intriguing, and also a little baffling, that the founders would give such weight to a term that does not appear to have been in common currency at the time. In retrospect, they seem to have been expressing a quiet confidence that their readers would know instinctively what they had in mind.

Even if the term "the American idea" was not part of the lingua franca of the mid-1850s, concerns about national identity were then very much on the minds of many Americans. Waves of westward expansion had stoked nationalistic sentiments, setting off a groundswell of support for a stronger federal government to supplant the loose and decentralized confederation of states that had been in place for decades. At the same time, antagonisms between the North and the South were intensifying over widening economic disparity and the corrosive issue of slavery. The collision of these two powerful forces would soon lead to the Civil War, four years of almost unimaginable carnage that would tear the country apart. *The Atlantic Monthly* was born into a world in which the very idea of America seemed imperiled.

Americans today doubtless have somewhat different associations with the term. For better or worse, we are far more engaged than our mid-nineteenth-century forebears were with spreading democracy and consumer capitalism to the rest of the world, and yet we are increasingly aware of the dangers of our messianism and fearful of our power's boomerang effects. Many (but by no means all) of our citizens are blessed with unparalleled wealth, comfort, and material choice, and yet we still feel the pangs of instability, disharmony, and spiritual emptiness. "The American idea" continues to represent not only great opportunity but also grave risk.

As this final section of the book demonstrates, *The Atlantic* remains singularly preoccupied with trying to define the changing character of the country and the country's changing relations with the world. This preoccupation is at the core of who we are as a magazine, a major part of our genetic heritage. It connects our labors with the work of the founders—and with that of all the other contributors to the magazine over the course of its history.

One hundred and forty-nine years after the founders first invoked their unembellished phrase, a latter-day group of *Atlantic* editors, preparing for the magazine's relocation to Washington, D.C., from Boston, put forward their own definition. One thing "the American idea" was not, proclaimed an editors' note that appeared in the magazine's January/February 2006 issue, was "some saccharine notion of American exceptionalism or a hyper-patriotic boosterism. It was a recognition that America was an experiment, based on certain principles—an experiment that could fail, but would if successful offer a rare kind of hope."

"What is 'the American idea'?" the editors' note concluded. "It is the fractious, maddening approach to the conduct of human affairs that values equality despite its elusiveness, that values democracy despite its debasement, that values pluralism despite its messiness, that values the institutions of civic culture despite their flaws, and that values public life as something higher and greater than the sum of all our private lives. The founders of the magazine valued these things—and they valued the immense amount of effort it takes to preserve them from generation to generation."

Robert Vare
Litchfield, Connecticut
June 2007

FIRSTS

The Election in November

JAMES RUSSELL LOWELL || 1860

The editorial principles set forth in The Atlantic's *inaugural issue pledged that the magazine would be "the organ of no party or clique," and for almost all of its 150 years that promise has been kept. The grand exception was over the issue of slavery. Among* The Atlantic's *staunch abolitionist founders, none was more dedicated to the antislavery cause and none more persuasive in articulating the case for manumission than the magazine's first editor, James Russell Lowell (1819–1891). Writing on the eve of the 1860 presidential election, Lowell, a respected poet, essayist and Harvard professor (and a future ambassador to England and Spain), viewed the political moment as a titanic struggle for the soul of the nation. The upcoming election, he wrote, more prophetically than he could have known, "is a turning-point in our history," in which only the Republican Party could pull the country out of the deepening moral morass that slavery had created. Lowell's words—confident, stirring, and biblical in force—helped to propel Abraham Lincoln into the White House, shoring up support for the obscure, untried congressman from Illinois among key northern abolitionists. A month into Lincoln's presidency, America was at war.*

It is a proverb, that to turn a radical into a conservative there needs only to put him into office, because then the license of speculation or sentiment is limited by a sense of responsibility,—then for the first time he becomes capable of that comparative view which sees principles and measures, not in the narrow abstract, but in the full breadth of their relations to each other and to political consequences. The theory of democracy presupposes something of these results of official position in the individual voter, since in exercising his right he becomes for the moment an integral part of the governing power.

How very far practice is from any likeness to theory a week's experience of our politics suffices to convince us. The very government itself seems an organized scramble, and Congress a boys' debating-club, with the disadvantage of being reported. As our party-creeds are commonly represented less by ideas than by persons (who are assumed, without too close a scrutiny, to be the exponents of certain ideas), our politics become personal and narrow to a degree never paralleled, unless in ancient Athens or mediaeval Florence. Our Congress debates and our newspapers discuss, sometimes for day after day, not questions of national interest, not what is wise and right, but what the Honorable Lafayette Skreemer said on the stump, or bad whiskey said for him, half a dozen years ago. The next Presidential Election looms always in advance, so that we seem never to have an actual Chief Magistrate, but a prospective one, looking to the chances of reelection, and mingling in all the dirty intrigues of provincial politics with an unhappy talent for making them dirtier. We are kept normally in that most unprofitable of predicaments, a state of transition, and politicians measure their words and deeds by a standard of immediate and temporary expediency,—an expediency not as concerning the nation, but which, if more than merely personal, is no wider than the interests of party.

Is all this a result of the failure of democratic institutions? Rather of the fact that those institutions have never yet had a fair trial, and that for the last thirty years an abnormal element has been acting adversely with continually increasing strength. Whatever be the effect of slavery upon the States where it exists, there can be no doubt that its moral influence upon the North has been most disastrous. It has compelled our politicians into that first fatal compromise with their moral instincts and hereditary principles which makes all consequent ones easy; it has accustomed us to makeshifts instead of statesmanship, to subterfuge instead of policy, to party-platforms for opinions, and to a defiance of the public sentiment of the civilized world for patriotism. We have been asked to admit, first, that it was a necessary evil; then that it was a good both to master and slave; then that it was the corner-stone of free institutions; then that it was a system divinely instituted under the Old Law and sanctioned under the New. With a representation, three-fifths of it based on the assumption that negroes are men, the South turns upon us and insists on our acknowledging that they are things. After compelling her Northern allies to pronounce the "free and equal" clause of the preamble to the Declaration of Independence (because it stood in the way of enslaving men) a manifest absurdity, she has declared, through the Supreme Court of the United States, that negroes are not men in the ordinary meaning of the word. To eat dirt is bad enough, but to find that we have eaten more than was necessary may chance to give us an indigestion. The slaveholding interest has gone on step by step, forcing concession after concession, till it needs but little to secure it forever in the political supremacy of the country. Yield to its latest demand,—let it mould the evil destiny of the Territories,—and the thing is done past recall. The next Presidential Election is to say *Yes* or *No*.

We believe that this election is a turning-point in our history; for, although there are four candidates, there are really, as everyone knows, but two parties, and a single question divides them. To be told that we ought not to agitate the question of Slavery, when it is that which is forever agitating us, is like telling a man with the fever and ague on him to stop shaking and he will be cured. [The] Slave-System is one of those fearful blunders in political economy which are sure, sooner or later, to work their own retribution. The inevitable tendency of slavery is to concentrate in a few hands the soil, the capital, and the power of the countries where it exists, to reduce the non-slaveholding class to a continually lower and lower level of property, intelligence, and enterprise,—their increase in number adding much to the economical hardship of their position and nothing to their political weight in the communities where education induces refinement, where facility of communication stimulates invention and variety of enterprise, where newspapers make every man's improvement in tools, machinery, or culture of the soil an incitement to all, and bring all the thinkers of the world to teach in the cheap university of the people. We do not, of course, mean to say that slaveholding states may not and do not produce fine men; but they fail, by the inherent vice of their constitution and its attendant consequences, to create enlightened, powerful, and advancing communities of men, which is the true object of all political organizations, and which is essential to the prolonged existence of all those whose life and spirit are derived directly from the people.

The election in November turns on the single and simple question, Whether we shall consent to the indefinite multiplication of [slave communities]; and the only party which stands plainly and unequivocally pledged against such a policy, nay, which is not either openly or impliedly in favor of it, is the Republican party. It is in a moral aversion to slavery as a great wrong that the chief strength of the Republican party lies. No man pretends that under the Constitution there is any possibility of interference with the domestic relations of the individual States; no party has ever remotely hinted at any such interference; but what the Republicans affirm is, that in every contingency where the Constitution can be construed in favor of freedom, it ought to be and shall be so construed. The object of the Republican party is not the abolition of African slavery, but the utter extirpation of dogmas which are the logical sequence of the attempts to establish its righteousness and wisdom, and which would serve equally well to justify the enslavement of every white man unable to protect himself. They believe that slavery is a wrong morally, a mistake politically, and a misfortune practically, wherever it exists; that it has nullified our influence abroad and forced us to compromise with our better instincts at home;

that it has perverted our government from its legitimate objects, weakened the respect for the laws by making them the tools of its purposes, and sapped the faith of men in any higher political morality than interest or any better statesmanship than chicane. They mean in every lawful way to hem it within its present limits.

We are persuaded that the election of Mr. Lincoln will do more than anything else to appease the excitement of the country. He has proved both his ability and his integrity; he has had experience enough in public affairs to make him a statesman, and not enough to make him a politician. That he has not had more will be no objection to him in the eyes of those who have seen the administration of the experienced public functionary whose term of office is just drawing to a close. He represents a party who know that true policy is gradual in its advances, that it is conditional and not absolute, that it must deal with fact and not with sentiments, but who know also that it is wiser to stamp out evil in the spark than to wait till there is no help but in fighting fire with fire. They are the only conservative party, because they are the only one based on an enduring principle, the only one that is not willing to pawn tomorrow for the means to gamble with today. They have no hostility to the South, but a determined one to doctrines of whose ruinous tendency every day more and more convinces them.

The encroachments of Slavery upon our national policy have been like those of a glacier in a Swiss valley. Inch by inch, the huge dragon with his glittering scales and crests of ice coils itself onward, an anachronism of summer, the relic of a bygone world where such monsters swarmed. But it has its limit, the kindlier forces of Nature work against it, and the silent arrows of the sun are still, as of old, fatal to the frosty Python. Geology tells us that such enormous devastators once covered the face of the earth, but the benignant sunlight of heaven touched them, and they faded silently, leaving no trace but here and there the scratches of their talons, and the gnawed boulders scattered where they made their lair. We have entire faith in the benignant influence of Truth, the sunlight of the moral world, and believe that slavery, like other worn-out systems, will melt gradually before it.

The Stereoscope and the Stereograph

OLIVER WENDELL HOLMES || 1859

Physician, poet, novelist, father of a Supreme Court justice (and co-founder of The Atlantic*), Oliver Wendell Holmes (1809–1894) is still widely celebrated as the classic nineteenth-century man of many parts. Less well known, perhaps, is Holmes's crucial role in championing a new technology called stereoscopy and ushering in the age of photography. Although in the late 1850s the technology was still in its early stages— Louis Daguerre had invented the daguerreotype twenty years before— Holmes had the foresight and aesthetic vision to understand the new medium's vast potential to alter our perceptions of the physical universe. In a series of essays for* The Atlantic, *Holmes described the powerful impact of a visual art in which "form is . . . divorced from matter" and which "produces a dream-like exaltation." With extraordinary prescience, he proclaimed the camera to be an invention comparable to the printing press—a democratizing force that would enable the reproduction of documents, advance our understanding of war, and even influence our personal relationships. Somewhat less presciently, Holmes also predicted great things for the 3-D stereoscopic viewer, a handheld version of which he himself had invented. The Holmes Stereoscope had a brief burst of popularity and swiftly faded into oblivion.*

Theoretically, a perfect photograph is absolutely inexhaustible. In a picture you can find nothing which the artist has not seen before you; but in a perfect photograph there will be as many beauties lurking, unobserved, as there are flowers that blush unseen in forests and meadows. It is a mistake to suppose one knows a stereoscopic picture when he has studied it a hundred times by the aid of the best of our common instruments. Do we know all that there is in a landscape by looking out at it from our parlor-windows? In one of the glass stereoscopic views of Table Rock, two figures, so minute as to be mere objects of comparison with the surrounding vastness, may be seen standing side by side. Look at the two faces with a strong magnifier, and you could identify their owners, if you met them in a court of law.

Many persons suppose that they are looking on miniatures of the objects represented, when they see them in the stereoscope. They will be surprised to be told that they see most objects as large as they appear in

Nature. A few simple experiments will show how what we see in ordinary vision is modified in our perceptions by what we think we see. We made a sham stereoscope, the other day, with no glasses, and an opening in the place where the pictures belong, about the size of one of the common stereoscopic pictures. Through this we got a very ample view of the town of Cambridge, including Mount Auburn and the Colleges, in a single field of vision. We do not recognize how minute distant objects really look to us, without something to bring the fact home to our conceptions. A man does not deceive us as to his real size when we see him at the distance of the length of Cambridge Bridge. But hold a common black pin before the eyes at the distance of distinct vision, and one-twentieth of its length, nearest the point, is enough to cover him so that he cannot be seen. The head of the same pin will cover one of the Cambridge horse-cars at the same distance, and conceal the tower of Mount Auburn, as seen from Boston.

We are near enough to an edifice to see it well, when we can easily read an inscription upon it. The stereoscopic views of the arches of Constantine and of Titus give not only every letter of the old inscriptions, but render the grain of the stone itself. On the pediment of the Pantheon may be read, not only the words traced by Agrippa, but a rough inscription above it, scratched or hacked into the stone by some wanton hand during an insurrectionary tumult.

This distinctness of the lesser details of a building or a landscape often gives us incidental truths which interest us more than the central object of the picture. Here is Alloway Kirk, in the churchyard of which you may read a real story by the side of the ruin that tells of more romantic fiction. There stands the stone "Erected by James Russell, seedsman, Ayr, in memory of his children,"—three little boys, James, and Thomas, and John, all snatched away from him in the space of three successive summer-days, and lying under the matted grass in the shadow of the old witch-haunted walls. It was Burns's Alloway Kirk we paid for, and we find we have bought a share in the griefs of James Russell, seedsman; for is not the stone that tells this blinding sorrow of real life the true center of the picture, and not the roofless pile which reminds us of an idle legend?

We have often found these incidental glimpses of life and death running away with us from the main object the picture was meant to delineate. The more evidently accidental their introduction, the more trivial they are in themselves, the more they take hold of the imagination. It is common to find an object in one of the twin pictures which we miss in the other; the person or the vehicle having moved in the interval of taking the two photographs. There is before us a view of the Pool of David at Hebron, in which a shadowy figure appears at the water's edge, in the right-hand far-ther corner of the right-hand picture only. This muffled shape stealing silently into the solemn scene has already written a hundred biographies in our imagination. In the lovely glass stereograph of the Lake of Brienz, on the left-hand side, a vaguely hinted female figure stands by the margin of the fair water; on the other side of the picture she is not seen. This is life; we seem to see her come and go. All the longings, passions, experiences, possibilities of womanhood animate that gliding shadow which has flitted through our consciousness, nameless, dateless, featureless, yet more pro-foundly real than the sharpest of portraits traced by a human hand.

Oh, infinite volumes of poems that I treasure in this small library of glass and pasteboard! I creep over the vast features of Rameses, on the face of his rockhewn Nubian temple; I scale the huge mountain-crystal that calls itself the Pyramid of Cheops. I pace the length of the three Titanic stones of the wall of Baalbec,—mightiest masses of quarried rock that man has lifted into the air; and then I dive into some mass of foliage with my microscope, and trace the veinings of a leaf so delicately wrought in the painting not made with hands, that I can almost see its down and the green aphis that sucks its juices. I look into the eyes of the caged tiger, and on the scaly train of the crocodile, stretched on the sands of the river that has mir-rored a hundred dynasties. I stroll through Rhenish vineyards, I sit under Roman arches, I walk the streets of once buried cities, I look into the chasms of Alpine glaciers, and on the rush of wasteful cataracts. I pass, in a moment, from the banks of the Charles to the ford of the Jordan, and leave my outward frame in the arm-chair at my table, while in spirit I am looking down upon Jerusalem from the Mount of Olives.

What is to come of the stereoscope and the photograph we are almost afraid to guess, lest we should seem extravagant. But, premising that we are to give a colored stereoscopic mental view of their prospects, we will ven-ture on a few glimpses at a conceivable, if not a possible future.

Form is henceforth divorced from matter. In fact, matter as a visible object is of no great use any longer, except as the mould on which form is shaped. Give us a few negatives of a thing worth seeing, taken from differ-ent points of view, and that is all we want of it. Pull it down or burn it up, if you please. We must, perhaps, sacrifice some luxury in the loss of color; but form and light and shade are the great things, and even color can be added, and perhaps by and by may be got direct from Nature.

There is only one Coliseum or Pantheon; but how many millions of potential negatives have they shed,—representatives of billions of pic-tures,—since they were erected! Matter in large masses must always be fixed and dear; form is cheap and transportable. We have got the fruit of creation now, and need not trouble ourselves with the core. Every conceivable object of Nature and Art will soon scale off its surface for us. Men will hunt all curious, beautiful, grand objects, as they hunt the cattle in South America, for their skins, and leave the carcasses as of little worth.

The next European war will send us stereographs of battles. It is asserted that a bursting shell can be photographed. The time is perhaps at hand when a flash of light, as sudden and brief as that of the lightning which shows a whirling wheel standing stock still, shall preserve the very instant of the shock of contact of the mighty armies that are even now gathering. The lightning from heaven does actually photograph natural objects on the bodies of those it has just blasted,—so we are told by many witnesses. The lightning of clashing sabres and bayonets may be forced to stereotype itself in a stillness as complete as that of the tumbling tide of Niagara as we see it self-pictured.

We should be led on too far, if we developed our belief as to the transformations to be wrought by this greatest of human triumphs over earthly conditions, the divorce of form and substance. Let our readers fill out a blank check on the future as they like,—we give our endorsement to their imaginations beforehand. We are looking into stereoscopes as pretty toys, and wondering over the photograph as a charming novelty; but before another generation has passed away, it will be recognized that a new epoch in the history of human progress dates from the time when He who

> never but in uncreated light
> Dwelt from eternity—

took a pencil of fire from the hand of the "angel standing in the sun," and placed it in the hands of a mortal.

Darwin and His Critics

ASA GRAY || 1860

A year after the publication of The Origin of Species, *Asa Gray (1810–1888), an eminent Harvard botanist, published three articles in the magazine defending Charles Darwin and his epochal theory of evolution, which had created a firestorm on both sides of the Atlantic. Gray was an unlikely ally for the embattled British naturalist. Conservative and deeply religious, he harbored profound misgivings about the compatibility of evolutionary and scriptural truth. Nevertheless, he immediately recognized the scientific merit of Darwin's work, and even wrote to him in London with the pledge, "You shall have fair play here." The fulfillment of Gray's promise has earned him a place in history as the first American exponent of the Darwinian revolution—and one of the most pivotal. Darwin himself was so pleased with Gray's support that he arranged to have the three* Atlantic *articles reprinted in England as a direct rebuttal to his enemies in the church. And yet even Darwin realized that Gray's backing was not unqualified. As Darwin wrote in a letter to a colleague, "No one person understands my views & has defended them so well as A. Gray;—though he does not by any means go all the way with me."*

Two hypotheses divide the scientific world, very unequally, upon the origin of the existing diversity of the plants and animals which surround us. One assumes that the actual kinds are primordial; the other, that they are derivative. One, that all kinds originated supernaturally and directly as such, and have continued unchanged in the order of Nature; the other, that the present kinds appeared in some sort of genealogical connection with other and earlier kinds, that they became what they now are in the course of time and in the order of Nature.

Or, bringing in the word *species*, which is well defined as "the perennial succession of individuals," and reducing the question to mathematical simplicity of statement: species are lines of individuals coming down from the past and running on to the future,—lines receding, therefore, from our view in either direction. Within our limited view they appear to be parallel lines, as a general thing neither approaching to nor diverging from each other. The first hypothesis assumes that they were parallel from the unknown beginning and will be to the unknown end. The second hypothesis assumes that the apparent parallelism is not real and complete, at least aboriginally, but approximate or temporary; that we should find the lines convergent in the past, if we could trace them far enough.

To us the present revival of the derivative hypothesis, in a more winning shape than it ever before had, was not unexpected. We wonder that any thoughtful observer of the course of investigation and of speculation in science should not have foreseen it, and have learned at length to take its inevitable coming patiently the more so as in Darwin's treatise it comes in a purely scientific form, addressed only to scientific men. The notoriety and wide popular perusal of this treatise appear to have astonished the author even more than the book itself has astonished the reading world. Coming, as the new presentation does, from a naturalist of acknowledged character and ability, and marked by a conscientiousness and candor which have not always been reciprocated, we have thought it simply right to set forth the doctrine as fairly and as favorably as we could. There are plenty to decry it, and the whole theory is widely exposed to attack. For the arguments on the other side we may look to the numerous adverse publications which Darwin's volume has already called out, and especially to those reviews which propose directly to refute it. Taking various lines and reflecting very diverse modes of thought, these hostile critics may be expected to concentrate and enforce the principal objections which can be brought to bear against the derivative hypothesis in general, and Darwin's new exposition of it in particular.

In our survey of the lively discussion which has been raised, it matters little how our own particular opinions may incline. But we may confess to an impression, thus far, that the doctrine of the permanent and complete immutability of species has not been established, and may fairly be doubted. We believe that species vary, and that "Natural Selection" works; but we suspect that its operation, like every analogous natural operation, may be limited by something else. Just as every species by its natural rate of reproduction would soon fill any country it could live in, but does not, being checked by some other species or some other condition;—so it may be surmised that Variation and Natural Selection have their Struggle and consequent Check, or are limited by something inherent in the constitution of organic beings. We are disposed to rank the derivative hypothesis in its fullness with the nebular hypothesis [a long-standing theory, first formulated by Immanuel Kant, regarding the formation of the solar system], and to regard both as allowable, as not unlikely to prove tenable in spite of some strong objections, but as not therefore demonstrably true. Those, if any there be, who regard the derivative hypothesis as satisfactorily proved must have loose notions as to what proof is. Those who imagine it can be easily refuted and cast aside must, we think, have [an] imperfect or very prejudiced conception of the facts concerned and of the questions at issue.

The proposition, that things and events in Nature were not designed to be so, if logically carried out, is doubtless tantamount to atheism. Yet most people believe that some were designed and others were not, although they fall into a hopeless maze whenever they undertake to define their position. Whatever might be thought of Darwin's doctrine, we are surprised that he should be charged with *scorning* or *sneering* at the opinions of others, upon such a subject. Perhaps Darwin's view is incompatible with final causes, but as to the charge that he "sneers at the idea of any manifestation of design in the material universe," we are confident that it is not at all warranted.

[It] is undeniable that Mr. Darwin has purposely been silent upon the philosophical and theological applications of his theory. This reticence, under the circumstances, argues design, and raises inquiry as to the final cause or reason why. Perhaps the author is more familiar with natural-historical than with philosophical inquiries, and, not having decided which particular theory about efficient cause is best founded, he meanwhile argues the scientific questions concerned—all that relates to secondary causes—upon purely scientific grounds, as he must do in any case. Perhaps, confident, as he evidently is, that his view will finally be adopted, he may enjoy a sort of satisfaction in hearing it denounced as sheer atheism by the inconsiderate, and afterwards, when it takes its place with the neb-ular hypothesis and the like, see this judgment reversed, as we suppose it would be in such event.

Whatever Mr. Darwin's philosophy may be, or whether he has any, is a matter of no consequence at all, compared with the important questions, whether a theory to account for the origination and diversification of ani-mal and vegetable forms through the operation of secondary causes does or does not exclude design; and whether the establishment by adequate ev-idence of Darwin's particular theory of diversification through variation and natural selection would essentially alter the present scientific and philosophical grounds for theistic views of Nature. We hesitate to advance our conclusions in opposition to [Darwin's critics]. But, after full and seri-ous consideration, we are constrained to say, that, in our opinion, the adoption of a derivative hypothesis, and of Darwin's particular hypothesis, if we understand it, would leave the doctrines of final causes, utility, and special design just where they were before. We do not pretend that the sub-ject is not environed with difficulties. Every view is so environed; and every shifting of the view is likely, if it removes some difficulties, to bring others into prominence. But we cannot perceive that Darwin's theory brings in any new kind of scientific difficulty, that is, any with which philosophical naturalists were not already familiar.

Since natural science deals only with secondary or natural causes, the scientific terms of a theory of derivation of species—no less than of a theory of dynamics—must needs be the same to the theist as to the atheist. The difference appears only when the inquiry is carried up to the question of primary cause,—a question which belongs to philosophy. Wherefore, Darwin's reticence about efficient cause does not disturb us. He considers only the scientific questions. [We] think that a theistic view of Nature is implied in his Book, and we must charitably refrain from suggesting the contrary until the contrary is logically deduced from his positions.

Battle Hymn of the Republic

JULIA WARD HOWE ‖ 1862

Julia Ward Howe (1819–1910) wrote "Battle Hymn of the Republic" in a burst of early-morning inspiration. Howe, who had already published two volumes of poetry despite having a husband who disapproved of her literary aspirations, had been traveling in Virginia and had just witnessed a Confederate raid on a Union army camp. She had heard the Union soldiers singing an impassioned tribute to the recently hanged abolitionist John Brown and decided to craft new verses and set them to the same rousing cadences. Howe's poem was quickly published by the editors of The Atlantic, *who gave it prominent display on the first page of the February 1862 issue. The response was overwhelming. The verses swiftly evolved into a Union anthem—when President Lincoln first heard it, shortly after the Battle of Gettysburg, he reportedly cried out, "Sing it again!"—and have become a permanent feature of American public life, inspiring millions, from World War II soldiers to civil rights activists to mourners at the funerals of Robert Kennedy and Ronald Reagan.*

Mine eyes have seen the glory of the coming of the Lord:
He is trampling out the vintage where the grapes of wrath are stored;
He hath loosed the fateful lightning of His terrible swift sword:
　　His truth is marching on.

I have seen Him in the watch-fires of a hundred circling camps,
They have builded Him an altar in the evening dews and damps;
I can read His righteous sentence by the dim and flaring lamps:
　　His day is marching on.

I have read a fiery gospel writ in burnished rows of steel:
"As ye deal with my contemners, so with you my grace shall deal;
Let the Hero, born of woman, crush the serpent with his heel,
　　Since God is marching on."

He has sounded forth the trumpet that shall never call retreat;
He is sifting out the hearts of men before His judgment-seat:

Oh, be swift, my soul, to answer Him! be jubilant, my feet!
Our God is marching on.

In the beauty of the lilies Christ was born across the sea,
With a glory in his bosom that transfigures you and me:
As he died to make men holy, let us die to make men free,
While God is marching on.

The Story of a Year

HENRY JAMES ‖ 1865

Henry James (1843–1916) was the first member of his celebrated literary family to write for The Atlantic, *but he wasn't the only one. Both his brother, the psychologist and philosopher William James, and his father, the theologian Henry James, Sr., published essays in the magazine's pages. On more than one occasion, Henry James, Jr., and Henry James, Sr., even appeared in the same table of contents—a coincidence that rankled the ambitious, young writer. He wouldn't have to share the spotlight for long. With the enthusiastic support of the magazine's editors, especially a young assistant with an eye for talent named William Dean Howells (who would become a lifelong champion and friend), James became a literary fixture at* The Atlantic, *contributing dozens of reviews, travel pieces, and, most important, works of fiction. The magazine serialized not only James's first four novels—*Watch and Ward *(1871),* Roderick Hudson *(1875),* The American *(1876), and* The Europeans *(1878)—but also three of his best:* Daisy Miller *(1879),* The Portrait of a Lady *(1881), and* The Spoils of Poynton *(1897). "The Story of a Year," James's first short story published under his own name—written when he was twenty-one—tells the tale of a young woman torn between her loyalty to her fiancé, a Union soldier who has been badly wounded, and her infatuation with an aggressive local suitor. This excerpt puts on display, albeit in not yet fully developed form, some of the hallmarks of James's top-flight fiction: a sharp attention to detail and to psychological nuance, a polished, lapidary prose, and a fascination with the anguish of moral choice.*

It was a week before Lizzie heard from Mrs. Ford. The letter, when it came, was very brief. Jack still lived. The wounds were three in number, and very serious; he was unconscious; he had not recognized her; but still the chances either way were thought equal. They would be much greater for his recovery nearer home; but it was impossible to move him. "I write from the midst of horrible scenes," said the poor lady. Subjoined was a list of necessary medicines, comforts, and delicacies, to be boxed up and sent.

For a while Lizzie found occupation in writing a letter to Jack, to be read in his first lucid moment, as she told Mrs. Ford. This lady's man-of-business came up from the village to superintend the packing of the boxes.

Her directions were strictly followed; and in no point were they found wanting. Mr. Mackenzie bespoke Lizzie's admiration for their friend's wonderful clearness of memory and judgment. "I wish we had that woman at the head of affairs," said he. "Gad, I'd apply for a Brigadier-Generalship."—"I'd apply to be sent South," thought Lizzie. When the boxes and letter were despatched, she sat down to await more news. Sat down, say I? Sat down, and rose, and wondered, and sat down again. These were lonely, weary days. Very different are the idleness of love and the idleness of grief. Very different is it to be alone with your hope and alone with your despair. Lizzie failed to rally her musings. I do not mean to say that her sorrow was very poignant, although she fancied it was. Habit was a great force in her simple nature; and her chief trouble now was that habit refused to work. Lizzie had to grapple with the stern tribulation of a decision to make, a problem to solve. She felt that there was some spiritual barrier between herself and repose. So she began in her usual fashion to build up a false repose on the hither side of belief. She might as well have tried to float on the Dead Sea. Peace eluding her, she tried to resign herself to tumult. She drank deep at the well of self-pity, but found its waters brackish. People are apt to think that they may temper the penalties of misconduct by self-commiseration, just as they season the long aftertaste of beneficence by a little spice of self-applause. But the Power of Good is a more grateful master than the Devil. What bliss to gaze into the smooth gurgling wake of a good deed, while the comely bark sails on with floating pennon! What horror to look into the muddy sediment which floats round the piratic keel! Go, sinner, and dissolve it with your tears! And you, scoffing friend, there is the way out! Or would you prefer the window? I'm an honest man forevermore.

One night Lizzie had a dream,—a rather disagreeable one,—which haunted her during many waking hours. It seemed to her that she was walking in a lonely place, with a tall, dark-eyed man who called her wife. Suddenly, in the shadow of a tree, they came upon an unburied corpse. Lizzie proposed to dig him a grave. They dug a great hole and took hold of the corpse to lift him in; when suddenly he opened his eyes. Then they saw that he was covered with wounds. He looked at them intently for some time, turning his eyes from one to the other. At last he solemnly said, "Amen!" and closed his eyes. Then she and her companion placed him in the grave, and shovelled the earth over him, and stamped it down with their feet.

He of the dark eyes and he of the wounds were the two constantly recurring figures of Lizzie's reveries. She could never think of John without thinking of the courteous Leatherborough gentleman, too. These were the *data* of her problem. These two figures stood like opposing knights (the black and the white), foremost on the great chess-board of fate. Lizzie was the wearied, puzzled player. She would idly finger the other pieces, and shift them carelessly hither and thither; but it was of no avail: the game lay between the two knights. She would shut her eyes and long for some kind hand to come and tamper with the board; she would open them and see the two knights standing immovable, face to face. It was nothing new. A fancy had come in and offered defiance to a fact; they must fight it out. Lizzie generously inclined to the fancy, the unknown champion, with a reputation to make. Call her *blasée*, if you like, this little girl, whose record told of a couple of dances and a single lover, heartless, old before her time. Perhaps she deserves your scorn. I confess she thought herself ill-used. By whom? by what? wherein? These were questions Miss Crowe was not prepared to answer. Her intellect was unequal to the stern logic of human events. She expected two and two to make five: as why should they not for the nonce? She was like an actor who finds himself on the stage with a half-learned part and without sufficient wit to extemporize. Pray, where is the prompter? Alas, Elizabeth, that you had no mother! Young girls are prone to fancy that when once they have a lover, they have everything they need: a conclusion inconsistent with the belief entertained by many persons, that life begins with love. Lizzie's fortunes became old stories to her before she had half read them through. Jack's wounds and danger were an old story. Do not suppose that she had exhausted the lessons, the suggestions of these awful events, their inspirations, exhortations,—that she had wept as became the horror of the tragedy. No: the curtain had not yet fallen, yet our young lady had begun to yawn. To yawn? Ay, and to long for the afterpiece. Since the tragedy dragged, might she not divert herself with that well-bred man beside her?

Elizabeth was far from owning to herself that she had fallen away from her love. For my own part, I need no better proof of the fact than the dull persistency with which she denied it. What accusing voice broke out of the stillness? Jack's nobleness and magnanimity were the hourly theme of her clogged fancy. Again and again she declared to herself that she was unworthy of them, but that, if he would only recover and come home, she would be his eternal bond-slave. So she passed a very miserable month. Let us hope that her childish spirit was being tempered to some useful purpose. Let us hope so.

She roamed about the empty house with her footsteps tracked by an unlaid ghost. She cried aloud and said that she was very unhappy; she groaned and called herself wicked. Then, sometimes, appalled at her moral perplexities, she declared that she was neither wicked nor unhappy; she was contented, patient, and wise. Other girls had lost their lovers: it was the present way of life. Was she weaker than most women? Nay, but Jack was the best of men. If he would only come back directly, without delay, as he was, senseless, crying even, that she might look at him, touch him, speak to him! Then she would say that she could no longer answer for herself, and wonder (or pretend to wonder) whether she were not going mad. Suppose Mrs. Ford should come back and find her in an unswept room, pallid and insane? or suppose she should die of her troubles? What if she should kill herself?—dismiss the servants, and close the house, and lock herself up with a knife? Then she would cut her arm to escape from dismay at what she had already done; and then her courage would ebb away with her blood, and, having so far pledged herself to despair, her life would ebb away with her courage; and then, alone, in darkness, with none to help her, she would vainly scream, and thrust the knife into her temple, and swoon to death. And Jack would come back, and burst into the house, and wander through the empty rooms, calling her name, and for all answer get a death-scent! These imaginings were the more creditable or discreditable to Lizzie, that she had never read "Romeo and Juliet." At any rate, they served to dissipate time,—heavy, weary time,—the more heavy and weary as it bore dark foreshadowings of some momentous event. If that event would only come, whatever it was, and sever this Gordian knot of doubt!

The days passed slowly: the leaden sands dropped one by one. The roads were too bad for walking; so Lizzie was obliged to confine her restlessness to the narrow bounds of the empty house, or to an occasional journey to the village, where people sickened her by their dull indifference to her spiritual agony. Still they could not fail to remark how poorly Miss Crowe was looking. This was true, and Lizzie knew it. I think she even took a certain comfort in her pallor and in her failing interest in her dress. There was some satisfaction in displaying her white roses amid the apple-checked prosperity of Main Street. At last Miss Cooper, the Doctor's sister, spoke to her:—

"How is it, Elizabeth, you look so pale, and thin, and worn out? What you been doing with yourself? Falling in love, eh? It isn't right to be so much alone. Come down and stay with us awhile,—till Mrs. Ford and John come back," added Miss Cooper, who wished to put a cheerful face on the matter.

For Miss Cooper, indeed, any other face would have been difficult. Lizzie agreed to come. Her hostess was a busy, unbeautiful old maid, sister and housekeeper of the village physician. Her occupation here below was to perform the forgotten tasks of her fellowmen,—to pick up their dropped stitches, as she herself declared. She was never idle, for her general cleverness was commensurate with mortal needs. Her own story was that she kept moving, so that folks couldn't see how ugly she was. And, in fact, her existence was manifest through her long train of good deeds,—just as the presence of a comet is shown by its tail. It was doubtless on the above principle that her visage was agitated by a perpetual laugh.

Meanwhile more news had been coming from Virginia. "What an absurdly long letter you sent John," wrote Mrs. Ford, in acknowledging the receipt of the boxes. "His first lucid moment would be very short, if he were to take upon himself to read your effusions. Pray keep your long stories till he gets well." For a fortnight the young soldier remained the same,—feverish, conscious only at intervals. Then came a change for the worse, which, for many weary days, however, resulted in nothing decisive. "If he could only be moved to Glenham, home, and old sights," said his mother, "I should have hope. But think of the journey!" By this time Lizzie had stayed out ten days of her visit.

One day Miss Cooper came in from a walk, radiant with tidings. Her face, as I have observed, wore a continual smile, being dimpled and punctured all over with merriment,—so that, when an unusual cheerfulness was super-diffused, it resembled a tempestuous little pool into which a great stone has been cast.

"Guess who's come," said she, going up to the piano, which Lizzie was carelessly fingering, and putting her hands on the young girl's shoulders. "Just guess!" Lizzie looked up.

"Jack," she half gasped.

"Oh, dear, no, not that! How stupid of me! I mean Mr. Bruce, your Leatherborough admirer."

"Mr. Bruce! Mr. Bruce!" said Lizzie. "Really?"

"True as I live. He's come to bring his sister to the Water-Cure. I met them at the post-office."

Lizzie felt a strange sensation of good news. Her finger-tips were on fire. She was deaf to her companion's rattling chronicle. She broke into the midst of it with a fragment of some triumphant, jubilant melody. The keys rang beneath her flashing hands. And then she suddenly stopped, and Miss Cooper, who was taking off her bonnet at the mirror, saw that her face was covered with a burning flush.

That evening, Mr. Bruce presented himself at Doctor Cooper's, with whom he had a slight acquaintance. To Lizzie he was infinitely courteous and tender. He assured her, in very pretty terms, of his profound sympathy with her in her cousin's danger;—her cousin he still called him,—and it seemed to Lizzie that until that moment no one had begun to be kind. And then he began to rebuke her, playfully and in excellent taste, for her pale cheeks.

"Isn't it dreadful?" said Miss Cooper. "She looks like a ghost. I guess she's in love."

"He must be a good-for-nothing lover to make his mistress look so sad. If I were you, I'd give him up, Miss Crowe."

"I didn't know I looked sad," said Lizzie.

"You don't now," said Miss Cooper. "You're smiling and blushing. A'n't she blushing, Mr. Bruce?"

"I think Miss Crowe has no more than her natural color," said Bruce, dropping his eye-glass. "What have you been doing all this while since we parted?"

"All this while? It's only six weeks. I don't know. Nothing. What have you?"

"I've been doing nothing, too. It's hard work."

"Have you been to any more parties?"

"Not one."

"Any more sleigh-rides?"

"Yes. I took one more dreary drive all alone,—over that same road, you know. And I stopped at the farm-house again, and saw the old woman we had the talk with. She remembered us, and asked me what had become of the young lady who was with me before. I told her you were gone home, but that I hoped soon to go and see you. So she sent you her love."

"Oh, how nice!" exclaimed Lizzie.

"Wasn't it? And then she made a certain little speech; I won't repeat it, or we shall have Miss Cooper talking about your blushes again."

"I know," cried the lady in question: "she said she was very"—

"Very what?" said Lizzie.

"Very h-a-n-d—what every one says."

"Very handy?" asked Lizzie. "I'm sure no one ever said that."

"Of course," said Bruce; "and I answered what every one answers."

"Have you seen Mrs. Littlefield lately?"

"Several times. I called on her the day before I left town, to see if she had any messages for you."

"Oh, thank you! I hope she's well."

"Oh, she's as jolly as ever. She sent you her love, and hoped you would come back to Leatherborough very soon again. I told her, that, however it might be with the first message, the second should be a joint one from both of us."

"You're very kind. I should like very much to go again.—Do you like Mrs. Littlefield?"

"Like her? Yes. Don't you? She's thought a very pleasing woman."

"Oh, she's very nice.—I don't think she has much conversation."

"Ah, I'm afraid you mean she doesn't backbite. We've always found plenty to talk about."

"That's a very significant tone. What, for instance?"

"Well, we *have* talked about Miss Crowe."

"Oh, you have? Do you call that having plenty to talk about?"

"We *have* talked about Mr. Bruce,—haven't we, Elizabeth?" said Miss Cooper, who had her own notion of being agreeable.

It was not an altogether bad notion, perhaps; but Bruce found her interruptions rather annoying, and insensibly allowed them to shorten his visit. Yet, as it was, he sat till eleven o'clock,—a stay quite unprecedented at Glenham.

When he left the house, he went splashing down the road with a very elastic tread, springing over the starlit puddles, and trolling out some sentimental ditty. He reached the inn, and went up to his sister's sitting-room.

"Why, Robert, where have you been all this while?" said Miss Bruce.

"At Dr. Cooper's."

"Dr. Cooper's? I should think you had! Who's Dr. Cooper?"

"Where Miss Crowe's staying."

"Miss Crowe? Ah, Mrs. Littlefield's friend! Is she as pretty as ever?"

"Prettier,—prettier,—prettier. *Ta-ra-ta! Ta-ra-ta!*"

"Oh, Robert, do stop that singing! You'll rouse the whole house."

One fall day in 1869, a flashy, hyperkinetic young writer, sporting a bushy mustache and a sealskin coat, paid an unannounced visit to The Atlantic's *offices. Under the byline Mark Twain (1835–1910), Samuel Langhorne Clemens was by then an established newspaper correspondent and a humorist of some renown, and he had come in person to express his gratitude for a rave review of his first full-length book,* The Innocents Abroad. *That the magazine had even chosen to review Twain's book, let alone sing its praises, was unusual. A satirical first-person account of his misadventures traveling aboard a cruise ship and through Europe and the Holy Land, it had been distributed not by a reputable publisher but by a small outfit that peddled copies door to door. Yet the author of the review, William Dean Howells (then an assistant editor), had detected something fresh and bracingly American in the book's conversational style and acerbic observations. Twain and Howells had much in common: a western, rather than an East Coast, upbringing; an early apprenticeship in newspapers; extraordinary literary ambition; and a fascination with the new wave of realism that was then starting to take hold in the American novel. Their meeting in* The Atlantic's *offices that day sparked a four-decade-long friendship and one of the magazine's most consequential editorial relationships. In the coming years, eighteen of Twain's essays and short stories, including the seven-part series of tales that would be shaped into the immensely popular* Life on the Mississippi *(1883), appeared in* The Atlantic's *pages. And although he could usually make more money elsewhere, Twain always preferred to be in* The Atlantic—*first, because of Howells and, second, because of the magazine's astute readership. As Twain wrote Howells in an appreciative 1874 letter, "The Atlantic audience is the only audience that I sit down before with perfect serenity (for the simple reason that it don't require a 'humorist' to paint himself stripèd and stand on his head every fifteen minutes)."*

The Innocents Abroad, or the New Pilgrim's Progress

WILLIAM DEAN HOWELLS ‖ 1869

The character of American humor, and its want of resemblance to the humor of Kamtschatka and Patagonia,—will the reader forgive us if we fail to set down here the thoughts suggested by these fresh and apposite topics? Will he credit us with a self-denial proportioned to the vastness of Mr. Clemens's very amusing book, if we spare to state why he is so droll, or—which is as much to the purpose—why we do not know? This reticence will leave us very little to say by way of analysis; and, indeed, there is very little to say of "The Innocents Abroad" which is not of the most obvious and easy description. The idea of a steamer-load of Americans going on a prolonged picnic to Europe and the Holy Land is itself almost sufficiently delightful, and it is perhaps praise enough for the author to add that it suffers nothing from his handling. If one considers the fun of making a volume of six hundred octavo pages upon this subject, in compliance with one of the main conditions of a subscription book's success, bigness namely, one has a tolerably fair piece of humor, without troubling Mr. Clemens further. It is out of the bounty and abundance of his own nature that he is as amusing in the execution as in the conception of his work. And it is always good-humored humor, too, that he lavishes on his reader, and even in its impudence it is charming; we do not remember where it is indulged at the cost of the weak or helpless side, or where it is insolent, with all its sauciness and irreverence. The standard shams of travel which everybody sees through suffer possibly more than they ought, but not so much as they might; and one readily forgives the harsh treatment of them in consideration of the novel piece of justice done on such a traveller as suffers under the pseudonym of Grimes. It is impossible also that the quality of humor should not sometimes be strained in the course of so long a narrative; but the wonder is rather in the fact that it is strained so seldom.

Mr. Clemens gets a good deal of his fun out of his fellow-passengers, whom he makes us know pretty well, whether he presents them somewhat caricatured, as in the case of the "Oracle" of the ship, or carefully and exactly done, as in the case of such a shrewd, droll, business-like, sensible, kindly type of the American young man as "Dan."

Of course the instructive portions of Mr. Clemens's book are of a general rather than particular character, and the reader gets as travel very little besides series of personal adventures and impressions; he is taught next to nothing about the population of the cities and the character of the rocks in the different localities. Yet the man who can be honest enough to let himself see the realities of human life everywhere, or who has only seen Americans as they are abroad, has not travelled in vain and is far from a useless guide. The very young American who told the English officers that a couple of our gunboats could come and knock Gibraltar into the Mediterranean Sea; the American who at a French restaurant "talked very loudly and coarsely, and laughed boisterously, where all others were so quiet and well behaved," and who ordered "wine, sir!" adding, to raise admiration in a country where wine is as much a matter of course as soup, "I never dine without wine, sir"; the American who had to be addressed several times as Gordon, being so accustomed to hear the name pronounced Gorrdong, and who had forgotten most English words during a three months' sojourn in Paris; the Americans who pitilessly made a three days' journey in Palestine within two days, cruelly overworking the poor beasts they rode, and overtaxing the strength of their comrades, in order not to break the Sabbath; the American Pilgrims who travelled half round the world to be able to take a sail on the Sea of Galilee, and then missed their sole opportunity because they required the boatman to take them for one napoleon when he wanted two;—these are all Americans who are painted to peculiar advantage by Mr. Clemens, and who will be easily recognized by such as have had the good fortune to meet them abroad.

The didactic, however, is not Mr. Clemens's prevailing mood, nor his best, by any means. The greater part of his book is in the vein of irony, which, with a delicious impudence, he attributes to Saint Luke, declaring that Luke, in speaking of the winding "street, called Straight" in Damascus, "is careful not to commit himself; he does not say it is the street which *is* straight, but the 'street which is *called* Straight.' It is a fine piece of irony; it is the only facetious remark in the Bible, I believe." At Tiberias our author saw the women who wear their dowry in their head-dresses of coins. "Most of these maidens were not wealthy, but some few have been kindly dealt with by fortune. I saw heiresses there, worth, in their own right,—worth, well, I suppose I might venture to say as much as nine dollars and a half. But such cases are rare. When you come across one of these, she naturally puts on airs." He thinks the owner of the horse "Jericho," on which he travelled towards Jerusalem, "had a wrong opinion about him. He had an idea that he was one of those fiery, untamed steeds, but he is not of that character. I know the Arab had this idea, because when he brought the horse out for inspection in Beirout, he kept jerking at the bridle and shouting in

Arabic, 'Ho! Will you? Do you want to run away, you ferocious beast, and break your neck?' when all the time the horse was not doing anything in the world, and only looked like he wanted to lean up against something and think. Whenever he is not shying at things or reaching after a fly, he wants to do that yet. How it would surprise his owner to know this!" In this vein of ironical drollery is that now celebrated passage in which Mr. Clemens states that he was affected to tears on coming, a stranger in a strange land, upon the grave of a blood-relation,—the tomb of Adam; but that passage is somewhat more studied in tone than most parts of the book, which are written with a very successful approach in style to colloquial drolling. As Mr. Clemens writes of his experiences, we imagine he would talk of them; and very amusing talk it would be: often not at all fine in matter or manner, but full of touches of humor,—which if not delicate are nearly always easy,—and having a base of excellent sense and good feeling. There is an amount of pure human nature in the book, that rarely gets into literature; the depths of our poor unregeneracy—dubious even of the blissfulness of bliss—are sounded by such a simple confession as Mr. Clemens makes in telling of his visit to the Emperor of Russia: "I would as soon have thought of being cheerful in Abraham's bosom as in the palace of an Emperor." Almost any topic, and any event of the author's past life, he finds pertinent to the story of European and Oriental travel, and if the reader finds it impertinent, he does not find it the less amusing. The effect is dependent in so great degree upon this continuous incoherence, that no chosen passage can illustrate the spirit of the whole.

Under his *nom de plume* of Mark Twain, Mr. Clemens is well known to the very large world of newspaper-readers; and this book ought to secure him something better than the uncertain standing of a popular favorite. It is no business of ours to fix his rank among the humorists California has given us, but we think he is, in an entirely different way from all the others, quite worthy of the company of the best.

A True Story, Repeated
Word for Word as I Heard It

MARK TWAIN ‖ 1874

Despite Twain's gratitude for The Atlantic's *early support, it took How-ells five years to coax a submission out of his good friend. The sticking point was money: Twain's fame was growing exponentially, and* The Atlantic *was unable to afford his soaring fees. Howells, who ascended to the post of editor-in-chief in 1871, finally prevailed upon the magazine's publisher to pay Twain twenty dollars per page—twice as much as other contributors received at the time and the highest rate* The Atlantic *had ever offered a writer. That did the trick, and in 1874 Twain sent the first of his many contributions to the magazine. "A True Story, Repeated Word for Word as I Heard It" is a fictional portrait of a former slave who presages one of the most beloved characters in American literature—the runaway slave Jim, from* Huckleberry Finn. *Through the monologue of "Aunt Rachel," who spins a tale in a dialect that is authentic but never opaque, Twain offers up an implicit denunciation of the cruelties of slav-ery and one of the most poignant sketches he ever produced.*

It was summer time, and twilight. We were sitting on the porch of the farm-house, on the summit of the hill, and "Aunt Rachel" was sitting re-spectfully below our level, on the steps,—for she was our servant, and col-ored. She was of mighty frame and stature; she was sixty years old, but her eye was undimmed and her strength unabated. She was a cheerful, hearty soul, and it was no more trouble for her to laugh than it is for a bird to sing. She was under fire, now, as usual when the day was done. That is to say, she was being chaffed without mercy, and was enjoying it. She would let off peal after peal of laughter, and then sit with her face in her hands and shake with throes of enjoyment which she could no longer get breath enough to express. At such a moment as this a thought occurred to me, and I said:—

"Aunt Rachel, how is it that you've lived sixty years and never had any trouble?"

She stopped quaking. She paused, and there was a moment of silence. She turned her face over her shoulder toward me, and said, without even a smile in her voice:—

"Misto C——, is you in 'arnest?"

It surprised me a good deal; and it sobered my manner and my speech, too. I said:—

"Why, I thought—that is, I meant—why, you *can't* have had any trouble. I've never heard you sigh, and never seen your eye when there wasn't a laugh in it."

She faced fairly around, now, and was full of earnestness.

"Has I had any trouble? Misto C—, I's gwyne to tell you, den I leave it to you. I was bawn down 'mongst de slaves; I knows all 'bout slavery, 'case I ben one of 'em my own se'f. Well, sah, my ole man—dat's my husban'—he was lovin' an' kind to me, jist as kind as you is to yo' own wife. An' we had children—seven chil'en—an' we loved dem chil'en jist de same as you loves yo' chil'en. Dey was black, but de Lord can't make no chil'en so black but what dey mother loves 'em an' wouldn't give 'em up, no, not for anything dat's in dis whole world.

"Well, sah, I was raised in Ole Fo'-ginny, but my mother she was raised in Maryland; an' my *souls*! she was turrible when she'd git started! My *lan*'! but she'd make de fur fly! When she'd git into dem tantrums, she always had one word dat she said. She'd straighten herse'f up an' put her fists in her hips an' say, 'I want you to understan' dat I wan't bawn in de mash to be fool' by trash! I's one o' de ole Blue Hen's Chickens, *I* is!' 'Ca'se, you see, dat's what folks dat's bawn in Maryland calls deyselves, an' dey's proud of it. Well, dat was her word. I don't ever forgit it, beca'se she said it so much, an' beca'se she said it one day when my little Henry tore his wris' awful, an' most busted his head, right up at de top of his forehead, an' de niggers didn't fly aroun' fas' enough to 'tend to him. An' when dey talk' back at her, she up an' she says, 'Look-a-heah!' she says, 'I want you niggers to understan' dat I wa'n't bawn in de mash to be fool' by trash! I's one o' de ole Blue Hen's Chickens, *I* is!' an' den she clar' dat kitchen an' bandage' up de chile herse'f. So I says dat word, too, when I's riled.

"Well, bymeby my ole mistis say she's broke, an' she got to sell all de niggers on de place. An' when I heah dat dey gwyne to sell us all off at action in Richmon', oh de good gracious! I know what dat mean!"

Aunt Rachel had gradually risen, while she warmed to her subject, and now she towered above us, black against the stars.

"Dey put chains on us an' put us on a stan' as high as dis po'ch,—twenty foot high,—an' all de people stood aroun', crowds an' crowds. An' dey'd come up dah an' look at us all roun', an' squeeze our arm, an' make us git up an' walk, an' den say, 'Dis one don't 'mount to much.' An' dey sole my ole man, an' took him away, an' dey begin to sell my chil'en an' take *dem* away, an' I begin to cry; an' de man say, 'Shet up yo' dam blubberin',' an' hit me on de mouf wid his han'. An' when de las' one was gone but my little Henry, I grab' *him* clost up to my breas' so, an' I ris up an' says, 'You shan't take him away,' I says; 'I'll kill de man dat tetches him!' I says. But my little Henry whisper an' say, 'I gwyne to run away, an' den I work an' buy yo' freedom.' Oh, bless de chile, he always so good! But dey got him—dey got him, de men did; but I took and tear de clo'es mos' off of 'em, an' beat 'em over de head wid my chain; an' *dey* give it to *me*, too, but I didn't mine dat.

"Well, dah was my ole man gone, 'an all my chil'en, all my seven chil'en—an' six of 'em I hain't set eyes on ag'in to dis day, an' dat's twenty-two year ago las' Easter. De man dat bought me b'long' in Newbern, an' he took me dah. Well, bymeby de years roll on an' de waw come. My marster he was a Confedrit colonel, an' I was his family's cook. So when de Unions took dat town, dey all run away an' lef' me all by myse'f wid de other niggers in dat mons'us big house. So de big Union officers move in dah, an' dey ask would I cook for *dem*. 'Lord bless you,' says I, 'dat's what I's *for*.'

"Dey wa'n't no small-fry officers, mine you, dey was de biggest dey is; an' de way dey made dem sojers mosey roun'! De Gen'l he tole me to boss dat kitchen; an' he say, 'If anybody come meddlin' wid you, you jist make 'em walk chalk; don't you be afeard,' he say; 'you's 'mong frens, now.'

"Well, I thinks to myse'f, if my little Henry ever got a chance to run away, he'd make to de Norf, o'course. So one day I comes in dah whah de big officers was, in de parlor, an' I drops a kurtchy, so, an' I up an' tole 'em 'bout my Henry, dey a-listenin' to my troubles jist de same as if I was white folks; an' I says, 'What I come for is beca'se if he got away and got up Norf whah you gemmen comes from, you might 'a' seen him, maybe, an' could tell me so as I could fine him ag'in; he was very little, an' he had a sk-yar on his lef' wris', an' at de top of his forehead.' Den dey mournful, an' de Gen'l say, 'How long sence you los' him?' an' I say, 'Thirteen year.' Den de Gen'l say, 'He wouldn't be little no mo', now—he's a man!'

"I never thought o' dat befo'! He was only dat little feller to *me*, yit. I never thought 'bout him growin' up an' bein' big. But I see it den. None o' de gemmen had run acrost him, so dey couldn't do nothin' for me. But all dat time, do' I didn't know it, my Henry *was* run off to de Norf, years an' years, an' he was a barber, too, an' worked for hisse'f. An' bymeby, when de waw come, he ups an' he says, 'I's done barberin',' he says; 'I's gwyne to fine my ole mammy, less'n she's dead.' So he sole out an' went to whah dey was recruitin', an' hired hisse'f out to de colonel for his servant; an' den he went froo de battles everywhah, huntin' his ole mammy; yes indeedy, he'd hire to fust one officer an' den another, tell he'd ransacked de whole Souf; but you see *I* didn't know nuffin 'bout *dis*. How was *I* gwyne to know it?

"Well, one night we had a big sojer ball; de sojers dah at Newbern was always havin' balls an' carryin' on. Dey had 'em in my kitchen, heaps o' times, 'ca'se it was so big. Mine you, I was *down* on sich doin's; beca'se my place was wid de officers, an' it rasp' me to have dem common sojers cavortin' roun' my kitchen like dat. But I alway' stood aroun' an' kep' things straight, I did; an' sometimes dey'd git my dander up, 'an den I'd make 'em clar dat kitchen, mine I *tell* you!

"Well, one night—it was a Friday night—dey comes a whole plattoon f'm a *nigger* ridgment dat was on guard at de house,—de house was headquarters, you know,—an' den I was jist a-*bilin'*! Mad? I was jist a-*boomin'*! I swelled aroun', an' swelled aroun'; I jist was a-itchin' for 'em to do somefin for to start me. An' dey was a-waltzin' an a-dancin'! *my!* but dey was havin' a time! an' I jist a-swellin' an' a-swellin' up! Pooty soon, 'long comes *sich* a spruce young nigger a-sailin' down de room wid a yaller wench roun' de wais'; an' roun' an' roun' an' roun' dey went, enough to make a body drunk to look at 'em; an' when dey got abreas' o' me, dey went to kin' o' balancin' aroun', fust on one leg, an' den on t'other, an' smilin' at my big red turban, an' makin' fun, an' I ups an' says, '*Git* along wid you!—rubbage!' De young man's face kin' o' changed, all of a sudden, for 'bout a second, but den he went to smilin' ag'in, same as he was befo'. Well, 'bout dis time, in comes some niggers dat played music an' b'long' to de ban', an' dey *never* could git along widout puttin' on airs. An' de very fust air dey put on dat night, I lit into 'em! Dey laughed, an' dat made me wuss. De res' o' de niggers got to laughin', an' den my soul *alive* but I was hot! My eye was jist a-blazin'! I jist straightened myself up, so,—jist as I is now, plum to de ceilin', mos',—an' I digs my fists into my hips, an' I says, 'Look-a-heah!' I says, 'I want you niggers to understan' dat I wa'n't bawn in de mash to be fool' by trash! I's one o' de ole Blue Hen's Chickens, *I* is!' an' den I see dat young man stan' a-starin' an' stiff, lookin' kin' o' up at de ceilin' like he fo'got somefin, an' couldn't 'member it no mo'. Well, I jist march' on dem niggers,—so, lookin' like a gen'l,—an' dey jist cave' away befo' me an' out at de do'. An' as dis young man was a-goin' out, I heah him say to another nigger, 'Jim,' he says, 'you go 'long an' tell de cap'n I be on han' 'bout eight o'clock in de mawnin'; dey's somefin on my mine,' he says; 'I don't sleep no mo' dis night. You go 'long,' he says, 'an' leave me by my own se'f.'

"Dis was 'bout one o'clock in de mawnin'. Well, 'bout seven, I was up an' on han', gittin' de officers' breakfast. I was a-stoopin' down by de stove,—jist so, same as if yo' foot was de stove,—an' I'd opened de stove do wid my right han',—so, pushin' it back, jist as I pushes yo' foot,—an' I'd jist got de pan o' hot biscuits in my han' an' was 'bout to raise up, when I see a black face come aroun' under mine, an' de eyes a-lookin' up into mine, jist as I's a-lookin' up clost under yo' face now; an' I jist stopped *right dah*, an' never budged! jist gazed, an' gazed, so; an' de pan begin to tremble, an' all of a sudden I *knowed*! De pan drop' on de flo' an' I grab his lef' han' an' shove back his sleeve,—jist so, as I's doin' to you,—an' den I goes for his forehead an' push de hair back, so, an' 'Boy!' I says, 'if you an't my Henry, what is you doin' wid dis welt on yo' wris' an' dat sk-yar on yo' forehead? De Lord God ob heaven be praise', I got my own ag'in!

"Oh, no, Misto C—, *I* hain't had no trouble. An' no *joy*!"

A Telephonic Conversation

MARK TWAIN ‖ 1880

*In 1880, four years after Alexander Graham Bell filed a patent for the
telephone, Twain—by then baronially ensconced in a Victorian mansion
in Hartford, Connecticut—became one of the first Americans to have the
revolutionary invention installed in his home. He was both amused and
irritated by the new device, which subjected him to "that queerest of all
the queer things in this world,—a conversation with only one end to it,"
and composed this brief dispatch to vent his befuddlement.*

I consider that a conversation by telephone—when you are simply sitting
by and not taking any part in that conversation—is one of the solemnest
curiosities of this modern life. Yesterday I was writing a deep article on a
sublime philosophical subject while such a conversation was going on in
the room. I notice that one can always write best when somebody is talking through a telephone close by. Well, the thing began in this way. A member of our household came in and asked me to have our house put into
communication with Mr. Bagley's, down town. I have observed, in many
cities, that the gentle sex always shrink from calling up the central office
themselves. I don't know why, but they do. So I touched the bell, and this
talk ensued:—

Central Office. [Gruffly.] Hello!

I. Is it the Central Office?

C. O. Of course it is. What do you want?

I. Will you switch me on to the Bagleys, please?

C. O. All right. Just keep your ear to the telephone.

Then I heard, *k-look, k-look, k'look—klook-klook-klook-look-look!* then
a horrible "gritting" of teeth, and finally a piping female voice: "Y-e-s? [Ris-
ing inflection.] Did you wish to speak to me?"

Without answering, I handed the telephone to the applicant, and sat
down. Then followed that queerest of all the queer things in this world,—
a conversation with only one end to it. You hear questions asked; you don't
hear the answer. You hear invitations given; you hear no thanks in return.
You have listening pauses of dead silence, followed by apparently irrelevant
and unjustifiable exclamations of glad surprise, or sorrow, or dismay. You
can't make head or tail of the talk, because you never hear anything that
the person at the other end of the wire says. Well, I heard the following

remarkable series of observations, all from the one tongue, and all shouted,—for you can't ever persuade the gentle sex to speak gently into a telephone:—

Yes? Why, how did *that* happen?

Pause.

What did you say?

Pause.

Oh, no, I don't think it was.

Pause.

No! Oh, no, I didn't mean *that*. I meant, put it in while it is still boiling,—or just before it *comes* to a boil.

Pause.

WHAT?

Pause.

I turned it over with a back stitch on the selvage edge.

Pause.

Yes, I like that way, too; but I think it's better to baste it on with Valenciennes or bombazine, or something of that sort. It gives it such an air,—and attracts so much notice.

Pause.

It's forty-ninth Deuteronomy, sixty-fourth to ninety-seventh inclusive. I think we ought all to read it often.

Pause.

Perhaps so; I generally use a hair-pin.

Pause.

What did you say? [*Aside*] Children, do be quiet!

Pause.

Oh! B *flat!* Dear me, I thought you said it was the cat!

Pause.

Since *when*?

Pause.

Why, *I* never heard of it.

Pause.

You astound me! It seems utterly impossible!

Pause.

Who did?

Pause.

Good-ness gracious!

Pause.

Well, what *is* this world coming to? Was it right in *church*?

Pause.

And was her *mother* there?

Pause.

Why, Mrs. Bagley, I should have died of humiliation! What did they *do*?

Long Pause.

I can't be perfectly sure, because I haven't the notes by me; but I think it goes something like this: te-rolly-loll-loll, loll lolly-loll-loll, O tolly-loll-loll-*lee-ly-li-i*-do! And then *repeat*, you know.

Pause.

Yes, I think it *is* very sweet,—and very solemn and impressive, if you get the andantino and the pianissimo right.

Pause.

Oh, gum-drops, gum-drops! But I never allow them to eat striped candy. And of course they *can't*, till they get their teeth, any way.

Pause.

What?

Pause.

Oh, not in the least,—go right on. He's here writing,—it doesn't bother *him*.

Pause.

Very well, I'll come if I can. [*Aside.*] Dear me, how it does tire a person's arm to hold this thing up so long! I wish she'd—

Pause.

Oh, no, not at all; I *like* to talk,—but I'm afraid I'm keeping you from your affairs.

Pause.

Visitors?

Pause.

No, we never use butter on them.

Pause.

Yes, that is a very good way; but all the cook-books say they are very unhealthy when they are out of season. And *he* doesn't like them, any way,—especially canned.

Pause.

Oh, I think that is too high for them; we have never paid over fifty cents a bunch.

Pause.

Must you go? Well, *good*-by.

Pause.

Yes, I think so. *Good*-by.

Pause.

Four, o'clock then—I'll be ready. *Good*-by.

Pause.

Thank you ever so much. *Good*-by.

Pause.

Oh, not at all!—just as fresh—*Which?* Oh, I'm glad to hear you say that. *Good*-by.

[Hangs up the telephone and says, "Oh, it *does* tire a person's arm so!"]

A man delivers a single brutal "Good-by," and that is the end of it. Not so with the gentle sex,—I say it in their praise; they cannot abide abruptness.

The American Forests

JOHN MUIR ‖ 1897

*John Muir (1838–1914) not only looked like an Old Testament prophet;
he sounded like one as well. His flowing white beard, deep-set eyes,
and wiry frame were a perfect match for the thunderclap cadences and
righteous urgency of his prose. It's not hard to understand how Muir
became the godfather of the American environmental movement. From
his childhood in the Scottish countryside, his readings of Thoreau, and
his lengthy travels through the American West, Muir developed a deep,
almost religious appreciation for the natural world and a horror of
any human power that would seek to exploit it for profit. His relentless
campaign to save the American wilderness—he was the founder of the
Sierra Club—had far-reaching effects, leading directly to the establishment of Yosemite National Park, in 1890, and the preservation of millions of acres of forests. The following is the first of seventeen essays that
Muir published in* The Atlantic *and is perhaps his most enduring clarion call for an immediate end to the destruction of the country's woodlands by logging companies and settlers. "The American Forests" helped
reawaken public support at a time when the conservation movement
faced intense political opposition in Congress and helped persuade President Theodore Roosevelt, who camped with Muir in Yosemite in 1903, to
create the U.S. Forest Service and expand the park to its present size of
more than 1,100 square miles.*

The forests of America, however slighted by man, must have been a great
delight to God; for they were the best he ever planted. The whole continent
was a garden, and from the beginning it seemed to be favored above all the
other wild parks and gardens of the globe. To prepare the ground, it was
rolled and sifted in seas with infinite loving deliberation and forethought,
lifted into the light, submerged and warmed over and over again, pressed
and crumpled into folds and ridges, mountains and hills, subsoiled with
heaving volcanic fires, ploughed and ground and sculptured into scenery
and soil with glaciers and rivers,—every feature growing and changing
from beauty to beauty, higher and higher. And in the fullness of time it was
planted in groves, and belts, and broad, exuberant, mantling forests, with
the largest, most varied, most fruitful, and most beautiful trees in the
world. Bright seas made its border with wave embroidery and icebergs;

gray deserts were outspread in the middle of it, mossy tundras on the north, savannas on the south, and blooming prairies and plains; while lakes and rivers shone through all the vast forests and openings, and happy birds and beasts gave delightful animation. Everywhere, everywhere over all the blessed continent, there were beauty, and melody, and kindly, wholesome, foodful abundance.

These forests were composed of about five hundred species of trees, all of them in some way useful to man, ranging in size from twenty-five feet in height and less than one foot in diameter at the ground to four hundred feet in height and more than twenty feet in diameter,—lordly monarchs proclaiming the gospel of beauty like apostles. For many a century after the ice-ploughs were melted, nature fed them and dressed them every day; working like a man, a loving, devoted, painstaking gardener; fingering every leaf and flower and mossy furrowed bole; bending, trimming, modeling, balancing, painting them with the loveliest colors; bringing over them now clouds with cooling shadows and showers, now sunshine; fanning them with gentle winds and rustling their leaves; exercising them in every fibre with storms, and pruning them; loading them with flowers and fruit, loading them with snow, and ever making them more beautiful as the years rolled by. Wide-branching oak and elm in endless variety, walnut and maple, chestnut and beech, ilex and locust, touching limb to limb, spread a leafy translucent canopy along the coast of the Atlantic over the wrinkled folds and ridges of the Alleghanies,—a green billowy sea in summer, golden and purple in autumn, pearly gray like a steadfast frozen mist of interlacing branches and sprays in leafless, restful winter.

To the southward stretched dark, level-topped cypresses in knobby, tangled swamps, grassy savannas in the midst of them like lakes of light, groves of gay sparkling spice-trees, magnolias and palms, glossy-leaved and blooming and shining continually. To the northward, over Maine and the Ottawa, rose hosts of spiry, rosiny evergreens,—white pine and spruce, hemlock and cedar, shoulder to shoulder, laden with purple cones, their myriad needles sparkling and shimmering, covering hills and swamps, rocky headlands and domes, ever bravely aspiring and seeking the sky; the ground in their shade now snow-clad and frozen, now mossy and flowery; beaver meadows here and there, full of lilies and grass; lakes gleaming like eyes, and a silvery embroidery of rivers and creeks watering and brightening all the vast glad wilderness.

Thence westward were oak and elm, hickory and tupelo, gum and liriodendron, sassafras and ash, linden and laurel, spreading on ever wider in glorious exuberance over the great fertile basin of the Mississippi, over damp level bottoms, low dimpling hollows, and round dotting hills, embosoming sunny prairies and cheery park openings, half sunshine, half shade; while a dark wilderness of pines covered the region around the Great Lakes. Thence still westward swept the forests to right and left around grassy plains and deserts a thousand miles wide: irrepressible hosts of spruce and pine, aspen and willow, nut-pine and juniper, cactus and yucca, caring nothing for drought, extending undaunted from mountain to mountain, over mesa and desert, to join the darkening multitudes of pines that covered the high Rocky ranges and the glorious forests along the coast of the moist and balmy Pacific, where new species of pine, giant cedars and spruces, silver firs and sequoias, kings of their race, growing close together like grass in a meadow, poised their brave domes and spires in the sky three hundred feet above the ferns and the lilies that enameled the ground; towering serene through the long centuries, preaching God's forestry fresh from heaven.

Here the forests reached their highest development. Hence they went wavering northward over icy Alaska, brave spruce and fir, poplar and birch, by the coasts and the rivers, to within sight of the Arctic Ocean. American forests! the glory of the world! Surveyed thus from the east to the west, from the north to the south, they are rich beyond thought, immortal, immeasurable, enough and to spare for every feeding, sheltering beast and bird, insect and son of Adam; and nobody need have cared had there been no pines in Norway, no cedars and deodars on Lebanon and the Himalayas, no vine-clad selvas in the basin of the Amazon. With such variety, harmony, and triumphant exuberance, even nature, it would seem, might have rested content with the forests of North America, and planted no more.

So they appeared a few centuries ago when they were rejoicing in wildness. The Indians with stone axes could do them no more harm than could gnawing beavers and browsing moose. Even the fires of the Indians and the fierce shattering lightning seemed to work together only for good in clearing spots here and there for smooth garden prairies, and openings for sunflowers seeking the light. But when the steel axe of the white man rang out in the startled air their doom was sealed. Every tree heard the bodeful sound, and pillars of smoke gave the sign in the sky.

I suppose we need not go mourning the buffaloes. In the nature of things they had to give place to better cattle, though the change might have been made without barbarous wickedness. Likewise many of nature's five hundred kinds of wild trees had to make way for orchards and cornfields. In the settlement and civilization of the country, bread more than timber or beauty was wanted; and in the blindness of hunger, the early settlers, claiming Heaven as their guide, regarded God's trees as only a larger kind of pernicious weeds, extremely hard to get rid of. Accordingly, with no eye to the future, these pious destroyers waged interminable forest wars; chips flew thick and fast; trees in their beauty fell crashing by millions, smashed to confusion, and the smoke of their burning has been rising to heaven more than two hundred years. After the Atlantic coast from Maine to Georgia had been mostly cleared and scorched into melancholy ruins, the overflowing multitude of bread and money seekers poured over the Alleghanies into the fertile middle West, spreading ruthless devastation ever wider and farther over the rich valley of the Mississippi and the vast shadowy pine region about the Great Lakes. Thence still westward the invading horde of destroyers called settlers made its fiery way over the broad Rocky Mountains, felling and burning more fiercely than ever, until at last it has reached the wild side of the continent, and entered the last of the great aboriginal forests on the shores of the Pacific.

Surely, then, it should not be wondered at that lovers of their country, bewailing its baldness, are now crying aloud, "Save what is left of the forests!" Clearing has surely now gone far enough; soon timber will be scarce, and not a grove will be left to rest in or pray in. The remnant protected will yield plenty of timber, a perennial harvest for every right use, without further diminution of its area, and will continue to cover the springs of the rivers that rise in the mountains and give irrigating waters to the dry valleys at their feet, prevent wasting floods and be a blessing to everybody forever.

Every other civilized nation in the world has been compelled to care for its forests, and so must we if waste and destruction are not to go on to the bitter end, leaving America as barren as Palestine or Spain. In its calmer moments in the midst of bewildering hunger and war and restless over-industry, Prussia has learned that the forest plays an important part in human progress, and that the advance in civilization only makes it more indispensable. . . . But the state woodlands are not allowed to lie idle. On the contrary, they are made to produce as much timber as is possible without spoiling them. In the administration of its forests, the state righteously considers itself bound to treat them as a trust for the nation as a whole, and to keep in view the common good of the people for all time.

So far our government has done nothing effective with its forests, though the best in the world, but is like a rich and foolish spendthrift who has inherited a magnificent estate in perfect order, and then has left his rich fields and meadows, forests and parks, to be sold and plundered and wasted at will, depending on their inexhaustible abundance. Now it is plain that the forests are not inexhaustible, and that quick measures must be taken if ruin is to be avoided. Year by year the remnant is growing smaller before the axe and fire, while the laws in existence provide neither for the protection of the timber from destruction nor for its use where it is most needed.

It is not generally known that, notwithstanding the immense quantities of timber cut every year for foreign and home markets and mines, from five to ten times as much is destroyed as is used, chiefly by running forest fires that only the federal government can stop. Travelers through the West in summer are not likely to forget the fire-work displayed along the various railway tracks. Thoreau, when contemplating the destruction of the forests on the east side of the continent, said that soon the country would be so bald that every man would have to grow whiskers to hide its nakedness, but he thanked God that at least the sky was safe. Had he gone West he would have found out that the sky was not safe; for all through the summer months, over most of the mountain regions, the smoke of mill and forest fires is so thick and black that no sunbeam can pierce it. The whole sky, with clouds, sun, moon, and stars, is simply blotted out. There is no real sky and no scenery. Not a mountain is left in the landscape. At least none is in sight from the lowlands, and they all might as well be on the moon, as far as scenery is concerned.

The half dozen transcontinental railroad companies advertise the beauties of their lines in gorgeous many-colored folders, each claiming its as the "scenic route." "The route of superior desolation"—the smoke, dust, and ashes route—would be a more truthful description. Every train rolls on through dismal smoke and barbarous melancholy ruins; and the companies might well cry in their advertisements: "Come! travel our way. Ours is the blackest. . . . The sky is black and the ground is black, and on either side there is a continuous border of black stumps and logs and blasted trees appealing to heaven for help as if still half alive, and their mute eloquence is most interestingly touching."

Of course a way had to be cleared through the woods. But the felled timber is not worked up into firewood for the engines and into lumber for the company's use; it is left lying in vulgar confusion, and is fired from time to time by sparks from locomotives or by the workmen camping along the line. The fires, whether accidental or set, are allowed to run into the woods as far as they may, thus assuring comprehensive destruction.

Notwithstanding all the waste and use which have been going on unchecked like a storm for more than two centuries, it is not yet too late, though it is high time, for the government to begin a rational administration of its forests. About seventy million acres it still owns,—enough for all the country, if wisely used. These residual forests are generally on mountain slopes, just where they are doing the most good, and where their removal would be followed by the greatest number of evils; the lands they cover are too rocky and high for agriculture, and can never be made as valuable for any other crop as for the present crop of trees. It has been shown over and over again that if these mountains were to be stripped of their trees and underbrush, and kept bare and sodless by hordes of sheep and the innumerable fires the shepherds set, besides those of the millmen, prospectors, shake-makers, and all sorts of adventurers, both lowlands and mountains would speedily become little better than deserts, compared with their present beneficent fertility. During heavy rainfalls and while the winter accumulations of snow were melting, the larger streams would swell into destructive torrents; cutting deep, rugged-edged gullies, carrying away the fertile humus and soil as well as sand and rocks, filling up and overflowing their lower channels, and covering the lowland fields with raw detritus. Drought and barrenness would follow.

Yet the dawn of a new day in forestry is breaking. Honest citizens see that only the rights of the government are being trampled, not those of the settlers. Merely what belongs to all alike is reserved, and every acre that is left should be held together under the federal government as a basis for a general policy of administration for the public good. The people will not always be deceived by selfish opposition, whether from lumber and mining corporations or from sheepmen and prospectors, however cunningly brought forward underneath fables and gold.

Emerson says that things refuse to be mismanaged long. An exception would seem to be found in the case of our forests, which have been mismanaged rather long, and now come desperately near being like smashed eggs and spilt milk. Still, in the long run the world does not move backward. The wonderful advance made in the last few years, in creating four national parks in the West, and thirty forest reservations, embracing nearly forty million acres; and in the planting of the borders of streets and highways and spacious parks in all the great cities, to satisfy the natural taste and hunger for landscape beauty and righteousness that God has put, in some measure, into every human being and animal, shows the trend of awakening public opinion. The making of the far-famed New York Central Park was opposed by even good men, with misguided pluck, perseverance, and ingenuity; but straight right won its way, and now that park is appreciated. So we confidently believe it will be with our great national parks and forest reservations. There will be a period of indifference on the part of the rich, sleepy with wealth, and of the toiling millions, sleepy with poverty, most of whom never saw a forest; a period of screaming protest and objection from the plunderers, who are as unconscionable and enterprising as Satan. But light is surely coming, and the friends of destruction will preach and bewail in vain.

Any fool can destroy trees. They cannot run away; and if they could, they would still be destroyed,—chased and hunted down as long as fun or a dollar could be got out of their bark hides, branching horns, or magnificent bole backbones. Few that fell trees plant them; nor would planting avail much towards getting back anything like the noble primeval forests. During a man's life only saplings can be grown, in the place of the old trees—tens of centuries old—that have been destroyed. It took more than three thousand years to make some of the trees in these Western woods,— trees that are still standing in perfect strength and beauty, waving and singing in the mighty forests of the Sierra. Through all the wonderful, eventful centuries since Christ's time—and long before that—God has cared for these trees, saved them from drought, disease, avalanches, and a thousand straining, leveling tempests and floods; but he cannot save them from fools,—only Uncle Sam can do that.

Can a Catholic Be President?

ALFRED E. SMITH ‖ 1927

In 1927, Ellery Sedgwick, the eighth editor of The Atlantic, *instigated a seminal debate in American political history. Prompted by the likelihood that the Democratic governor of New York, Al Smith, would become the first Roman Catholic to secure a major party's nomination for president—and by the deep reserves of antipathy in some parts of the country to the idea of a Catholic in the White House—Sedgwick invited a prominent Episcopalian lawyer, Charles Marshall, to argue the church–state issue in the magazine's pages. Marshall obliged with "An Open Letter to the Honorable Alfred E. Smith," a scholarly discourse that used an array of papal bulls, encyclicals, and other church documents to make the case that "there is a conflict between authoritative Roman Catholic claims on one side and our constitutional law and principles on the other." At first Governor Smith, who was not exactly a devout Catholic, declined to reply: "What the hell is an encyclical?" he reportedly asked aides. But his staff persuaded him to join the debate, and with the help of Francis Duffy, a well-known World War I chaplain, he produced this historic affirmation of the fundamental compatibility of political service and religious belief. Smith's essay was widely praised as a brilliant rearticulation of the Fourth Amendment, but it fell short politically. In 1928, Smith won the Democratic nomination but lost the general election by a landslide to the Republican Herbert Hoover. Nevertheless, the article helped change the attitudes of many Americans about having a Catholic in the White House, and it is difficult to imagine John F. Kennedy's successful presidential run, thirty-two years later, without Smith's trailblazing example.*

CHARLES C. MARSHALL, ESQ.

Dear Sir:—

In your open letter to me in the April *Atlantic Monthly* you "impute" to American Catholics views which, if held by them, would leave open to question the loyalty and devotion to this country and its Constitution of more than twenty million American Catholic citizens. I am grateful to you for defining this issue in the open and for your courteous expression of the satisfaction it will bring to my fellow citizens for me to give "a disclaimer of the convictions" thus imputed. Without mental reservation I can and do make that disclaimer. These convictions are held neither by me nor by any other American Catholic, as far as I know. I should be a poor American and a poor Catholic alike if I injected religious discussion into a political campaign. Therefore I would ask you to accept this answer from me not as a candidate for any public office but as an American citizen, honored with high elective office, meeting a challenge to his patriotism and his intellectual integrity.

Taking your letter as a whole and reducing it to commonplace English, you imply that there is conflict between religious loyalty to the Catholic faith and patriotic loyalty to the United States. Everything that has actually happened to me during my long public career leads me to know that no such thing as that is true. I have taken an oath of office in this State nineteen times. Each time I swore to defend and maintain the Constitution of the United States. All of this represents a period of public service in elective office almost continuous since 1903. I have never known any conflict between my official duties and my religious belief. No such conflict could exist. Certainly the people of this State recognize no such conflict. They have testified to my devotion to public duty by electing me to the highest office within their active gift four times. If there were conflict, I, of all men, could not have escaped it, because I have not been a silent man, but a battler for social and political reform. These battles would in their very nature disclose this conflict if there were any. Moreover, I am unable to understand how anything that I was taught to believe as a Catholic could possibly be in conflict with what is good citizenship. The essence of my faith is built upon the Commandments of God. The law of the land is built upon the Commandments of God. There can be no conflict between them.

I come now to the speculation with which theorists have played for generations as to the respective functions of Church and State. You claim that the Roman Catholic Church holds that, if conflict arises, the Church must prevail over the State. You write as though there were some Catholic authority or tribunal to decide with respect to such conflict. Of course there is no such thing. As Dr. Ryan [John A. Ryan, professor of moral theology at the Catholic University of America] writes: "The Catholic doctrine concedes, nay, maintains, that the State is coordinate with the Church and equally independent and supreme in its own distinct sphere."

What is the Protestant position? The Articles of Religion of your Protestant Episcopal Church (XXXVII) declare: "The Power of the Civil Magistrate extendeth to all men, as well Clergy as Laity, in all things temporal; but hath no authority in things purely spiritual."

Your Church, just as mine, is voicing the injunction of our common Saviour to render unto Caesar the things that are Caesar's and unto God the things that are God's.

What is this conflict about which you talk? It may exist in some lands which do not guarantee religious freedom. But in the wildest dreams of your imagination you cannot conjure up a possible conflict between religious principle and political duty in the United States, except on the unthinkable hypothesis, that some law were to be passed which violated the common morality of all God-fearing men. And if you can conjure up such a conflict, how would a Protestant resolve it? Obviously by the dictates of his conscience. That is exactly what a Catholic would do. There is no ecclesiastical tribunal which would have the slightest claim upon the obedience of Catholic communicants in the resolution of such a conflict. As Cardinal Gibbons [James Gibbons, archbishop of Baltimore from 1877 to 1921] said of the supposition that "the Pope were to issue commands in purely civil matters":—

"He would be offending not only against civil society, but against God, and violating an authority as truly from God as his own. Any Catholic who clearly recognized this would not be bound to obey the Pope; or rather his conscience would bind him absolutely to disobey, because with Catholics conscience is the supreme law which under no circumstances can we ever lawfully disobey."

Under our system of government the electorate entrusts to its officers of every faith the solemn duty of action according to the dictates of conscience. I may fairly refer once more to my own record to support these truths. No man, cleric or lay, has ever directly or indirectly attempted to exercise Church influence on my administration of any office I have ever held, nor asked me to show special favor to Catholics or exercise discrimination against non-Catholics. It is a well-known fact that I have made all of my appointments to public office on the basis of merit and have never asked any man about his religious belief.

I summarize my creed as an American Catholic. I believe in the worship of God according to the faith and practice of the Roman Catholic Church. I recognize no power in the institutions of my Church to interfere with the operations of the Constitution of the United States or the enforcement of the law of the land. I believe in absolute freedom of conscience for all men and in equality of all churches, all sects, and all beliefs before the law as a matter of right and not as a matter of favor. I believe in the absolute separation of Church and State and in the strict enforcement of the provisions of the Constitution that Congress shall make no law respecting an establishment of religion or prohibiting the free exercise thereof. I believe that no tribunal of any church has any power to make any decree of any force in the law of the land, other than to establish the status of its own communicants within its own church. I believe in the support of the public school as one of the cornerstones of American liberty. I believe in the right of every parent to choose whether his child shall be educated in the public school or in a religious school supported by those of his own faith. I believe in the principled noninterference by this country in the internal affairs of other nations and that we should stand steadfastly against any such interference by whomsoever it may be urged. And I believe in the common brotherhood of man under the common fatherhood of God.

In this spirit I join with fellow Americans of all creeds in a fervent prayer that never again in this land will any public servant be challenged because of the faith in which he has tried to walk humbly with his God.

Very truly yours,
Alfred E. Smith

Fifty Grand

ERNEST HEMINGWAY || 1927

To hear Ernest Hemingway (1899–1961) tell it, his first appearance in
The Atlantic *represented a career watershed. "From 1919 to 1927 he sent
stories to American magazines without being able to sell one until the*
Atlantic Monthly *published a story called 'Fifty Grand,' " Hemingway
recalled in a 1936 autobiographical sketch, referring to himself (characteristically) in the third person. Although Hemingway had published*
The Sun Also Rises *the year before, he was still a struggling writer living
in Paris when he wrote this landmark tale of greed, brutality, and betrayal in the boxing world. "Fifty Grand," which came to* The Atlantic
*after being rejected by at least half a dozen other respected magazines—
including* Collier's, Scribner's, *and* The Saturday Evening Post—*was
the first of Hemingway's lengthy stories to appear in an American publication and is considered by critics to be one of his finest. With its
machine-gun dialogue and stripped-down prose, the story helped establish its author as a new and original talent and propelled a career that
would encompass both the Nobel and Pulitzer Prizes.*

"How are you going yourself, Jack?" I asked him.

"You see this Walcott?" he says.

"Just in the gym."

"Well," Jack says, "I'm going to need a lot of luck with that boy."

"He can't hit you, Jack," Soldier said.

"I wish to hell he couldn't."

"He couldn't hit you with a handful of birdshot."

"Birdshot'd be all right," Jack says. "I wouldn't mind birdshot any."

"He looks easy to hit," I said.

"Sure," Jack says, "he ain't going to last long. He ain't going to last like
you and me, Jerry. But right now he's got everything."

"You'll left-hand him to death."

"Maybe," Jack says. "Sure. I got a chance to."

"Handle him like you handled Kid Lewis."

"Kid Lewis," Jack said. "That kike!"

The three of us, Jack Brennan, Soldier Bartlett, and I, were in Handley's. There were a couple of broads sitting at the next table to us. They had
been drinking.

"What do you mean, kike?" one of the broads says. "What do you mean, kike, you big Irish bum!"

"Sure," Jack says. "That's it."

"Kikes," this broad goes on. "They're always talking about kikes, these big Irishmen. What do you mean, kikes?"

"Come on. Let's get out of here."

"Kikes," this broad goes on. "Whoever saw you ever buy a drink? Your wife sews your pockets up every morning. These Irishmen and their kikes. Ted Lewis could lick you, too."

"Sure," Jack says. "And you give away a lot of things free, too, don't you?"

We went out. That was Jack. He could say what he wanted to when he wanted to say it.

Jack started training out at Danny Hogan's health farm over in Jersey. It was nice out there, but Jack didn't like it much. He didn't like being away from his wife and the kids, and he was sore and grouchy most of the time. He liked me and we got along fine together; and he liked Hogan, but after a while Soldier Bartlett commenced to get on his nerves. A kidder gets to be an awful thing around a camp if his stuff goes sort of sour. Soldier was always kidding Jack, just sort of kidding him all the time. It wasn't very funny and it wasn't very good, and it began to get to Jack.

It was sort of stuff like this. Jack would finish up with the weights and the bag and pull on the gloves. "You want to work?" he'd say to Soldier.

"Sure. How you want me to work?" Soldier would ask. "Want me to treat you rough like Walcott? Want me to knock you down a few times?"

"That's it," Jack would say. He didn't like it any, though.

One morning we were all out on the road. We'd been out quite a way and now we were coming back. We'd go along fast for three minutes and then walk a minute, and then go fast for three minutes again. Jack wasn't ever what you would call a sprinter. He'd move around fast enough in the ring if he had to, but he wasn't any too fast on the road. All the time we were walking Soldier Bartlett was kidding him. We came up the hill to the farmhouse.

"Well," says Jack, "you better go back to town, Soldier."

"What do you mean?"

"You better go back to town and stay there."

"What's the matter?"

"I'm sick of hearing you talk."

"Yes?" says Soldier.

"Yes," says Jack.

"You'll be a damn sight sicker when Walcott gets through with you."

"Sure," says Jack, "maybe I will. But I know I'm sick of you."

So Soldier went off on the train to town that same morning. I went down with him to the train. He was good and sore.

"I was just kidding him," he said. We were waiting on the platform. "He can't pull that stuff with me, Jerry."

"He's nervous and crabby," I said. "He's a good fellow, Soldier."

"The hell he is. The hell he's ever been a good fellow."

"Well," I said, "so long, Soldier."

The train had come in. He climbed up with his bag.

"So long, Jerry," he says. "You be in town before the fight?"

"I don't think so."

"See you then."

He went in and the conductor swung up and the train went out. I rode back to the farm in the cart. Jack was on the porch writing a letter to his wife. The mail had come and I got the papers and went over on the other side of the porch and sat down to read. Hogan came out the door and came over to me.

"Did he have a jam with Soldier?"

"Not a jam," I said. "He just told him to go back to town."

"I could see it coming," Hogan said. "He never liked Soldier much."

"No. He don't like many people."

"He's a pretty cold one," Hogan said.

"Well, he's always been fine to me."

"Me too," Hogan said. "I got no kick on him. He's a cold one, though."

Hogan went in through the screen door and I sat there on the porch and read the papers. It was just starting to get fall weather and it's nice country there in Jersey up in the hills, and after I read the paper through I sat there and looked out at the country and the road down below against the woods, with a car going along it, lifting the dust up. It was fine weather and pretty nice-looking country. Hogan came to the door and I said, "Say, Hogan, haven't you got anything to shoot out here?"

"No," Hogan said. "Only sparrows."

"Seen the paper?" I said to Hogan.

"What's in it?"

"Sande booted three of them in yesterday."

"I got that on the telephone last night."

"You follow them pretty close, Hogan?" I asked.

"Oh, I keep in touch with them."

"How about Jack?" I says. "Does he still play them?"

"Him?" said Hogan. "Can you see him doing it?"

Just then Jack came around the corner with the letter in his hand. He's wearing a sweater and an old pair of pants and boxing shoes.

"Got a stamp, Hogan?" he asks.

"Give me the letter," Hogan said. "I'll mail it for you."

"Say, Jack," I said. "Didn't you used to play the ponies?"

"Sure."

"I knew you did. I knew I used to see you out at Sheepshead."

"What did you lay off them for?" Hogan asked.

"Lost money."

Jack sat down on the porch by me. He leaned back against a post. He shut his eyes in the sun.

"Want a chair?" Hogan asked.

"No," said Jack. "This is fine."

"It's a nice day," I said. "It's pretty nice out in the country."

"I'd a damn sight rather be in town with the wife."

"Well, you only got another week."

"Yes," Jack says. "That's so."

We sat there on the porch. Hogan was inside at the office.

"What do you think about the shape I'm in?" Jack asked me.

"Well, you can't tell," I said. "You got a week to get around into form."

"Don't stall me."

"Well," I said, "you're not right."

"I'm not sleeping," Jack said.

"You'll be all right in a couple of days."

"No," says Jack, "I got the insomnia."

"What's on your mind?"

"I miss the wife."

"Have her come out."

"No. I'm too old for that."

"We'll take a long walk before you turn in, and get you good and tired."

"Tired!" Jack says. "I'm tired all the time."

He was that way all week. He wouldn't sleep at night and he'd get up in the morning feeling that way—you know, when you can't shut your hands.

"He's stale as poorhouse cake," Hogan said. "He's nothing."

"I never seen Walcott," I said.

"He'll kill him," said Hogan. "He'll tear him in two."

"Well," I said, "everybody's got to get it sometime."

"Not like this, though," Hogan said. "They'll think he never trained. It gives the farm a black eye."

"You hear what the reporters said about him?"

"Didn't I! They said he was awful. The said they oughtn't to let him fight."

"Well," I said, "they're always wrong, ain't they?"

"Yes," said Hogan. "But this time they're right."

"What the hell do they know about whether a man's right or not?"

"Well," said Hogan, "they're not such fools."

"All they did was pick Willard at Toledo. This Lardner, he's so wise now, ask him about when he picked Willard at Toledo."

"Aw, he wasn't out," Hogan said. "He only writes the big fights."

"I don't care who they are," I said. "What the hell do they know? They can write, maybe, but what the hell do they know?"

"You don't think Jack's in any shape, do you?" Hogan asked.

"No. He's through. All he needs is to have Corbett pick him to win for it to be all over."

"Well, Corbett'll pick him," Hogan says.

"Sure. He'll pick him."

That night Jack didn't sleep any either. The next morning was the last day before the fight. After breakfast we were out on the porch again.

"What do you think about, Jack, when you can't sleep?" I said.

"Oh, I worry," Jack says. "I worry about property I got up in the Bronx. I worry about property I got in Florida. I worry about the kids. I worry about the wife. Sometimes I think about fights. I think about that kike Ted Lewis and I get sore. I got some stocks and I worry about them. What the hell don't I think about?"

"Well," I said, "to-morrow night it'll all be over."

"Sure," said Jack. "That always helps a lot, don't it? That just fixes everything all up, I suppose. Sure."

He was sore all day. We didn't do any work. Jack just moved around a little to loosen up. He shadow-boxed a few rounds. He didn't even look good doing that. He skipped the rope a little while. He couldn't sweat.

"He'd be better not to do any work at all," Hogan said. We were standing watching him skip rope. "Don't he ever sweat at all any more?"

"He can't sweat."

"Do you suppose he's got the con? He never had any trouble making weight, did he?"

"No, he hasn't got any con. He just hasn't got anything inside any more."

"He ought to sweat," said Hogan.

Jack came over skipping the rope. He was skipping up and down in front of us, forward and back, crossing his arms every third time.

"Well," he says, "what are you buzzards talking about?"

"I don't think you ought to work any more," Hogan says. "You'll be stale."

"Wouldn't that be awful?" Jack says and skips away down the floor, slapping the rope hard.

THAT AFTERNOON John Collins showed up out at the farm. Jack was up in his room. John came out in a car from town. He had a couple of friends with him. The car stopped and they all got out.

"Where's Jack?" John asked me.

"Up in his room, lying down."

"Lying down?"

"Yes," I said.

"How is he?"

I looked at the two fellows that were with John.

"They're friends of his," John said.

"He's pretty bad," I said.

"What's the matter with him?"

"He don't sleep."

"Hell," John said. "That Irishman could never sleep."

"He isn't right," I said.

"Hell," John said. "He's never right. I've had him for ten years and he's never been right yet."

The fellows with him laughed.

"I want you to shake hands with Mr. Morgan and Mr. Steinfelt," John said. "This is Mr. Doyle. He's been training Jack."

"Glad to meet you," I said.

"Let's go up and see the boy," the fellow called Morgan said.

"Let's have a look at him," Steinfelt said.

We all went upstairs.

"Where's Hogan?" John asked.

"He's out in the barn with a couple of customers," I said.

"He got many people out here now?"

"Just two."

"Pretty quiet, ain't it?" Morgan said.

"Yes," I said. "It's pretty quiet."

We were outside Jack's room. John knocked on the door. There wasn't any answer.

"Maybe he's asleep," I said.

"What the hell's he sleeping in the daytime for?"

John turned the handle and we all went in. Jack was lying asleep on the bed. He was face down and his face was in the pillow. Both his arms were around the pillow.

"Hey, Jack!" John said to him.

Jack's head moved a little on the pillow. "Jack!" John says, leaning over him. Jack just dug a little deeper in the pillow. John touched him on the shoulder. Jack sat up and looked at us. He hadn't shaved and he was wearing an old sweater.

"Hell! Why can't you let me sleep?" he says to John.

"Don't be sore," John says. "I didn't mean to wake you up."

"Oh no," Jack says. "Of course not."

"You know Morgan and Steinfelt," John said.

"Glad to see you," Jack says.

"How do you feel, Jack?" Morgan asks him.

"Fine," Jack says. "How the hell would I feel?"

"You look fine," Steinfelt says.

"Yes, don't I?" says Jack. "Say," he says to John. "You're my manager. You get a big enough cut. Why the hell didn't you come out here when the reporters was out? You want Jerry and me to talk to them?"

"I had Lew fighting in Philadelphia."

"What the hell's that to me?" Jack says. "You're my manager. You get a big enough cut, don't you? You aren't making me any money in Philadelphia, are you? Why the hell aren't you out here when I ought to have you?"

"Hogan was here."

"Hogan," Jack says. "Hogan's as dumb as I am."

"Soldier Bahtlett was out here wukking with you for a while, wasn't he?" Steinfelt says, to change the subject.

"Yes, he was out here," Jack says. "He was out here, all right."

"Say, Jerry," John said to me. "Would you go and find Hogan and tell him we want to see him in about half an hour?"

"Sure," I said.

"Why the hell can't he stick around?" Jack says. "Stick around, Jerry."

Morgan and Steinfelt looked at each other.

"Quiet down, Jack," John said to him.

"I better go find Hogan," I said.

"All right, if you want to go," Jack says. "None of these guys are going to send you away, though."

"I'll go find Hogan," I said.

Hogan was out in the gym in the barn. He had a couple of his health-farm patients with the gloves on. They neither one wanted to hit the other for fear the other would come back and hit him.

"That'll do," Hogan said when he saw me come in. "You can stop the slaughter. You gentlemen take a shower and Bruce will rub you down."

They climbed out through the ropes and Hogan came over to me.

"John Collins is out with a couple of friends to see Jack," I said.

"I saw them come up in the car."

"Who are the two fellows with John?"

"They're what you call wise boys," Hogan said. "Don't you know them two?"

"No," I said.

"That's Happy Steinfelt and Lew Morgan. They got a pool room."

"I been away a long time," I said.

"Sure," said Hogan. "That Happy Steinfelt's a big operator."

"I've heard his name," I said.

"He's a pretty smooth boy," Hogan said. "They're a couple of sharp-shooters."

"Well," I said, "they want to see us in half an hour."

"You mean they don't want to see us until a half an hour?"

"That's it."

"Come on in the office," Hogan said. "To hell with those sharpshooters."

After about thirty minutes or so Hogan and I went upstairs. We knocked on Jack's door. They were talking inside the room.

"Wait a minute," somebody said.

"To hell with that stuff," Hogan said. "When you want to see me I'm down in the office."

We heard the door unlock. Steinfelt opened it.

"Come on in, Hogan," he says. "We're all going to have a drink."

"Well," says Hogan, "that's something."

We went in. Jack was sitting on the bed. John and Morgan were sitting on a couple of chairs. Steinfelt was standing up.

"You're a pretty mysterious lot of boys," Hogan said.

"Hello, Danny," John says.

"Hello, Danny," Morgan says and shakes hands.

Jack doesn't say anything. He just sits there on the bed. He ain't with the others. He's all by himself. He was wearing an old blue jersey and an old pair of pants and had on boxing shoes. He needed a shave. Steinfelt and Morgan were dressers. John was quite a dresser, too. Jack sat there looking Irish and tough.

Steinfelt brought out a bottle and Hogan brought in some glasses and everybody had a drink. Jack and I took one and the rest of them went on and had two or three each.

"Better save some for your ride back," Hogan said.

"Don't you worry. We got plenty," Morgan said.

Jack hadn't drunk anything since the one drink. He was standing up and looking at them. Morgan was sitting on the bed where Jack had sat.

"Have a drink, Jack," John said and handed him the glass and the bottle.

"No," Jack said, "I never liked to go to these wakes."

They all laughed. Jack didn't laugh.

They were all feeling pretty good when they left. Jack stood on the porch when they got into the car. They waved to him.

"So long," Jack said.

We had supper. Jack didn't say anything at all during the meal except "Will you pass me this?" or "Will you pass me that?" The two health-farm patients ate at the same table with us. They were pretty nice fellas. After we finished eating we went out on the porch. It was dark early.

"Like to take a walk, Jerry?" Jack asked.

"Sure," I said.

We put on our coats and started out. It was quite a way down to the main road, and then we walked along the main road about a mile and a half. Cars kept going by and we would pull out to the side until they were past. Jack didn't say anything. After we had stepped out into the bushes to let a big car go by, Jack said, "To hell with this walking. Come on back to Hogan's."

We went along a side road that cut up over the hill and cut across the field back to Hogan's. We could see the lights of the house up on the hill. We came around to the front of the house and there, standing in the doorway, was Hogan.

"Have a good walk?" Hogan asked.

"Oh, fine," Jack said. "Listen, Hogan. Have you got any liquor?"

"Sure," says Hogan. "What's the idea?"

"Send it up to the room," Jack says. "I'm going to sleep to-night."

"You're the doctor," Hogan says.

"Come on up to the room, Jerry," Jack says.

Upstairs Jack sat on the bed with his head in his hands.

"Ain't it a life?" Jack says.

Hogan brought in a quart of liquor and two glasses.

"Want some ginger ale?"

"What do you think I want to do—get sick?"

"I just asked you," said Hogan.

"Have a drink?" said Jack.

"No, thanks," said Hogan. He went out.

"How about you, Jerry?"

"I'll have one with you," I said.

Jack poured out a couple of drinks. "Now," he said, "I want to take it slow and easy."

"Put some water in it," I said.

"Yes," Jack said. "I guess that's better."

We had a couple of drinks without saying anything. Jack started to pour me another.

"No," I said, "that's all I want."

"All right," Jack said. He poured himself out another big shot and put water in it. He was lighting up a little.

"That was a fine bunch out here this afternoon," he said. "They don't take any chances, those two."

Then a little later, "Well," he says, "they're right. What the hell's the good in taking chances?"

"Don't you want another, Jerry?" he said. "Come on, drink along with me."

"I don't need it, Jack," I said. "I feel all right."

"Just have one more," Jack said. It was softening him up.

"All right," I said.

Jack poured one for me and another one for himself.

"You know," he said, "I like liquor pretty well. If I hadn't been boxing I would have drunk quite a lot."

"Sure," I said.

"You know," he said, "I missed a lot, boxing."

"You made plenty of money."

"Sure, that's what I'm after. You know I miss a lot, Jerry."

"How do you mean?"

"Well," he says, "like about the wife. And being away from home so much. It don't do my girls any good. 'Who's your old man?' some of these society kids'll say to them. 'My old man's Jack Brennan.' That don't do them any good."

"Hell," I said. "All that makes a difference is if they got dough."

"Well," says Jack, "I got the dough for them all right."

He poured out another drink. The bottle was about empty.

"Put some water in it," I said. Jack poured in some water.

"You know," he says, "you ain't got any idea how I miss the wife."

"Sure."

"You ain't got any idea. You can't have any idea what it's like."

"It ought to be better out in the country than in town."

"With me now," Jack said, "it don't make any difference where I am. You can't have an idea what it's like."

"Have another drink."

"Am I getting soused? Do I talk funny?"

"You're coming on all right."

"You can't have an idea what it's like. They ain't anybody can have an idea what it's like."

"Except the wife," I said.

"She knows," Jack said. "She knows, all right. She knows. You bet she knows."

"Put some water in that," I said.

"Jerry," says Jack, "you can't have an idea what it gets to be like."

He was good and drunk. He was looking at me steady. His eyes were sort of too steady.

"You'll sleep, all right," I said.

"Listen, Jerry," Jack says. "You want to make some money? Get some dough down on Walcott."

"Yes?"

"Listen, Jerry." Jack put down the glass. "I'm not drunk now, see? You know what I'm betting on him? Fifty grand."

"That's a lot of dough."

"Fifty grand," Jack says, "at two to one. I'll get twenty-five thousand bucks. Get some money on him, Jerry."

"It sounds good," I said.

"How can I beat him?" Jack says. "It ain't crooked. How can I beat him? Why not make money on it?"

"Put some water in that," I said.

"I'm through after this fight," Jack says. "I'm through with it. I got to take a beating. Why shouldn't I make money on it?"

"Sure."

"I ain't slept for a week," Jack says. "All night I lay awake and worry my can off. I can't sleep, Jerry. You ain't got an idea what it's like when you can't sleep."

"Sure."

"I can't sleep. That's all. I just can't sleep. What's the use of taking care of yourself all these years when you can't sleep?"

"It's bad."

"You ain't got an idea what it's like, Jerry, when you can't sleep."

"Put some water in that," I said.

Well, about eleven o'clock Jack passes out and I put him to bed. Finally he's so he can't keep from sleeping. I helped him get his clothes off and got him into bed.

"You'll sleep, all right, Jack," I said.

"Sure," Jack says, "I'll sleep now."

"Good night, Jack," I said.

"Good night, Jerry," Jack says. "You're the only friend I got."

"Oh, hell," I said.

"You're the only friend I got," Jack says. "The only friend I got."

"Go to sleep," I said.

"I'll sleep," Jack says.

Downstairs Hogan was sitting at the desk in the office reading the papers. He looked up.

"Well, you get your boy friend to sleep?" he asks.

"He's off."

"It's better for him than not sleeping," Hogan said.

"Sure."

"You'd have a hell of a time explaining that to these sport writers, though," Hogan said.

"Well, I'm going to bed myself," I said.

"Good night," said Hogan.

IN THE MORNING I came downstairs about eight o'clock and got some breakfast. Hogan had his two customers out in the barn doing exercises. I went out and watched them.

"One! Two! Three! Four!" Hogan was counting for them. "Hello, Jerry," he said. "Is Jack up yet?"

"No. He's still sleeping."

I went back to my room and packed up to go in to town. About nine-thirty I heard Jack getting up in the next room. When I heard him go downstairs I went down after him. Jack was sitting at the breakfast table. Hogan had come in and was standing beside the table.

"How do you feel, Jack?" I asked him.

"Not so bad."

"Sleep well?" Hogan asked.

"I slept, all right," Jack said. "I got a thick tongue, but I ain't got a head."

"Good," said Hogan. "That was good liquor."

"Put it on the bill," Jack says.

"What time you want to go in to town?" Hogan asked.

"Before lunch," Jack says. "The eleven o'clock train."

Hogan went out.

"Sit down, Jerry," Jack said.

I sat down at the table. Jack was eating a grapefruit. When he'd find a seed he'd spit it out in the spoon and dump it on the plate.

"I guess I was pretty stewed last night," he started.

"You drank some liquor."

"I guess I said a lot of fool things."

"You weren't bad."

"Where's Hogan?" he asked. He was through with the grapefruit.

"He's out in front in the office."

"What did I say about betting on the fight?" Jack asked. He was holding the spoon and sort of poking at the grapefruit with it.

The girl came in with some ham and eggs and took away the grapefruit.

"Bring me another glass of milk," Jack said to her. She went out.

"You said you had fifty grand on Walcott," I said.

"That's right," Jack said.

"That's a lot of money."

"I don't feel too good about it," Jack said.

"Something might happen."

"No," Jack said. "He wants the title bad. They'll be shooting with him, all right."

"You can't ever tell."

"No. He wants the title. It's worth a lot of money to him."

"Fifty grand is a lot of money," I said.

"It's business," said Jack. "I can't win. You know I can't win anyway."

"As long as you're in there you got a chance."

"No," Jack says. "I'm all through. It's just business."

"How do you feel?"

"Pretty good," Jack said. "The sleep was what I needed."

"You might go good."

"I'll give them a good show," Jack said.

After breakfast Jack called up his wife on the long distance. He was inside the booth telephoning.

"That's the first time he's called her up since he's out here," Hogan said.

"He writes her every day."

"Sure," Hogan says. "A letter only costs two cents."

Hogan said good-bye to us, and Bruce, the nigger rubber, drove us down to the train in the cart.

"Good-bye, Mr. Brennan," Bruce said at the train. "I sure hope you knock his can off."

"So long," Jack said. He gave Bruce two dollars. Bruce had worked on him a lot. He looked kind of disappointed. Jack saw me looking at Bruce holding the two dollars.

"It's all in the bill," he said. "Hogan charged me for the rubbing."

On the train going into town Jack didn't talk. He sat in the corner of the seat with his ticket in his hatband and looked out of the window. Once he turned and spoke to me.

"I told the wife I'd take a room at the Shelby to-night," he said. "It's just around the corner from the Garden. I can go up to the house to-morrow morning."

"That's a good idea," I said. "Your wife ever see you fight, Jack?"

"No," Jack says. "She never seen me fight."

I thought, he must be figuring on taking an awful beating if he doesn't want to go home afterward. In town we took a taxi up to the Shelby. A boy came out and took our bags and we went in to the desk.

"How much are the rooms?" Jack asked.

"We only have double rooms," the clerk says. "I can give you a nice double room for ten dollars."

"That's too steep."

"I can give a double room for seven dollars."

"With a bath?"

"Certainly."

"You might as well bunk with me, Jerry," Jack says.

"Oh," I said, "I'll sleep down at my brother-in-law's."

"I don't mean for you to pay it," Jack says. "I just want to get my money's worth."

"Will you register, please?" the clerk says.

He looked at the names. "Number 238, Mr. Brennan."

We went up in the elevator. It was a nice big room with two beds and a door opening into a bathroom.

"This is pretty good," Jack says.

The boy who brought us up pulled up the curtains and brought in our bags. Jack didn't make any move, so I gave the boy a quarter. We washed up and Jack said we better go out and get something to eat.

We ate a lunch at Jimmy Handley's place. Quite a lot of the boys were there. When we were about half through eating, John came in and sat down with us. Jack didn't talk much.

"How are you on the weight, Jack?" John asked him. Jack was putting away a pretty good lunch.

"I could make it with my clothes on," Jack said. He never had to worry about taking off weight. He was a natural welterweight and he'd never gotten fat. He'd lost weight out at Hogan's.

"Well, that's one thing you never had to worry about," John said.

"That's one thing," Jack says.

We went around to the Garden to weigh in after lunch. The match was made at a hundred forty-seven pounds at three o'clock. Jack stepped on the scales with a towel around him. The bar didn't move. Walcott had just weighed and was standing with a lot of people around him.

"Let's see what you weigh, Jack," Freedman, Walcott's manager, said.

"All right, weigh *him* then," Jack jerked his head toward Walcott.

"Drop the towel," Freedman said.

"What do you make it?" Jack asked the fellows who were weighing.

"Hundred and forty-three pounds," the fat man who was weighing said.

"You're down fine, Jack," Freedman says.

"Weigh *him*," Jack says.

Walcott came over. He was a blond with wide shoulders and arms like a heavyweight. He didn't have much legs. Jack stood about half a head taller than he did.

"Hello, Jack," he said. His face was plenty marked up.

"Hello," said Jack. "How you feel?"

"Good," Walcott says. He dropped the towel from around his waist and stood on the scales. He had the widest shoulders and back you ever saw.

"One hundred and forty-six pounds and twelve ounces."

Walcott stepped off and grinned at Jack.

"Well," John says to him, "Jack's spotting you about four pounds."

"More than that when I come in, Kid," Walcott says. "I'm going to go and eat now."

We went back and Jack got dressed. "He's a pretty tough-looking boy," Jack says to me.

"He looks as though he'd been hit plenty of times."

"Oh yes," Jack says. "He ain't hard to hit."

"Where are you going?" John asked when Jack was dressed.

"Back to the hotel," Jack says. "You looked after everything?"

"Yes," John says. "It's all looked after."

"I'm going to lie down a while," Jack says.

"I'll come around for you about a quarter to seven and we'll go and eat."

"All right."

Up at the hotel Jack took off his shoes and his coat and lay down for a while. I wrote a letter. I looked over a couple of times and Jack wasn't sleeping. He was lying perfectly still, but every once in a while his eyes would open. Finally he sits up.

"Want to play some cribbage, Jerry?" he says.

"Sure," I said.

He went over to his suitcase and got out the cards and the cribbage board. We played cribbage and he won three dollars off me. John knocked at the door and came in.

"Want to play some cribbage, John?" Jack asked him.

John put his hat down on the table. It was all wet. His coat was wet, too.

"Is it raining?" Jack asks.

"It's pouring," John says. "The taxi I had got tied up in the traffic and I got out and walked."

"Come on, play some cribbage," Jack says.

"You ought to go and eat."

"No," says Jack. "I don't want to eat yet."

So they played cribbage for about half an hour and Jack won a dollar and a half off him.

"Well, I suppose we got to go eat," Jack says. He went to the window and looked out.

"Is it still raining?"

"Yes."

"Let's eat in the hotel," John says.

"All right," Jack says. "I'll play you once more to see who pays for the meal."

After a little while Jack gets up and says, "You buy the meal, John," and we went downstairs and ate in the big dining room.

After we ate we went upstairs and Jack played cribbage with John again and won two dollars and a half off him. Jack was feeling pretty good. John had a bag with him with all his stuff in it. Jack took off his shirt and collar and put on a jersey and a sweater, so he wouldn't catch cold when he came out, and put his ring clothes and his bathrobe in a bag.

"You all ready?" John asks him. "I'll call up and have them get a taxi."

Pretty soon the telephone rang and they said the taxi was waiting.

We rode down in the elevator and went out through the lobby, and got in the taxi and rode around to the Garden. It was raining hard, but there was a lot of people outside on the streets. The Garden was sold out. As we came in on our way to the dressing room I saw how full it was. It looked like half a mile down to the ring. It was all dark. Just the lights over the ring.

"It's a good thing, with this rain, they didn't try and pull this fight in the ball park," John said.

"They got a good crowd," Jack says.

"This is a fight that would draw a lot more than the Garden could hold."

"You can't tell about the weather," Jack says.

John came to the door of the dressing room and poked his head in. Jack was sitting there with his bathrobe on; he had his arms folded and was looking at the floor. John had a couple of handlers with him. They looked over his shoulder. Jack looked up.

"Is he in?" he asked.

"He's just gone down," John said.

We started down. Walcott was just getting into the ring. The crowd gave him a big hand. He climbed through between the ropes and put his two fists together and smiled and shook them at the crowd, first at one side of the ring, then at the other, and then sat down. Jack got a good hand coming down through the crowd. Jack is Irish, and the Irish always get a pretty good hand. An Irishman don't draw in New York like a Jew or an Eyetalian, but they always get a good hand. Jack climbed up and bent down to go through the ropes, and Walcott came over from his corner and pushed the rope down for Jack to go through. Walcott put his hand on Jack's shoulder and they stood there just for a second.

"So you're going to be one of these popular champions," Jack says to him. "Take your goddam hand off my shoulder."

"Be yourself," Walcott says.

This is all great for the crowd. How gentlemanly the boys are before the fight! How they wish each other luck!

Solly Freedman comes over to our corner while Jack is bandaging his hands and John is over in Walcott's corner. Jack put his thumb through the slit in the bandage and then wrapped his hand nice and smooth. I taped it around the wrist and twice across the knuckles.

"Hey," Freedman says. "Where do you get all that tape?"

"Feel of it," Jack says. "It's soft, ain't it? Don't be a hick."

Freedman stands there all the time while Jack bandages the other hand, and one of the boys that's going to handle him brings the gloves and I pull them on and work them around.

"Say, Freedman," Jack asks. "What nationality is Walcott?"

"I don't know," Solly says. "He's some sort of a Dane."

"He's a Bohemian," the lad who brought the gloves said.

The referee called them out to the center of the ring and Jack walks out. Walcott comes out smiling. They met and the referee put his arm on each of their shoulders.

"Hello, Popularity," Jack says to Walcott.

"Be yourself."

"What do you call yourself Walcott for," Jack says. "Didn't you know he was a nigger?"

"Listen—" says the referee, and he gives them the same old line. Once Walcott interrupts him. He grabs Jack's arm and says, "Can I hit when he's got me like this?"

"Keep your hands off me," Jack says. "There ain't no moving picture of this."

They went back to their corners. I lifted the bathrobe off Jack and he leaned on the ropes and flexed his knees a couple of times and scuffed his shoes in the rosin. The gong rang and Jack turned quick and went out. Walcott came toward him and they touched gloves, and as soon as Walcott dropped his hands Jack jumped his left into his face twice. There wasn't anybody ever boxed better than Jack. Walcott was after him, going forward all the time with his chin on his chest. He's a hooker and he carries his hands pretty low. All he knows is to get in there and sock. But every time he gets in there close, Jack has the left hand in his face. It's just as though it's automatic. Jack just raises his left hand up and it's in Walcott's face. Three or four times Jack brings the right over, but Walcott gets it on the shoulder or high up on the head. He's just like all these hookers. The only thing he's afraid of is another one of the same kind. He's covered every-where you can hurt him. He don't care about a left hand in his face.

After about four rounds Jack has him bleeding bad and his face all cut up, but every time Walcott's got in close he's socked so hard he's got two big red patches on both sides just below Jack's ribs. Every time he gets in close, Jack ties him up, then gets one hand loose and uppercuts him, but when Walcott gets his hands loose he socks Jack in the body so they can hear it outside in the street. He's a socker.

It goes along like that for three rounds more. They don't talk any. They're working all the time. We worked over Jack plenty, too, in between the rounds. He don't look good at all, but he never does much work in the ring. He don't move around much, and that left hand is just automatic. It's just like it was connected with Walcott's face and Jack just had to wish it in every time. Jack is always calm in close, and he doesn't waste any juice. He knows everything about working in close, too, and he's getting away with a lot of stuff. While they were in our corner I watched him tie Walcott up, get his right hand loose, turn it, and come up with an uppercut that got Walcott's nose with the heel of the glove. Walcott was bleeding bad and leaned his nose on Jack's shoulder so as to give Jack some of it, too, and Jack sort of lifted his shoulder sharp and caught him against the nose, and then brought down the right hand and uppercut him again.

Walcott was sore as hell. By the time they'd gone five rounds he hated Jack's guts. Jack wasn't sore; that is, he wasn't any sorer than he always was. He certainly did used to make the fellows he fought hate boxing. That was why he hated Kid Lewis so. He never got the Kid's goat. Kid Lewis always had about three new dirty things Jack couldn't do. Jack was as safe as a church all the time he was in there as long as he was strong. He certainly was treating Walcott rough. The funny thing was, it looked as though Jack was an open classic boxer. That was because he had all that stuff, too.

After the seventh round Jack says, "My left's getting heavy."

From then he started to take a beating. It didn't show at first. But instead of him running the fight it was Walcott running it. Instead of being safe all the time, now he was in trouble. He couldn't keep Walcott out with the left hand now. It looked as though it was the same as ever, only now, instead of Walcott's punches just missing him, they were just hitting him. He took an awful beating in the body.

"What's the round?" Jack asked.

"The eleventh."

"I can't stay," Jack says. "My legs are going bad."

Walcott had been just hitting him for a long time. It was like a baseball catcher pulls the ball and takes some of the shock off. From now on Walcott commenced to land solid. He certainly was a socking machine. Jack was just trying to block everything now. It didn't show what an awful beating he was taking. In between the rounds I worked on his legs. The muscles would flutter under my hands all the time I was rubbing them. He was sick as hell.

"How's it go?" he asked John, turning around, his face all swollen.

"It's his fight."

"I think I can last," Jack says. "I don't want this bohunk to stop me."

It was going just the way he thought it would. He knew he couldn't beat Walcott. He wasn't strong any more. He was all right, though. His money was all right and now he wanted to finish it off right to please himself. He didn't want to be knocked out.

The gong rang and we pushed him out. He went out slow. Walcott came right out after him. Jack put the left in his face and Walcott took it, came in under it, and started working on Jack's body. Jack tried to tie him up and it was just like trying to hold on to a buzz saw. Jack broke away from it and missed with the right. Walcott clipped him with a left hook and Jack went down. He went down on his hands and knees and looked at us. The referee started counting. Jack was watching us and shaking his head. At eight John motioned to him. You couldn't hear on account of the crowd. Jack got up. The referee had been holding Walcott back with one arm while he counted.

When Jack was on his feet Walcott started toward him.

"Watch yourself, Jimmy," I heard Solly Freedman yell to him.

Walcott came up to Jack looking at him. Jack stuck the left hand at him. Walcott just shook his head. He backed Jack up against the ropes, measured him, and then hooked the left very light to the side of Jack's head and socked the right into the body as hard as he could sock just as low as he could get it. He must have hit him five inches below the belt. I thought the eyes would come out of Jack's head. They stuck way out. His mouth came open.

The referee grabbed Walcott. Jack stepped forward. If he went down, there went fifty thousand bucks. He walked as though all his insides were going to fall out.

"It wasn't low," he said. "It was a accident."

The crowd were yelling so you couldn't hear anything.

"I'm all right," Jack says. They were right in front of us.

The referee looks at John and then he shakes his head.

"Come on, you dirty Polack," Jack says to Walcott.

John was hanging on to the ropes. He had the towel ready to chuck in. Jack was standing just a little way out from the ropes. He took a step forward. I saw the sweat come out on his face like somebody had squeezed it, and a big drop went down his nose.

"Come on and fight," Jack says to Walcott.

The referee looked at John and waved Walcott on.

"Go in there, you slob," he says.

Walcott went in. He didn't know what to do either. He never thought Jack could have stood it. Jack put the left in his face. There was all this yelling going on. They were right in front of us. Walcott hit him twice. Jack's face was the worst thing I ever saw—the look on it. He was holding himself and all his body together, and it all showed on his face. All the time he was thinking and holding his body in where it was busted.

Then he started to sock. His face looked awful all the time. He started to sock with his hands low down by his side, swinging at Walcott. Walcott covered up and Jack was swinging wild at Walcott's head. Then he swung the left and it hit Walcott in the groin and the right hit Walcott right bang where he'd hit Jack. Way low. Walcott went down and grabbed himself there and rolled and twisted around.

The referee grabbed Jack and pushed him toward his corner. John jumps into the ring. There was all this yelling going on. The referee was talking with the judges and then the announcer got into the ring with the megaphone and says, "Walcott on a foul."

The referee is talking to John and he says, "What could I do? Jack wouldn't take the foul. Then when he's groggy he fouls him."

"He'd lost it anyway," John says.

Jack's sitting on the chair. I've got his gloves off and he's holding himself in down there with both hands.

"Go over and say you're sorry," John says into his ear. "It'll look good."

Jack stands up and the sweat comes out all over his face. I put the bathrobe around him and he holds himself in with one hand under the bathrobe and goes across the ring. They've picked Walcott up and they're working on him. There's a lot of people in Walcott's corner. Nobody speaks to Jack. He leans over Walcott.

"I'm sorry," Jack says. "I didn't mean to foul you."

Walcott doesn't say anything. He looks too damned sick.

"Well, you're the champion now," Jack says to him. "I hope you get a hell of a lot of fun out of it."

"Leave the kid alone," Solly Freedman says.

"Hello, Solly," Jack says. "I'm sorry I fouled your boy."

Freedman just looks at him.

Jack went over to his corner walking that funny jerky way, and we got him down through the ropes and through the reporters' tables and out down the aisle. A lot of people want to slap Jack on the back. He goes out through all that mob in his bathrobe to the dressing room. It's a popular win for Walcott. That's the way the money was bet in the Garden.

Once we got inside the dressing room Jack lay down and shut his eyes.

"We want to get to the hotel and get a doctor," John says.

"I'm all busted inside," Jack says.

"I'm sorry as hell, Jack," John says.

"It's all right," Jack says.

He lies there with his eyes shut.

"They certainly tried a nice double cross," John said.

"Your friends Morgan and Steinfelt," Jack said. "You got nice friends."

He lies there; his eyes are open now. His face has still got that awful drawn look.

"It's funny how fast you can think when it means that much money," Jack says.

"You're some boy, Jack," John says.

"No," Jack says. "It was nothing."

Cloud, Castle, Lake

VLADIMIR NABOKOV ‖ 1941

"Cloud, Castle, Lake" was the first short story to be published in English by Vladimir Nabokov (1899–1977). Even before the Russian novelist, poet, professor, and lepidopterist immigrated to the United States, in 1941, he had struggled to find an American outlet for his work. Nabokov had been a cult favorite among the flourishing Russian émigré community in Berlin—the city to which he had fled to escape the Communists and from which he would flee to escape the Nazis—but American editors invariably balked at his rich, prankish, often surreal concoctions. The first exception was The Atlantic's ninth editor-in-chief, Edward Weeks. The two men were introduced in 1941 by the critic Edmund Wilson and began to meet regularly for lunch at the Ritz Hotel in Boston. Weeks was enchanted by Nabokov. As Weeks recalled years later in an interview: "He would come in a shabby tweed coat, trousers bulging at the knee, but be quite the most distinguished man in the room, with his perfectly beautiful hazel eyes, his fine brown hair, the elan, the spark. . . . He just had to walk into the room and the girls looked around." Weeks was equally enthralled by the first short story Nabokov offered—a nightmarish fable about a gentle Russian émigré who takes an ill-fated holiday trip to the countryside. At the time he wrote the story, Nabokov had been entangled in an adulterous affair—unable to choose between his wife, on whom he utterly depended, and his mistress, with whom he was obsessed. The themes of "Cloud, Castle, Lake"—the elusiveness of happiness and the obstacles posed by "traveling companions" to our individual contentment—masterfully reflected that sense of entrapment. Over the next five years, six more Nabokov short stories, as well as two poems, would appear in The Atlantic's pages, but this would always be one of his favorites.

One of my representatives—a modest, mild bachelor, very efficient—happened to win a pleasure trip at a charity ball given by Russian refugees. The Berlin summer was in full flood (it was the second week of damp and cold, so that it was a pity to look at everything which had turned green in vain, and only the sparrows kept cheerful); he did not care to go anywhere, but when he tried to sell his ticket at the office of the Bureau of Pleasantrips he was told that to do so he would have to have special permission from the Ministry of Transportation; when he tried them, it turned out that first he would have to draw up a complicated petition at a notary's on stamped paper; and besides, a so-called "certificate of non-absence from the city for the summertime" had to be obtained from the police.

So he sighed a little, and decided to go. He borrowed an aluminum flask from friends, repaired his soles, bought a belt and a fancy-style flannel shirt—one of those cowardly things which shrink in the first wash. Incidentally, it was too large for that likable little man, his hair always neatly trimmed, his eyes so intelligent and kind. I cannot remember his name at the moment. I think it was Vasili Ivanovich.

He slept badly the night before the departure. And why? Because he had to get up unusually early, and hence took along into his dreams the delicate face of the watch ticking on his night table; but mainly because that very night, for no reason at all, he began to imagine that this trip, thrust upon him by a feminine Fate in a low-cut gown, this trip which he had accepted so reluctantly, would bring him some wonderful, tremulous happiness. This happiness would have something in common with his childhood, and with the excitement aroused in him by Russian lyrical poetry, and with some evening sky line once seen in a dream, and with that lady, another man's wife, whom he had hopelessly loved for seven years— but it would be even fuller and more significant than all that. And besides, he felt that the really good life must be oriented toward something or someone.

The morning was dull, but steam-warm and close, with an inner sun, and it was quite pleasant to rattle in a streetcar to the distant railway station where the gathering place was: several people, alas, were taking part in the excursion. Who would they be, these drowsy beings, drowsy as seem all creatures still unknown to us? By Window No. 6, at 7 A.M., as was indicated in the directions appended to the ticket, he saw them (they were already waiting; he had managed to be late by about three minutes).

A lanky blond young man in Tyrolese garb stood out at once. He was burned the color of a cock's comb, had huge brick-red knees with golden hairs, and his nose looked lacquered. He was the leader furnished by the Bureau, and as soon as the newcomer had joined the group (which consisted of four women and as many men) he led it off toward a train lurking behind other trains, carrying his monstrous knapsack with terrifying ease, and firmly clanking with his hobnailed boots.

Everyone found a place in an empty car, unmistakably third-class, and Vasili Ivanovich, having sat down by himself and put a peppermint into his mouth, immediately opened a little volume of Tiutchev, whom he had long intended to reread, but he was requested to put the book aside and join the group. An elderly bespectacled post-office clerk, with skull, chin, and upper lip a bristly blue as if he had shaved off some extraordinarily luxuriant and tough growth especially for this trip, immediately announced that he had been to Russia and knew some Russian,—for instance, *patzlui*,—and, recalling philanderings in Tsaritsyn, winked in such a manner that his fat wife sketched out in the air the preface of a backhand box on the ear. The company was getting noisy. Four employees of the same building firm were tossing each other heavyweight jokes: a middle-aged man, Schultz; a younger man, Schultz also, and two fidgety young women with big mouths and big rumps. The red-headed, rather burlesque widow in a sport skirt knew something too about Russia (the Riga beaches). There was also a dark young man by the name of Schramm, with lustreless eyes and a vague velvety vileness about his person and manners, who constantly switched the conversation to this or that attractive aspect of the excursion, and who gave the first signal for rapturous appreciation; he was, as it turned out later, a special stimulator from the Bureau of Pleasantrips.

The locomotive, working rapidly with its elbows, hurried through a pine forest, then—with relief—among fields. Only dimly realizing as yet all the absurdity and horror of the situation, and perhaps attempting to persuade himself that everything was very nice, Vasili Ivanovich contrived to enjoy the fleeting gifts of the road. And indeed, how enticing it all is, what charm the world acquires when it is wound up and moving like a merry-go-round! The burning sun crept toward a corner of the window and suddenly spilled over the yellow bench. The badly pressed shadow of the car sped madly along the grassy bank, where flowers blended into colored streaks. A crossing: a cyclist was waiting, one foot resting on the ground. Trees appeared in groups and singly, revolving coolly and blandly, displaying the latest fashions. The blue dampness of a ravine. A memory of love, disguised as a meadow. Wispy clouds—greyhounds of heaven.

We both, Vasili Ivanovich and I, have always been impressed by the anonymity of all the parts of a landscape, so dangerous for the soul, the impossibility of ever finding out where that path you see leads—and look, what a tempting thicket! It happened that on a distant slope or in a gap in the trees there would appear and, as it were, stop for an instant, like air retained in the lungs, a spot so enchanting—a lawn, a terrace—such perfect expression of tender, well-meaning beauty—that it seemed that if one could stop the train and go thither, forever, to you, my love . . . But a thousand beech trunks were already madly leaping by, whirling in a sizzling sun pool, and again the chance for happiness was gone.

At the stations, Vasili Ivanovich would look at the configuration of some entirely insignificant objects—a smear on the platform, a cherry stone, a cigarette butt—and would say to himself that never, never would he remember these three little things here in that particular interrelation, this pattern, which he now could see with such deathless precision; or again, looking at a group of children waiting for a train, he would try with all his might to single out at least one remarkable destiny—in the form of a violin or a crown, a propeller or a lyre—and would gaze until the whole party of village schoolboys appeared as on an old photograph, now reproduced with a little white cross above the face of the last boy on the right: the hero's childhood.

But one could look out of the window only by snatches. All had been given sheet music with verses from the Bureau:—

Stop that worrying and moping,
Take a knotted stick and rise,
Come a-tramping in the open
With the good, the hearty guys!

Tramp your country's grass and stubble,
With the good, the hearty guys,
Kill the hermit and his trouble
And to hell with doubts and sighs!

One mile, two miles, five and twenty,
Sunny skies and wind in plenty . . .
Come a-tramping with the guys!

This was to be sung in chorus. Vasili Ivanovich, who not only could not sing, but could not even pronounce German words clearly, took advantage of the drowning roar of mingling voices and merely opened his mouth while swaying slightly, as if he were really singing—but the leader, at a sign from the subtle Schramm, suddenly stopped the general singing and, squinting askance at Vasili Ivanovich, demanded that he sing solo. Vasili Ivanovich cleared his throat, timidly began, and after a minute of solitary torment all joined in; but he did not dare thereafter to drop out.

He had with him his favorite cucumber from the Russian store, a loaf of bread, and three eggs. When evening came, and the low crimson sun entered wholly the soiled seasick car, stunned by its own din, all were invited to hand over their provisions, in order to divide them evenly—this was particularly easy, as all except Vasili Ivanovich had the same things. The cucumber amused everybody, was pronounced inedible, and was thrown out of the window. In view of the insufficiency of his contribution, Vasili Ivanovich got a smaller portion of sausage.

He was made to play cards. They pulled him about, questioned him, verified whether he could show the route of the trip on a map—in a word, all busied themselves with him, at first good-naturedly, then with malevolence, which grew with the approach of night. Both girls were called Greta; the red-headed widow somehow resembled the rooster-leader; Schramm, Schultz, and the other Schultz, the post-office clerk and his wife, all gradually melted together, merged together, forming one collective, wobbly, many-handed being, from which one could not escape. It pressed upon him from all sides. But suddenly at some station all climbed out, and it was already dark, although in the west there still hung a very long, very pink cloud, and farther along the track, with a soul-piercing light, the star of a lamp trembled through the slow smoke of the engine, and crickets chirped in the dark, and from somewhere there came the odor of jasmine and hay, my love.

They spent the night in a tumbledown inn. A mature bedbug is awful, but there is a certain grace in the motions of silky wood lice. The post-office clerk was separated from his wife, who was put with the widow; he was given to Vasili Ivanovich for the night. The two beds took up the whole room. Quilt on top, chamber pot below. The clerk said that somehow he did not feel sleepy, and began to talk of his Russian adventures, rather more circumstantially than in the train. He was a great bully of a man, thorough and obstinate, clad in long cotton drawers, with mother-of-pearl claws on his dirty toes, and bear's fur between fat breasts. A moth dashed about the ceiling, hobnobbing with its shadow. "In Tsaritsyn," the clerk was saying, "there are now three schools, a German, a Czech, and a Chinese one. At any rate, that is what my brother-in-law says; he went there to build tractors."

Next day, from early morning to five o'clock in the afternoon, they raised dust along a highway, which undulated from hill to hill; then they took a green road through a dense fir wood. Vasili Ivanovich, as the least burdened, was given an enormous round loaf of bread to carry under his arm. How I hate you, our daily! But still his precious, experienced eyes noted what was necessary. Against the background of fir-tree gloom a dry needle was hanging vertically on an invisible thread.

Again they piled into a train, and again the small partitionless car was empty. The other Schultz began to teach Vasili Ivanovich how to play the mandolin. There was much laughter. When they got tired of that, they thought up a capital game, which was supervised by Schramm. It consisted of the following: the women would lie down on the benches they chose, under which the men were already hidden, and when from under one of the benches there would emerge a ruddy face with ears, or a big outspread hand, with a skirt-lifting curve of the fingers (which would provoke much squealing), then it would be revealed who was paired off with whom. Three times Vasili Ivanovich lay down in filthy darkness, and three times it turned out that there was no one on the bench when he crawled out from under. He was acknowledged the loser and was forced to eat a cigarette butt.

They spent the night on straw mattresses in a barn, and early in the morning set out again on foot. Firs, ravines, foamy streams. From the heat, from the songs which one had constantly to bawl, Vasili Ivanovich became so exhausted that during the midday halt he fell asleep at once, and awoke only when they began to slap at imaginary horseflies on him. But after another hour of marching, that very happiness of which he had once half-dreamt was suddenly discovered.

It was a pure, blue lake, with an unusual expression of its water. In the middle, a large cloud was reflected in its entirety. On the other side, on a hill thickly covered with verdure (and the darker the verdure, the more poetic it is), towered, arising from dactyl to dactyl, an ancient black castle. Of course, there are plenty of such views in Central Europe, but just this one, in the inexpressible and unique harmoniousness of its three principal parts, in its smile, in some mysterious innocence it had,—my love! my obedient one!—was something so unique, and so familiar, and so long-promised, and it so understood the beholder, that Vasili Ivanovich even pressed his hand to his heart, as if to see whether his heart was there in order to give it away.

At some distance, Schramm, poking into the air with the leader's alpenstock, was calling the attention of the excursionists to something or other; they had settled themselves around on the grass in poses seen in amateur snapshots, while the leader sat on a stump, his behind to the lake, and was having a snack. Quietly, concealing himself behind his own back, Vasili Ivanovich followed the shore, and came to a kind of inn. A dog still quite young greeted him; it crept on its belly, its jaws laughing, its tail fervently beating the ground. Vasili Ivanovich accompanied the dog into the house, a piebald two-storied dwelling with a winking window beneath a convex tiled eyelid, and he found the owner, a tall old man vaguely resembling a Russian war veteran, who spoke German so poorly and with such a soft

drawl that Vasili Ivanovich changed to his own tongue, but the man understood as in a dream, and continued in the language of his environment, his
family.

Upstairs was a room for travelers. "You know, I shall take it for the rest
of my life," Vasili Ivanovich is reported to have said as soon as he had entered it. The room itself had nothing remarkable about it. On the contrary,
it was a most ordinary room, with a red floor, daisies daubed on the white
walls, and a small mirror half filled with the yellow infusion of the reflected
flowers—but from the window one could clearly see the lake with its cloud
and its castle, in a motionless and perfect correlation of happiness. Without reasoning, without considering, only entirely surrendering to an attraction the truth of which consisted in its own strength, a strength which
he had never experienced before, Vasili Ivanovich in one radiant second realized that here in this little room with that view, beautiful to the verge of
tears, life would at last be what he had always wished it to be. What exactly
it would be like, what would take place here, that of course he did not
know, but all around him were help, promise, and consolation—so that
there could not be any doubt that he must live here. In a moment he figured out how he would manage it so as not to have to return to Berlin
again, how to get the few possessions that he had—books, the blue suit, her
photograph. How simple it was turning out! As my representative, he was
earning enough for the modest life of a refugee Russian.

"My friends," he cried, having run down again to the meadow by the
shore, "my friends, good-bye. I shall remain for good in that house over
there. We can't travel together any longer. I shall go no farther. I am not going anywhere. Good-bye!"

"How is that?" said the leader in a queer voice, after a short pause, during which the smile on the lips of Vasili Ivanovich slowly faded, while the
people who had been sitting on the grass half-rose and stared at him with
stony eyes.

"But why?" he faltered. "It is here that . . ."

"Silence!" the post-office clerk suddenly bellowed with extraordinary
force. "Come to your senses, you drunken swine!"

"Wait a moment, gentlemen," said the leader, and, having passed his
tongue over his lips, he turned to Vasili Ivanovich.

"You probably have been drinking," he said quietly. "Or have gone out
of your mind. You are taking a pleasure trip with us. Tomorrow, according
to the appointed itinerary,—look at your ticket,—we are all returning to
Berlin. There can be no question of anyone—in this case you—refusing to
continue this communal journey. We were singing today a certain song—

try and remember what it said. That's enough now! Come, children, we are going on."

"There will be beer at Ewald," said Schramm in a caressing voice. "Five hours by train. Walks. A hunting lodge. Coal mines. Lots of interesting things."

"I shall complain," wailed Vasili Ivanovich. "Give me back my bag. I have the right to remain where I want. Oh, but this is nothing less than an invitation to a beheading"—he told me he cried when they seized him by the arms.

"If necessary we shall carry you," said the leader grimly, "but that is not likely to be pleasant for you. I am responsible for each of you, and shall bring back each of you, alive or dead."

Swept along a forest road as in a hideous fairy tale, squeezed, twisted, Vasili Ivanovich could not even turn around, and only felt how the radiance behind his back receded, fractured by trees, and then it was no longer there, and all around the dark firs fretted but could not interfere. As soon as everyone had got into the car and the train had pulled off, they began to beat him—they beat him a long time, and with a good deal of inventiveness. It occurred to them, among other things, to use a corkscrew on his palms; then on his feet. The post-office clerk, who had been to Russia, fashioned a knout out of a stick and a belt, and began to use it with devilish dexterity. Atta boy! The other men relied more on their iron heels, whereas the women were satisfied to pinch and to slap. All had a wonderful time.

After returning to Berlin, he called on me; was much changed; sat down quietly, putting his hands on his knees; told his story; kept on repeating that he must resign his position, begged me to let him go, insisted that he could not continue, that he had not the strength to belong to mankind any longer. Of course, I let him go.

As We May Think

VANNEVAR BUSH || 1945

When this visionary essay appeared in The Atlantic *near the end of World War II, it was introduced by an editor's note that likened it to Ralph Waldo Emerson's famous 1837 address, "The American Scholar." The comparison was apt. Though men of vastly different eras and areas of expertise, Vannevar Bush (1890–1974) and Emerson were once-in-a-generation polymaths with unusual abilities to see beyond the horizon. Bush's celebrity has faded somewhat over the years, but as the founder and director of the Office of Scientific Research and Development, the federal agency that coordinated all technology research for the war effort, including the Manhattan Project, he was at midcentury an enormously important figure in American public life—the chief architect of the burgeoning military-industrial complex, a close confidant of President Franklin D. Roosevelt, and the subject of adoring press coverage. With the war drawing to a close, Bush turned his attentions from military strategy and weapons advancement to a new challenge: the development of technology to reckon with the exponential growth and rapid specialization of human knowledge. He was among the first to recognize that innovative new tools would be required to store, manage, and access information efficiently, and in "As We May Think," he envisioned a number of revolutionary devices and systems that would accomplish these tasks. Bush was not perfectly clairvoyant—he was, for example, unable to make the leap from analog to digital technology—but it is amazing to see how much of our future he managed to conjure a half century ahead of his time: the personal computer, the computer workstation, voice-recognition software, hypertext, and even the World Wide Web. Small wonder that technorati now widely regard "As We May Think" as the essential early road map to the Internet age and Bush as its founding father.*

Of what lasting benefit has been man's use of science and of the new instruments which his research brought into existence? First, they have increased his control of his material environment. They have improved his food, his clothing, his shelter; they have increased his security and released him partly from the bondage of bare existence. They have given him increased knowledge of his own biological processes so that he has had a progressive freedom from disease and an increased span of life. They are illuminating the interactions of his physiological and psychological functions, giving the promise of an improved mental health.

Science has provided the swiftest communication between individuals; it has provided a record of ideas and has enabled man to manipulate and to make extracts from that record so that knowledge evolves and endures throughout the life of a race rather than that of an individual.

There is a growing mountain of research. But there is increased evidence that we are being bogged down today as specialization extends. The investigator is staggered by the findings and conclusions of thousands of other workers—conclusions which he cannot find time to grasp, much less to remember, as they appear. Yet specialization becomes increasingly necessary for progress, and the effort to bridge between disciplines is correspondingly superficial.

Professionally our methods of transmitting and reviewing the results of research are generations old and by now are totally inadequate for their purpose. If the aggregate time spent in writing scholarly works and in reading them could be evaluated, the ratio between these amounts of time might well be startling. Mendel's concept of the laws of genetics was lost to the world for a generation because his publication did not reach the few who were capable of grasping and extending it; and this sort of catastrophe is undoubtedly being repeated all about us, as truly significant attainments become lost in the mass of the inconsequential.

The difficulty seems to be, not so much that we publish unduly in view of the extent and variety of present day interests, but rather that publication has been extended far beyond our present ability to make real use of the record. The summation of human experience is being expanded at a prodigious rate, and the means we use for threading through the consequent maze to the momentarily important item is the same as was used in the days of square-rigged ships.

Our ineptitude in getting at the record is largely caused by the artificiality of systems of indexing. When data of any sort are placed in storage, they are filed alphabetically or numerically, and information is found (when it is) by tracing it down from subclass to subclass. It can be in only one place, unless duplicates are used; one has to have rules as to which path will locate it, and the rules are cumbersome. Having found one item, moreover, one has to emerge from the system and re-enter on a new path.

The human mind does not work that way. It operates by association. With one item in its grasp, it snaps instantly to the next that is suggested by the association of thoughts, in accordance with some intricate web of trails carried by the cells of the brain. It has other characteristics, of course; trails that are not frequently followed are prone to fade, items are not fully permanent, memory is transitory. Yet the speed of action, the intricacy of trails, the detail of mental pictures, is awe-inspiring beyond all else in nature.

Man cannot hope fully to duplicate this mental process artificially, but he certainly ought to be able to learn from it. In minor ways he may even improve, for his records have relative permanency. The first idea, however, to be drawn from the analogy concerns selection. Selection by association, rather than indexing, may yet be mechanized. One cannot hope thus to equal the speed and flexibility with which the mind follows an associative trail, but it should be possible to beat the mind decisively in regard to the permanence and clarity of the items resurrected from storage.

Consider a future device for individual use, which is a sort of mechanized private file and library. It needs a name, and, to coin one at random, "memex" will do. A memex is a device in which an individual stores all his books, records, and communications, and which is mechanized so that it may be consulted with exceeding speed and flexibility. It is an enlarged intimate supplement to his memory.

It consists of a desk, and while it can presumably be operated from a distance, it is primarily the piece of furniture at which he works. On the top are slanting translucent screens, on which material can be projected for convenient reading. There is a keyboard, and sets of buttons and levers. Otherwise it looks like an ordinary desk.

In one end is the stored material. The matter of bulk is well taken care of by improved microfilm. Only a small part of the interior of the memex is devoted to storage, the rest to mechanism. Yet if the user inserted 5,000 pages of material a day it would take him hundreds of years to fill the repository, so he can be profligate and enter material freely.

Most of the memex contents are purchased on microfilm ready for insertion. Consider film of the same thickness as paper, although thinner film will certainly be usable. Even under these conditions there would be a total factor of 10,000 between the bulk of the ordinary record on books, and its microfilm replica. The *Encyclopoedia Britannica* could be reduced to the volume of a matchbox. A library of a million volumes could be compressed into one end of a desk. If the human race has produced since the invention of movable type a total record, in the form of magazines, newspapers, books, tracts, advertising blurbs, correspondence, having a volume corresponding to a billion books, the whole affair, assembled and compressed, could be lugged off in a moving van.

Books of all sorts, pictures, current periodicals, newspapers, are thus obtained and dropped into place. Business correspondence takes the same path. And there is provision for direct entry. On the top of the memex is a transparent platen. On this are placed longhand notes, photographs, memoranda, all sorts of things. When one is in place, the depression of a lever causes it to be photographed onto the next blank space in a section of the memex film, dry photography being employed.

There is, of course, provision for consultation of the record by the usual scheme of indexing. If the user wishes to consult a certain book, he taps its code on the keyboard, and the title page of the book promptly appears before him, projected onto one of his viewing positions. Frequently-used codes are mnemonic, so that he seldom consults his code book; but when he does, a single tap of a key projects it for his use. Moreover, he has supplemental levers. On deflecting one of these levers to the right he runs through the book before him, each page in turn being projected at a speed which just allows a recognizing glance at each. If he deflects it further to the right, he steps through the book 10 pages at a time; still further at 100 pages at a time. Deflection to the left gives him the same control backwards.

A special button transfers him immediately to the first page of the index. Any given book of his library can thus be called up and consulted with far greater facility than if it were taken from a shelf. As he has several projection positions, he can leave one item in position while he calls up another. He can add marginal notes and comments, taking advantage of one possible type of dry photography, and it could even be arranged so that he can do this by a stylus scheme, . . . just as though he had the physical page before him.

All this is conventional, except for the projection forward of present-day mechanisms and gadgetry. It affords an immediate step, however, to associative indexing, the basic idea of which is a provision whereby any item may be caused at will to select immediately and automatically another. This is the essential feature of the memex. The process of tying two items together is the important thing.

When the user is building a trail, he names it, inserts the name in his code book, and taps it out on his keyboard. Before him are the two items to be joined, projected onto adjacent viewing positions. At the bottom of each there are a number of blank code spaces, and a pointer is set to indicate one of these on each item. The user taps a single key, and the items are permanently joined. In each code space appears the code word. Out of view, but also in the code space, is inserted a set of dots for photocell viewing; and on each item these dots by their positions designate the index number of the other item.

Thereafter, at any time, when one of these items is in view, the other can be instantly recalled merely by tapping a button below the corresponding code space. Moreover, when numerous items have been thus joined together to form a trail, they can be reviewed in turn, rapidly or slowly, by deflecting a lever like that used for turning the pages of a book. It is exactly as though the physical items had been gathered together from widely separated sources and bound together to form a new book. It is more than this, for any item can be joined into numerous trails.

The owner of the memex, let us say, is interested in the origin and properties of the bow and arrow. Specifically he is studying why the short Turkish bow was apparently superior to the English long bow in the skirmishes of the Crusades. He has dozens of possibly pertinent books and articles in his memex. First he runs through an encyclopedia, finds an interesting but sketchy article, leaves it projected. Next, in a history, he finds another pertinent item, and ties the two together. Thus he goes, building a trail of many items. Occasionally he inserts a comment of his own, either linking it into the main trail or joining it by a side trail to a particular item.

Wholly new forms of encyclopedias will appear [in this way], ready made with a mesh of associative trails running through them, ready to be dropped into the memex and there amplified. The lawyer has at his touch the associated opinions and decisions of his whole experience, and of the experience of friends and authorities. The patent attorney has on call the millions of issued patents, with familiar trails to every point of his client's interest. The physician, puzzled by a patient's reactions, strikes the trail established in studying an earlier similar case, and runs rapidly through analogous case histories, with side references to the classics for the pertinent anatomy and histology. The chemist, struggling with the synthesis of an organic compound, has all the chemical literature before him in his laboratory, with trails following the analogies of compounds, and side trails to their physical and chemical behavior.

The historian, with a vast chronological account of a people, parallels it with a skip trail which stops only on the salient items, and can follow at any time contemporary trails which lead him all over civilization at a particular epoch. There is a new profession of trail blazers, those who find delight in the task of establishing useful trails through the enormous mass of the common record. The inheritance from the master becomes, not only his additions to the world's record, but for his disciples the entire scaffolding by which they were erected.

Thus science may implement the ways in which man produces, stores, and consults the record of the race. Presumably man's spirit should be elevated if he can better review his shady past and analyze more completely and objectively his present problems. He has built a civilization so complex that he needs to mechanize his records more fully if he is to push his experiment to its logical conclusion and not merely become bogged down part way there by overtaxing his limited memory. His excursions may be more enjoyable if he can reacquire the privilege of forgetting the manifold things he does not need to have immediately at hand, with some assurance that he can find them again if they prove important.

The Captivity of Marriage

NORA JOHNSON ‖ 1961

Historians usually cite 1963, the year in which The Feminine Mystique
*was published, as the beginning of the modern feminist movement—a
two-decade-long explosion of political activism in support of the principle that women ought to have political, economic, and social rights equal
to those of men. Betty Friedan's indictment of the notion that women
could find fulfillment only through motherhood and homemaking inar-
guably had an enormous impact on American culture, uncovering deep
fissures of dissatisfaction in the lives of women. Yet Friedan was not,
as her disciples sometimes claim, the first to illuminate the existential
costs of domesticity. In 1961, the novelist and memoirist Nora Johnson
(1933–   ), had boldly plumbed the subject in* The Atlantic, *identifying
what she called "the housewife's syndrome"—the vague feeling, common
among educated wives and mothers, "that she is frittering away her days
and that a half-defined but important part of her ability is lying about
unused." The author of two comic novels, including* The World of
Henry Orient *(which was adapted by Johnson and her screenwriter/di-
rector father, Nunnally Johnson, into a movie starring Peter Sellers),
Johnson was the mother of two young daughters at the time she wrote
this essay, professing herself to be happily married and in love with her
husband. But she had begun to detect in her own life as well as in the
lives of those in her circle a chasm between expectation and reality in the
world of marriage and motherhood, which she memorably described as
"the simple, nerve-wracking, mindless, battering-ram process of trying to
teach a savage to use a fork." "The Captivity of Marriage" is a witty,
stylish essay that, despite its raw and tendentious subject matter, manages to be sharp without being angry and incisive without projecting a
trace of bitterness.*

Wives are lonelier now than they ever used to be. In older, gentler times,
when age still had its privileges, the old folks never harbored any guilt feelings about being a drag on the young. They either moved in, reasoning that
it was high time they were supported for a change, or else they lived nearby.
People moved less, and families stuck closer together. Grandma, never having become emancipated, was always around for advice and help. (Today
grandma is likely to be off fund raising or taking courses at Columbia.) I

know a Polish area in Chicago where everyone in the family lives within a few blocks of the others, and there are usually two generations in each house. They may have other problems, but loneliness isn't one of them.

The young college-educated mother with a medium amount of money is the one who reflects all the problems at once. In spite of her hopes for fulfillment through her children and contentment with woman's great career, she vaguely feels that she is frittering away her days and that a half-defined but important part of her ability is lying about unused; she is guilty about her feeling of futility because of her belief in the magic medicine of love. This is the housewife's syndrome, the vicious circle, the feeling of emptiness in the gap between what she thought marriage was going to be like and what it is really like.

Let's take a look at a fairly typical young mother. She married her husband because she loved him, and she still does. She has two children and is pregnant with a third. Whether in city or country, she is more or less surrounded by gadgets which free her from drudgery. If she is lucky, she has a cleaning woman once a week. She and her husband have enough money for a fairly comfortable life, but for time alone together are dependent on baby sitters and possibly a grandma who will help out in a pinch.

If the young mother is in the country, the children play in the yard, and she watches them from the window; if she is in the city, she takes them out once or twice a day, pushing a carriage and pulling a tricycle. Talking to her friends on these outings is her solution to loneliness. Her day is full of a thousand pressures, some miniature, some large. Two of the main worries are illness and money. If everyone in the family is healthy for two weeks at a stretch, she counts herself fortunate. Every cold goes the rounds of the family, and she sometimes feels that she supports the pediatrician single-handedly.

During the healthy periods she strives to improve her home, cook a new dish, do something about her looks, give a dinner party and a children's birthday party, go to the theater with her husband, catch up on her reading, have coffee with a friend. Her life vacillates between being very organized and completely disorganized, because she has the struggle of all women: to keep the house clean and in repair without being a shrew about people's messing it up. Because children are natural makers of havoc, she constantly strives to maintain the delicate line of balance.

Usually, when the first child starts school, she is drawn into community or P.T.A. work of some kind. If she is normally conscientious, she feels she should do something, but if she is normally realistic, she knows she doesn't have time. So she does it anyway. Joining things as a virtue is a hangover from college, where well-roundedness and abundant interests were considered rungs on the ladder to heaven.

The demands of her family and community cause her to feel, as one woman put it, like a pie with not enough pieces to go around. Depending on whether or not she is gregarious, she longs for time to talk to her friends or time to be alone; I should say, the busier she is, the greater her urge to be by herself, to feel unique and separate again. Great numbers of friends are a luxury she can no longer afford; old friends often diminish in importance, which she is sorry about. But there is a limit to her capacity for giving affection, and maintaining old friendships at their original intensity requires an effort she hardly has the energy for. Besides, she is often forced into unwanted and demanding friendships with the next-door neighbor, the boss's wife, or the ladies' club chairman, and she must learn to cover up her real feelings. (To her surprise, she often ends by liking these women.) Another group of demanding relationships is required with her in-laws, and if she gets along well with them, she is lucky. If her husband now lacks the mystery and fascination of the wedding night, he is now more loved and appreciated. The occasions when they have time alone together are among her precious jewels.

In spite of this full life, the old illusions of what life was supposed to hold, the restless remnants, the undefined dreams do not die as they were supposed to. Probably every educated wife has found herself staring at a mountain of dirty diapers and asking herself desperately, "Is this all there is?" And at the same time she is embarrassed by her dissatisfaction; she, of all people, with her intelligence and realistic view of life, should be able to rise above it. But the paradox is that it is she who is least able to. She lives for a better day. Things will be easier when this baby is born, or that one toilet-trained, or the children are all in school; and she will have time to be pretty and intelligent and young again. The mistake is in thinking that everything is going to solve itself by magic. What our girl must do, as she stares at the diapers, is to accept some of the truths about marriage and motherhood that her education and society conspired to keep from her, and go on from there. And if she would appreciate what she has, she must do it now, not next year or five years from now.

The first truth is that marriage does not automatically equal security and contentment. An unmarried friend of mine told me once that she did not see how any problem in marriage could be as bad as one outside of it, because if you had your man, anything else could be easily straightened out. We had a long argument about whether the heart sank more over a sick child or a departed boy friend, and neither of us won. She is one of a good many girls who think that three dates a week, secretarial jobs, and the responsibility of keeping themselves clothed are a nerve-shattering, frantic business, and who look forward to marriage and motherhood as a long, relaxing rest cure. "Getting married and settling down" is a valid notion for men, as it has been throughout history, but not for potential mothers. The day the doctor confirms one's pregnancy is the day to start bracing oneself for the really hard work. (I cannot convince my unmarried friends of this, but, of course, that is as it should be, or many babies might never be born.)

The truth is that, with the birth of the first child, marvelous changes take place. From that moment on, mama is no longer the center of attention; the baby is. Mama and papa will give—and willingly—and the baby will take. They will assume responsibility, earn money, employ their energy, change their lives, if necessary—all for the baby. This is no light undertaking, but the business of life is starting now, and every day of mama's life proves it to be so. And here her struggle starts. She wants to give everything to the baby; she wants equally to hold on to herself, her intelligence and uniqueness, while the baby constantly tries her patience, her strength, her nerves, and roots out of her the deepest emotions she has ever known in her life. This is a whole new process, and not one that provides built-in security.

IT IS A MISTAKE to assume that marriage is a cure-all, a miraculous bit of psychiatry that is going to banish all the old problems overnight and, like phenobarbital, put disturbingly violent instincts to sleep. The benediction of church and state is not enough to still the quality of excitement that comes from strangeness and the idealization of a still-unknown experience. These things, after all, were part and parcel of sex before marriage, and half its value. Sex in marriage makes up in intimacy what it loses in mystery, but this does not mean that mystery is no longer attractive. The most embarrassing lust for the least likely person can exist in the best-adjusted P.T.A. member in town. Whether or not anything is done about it is another story, but probably most of the time nothing is. We take marriage very seriously; our Puritan heritage is still very much with us; and we fear the wages of sin. Besides, the communities of young married couples are built for decency and togetherness, and the woman who considers taking a lover simply has no place to go.

All of the notions about peace being intrinsic in the state of marriage have to do with the happiness-togetherness cult, the great American dream, the return to the hearth. The peak of all earthly satisfaction is said to be found in the family, popping corn together in matching pajamas, not in hard work and self-denial, or even in the self-knowledge that came with the Freudian age. In our unending search for panaceas, we believe that happiness and "success"—which, loosely translated, means money—are the things to strive for. People are constantly surprised that, even though they have acquired material things, discontent still gnaws.

An Englishman said to me recently, "You Americans live on a much higher plane of expectancy than we do. You constantly work toward some impossible goal of happiness and perfection, and you unfortunately don't have our ability just to give up. Really, it's much easier to accept the fact that some things can't be solved." He is right; we never accept it, and we kill ourselves trying. The feeling of futility of the housewife is based on a history of high expectancy, a faith in external things, and an inability to see that the rewards are found within oneself. It is a paradox that the achievement of a home and family is so often regarded by women as the consummate solution for human ills, when actually the responsibilities it entails are enough to reduce some people to nervous wrecks. Marriage, entered upon maturely, is the only life for most women. But it *is* a way of life, not a magic bag of goodies at the end of the road.

The fact is that marriage and motherhood bring forth deeper and more staggering emotions than any experience before marriage. There is nothing soothing or secure about the feeling, familiar to all mothers, of wanting to murder one's child and really feeling capable of it, and then the next moment dissolving into the deepest love and repentance. There is nothing soothing about the insane annoyance that one can feel at some irritating habit of a loved one, or at loathing the knowledge of what he or she is going to say; one feels trapped by a total ability to see—mystery gone forever. It can be painful to find oneself isolated, in marriage, with problems that have always been shared with mother or girl friends, and to realize that there are some things that even one's husband cannot be told. This is the hard lesson of discretion. And there is nothing soothing to participants or onlookers about the spine-chilling habit of some couples who goad each other to a fever pitch of irritation, with repeated fingernail rasps on each other's well-known sensitive spots—all in the name of playful affection. It is frightening to see how close emotions are to the surface and how little it takes to make destruction.

And it is equally frightening to know suddenly how complete love is and how much one gives to it, to see how little one can really stand when someone in the family is sick, and to know how quickly one can be torn apart by nothing at all. A young mother said the other day, speaking of young mothers in general, "It always amazes me how vulnerable we are and how we, who are supposed to be so responsible, are such preys of our own feelings." In a family of love, one must become infinitely flexible to withstand the continuous jounce of emotion. This is the muscle that develops, not superefficiency or physical strength, and it is the weariness of this muscle that causes young mothers to want to run away and hide in a solitary place where nothing can jar the heart.

THE SECOND TRUTH is that a girl does not need a college education to take care of babies and keep house. I recall a lot of talk at college among engaged girls that bringing up children is a vastly complicated business which makes full use of a mother's brains and energy, and that no man on earth has a position as responsible and delicate as that of being totally in charge of the education of minds, souls, and bodies of two or three important human beings.

Well, for one thing, mother is not totally in charge, though she may like to think so. The influences of father, school, doctor, friends, neighborhood, city, or country are equally important. Besides, mother is not really in charge of herself enough to be in charge of her children. What the children learn is what mother *is*, not what she thinks she is. For another thing, the job is hardly complicated and delicate, at least at first. It is the simple, nerve-wracking, mindless, battering-ram process of trying to teach a savage to use a fork. It requires bloodless patience, a deadly will, enormous physical stamina, and a stable disposition, but no precision instruments. It takes strength and determination.

For the fact is that motherhood makes the heaviest demands in what might be called the areas of least experience. I would be surprised if there were a single college-educated mother who has not been struck by the total uselessness of her liberal education when it comes to housewifery. Instead of distilling pearls of knowledge from a large body of facts, she must now master a whole new set of domestic facts: how to roast a chicken, remove gum from the rug, take a child's temperature, keep the shine on the Sheraton table, iron a blouse, or even change a tire or build a bookcase. Some of these necessities are positively shocking. The care of dirty diapers and the job of keeping the oven clean call for a strong-minded unfastidiousness; even more does the whole process of having a baby, which is certainly nature at its rawest. Learning all of these things calls for a day-to-day resourcefulness and is a new and rather frightening responsibility.

Choosing a house and everything that goes into it, and a school, and a competent doctor are decisions that the young mother makes without adequate knowledge, and she can ill afford mistakes. If her husband is sympathetic, he helps her with these decisions. If not, she gropes her way along and takes the blame when that lovely color for the living-room walls turns out to be bilious salmon pink in the sunlight. And this calls for a brand-new virtue, too: the ability to adapt oneself completely, in about thirty seconds flat, to an entirely new viewpoint. Around a house, no achievement is very permanent, and the day can turn inside out before one's eyes. The salmon-pink walls must suddenly be repainted, the baby sitter suddenly fails, the clean living room is no longer clean, the elevator in the apartment building breaks down, and mother and baby carriage are trapped for the day on the seventh floor.

THE THIRD TRUTH is that there are only twenty-four hours in a day. The pressure to join is apparently very heavy in the suburbs; in New York, and, I suppose, other large cities, one can do as one pleases. Joining things is one solution to the vaguely frustrated, my-mind-is-rotting feeling. As at college, it is often considered a virtue in itself for a group of women to get together and form a committee, to do something useful, to pursue culture or play bridge. If the activities get out of hand, they can run mother and father into ulcers. Besides, joining things contradicts the real need, which is to be alone and feel unique again, to be less urgent and more cerebral.

It is important to have a solid grasp of time. The makers of household appliances say that they have given the modern housewife great amounts of free time, such as her mother and grandmother never had. This, of course, is nonsense. The truth is that mama is freed from the hard work that used to be done by grandma's maid. The free time comes in dribs and drabs, fifteen minutes here, half an hour there. The bogey of the young mother is in believing that she is simply abounding in leisure and so she really ought to cram in a few more activities and be a better wife than ever.

The young mother also seems to feel that she ought to have a few more children. This is a fairly recent development and quite a change from our parents' generation, when married couples had one or two children at the most. Women who had more were deprecatingly referred to as brood mares. Now that women have stopped trying to prove how emancipated they are, some of them think that a lovely family of six is a step toward utopia. Other women, for some private neurotic reason, are only happy when pregnant or nursing a baby; the rest of the time they feel useless. And some women just stumble into pregnancy. Even in these advanced times, there are a great many women, B.A.'s included, who, though hardheaded enough about most things, occasionally forget the facts of life in the romance of the moment. (A small and admittedly inconclusive survey in my neighborhood revealed that half the children in the park were unplanned.) However, the explanation for large families apparently lies in some notion that the world is cold, lonely, and dangerous, and children will make it less so, or shield us from it. It is a strange notion for such a practical generation in a dangerous world; one would think it would be exactly the opposite.

Young wives, particularly those who feel that their minds are rotting and their backs are aching, should remind themselves that maturity is more than simply accepting one's present condition and somehow muddling through until things are better. The beginning of wisdom comes with looking at one's life from the viewpoint of eternity and realizing that the hard years are part and parcel of loving and having children, and that rather than just getting through them, the thing to do is appreciate them. The happiest women are the ones who can do that. No magic is going to happen when this child is out of diapers or that one in school. Things certainly get easier as children get older, but this does not solve the personal problem.

Young mothers need time more than anything else, time for whatever fancy suits them. Time to have lunch with a friend and talk over the problems of the world; time to see a play, browse in a library, or simply sit and stare out the window. A lot of women feel vaguely guilty about doing these things, as though one got points of virtue for simply staying around the house. But the restoring effect of simply going off by oneself is more important than they realize. It restores joy to our lives and reminds us that we are not only part of a family but part of a community or a city or a society. This wider view gives us a feeling of personal importance and causes us to greet our children with greater affection than usual when we come home, because we have been reminded that we are the ones who know the world and sort out its complexities for them, who clarify its diffusiveness for them, and who gradually lead them out into it.

The Education of David Stockman

WILLIAM GREIDER || 1981

Among the lead insurgents of the so-called Reagan Revolution—Ronald Reagan's program to slash the size of the federal government—none was more dedicated to the cause than David Stockman. A two-term Republican congressman from Michigan, Stockman became the youngest cabinet member of the twentieth century when Reagan chose him shortly after the 1980 election to head the Office of Management and Budget, the small but powerful White House agency that is charged with setting national fiscal policy and riding herd on the far-flung federal bureaucracy. Over the course of fifteen years, Stockman had morphed from antiwar liberal to radical conservative; he had embraced, with evangelical fervor, the theory of "supply-side economics," which contends that tax cuts are the golden path to economic growth. As Stockman set off to mount the most sweeping attack on the status quo since the New Deal, he agreed to a series of interviews for The Atlantic *with William Greider (1936–   ), a longtime* Washington Post *reporter and editor, about how the mission was going. Rarely, if ever, has a cabinet member (while still in office) spoken on the record with such remarkable candor about his growing disillusionment with his own administration's policies. Among the article's more startling admissions: Stockman acknowledged that budget deficits would rapidly increase, not decrease, because of his boss's policies, and that even he did not understand the budget figures that the president was so confidently touting to the nation. Despite the political furor that followed the publication of Greider's article, Stockman somehow managed to keep his job for another four years—even after being allegedly "taken to the woodshed" by Reagan. And time proved his very publicly voiced fears right. By the time Reagan left office, in 1988, the federal budget deficit was at an all-time high under a peacetime president. Big government was bigger than ever.*

Three weeks before the Inauguration, Stockman and his transition team of a dozen or so people were already established at the OMB office in the Old Executive Office Building. When his appointment as budget director first seemed likely, he had agreed to meet with me from time to time and relate, off the record, his private account of the great political struggle ahead. The particulars of these conversations were not to be reported until later, after the season's battles were over, but a cynic familiar with how Washington works would understand that the arrangement had obvious symbiotic value. As an assistant managing editor at *The Washington Post*, I benefited from an informed view of policy discussions of the new administration; Stockman, a student of history, was contributing to history's record and perhaps influencing its conclusions. For him, our meetings were another channel—among many he used—to the press. The older generation of orthodox Republicans distrusted the press; Stockman was one of the younger "new" conservatives who cultivated contacts with columnists and reporters, who saw the news media as another useful tool in political combat. In any case, for the eight months that followed, Stockman kept the agreement, and our regular conversations, over breakfast at the Hay-Adams, provided the basis of the account that follows.

In early January, Stockman and his staff were assembling dozens of position papers on program reductions and studying the internal forecasts for the federal budget and the national economy. The initial figures were frightening—"absolutely shocking," he confided—yet he seemed oddly exhilarated by the bad news, and was bubbling with new plans for coping with these horrendous numbers. An OMB computer, programmed as a model of the nation's economic behavior, was instructed to estimate the impact of Reagan's program on the federal budget. It predicted that if the new President went ahead with his promised three-year tax reduction and his increase in defense spending, the Reagan Administration would be faced with a series of federal deficits without precedent in peacetime—ranging from $82 billion in 1982 to $116 billion in 1984. Even Stockman blinked. If those were the numbers included in President Reagan's first budget message, the following month, the financial markets that Stockman sought to reassure would instead be panicked. Interest rates, already high, would go higher; the expectation of long-term inflation would be confirmed.

Stockman saw opportunity in these shocking projections. "All the conventional estimates just wind up as mud," he said. "As absurdities. What they basically say, to boil it down, is that the world doesn't work."

Stockman set about doing two things. First, he changed the OMB computer. Assisted by like-minded supply-side economists, the new team discarded orthodox premises of how the economy would behave. Instead of a continuing double-digit inflation, the new computer model assumed a swift decline in prices and interest rates. Instead of the continuing pattern of slow economic growth, the new model was based on a dramatic surge in the nation's productivity. New investment, new jobs, and growing profits— and Stockman's historic bull market. "It's based on valid economic analysis," he said, "but it's the inverse of the last four years. When we go public, this is going to set off a wide-open debate on how the economy works, a great battle over the conventional theories of economic performance."

The original apostles of supply-side, particularly Representative Jack Kemp, of New York, and the economist Arthur B. Laffer, dismissed budget-cutting as inconsequential to the economic problems, but Stockman was trying to fuse new theory and old. "Laffer sold us a bill of goods," he said, then corrected his words: "Laffer wasn't wrong—he didn't go far enough."

The great debate never quite took hold in the dimensions that Stockman had anticipated, but the Reagan Administration's economic projections did become the source of continuing controversy. In defense of their counter-theories, Stockman and his associates would argue, correctly, that conventional forecasts, particularly by the Council of Economic Advisers in the preceding administration, had been consistently wrong in the past. His critics would contend that the supply-side premises were based upon wishful thinking, not sound economic analysis.

But, second, Stockman used the appalling deficit projections as a valuable talking point in the policy discussions that were under way with the President and his principal advisers. Nobody in that group was the least bit hesitant about cutting federal programs, but Reagan had campaigned on the vague and painless theme that eliminating "waste, fraud, and mismanagement" would be sufficient to balance the accounts. Now, as Stockman put it, "the idea is to try to get beyond the waste, fraud, and mismanagement modality and begin to confront the real dimensions of budget reduction."

No President had balanced the budget in the past twelve years. Still, Stockman thought it could be done, by 1984, if the Reagan Administration adhered to the principle of equity, cutting weak claims, not merely weak clients, and if it shocked the system sufficiently to create a new political climate. Eliminate Social Security minimum benefits. Cap the runaway costs of Medicaid. Tighten eligibility for food stamps. Merge the trade adjustment assistance for unemployed industrial workers with standard unemployment compensation and shrink it. Cut education aid by a quarter. Cut grants for the arts and humanities in half. "Zero out" CETA [the Comprehensive Employment and Training Act] and the Community Services Administration and National Consumer Cooperative Bank. And so forth. "Zero out" became a favorite phrase of Stockman's; it meant closing down a program "cold turkey," in one budget year.

THE REACTIONS FROM CAPITOL HILL were clamorous, as expected, but the budget director was more impressed by the silences, the stutter and hesitation of the myriad interest groups. Stockman was becoming a favorite caricature for newspaper cartoonists—the grim reaper of the Reagan Administration, the Republican Robespierre.

Even by Washington standards, where overachieving young people with excessive adrenaline are commonplace, Stockman was busy. Back and forth, back and forth he went, from his vast office at the Old Executive Office Building, with its classic high ceilings and its fireplace, to the cloakrooms and hideaway offices and hearing chambers of the Capitol, to the West Wing of the White House. Usually, he carried an impossible stack of books and papers under his arm, like a harried high school student who has not been given a locker. He promised friends he would relax—take a day off, or at least sleep later than 5 A.M., when he usually arose to read policy papers before breakfast. But he did not relax easily. What was social life compared with the thrill of reshaping the federal establishment?

The Democrats [who controlled Congress at the time], by Stockman's analysis ... were really three groups: the old-line liberal faithful, who would follow the party leadership and defend against any or all budget cuts; a middle group, including Jim Jones, the Democratic chairman of the House Budget Committee, and other younger members, who recognized that federal deficits were out of control and were willing to confront the problem (Stockman referred to them as "the progressives"); and, finally, the "boll weevils," the thirty-eight southerners who were pulled toward Reagan both in conservative philosophy and by the politics of their home districts, which had voted overwhelmingly for the President. Jones was drawing up a resolution that would restore some funds to social programs, to keep the liberals happy; that projected a smaller deficit than Stockman's, to appear more responsible in fiscal terms; and that did not touch the defense budget, which would offend the southerners.

Artful as it was, the Jones resolution was, according to Stockman, a series of gimmicks: economic estimates and accounting tricks. "Political numbers," he called them. But Stockman was not critical of Jones for these budget ploys, because he cheerfully conceded that the administration's own budget numbers were constructed on similar shaky premises, mixing cuts from the original 1981 budget left by Jimmy Carter with new baseline projections from the Congressional Budget Office in a way that, fundamentally, did not add up. The budget politics of 1981, which produced such clear and dramatic rhetoric from both sides, was, in fact, based upon a bewildering set of numbers that confused even those, like Stockman, who produced them.

"None of us really understands what's going on with all these numbers," Stockman confessed at one point. "You've got so many different budgets out and so many different baselines and such complexity now in the interactive parts of the budget between policy action and the economic environment and all the internal mysteries of the budget, and there are a lot of them. People are getting from A to B and it's not clear how they are getting there. It's not clear how we got there and it's not clear how Jones is going to get there."

Stockman was privately staring at another reality—a gloomy portent that the economic theory behind the President's program wasn't working. While it was winning in the political arena, the plan was losing on Wall Street. The financial markets, which Stockman had thought would be reassured by the new President's bold actions, and which were supposed to launch a historic "bull market" in April, failed to respond in accordance with Stockman's script. The markets not only failed to rally, they went into a new decline. Interest rates started up again; the bond market slumped. Investment analysts . . . were looking closely at the Stockman budget figures, looking beyond the storm of political debate and the President's winning style, and what they saw were enormous deficits ahead—the same numbers that had shocked David Stockman when he came into office in January. Stockman . . . conceded that his own original conception—that dramatic political action would somehow alter the marketplace expectations of continuing inflation—had been wrong.

Stockman thought he had taken care of embarrassing questions about future deficits with a device he referred to as the "magic asterisk." (Senator Howard Baker had dubbed it that in strategy sessions, Stockman said.) The "magic asterisk" would blithely denote all of the future deficit problems that were to be taken care of with additional budget reductions, to be announced by the President at a later date. Thus, everyone could finesse the hard questions, for now.

But the real problem, as Stockman conceded, was still unsolved. Indeed, pondering the reactions of financial markets, the budget director made an extraordinary confession in private: the original agenda of budget reductions, which had seemed so radical in February, was exposed by May as inadequate. The "magic asterisk" might suffice for the political debate in Congress, but it would not answer the fundamental question asked by Wall Street: How, in fact, did Ronald Reagan expect to balance the federal budget?

"It means," Stockman said, "that you have to have some recalibration in the policy. The thing was put together so fast that it probably should have been put together differently." . . . Stockman looked back at what had gone wrong: "The defense numbers got out of control and we were doing that whole budget-cutting exercise so frenetically. In other words, you were juggling details, pushing people, and going from one session to another, trying to cut housing programs here and rural electric there, and we were doing it so fast, we didn't know where we were ending up for sure. . . . In other words, we should have designed those pieces to be more compatible. But the pieces were moving on independent tracks—the tax program, where we were going on spending, and the defense program, which was just a bunch of numbers written on a piece of paper. And it didn't quite mesh."

Reagan's policy-makers knew that their plan was wrong, or at least inadequate to its promised effects, but the President went ahead and conveyed the opposite impression to the American public. With the cool sincerity of an experienced television actor, Reagan appeared on network TV to rally the nation . . . , promising a new era of fiscal control and balanced budgets, when Stockman knew they still had not found the solution.

In short, the fundamental arithmetic of the federal budget, which Stockman and others had brushed aside in the heady days of January, was now back to haunt them. If the new administration would not cut defense or Social Security or major "safety-net" programs that Reagan had put off limits, then it must savage the smaller slice remaining. Otherwise, balancing the budget in 1984 became an empty promise. The political pain of taking virtually all of the budget savings from government grants and operations would be too great, Stockman believed; Congress would never stand for it.

Without recognizing it at the time, the budget director was headed into a summer in which not only financial markets but life itself seemed to be absolutely perverse. The Reagan program kept winning in public, a series of well-celebrated political victories in Congress—yet privately Stockman was losing his struggle.

Stockman was changing, in a manner that perhaps he himself did not recognize. His conversations began to reflect a new sense of fatalism, a brittle edge of uncertainty.

"There was a certain dimension of our theory that was unrealistic . . ."

"The system has an enormous amount of inertia . . ."

"I don't believe too much in the momentum theory any more . . ."

"I have a new theory—there are no real conservatives in Congress . . ."

STOCKMAN HIMSELF HAD BEEN a late convert to supply-side theology, and now he was beginning to leave the church. The theory of "expectations" wasn't working. He could see that. And Stockman's institutional role as budget director forced him to look constantly at aspects of the political economy that the other supply-siders tended to dismiss. Whatever the reason, Stockman was creating some distance between himself and the supply-side purists; eventually, he would become the target of their nasty barbs. For his part, Stockman began to disparage the grand theory as a kind of convenient illusion—new rhetoric to cover old Republican doctrine.

"The hard part of the supply-side tax cut is dropping the top rate from 70 to 50 percent—the rest of it is a secondary matter," Stockman explained. "The original argument was that the top bracket was too high, and that's having the most devastating effect on the economy. Then, the general argument was that, in order to make this palatable as a political matter, you had to bring down all the brackets."

Yet he was conceding what the liberal Keynesian critics had argued from the outset—the supply-side theory was not a new economic theory at all but only new language and argument to conceal a hoary old Republican doctrine: give the tax cuts to the top brackets, the wealthiest individuals and largest enterprises, and let the good effects "trickle down" through the economy to reach everyone else. Yes, Stockman conceded, when one stripped away the new rhetoric emphasizing across-the-board cuts, the supply-side theory was really new clothes for the unpopular doctrine of the old Republican orthodoxy. "It's kind of hard to sell 'trickle down,'" he explained, "so the supply-side formula was the only way to get a tax policy that was really 'trickle down.' Supply-side is 'trickle-down' theory."

The economy might start to respond, eventually, to the stimulation of the tax cuts. "Who knows?" Stockman said. From David Stockman, it was a startling remark. He would continue to invent new scenarios for success, but they would be more complicated and cloudy than his original optimism. "Who knows?" The world was less manageable than he had imagined; this machine had too many crazy moving parts to incorporate in a single lucid theory. The random elements of history—politics, the economy, the anarchical budget numbers—were out of control.

Broken Windows

JAMES Q. WILSON AND GEORGE L. KELLING ‖ 1982

In late 1993, when former New York City mayor Rudolph Giuliani hired William Bratton to run his police department, violent crime in the city was near an all-time high, with 2,420 murders recorded that year. By the end of the decade, violent crime had plunged to its lowest point in thirty-five years, with the total number of recorded murders in 1999 falling to 903. A number of possible explanations for the spectacular turnaround have been offered up over the years—the decline of crack cocaine abuse, significant drops in the unemployment rate, even the demographic consequences of legalized abortion. But many criminologists, as well as Giuliani and Bratton themselves, contend that the city's radically improved crime picture emanated directly from the ideas expressed in this groundbreaking Atlantic essay, "Broken Windows."

James Q. Wilson (1931–), who was then a professor of government at Harvard, and George L. Kelling (1935–), a professor of criminal justice at Rutgers University, teamed up to write their article out of a deep concern about the shifting role of the police from crime preventers to crime solvers—from maintaining law and order on the streets to investigating crimes that had already been committed. They argued that this crucial metamorphosis in police responsibility, which had begun in the 1960s, contravened what social scientists had long observed about the dangerous effects that are unleashed when society tacitly accepts even minor crimes, such as aggressive panhandling and graffiti: they quickly proliferate into major ones. "Social psychologists and police officers tend to agree that if a window in a building is broken and is left unrepaired, all the rest of the windows will soon be broken," Wilson and Kelling observed, adding that "serious street crime flourishes in areas in which disorderly behavior goes unchecked." Under the rubric of "community policing" and "zero tolerance," Wilson and Kelling's crime-fighting prescriptions have been successfully adopted not only by New York City but by police departments in Los Angeles, Boston, Denver, and other cities throughout the country. "If there were a Hall of Fame for influential public-policy ideas," said a 2001 article in The Chronicle of Higher Education, *"then the 'broken windows' thesis would probably have its own exhibit."*

Social psychologists and police officers tend to agree that if a window in a building is broken and is left unrepaired, all the rest of the windows will soon be broken. This is as true in nice neighborhoods as in rundown ones. Window-breaking does not necessarily occur on a large scale because some areas are inhabited by determined window-breakers whereas others are populated by window-lovers; rather, one unrepaired broken window is a signal that no one cares, and so breaking more windows costs nothing. (It has always been fun.)

We suggest that "untended" behavior also leads to the breakdown of community controls. A stable neighborhood of families who care for their homes, mind each other's children, and confidently frown on unwanted intruders can change, in a few years or even a few months, to an inhospitable and frightening jungle. A piece of property is abandoned, weeds grow up, a window is smashed. Adults stop scolding rowdy children; the children, emboldened, become more rowdy. Families move out, unattached adults move in. Teenagers gather in front of the corner store. The merchant asks them to move; they refuse. Fights occur. Litter accumulates. People start drinking in front of the grocery; in time, an inebriate slumps to the sidewalk and is allowed to sleep it off. Pedestrians are approached by panhandlers.

At this point it is not inevitable that serious crime will flourish or violent attacks on strangers will occur. But many residents will think that crime, especially violent crime, is on the rise, and they will modify their behavior accordingly. They will use the streets less often, and when on the streets will stay apart from their fellows, moving with averted eyes, silent lips, and hurried steps. "Don't get involved." For some residents, this growing atomization will matter little, because the neighborhood is not their "home" but "the place where they live." Their interests are elsewhere; they are cosmopolitans. But it will matter greatly to other people, whose lives derive meaning and satisfaction from local attachments rather than worldly involvement; for them, the neighborhood will cease to exist except for a few reliable friends whom they arrange to meet.

Such an area is vulnerable to criminal invasion. Though it is not inevitable, it is more likely that here, rather than in places where people are confident they can regulate public behavior by informal controls, drugs will change hands, prostitutes will solicit, and cars will be stripped. That the drunks will be robbed by boys who do it as a lark, and the prostitutes' customers will be robbed by men who do it purposefully and perhaps violently. That muggings will occur.

THE PROCESS WE CALL URBAN DECAY has occurred for centuries in every city. But what is happening today is different in at least two important respects. First, in the period before, say, World War II, city dwellers—because of money costs, transportation difficulties, familial and church connections—could rarely move away from neighborhood problems. When movement did occur, it tended to be along public-transit routes. Now mobility has become exceptionally easy for all but the poorest or those who are blocked by racial prejudice. Earlier crime waves had a kind of built-in self-correcting mechanism: the determination of a neighborhood or community to reassert control over its turf. Areas in Chicago, New York, and Boston would experience crime and gang wars, and then normalcy would return, as the families for whom no alternative residences were possible reclaimed their authority over the streets.

Second, the police in this earlier period assisted in that reassertion of authority by acting, sometimes violently, on behalf of the community. Young toughs were roughed up, people were arrested "on suspicion" or for vagrancy, and prostitutes and petty thieves were routed. "Rights" were something enjoyed by decent folk, and perhaps also by the serious professional criminal, who avoided violence and could afford a lawyer.

This pattern of policing was not an aberration or the result of occasional excess. From the earliest days of the nation, the police function was seen primarily as that of a night watchman: to maintain order against the chief threats to order—fire, wild animals, and disreputable behavior. Solving crimes was viewed not as a police responsibility but as a private one. In the March, 1969, *Atlantic*, one of us (Wilson) wrote a brief account of how the police role had slowly changed from maintaining order to fighting crimes. The change began with the creation of private detectives (often ex-criminals), who worked on a contingency-fee basis for individuals who had suffered losses. In time, the detectives were absorbed in municipal agencies and paid a regular salary simultaneously, the responsibility for prosecuting thieves was shifted from the aggrieved private citizen to the professional prosecutor. This process was not complete in most places until the twentieth century.

In the 1960s, when urban riots were a major problem, social scientists began to explore carefully the order maintenance function of the police, and to suggest ways of improving it—not to make streets safer (its original function) but to reduce the incidence of mass violence. Order maintenance became, to a degree, coterminous with "community relations." But, as the crime wave that began in the early 1960s continued without abatement throughout the decade and into the 1970s, attention shifted to the role of the police as crime-fighters. Studies of police behavior ceased, by and large, to be accounts of the order-maintenance function and became, instead, efforts to propose and test ways whereby the police could solve more crimes, make more arrests, and gather better evidence. If these things could be done, social scientists assumed, citizens would be less fearful.

A great deal was accomplished during this transition, as both police chiefs and outside experts emphasized the crime-fighting function in their plans, in the allocation of resources, and in deployment of personnel. The police may well have become better crime-fighters as a result. And doubtless they remained aware of their responsibility for order. But the link between order-maintenance and crime-prevention, so obvious to earlier generations, was forgotten.

That link is similar to the process whereby one broken window becomes many. The citizen who fears the ill-smelling drunk, the rowdy teenager, or the importuning beggar is not merely expressing his distaste for unseemly behavior; he is also giving voice to a bit of folk wisdom that happens to be a correct generalization—namely, that serious street crime flourishes in areas in which disorderly behavior goes unchecked. The unchecked panhandler is, in effect, the first broken window. Muggers and robbers, whether opportunistic or professional, believe they reduce their chances of being caught or even identified if they operate on streets where potential victims are already intimidated by prevailing conditions. If the neighborhood cannot keep a bothersome panhandler from annoying passersby, the thief may reason, it is even less likely to call the police to identify a potential mugger or to interfere if the mugging actually takes place.

Some police administrators concede that this process occurs, but argue that motorized-patrol officers can deal with it as effectively as foot patrol officers. We are not so sure. In theory, an officer in a squad car can observe as much as an officer on foot; in theory, the former can talk to as many people as the latter. But the reality of police-citizen encounters is powerfully altered by the automobile. An officer on foot cannot separate himself from the street people; if he is approached, only his uniform and his personality can help him manage whatever is about to happen. And he can never be certain what that will be—a request for directions, a plea for help, an angry denunciation, a teasing remark, a confused babble, a threatening gesture.

In a car, an officer is more likely to deal with street people by rolling down the window and looking at them. The door and the window exclude the approaching citizen; they are a barrier. Some officers take advantage of this barrier, perhaps unconsciously, by acting differently if in the car than they would on foot. We have seen this countless times. The police car pulls up to a corner where teenagers are gathered. The window is rolled down. The officer stares at the youths. They stare back. The officer says to one, "C'mere." He saunters over, conveying to his friends by his elaborately casual style the idea that he is not intimidated by authority. "What's your name?" "Chuck." "Chuck who?" "Chuck Jones." "What'ya doing, Chuck?" "Nothin'." "Got a P.O. [parole officer]?" "Nah." "Sure?" "Yeah." "Stay out of trouble, Chuckie." Meanwhile, the other boys laugh and exchange comments among themselves, probably at the officer's expense. The officer stares harder. He cannot be certain what is being said, nor can he join in and, by displaying his own skill at street banter, prove that he cannot be "put down." In the process, the officer has learned almost nothing, and the boys have decided the officer is an alien force who can safely be disregarded, even mocked.

Our experience is that most citizens like to talk to a police officer. Such exchanges give them a sense of importance, provide them with the basis for gossip, and allow them to explain to the authorities what is worrying them (whereby they gain a modest but significant sense of having "done something" about the problem). You approach a person on foot more easily, and talk to him more readily, than you do a person in a car. Moreover, you can more easily retain some anonymity if you draw an officer aside for a private chat. Suppose you want to pass on a tip about who is stealing handbags, or who offered to sell you a stolen TV. In the inner city, the culprit, in all likelihood, lives nearby. To walk up to a marked patrol car and lean in the window is to convey a visible signal that you are a "fink."

The essence of the police role in maintaining order is to reinforce the informal control mechanisms of the community itself. The police cannot, without committing extraordinary resources, provide a substitute for that informal control. On the other hand, to reinforce those natural forces the police must accommodate them. And therein lies the problem.

SHOULD POLICE ACTIVITY ON THE STREET be shaped, in important ways, by the standards of the neighborhood rather than by the rules of the state? Over the past two decades, the shift of police from order-maintenance to law enforcement has brought them increasingly under the influence of legal restrictions, provoked by media complaints and enforced by court decisions and departmental orders. As a consequence, the order-maintenance functions of the police are now governed by rules developed to control police relations with suspected criminals. This is, we think, an entirely new development. For centuries, the role of the police as watchmen was judged primarily not in terms of its compliance with appropriate procedures but rather in terms of its attaining a desired objective. The objective was order, an inherently ambiguous term but a condition that people in a given community recognized when they saw it. The means were the same as those the community itself would employ, if its members were sufficiently determined, courageous, and authoritative. Detecting and apprehending criminals, by contrast, was a means to an end, not an end in itself; a judicial determination of guilt or innocence was the hoped-for result of the law-enforcement mode. From the first, the police were expected to follow rules defining that process, though states differed in how stringent the rules should be. The criminal-apprehension process was always understood to involve individual rights, the violation of which was unacceptable because it meant that the violating officer would be acting as a judge and jury—and that was not his job. Guilt or innocence was to be determined by universal standards under special procedures.

Ordinarily, no judge or jury ever sees the persons caught up in a dispute over the appropriate level of neighborhood order. That is true not only because most cases are handled informally on the street but also because no universal standards are available to settle arguments over disorder, and thus a judge may not be any wiser or more effective than a police officer. Until quite recently in many states, and even today in some places, the police made arrests on such charges as "suspicious person" or "vagrancy" or "public drunkenness"—charges with scarcely any legal meaning. These charges exist not because society wants judges to punish vagrants or drunks but because it wants an officer to have the legal tools to remove undesirable persons from a neighborhood when informal efforts to preserve order in the streets have failed.

Once we begin to think of all aspects of police work as involving the application of universal rules under special procedures, we inevitably ask what constitutes an "undesirable person" and why we should "criminalize" vagrancy or drunkenness. A strong and commendable desire to see that people are treated fairly makes us worry about allowing the police to rout persons who are undesirable by some vague or parochial standard. A growing and not-so-commendable utilitarianism leads us to doubt that any behavior that does not "hurt" another person should be made illegal. And thus many of us who watch over the police are reluctant to allow them to perform, in the only way they can, a function that every neighborhood desperately wants them to perform.

This wish to "decriminalize" disreputable behavior that "harms no one"—and thus remove the ultimate sanction the police can employ to maintain neighborhood order—is, we think, a mistake. Arresting a single drunk or a single vagrant who has harmed no identifiable person seems unjust, and in a sense it is. But failing to do anything about a score of drunks or a hundred vagrants may destroy an entire community. A particular rule that seems to make sense in the individual case makes no sense when it is made a universal rule and applied to all cases. It makes no sense because it fails to take into account the connection between one broken window left untended and a thousand broken windows.

The concern about equity is more serious. We might agree that certain behavior makes one person more undesirable than another but how do we ensure that age or skin color or national origin or harmless mannerisms will not also become the basis for distinguishing the undesirable from the desirable? How do we ensure, in short, that the police do not become the agents of neighborhood bigotry?

We can offer no wholly satisfactory answer to this important question. We are not confident that there is a satisfactory answer except to hope that by their selection, training, and supervision, the police will be inculcated with a clear sense of the outer limit of their discretionary authority. That limit, roughly, is this—the police exist to help regulate behavior, not to maintain the racial or ethnic purity of a neighborhood.

[How] can the police strengthen the informal social-control mechanisms of natural communities in order to minimize fear in public places? Law enforcement, per se, is no answer: a gang can weaken or destroy a community by standing about in a menacing fashion and speaking rudely to passersby without breaking the law.

It may be their greater sensitivity to communal as opposed to individual needs that helps explain why the residents of small communities are more satisfied with their police than are the residents of similar neighborhoods in big cities. Elinor Ostrom and her co-workers at Indiana University compared the perception of police services in two poor, all-black Illinois towns—Phoenix and East Chicago Heights—with those of three comparable all-black neighborhoods in Chicago. The level of criminal victimization and the quality of police-community relations appeared to be about the same in the towns and the Chicago neighborhoods. But the citizens living in their own villages were much more likely than those living in the Chicago neighborhoods to say that they do not stay at home for fear of crime, to agree that the local police have "the right to take any action necessary" to deal with problems, and to agree that the police "look out for the needs of the average citizen." It is possible that the residents and the police of the small towns saw themselves as engaged in a collaborative effort to maintain a certain standard of communal life, whereas those of the big city felt themselves to be simply requesting and supplying particular services on an individual basis.

Until well into the nineteenth century, volunteer watchmen, not policemen, patrolled their communities to keep order. They did so, by and large, without taking the law into their own hands—without, that is, punishing persons or using force. Their presence deterred disorder or alerted the community to disorder that could not be deterred. There are hundreds of such efforts today in communities all across the nation.

THOUGH CITIZENS CAN DO A GREAT DEAL, the police are plainly the key to order maintenance. For one thing, many communities . . . cannot do the job by themselves. For another, no citizen in a neighborhood, even an organized one, is likely to feel the sense of responsibility that wearing a badge confers. Psychologists have done many studies on why people fail to go to the aid of persons being attacked or seeking help, and they have learned that the cause is not "apathy" or "selfishness" but the absence of some plausible grounds for feeling that one must personally accept responsibility. Ironically, avoiding responsibility is easier when a lot of people are standing about. On streets and in public places, where order is so important, many people are likely to be "around," a fact that reduces the chance of any one person acting as the agent of the community. The police officer's uniform singles him out as a person who must accept responsibility if asked.

But the police forces of America are losing, not gaining, members. Some cities have suffered substantial cuts in the number of officers available for duty. One way to stretch limited police resources is being tried in some public housing projects. Tenant organizations hire off-duty police officers for patrol work in their buildings. The costs are not high (at least not per resident), the officer likes the additional income, and the residents feel safer. Such arrangements are probably more successful than hiring private watchmen. . . . A private security guard may deter crime or misconduct by his presence, and he may go to the aid of persons needing help, but he may well not intervene—that is, control or drive away—someone challenging community standards. Being a sworn officer—a "real cop"—seems to give one the confidence, the sense of duty, and the aura of authority necessary to perform this difficult task.

But the most important requirement is to think that to maintain order in precarious situations is a vital job. The police know this is one of their functions, and they also believe, correctly, that it cannot be done to the exclusion of criminal investigation and responding to calls. We may have encouraged them to suppose, however, on the basis of our oft-repeated concerns about serious, violent crime, that they will be judged exclusively on their capacity as crime-fighters. To the extent that this is the case, police administrators will continue to concentrate police personnel in the highest-crime areas (though not necessarily in the areas most vulnerable to criminal invasion), emphasize their training in the law and criminal apprehension (and not their training in managing street life), and join too quickly in campaigns to decriminalize "harmless" behavior (though public drunkenness, street prostitution, and pornographic displays can destroy a community more quickly than any team of professional burglars).

Above all, we must return to our long-abandoned view that the police ought to protect communities as well as individuals. Our crime statistics and victimization surveys measure individual losses, but they do not measure communal losses. Just as physicians now recognize the importance of fostering health rather than simply treating illness, so the police—and the rest of us—ought to recognize the importance of maintaining, intact, communities without broken windows.

The Roots of Muslim Rage

BERNARD LEWIS || 1990

In the period of national shock and confusion that followed 9/11, a number of Americans, both in and out of government, turned to the work of one man, Bernard Lewis (1916–   ), to better understand the underlying reasons behind that day's devastating attacks. Over the course of a sixty-year career, Lewis, a Princeton historian emeritus who has authored some thirty books and numerous magazine articles, has become widely recognized as one of the world's leading authorities on Islamic history and culture. And nowhere in Lewis's voluminous writings has he put forth a more concise, cogent, and convincing explanation of the late-twentieth-century wave of Islamic fundamentalism than in his seminal
Atlantic *essay, "The Roots of Muslim Rage." More than a decade before September 11, Lewis told readers why the emerging radical Muslim movement was becoming a powerful and dangerous force in the world, an epidemic driven by a particularly virulent strain of anti-Americanism. Framing the issues dividing the countries of the West and of the Middle East as a new phase in an age-old "clash of civilizations" (three years before the political scientist Samuel Huntington popularized that term in a widely cited essay of the same title), Lewis contended that this conflict was driven, in large part, by a dramatic reversal of fortunes—with America and the West becoming firmly ensconced as the world's political, economic, and cultural center and with Islam suffering a commensurate, centuries-long decline in its global reach. In recent years, Lewis has become something of a controversial figure, thanks to his close ties to the Bush administration and to his staunch advocacy of the invasion of Iraq. Lewis's support for the Iraq War is all the more surprising, given the ominous warning he sounds toward the end of this essay: "But before this issue [Islamic moderates vs. fundamentalists] is decided there will be a hard struggle, in which we of the West can do little or nothing. Even the attempt might do harm, for these are issues that Muslims must decide among themselves. And in the meantime we must take great care on all sides to avoid the danger of a new era of religious wars, arising from the exacerbation of differences and the revival of ancient prejudices."*

In one of his letters Thomas Jefferson remarked that in matters of religion "the maxim of civil government" should be reversed and we should rather say, "Divided we stand, united, we fall." In this remark Jefferson was setting forth with classic terseness an idea that has come to be regarded as essentially American: the separation of Church and State. This idea was not entirely new; it had some precedents in the writings of Spinoza, Locke, and the philosophers of the European Enlightenment. It was in the United States, however, that the principle was first given the force of law and gradually, in the course of two centuries, became a reality.

If the idea that religion and politics should be separated is relatively new, dating back a mere three hundred years, the idea that they are distinct dates back almost to the beginnings of Christianity. Christians are enjoined in their Scriptures to "render . . . unto Caesar the things which are Caesar's and unto God the things which are God's." While opinions have differed as to the real meaning of this phrase, it has generally been interpreted as legitimizing a situation in which two institutions exist side by side, each with its own laws and chain of authority—one concerned with religion, called the Church, the other concerned with politics, called the State. And since they are two, they may be joined or separated, subordinate or independent, and conflicts may arise between them over questions of demarcation and jurisdiction.

This formulation of the problems posed by the relations between religion and politics, and the possible solutions to those problems, arise from Christian, not universal, principles and experience. There are other religious traditions in which religion and politics are differently perceived, and in which, therefore, the problems and the possible solutions are radically different from those we know in the West. Most of these traditions, despite their often very high level of sophistication and achievement, remained or became local—limited to one region or one culture or one people. There is one, however, that in its worldwide distribution, its continuing vitality, its universalist aspirations, can be compared to Christianity, and that is Islam.

Islam is one of the world's great religions. Let me be explicit about what I, as a historian of Islam who is not a Muslim, mean by that. Islam has brought comfort and peace of mind to countless millions of men and women. It has given dignity and meaning to drab and impoverished lives. It has taught people of different races to live in brotherhood and people of different creeds to live side by side in reasonable tolerance. It inspired a great civilization in which others besides Muslims lived creative and useful lives and which, by its achievement, enriched the whole world. But Islam, like other religions, has also known periods when it inspired in some of its followers a mood of hatred and violence. It is our misfortune that part, though by no means all or even most, of the Muslim world is now going through such a period, and that much, though again not all, of that hatred is directed against us.

We should not exaggerate the dimensions of the problem. The Muslim world is far from unanimous in its rejection of the West, nor have the Muslim regions of the Third World been the most passionate and the most extreme in their hostility. There are still significant numbers, in some quarters perhaps a majority, of Muslims with whom we share certain basic cultural and moral, social and political, beliefs and aspirations; there is still an imposing Western presence—cultural, economic, diplomatic—in Muslim lands, some of which are Western allies. But there is . . . a surge of hatred that distresses, alarms, and above all baffles Americans.

At times this hatred goes beyond hostility to specific interests or actions or policies or even countries and becomes a rejection of Western civilization as such, not only what it does but what it is, and the principles and values that it practices and professes. These are indeed seen as innately evil, and those who promote or accept them as the "enemies of God."

This phrase . . . must seem very strange to the modern outsider, whether religious or secular. The idea that God has enemies, and needs human help in order to identify and dispose of them, is a little difficult to assimilate. It is not, however, all that alien. The concept of the enemies of God is familiar in preclassical and classical antiquity, and in both the Old and New Testaments, as well as in the Koran. The Koran is of course strictly monotheistic, and recognizes one God, one universal power only. There is a struggle in human hearts between good and evil, between God's commandments and the tempter, but this is seen as a struggle ordained by God, with its outcome preordained by God, serving as a test of mankind, and not, as in some of the old dualist religions, a struggle in which mankind has a crucial part to play in bringing about the victory of good over evil. Despite this monotheism, Islam, like Judaism and Christianity, was at various stages influenced, especially in Iran, by the dualist idea of a cosmic clash of good and evil, light and darkness, order and chaos, truth and falsehood, God and the Adversary, variously known as devil, Iblis, Satan, and by other names.

IN ISLAM THE STRUGGLE OF GOOD AND EVIL very soon acquired political and even military dimensions. Muhammad, it will be recalled, was not only a prophet and a teacher, like the founders of other religions; he was also the head of a polity and of a community, a ruler and a soldier. Hence his struggle involved a state and its armed forces. If the fighters in the war for Islam, the holy war "in the path of God," are fighting for God, it follows that their opponents are fighting against God. And since God is in principle the sovereign, the supreme head of the Islamic state—and the Prophet and, after the Prophet, the caliphs are his vicegerents—then God as sovereign commands the army. The army is God's army and the enemy is God's enemy. The duty of God's soldiers is to dispatch God's enemies as quickly as possible to the place where God will chastise them—that is to say, the afterlife.

In the classical Islamic view, to which many Muslims are beginning to return, the world and all mankind are divided into two: the House of Islam, where the Muslim law and faith prevail, and the rest, known as the House of Unbelief or the House of War, which it is the duty of Muslims ultimately to bring to Islam. But the greater part of the world is still outside Islam, and even inside the Islamic lands, according to the view of the Muslim radicals, the faith of Islam has been undermined and the law of Islam has been abrogated. The obligation of holy war therefore begins at home and continues abroad, against the same infidel enemy.

Like every other civilization known to human history, the Muslim world in its heyday saw itself as the center of truth and enlightenment, surrounded by infidel barbarians whom it would in due course enlighten and civilize. But between the different groups of barbarians there was a crucial difference. The barbarians to the east and the south were polytheists and idolaters, offering no serious threat and no competition at all to Islam. In the north and west, in contrast, Muslims from an early date recognized a genuine rival—a competing world religion, a distinctive civilization inspired by that religion, and an empire that, though much smaller than theirs, was no less ambitious in its claims and aspirations. This was the entity known to itself and others as Christendom, a term that was long almost identical with Europe.

The struggle between these rival systems has now lasted for some fourteen centuries. It began with the advent of Islam, in the seventh century, and has continued virtually to the present day. It has consisted of a long series of attacks and counterattacks, jihads and crusades, conquests and reconquests. For the first thousand years Islam was advancing, Christendom in retreat and under threat. The new faith conquered the old Christian lands of the Levant and North Africa, and invaded Europe, ruling for a while in Sicily, Spain, Portugal, and even parts of France. The attempt by the Crusaders to recover the lost lands of Christendom in the east was held and thrown back, and even the Muslims' loss of southwestern Europe to the Reconquista was amply compensated by the Islamic advance into southeastern Europe, which twice reached as far as Vienna. For the past three hundred years, since the failure of the second Turkish siege of Vienna in 1683 and the rise of the European colonial empires in Asia and Africa, Islam has been on the defensive, and the Christian and post-Christian civilization of Europe and her daughters has brought the whole world, including Islam, within its orbit.

FOR A LONG TIME NOW there has been a rising tide of rebellion against this Western paramountcy, and a desire to reassert Muslim values and restore Muslim greatness. The Muslim has suffered successive stages of defeat. The first was his loss of domination in the world, to the advancing power of Russia and the West. The second was the undermining of his authority in his own country, through an invasion of foreign ideas and laws and ways of life and sometimes even foreign rulers or settlers, and the enfranchisement of native non-Muslim elements. The third—the last straw—was the challenge to his mastery in his own house, from emancipated women and rebellious children. It was too much to endure, and the outbreak of rage against these alien, infidel, and incomprehensible forces that had subverted his dominance, disrupted his society, and finally violated the sanctuary of his home was inevitable. It was also natural that this rage should be directed primarily against the millennial enemy and should draw its strength from ancient beliefs and loyalties.

Europe and her daughters? The phrase may seem odd to Americans, whose national myths, since the beginning of their nationhood and even earlier, have usually defined their very identity in opposition to Europe, as something new and radically different from the old European ways. This is not, however, the way that others have seen it. . . . Though people of other races and cultures participated, for the most part involuntarily, in the discovery and creation of the Americas, this was, and in the eyes of the rest of the world long remained, a European enterprise, in which Europeans predominated and dominated and to which Europeans gave their languages, their religions, and much of their way of life.

For a very long time voluntary immigration to America was almost exclusively European. There were indeed some who came from the Muslim lands in the Middle East and North Africa, but few were Muslims; most were members of the Christian and to a lesser extent the Jewish minorities in those countries. Their departure for America, and their subsequent presence in America, must have strengthened rather than lessened the European image of America in Muslim eyes.

In the lands of Islam remarkably little was known about America. The Second World War, the oil industry, and postwar developments brought many Americans to the Islamic lands; increasing numbers of Muslims also came to America, first as students, then as teachers or businessmen or other visitors, and eventually as immigrants. Cinema and later television brought the American way of life, or at any rate a certain version of it, before countless millions to whom the very name of America had previously been meaningless or unknown. A wide range of American products, particularly in the immediate postwar years, when European competition was virtually eliminated and Japanese competition had not yet arisen, reached into the remotest markets of the Muslim world, winning new customers and, perhaps more important, creating new tastes and ambitions. For some, America represented freedom and justice and opportunity. For many more, it represented wealth and power and success, at a time when these qualities were not regarded as sins or crimes.

And then came the great change, when the leaders of a widespread and widening religious revival sought out and identified their enemies as the enemies of God, and gave them a local habitation and a name in the Western Hemisphere. Suddenly, or so it seemed, America had become the archenemy, the incarnation of evil, the diabolic opponent of all that is good, and specifically, for Muslims, of Islam. Why?

AT FIRST THE MUSLIM RESPONSE to Western civilization was one of admiration and emulation—an immense respect for the achievements of the West, and a desire to imitate and adopt them. This desire arose from a keen and growing awareness of the weakness, poverty, and backwardness of the Islamic world as compared with the advancing West. The disparity first became apparent on the battlefield but soon spread to other areas of human activity. Muslim writers observed and described the wealth and power of the West, its science and technology, its manufactures, and its forms of government. For a time the secret of Western success was seen to lie in two achievements: economic advancement and especially industry; political institutions and especially freedom. Several generations of reformers and modernizers tried to adapt these and introduce them to their own countries, in the hope that they would thereby be able to achieve equality with the West and perhaps restore their lost superiority.

In our own time this mood of admiration and emulation has, among many Muslims, given way to one of hostility and rejection. In part this mood is surely due to a feeling of humiliation—a growing awareness, among the heirs of an old, proud, and long dominant civilization, of having been overtaken, overborne, and overwhelmed by those whom they regarded as their inferiors. The introduction of Western commercial, financial, and industrial methods did indeed bring great wealth, but it accrued to transplanted Westerners and members of Westernized minorities, and to only a few among the mainstream Muslim population. In time these few became more numerous, but they remained isolated from the masses, differing from them even in their dress and style of life. Inevitably they were seen as agents of and collaborators with what was once again regarded as a hostile world. Even the political institutions that had come from the West were discredited, being judged not by their Western originals but by their local imitations, installed by enthusiastic Muslim reformers. These, operating in a situation beyond their control, using imported and inappropriate methods that they did not fully understand, were unable to cope with the rapidly developing crises and were one by one overthrown. For vast numbers of Middle Easterners, Western-style economic methods brought poverty, Western-style political institutions brought tyranny, even Western-style warfare brought defeat. It is hardly surprising that so many were willing to listen to voices telling them that the old Islamic ways were best and that their only salvation was to throw aside the pagan innovations of the reformers and return to the True Path that God had prescribed for his people.

Ultimately, the struggle of the fundamentalists is against two enemies, secularism and modernism. The war against secularism is conscious and explicit, and there is by now a whole literature denouncing secularism as an evil neo-pagan force in the modern world and attributing it variously to the Jews, the West, and the United States. The war against modernity is for the most part neither conscious nor explicit, and is directed against the whole process of change that has taken place in the Islamic world in the past century or more and has transformed the political, economic, social, and even cultural structures of Muslim countries. Islamic fundamentalism has given an aim and a form to the otherwise aimless and formless resentment and anger of the Muslim masses at the forces that have devalued their traditional values and loyalties and, in the final analysis, robbed them of their beliefs, their aspirations, their dignity, and to an increasing extent even their livelihood.

There is something in the religious culture of Islam which inspired, in even the humblest peasant or peddler, a dignity and a courtesy toward others never exceeded and rarely equalled in other civilizations. And yet, in moments of upheaval and disruption, when the deeper passions are stirred, this dignity and courtesy toward others can give way to an explosive mixture of rage and hatred which impels even the government of an ancient and civilized country—even the spokesman of a great spiritual and ethical religion—to espouse kidnapping and assassination, and try to find, in the life of their Prophet, approval and indeed precedent for such actions.

The instinct of the masses is not false in locating the ultimate source of these cataclysmic changes in the West and in attributing the disruption of their old way of life to the impact of Western domination, Western influence, or Western precept and example. And since the United States is the legitimate heir of European civilization and the recognized and unchallenged leader of the West, the United States has inherited the resulting grievances and become the focus for the pent-up hate and anger. It should by now be clear that we are facing a mood and a movement far transcending the level of issues and policies and the governments that pursue them. This is no less than a clash of civilizations—the perhaps irrational but surely historic reaction of an ancient rival against our Judeo-Christian heritage, our secular present, and the worldwide expansion of both. It is crucially important that we on our side should not be provoked into an equally historic but also equally irrational reaction against that rival.

The movement nowadays called fundamentalism is not the only Islamic tradition. There are others, more tolerant, more open, that helped to inspire the great achievements of Islamic civilization in the past, and we may hope that these other traditions will in time prevail. But before this issue is decided there will be a hard struggle, in which we of the West can do little or nothing. Even the attempt might do harm, for these are issues that Muslims must decide among themselves. And in the meantime we must take great care on all sides to avoid the danger of a new era of religious wars, arising from the exacerbation of differences and the revival of ancient prejudices.

Who Was Deep Throat?

JAMES MANN ‖ 1992

> *It was one of the great mysteries in the history of American journalism:
> the identity of the man who, obscured by midnight shadows in an under-
> ground parking garage, meted out crucial Delphic clues ("Follow the
> money") to a young reporter named Bob Woodward. Who was Deep
> Throat, the legendary anonymous source who helped Woodward and his*
> Washington Post *colleague, Carl Bernstein, crack the Watergate scandal
> and end the presidency of Richard Nixon? From the moment Woodward
> and Bernstein, in their 1974 book* All the President's Men, *attached that
> famous moniker (wittily appropriated from a hit porno film) to their high-
> placed government source, answering this question became not just a na-
> tional parlor game but a question of historical import—the last missing
> piece of the Watergate puzzle. And yet in May of 2005, when the former
> FBI associate director W. Mark Felt came forward, at the age of ninety-one,
> and identified himself, almost all those who had hazarded guesses over the
> years were proved to be off the mark, often wildly so. One of the few excep-
> tions was James Mann (1946–   ), who offered his own theory of the case in*
> The Atlantic *on the twentieth anniversary of the Watergate break-in.*
>
> *In retrospect, it is not surprising that Mann succeeded in unraveling
> much of the enigma that had confounded so many for so long. A reporter
> for the* Post *at the time of Watergate, he was a friend of Woodward's and
> was well positioned to pick up telltale evidence. More important, Mann,
> a distinguished diplomatic and foreign-affairs correspondent, possessed
> an intimate understanding of institutional infighting in Washington. It
> was this insider's knowledge that he marshaled to such impressive effect
> in his* Atlantic *article, determining with careful, convincing analysis that
> Deep Throat must have been an FBI higher-up. From there, only a few
> candidates seemed plausible; the most probable, Mann says point blank,
> was Mark Felt. Mann was too conscientious a journalist to declare the
> mystery solved, so at the time his article did not gain the widespread
> attention it deserved. But when the identity of Deep Throat was finally
> revealed, the legions of Watergate sleuths could only agree that, among
> them, James Mann had come closest to getting it right.*

With the anniversary of Watergate approaching, one question about the
affair remains as haunting today as it was at the time: Who was Deep

Throat, the mysterious source within the federal government who repeatedly met *The Washington Post*'s Bob Woodward in a parking garage in the early morning hours to guide the *Post*'s inquiries into the scandal, to pass on information about the federal investigation, and to thwart the Nixon Administration's efforts to rein in that investigation?

Beyond mere curiosity, the answer to the question is of considerable historical interest. Identifying Deep Throat would clarify our view of the Nixon Administration and would enhance our understanding of the underlying institutional forces at work in Washington during the late 1960s and early 1970s. In the common imagination, the executive branch is run by the President, his Cabinet, and his White House advisers. Thus much of the speculation about Deep Throat over the past two decades has focused on known names within Nixon's White House, such as Haig, the press spokesman Ronald Ziegler, and the White House adviser Leonard Garment. Rarely is it asked whether these people had the regular, immediate access to the federal investigation of Watergate which provided the backdrop to the *Post*'s stories. Even more rarely is it asked whether White House aides like Haig, Ziegler, and Garment were the sort of people willing to hold 2:00 A.M. meetings in a parking garage, or whether they were able to arrange the circling of the page number 20 of Bob Woodward's copy of *The New York Times*, which was delivered to his apartment by 7:00 A.M.—the signal that Deep Throat wanted a meeting.

During any Administration, institutions and bureaucracies are powerful entities within themselves, sometimes with more clout than the White House personalities who theoretically govern them. And among these powerful bureaucracies are the U.S. intelligence and investigative agencies: the CIA and the FBI. In what follows I will explore some of these matters. I cannot reveal who Deep Throat was, because I do not know. I do know, however, the part of the government in which Deep Throat worked, and I can speculate with some conviction about what Deep Throat's institutional motivations may have been.

THE YEAR 1972 WAS THE MOST TUMULTUOUS ONE in the history of the FBI. On May 2, J. Edgar Hoover, the director of the FBI, died at the age of seventy-seven. Over a period of nearly five decades he had built up the organization from scratch, had ruled it in an autocratic fashion, and had filled its upper ranks with men acceptable to him.

To these men of the Bureau, Presidents were temporary and Hoover's FBI was permanent. Hoover had dealt with and outlasted every President since Calvin Coolidge. He and his associates had fended off the Kennedys and Lyndon Johnson, and they believed they would survive Richard Nixon, too. This was a matter of pride, of virtue: although it occasionally provided a bit of clandestine help to occupants of the Oval Office, the FBI saw itself as fearlessly independent—outside politics and ultimately beyond the control of the White House. Unlike, say, the Justice Department or the State Department, the FBI did not get a new leader with each new President.

This tradition was suddenly thrown into question with Hoover's death. Officials at the Bureau believed that Hoover's successor would be appointed from within their ranks. W. Mark Felt, the FBI's deputy associate director, the No. 3 man in Hoover's hierarchy, wrote in a 1979 memoir, *The FBI Pyramid*:

> It did not cross my mind that the President would appoint an outsider to replace Hoover. Had I known this, I would not have been hopeful about the future. There were many trained executives in the FBI who could have effectively handled the job of Director. My own record was good and I allowed myself to think I had an excellent chance.

When Hoover died, FBI officials like Felt did not have much time to think. On May 3, while Hoover's body was lying in state in the Capitol Rotunda, Assistant Attorney General L. Patrick Gray III appeared at FBI headquarters and asked to see Hoover's secret files. FBI officials refused, insisting that there were no such documents, and after a nasty face-off Gray left. A few hours later Gray was appointed by the Nixon Administration to be the FBI's acting director.

Nixon and his aides had many reasons for wanting to appoint an outsider to head the FBI—some of them honorable, some not. They felt, as had some of their predecessors in the White House, that the FBI was too tradition-bound, and badly needed to adopt more modern law-enforcement techniques. They also wanted the FBI to be subject to much greater political direction from the White House and the Justice Department than had been possible under Hoover.

The FBI had resisted several law-enforcement and domestic intelligence-gathering initiatives by the Nixon White House, notably the famous "Huston plan"—the effort, led by the White House aide Tom Charles Huston, to expand intelligence-gathering through a network of informants along with a campaign of wiretapping, bugging, mail opening, and burglaries. Moreover, White House officials feared that if the FBI retained the independence it had had under Hoover, it would never go along with the Nixon Administration's continuing efforts to use the federal bureaucracy to reward friends and punish enemies.

In short, Hoover's death presented the Nixon Administration with a long-sought opportunity to gain political control of the FBI. Traumatized by Hoover's death, and anxious to preserve the Bureau's traditions, the FBI's leadership resented and resisted the Administration's efforts. By coincidence, the Watergate break-in occurred on June 17, less than seven weeks after Hoover's death and Gray's appointment. The FBI took charge of the federal investigation at the same time that the Administration was trying to limit its scope.

Therein lies the origin of Deep Throat.

WHEN BOB WOODWARD ARRIVED in the *Post* newsroom, less than a year before Watergate, he quickly established himself as one of the top investigative reporters on the local staff. Other reporters might spend weeks, months, or even years on a single project (as, indeed, Woodward himself does now). Woodward distinguished himself by delivering stories fast, sometimes coming up with new information on the controversy of the week. I was a *Post* reporter at the time of his arrival, and because I was covering Washington's federal courthouse, Woodward and I often worked closely together. We were friends, reporting alongside each other on the *Post*'s metro staff.

During the late winter and early spring of 1972, the story that occupied much of his time was a running local scandal involving corruption within the District of Columbia police department. Some members of the D.C. vice squad had been found to have been involved in gambling and prostitution, and there were allegations that others had ties to narcotics figures. Woodward monitored the developing investigation—reporting, for example, in a front-page story on February 3, "Two grand juries here are conducting separate investigations into police corruption and major drug dealers, it has been learned. Sources say the probes may lead to the most sweeping criminal indictments in the city in recent years."

This was a natural subject for a new investigative reporter on the *Post*'s local staff. Yet in writing about the D.C. police, Woodward happened to step onto one of the main political battlegrounds in the ongoing struggle between the Nixon Administration and the FBI. At that time the District of Columbia Police Department was favored by Nixon and particularly by his Attorney General, John Mitchell. Top FBI officials suspected, rightly, that

Nixon and Mitchell would have liked to name the D.C. police chief, Jerry V. Wilson, to be the next FBI director. Wilson's police force was everything the FBI was not: it espoused a belief in the need for more progressive law-enforcement techniques, and it got along well with the Administration. The D.C. police hired minority members, women, and even a handful of "Ivy League cops"—young college graduates who were eager to learn about law enforcement at the street level. These personnel practices were intensely mistrusted by the FBI.

In one particular crisis, the sweeping anti-war demonstrations that had threatened to close down Washington on May 3, 1971, the White House and the Justice Department had worked closely with Wilson's police in arranging the arrest of some 12,000 people.

In short, the FBI viewed the D.C. police force as an ally of the Nixon Administration and thus an implied rebuke to the Bureau and its independent tradition. The symbolic value of the investigation into police corruption was openly discussed and debated at the time. Here is how Woodward himself put it in an article on January 13, 1972:

> Because Washington is the nation's capital and since President
> Nixon has said he wants to make Washington a model city of law
> enforcement, the allegation of police corruption has political
> overtones.
>
> Some investigators say political pressure has been brought to find
> widespread corruption. They conjecture it is perhaps to discredit
> the President. On the other hand, some other investigators say
> pressure has been exerted to not uncover too much and protect the
> Administration.

Only days after this story appeared, the White House moved to lend political support to the police department. "President Nixon yesterday opposed any outside investigation of alleged corruption in the metropolitan police department," the *Post* reported on its front page. It quoted Egil (Bud) Krogh, the White House adviser responsible for the District of Columbia (and one of the Nixon "plumbers"), as saying that Nixon believed the D.C. police themselves should be allowed to uncover and correct any corruption that might exist.

The FBI had been in charge of the investigation of the D.C. police, and Woodward would have dealt with FBI officials in the course of his reporting. Then, in mid-May of 1972, with the investigations winding down, the

Post's metropolitan staff, and Woodward in particular, shifted their attention to a new story: the attempted assassination of Alabama Governor George Wallace. By this time Woodward was clearly making considerable and frequent use of a source at the FBI.

As the former *Post* city editor Barry Sussman has disclosed in his Watergate book, *The Great Cover-Up*, within hours of the Wallace shooting, when the identity of the assailant was still not publicly known, Woodward volunteered that he had a "friend" who might be able to help. And indeed, on that day and over the following two weeks, working as part of a team of *Post* reporters, Woodward was able to come up with details about the life and travels of Arthur Bremer, the man who stalked and finally shot Wallace, virtually as soon as FBI investigators uncovered them.

> High federal officials who have reviewed investigative reports on the Wallace shooting said yesterday that there is no evidence whatsoever to indicate that Bremer was a hired killer.
>
> At least 200 FBI agents still were following leads across the country and have found no indication of a conspiracy in the Wallace shooting, federal sources here in Washington said. . . . *Officially* the FBI declined to comment on the search.
>
> —BOB WOODWARD, MAY 18, ITALICS MINE.

> A reliable federal source close to the investigation termed "incredible" the picture of Bremer's travels being assembled by federal investigators.
>
> Bremer has been positively placed in the following places . . .
>
> —HEDLEY BURRELL AND BOB WOODWARD, MAY 25.

> The Federal Bureau of Investigation has finished its investigation into the life and travels of suspect Arthur Herman Bremer and has found no evidence of any conspiracy or accomplices in the May 15 shooting of Alabama Gov. George C. Wallace, federal sources said yesterday.
>
> —PHILIP MCCOMBS AND BOB WOODWARD, JUNE 3.

Two weeks after the last of the above stories on the Wallace shooting, five men were arrested inside the Democratic National Committee headquarters at the Watergate. Immediately, on Monday, June 19, Woodward turned to his source at the FBI for help: "Federal sources close to the investigation said the address books contain the name and home telephone number of Howard E. Hunt [sic], with the notations 'W. House' and 'W.H.'" (Bob Woodward and E. J. Bachinski, June 20.)

By Woodward's own description, in *All the President's Men*, this source was Deep Throat. "It was he who had advised Woodward on June 19 that Howard Hunt was definitely involved in Watergate," Woodward wrote.

At the time of the Watergate break-in, of course, "Deep Throat" was not yet the name of a Watergate source but merely the name of a recently released pornographic movie. Rather, during the summer and early fall of 1972, Woodward spoke to me repeatedly of "my source at the FBI," or, alternatively, of "my friend at the FBI"—each time making it plain that this was a special, and unusually well-placed, source.

Writing much later, in *All the President's Men*, Woodward noted that "Deep Throat had access to information from the White House, Justice, the FBI, and CRP [Committee for the Re-election of the President]. What he knew represented an aggregate of hard information flowing in and out of many stations." FBI officials, in their investigations of Watergate, were collecting information about the CRP and the White House. At the same time, they were working with prosecutors at the Justice Department and were trying to deal with, and fend off, efforts by Nixon and his aides to restrict the Watergate investigation.

My conviction that Woodward's FBI source was the man later called Deep Throat was buttressed by the following incident. On September 15 the first Watergate indictments were handed down, against the original burglary team. At the time I had just left the *Post* and was emptying out my Washington apartment before spending a year in Italy. The day after the indictments were handed down, I called Woodward to say good-bye. I raised the subject of the indictments and asked what was new. "I just talked to my friend at the FBI," Woodward answered. "I think we're on to a whole new level on this thing."

In *All the President's Men*, Woodward and Bernstein wrote,

> The day after the indictments were handed down Woodward broke the rule about telephone contact. Deep Throat sounded nervous, but listened as the draft of a story was read to him. . . . "Too soft," Deep Throat said. "You can go much stronger."

On September 18 the *Post* published the first story broadening the investigation beyond the Watergate break-in. "SECRET FUND TIED TO INTELLIGENCE USE," the front-page story said.

Two of President Nixon's top campaign officials each withdrew more than $50,000 from a secret fund that financed intelligence gathering activities against the Democrats, according to sources close to the Watergate investigation.

The two officials, both former White House aides, are Jeb Stuart Magruder, deputy director of the Committee for the Re-election of the President, and Herbert L. Porter, scheduling director of the committee.

WITH THE BENEFIT OF HINDSIGHT, it becomes abundantly clear why someone at the FBI would have an interest in leaking information about Watergate to *The Washington Post*. In the very first week after the Watergate arrests, FBI investigators found that the White House was putting obstacles in the way of its investigation of the case. White House counsel John Dean insisted on sitting in on the FBI's interviews. The Bureau's efforts to interview witnesses and to obtain various records were being stalled or blocked. L. Patrick Gray, who was working closely with Dean, ordered FBI agents to call off a proposed interview with Miguel Ogarrio, a lawyer whose checks totalling $89,000 had been deposited in the bank account of one of the arrested men; Gray said the interview might jeopardize existing CIA operations in Mexico.

Nixon's White House tapes later demonstrated that, in one of the key acts of the Watergate cover-up, Nixon and his chief of staff, H. R. Haldeman, had ordered the CIA deputy director, Vernon Walters, to ask the FBI not to pursue its inquiries in Mexico. Of course, FBI officials other than Gray did not know this at the time. All they knew in late June of 1972, little more than a month after Hoover's death and Gray's appointment, was that the White House was impeding their investigation. And these White House efforts seemed to validate their worst fear: that the Nixon White House intended to use the FBI for political purposes.

FBI officials were furious. According to Mark Felt, on July 5 three top FBI officials asked for a meeting with Gray to protest White House obstruction of the Watergate investigation. The three were Felt, Charles W. Bates, the assistant director in charge of the FBI's General Investigative Division, and Robert Kunkel, the special agent in charge of the Washington field office, which was conducting the investigation. As Felt recounted in his memoir,

"Look," I told Gray, "the reputation of the FBI is at stake. . . . We can't delay the Ogarrio interview any longer! I hate to make this sound like an ultimatum, but unless we get a request in writing from [CIA] Director Helms to forego the Ogarrio interview, we're going ahead anyway. . . .

"That's not all," I went on. "We must do something about the complete lack of cooperation from John Dean and the Committee to Reelect the President. It's obvious they're holding back—delaying and leading us astray in every way they can."

Invoking Hoover's name, Felt made clear that he and his colleagues believed that the FBI's traditions and its future were at stake:

In fact, no one could have stopped the driving force of the investigation without an explosion in the Bureau—not even J. Edgar Hoover. For me, as well as for all the Agents who were involved, it had become a question of our integrity. We were under attack for dragging our feet and as professional law enforcement officers we were determined to go on.

For a senior FBI official like Deep Throat, talking to Woodward and the *Post* about Watergate was a way to fend off White House interference with the investigation. The contacts with the press guaranteed that information developed by the FBI's Watergate investigative team would not be suppressed or altered by Nixon Administration officials. And, more broadly, the leaks furthered the cause of an independent FBI unfettered by political control.

AS I SAID AT THE OUTSET, I didn't know who Deep Throat was. I know from conversation with Bob Woodward at the time only that he was from the FBI.

He could well have been Mark Felt, who admitted that he harbored ambitions to be the FBI director—not only at the time of Hoover's death but also in the spring of 1973, when Gray's nomination as permanent director failed to win confirmation and Nixon named William Ruckelshaus acting director. Felt was known in Washington as a person willing to talk to the press. He has denied that he was Deep Throat. "I never leaked information to Woodward and Bernstein or to anyone else!" he wrote in his 1979 book. Felt retired from the FBI in 1973, not long after Ruckelshaus's appointment.

Perhaps he was Charles Bates, whose job as assistant director of the General Investigative Division would have given him direct supervisory authority over the police-corruption investigation, over the investigation into Arthur Bremer's shooting of George Wallace, and over the investigation into the Watergate break-in. In the midst of the Watergate investigation Bates asked to be reassigned as special agent in charge of the FBI's field office in San Francisco, where he later headed the Bureau's investigation into the kidnapping of Patty Hearst.

Perhaps Deep Throat was Robert Kunkel or one of the other FBI agents in the Washington field office who were working on Watergate. That seems less likely, however. Gray ousted Kunkel from his job and assigned him to be head of the St. Louis office in the middle of Watergate; FBI agents attributed the demotion to Kunkel's aggressive direction of the Watergate investigation. And the Washington field office didn't have direct responsibility for the investigation of the Wallace shooting, about which Woodward's FBI source had proved so helpful.

Conceivably, Deep Throat was some other senior FBI official who was keeping track of the Watergate investigation and the Administration's efforts to thwart it—or acting as a messenger from top officials like Felt and Bates to Woodward.

By Woodward's account, in *All the President's Men*, Deep Throat passed on most of his crucial information from June of 1972 to early 1973. However, Woodward says in the book that he met with Deep Throat at least once in November of 1973, when his source provided him with some information on the gaps that investigators had found on Nixon's White House tapes. By that time Felt had officially retired from the FBI, and Bates and Kunkel were out of Washington. Still, all of them would have kept in close touch with the FBI's Watergate investigators, and would have been in a position to pass on information to Woodward. It is also possible that the FBI official who was Woodward's original source handed over the mantle of Deep Throat to a successor.

There has been considerable speculation that Deep Throat never existed, that he must have been either a complete fiction or a composite of several people. My memory of those early months of Watergate is otherwise: that there was a specific individual, from the FBI, and Woodward had special access to him.

What seems important, with two decades of hindsight, is that in our national preoccupation with personality and celebrity in the nation's capital, we have concentrated too much on Deep Throat as an individual and not enough on the underlying bureaucratic forces. To be sure, Deep Throat may have had personal motives for his parking-garage meetings with Woodward. Several top FBI officials, including Felt, hoped to take over

Hoover's job. Moreover, Woodward demonstrated great skill in cultivating and preserving Deep Throat as a source and a friend. But the institutional motivations at work would seem to have been at least as important as the personal interests or idiosyncrasies of an individual source and a newspaper reporter.

After Hoover's death, the FBI faced what its officials felt was a threat to its tradition of independence from political control. Top FBI officials were worried about the impact of Gray's appointment. And in less than seven weeks, White House interference with the Watergate investigation proved to them that their fears were justified. They responded—as FBI officials had often done during the Hoover era—by going to the press.

The Coming Anarchy

ROBERT D. KAPLAN || 1994

When Robert D. Kaplan's "The Coming Anarchy" was published as an
Atlantic cover story (illustrated by an image of the earth aflame and
deflating like a withered balloon), Bill Clinton declared the article
"stunning" and circulated it around the White House as must reading.
"[It] makes you really imagine a future that's like one of those Mel Gib-
son 'Road Warrior' movies," the president remarked. Soon, Kaplan's
dystopian vision was the talk of official Washington and beyond. (The
issue that featured the article became one of the best selling in Atlantic
history.) The cascade of admiration that greeted Kaplan's essay was
hardly to be expected for what was, in essence, a portrait of approaching
global collapse. By 1994, Kaplan (1952–   ), a prolific Atlantic correspon-
dent and the author of such acclaimed books as Balkan Ghosts *and* The
Ends of the Earth, *had already earned the recognition of decision mak-*
ers and academics alike with his unnerving travelogues—deftly reported,
historically informed, philosophically minded dispatches from the most
dangerous places on the planet. But "The Coming Anarchy" was jour-
nalism of a different order. Reporting principally from West Africa,
Kaplan set out to explore whether worsening Third World problems—
governmental breakdown, environmental degradation, rampant disease,
uncontrolled urbanization, ethnic and sectarian conflict—might be the
chronicle of a decline foretold about the rest of the world's geopolitical fu-
ture. Less than a decade into a new century, it is too early to tell whether
Kaplan's grim forecasts will be borne out. But the genocide in Rwanda,
which took place only six months after his article was published, as well
as unrelenting violence, poverty, and disease in Africa, the Middle East,
and other chronically troubled regions of the world provide chilling bal-
last for his thesis.

It is time to understand the environment for what it is: *the* national-
security issue of the early twenty-first century. The political and strategic impact of surging populations, spreading disease, deforestation and
soil erosion, water depletion, air pollution, and, possibly, rising sea levels
in critical, overcrowded regions like the Nile Delta and Bangladesh—
developments that will prompt mass migrations and, in turn, incite group
conflicts—will be the core foreign-policy challenge from which most others

will ultimately emanate, arousing the public and uniting assorted interests left over from the Cold War. In the twenty-first century water will be in dangerously short supply in such diverse locales as Saudi Arabia, Central Asia, and the southwestern United States. A war could erupt between Egypt and Ethiopia over Nile River water. Even in Europe tensions have arisen between Hungary and Slovakia over the damming of the Danube, a classic case of how environmental disputes fuse with ethnic and historical ones. The political scientist and erstwhile Clinton adviser Michael Mandelbaum has said, "We have a foreign policy today in the shape of a doughnut—lots of peripheral interests but nothing at the center." The environment, I will argue, is part of a terrifying array of problems that will define a new threat to our security, filling the hole in Mandelbaum's doughnut and allowing a post–Cold War foreign policy to emerge inexorably by need rather than by design.

Our Cold War foreign policy truly began with George F. Kennan's famous article, signed "X," published in *Foreign Affairs* in July of 1947, in which Kennan argued for a "firm and vigilant containment" of a Soviet Union that was imperially, rather than ideologically, motivated. It may be that our post–Cold War foreign policy will one day be seen to have had its beginnings in an even bolder and more detailed piece of written analysis: one that appeared in the journal *International Security*. The article, published in the fall of 1991 by Thomas Fraser Homer-Dixon, who is the head of the Peace and Conflict Studies Program at the University of Toronto, was titled "On the Threshold: Environmental Changes as Causes of Acute Conflict." Homer-Dixon has, more successfully than other analysts, integrated two hitherto separate fields—military-conflict studies and the study of the physical environment.

In Homer-Dixon's view, future wars and civil violence will often arise from scarcities of resources such as water, cropland, forests, and fish. Just as there will be environmentally driven wars and refugee flows, there will be environmentally induced praetorian regimes—or, as he puts it, "hard regimes." Countries with the highest probability of acquiring hard regimes, according to Homer-Dixon, are those that are threatened by a declining resource base yet also have "a history of state [read 'military'] strength." Candidates include Indonesia, Brazil, and . . . Nigeria. Though each of these nations has exhibited democratizing tendencies of late, Homer-Dixon argues that such tendencies are likely to be superficial "epiphenomena" having nothing to do with long-term processes that include soaring populations and shrinking raw materials. Democracy is problematic; scarcity is more certain.

Indeed, the Saddam Husseins of the future will have more, not fewer, opportunities. In addition to engendering tribal strife, scarcer resources will place a great strain on many peoples who never had much of a democratic or institutional tradition to begin with. Over the next fifty years the earth's population will soar from 5.5 billion to more than nine billion. Though optimists have hopes for new resource technologies and free-market development in the global village, they fail to note that, as the National Academy of Sciences has pointed out, 95 percent of the population increase will be in the poorest regions of the world, where governments now—just look at Africa—show little ability to function, let alone to implement even marginal improvements. Homer-Dixon writes, ominously, "Neo-Malthusians may underestimate human adaptability in today's environmental-social system, but as time passes their analysis may become ever more compelling."

While a minority of the human population will be, as Francis Fukuyama would put it, sufficiently sheltered so as to enter a "post-historical" realm, living in cities and suburbs in which the environment has been mastered and ethnic animosities have been quelled by bourgeois prosperity, an increasingly large number of people will be stuck in history, living in shantytowns where attempts to rise above poverty, cultural dysfunction, and ethnic strife will be doomed by a lack of water to drink, soil to till, and space to survive in. In the developing world environmental stress will present people with a choice that is increasingly among totalitarianism (as in Iraq), fascist-tending mini-states (as in Serb-held Bosnia), and road-warrior cultures (as in Somalia). Homer-Dixon concludes that "as environmental degradation proceeds, the size of the potential social disruption will increase."

Tad Homer-Dixon is an unlikely Jeremiah. Today a boyish thirty-seven, he grew up amid the sylvan majesty of Vancouver Island, attending private day schools. His speech is calm, perfectly even, and crisply enunciated. There is nothing in his background or manner that would indicate a bent toward pessimism. A Canadian Anglican who spends his summers canoeing on the lakes of northern Ontario, and who talks about the benign mountains, black bears, and Douglas firs of his youth, he is the opposite of the intellectually severe neoconservative, the kind at home with conflict scenarios. Nor is he an environmentalist who opposes development. "My father was a logger who thought about ecologically safe forestry before others," he says. As an only child whose playground was a virtually untouched wilderness and seacoast, Homer-Dixon has a familiarity with the natural world that permits him to see a reality that most policy analysts—children of suburbia and city streets—are blind to.

"We need to bring nature back in," he argues. "We have to stop separating politics from the physical world—the climate, public health, and the environment." Quoting Daniel Deudney, another pioneering expert on the security aspects of the environment, Homer-Dixon says that "for too long we've been prisoners of 'social-social' theory, which assumes there are only social causes for social and political changes, rather than natural causes, too. This social-social mentality emerged with the Industrial Revolution, which separated us from nature. But nature is coming back with a vengeance, tied to population growth. It will have incredible security implications.

"Think of a stretch limo in the potholed streets of New York City, where homeless beggars live. Inside the limo are the air-conditioned post-industrial regions of North America, Europe, the emerging Pacific Rim, and a few other isolated places, with their trade summitry and computer-information highways. Outside is the rest of mankind, going in a completely different direction."

We are entering a bifurcated world. Part of the globe is inhabited by Hegel's and Fukuyama's Last Man, healthy, well fed, and pampered by technology. The other, larger, part is inhabited by Hobbes's First Man, condemned to a life that is "poor, nasty, brutish, and short." Although both parts will be threatened by environmental stress, the Last Man will be able to master it; the First Man will not.

The Last Man will adjust to the loss of underground water tables in the western United States. He will build dikes to save Cape Hatteras and the Chesapeake beaches from rising sea levels, even as the Maldive Islands, off the coast of India, sink into oblivion, and the shorelines of Egypt, Bangladesh, and Southeast Asia recede, driving tens of millions of people inland where there is no room for them, and thus sharpening ethnic divisions.

Homer-Dixon points to a world map of soil degradation in his Toronto office. "The darker the map color, the worse the degradation," he explains. The West African coast, the Middle East, the Indian subcontinent, China, and Central America have the darkest shades, signifying all manner of degradation, related to winds, chemicals, and water problems. "The worst degradation is generally where the population is highest. The population is generally highest where the soil is the best. So we're degrading earth's best soil."

China, in Homer-Dixon's view, is the quintessential example of environmental degradation. Its current economic "success" masks deeper problems. "China's fourteen percent growth rate does not mean it's going to be a world power. It means that coastal China, where the economic growth is taking place, is joining the rest of the Pacific Rim. The disparity with inland China is intensifying." Referring to the environmental research of his colleague, the Czech-born ecologist Vaclav Smil, Homer-Dixon explains how the per capita availability of arable land in interior China has rapidly declined at the same time that the quality of that land has been destroyed by deforestation, loss of topsoil, and salinization. He mentions the loss and contamination of water supplies, the exhaustion of wells, the plugging of irrigation systems and reservoirs with eroded silt, and a population of 1.54 billion by the year 2025: it is a misconception that China has gotten its population under control. Large-scale population movements are under way, from inland China to coastal China and from villages to cities, leading to a crime surge like the one in Africa and to growing regional disparities and conflicts in a land with a strong tradition of warlordism and a weak tradition of central government—again as in Africa. "We will probably see the center challenged and fractured, and China will not remain the same on the map," Homer-Dixon says.

IN THE SUMMER, 1993, ISSUE OF *FOREIGN AFFAIRS*, Samuel P. Huntington, of Harvard's Olin Institute for Strategic Studies, published a thought-provoking article called "The Clash of Civilizations?" The world, he argues, has been moving during the course of this century from nation-state conflict to ideological conflict to, finally, cultural conflict. I would add that as refugee flows increase and as peasants continue migrating to cities around the world—turning them into sprawling villages—national borders will mean less, even as more power will fall into the hands of less educated, less sophisticated groups. In the eyes of these uneducated but newly empowered millions, the real borders are the most tangible and intractable ones: those of culture and tribe. Huntington writes, "First, differences among civilizations are not only real; they are basic," involving, among other things, history, language, and religion. "Second . . . interactions between peoples of different civilizations are increasing; these increasing interactions intensify civilization consciousness." Economic modernization is not necessarily a panacea, since it fuels individual and group ambitions while weakening traditional loyalties to the state. It is worth noting, for example, that it is precisely the wealthiest and fastest-developing city in India, Bombay, that has seen the worst intercommunal violence between Hindus and Muslims. Consider that Indian cities, like African and Chinese ones, are ecological time bombs—Delhi and Calcutta, and also Beijing, suffer the worst air quality of any cities in the world—and it is apparent how surging populations, environmental degradation, and ethnic conflict are deeply related.

Huntington points to interlocking conflicts among Hindu, Muslim, Slavic Orthodox, Western, Japanese, Confucian, Latin American, and possibly African civilizations: for instance, Hindus clashing with Muslims in India, Turkic Muslims clashing with Slavic Orthodox Russians in Central Asian cities, the West clashing with Asia. (Even in the United States, African-Americans find themselves besieged by an influx of competing Latinos.) Whatever the laws, refugees find a way to crash official borders, bringing their passions with them, meaning that Europe and the United States will be weakened by cultural disputes. Everywhere in the developing world at the turn of the twenty-first century these new men and women, rushing into the cities, are remaking civilizations and redefining their identities in terms of religion and tribal ethnicity that do not coincide with the borders of existing states.

Whereas rural poverty is age-old and almost a "normal" part of the social fabric, urban poverty is socially destabilizing. As Iran has shown, Islamic extremism is the psychological defense mechanism of many urbanized peasants threatened with the loss of traditions in pseudo-modern cities where their values are under attack, where basic services like water and electricity are unavailable, and where they are assaulted by a physically unhealthy environment. Beyond its stark, clearly articulated message, Islam's very militancy makes it attractive to the downtrodden. It is the one religion that is prepared to fight. A political era driven by environmental stress, increased cultural sensitivity, unregulated urbanization, and refugee migrations is an era divinely created for the spread and intensification of Islam, already the world's fastest-growing religion.

"OH, WHAT A RELIEF TO FIGHT, to fight enemies who defend themselves, enemies who are awake!" André Malraux wrote in *Man's Fate*. I cannot think of a more suitable battle cry for many combatants in the early decades of the twenty-first century. The intense savagery of the fighting in such diverse cultural settings as Liberia, Bosnia, the Caucasus, and Sri Lanka—to say nothing of what obtains in American inner cities—indicates something very troubling that those of us inside the stretch limo, concerned with issues like middle-class entitlements and the future of interactive cable television, lack the stomach to contemplate. It is this: a large number of people on this planet, to whom the comfort and stability of a middle-class life is utterly unknown, find war and a barracks existence a step up rather than a step down.

"Just as it makes no sense to ask 'why people eat' or 'what they sleep for,'" writes Martin van Creveld, a military historian at the Hebrew University in Jerusalem, in *The Transformation of War*, "so fighting in many ways is not a means but an end. Throughout history, for every person who has expressed his horror of war there is another who found in it the most marvelous of all the experiences that are vouchsafed to man, even to the point that he later spent a lifetime boring his descendants by recounting his exploits." When I asked Pentagon officials about the nature of war in the twenty-first century, the answer I frequently got was "Read Van Creveld." The top brass are enamored of this historian not because his writings justify their existence but, rather, the opposite: Van Creveld warns them that huge state military machines like the Pentagon's are dinosaurs about to go extinct, and that something far more terrible awaits us.

The degree to which Van Creveld's *Transformation of War* complements Homer-Dixon's work on the environment, Huntington's thoughts on cultural clash, my own realizations in traveling by foot, bus, and bush taxi in more than sixty countries, and America's sobering comeuppances in intractable-culture zones like Haiti and Somalia is startling. The book begins by demolishing the notion that men don't like to fight. "By compelling the senses to focus themselves on the here and now," Van Creveld writes, war "can cause a man to take his leave of them." As anybody who has had experience with Chetniks in Serbia, "technicals" in Somalia, Tontons Macoutes in Haiti, or soldiers in Sierra Leone can tell you, in places where the Western Enlightenment has not penetrated and where there has always been mass poverty, people find liberation in violence. In Afghanistan and elsewhere, I vicariously experienced this phenomenon: worrying about mines and ambushes frees you from worrying about mundane details of daily existence. If my own experience is too subjective, there is a wealth of data showing the sheer frequency of war, especially in the developing world since the Second World War. Physical aggression is a part of being human. Only when people attain a certain economic, educational, and cultural standard is this trait tranquilized. In light of the fact that 95 percent of the earth's population growth will be in the poorest areas of the globe, the question is not whether there will be war (there will be a lot of it) but what kind of war. And who will fight whom?

Debunking the great military strategist Carl von Clausewitz, Van Creveld, who may be the most original thinker on war since that early-nineteenth-century Prussian, writes, "Clausewitz's ideas . . . were wholly rooted in the fact that, ever since 1648, war had been waged overwhelmingly by states." But, as Van Creveld explains, the period of nation-states and, therefore, of state conflict is now ending, and with it the clear "three-fold division into government, army, and people" which state-directed wars enforce.

Because, as Van Creveld notes, the radius of trust within tribal societies is narrowed to one's immediate family and guerrilla comrades, truces arranged with one Bosnian commander, say, may be broken immediately by another Bosnian commander. The plethora of short-lived ceasefires in the Balkans and the Caucasus constitute proof that we are no longer in a world where the old rules of state warfare apply. More evidence is provided by the destruction of medieval monuments in the Croatian port of Dubrovnik: when cultures, rather than states, fight, then cultural and religious monuments are weapons of war, making them fair game.

Also, war-making entities will no longer be restricted to a specific territory. Loose and shadowy organisms such as Islamic terrorist organizations suggest why borders will mean increasingly little and sedimentary layers of tribalistic identity and control will mean more. "From the vantage point of the present, there appears every prospect that religious . . . fanaticisms will play a larger role in the motivation of armed conflict" in the West than at any time "for the last 300 years," Van Creveld writes. This is why analysts like Michael Vlahos are closely monitoring religious cults. Vlahos says, "An ideology that challenges us may not take familiar form, like the old Nazis or Commies. It may not even engage us initially in ways that fit old threat markings." Van Creveld concludes, "Armed conflict will be waged by men on earth, not robots in space. It will have more in common with the struggles of primitive tribes than with large-scale conventional war."

Van Creveld's . . . vision of worldwide low-intensity conflict is not a superficial "back to the future" scenario. First of all, technology will be used toward primitive ends. In Liberia the guerrilla leader Prince Johnson didn't just cut off the ears of President Samuel Doe before Doe was tortured to death in 1990—Johnson made a video of it, which has circulated throughout West Africa. In December of 1992, when plotters of a failed coup against the Strasser regime in Sierra Leone had their ears cut off at Freetown's Hamilton Beach prior to being killed, it was seen by many to be a copycat execution. Considering . . . that the Strasser regime is not really a government and that Sierra Leone is not really a nation-state, listen closely to Van Creveld: "Once the legal monopoly of armed force, long claimed by the state, is wrested out of its hands, existing distinctions between war and crime will break down much as is already the case today in . . . Lebanon, Sri Lanka, El Salvador, Peru, or Colombia."

If crime and war become indistinguishable, then "national defense" may in the future be viewed as a local concept. As crime continues to grow in our cities and the ability of state governments and criminal-justice systems to protect their citizens diminishes, urban crime may, according to Van Creveld, "develop into low-intensity conflict by coalescing along racial, religious, social, and political lines." As small-scale violence multiplies at home and abroad, state armies will continue to shrink, being gradually replaced by a booming private security business, as in West Africa, and by urban mafias, especially in the former communist world, who may be better equipped than municipal police forces to grant physical protection to local inhabitants.

Future wars will be those of communal survival, aggravated or, in many cases, caused by environmental scarcity. These wars will be subnational, meaning that it will be hard for states and local governments to protect their own citizens physically. This is how many states will ultimately die. As state power fades—and with it the state's ability to help weaker groups within society, not to mention other states—peoples and cultures around the world will be thrown back upon their own strengths and weaknesses, with fewer equalizing mechanisms to protect them. Whereas the distant future will probably see the emergence of a racially hybrid, globalized man, the coming decades will see us more aware of our differences than of our similarities.

The Medical Ordeals of JFK

ROBERT DALLEK || 2002

The presidency of John F. Kennedy is now remembered as much for its secrets as for its substance or style. Reports of Kennedy's tireless philandering in the White House have abraded his carefully cultivated image as a devoted family man. Another major Kennedy secret—painstakingly hidden from public view by friends and close aides for fear of the political fallout—concerned the state of his health. For years during and after his presidency, rumors circulated that Kennedy had been in less than robust medical condition, notwithstanding the countless images of him confidently romping through touch football games at Hyannis Port. But the full and frightening magnitude of Kennedy's medical problems did not become known until 2002, when The Atlantic *published this article by the eminent presidential historian Robert Dallek (1934–).*

The article's revelations, culled from Dallek's book An Unfinished Life: John F. Kennedy, 1917–1963, *led network and cable newscasts and were reported on the front pages of newspapers throughout the world. Granted unprecedented access to long-buried medical files at the Kennedy Library, Dallek, the author of much-praised books about Lyndon Johnson, Franklin Roosevelt, and Ronald Reagan, portrayed a man in almost constant pain since childhood and in daily need of a veritable pharmacopeia of prescription medications. ("I don't care if it's horse piss," the president was heard to remark about a particularly potent combination of amphetamines and painkillers he was taking. "It works.") Kennedy suffered, Dallek discovered, from a staggering array of ailments for a man so young, including life-threatening Addison's disease, colitis, urinary tract infections, anemia, low blood pressure, high cholesterol, depression, insomnia, and chronic fatigue—in addition to the degenerative back problems that had already come to light. For Dallek, JFK's many years of stonewalling about his medical history should be seen not so much as a betrayal of public trust but as a profile in courage—"a man struggling to endure extraordinary pain and distress and performing his presidential . . . duties largely undeterred by his physical suffering." And in the article's final observation, Dallek chillingly postulates that Kennedy might even have survived his assassination in Dallas had it not been for the back brace he was habitually forced to wear.*

The lifelong health problems of John F. Kennedy constitute one of the best-kept secrets of recent U.S. history—no surprise, because if the extent of those problems had been revealed while he was alive, his presidential ambitions would likely have been dashed. Kennedy, like so many of his predecessors, was more intent on winning the presidency than on revealing himself to the public. On one level this secrecy can be taken as another stain on his oft-criticized character, a deception maintained at the potential expense of the citizens he was elected to lead. Yet there is another way of viewing the silence regarding his health—as the quiet stoicism of a man struggling to endure extraordinary pain and distress and performing his presidential (and pre-presidential) duties largely undeterred by his physical suffering. Does this not also speak to his character, but in a more complex way?

Not only the extent of Kennedy's medical problems but the lengths to which he and his family went to conceal them were significant. According to Bill Walton, a Kennedy family friend, JFK was followed everywhere during the 1960 presidential campaign by an aide with a special bag containing the "medical support" that was needed all the time. When the bag was misplaced during a trip to Connecticut, Kennedy telephoned Governor Abe Ribicoff and said, "There's a medical bag floating around and it can't get in anybody's hands. . . . You have to find that bag." If the wrong people got hold of it, he said, "it would be murder." (The bag was recovered.)

In 1983 the Kennedy biographer Herbert Parmet observed that "dealing with the Kennedy medical history is in some ways like trying to uncover aspects of vital national-security operations." In 1995, when executors of Joseph P. Kennedy's estate made additional family papers available in the JFK Library, reports to Joe about Jack's medical condition remained closed. Before, during, and since his presidency, the Kennedys have guarded JFK's medical records from public view, apparently worrying that even posthumous revelations about his health would hurt his reputation for honest dealings with the public.

Of course, evidence of Kennedy's medical problems has been trickling out for years. In 1960, during the fight for the Democratic nomination, John Connally and India Edwards, aides to Lyndon B. Johnson, told the press—correctly—that Kennedy suffered from Addison's disease, a condition of the adrenal glands characterized by a deficiency of the hormones needed to regulate blood sugar, sodium and potassium, and the response to stress. They described the problem as life-threatening and requiring regular doses of cortisone. The Kennedys publicly denied the allegation. They released a letter from two of JFK's doctors describing his health as "excellent" and Kennedy as fully capable of serving as President. During his Administration, according to Admiral George Burkley, a physician on the White House staff, Kennedy was so determined not to give the impression that he was "physically impaired . . . and require[d] the constant supervision of a physician" that he shunned having "a medical man in the near proximity to him" in public.

It appears that Richard Nixon may have tried at one point to gain access to Kennedy's medical history. In the fall of 1960, as he and JFK battled in what turned out to be one of the closest presidential elections ever, thieves ransacked the office of Eugene J. Cohen, a New York endocrinologist who had been treating Kennedy for Addison's disease. When they failed to find Kennedy's records, which were filed under a code name, they tried unsuccessfully to break into the office of Janet Travell, an internist and pharmacologist who had been relieving Kennedy's back pain with injections of procaine (an agent similar to lidocaine). Although the thieves remain unidentified, it is reasonable to speculate that they were Nixon operatives; the failed robberies have the aura of Watergate and of the break-in at the Beverly Hills office of Daniel Ellsberg's psychiatrist.

Using personal letters, Navy records, and oral histories, biographers and historians over the past twenty years have begun to fill in a picture of Jack Kennedy as ill and ailment-ridden for his entire life—a far cry from the paragon of vigor (or "vigah," in the family's distinctive Massachusetts accent) that the Kennedys presented. After a sickly childhood he spent significant periods during his prep school and college years in the hospital for severe intestinal ailments, infections, and what doctors thought for a time was leukemia. He suffered from ulcers and colitis as well as Addison's disease, which necessitated the administration of regular steroid treatments. And it has been known for some time that Kennedy endured terrible back trouble. He wrote his book *Profiles in Courage* while recovering from back surgery in 1954 that almost killed him.

But the full extent of Kennedy's medical ordeals has not been known until now. Earlier this year a small committee of Kennedy Administration friends and associates agreed to open a collection of his papers for the years 1955–1963. I was given access to these newly released materials, which included x-rays and prescription records from Janet Travell's files. Together with recent research and a growing understanding of medical science, the newly available records allow us to construct an authoritative account of JFK's medical tribulations. And they add telling detail to a story of lifelong suffering, revealing that many of the various treatments doctors gave Kennedy, starting when he was a boy, did far more harm than good. In particular, steroid treatments that he may have received as a young man for his intestinal ailments could have compounded—and perhaps even caused—both the Addison's disease and the degenerative back trouble that plagued him later in life. Travell's prescription records also confirm that during his presidency—and in particular during times of stress, such as the Bay of Pigs fiasco, in April of 1961, and the Cuban Missile Crisis, in October of 1962—Kennedy was taking an extraordinary variety of medications: steroids for his Addison's disease; painkillers for his back; anti-spasmodics for his colitis; antibiotics for urinary-tract infections; antihistamines for allergies; and, on at least one occasion, an anti-psychotic (though only for two days) for a severe mood change that Jackie Kennedy believed had been brought on by the antihistamines.

Kennedy's charismatic appeal rested heavily on the image of youthful energy and good health he projected. This image was a myth. The real story, disconcerting though it would have been to contemplate at the time, is actually more heroic. It is a story of iron-willed fortitude in mastering the difficulties of chronic illness.

ONE THING IN PARTICULAR remained unknown until the Travell records were opened this year: from May of 1955 until October of 1957, as he tried to get the 1956 vice-presidential nomination and then began organizing his presidential campaign, Kennedy was hospitalized nine times, for a total of forty-five days, including one nineteen-day stretch and two week-long stays. The record of these two and a half years reads like the ordeal of an old man, not one in his late thirties, in the prime of life.

Kennedy's collective health problems were not enough to deter him from running for President. Though they were a considerable burden, no one of them impressed him as life-threatening. Nor did he believe that the many medications he took would reduce his ability to work effectively; on the contrary, he saw them as ensuring his competence to deal with the demands of the office. And apparently none of his many doctors told him that were he elevated to the presidency, his health problems (or the treatments for them) could pose a danger to the country.

After reaching the White House, Kennedy believed it was more essential than ever to hide his afflictions. The day after his election, in response to a reporter's question, he declared himself in "excellent" shape and dismissed the rumors of Addison's disease as false. An article based largely on information supplied by Bobby Kennedy echoed JFK's assertions. Published in *Today's Health,* an American Medical Association journal, and summarized in *The New York Times,* the article described JFK as being in "superb physical condition."

During his time in the White House, despite public indications of continuing back difficulties, Kennedy enjoyed an image of robust good health. But according to the Travell records, medical attention was a fixed part of his routine. He was under the care of an allergist, an endocrinologist, a gastroenterologist, an orthopedist, and a urologist, along with that of Janet Travell, Admiral George Burkley, and Max Jacobson, an émigré doctor from Germany who now lived in New York and had made a reputation by treating celebrities with "pep pills," or amphetamines, that helped to combat depression and fatigue. Jacobson, whom patients called "Dr. Feelgood," administered amphetamines and back injections of painkillers that JFK believed made him less dependent on crutches.

When Kennedy went to France, in June of 1961, to meet Charles de Gaulle, Travell and Burkley accompanied him on *Air Force One.* Unknown to Travell and Burkley, Jacobson flew on a chartered jet to Paris, where he continued giving the President back injections. In addition Travell was injecting him with procaine two or three times a day to relieve his suffering, which in the spring and summer of 1961 had become unbearable. On August 27 she noted in her records that Kennedy's cry of pain in response to the injections brought Jackie in from another room to see what was wrong. In June of 1961, after Senator George McGovern had expressed sympathy to Bobby about JFK's suffering, Bobby acknowledged its seriousness. If it were not for Travell's care during the previous several years, Bobby wrote in response, his brother "would not presently be President of the United States."

The Travell records reveal that during the first six months of his term, Kennedy suffered stomach, colon, and prostate problems, high fevers, occasional dehydration, abscesses, sleeplessness, and high cholesterol, in addition to his ongoing back and adrenal ailments. His physicians administered large doses of so many drugs that Travell kept a "Medicine Administration Record," cataloguing injected and ingested corticosteroids for his adrenal insufficiency; procaine shots and ultrasound treatments and hot packs for his back; Lomotil, Metamucil, paregoric, phenobarbital, testosterone, and trasentine to control his diarrhea, abdominal discomfort, and weight loss; penicillin and other antibiotics for his urinary-tract infections and an abscess; and Tuinal to help him sleep. Before press conferences and nationally televised speeches his doctors increased his cortisone dose to deal with tensions harmful to someone unable to produce his own corticosteroids in response to stress. Though the medications occasionally made Kennedy groggy and tired, he did not see them as a problem. He dismissed questions about Jacobson's injections, saying, "I don't care if it's horse piss. It works."

In 1961 Burkley concluded that the injections, along with back braces and positioning devices that immobilized Kennedy, were doing him more harm than good. Burkley and some Secret Service men, who observed the President's difficulties getting up from a sitting position and his reliance on crutches, feared that he would soon be unable to walk and might end up in a wheelchair. Out of sight of the press, Kennedy went up and down helicopter stairs one at a time. After a meeting with JFK, in Bermuda in December of 1961, British Prime Minister Harold Macmillan recorded, "In health, I thought the President *not* in good shape. His back is hurting. He cannot sit long without pain."

In the fall of 1961 Burkley insisted to Travell that Kennedy consult Hans Kraus, an orthopedic surgeon who, like Jacobson, was a European émigré. When Travell resisted the idea, Burkley threatened to go to the President. Kraus, a brusque Austrian, confirmed Burkley's worst suspicions: he told Kennedy that if he continued the injections and did not begin regular exercise therapy to strengthen his back and abdominal muscles, he would become a cripple. Fearful that frequent visits by Kraus to supervise such therapy might trigger press inquiries and unwanted speculation, Kennedy was initially reluctant to accept the recommendation. The lost medical kit and the apparent attempts to steal his medical records during the 1960 campaign had put Kennedy on edge about the potential political damage from opponents armed with information about his health problems.

Nevertheless, Kennedy continued to need extensive medication. His condition at the time of the Cuban Missile Crisis is a case in point. The Travell records show that during the thirteen days in October of 1962 when Moscow and Washington brought the world to the brink of a nuclear war, Kennedy took his usual doses of anti-spasmodics to control his colitis, antibiotics for a flare-up of his urinary-tract problem and a bout of sinusitis, and increased amounts of hydrocortisone and testosterone, along with salt tablets, to control his Addison's disease and boost his energy. Judging from the tape recordings made of conversations during this time, the medications were no impediment to lucid thought during these long days; on the contrary, Kennedy would have been significantly less effective without them, and might even have been unable to function. But these medications were only one element in helping Kennedy to focus on the crisis; his extraordinary strength of will cannot be underestimated.

This is not to suggest that Kennedy was superhuman, or to exaggerate his ability to endure physical and emotional ills. On November 2, 1962, he took ten additional milligrams of hydrocortisone and ten grains of salt to boost himself before giving a brief report to the American people on the dismantling of the Soviet missile bases in Cuba. In December, Jackie complained to the President's gastroenterologist, Russell Boles, that the antihistamines for food allergies had a "depressing action" on the President. She asked Boles to prescribe something that would assure "mood elevation without irritation to the gastrointestinal tract." The Travell records reveal that Boles prescribed one milligram twice a day of Stelazine, an anti-psychotic that was also used as a treatment for anxiety. In two days, Kennedy showed marked improvement, and he apparently never needed the drug again.

From the start of his presidency John F. Kennedy had the example of FDR, who had functioned brilliantly despite his paralysis. Roosevelt, however, never needed the combination of medicines on which Kennedy relied to get through the day. When Kennedy ran for and won the presidency, he was in fact gambling that his health problems would not prevent him from handling the job. By hiding the extent of his ailments he denied voters the chance to decide whether they wanted to share this gamble. It is hard to believe that he could have been nominated, much less elected, if the public had known what we now know about his health.

There is no evidence that JFK's physical torments played any significant part in shaping the successes or shortcomings of his public actions, either before or during his presidency. Prescribed medicines and the program of exercises begun in the fall of 1961, combined with his intelligence, knowledge of history, and determination to manage presidential challenges, allowed him to address potentially disastrous problems sensibly. His presidency was not without failings (the invasion of Cuba at the Bay of Pigs and his slowness to act on civil rights were glaring lapses of judgment), but they were not the result of any physical or emotional impairment.

Lee Harvey Oswald killed Kennedy before the President's medical ailments could. But the evidence suggests that Kennedy's physical condition contributed to his demise. On November 22, 1963, Kennedy was, as always, wearing a corsetlike back brace as he rode through Dallas. Oswald's first bullet struck him in the back of the neck. Were it not for the back brace, which held him erect, the second, fatal shot to the head might not have found its mark.

The Fifty-first State

JAMES FALLOWS || 2002

The run-up to the Iraq War was not the American media's finest hour. In the months preceding the conflict, much of the reportage emanating from the major news organizations sounded a loud and steady amen chorus for the Bush administration's unannounced but readily apparent invasion plans. One of the few journalists who declined to buy into the conventional wisdom about the blessings that "regime change" would bring to Iraq was The Atlantic's longtime national correspondent James Fallows (1949–   ). In this remarkably prescient cover story, published six months before the start of the war, Fallows leapfrogged over the question that seemed to preoccupy most other journalists at the time—How quickly would Saddam Hussein be deposed?—and raised the larger question that no one, including the chief architects of the war, seemed to be asking: What would happen next? Fallows, drawing on dozens of interviews with military strategists and Middle East experts, was able to construct elaborate scenarios that prefigured, with extraordinary accuracy, nearly the entire catalog of difficulties and dangers that the American-led occupation has had to face since the overthrow of Saddam: the breakdown of security and civil order; the paucity of political power needed to control potential insurgencies; the decimation of infrastructure providing electricity and water; the looming threat of civil war due to rising sectarian violence; the probability of a protracted occupation in the absence of clear goals for withdrawal. "The day after a war ended, Iraq would become America's problem," Fallows writes. "Because we would have destroyed the political order and done physical damage in the process, the claims on American resources and attention would be comparable to those of any U.S. state."

As a follow-up to "The Fifty-first State," which won a National Magazine Award in 2003, Fallows went on to produce a series of related articles for The Atlantic that, taken as a whole, represent one of the most comprehensive indictments of the Bush administration's conduct of the war. These articles, collected in Blind into Baghdad *(2006), have brought Fallows's uncommon gifts for interviewing, document sifting, and synthesizing to a large national stage. As David Shaw, the Los Angeles Times's veteran media critic, observed in a 2004 column, "If Fallows is not the best journalist of his generation, he is certainly in the top half-dozen."*

Over the past few months I interviewed several dozen people about what could be expected in Iraq after the United States dislodged Saddam Hussein. An assumption behind the question was that sooner or later the United States would go to war—and would go with at best a fraction of the support it enjoyed eleven years ago when fighting Iraq during the Gulf War. Most nations in the region and traditional U.S. allies would be neutral or hostile unless the Bush Administration could present new evidence of imminent danger from Iraq.

A further assumption was that even alone, U.S. forces would win this war. The victory might be slower than in the last war against Iraq, and it would certainly cost more American lives. But in the end U.S. tanks, attack airplanes, precision-guided bombs, special-operations forces, and other assets would crush the Iraqi military. The combat phase of the war would be over when the United States destroyed Saddam Hussein's control over Iraq's government, armed forces, and stockpile of weapons.

What then?

The people I asked were spies, Arabists, oil-company officials, diplomats, scholars, policy experts, and many active-duty and retired soldiers. They were from the United States, Europe, and the Middle East. Some firmly supported a pre-emptive war against Iraq; more were opposed. As of late summer, before the serious domestic debate had begun, most of the people I spoke with expected a war to occur.

I began my research sharing the view, prevailing in Washington this year, that forcing "regime change" on Iraq was our era's grim historical necessity: starting a war would be bad, but waiting to have war brought to us would be worse. This view depended to some degree on trusting that the U.S. government had information not available to the public about exactly how close Saddam Hussein is to having usable nuclear warheads or other weapons of mass destruction. It also drew much of its power from an analogy every member of the public could understand—to Nazi Germany. In retrospect, the only sin in resisting Hitler had been waiting too long. Thus would it be in dealing with Saddam Hussein today. Richard Perle, a Reagan-era Defense Department official who is one of the most influential members outside government of what is frequently called the "war party," expressed this thought in representative form in an August column for the London *Daily Telegraph*: "A pre-emptive strike against Hitler at the time of Munich would have meant an immediate war, as opposed to the one that came later. Later was much worse."

Nazi and Holocaust analogies have a trumping power in many arguments, and their effect in Washington was to make doubters seem weak—Neville Chamberlains, versus the Winston Churchills who were ready to face the truth. The most experienced military figure in the Bush Cabinet, Secretary of State Colin Powell, was cast as the main "wet," because of his obvious discomfort with an effort that few allies would support. His instincts fit the general sociology of the Iraq debate: As a rule, the strongest advocates of pre-emptive attack, within the government and in the press, had neither served in the military nor lived in Arab societies. Military veterans and Arabists were generally doves. For example: Paul Wolfowitz, the deputy secretary of defense and the intellectual leader of the war party inside the government, was in graduate school through the late 1960s. Richard Armitage, his skeptical counterpart at the State Department and Powell's ally in pleading for restraint, is a Naval Academy graduate who served three tours in Vietnam.

I ended up thinking that the Nazi analogy paralyzes the debate about Iraq rather than clarifying it. Like any other episode in history, today's situation is both familiar and new. In the ruthlessness of the adversary it resembles dealing with Adolf Hitler. But Iraq, unlike Germany, has no industrial base and few military allies nearby. It is split by regional, religious, and ethnic differences that are much more complicated than Nazi Germany's simple mobilization of "Aryans" against Jews. Hitler's Germany constantly expanded, but Iraq has been bottled up, by international sanctions, for more than ten years. As in the early Cold War, America faces an international ideology bent on our destruction and a country trying to develop weapons to use against us. But then we were dealing with another superpower, capable of obliterating us. Now there is a huge imbalance between the two sides in scale and power.

If we had to choose a single analogy to govern our thinking about Iraq, my candidate would be World War I. The reason is not simply the one the historian David Fromkin advanced in his book *A Peace to End All Peace*: that the division of former Ottoman Empire territories after that war created many of the enduring problems of modern Iraq and the Middle East as a whole. The Great War is also relevant as a powerful example of the limits of human imagination: specifically, imagination about the long-term consequences of war.

The importance of imagination was stressed to me by Merrill McPeak, a retired Air Force general with misgivings about a pre-emptive attack. When America entered the Vietnam War, in which McPeak flew combat missions over the jungle, the public couldn't imagine how badly combat against a "weak" foe might turn out for the United States. Since that time, and because of the Vietnam experience, we have generally overdrawn the risks of combat itself. America's small wars of the past generation, in Grenada, Haiti, and Panama, have turned out far better—tactically, at least—than many experts dared to predict. The larger ones, in the Balkans, the Persian Gulf, and Afghanistan, have as well. The "Black Hawk Down" episode in Somalia is the main exception, and it illustrates a different rule: when fighting not organized armies but stateless foes, we have underestimated our vulnerabilities.

There is an even larger realm of imagination, McPeak suggested to me. It involves the chain of events a war can set off. Wars change history in ways no one can foresee. The Egyptians who planned to attack Israel in 1967 could not imagine how profoundly what became the Six Day War would change the map and politics of the Middle East. After its lightning victory Israel seized neighboring territory, especially on the West Bank of the Jordan River, that is still at the heart of disputes with the Palestinians. Fifty years before, no one who had accurately foreseen what World War I would bring could have rationally decided to let combat begin. The war meant the collapse of three empires, the Ottoman, the Austro-Hungarian, and the Russian; the cresting of another, the British; the eventual rise of Hitler in Germany and Mussolini in Italy; and the drawing of strange new borders from the eastern Mediterranean to the Persian Gulf, which now define the battlegrounds of the Middle East. Probably not even the United States would have found the war an attractive bargain, even though the U.S. rise to dominance began with the wounds Britain suffered in those years.

In 1990, as the United States prepared to push Iraqi troops out of Kuwait, McPeak was the Air Force chief of staff. He thought that war was necessary and advocated heavy bombing in Iraq. Now he opposes an invasion, largely because of how hard it is to imagine the full consequences of America's first purely pre-emptive war—and our first large war since the Spanish-American War in which we would have few or no allies.

We must use imagination on both sides of the debate: about the risks of what Saddam Hussein might do if left in place, and also about what such a war might unleash. Some members of the war party initially urged a quick in-and-out attack. Their model was the three-part formula of the "Powell doctrine": First, line up clear support—from America's political leadership, if not internationally. Then assemble enough force to leave no doubt about the outcome. Then, before the war starts, agree on how it will end and when to leave.

The in-and-out model has obviously become unrealistic. If Saddam Hussein could be destroyed by a death ray or captured by a ninja squad that sneaked into Baghdad and spirited him away, the United States might plausibly call the job done. It would still have to wonder what Iraq's next leader might do with the weapons laboratories, but the immediate problem would be solved.

Absent ninjas, getting Saddam out will mean bringing in men, machinery, and devastation. If the United States launched a big tank-borne campaign, as suggested by some of the battle plans leaked to the press, tens of thousands of soldiers, with their ponderous logistics trail, would be in the middle of a foreign country when the fighting ended. If the U.S. military relied on an air campaign against Baghdad, as other leaked plans have implied, it would inevitably kill many Iraqi civilians before it killed Saddam. One way or another, America would leave a large footprint on Iraq, which would take time to remove.

And logistics wouldn't be the only impediment to quick withdrawal. Having taken dramatic action, we would no doubt be seen—by the world and ourselves, by al Jazeera and CNN—as responsible for the consequences. The United States could have stopped the Khmer Rouge slaughter in Cambodia in the 1970s, but it was not going to, having spent the previous decade in a doomed struggle in Vietnam. It could have prevented some of the genocide in Rwanda in the 1990s, and didn't, but at least it did not trigger the slaughter by its own actions. "It is quite possible that if we went in, took out Saddam Hussein, and then left quickly, the result would be an extremely bloody civil war," says William Galston, the director of the Institute for Philosophy and Public Policy at the University of Maryland, who was a Marine during the Vietnam War. "That blood would be directly on our hands." Most people I spoke with, whether in favor of war or not, recognized that military action is a barbed hook: once it goes in, there is no quick release.

The tone of the political debate reflects a dawning awareness of this reality. Early this year, during the strange "phony war" stage of Iraq discussions, most people in Washington assumed that war was coming, but there was little open discussion of exactly why it was necessary and what consequences it would bring. The pro-war group avoided questions about what would happen after a victory, because to consider postwar complications was to weaken the case for a pre-emptive strike. Some war advocates even said, if pressed, that the details of postwar life didn't matter. With the threat and the tyrant eliminated, the United States could assume that whatever regime emerged would be less dangerous than the one it replaced.

As the swirl of leaks, rumors, and official statements made an attack seem alternately more and less imminent, the increasing chaos in Afghanistan underscored a growing consensus about the in-and-out scenario for Iraq: it didn't make sense. The war itself might be quick, perhaps even quicker than the rout of the Taliban. But the end of the fighting would hardly mean the end of America's commitment. In August, as warlords reasserted their power in Afghanistan, General Tommy Franks, the U.S. commander, said that American troops might need to stay in Afghanistan for many years.

If anything, America's involvement in Afghanistan should have been cleaner and more containable than what would happen in Iraq. In Afghanistan the United States was responding to an attack, rather than initiating regime change. It had broad international support; it had the Northern Alliance to do much of the work. Because the Taliban and al Qaeda finally chose to melt away rather than stand and fight, U.S. forces took control of the major cities while doing relatively little unintended damage. And still, getting out will take much longer than getting in.

Some proponents of war viewed the likelihood of long involvement in Iraq as a plus. If the United States went in planning to stay, it could, they contended, really make a difference there. Richard Perle addressed a major anti-war argument—that Arab states would flare up in resentment—by attempting to turn it around. "It seems at least as likely," he wrote in his *Daily Telegraph* column, "that Saddam's replacement by a decent Iraqi regime would open the way to a far more stable and peaceful region. A democratic Iraq would be a powerful refutation of the patronizing view that Arabs are incapable of democracy."

Some regional experts made the opposite point: that a strong, prosperous, confident, stable Iraq was the last thing its neighbors, who prefer it in its bottled-up condition, wanted to see. Others pooh-poohed the notion that any Western power, however hard it tried or long it stayed, could bring about any significant change in Iraq's political culture.

Regardless of these differences, the day after a war ended, Iraq would become America's problem, for practical and political reasons. Because we would have destroyed the political order and done physical damage in the process, the claims on American resources and attention would be comparable to those of any U.S. state. Conquered Iraqis would turn to the U.S. government for emergency relief, civil order, economic reconstruction, and protection of their borders. They wouldn't be able to vote in U.S. elections, of course—although they might after they emigrated. (Every American war has created a refugee-and-immigrant stream.) But they would be part of us.

BLACK AND WHITE

Reconstruction

FREDERICK DOUGLASS || 1866

Throughout the Civil War, in such highly charged essays as Ralph Waldo Emerson's "American Civilization" (see p. 542), The Atlantic's editors stepped up their campaign to abolish slavery. Once the war ended and emancipation became reality, however, the editors reset their sights on a different racial cause and began to press for legislative reforms that would put black and white Americans on equal footing. The Atlantic's drive to secure enfranchisement and other basic civil rights for African Americans antagonized many Southerners, but at the same time it began to attract some of the country's preeminent black writers to the magazine's pages. Among the most influential of these early contributors was the memoirist, newspaperman, lecturer, diplomat, and former slave Frederick Douglass (1818–1895). Born in the backcountry of Maryland to a slave named Harriet Bailey and an unknown white man, Douglass escaped from a brutal owner in 1838 and took refuge in the thriving black community of New Bedford, Massachusetts. His rhetorical brilliance quickly made him a mainstay on the abolitionist lecture circuit, and, in 1845, his Narrative of the Life of Frederick Douglass *became one of the bestselling books of the day, transforming him into an international celebrity and a much-sought-after spokesman on the subject of race. Douglass had spent more than half of his life fighting to banish slavery from the country, but, as with* The Atlantic, *once that goal had been achieved he immediately reordered his priorities. In this excerpt from the first half of a two-part article, he called upon Congress to pass a civil rights amendment, arguing that only by the establishment of equal rights for blacks could the fruits of victory in the war be reaped. Four years later, the Fifteenth Amendment granted blacks the right to vote, but that historic breakthrough was soon nullified by numerous acts of intimidation, violence, and fraud against black voters in the South.*

The assembling of the Second Session of the Thirty-ninth Congress may very properly be made the occasion of a few earnest words on the already much-worn topic of reconstruction.

Seldom has any legislative body been the subject of a solicitude more intense, or of aspirations more sincere and ardent. There are the best of reasons for this profound interest. Questions of vast moment, left undecided by the last session of Congress, must be manfully grappled with by this. No political skirmishing will avail. The occasion demands statesmanship.

Whether the tremendous war so heroically fought and so victoriously ended shall pass into history a miserable failure, barren of permanent results,—a scandalous and shocking waste of blood and treasure,—a strife for empire, of no value to liberty or civilization,—an attempt to re-establish a Union by force, which must be the merest mockery of a Union . . . or whether, on the other hand, we shall, as the rightful reward of victory over treason, have a solid nation, entirely delivered from all contradictions and social antagonisms, based upon loyalty, liberty, and equality, must be determined one way or the other by the present session of Congress.

Slavery, like all other great systems of wrong, founded in the depths of human selfishness, and existing for ages, has not neglected its own conservation. It has steadily exerted an influence upon all around it favorable to its own continuance. And today it is so strong that it could exist, not only without law, but even against law. Custom, manners, morals, religion, are all on its side everywhere in the South; and when you add the ignorance and servility of the ex-slave to the intelligence and accustomed authority of the master, you have the conditions, not out of which slavery will again grow, but under which it is impossible for the Federal government to wholly destroy it, unless the Federal government be armed with despotic power, to blot out State authority, and to station a Federal officer at every cross-road. This, of course, cannot be done, and ought not even if it could. The true way and the easiest way is to make our government entirely consistent with itself, and give to every loyal citizen the elective franchise,—a right and power which will be ever present, and will form a wall of fire for his protection.

One of the invaluable compensations of the late Rebellion is the highly instructive disclosure it made of the true source of danger to republican government. Whatever may be tolerated in monarchical and despotic governments, no republic is safe that tolerates a privileged class, or denies to any of its citizens equal rights and equal means to maintain them. What was theory before the war has been made fact by the war.

At any rate, to this grand work of national regeneration and entire purification Congress must now address itself, with full purpose that the work shall this time be thoroughly done. The deadly upas, root and branch, leaf and fibre, body and sap, must be utterly destroyed. The country is evidently not in a condition to listen patiently to pleas for postponement, however plausible, nor will it permit the responsibility to be shifted to other shoulders. Authority and power are here commensurate with the duty imposed. There are no cloud-flung shadows to obscure the way. Truth shines with brighter light and intenser heat at every moment, and a country torn and rent and bleeding implores relief from its distress and agony.

If time was at first needed, Congress has now had time. All the requisite materials from which to form an intelligent judgment are now before it. Whether its members look at the origin, the progress, the termination of the war, or at the mockery of a peace now existing, they will find only one unbroken chain of argument in favor of a radical policy of reconstruction. For the omissions of the last session, some excuses may be allowed. A treacherous President [Andrew Johnson] stood in the way; and it can be easily seen how reluctant good men might be to admit an apostasy which involved so much of baseness and ingratitude. It was natural that they should seek to save him by bending to him even when he leaned to the side of error. But all is changed now. Congress knows now that it must go on without his aid, and even against his machinations. The advantage of the present session over the last is immense. Where that investigated, this has the facts. Where that walked by faith, this may walk by sight. Where that halted, this must go forward, and where that failed, this must succeed, giving the country whole measures where that gave us half-measures, merely as a means of saving the elections in a few doubtful districts. That Congress saw what was right, but distrusted the enlightenment of the loyal masses; but what was forborne in distrust of the people must now be done with a full knowledge that the people expect and require it.

In every considerable public meeting, and in almost every conceivable way, whether at court-house, school-house, or cross-roads, indoors and out, the subject has been discussed, and the people have emphatically pronounced in favor of a radical policy. Listening to the doctrines of expediency and compromise with pity, impatience, and disgust, they have everywhere broken into demonstrations of the wildest enthusiasm when a brave word has been spoken in favor of equal rights and impartial suffrage. Radicalism, so far from being odious, is now the popular passport to power. The men most bitterly charged with it go to Congress with the largest majorities, while the timid and doubtful are sent by lean majorities, or else left at home.

[It] is obvious to common sense that the rebellious States stand to-day, in point of law, precisely where they stood when, exhausted, beaten, conquered, they fell powerless at the feet of Federal authority. Their State governments were overthrown, and the lives and property of the leaders of the Rebellion were forfeited. In reconstructing the institutions of these shattered and overthrown States, Congress should begin with a clean slate, and make clean work of it. Let there be no hesitation. It would be a cowardly deference to a defeated and treacherous President, if any account were made of the illegitimate, one-sided, sham governments hurried into existence for a malign purpose in the absence of Congress. These pretended governments, which were never submitted to the people, and from participation in which four millions of the loyal people were excluded by Presidential order, should now be treated according to their true character, as shams and impositions, and supplanted by true and legitimate governments, in the formation of which loyal men, black and white, shall participate.

It is not, however, within the scope of this paper to point out the precise steps to be taken, and the means to be employed. The people are less concerned about these than the grand end to be attained. They demand such a reconstruction as shall put an end to the present anarchical state of things in the late rebellious States,—where frightful murders and wholesale massacres are perpetrated in the very presence of Federal soldiers. This horrible business they require shall cease. They want a reconstruction such as will protect loyal men, black and white, in their persons and property; such a one as will cause Northern industry, Northern capital, and Northern civilization to flow into the South, and make a man from New England as much at home in Carolina as elsewhere in the Republic. No Chinese wall can now be tolerated. The South must be opened to the light of law and liberty, and this session of Congress is relied upon to accomplish this important work.

The plain, common-sense way of doing this work, as intimated at the beginning, is simply to establish in the South one law, one government, one administration of justice, one condition to the exercise of the elective franchise, for men of all races and colors alike. This great measure is sought as earnestly by loyal white men as by loyal blacks, and is needed alike by both. Let sound political prescience but take the place of an unreasoning prejudice, and this will be done.

The policy that emancipated and armed the negro—now seen to have been wise and proper by the dullest—was not certainly more sternly demanded than is now the policy of enfranchisement. If with the negro was success in war, and without him failure, so in peace it will be found that the nation must fall or flourish with the negro.

Fortunately, the Constitution of the United States knows no distinction between citizens on account of color. Neither does it know any difference between a citizen of a State and a citizen of the United States.

Citizenship evidently includes all the rights of citizens, whether State or national. If the Constitution knows none, it is clearly no part of the duty of a Republican Congress now to institute one. The mistake of the last session was the attempt to do this very thing, by a renunciation of its power to secure political rights to any class of citizens, with the obvious purpose to allow the rebellious States to disfranchise, if they should see fit, their colored citizens. This unfortunate blunder must now be retrieved, and the emasculated citizenship given to the negro supplanted by that contemplated in the Constitution of the United States, which declares that the citizens of each State shall enjoy all the rights and immunities of citizens of the several States,—so that a legal voter in any State shall be a legal voter in all the States.

The Awakening of the Negro

BOOKER T. WASHINGTON || 1896

*Few African American public figures have been more influential,
more vilified, and more misunderstood than Booker T. Washington
(1856–1915). Washington's rise to prominence in the late nineteenth century coincided with the arrival of Jim Crow—the systematic legalization
of racial segregation in the South that culminated with the Supreme
Court's enshrinement of the "separate but equal" doctrine in its 1896*
Plessy v. Ferguson *ruling. Two decades earlier, southern blacks had seen
their hopes for political and economic equality dashed as the gains they
had achieved in the post–Civil War era of Reconstruction were rolled
back and, in some cases, obliterated by white vigilante attacks. Against
this backdrop came Washington, with a message that emphasized black
economic empowerment and self-help. An educator and a former slave,
Washington was often compared to Frederick Douglass, but unlike the
fiery abolitionist, he attempted to downplay the horrors of slavery, advocating instead a comprehensive program of vocational and agricultural
training, the goal of which was to transform impoverished African
Americans into a stable, albeit segregated, working class. Washington
wanted to wipe the slave past clean, to liberate African Americans from
what he saw as a self-destructive preoccupation with their victimization,
and even to turn Frederick Douglass's legacy on its head by suggesting
that slavery, though evil, had taught blacks valuable life lessons. To accel-
erate black economic development, he was willing to postpone the fight
for full racial equality, and he used his own life story as Exhibit A. As he
recalls in "The Awakening of the Negro"—and later in his autobiography*
Up from Slavery—*he had lifted himself out of plantation slavery and
West Virginia coal mines to become an entrepreneurial educator: the first
director of an all-black vocational school called the Tuskegee Normal and
Industrial Institute, which later expanded into Tuskegee University.*

This Atlantic *article represents one of the earliest and best distilla-
tions not only of the principles by which Washington ran Tuskegee but
also of his racial philosophy. Washington's worldview won him many
black followers as well as some powerful white ones, including Theodore
Roosevelt and Andrew Carnegie. But his gradualist approach and his
seemingly forgiving attitude toward slavery infuriated many blacks in
the North, who ridiculed him as an "Uncle Tom" and "The Great Ac-
commodator." The latter epithet was coined by W.E.B. Du Bois, the bril-*

liant black historian and sociologist who would emerge as Washington's chief rival for Frederick Douglass's crown. The war between the two men's ideologies—Bookerite pragmatism and DuBoisian political activism—would play out directly in the pages of The Atlantic *over the next decade and remains to this day the great schism in African American thought.*

My earliest recollection is of a small one-room log hut on a large slave plantation in Virginia. After the close of the war, while working in the coalmines of West Virginia for the support of my mother, I heard in some accidental way of the Hampton Institute. When I learned that it was an institution where a black boy could study, could have a chance to work for his board, and at the same time be taught how to work and to realize the dignity of labor, I resolved to go there. Bidding my mother good-by, I started out one morning to find my way to Hampton, though I was almost penniless and had no definite idea where Hampton was. By walking, begging rides, and paying for a portion of the journey on the steam-cars, I finally succeeded in reaching the city of Richmond, Virginia. I was without money or friends. I slept under a sidewalk, and by working on a vessel the next day I earned money to continue my way to the institute, where I arrived with a surplus of fifty cents. At Hampton I found the opportunity—in the way of buildings, teachers, and industries provided by the generous—to get training in the class-room and by practical touch with industrial life, to learn thrift, economy, and push. I was surrounded by an atmosphere of business, Christian influence, and a spirit of self-help that seemed to have awakened every faculty in me, and caused me for the first time to realize what it meant to be a man instead of a piece of property.

While there I resolved that when I had finished the course of training I would go into the far South, into the Black Belt of the South, and give my life to providing the same kind of opportunity for self-reliance and self-awakening that I had found provided for me at Hampton. My work began at Tuskegee, Alabama, in 1881, in a small shanty and church, with one teacher and thirty students, without a dollar's worth of property. The spirit of work and of industrial thrift, with aid from the State and generosity from the North, has enabled us to develop an institution of eight hundred students gathered from nineteen States, with seventy-nine instructors, fourteen hundred acres of land, and thirty buildings, including large and small; in all, property valued at $280,000. Twenty-five industries have been organized, and the whole work is carried on at an annual cost of about

$80,000 in cash; two fifths of the annual expense so far has gone into permanent plant.

What is the object of all this outlay? First, it must be borne in mind that we have in the South a peculiar and unprecedented state of things. It is of the utmost importance that our energy be given to meeting conditions that exist right about us rather than conditions that existed centuries ago or that exist in countries a thousand miles away. What are the cardinal needs among the colored people in the South, most of whom are to be found on the plantations? Roughly, these needs may be stated as food, clothing, shelter, education, proper habits, and a settlement of race relations. The seven millions of colored people of the South cannot be reached directly by any missionary agency, but they can be reached by sending out among them strong selected young men and women, with the proper training of head, hand, and heart, who will live among these masses and show them how to lift themselves up.

The problem that the Tuskegee Institute keeps before itself constantly is how to prepare these leaders. From the outset, in connection with religious and academic training, it has emphasized industrial or hand training as a means of finding the way out of present conditions. First, we have found the industrial teaching useful in giving the student a chance to work out a portion of his expenses while in school. Second, the school furnishes labor that has an economic value, and at the same time gives the student a chance to acquire knowledge and a skill while performing the labor. Most of all, we find the industrial system valuable in teaching economy, thrift, and the dignity of labor, and in giving moral backbone to students. The fact that a student goes out into the world conscious of his power to build a house or a wagon, or to make a harness, gives him a certain confidence and moral independence that he would not possess without such training.

A more detailed example of our methods at Tuskegee may be of interest. For example, we cultivate by student labor six hundred and fifty acres of land. The object is not only to cultivate the land in a way to make it pay our boarding department, but at the same time to teach the students, in addition to the practical works, something of the chemistry of the soil, the best methods of drainage, dairying, the cultivation of fruit, the care of livestock and tools, and scores of other lessons needed by a people whose main dependence is on agriculture. Notwithstanding that eighty-five per cent of the colored people in the South live by agriculture in some form, aside from what has been done by Hampton, Tuskegee, and one or two other institutions practically nothing has been attempted in the direction of teaching them about the very industry from which the masses of our people must get their subsistence. Friends have recently provided means for the erection of a large new chapel at Tuskegee. Our students have made the bricks for this chapel. A large part of the timber is sawed by students at our own sawmill, the plans are drawn by our teacher of architecture and mechanical drawing, and students do the brick-masonry, plastering, painting, carpentry work, tinning, slatting, and make most of the furniture. Practically, the whole chapel will be built and furnished by student labor; in the end the school will have the building for permanent use, and the students will have a knowledge of the trades employed in its construction. In this way all but three of the thirty buildings on the grounds have been erected. While the young men do the kinds of work I have mentioned, the young women to a large extent make, mend, and launder the clothing of the young men, and thus are taught important industries.

One of the objections sometimes urged against industrial education for the negro is that it aims merely to teach him to work on the same plan that he was made to follow when in slavery. This is far from being the object at Tuskegee. At the head of each of the twenty-five industrial departments we have an intelligent and competent instructor, just as we have in our history classes, so that the student is taught not only practical brick-masonry, for example, but also the underlying principles of that industry, the mathematics and the mechanical and architectural drawing. Or he is taught how to become master of the forces of nature so that, instead of cultivating corn in the old way, he can use a corn cultivator, that lays off the furrows, drops the corn into them, and covers it, and in this way he can do more work than three men by the old process of corn-planting; at the same time much of the toil is eliminated and labor is dignified. In a word, the constant aim is to show the student how to put brains into every process of labor; how to bring his knowledge of mathematics and the sciences into farming, carpentry, forging, foundry work; how to dispense as soon as possible with the old form of ante-bellum labor. In the erection of the chapel just referred to, instead of letting the money which was given us go into outside hands, we make it accomplish three objects: first, it provides the chapel; second, it gives the students a chance to get a practical knowledge of the trades connected with building; and third, it enables them to earn something toward the payment of board while receiving academic and industrial training. Having been fortified at Tuskegee by education of mind, skill of hand, Christian character, ideas of thrift, economy, and push, and a spirit of independence, the student is sent out to become a center of influence and light in showing the masses of our people in the Black Belt of the South how to lift themselves up.

Nothing else so soon brings about right relations between the two races in the South as the industrial progress of the negro. Friction between the races will pass away in proportion as the black man, by reason of his skill, intelligence, and character, can produce something that the white man wants or respects in the commercial world. This is another reason why at Tuskegee we push the industrial training. We find that as every year we put into a Southern community colored men who can start a brick-yard, a sawmill, a tin-shop, or a printing-office,—men who produce something that makes the white man partly dependent upon the negro, instead of all the dependence being on the other side,—a change takes place in the relations of the races.

Let us go on for a few more years knitting our business and industrial relations into those of the white man, till a black man gets a mortgage on a white man's house that he can foreclose at will. The white man on whose house the mortgage rests will not try to prevent that negro from voting when he goes to the polls. It is through the dairy farm, the truck garden, the trades, and commercial life, largely, that the negro is to find his way to the enjoyment of all his rights. Whether he will or not, a white man respects a negro who owns a two-story brick house.

What is the permanent value of the Tuskegee system of training to the South in a broader sense? In connection with this, it is well to bear in mind that slavery taught the white man that labor with the hands was something fit for the negro only, and something for the white man to come into contact with just as little as possible. It is true that there was a large class of poor white people who labored with the hands, but they did it because they were not able to secure negroes to work for them; and these poor whites were constantly trying to imitate the slave-holding class in escaping labor, and they too regarded it as anything but elevating. The negro in turn looked down upon the poor whites with a certain contempt because they had to work. The negro, it is to be borne in mind, worked under constant protest, because he felt that his labor was being unjustly required, and he spent almost as much effort in planning how to escape work as in learning how to work. Labor with him was a badge of degradation. The white man was held up before him as the highest type of civilization, but the negro noted that this highest type of civilization himself did not labor; hence he argued that the less work he did, the more nearly he would be like a white man. Then, in addition to these influences, the slave system discouraged labor-saving machinery. To use labor-saving machinery intelligence was required, and intelligence and slavery were not on friendly terms; hence the negro always associated labor with toil, drudgery, something to be escaped.

When the negro first became free, his idea of education was that it was something that would soon put him in the same position as regards work that his recent master had occupied. Out of these conditions grew the Southern habit of putting off till to-morrow and the day after the duty that should be done promptly to-day. The leaky house was not repaired while the sun shone, for then the rain did not come through. While the rain was falling, no one cared to expose himself to stop the leak. The plough, on the same principle, was left where the last furrow was run, to rot and rust in the field during the winter. There was no need to repair the wooden chimney that was exposed to the fire, because water could be thrown on it when it was on fire. There was no need to trouble about the payment of a debt to-day, for it could just as well be paid next week or next year. Besides these conditions, the whole South, at the close of the war, was without proper food, clothing, and shelter,—was in need of habits of thrift and economy and of something laid up for a rainy day.

At Tuskegee we became convinced that the thing to do was to make a careful systematic study of the condition and needs of the South, especially the Black Belt, and to bend our efforts in the direction of meeting these needs, whether we were following a well-beaten track, or were hewing out a new path to meet conditions probably without a parallel in the world. After fourteen years of experience and observation, what is the result? Gradually but surely, we find that all through the South the disposition to look upon labor as a disgrace is on the wane, and the parents who themselves sought to escape work are so anxious to give their children training in intelligent labor that every institution which gives training in the handicrafts is crowded, and many (among them Tuskegee) have to refuse admission to hundreds of applicants. The influence of the Tuskegee system is shown again by the fact that almost every little school at the remotest cross-roads is anxious to be known as an industrial school, or, as some of the colored people call it, an "industrious" school.

The social lines that were once sharply drawn between those who labored with the hand and those who did not are disappearing. Those who formerly sought to escape labor, now when they see that brains and skill rob labor of the toil and drudgery once associated with it, instead of trying to avoid it are willing to pay to be taught how to engage in it. The South is beginning to see labor raised up, dignified and beautified, and in this sees its salvation. In proportion as the love of labor grows, the large idle class which has long been one of the curses of the South disappears. As its members become absorbed in occupations, they have less time to attend to everybody else's business, and more time for their own.

The South is still an undeveloped and unsettled country, and for the next half century and more the greater part of the energy of the masses will be needed to develop its material opportunities. Any force that brings the rank and file of the people to a greater love of industry is therefore especially valuable. This result industrial education is surely bringing about. It stimulates production and increases trade,—trade between the races,— and in this new and engrossing relation both forget the past.

Strivings of the Negro People

W.E.B. DU BOIS ‖ 1897

Booker T. Washington could not have had a more formidable adversary than William Edward Burghardt Du Bois (1868–1963)—unquestionably the reigning black intellectual of the last one hundred fifty years. A native New Englander who earned three degrees from Harvard, Du Bois became, in 1895, the first African American to be awarded a PhD by that institution. He was an imposing polymath, writing electrifying essays and polemics as well as history, memoir, fiction, and poetry; authoring the first sociological study in America, The Philadelphia Negro; *and co-founding the National Association for the Advancement of Colored People. It seems extraordinary, in retrospect, that so soon after Washington published "The Awakening of the Negro" in* The Atlantic, *Du Bois would follow suit with "Strivings of the Negro People," the essay that would give him his first taste of national attention and become the first chapter of his most canonical work,* The Souls of Black Folk.

Published only eleven months apart, these two essays are light-years distant from each other in viewpoint, sensibility, and style. If Washington was the apostle of industrial education and incremental assimilation, Du Bois was the apostle of academic education and urgent racial realignment. In "Strivings of the Negro People," which exudes an aura of out-and-out modernity, Du Bois sets forth for the first time his bold psychological theory that blacks are cursed by a kind of split personality, a "double consciousness" that prevents them from achieving genuine self-awareness and realizing their full human potential. In one of the most quoted lines in African American literature, he observes: "One feels his two-ness—an American, a Negro; two souls, two thoughts, two unreconciled strivings; two warring ideals in one dark body." Absent a resolution of these painfully divided loyalties, Du Bois argues, blacks will remain consigned to the shadows of American life—always thwarted in their attempts to attain political and economic parity, always measuring themselves through the eyes of others, always fated to live behind "the veil," his powerful metaphor for black isolation from and subjugation to the white world. Du Bois's mission in this essay is to sweep away the veil, to broker a marriage of the two conflicting black identities into a proud union that would later be evoked by the term "African American."

Betcween me and the other world there is ever an unasked question: unasked by some through feelings of delicacy; by others through the difficulty of rightly framing it. All, nevertheless, flutter round it. They approach me in a half-hesitant sort of way, eye me curiously or compassionately, and then, instead of saying directly, How does it feel to be a problem? they say, I know an excellent colored man in my town; or I fought at Mechanicsville; or, Do not these Southern outrages make your blood boil? At these I smile, or am interested, or reduce the boiling to a simmer, as the occasion may require. To the real question, How does it feel to be a problem? I answer seldom a word.

And yet, being a problem is a strange experience,—peculiar even for one who has never been anything else, save perhaps in babyhood and in Europe. It is in the early days of rollicking boyhood that the revelation first burst upon one, all in a day, as it were. I remember well when the shadow swept across me. I was a little thing, away up in the hills of New England, where the dark Housatonic winds between Hoosac and Taghanic to the sea. In a wee wooden schoolhouse, something put it into the boys' and girls' heads to buy gorgeous visiting-cards—ten cents a package—and exchange. The exchange was merry, till one girl, a tall newcomer, refused my card,—refused it peremptorily, with a glance. Then it dawned upon me with a certain suddenness that I was different from the others; or like, mayhap, in heart and life and longing, but shut out from their world by a vast veil. I had thereafter no desire to tear down that veil, to creep through; I held all beyond it in common contempt, and lived above it in a region of blue sky and great wandering shadows. That sky was bluest when I could beat my mates at examination-time, or beat them at a foot-race, or even beat their stringy heads. Alas, with the years all this fine contempt began to fade; for the world I longed for, and all its dazzling opportunities, were theirs, not mine. But they should not keep these prizes, I said; some, all, I would wrest from them. Just how I would do it I could never decide: by reading law, by healing the sick, by telling the wonderful tales that swam in my head,—some way. With other black boys the strife was not so fiercely sunny: their youth shrunk into tasteless sycophancy, or into silent hatred of the pale world about them and mocking distrust of everything white; or wasted itself in a bitter cry, Why did God make me an outcast and a stranger in mine own house? The "shades of the prison-house" closed round about us all: walls strait and stubborn to the whitest, but relentlessly narrow, tall, and unscalable to sons of night who must plod darkly against the stone, or steadily, half hopelessly watch the streak of blue above.

After the Egyptian and Indian, the Greek and Roman, the Teuton and Mongolian, the Negro is a sort of seventh son, born with a veil, and gifted with second-sight in this American world,—a world which yields him no self-consciousness, but only lets him see himself through the revelation of the other world. It is a peculiar sensation, this double-consciousness, this sense of always looking at one's self through the eyes of others, of measuring one's soul by the tape of a world that looks on in amused contempt and pity. One feels his two-ness,—an American, a Negro; two souls, two thoughts, two unreconciled strivings; two warring ideals in one dark body, whose dogged strength alone keeps it from being torn asunder. The history of the American Negro is the history of this strife,—this longing to attain self-conscious manhood, to merge his double self into a better and truer self. In this merging he wishes neither of the older selves to be lost. He does not wish to Africanize America, for America has too much to teach the world and Africa; he does not wish to bleach his Negro blood in a flood of white Americanism, for he believes—foolishly, perhaps, but fervently—that Negro blood has yet a message for the world. He simply wishes to make it possible for a man to be both a Negro and an American without being cursed and spit upon by his fellows, without losing the opportunity of self-development.

This is the end of his striving: to be a co-worker in the kingdom of culture, to escape both death and isolation, and to husband and use his best powers. These powers, of body and of mind, have in the past been so wasted and dispersed as to lose all effectiveness, and to seem like absence of all power, like weakness. The double-aimed struggle of the black artisan, on the one hand to escape white contempt for a nation of mere hewers of wood and drawers of water, and on the other hand to plough and nail and dig for a poverty-stricken horde, could only result in making him a poor craftsman, for he had but half a heart in either cause. By the poverty and ignorance of his people the Negro lawyer or doctor was pushed toward quackery and demagogism, and by the criticism of the other world toward an elaborate preparation that overfitted him for his lowly tasks. The would-be black-savant was confronted by the paradox that the knowledge his people needed was a twice-told tale to his white neighbors, while the knowledge which would teach the white world was Greek to his own flesh and blood. The innate love of harmony and beauty that set the ruder souls of his people a-dancing, a-singing, and a-laughing raised but confusion and doubt in the soul of the black artist; for the beauty revealed to him was the soul-beauty of a race which his larger audience despised, and he could not articulate the message of another people.

This waste of double aims, this seeking to satisfy two unreconciled ideals, has wrought sad havoc with the courage and faith and deeds of eight thousand people, has sent them often wooing false gods and invoking false means of salvation, and has even at times seemed destined to make them ashamed of themselves. In the days of bondage they thought to see in one divine event the end of all doubt and disappointment; eighteenth-century Rousseauism never worshiped freedom with half the unquestioning faith that the American Negro did for two centuries. To him slavery was, indeed, the sum of all villainies, the cause of all sorrow, the root of all prejudice; emancipation was the key to a promised land of sweeter beauty than ever stretched before the eyes of wearied Israelites. In his songs and exhortations swelled one refrain, liberty; in his tears and curses the god he implored had freedom in his right hand. At last it came,—suddenly, fearfully, like a dream. With one wild carnival of blood and passion came the message in his own plaintive cadences:—

"Shout, O children!
  Shout, you're free!
The Lord has bought your liberty!"

Years have passed away, ten, twenty, thirty. Thirty years of national life, thirty years of renewal and development, and yet the swarthy ghost of Banquo sits in its old place at the national feast. In vain does the nation cry to its vastest problem,—

"Take any shape but that, and my firm nerves
Shall never tremble!"

The freedman has not yet found in freedom his promised land. Whatever of lesser good may have come in these years of change, the shadow of a deep disappointment rests upon the Negro people,—a disappointment all the more bitter because the unattained ideal was unbounded save by the simple ignorance of a lowly folk.

The first decade was merely a prolongation of the vain search for freedom, the boon that seemed ever barely to elude their grasp,—like a tantalizing will-o'-the wisp, maddening and misleading the headless host. The holocaust of war, the terrors of the Kuklux Klan, the lies of carpet-baggers, the disorganization of industry, and the contradictory advice of friends and foes left the bewildered serf with no new watchword beyond the old cry for freedom. As the decade closed, however, he began to grasp a new idea. The ideal of liberty demanded for its attainment powerful means, and these the Fifteenth Amendment gave him. The ballot, which before he had looked upon as a visible sign of freedom, he now regarded as the chief means of gaining and perfecting the liberty with which war had partially endowed him. And why not? Had not votes made war and emancipated millions? Had not votes enfranchised the freedmen? Was anything impossible to a power that had done all this? A million black men started with renewed zeal to vote themselves into the kingdom. The decade fled away,—a decade containing, to the freedman's mind, nothing but suppressed votes, stuffed ballot-boxes, and election outrages that nullified his vaunted right of suffrage. And yet that decade from 1875 to 1885 held another powerful movement, the rise of another ideal to guide the unguided, another pillar of fire by night after a clouded day. It was the ideal of "book-learning"; the curiosity, born of compulsory ignorance, to know and test the power of the cabalistic letters of the white man, the longing to know. Mission and night schools began in the smoke of battle, ran the gauntlet of reconstruction and at last developed into permanent foundations. Here at last seemed to have been discovered the mountain path to Canaan; longer than the highway of emancipation and law, steep and rugged, but straight, leading to heights high enough to overlook life.

Up the new path the advance guard toiled, slowly, heavily, doggedly; only those who have watched and guided the faltering feet, the misty minds, the dull understandings, of the dark pupils of these schools know how faithfully, how piteously, this people strove to learn. It was weary work. The cold statistician wrote down the inches of progress here and there, noted also where here and there a foot had slipped or some one had fallen. To the tired climbers, the horizon was ever dark, the mists were often cold, the Canaan was always dim and far away. If, however, the vistas disclosed as yet no goal, no resting-place, little but flattery and criticism, the journey at least gave leisure for reflection and self-examination; it changed the child of emancipation to the youth with dawning self-consciousness, self-realization, self-respect. In those sombre forests of his striving his own soul rose before him, and he saw himself,—darkly as through a veil; and yet he saw in himself some faint revelation of his power, of his mission. He began to have a dim feeling that, to attain his place in the world, he must be himself, and not another. For the first time he sought to analyze the burden he bore upon his back, that dead-weight of social degradation partially masked behind a half-named Negro problem. He felt his poverty; without a cent, without a home, without land, tools, or savings, he had entered into competition with rich landed, skilled neighbors.

To be a poor man is hard, but to be a poor race in a land of dollars is the very bottom of hardships. He felt the weight of his ignorance,—not simply of letters, but of life, of business, of the humanities; the accumulated sloth and shirking and awkwardness of decades and centuries shackled his hands and feet. Nor was his burden all poverty and ignorance. The red stain of bastardy, which two centuries of systematic legal defilement of Negro women had stamped upon his race, meant not only the loss of ancient African chastity, but also the hereditary weight of a mass of filth from white whoremongers and adulterers, threatening almost the obliteration of the Negro home.

A people thus handicapped ought not to be asked to race with the world, but rather allowed to give all its time and thought to its own social problems. But alas! while sociologists gleefully count his bastards and his prostitutes, the very soul of the toiling, sweating black man is darkened by the shadow of a vast despair. Men call the shadow prejudice, and learnedly explain it as the natural defense of culture against barbarism, learning against ignorance, purity against crime, the "higher" against the "lower" races. To which the Negro cries Amen! and swears that to so much of this strange prejudice as is founded on just homage to civilization, culture, righteousness, and progress he humbly bows and meekly does obeisance. But before that nameless prejudice that leaps beyond all this he stands helpless, dismayed, and well-nigh speechless; before that personal disrespect and mockery, the ridicule and systematic humiliation, the distortion of fact and wanton license of fancy, the cynical ignoring of the better and boisterous welcoming of the worse, the all-pervading desire to inculcated disdain for everything black, from Toussaint to the devil,—before this there rises a sickening despair that would disarm and discourage any nation save that black host to whom "discouragement" is an unwritten word.

They still press on, they still nurse the dogged hope,—not a hope of nauseating patronage, not a hope of reception into charmed social circles of stock-jobbers, pork-packers, and earl-hunters, but the hope of a higher synthesis of civilization and humanity, a true progress, with which the chorus "Peace, good will to men,"

"May make one music as before,
But vaster."

Thus the second decade of the American Negro's freedom was a period of conflict, of inspiration and doubt, of faith and vain questionings, of *Sturm und Drang*. The ideals of physical freedom, of political power, of school training, as separate all-sufficient panaceas for social ills, became in the third decade dim and overcast. They were the vain dreams of credulous race childhood; not wrong, but incomplete and over-simple. The training of the schools we need to-day more than ever,—the training of deft hands, quick eyes and ears, and the broader, deeper, higher culture of gifted minds. The power of the ballot we need in sheer self-defense, and as a guarantee of good faith. We may misuse it, but we can scarce do worse in this respect than our whilom masters. Freedom, too, the long-sought, we still seek;—the freedom of life and limb, the freedom to work and think. Work, culture, and liberty—all these we need, not singly, but together; for today these ideals among the Negro people are gradually coalescing, and finding a higher meaning in the unifying ideal of race,—the ideal of foster-ing the traits and talents of the Negro, not in opposition to, but in con-formity with, the greater ideals of the American republic, in order that some day, on American soil, two world races may give each to each those characteristics which both so sadly lack. Already we come not altogether empty-handed: there is to-day no true American music but the sweet wild melodies of the Negro slave; the American fairy tales are Indian and African; we are the sole oasis of simple faith and reverence in a dusty desert of dollars and smartness. Will America be poorer if she replace her brutal, dyspeptic blundering with the light-hearted but determined Negro humil-ity; or her coarse, cruel wit with loving, jovial good humor; or her Annie Rooney with Steal Away?

Merely a stern concrete test of the underlying principles of the great republic is the Negro problem, and the spiritual striving of the freedmen's sons is the travail of souls whose burden is almost beyond the measure of their strength, but who bear it in the name of an historic race, in the name of this the land of their fathers' fathers, and in the name of human opportunity.

Letter from Birmingham Jail

MARTIN LUTHER KING, JR. ‖ 1963

Many historians believe that "Letter from Birmingham Jail" (published in The Atlantic *under the title "The Negro Is Your Brother") was the tide-turning document of the American civil rights movement. At the time the "Letter" was written, the movement seemed dispirited and out of gas: its top organizations had run dangerously low on funds; its tactics of nonviolent but disruptive demonstrations had become a growing source of irritation inside the Kennedy White House; and its leaders had failed to score a decisive public relations victory since the Montgomery, Alabama, bus boycott of eight years before. Then in April 1963, Martin Luther King, Jr. (1929–1968), the young Baptist minister who headed the key civil rights organization, the Southern Christian Leadership Conference, decided to join a local antisegregation protest already under way in Birmingham, Alabama—a city so infamous for its history of violence against blacks that it had been nicknamed "Bombingham." By defying a local ordinance against marching without a permit, King engineered his own arrest, and although the authorities immediately locked him away in solitary confinement, he was able to follow the press coverage of his campaign in newspapers smuggled in by his lawyers. On the second page of the local daily, the* Birmingham News, *King found an open letter to him from a group of white Alabama clergymen that raised his indignation to the boiling point. The letter, signed by seven Protestant ministers and one rabbi—all regarded as moderates—urged King and his demonstrators to abandon their pacifist resistance in favor of pursuing their goals in the courts. Exasperated by the go-slow approach advocated by his presumed brethren, King began furiously scribbling a response—first in the margins of the newspaper, then on paper slipped to him by a black jail trusty, and even on scraps of toilet paper. Piece by piece, King's aides visiting him in his narrow cell spirited his words beyond the prison gates and reassembled them at a nearby hotel. What emerged from these labors was a twenty-page, typewritten statement that represented nothing less than a grand* summa *of King's political and theological philosophy. In one of the most famous passages, he writes: "I cannot sit idly by in Atlanta and not be concerned about what happens in Birmingham. Injustice anywhere is a threat to justice everywhere. We are caught in an inescapable network of mutuality, tied in a single garment of destiny."*

When the "Letter" was first published, it received little media cover-

age and seemed to have little impact. But as images of attack dogs and high-power water hoses used against the Birmingham protesters jolted the nation's conscience, King's words started to find their way into newspapers and magazines as well as Sunday sermons around the country. With public opinion rallying around the black civil rights struggle, President Kennedy announced in June 1963 that he was submitting to Congress a long-overdue civil rights bill. That bill would not become law until Lyndon Johnson's presidency, but later that summer King, newly reenergized by the cataract of financial and emotional support his "Letter" had unleashed, presided over the historic March on Washington that culminated with his "I Have a Dream" speech. As Andrew Young, King's close aide and confidant, wrote in his memoir of the civil rights movement: "More than any other document or statement, Martin's letter helped to lay a strong moral and intellectual basis not only for our struggle in Birmingham, but for all subsequent movement campaigns in the South. It has become a classic in American literature."

While confined here in the Birmingham city jail, I came across your recent statement calling our present activities "unwise and untimely." Seldom, if ever, do I pause to answer criticism of my work and ideas. If I sought to answer all of the criticisms that cross my desk, my secretaries would be engaged in little else in the course of the day, and I would have no time for constructive work. But since I feel that you are men of genuine good will and your criticisms are sincerely set forth, I would like to answer your statement in what I hope will be patient and reasonable terms.

I think I should give the reason for my being in Birmingham, since you have been influenced by the argument of "outsiders coming in." I have the honor of serving as president of the Southern Christian Leadership Conference, an organization operating in every Southern state, with headquarters in Atlanta, Georgia. We have some eighty-five affiliate organizations all across the South, one being the Alabama Christian Movement for Human Rights. Whenever necessary and possible, we share staff, educational and financial resources with our affiliates. Several months ago our local affiliate here in Birmingham invited us to be on call to engage in a nonviolent direct-action program if such were deemed necessary. We readily consented, and when the hour came we lived up to our promises. So I am here, along with several members of my staff, because we were invited here. I am here because I have basic organizational ties here.

Beyond this, I am in Birmingham because injustice is here. Just as the eighth-century prophets left their little villages and carried their "thus saith the Lord" far beyond the boundaries of their home towns; and just as the Apostle Paul left his little village of Tarsus and carried the gospel of Jesus Christ to practically every hamlet and city of the Graeco-Roman world, I too am compelled to carry the gospel of freedom beyond my particular home town. Like Paul, I must constantly respond to the Macedonian call for aid.

Moreover, I am cognizant of the interrelatedness of all communities and states. I cannot sit idly by in Atlanta and not be concerned about what happens in Birmingham. Injustice anywhere is a threat to justice everywhere. We are caught in an inescapable network of mutuality, tied in a single garment of destiny. Whatever affects one directly affects all indirectly. Never again can we afford to live with the narrow, provincial "outside agitator" idea. Anyone who lives inside the United States can never be considered an outsider.

You deplore the demonstrations that are presently taking place in Birmingham. But I am sorry that your statement did not express a similar concern for the conditions that brought the demonstrations into being. I am sure that each of you would want to go beyond the superficial social analyst who looks merely at effects and does not grapple with underlying causes. I would not hesitate to say that it is unfortunate that so-called demonstrations are taking place in Birmingham at this time, but I would say in more emphatic terms that it is even more unfortunate that the white power structure of this city left the Negro community with no other alternative.

IN ANY NONVIOLENT CAMPAIGN there are four basic steps: collection of the facts to determine whether injustices are alive, negotiation, self-purification, and direct action. We have gone through all of these steps in Birmingham. There can be no gainsaying of the fact that racial injustice engulfs this community. Birmingham is probably the most thoroughly segregated city in the United States. Its ugly record of police brutality is known in every section of this country. Its unjust treatment of Negroes in the courts is a notorious reality. There have been more unsolved bombings of Negro homes and churches in Birmingham than in any other city in this nation. These are the hard, brutal, and unbelievable facts. On the basis of them, Negro leaders sought to negotiate with the city fathers. But the political leaders consistently refused to engage in good-faith negotiation.

Then came the opportunity last September to talk with some of the leaders of the economic community. In these negotiating sessions certain promises were made by the merchants, such as the promise to remove the humiliating racial signs from the stores. On the basis of these promises, Reverend Shuttlesworth and the leaders of the Alabama Christian Movement for Human Rights agreed to call a moratorium on any type of demonstration. As the weeks and months unfolded, we realized that we were the victims of a broken promise. The signs remained. As in so many experiences of the past, we were confronted with blasted hopes, and the dark shadow of a deep disappointment settled upon us. So we had no alternative except that of preparing for direct action, whereby we would present our very bodies as a means of laying our case before the conscience of the local and national community. We were not unmindful of the difficulties involved. So we decided to go through a process of self-purification. We started having workshops on nonviolence and repeatedly asked ourselves the questions, "Are you able to accept blows without retaliating?" and "Are you able to endure the ordeals of jail?" We decided to set our direct-action program around the Easter season, realizing that, with exception of Christmas, this was the largest shopping period of the year. Knowing that a strong economic withdrawal program would be the by-product of direct action, we felt that this was the best time to bring pressure on the merchants for the needed changes. Then it occurred to us that the March election was ahead, and so we speedily decided to postpone action until after election day. When we discovered that Mr. Connor was in the runoff, we decided again to postpone action so that the demonstration could not be used to cloud the issues. At this time we agreed to begin our nonviolent witness the day after the runoff.

This reveals that we did not move irresponsibly into direct action. We, too, wanted to see Mr. Connor defeated, so we went through postponement after postponement to aid in this community need. After this we felt that direct action could be delayed no longer.

You may well ask, "Why direct action, why sit-ins, marches, and so forth? Isn't negotiation a better path?" You are exactly right in your call for negotiation. Indeed, this is the purpose of direct action. Nonviolent direct action seeks to create such a crisis and establish such creative tension that a community that has consistently refused to negotiate is forced to confront the issue. It seeks so to dramatize the issue that it can no longer be ignored. I just referred to the creation of tension as a part of the work of the nonviolent resister. This may sound rather shocking. But I must confess that I am not afraid of the word "tension." I have earnestly worked and preached against violent tension, but there is a type of constructive nonviolent tension that is necessary for growth. Just as Socrates felt that it was necessary to create a tension in the mind so that individuals could rise from the bondage of myths and half-truths to the unfettered realm of creative analysis and objective appraisal, we must see the need of having non-violent gadflies to create the kind of tension in society that will help men to rise from the dark depths of prejudice and racism to the majestic heights of understanding and brotherhood. So, the purpose of the direct action is to create a situation so crisis-packed that it will inevitably open the door to negotiation. We therefore concur with you in your call for negotiation. Too long has our beloved Southland been bogged down in the tragic attempt to live in monologue rather than dialogue.

One of the basic points in your statement is that our acts are untimely. Some have asked, "Why didn't you give the new administration time to act?" The only answer that I can give to this inquiry is that the new administration must be prodded about as much as the outgoing one before it acts. We will be sadly mistaken if we feel that the election of Mr. Boutwell will bring the millennium to Birmingham. While Mr. Boutwell is much more articulate and gentle than Mr. Connor, they are both segregationists, dedicated to the task of maintaining the status quo. The hope I see in Mr. Boutwell is that he will be reasonable enough to see the futility of massive resistance to desegregation. But he will not see this without pressure from the devotees of civil rights. My friends, I must say to you that we have not made a single gain in civil rights without determined legal and nonviolent pressure. History is the long and tragic story of the fact that privileged groups seldom give up their privileges voluntarily. Individuals may see the moral light and voluntarily give up their unjust posture; but, as Reinhold Niebuhr has reminded us, groups are more immoral than individuals.

We know through painful experience that freedom is never voluntarily given by the oppressor; it must be demanded by the oppressed. Frankly, I have never yet engaged in a direct-action movement that was "well timed" according to the timetable of those who have not suffered unduly from the disease of segregation. For years now I have heard the word "wait." It rings in the ear of every Negro with a piercing familiarity. This "wait" has almost always meant "never." It has been a tranquilizing thalidomide, relieving the emotional stress for a moment, only to give birth to an ill-formed infant of frustration. We must come to see with the distinguished jurist of yesterday that "justice too long delayed is justice denied." We have waited for more than three hundred and forty years for our God-given and constitutional rights. The nations of Asia and Africa are moving with jetlike speed toward the goal of political independence, and we still creep at horse-and-buggy pace toward the gaining of a cup of coffee at a lunch counter. I guess it is easy for those who have never felt the stinging darts of segregation to say "wait." But when you have seen vicious mobs lynch your mothers and fathers at will and drown your sisters and brothers at whim; when you have seen hate-filled policemen curse, kick, brutalize, and even kill your black brothers and sisters with impunity; when you see the vast majority of your twenty million Negro brothers smothering in an airtight cage of poverty in the midst of an affluent society; when you suddenly find your tongue twisted and your speech stammering as you seek to explain to your six-year-old daughter why she cannot go to the public amusement park that has just been advertised on television, and see tears welling up in her little eyes when she is told that Funtown is closed to colored children, and see the depressing clouds of inferiority begin to form in her little mental sky, and see her begin to distort her little personality by unconsciously developing a bitterness toward white people; when you have to concoct an answer for a five-year-old son asking in agonizing pathos, "Daddy, why do white people treat colored people so mean?"; when you take a cross-country drive and find it necessary to sleep night after night in the uncomfortable corners of your automobile because no motel will accept you; when you are humiliated day in and day out by nagging signs reading "white" and "colored"; when your first name becomes "nigger" and your middle name becomes "boy" (however old you are) and your last name becomes "John," and when your wife and mother are never given the respected title "Mrs."; when you are harried by day and haunted by night by the fact that you are a Negro, living constantly at tiptoe stance, never quite knowing what to expect next, and plagued with inner fears and outer resentments; when you are forever fighting a degenerating sense of "nobodyness"—then you will understand why we find it difficult to wait. There comes a time when the cup of endurance runs over and men are no longer willing to be plunged into an abyss of injustice where they experience the bleakness of corroding despair. I hope, sirs, you can understand our legitimate and unavoidable impatience.

YOU EXPRESS A GREAT DEAL OF ANXIETY over our willingness to break laws. This is certainly a legitimate concern. Since we so diligently urge people to obey the Supreme Court's decision of 1954 outlawing segregation in the public schools, it is rather strange and paradoxical to find us consciously breaking laws. One may well ask, "How can you advocate breaking some laws and obeying others?" The answer is found in the fact that there are two types of laws: there are just laws, and there are unjust laws. I would agree with St. Augustine that "An unjust law is no law at all."

Now, what is the difference between the two? How does one determine when a law is just or unjust? A just law is a man-made code that squares with the moral law or the law of God. An unjust law is a code that is out of harmony with the moral law. To put it in the terms of St. Thomas Aquinas, an unjust law is a human law that is not rooted in eternal and natural law. Any law that uplifts human personality is just. Any law that degrades human personality is unjust. All segregation statutes are unjust because segregation distorts the soul and damages the personality. It gives the segregator a false sense of superiority and the segregated a false sense of inferiority. To use the words of Martin Buber, the great Jewish philosopher, segregation substitutes an "I–it" relationship for an "I–thou" relationship and ends up relegating persons to the status of things. So segregation is not only politically, economically and sociologically unsound, but it is morally wrong and sinful. Paul Tillich has said that sin is separation. Isn't segregation an existential expression of man's tragic separation, an expression of his awful estrangement, his terrible sinfulness? So I can urge men to obey the 1954 decision of the Supreme Court because it is morally right, and I can urge them to disobey segregation ordinances because they are morally wrong.

Let us turn to a more concrete example of just and unjust laws. An unjust law is a code that a majority inflicts on a minority that is not binding on itself. This is difference made legal. On the other hand, a just law is a code that a majority compels a minority to follow, and that it is willing to follow itself. This is sameness made legal.

Let me give another explanation. An unjust law is a code inflicted upon a minority which that minority had no part in enacting or creating because it did not have the unhampered right to vote. Who can say that the legislature of Alabama which set up the segregation laws was democratically elected? Throughout the state of Alabama all types of conniving methods are used to prevent Negroes from becoming registered voters, and there are some counties without a single Negro registered to vote, despite the fact that the Negroes constitute a majority of the population. Can any law set up in such a state be considered democratically structured?

These are just a few examples of unjust and just laws. There are some instances when a law is just on its face and unjust in its application. For instance, I was arrested Friday on a charge of parading without a permit. Now, there is nothing wrong with an ordinance which requires a permit for a parade, but when the ordinance is used to preserve segregation and to deny citizens the First Amendment privilege of peaceful assembly and peaceful protest, then it becomes unjust.

Of course, there is nothing new about this kind of civil disobedience. It was seen sublimely in the refusal of Shadrach, Meshach, and Abednego to obey the laws of Nebuchadnezzar because a higher moral law was involved. It was practiced superbly by the early Christians, who were willing to face hungry lions and the excruciating pain of chopping blocks before submitting to certain unjust laws of the Roman Empire. To a degree, academic freedom is a reality today because Socrates practiced civil disobedience.

We can never forget that everything Hitler did in Germany was "legal" and everything the Hungarian freedom fighters did in Hungary was "illegal." It was "illegal" to aid and comfort a Jew in Hitler's Germany. But I am sure that if I had lived in Germany during that time, I would have aided and comforted my Jewish brothers even though it was illegal. If I lived in a Communist country today where certain principles dear to the Christian faith are suppressed, I believe I would openly advocate disobeying these anti-religious laws.

I MUST MAKE TWO HONEST CONFESSIONS TO YOU, my Christian and Jewish brothers. First, I must confess that over the last few years I have been gravely disappointed with the white moderate. I have almost reached the regrettable conclusion that the Negro's great stumbling block in the stride toward freedom is not the White Citizens Councillor or the Ku Klux Klanner but the white moderate who is more devoted to order than to justice; who prefers a negative peace which is the absence of tension to a positive peace which is the presence of justice; who constantly says, "I agree with you in the goal you seek, but I can't agree with your methods of direct action"; who paternalistically feels that he can set the timetable for another man's freedom; who lives by the myth of time; and who constantly advises the Negro to wait until a "more convenient season." Shallow understanding from people of good will is more frustrating than absolute misunderstanding from people of ill will. Lukewarm acceptance is much more bewildering than outright rejection.

In your statement you asserted that our actions, even though peaceful, must be condemned because they precipitate violence. But can this assertion be logically made? Isn't this like condemning the robbed man because his possession of money precipitated the evil act of robbery? Isn't this like condemning Socrates because his unswerving commitment to truth and his philosophical delvings precipitated the misguided popular mind to make him drink the hemlock? Isn't this like condemning Jesus because His unique God-consciousness and never-ceasing devotion to His will precipitated the evil act of crucifixion? We must come to see, as federal courts have consistently affirmed, that it is immoral to urge an individual to withdraw his efforts to gain his basic constitutional rights because the quest precipitates violence. Society must protect the robbed and punish the robber.

I had also hoped that the white moderate would reject the myth of time. I received a letter this morning from a white brother in Texas which said, "All Christians know that the colored people will receive equal rights eventually, but is it possible that you are in too great of a religious hurry? It has taken Christianity almost 2000 years to accomplish what it has. The teachings of Christ take time to come to earth." All that is said here grows out of a tragic misconception of time. It is the strangely irrational notion that there is something in the very flow of time that will inevitably cure all ills. Actually, time is neutral. It can be used either destructively or constructively. I am coming to feel that the people of ill will have used time much more effectively than the people of good will. We will have to repent in this generation not merely for the vitriolic words and actions of the bad people, but for the appalling silence of the good people. We must come to see that human progress never rolls in on wheels of inevitability. It comes through the tireless efforts and persistent work of men willing to be coworkers with God, and without this hard work time itself becomes an ally of the forces of social stagnation.

YOU SPOKE OF OUR ACTIVITY in Birmingham as extreme. At first I was rather disappointed that fellow clergymen would see my nonviolent efforts as those of an extremist. I started thinking about the fact that I stand in the middle of two opposing forces in the Negro community. One is a force of complacency made up of Negroes who, as a result of long years of oppression, have been so completely drained of self-respect and a sense of "somebodyness" that they have adjusted to segregation, and, on the other hand, of a few Negroes in the middle class who, because of a degree of academic and economic security and because at points they profit by segregation, have unconsciously become insensitive to the problems of the masses. The other force is one of bitterness and hatred and comes perilously close to advocating violence. It is expressed in the various black nationalist groups that are springing up over the nation, the largest and best known being Elijah Muhammad's Muslim movement. This movement is nourished by the contemporary frustration over the continued existence of racial discrimination. It is made up of people who have lost faith in America, who have absolutely repudiated Christianity, and who have concluded that the white man is an incurable devil. I have tried to stand between these two forces, saying that we need not follow the do-nothingism of the complacent or the hatred and despair of the black nationalist. There is a more excellent way, of love and nonviolent protest. I'm grateful to God that, through the Negro church, the dimension of nonviolence entered our struggle. If this philosophy had not emerged, I am convinced that by now many streets of the South would be flowing with floods of blood. And I am further convinced that if our white brothers dismiss as "rabble-rousers" and "outside agitators" those of us who are working through the channels of nonviolent direct action and refuse to support our nonviolent efforts, millions of Negroes, out of frustration and despair, will seek solace and security in black nationalist ideologies, a development that will lead inevitably to a frightening racial nightmare.

Oppressed people cannot remain oppressed forever. The urge for freedom will eventually come. This is what has happened to the American Negro. Something within has reminded him of his birthright of freedom; something without has reminded him that he can gain it. Consciously and unconsciously, he has been swept in by what the Germans call the *Zeitgeist*, and with his black brothers of Africa, and his brown and yellow brothers of Asia, South America, and the Caribbean, he is moving with a sense of cosmic urgency toward the promised land of racial justice. Recognizing this vital urge that has engulfed the Negro community, one should readily understand public demonstrations. The Negro has many pent-up resentments and latent frustrations. He has to get them out. So let him march sometime; let him have his prayer pilgrimages to the city hall; understand why he must have sit-ins and freedom rides. If his repressed emotions do not come out in these nonviolent ways, they will come out in ominous expressions of violence. This is not a threat; it is a fact of history. So I have not said to my people, "Get rid of your discontent." But I have tried to say that this normal and healthy discontent can be channeled through the creative outlet of nonviolent direct action. Now this approach is being dismissed as extremist. I must admit that I was initially disappointed in being so categorized.

But as I continued to think about the matter, I gradually gained a bit of satisfaction from being considered an extremist. Was not Jesus an extremist in love?—"Love your enemies, bless them that curse you, pray for them that despitefully use you." Was not Amos an extremist for justice?— "Let justice roll down like waters and righteousness like a mighty stream." Was not Paul an extremist for the gospel of Jesus Christ?—"I bear in my body the marks of the Lord Jesus." Was not Martin Luther an extremist?— "Here I stand; I can do no other so help me God." Was not John Bunyan an extremist?—"I will stay in jail to the end of my days before I make a mockery of my conscience." Was not Abraham Lincoln an extremist?—"This nation cannot survive half slave and half free." Was not Thomas Jefferson an extremist?—"We hold these truths to be self-evident, that all men are created equal." So the question is not whether we will be extremist, but what kind of extremists we will be. Will we be extremists for hate, or will we be extremists for love? Will we be extremists for the preservation of injustice, or will we be extremists for the cause of justice?

I had hoped that the white moderate would see this. Maybe I was too optimistic. Maybe I expected too much. I guess I should have realized that few members of a race that has oppressed another race can understand or appreciate the deep groans and passionate yearnings of those that have been oppressed, and still fewer have the vision to see that injustice must be rooted out by strong, persistent, and determined action. I am thankful, however, that some of our white brothers have grasped the meaning of this social revolution and committed themselves to it. They are still all too small in quantity, but they are big in quality. Some, like Ralph McGill, Lillian Smith, Harry Golden, and James Dabbs, have written about our struggle in eloquent, prophetic, and understanding terms. Others have marched with us down nameless streets of the South. They sat in with us at lunch counters and rode in with us on the freedom rides. They have languished in filthy roach-infested jails, suffering the abuse and brutality of angry policemen who see them as "dirty nigger lovers." They, unlike many of their moderate brothers, have recognized the urgency of the moment and sensed the need for powerful "action" antidotes to combat the disease of segregation.

LET ME RUSH ON TO MENTION my other disappointment. I have been disappointed with the white church and its leadership. Of course, there are some notable exceptions. I am not unmindful of the fact that each of you has taken some significant stands on this issue. I commend you, Reverend Stallings, for your Christian stand this past Sunday, in welcoming Negroes to your Baptist church worship service on a nonsegregated basis. I commend the Catholic leaders of this state for integrating Springhill College several years ago.

But despite these notable exceptions, I must honestly reiterate that I have been disappointed with the church. I do not say that as one of those negative critics who can always find something wrong with the church. I say it as a minister of the gospel who loves the church, who was nurtured in its bosom, who has been sustained by its spiritual blessings, and who will remain true to it as long as the cord of life shall lengthen.

I had the strange feeling when I was suddenly catapulted into the leadership of the bus protest in Montgomery several years ago that we would have the support of the white church. I felt that the white ministers, priests, and rabbis of the South would be some of our strongest allies. Instead, some few have been outright opponents, refusing to understand the freedom movement and misrepresenting its leaders; all too many others have been more cautious than courageous and have remained silent behind the anesthetizing security of stained-glass windows.

In spite of my shattered dreams of the past, I came to Birmingham with the hope that the white religious leadership of this community would see the justice of our cause and with deep moral concern serve as the channel through which our just grievances would get to the power structure. I had hoped that each of you would understand. But again I have been disappointed.

I have heard numerous religious leaders of the South call upon their worshippers to comply with a desegregation decision because it is the law, but I have longed to hear white ministers say, follow this decree because integration is morally right and the Negro is your brother. In the midst of blatant injustices inflicted upon the Negro, I have watched white churches stand on the sideline and merely mouth pious irrelevancies and sanctimonious trivialities. In the midst of a mighty struggle to rid our nation of racial and economic injustice, I have heard so many ministers say, "Those are social issues which the gospel has nothing to do with," and I have watched so many churches commit themselves to a completely otherworldly religion which made a strange distinction between bodies and souls, the sacred and the secular.

There was a time when the church was very powerful. It was during that period that the early Christians rejoiced when they were deemed worthy to suffer for what they believed. In those days the church was not merely a thermometer that recorded the ideas and principles of popular opinion; it was the thermostat that transformed the mores of society. Wherever the early Christians entered a town the power structure got disturbed and immediately sought to convict them for being "disturbers of the peace" and "outside agitators." But they went on with the conviction that they were "a colony of heaven" and had to obey God rather than man. They were small in number but big in commitment. They were too God-intoxicated to be "astronomically intimidated." They brought an end to such ancient evils as infanticide and gladiatorial contest.

Things are different now. The contemporary church is so often a weak, ineffectual voice with an uncertain sound. It is so often the arch supporter of the status quo. Far from being disturbed by the presence of the church, the power structure of the average community is consoled by the church's often vocal sanction of things as they are.

But the judgment of God is upon the church as never before. If the church of today does not recapture the sacrificial spirit of the early church, it will lose its authentic ring, forfeit the loyalty of millions, and be dismissed as an irrelevant social club with no meaning for the twentieth century. I meet young people every day whose disappointment with the church has risen to outright disgust.

I hope the church as a whole will meet the challenge of this decisive hour. But even if the church does not come to the aid of justice, I have no despair about the future. I have no fear about the outcome of our struggle in Birmingham, even if our motives are presently misunderstood. We will reach the goal of freedom in Birmingham and all over the nation, because the goal of America is freedom. Abused and scorned though we may be, our destiny is tied up with the destiny of America. Before the Pilgrims landed at Plymouth, we were here. Before the pen of Jefferson scratched across the pages of history the majestic word of the Declaration of Independence, we were here. For more than two centuries our foreparents labored in this country without wages; they made cotton king; and they built the homes of their masters in the midst of brutal injustice and shameful humiliation—and yet out of a bottomless vitality our people continue to thrive and develop. If the inexpressible cruelties of slavery could not stop us, the opposition we now face will surely fail. We will win our freedom because the sacred heritage of our nation and the eternal will of God are embodied in our echoing demands.

I must close now. But before closing I am impelled to mention one other point in your statement that troubled me profoundly. You warmly commended the Birmingham police force for keeping "order" and "preventing violence." I don't believe you would have so warmly commended the police force if you had seen its angry violent dogs literally biting six unarmed, nonviolent Negroes. I don't believe you would so quickly commend the policemen if you would observe their ugly and inhuman treatment of Negroes here in the city jail; if you would watch them push and curse old Negro women and young Negro girls; if you would see them slap and kick old Negro men and young boys; if you would observe them, as they did on two occasions, refusing to give us food because we wanted to sing our grace together. I'm sorry that I can't join you in your praise for the police department.

It is true that they have been rather disciplined in their public handling of the demonstrators. In this sense they have been publicly "nonviolent." But for what purpose? To preserve the evil system of segregation. Over the last few years I have consistently preached that nonviolence demands that the means we use must be as pure as the ends we seek. So I have tried to make it clear that it is wrong to use immoral means to attain moral ends. But now I must affirm that it is just as wrong, or even more, to use moral means to preserve immoral ends.

I wish you had commended the Negro demonstrators of Birmingham for their sublime courage, their willingness to suffer, and their amazing discipline in the midst of the most inhuman provocation. One day the South will recognize its real heroes. They will be the James Merediths,* courageously and with a majestic sense of purpose facing jeering and hostile mobs and with the agonizing loneliness that characterizes the life of the pioneer. They will be old, oppressed, battered Negro women, symbolized in a seventy-two-year-old woman of Montgomery, Alabama, who rose up with a sense of dignity and with her people decided not to ride the segregated buses, and responded to one who inquired about her tiredness with ungrammatical profundity, "My feets is tired, but my soul is rested." They will be young high school and college students, young ministers of the gospel and a host of their elders courageously and nonviolently sitting in at lunch counters and willingly going to jail for conscience's sake. One day the South will know that when these disinherited children of God sat down at lunch counters they were in reality standing up for the best in the American dream and the most sacred values in our Judeo-Christian heritage.

Never before have I written a letter this long—or should I say a book? I'm afraid that it is much too long to take your precious time. I can assure you that it would have been much shorter if I had been writing from a comfortable desk, but what else is there to do when you are alone for days in the dull monotony of a narrow jail cell other than write long letters, think strange thoughts, and pray long prayers?

If I have said anything in this letter that is an overstatement of the truth and is indicative of an unreasonable impatience, I beg you to forgive me. If I have said anything in this letter that is an understatement of the truth and is indicative of my having a patience that makes me patient with anything less than brotherhood, I beg God to forgive me.

Yours for the cause of Peace and Brotherhood,
Martin Luther King, Jr.

---

*In 1962, James Meredith (1933–), a civil rights activist and air force veteran, became the first African American to attend the University of Mississippi. His attempts to enroll set off campus-wide race riots. (See Archibald MacLeish's "Must We Hate?," p. 601.)

Say Good-bye to Big Daddy

RANDALL JARRELL || 1967

Eugene "Big Daddy" Lipscomb, the legendary defensive tackle who men-
aced opposing quarterbacks and running backs when he starred on the
championship Baltimore Colts teams of the late 1950s and early 1960s,
was the prototype of the modern football lineman. Standing six foot six
and weighing more than three hundred adamantine pounds, Lipscomb
was quite simply an order of magnitude larger, stronger, faster, and nim-
bler than any of the opposing linemen of his day. (Hunter S. Thompson
once described him as "arguably the cruelest pass rusher in NFL his-
tory.") But he was also outsized in another arena, setting superhuman
records for after-hours debauchery with women, alcohol, and drugs.
As the American poet and literary critic Randall Jarrell (1914–1965) so
memorably sums up Lipscomb's predicament in this lament for a lost life,
Big Daddy "found football easy enough, life hard enough." A complex
man who'd grown up in one of Detroit's toughest ghettos—he never
knew his father, and his mother was murdered by a boyfriend when Eu-
gene was only eleven—he was equally capable of unexpected tenderness
and terrifying rage. When he died of a heroin overdose at the age of
thirty-one, the tragic story of his life and death became a cautionary tale
of the struggles that have beset many black star athletes. At the time The
Atlantic *published "Say Good-bye to Big Daddy," just after the start of*
the 1967 fall football season, the poem evoked an extra level of elegiac
frisson as a posthumous tribute to the poet himself: Randall Jarrell, an
avid pro football fan, had died two years earlier from injuries sustained
after being struck by a car on a dark North Carolina road, just a few
months after the publication of his valedictory collection, The Lost
World. *"Say Good-bye to Big Daddy" is a poem rife with the bittersweet*
poignancy that prompted Jarrell's old friend Robert Lowell to hail him as
"the most heartbreaking English poet of his generation."

Big Daddy Lipscomb, who used to help them up
After he'd pulled them down, so that "the children
Won't think Big Daddy's mean"; Big Daddy Lipscomb,
Who stood unmoved by the blockers, like the Rock
Of Gibraltar in a life insurance ad,
Until the ball carrier came, and Daddy got him;

Big Daddy Lipscomb, being carried down an aisle
Of women by Night Train Lane, John Henry Johnson,
And Lenny Moore; Big Daddy, his three ex-wives,
His fiancée, and the grandfather who raised him
Going to his grave in five big Cadillacs;
Big Daddy, who found football easy enough, life hard enough
To—after his last night cruising Baltimore
In his yellow Cadillac—to die of heroin;
Big Daddy, who was scared, he said: "I've been scared
Most of my life. You wouldn't think so to look at me.
It gets so bad I cry myself to sleep—" his size
Embarrassed him, so that he was helped by smaller men
And hurt by smaller men; Big Daddy Lipscomb
Has helped to his feet the last ball carrier, Death.

The big black man in the television set
Whom the viewers stared at—sometimes, almost were—
Is a blur now; when we get up to adjust the set,
It's not the set, but a NETWORK DIFFICULTY.
The world won't be the same without Big Daddy.
Or else it will be.

The Barber

FLANNERY O'CONNOR ‖ 1970

Flannery O'Connor (1925–1964) might well have disapproved of the posthumous publication of this short story. Written when O'Connor was only twenty-two years old as part of her graduate thesis for the University of Iowa Writers' Workshop, "The Barber" was seen by its author as an "apprentice" work, and it has certainly never received the critical acclaim accorded her best-known fiction. Yet when O'Connor's literary executor, the poet and translator Robert Fitzgerald, offered "The Barber" to The Atlantic *in 1970, the magazine's editors instantly recognized its literary vitality. "The Barber" is the tale of a well-meaning but ineffectual college professor (an "interleckchul," as O'Connor liked to call the type) who attempts to talk a Southern haircutter and his customers out of their racial prejudices, and it is a mortar and pestle for the author's perennial themes: the dangerous chemistry of human interaction, the tendency of banal situations to erupt into violence. As much as any of her subsequent stories, "The Barber" also encapsulates, in a single dramatic narrative, O'Connor's views on race. O'Connor, who grew up and settled in rural Georgia, was pessimistic about the prospects for rapid improvement in race relations in the South, and she was critical of those who, like her story's protagonist, believed that prejudice could be easily vanquished by law, reason, or moral suasion. As she told an interviewer in 1963, only a year before she died, in her prime, of lupus: "For the rest of the country, the race problem is settled when the Negro has his rights, but for the Southerner, whether he's white or colored, that's only the beginning. The South has to evolve a way of life in which the two races can live together with mutual forbearance. You don't form a committee to do this or pass a resolution; both races have to work it out the hard way."*

It is trying on liberals in Dilton. After the Democratic White Primary, Rayber changed his barber. Three weeks before it, while he was shaving him, the barber asked, "Who you gonna vote for?"

"Darmon," Rayber said.

"You a nigger-lover?"

Rayber started in the chair. He had not expected to be approached so brutally. "No," he said. If he had not been taken off-balance, he would have said, "I am neither a Negro- nor a white-lover." He had said that before to

Jacobs, the philosophy man, and, to show you how trying it is for liberals in Dilton, Jacobs—a man of his education—had muttered, "That's a poor way to be."

"Why?" Rayber had asked bluntly. He knew he could argue Jacobs down.

Jacobs had said, "Skip it." He had a class. His classes frequently occurred, Rayber noticed, when Rayber was about to get him in an argument.

"I am neither a Negro- nor a white-lover," Rayber would have said to the barber.

The barber drew a clean path through the lather and then pointed the razor at Rayber. "I'm tellin' you," he said, "there ain't but two sides now, white and black. Anybody can see that from this campaign. You know what Hawk said? Said a hunnert and fifty years ago, they was runnin' each other down eatin' each other—throwin' jewel rocks at birds, skinnin' horses with their teeth. A nigger come in a white barbershop in Atlanta and says, 'Gimme a haircut.' They throwed him out but it just goes to show you. Why listen, three black hyenas over in Mulford last month shot a white man and took half of what was in his house and you know where they are now? Settin' in their county jail eatin' like the President of the United States—they might get dirty in the chain gaing' or some damn nigger-lover might come by and be heartbroke to see 'em pickin' rock. Why, lemme tell you this—ain't nothin' gonna be good again until we get rid of them Mother Hubbards and get us a man can put these niggers in their places. Shuh."

"You hear that, George?" he shouted to the colored boy wiping up the floor around the basins.

"Sho do," George said.

It was time for Rayber to say something, but nothing appropriate would come. He wanted to say something that George would understand. He was startled that George had been brought into the conversation. He remembered Jacobs telling about lecturing at a Negro college for a week. They couldn't say Negro—nigger—colored—black. Jacobs said he had come home every night and shouted, "NIGGER NIGGER NIGGER" out the back window. Rayber wondered what George's leanings were. He was a trim-looking boy.

"If a nigger come in my shop with any of that haircut sass, he'd get it cut all right." The barber made a noise between his teeth. "You a Mother Hubbard?" he asked.

"I'm voting for Darmon, if that's what you mean," Rayber said.

"You ever heard Hawkson talk?"

"I've had that pleasure," Rayber said.

"You heard his last one?"

"No, I understand his remarks don't alter from speech to speech," Rayber said curtly.

"Yeah?" the barber said. "Well, this last speech was a killeroo! Ol' Hawk let them Mother Hubbards have it."

"A good many people," Rayber said, "consider Hawkson a demagogue." He wondered if George knew what demagogue meant. Should have said, "lying politician."

"Demagogue!" The barber slapped his knee and whooped. "That's what Hawk said!" he howled. "Ain't that a shot! 'Folks,' he says, 'them Mother Hubbards says I'm a demagogue.' Then he rears back and says sort of softlike, 'Am I a demagogue, you people?' And they yells, 'Naw, Hawk, you ain't no demagogue!' And he comes forward shouting, 'Oh yeah I am, I'm the best damn demagogue in this state!' And you should hear them people roar! Whew!"

"Quite a show," Rayber said, "but what is it but a . . ."

"Mother Hubbard," the barber muttered. "You been taken in by 'em all right. Lemme tell you somethin'. . . ." He reviewed Hawkson's Fourth of July speech. It had been another killeroo, ending with poetry. Who was Darmon? Hawk wanted to know. Yeah, who was Darmon? the crowd had roared. Why, didn't they know? Why, he was Little Boy Blue, blowin' his horn. Yeah. Babies in the meadow and niggers in the corn. Man! Rayber should have heard that one. No Mother Hubbard could have stood up under it.

Rayber thought that if the barber would read a few . . .

Listen, he didn't have to read nothin'. All he had to do was think. That was the trouble with people these days—they didn't think, they didn't use their horse sense. Why wasn't Rayber thinkin'? Where was his horse sense?

Why am I straining myself? Rayber thought irritably.

"Nossir!" the barber said. "Big words don't do nobody no good. They don't take the place of thinkin'."

"Thinking!" Rayber shouted. "You call yourself thinking?"

"Listen," the barber said, "do you know what Hawk told them people at Tilford?" At Tilford Hawk had told them that he liked niggers fine in their place and if they didn't stay in that place, he had a place to put 'em. "How about that?"

Rayber wanted to know what that had to do with thinking.

The barber thought it was plain as a pig on a sofa what that had to do with thinking. He thought a good many other things too, which he told

Rayber. He said Rayber should have heard the Hawkson speeches at Mullin's Oak, Bedford, and Chickerville.

Rayber settled down in his chair again and reminded the barber that he had come in for a shave.

The barber started back shaving him. He said Rayber should have heard the one at Spartasville. "There wasn't a Mother Hubbard left standin', and all the Boy Blues got their horns broke. Hawk said," he said, "that the time had come when you had to sit on the lid with . . ."

"I have an appointment," Rayber said. "I'm in a hurry." Why should he stay and listen to that tripe?

As much rot as it was, the whole asinine conversation stuck with him the rest of the day and went through his mind in persistent detail after he was in bed that night. To his disgust, he found that he was going through it, putting in what he would have said if he'd had an opportunity to prepare himself. He wondered how Jacobs would have handled it. Jacobs had a way about him that made people think he knew more than Rayber thought he knew. It was not a bad trick in his profession. Rayber often amused himself analyzing it. Jacobs would have handled the barber calmly enough. Rayber started through the conversation again, thinking how Jacobs would have done it. He ended doing it himself.

The next time he went to the barber's, he had forgotten about the argument. The barber seemed to have forgotten it too. He disposed of the weather and stopped talking. Rayber was wondering what was going to be for supper. Oh. It was Tuesday. On Tuesday his wife had canned meat. Took canned meat and baked it with cheese, slice of meat and a slice of cheese, turned out striped—why do we have to have this stuff every Tuesday?—if you don't like it you don't have to—

"You still a Mother Hubbard?"

Raybor's head jerked. "What?"

"You still for Darmon?"

"Yes," Rayber said, and his brain darted to its store of preparations.

"Well, look-a-here, you teachers, you know, looks like, well . . ." He was confused. Rayber could see that he was not so sure of himself as he'd been the last time. He probably thought he had a new point to stress. "Looks like you fellows would vote for Hawk on account of you know what he said about teachers' salaries. Seems like you would now. Why not? Don't you want more money?"

"More money!" Rayber laughed. "Don't you know that with a rotten governor I'd lose more money than he'd give me?" He realized that he was finally on the barber's level. "Why, he dislikes too many different kinds of people," he said. "He'd cost me twice as much as Darmon."

"So what if he would?" the barber said. "I ain't one to pinch money when it does some good. I'll pay for quality any day."

"That's not what I meant!" Rayber began. "That's not . . ."

"That raise Hawk's promised don't apply to teachers like him anyway," somebody said from the back of the room. A fat man with an air of executive assurance came over near Rayber. "He's a college teacher, ain't he?"

"Yeah," the barber said, "that's right. He wouldn't get Hawk's raise; but say, he wouldn't get one if Darmon was elected neither."

"Ahh, he'd get something. All the schools are supporting Darmon. They stand to get their cut; free textbooks or new desks or something. That's the rules of the game."

"Better schools," Rayber sputtered, "benefit everybody."

"Seems like I been hearin' that a long time," the barber said.

"You see," the man explained, "you can't put nothing over on the schools. That's the way they throw it off—benefits everybody."

The barber laughed. "If you ever thought . . ." Rayber began.

"Maybe there'd be a new desk at the head of the room for you," the man chortled. "How about that, Joe?" He nudged the barber.

Rayber wanted to lift his foot under the man's chin. "You ever heard about reasoning?" he muttered.

"Listen," the man said, "you can talk all you want. What you don't realize is, we've got an issue here. How'd you like a couple of black faces looking at you from the back of your classroom?"

Rayber had a blind moment when he felt as if something that wasn't there were bashing him to the ground. George came in and began washing basins. "Willing to teach any person willing to learn—black or white," Rayber said. He wondered if George had looked up.

"All right," the barber agreed, "but not mixed up together, huh? How'd you like to go to a white school, George?" he shouted.

"Wouldn't like that," George said. "We needs sommo powders. These here the las' in this box." He dusted them out into the basin.

"Go get some, then," the barber said.

"The time has come," the executive went on, "just like Hawkson said, when we got to sit on the lid with both feet and a mule." He went on to review Hawkson's Fourth of July speech.

Rayber would like to have pushed him into the basin. The day was hot and full enough of flies without having to spend it listening to a fat fool. He could see the courthouse square, blue-green cool, through the tinted glass window. He wished to hell the barber would hurry. He fixed his attention on the square outside, feeling himself there where, he could tell from the trees, the air was moving slightly. A group of men sauntered up the courthouse walk. Rayber looked more closely and thought he recognized Jacobs. But Jacobs had a late-afternoon class. It was Jacobs, though. Or was it? If it was, who was he talking to? Blakeley? Or was that Blakeley? He squinted. Three colored boys in zoot suits strolled by on the sidewalk. One dropped down on the pavement so that only his head was visible to Rayber, and the other two lounged over him, leaning against the barbershop window and making a hole in the view. Why the hell can't they park somewhere else? Rayber thought fiercely. "Hurry up," he said to the barber, "I have an appointment."

"What's your hurry?" the fat man said. "Yon better stay and stick up for Boy Blue."

"You know you never told us why you're gonna vote for him," the barber chuckled, taking the cloth from around Rayber's neck.

"Yeah," the fat man said, "see can you tell us without sayin' goodgovermint."

"I have an appointment," Rayber said. "I can't stay."

"You just know Darmon is so sorry you won't be able to say a good word for him," the fat man howled.

"Listen," Rayber said, "I'll be back in here next week, and I'll give you as many reasons for voting for Darmon as you want—better reasons than you've given me for voting for Hawkson."

"I'd like to see you do that," the barber said. "Because I'm telling you, it can't be done."

"All right, we'll see," Rayber said.

"Remember," the fat man carped, "you ain't gonna say goodgovermint."

"I won't say anything you can't understand," Rayber muttered, and then felt foolish for showing his irritation. The fat man and the barber were grinning. "I'll see you Tuesday," Rayber said and left. He was disgusted with himself for saying he would give them reasons. Reasons would have to be worked out—systematically. He couldn't open his head in a second like they did. He wished to hell he could. He wished to hell "Mother Hubbard" weren't so accurate. He wished to hell Darmon spit tobacco juice. The reasons would have to be worked out—time and trouble. What was the matter with him? Why not work them out? He could make everything in that shop squirm if he put his mind to it.

By the time he got home, he had the beginnings of an outline for an argument. It would be filled in with no waste words, no big words—no easy job, he could see. He got right to work on it. He worked on it until suppertime and had four sentences, all crossed out. He got up once in the middle of the meal to go to his desk and change one. After supper he crossed the correction out.

"What is the matter with you?" his wife wanted to know.

"Not a thing," Rayber said, "not a thing. I just have to work."

"I'm not stopping you," she said.

When she went out, he kicked the board loose, on the bottom of the desk. By eleven o'clock he had one page. The next morning it came easier, and he finished it by noon. He thought it was blunt enough. It began, "For two reasons, men elect other men to power," and it ended, "Men who use ideas without measuring them are walking on wind." He thought the last sentence was pretty effective. He thought the whole thing was effective enough.

In the afternoon he took it around to Jacobs' office. Blakeley was there, but he left. Rayber read the paper to Jacobs.

"Well," Jacobs said, "so what? What do you call yourself doing?" He had been jotting figures down on a record sheet all the time Rayber was reading.

Rayber wondered if he was busy. "Defending myself against barbers," he said. "You ever tried to argue with a barber?"

"I never argue," Jacobs said.

"That's because you don't know this kind of ignorance," Rayber explained. "You've never experienced it."

Jacobs snorted. "Oh, yes, I have," he said.

"What happened?"

"I never argue."

"But you know you're right," Rayber persisted.

"I never argue."

"Well, I'm going to argue," Rayber said. "I'm going to say the right thing as fast as they can say the wrong. It'll be a question of speed. Understand," he went on, "this is no mission of conversion; I'm defending myself."

"I understand that," Jacobs said. "I hope you're able to do it."

"I've already done it! You read the paper. There it is." Rayber wondered if Jacobs was dense or preoccupied.

"OK, then leave it there. Don't spoil your complexion arguing with barbers."

"It's got to be done," Rayber said.

Jacobs shrugged.

Rayber had counted on discussing it with him at length. "Well, I'll see you," he said.

"OK," Jacobs said.

Rayber wondered why he had ever read the paper to him in the first place.

BEFORE HE LEFT for the barber's Tuesday afternoon, Rayber was nervous, and he thought that by way of practice, he'd try the paper out on his wife. He didn't know but what she was for Hawkson herself. Whenever he mentioned the election, she made it a point to say, "Just because you teach doesn't mean you know everything." Did he ever say he knew anything at all? Maybe he wouldn't call her. But he wanted to hear how the thing was actually going to sound said casually. It wasn't long; wouldn't take up much of her time. She would probably dislike being called. Still, she might possibly be affected by what he said. Possibly. He called her.

She said all right, but he'd just have to wait until she got through what she was doing; it looked like every time she got her hands in something, she had to leave and go do something else.

He said he didn't have all day to wait—it was only forty-five minutes until the shop closed—and would she please hurry up?

She came in wiping her hands and said all right; all right, she was there, wasn't she? Go ahead.

He began saying it very easily and casually, looking over her head. The sound of his voice playing over the words was not bad. He wondered if it was the words themselves or his tones that made them sound the way they did. He paused in the middle of a sentence and glanced at his wife to see if her face would give him any clue. Her head was turned slightly toward the table by her chair where an open magazine was lying. As he paused, she got up. "That was very nice," she said, and went back to the kitchen. Rayber left for the barber's.

He walked slowly, thinking what he was going to say in the shop and now and then stopping to look absently at a store window. Block's Feed Company had a display of automatic chicken-killers: "So Timid Persons Can Kill Their Own Fowl," the sign over them read. Rayber wondered if many timid persons used them. As he neared the barber's, he could see obliquely through the door that the man with the executive assurance was sitting in the corner reading a newspaper. Rayber went in and hung up his hat.

"Howdy," the barber said, "ain't this the hottest day in the year, though!"

"It's hot enough," Rayber said.

"Hunting season soon be over," the barber commented.

All right, Rayber wanted to say, let's get this thing going. He thought he would work into his argument from their remarks. The fat man hadn't noticed him.

"You should have seen the covey this dog of mine flushed the other day," the barber went on as Rayber got in the chair. "The birds spread once and we got four, and they spread again and we got two. That ain't bad."

"Never hunted quail," Rayber said hoarsely.

"There ain't nothing like taking a nigger and a hound dog and a gun and going after quail," the barber said. "You missed a lot out of life if you ain't had that."

Rayber cleared his throat, and the barber went on working. The fat man in the corner turned a page. What do they think I came in here for? Rayber thought. They couldn't have forgotten. He waited, hearing the noises flies make and the mumble of the men talking in the back. The fat man turned another page. Rayber could hear George's broom slowly stroking the floor somewhere in the shop, then stop, then scrape, then—"You, er, still a Hawkson man?" Rayber asked the barber.

"Yeah!" the barber laughed. "Yeah! You know I had forgot. You was gonna tell us why you are voting for Darmon. Hey, Roy!" he yelled to the fat man, "come over here. We gonna hear why we should vote for Boy Blue."

Roy grunted and turned another page. "Be there when I finish this piece," he mumbled.

"What you got there, Joe," one of the men in the back called. "One of them goodgovermint boys?"

"Yeah," the barber said. "He's gonna make a speech."

"I've heard too many of that kind already," the man said.

"You ain't heard one by Rayber," the barber said. "Rayber's all right. He don't know how to vote, but he's all right."

Rayber reddened. Two of the men strolled up. "This is no speech," Rayber said. "I only want to discuss it with you—sanely."

"Come on over here, Roy," the barber yelled.

"What are you trying to make of this?" Rayber muttered; then he said suddenly, "If you're calling everybody else, why don't you call your boy, George. You afraid to have him listen?"

The barber looked at Rayber for a second without saying anything.

Rayber felt as if he had made himself too much at home.

"He can hear," the barber said. "He can hear back where he is."

"I just thought he might be interested," Rayber said.

"He can hear," the barber repeated. "He can hear what he hears, and he can hear two times that much. He can hear what you don't say as well as what you do."

Roy came over folding his newspaper. "Howdy, boy," he said, putting his hand on Rayber's head, "let's get on with this speech."

Rayber felt as if he were fighting his way out of a net. They were over him with their red faces grinning. He heard the words drag out: "Well, the way I see it, men elect . . ." He felt them pull out of his mouth like freight cars, jangling, backing up on each other, grating to a halt, sliding, clinching back, jarring, and then suddenly stopping as roughly as they had begun. It was over. Rayber was jarred that it was over so soon. For a second, as if they were expecting him to go on, no one said anything.

Then, "How many yawl gonna vote for Boy Blue!" the barber yelled.

Some of the men turned around and snickered. One doubled over.

"Me," Roy said. "I'm gonna run right down there now so I'll be first to vote for Boy Blue tomorrow morning."

"Listen!" Rayber shouted, "I'm not trying . . ."

"George," the barber yelled, "you heard that speech?"

"Yessir," George said.

"Who you gonna vote for, George?"

"I'm not trying to . . ." Rayber yelled.

"I don't know is they gonna let me vote," George said. "Do, I gonna vote for Mr. Hawkson."

"Listen!" Rayber yelled. "Do you think I'm trying to change your fat minds? What do you think I am?" He jerked the barber around by the shoulder. "Do you think I'd tamper with your damn-fool ignorance?"

The barber shook Rayber's grip off his shoulder. "Don't get excited," he said, "we all thought it was a fine speech. That's what I been saying all along—you got to think, you got to . . ." He lurched backward when Rayber hit him, and landed sitting on the footrest of the next chair. "Thought it was fine," he finished, looking steadily at Rayber's white, half-lathered face glaring down at him. "It's what I been saying all along."

The blood began pounding up Rayber's neck just under his skin. He turned and pushed quickly through the men around him to the door. Outside, the sun was suspending everything in a pool of heat and before he had turned the first corner, almost running, lather began to drip inside his collar and down the barber's bib, dangling to his knees.

The Origins of the Underclass

NICHOLAS LEMANN || 1986

In the fall of 1980, the journalist Nicholas Lemann (1954–   ) was driving around the blighted neighborhoods of South Philadelphia for a newspaper series he was researching on welfare when a loud bell went off in his head. "I suddenly realized that these communities had gone through incredibly rapid changes in the space of one generation," Lemann subsequently recalled in an interview with The New York Times. *"They had been white, and they had become black almost overnight. And I thought there was a story there." Eleven years later, the largest mass migration in United States history—the relocation of more than five million African Americans from the rural South to the urban North between the early 1940s and late 1960s—became the monumental subject of Lemann's bestselling book* The Promised Land: The Great Black Migration and How It Changed America *(1991). The book won a number of awards and was selected by a New York University panel of journalists and scholars as one of the top one hundred works of twentieth-century American journalism.*

The Promised Land *first came to fruition five years earlier as an ambitious two-part series in* The Atlantic, *where Lemann had worked as a national correspondent from 1983 to 1998. Lemann wrote "The Origins of the Underclass" out of a conviction that traditional economic arguments, whether liberal or conservative, did not adequately explain why, two decades after the civil rights movement, millions of African Americans continued to live under conditions of unendurable poverty. With an unusual combination of on-street reporting and intellectual analysis, of narrative artistry and social history, he chronicles not one but two tectonic shifts in American racial demography—first, the great migration of blacks to the cities of the North, and second, the flight, starting in the late 1960s, of middle- and working-class blacks out of the ghettos to the suburbs. Those who remained behind, Lemann argues in "The Origins of the Underclass" (the first installment is excerpted here), have been trapped in a "culture of poverty"—a way of life that had first gained a foothold among black sharecroppers in the South and that had continued to exert a powerful influence after the migration to the North. Such a provocative thesis, coming from a white journalist, was fated to be controversial; the Harvard sociologist William Julius Wilson, for one, called Lemann's hypothesis "fundamentally incorrect." But Le-*

mann's reporting was so exhaustively researched and so deeply rooted in real-life characters that it drew plaudits from both ends of the political spectrum—from Garry Wills to George Will. Lemann, who is now the dean of the Columbia University Graduate School of Journalism and a staff writer for The New Yorker, *continues to write about race in America. But he remains best known for his book on the black underclass—a work that, as the critic James Wood observed (echoing Ralph Ellison's* Invisible Man*), "speaks to all of us on the lowest frequencies; its sadnesses and triumphs may yet pierce us all into action."*

"Stand in the center of the black belt—at Chicago's 47th St. and South Parkway. Around you swirls a continuous eddy of faces—black, brown, olive, yellow, and white. . . . In the nearby drugstore colored clerks are bustling about. (They are seldom seen in other neighborhoods.) In most of the other stores, too, there are colored salespeople, although a white proprietor or manager usually looms in the offing. In the offices around you, colored doctors, dentists, and lawyers go about their duties. And a brown-skinned policeman saunters along swinging his club and glaring sternly at the urchins who dodge in and out among the shoppers. . . . There is continuous and colorful movement here—shoppers streaming in and out of stores; insurance agents turning in their collections at a funeral parlor; club reporters rushing into a newspaper office with their social notes; irate tenants filing complaints with the Office of Price Administration; job-seekers moving in and out of the United States Employment Office."

So begins a chapter called "Bronzeville" in *Black Metropolis*, by St. Clair Drake and Horace Cayton, a study of the Chicago ghetto published in 1945. It's impossible to stand at the same corner today without wondering what went wrong. There's hardly ever any bustle at Forty-seventh and King Drive (as South Parkway is now called), especially during the day. The shopping strip still exists, though as a shadow of what it obviously once was, and there are heavy metal grates on virtually every storefront that has not been abandoned. Many of the landmarks of the neighborhood—the Regal Theater, the Savoy Ballroom, the Hotel Grand, the legendary blues clubs—are boarded up or gone entirely. The Michigan Boulevard Garden Apartments, a large complex that Drake and Cayton called "a symbol of good living on a relatively high income level," is a housing project populated by people on welfare. Prostitutes cruise Forty-seventh Street in the late afternoon. In cold weather middle-aged men stand in knots around fires built in garbage cans. Drake and Cayton's idea of the corner as the heart of a "Little Harlem," where one might glimpse Lena Horne or Joe Louis—or white people—sitting in a restaurant, seems ludicrous.

I recently spent some time in and around the black sections of Chicago: the South Side, roughly eight miles long and four wide, the single largest black neighborhood in America, of which Forty-seventh and South Parkway used to be the nerve center; and the West Side, a few miles away, a smaller and rougher area. It wasn't just at Forty-seventh and King Drive that the decline of the ghetto over two generations was striking. This is something that black people in Chicago talk about frequently, wondering why the working-poor neighborhoods where they grew up became terrible. Many others wonder the same thing, and they are weary of the standard explanations for the ghettos, which are intellectually neat but don't seem to fit the magnitude of what has gone wrong. It stands to reason that there is another answer to the terrible question of the ghettos. During my time in Chicago I became convinced that there is one.

When Drake and Cayton were writing, virtually all black Americans lived in segregated areas, though not necessarily in the urban North. By the sixties, when race relations had become a central national concern, the northern ghettos had received a large influx of migrants from the South, and they were portrayed as overcrowded, desperately poor slums stunted by racism. Today, after years of efforts to end poverty and discrimination, the ghettos are worse, much worse, than they were in the sixties. A few blocks from Forty-seventh and King Drive is a housing project called the Robert Taylor Homes, a two-mile-long row of 28 sixteen-story buildings housing more than 20,000 people. The four-block stretch of the Robert Taylor Homes between Forty-seventh and Fifty-first Streets has the distinction of being the poorest neighborhood in the United States. In the forties the strip of land where the Robert Taylor Homes now stand was the poorest part of the traditional black belt in Chicago, but it had many fewer residents and was just the bad part of the neighborhood. Today the project dominates it physically and demographically.

For a decade after the burst of attention paid to ghettos in the 1960s there was a feeling that blacks were steadily moving up in America. The distance between black and white incomes was continually narrowing. Black education levels were rising sharply. Middle-class blacks were becoming more and more visible on television and in public places. There was a long string of black "firsts," especially and most impressively in elective politics.

In the past few years there has been a steady stream of news indicating that at the same time there was another side to the story: a way of life in the ghettos utterly different from that in the American mainstream. One statistic had a tremendous impact on the public perception of black progress: starting in the late seventies, the U.S. National Center for Health Statistics began to report that more than half of black babies were born out of wedlock, up from 17 percent in 1950. Today the figure is thought to be 60 percent nationwide; in Chicago it is 75 percent. Urban school systems have become increasingly segregated, with a large gap in achievement levels between black and white schools. Black unemployment is nearly triple white unemployment. Black crime rates have soared—in Chicago, which is less than half black, about four times as many blacks as whites are arrested for violent crimes. The infant mortality rate, which is considered one of the basic indicators of how advanced a society is, is rising in the ghettos.

The way that the two versions of black life since the sixties fit together is through the idea of the bifurcation of black America, in which blacks are splitting into a middle class and an underclass that seems likely never to make it. The clearest line between the two groups is family structure. Black husband-wife families continue to close the gap with whites; their income is now 78 percent as high. But the income of black female-headed families, adjusted for inflation, has been dropping. The black female-headed family represents an ever larger share of the population of poor people in America: 7.3 percent in 1959 and 19.3 percent in 1984.

Why, during a period of relative prosperity and of national commitment to black progress, has the bifurcation taken place? The question should be urgent for anyone who thinks it wrong that millions of people in the black underclass lead destroyed lives or who, because of the problems of the ghettos, has had to give up the idea of an open, democratic city life built around public education and safe streets.

There are two answers prevalent right now, both of which explain the slide in the ghettos using the shifting of economic incentives.

The conservative answer is that welfare and the whole Great Society edifice of compensatory programs for blacks do exactly the opposite of what they're supposed to: they make blacks worse off by encouraging them to become dependent on government checks and favors. Poor blacks have children out of wedlock and don't work, so that they can get money from liberal programs.

The liberal answer is built around unemployment. At the time that the ghettos began getting worse, unemployment was very low, but blacks, by then heavily concentrated in the northern industrial cities, were dependent on the one part of the economy that was falling apart—inner-city unskilled heavy labor. In Chicago the harbinger of the change was the closing in the late fifties of the stockyards, which for half a century were the *sine qua non* of lower-class grunt work and a heavy employer of blacks. Chicago lost 200,000 jobs in the seventies; small shut-down redbrick factories that used to make products like boxes and ball bearings dot the city, especially the West Side. The lack of jobs, the argument continues, caused young men in the ghetto to adopt a drifting, inconstant life; to turn to crime; to engage in exaggeratedly macho behavior—acting tough, not studying, bullying women for money—as a way to get the sense of male strength that their fathers had derived from working and supporting families. As [conservatives] believe that one simple step, ending all welfare programs, would heal the ghettos, the unemployment school believes that another simple step, jobs, would heal them.

Among poverty experts the debate is raging, and though it is quite abstruse (it is based almost entirely on analysis of government statistics), the stakes are large. The country seems to be gearing up for another run at the problems of the ghettos; President Reagan has commissioned a major study of welfare reform, which is a polite way of asking what we should do about the black underclass. With the discussions of the issue so exclusively reliant on statistics, I thought that studying a ghetto at first hand would yield something new. Here, in brief, is what I found:

The black underclass did not just spring into being over the past twenty years. Every aspect of the underclass culture in the ghettos is directly traceable to roots in the South—and not the South of slavery but the South of a generation ago. In fact, there seems to be a strong correlation between underclass status in the North and a family background in the nascent underclass of the sharecropper South.

What happened to make the underclass grow so much in the seventies can best be understood by thinking less about welfare or unemployment than about demographics—specifically, two mass migrations of black Americans.

The first was from the rural South to the urban North, and numbered in the millions during the forties, fifties, and sixties, before ending in the early 1970s. This migration brought the black class system to the North virtually intact, though the underclass became more pronounced in the cities. The second migration began in the late sixties—a migration out of the ghettos by members of the black working and middle classes, who had been freed from housing discrimination by the civil-rights movement. Until then the strong leaders and institutions of the ghettos had promoted an ethic of assimilation (if not into white society, at least into a black middle class) for the underclass, which worked up to a point. Suddenly most of the leaders and institutions (except criminal ones) left, and the preaching of assimilation by both blacks and whites stopped. What followed was a kind of free fall into what sociologists call social disorganization. The result of the exodus from the ghettos is dramatic, both in the statistics and on the streets—the ghettos have lost considerable population, and they look not just bad today but also empty. As the population of the ghettos has dropped, the indices of disorganization there (crime, illegitimate births) have risen. The underclass flourished when in the seventies it was completely disengaged from the rest of society—when there were no brakes on it.

This argument is anthropological, not economic; it emphasizes the power over people's behavior that culture, as opposed to economic incentives, can have. Ascribing a society's conditions in part to the culture that prevails there seems benign when the society under discussion is England or California. But as a way of thinking about black ghettos it has become unpopular. Twenty years ago ghettos were often said to have a self-generating, destructive culture of poverty (the term has an impeccable source, the anthropologist Oscar Lewis). But then the left equated cultural discussions of the ghetto with accusing poor blacks of being in a bad situation that was of their own making; thus they would deserve no special help or sympathy from society. The left succeeded in limiting the terms of debate to purely economic ones, and today the right also discusses the ghetto in terms of economic "incentives to fail," provided by the welfare system. Both sides call apparently irrational behavior like bearing children out of wedlock and dropping out of school simply a rational response to conditions created by society.

In the ghettos, though, it appears that the distinctive culture is now the greatest barrier to progress by the black underclass, rather than either unemployment or welfare. Today the bedrock of the economic arguments of both left and right is eroding: the value of welfare benefits is declining, and the northern industrial cities are not rapidly losing jobs anymore. Still the ghettos get worse, and the power of culture seems to be the reason why. The new immigrants of the eighties (Koreans, Vietnamese, West Indians) have in many cases settled in the ghettos, and so should have experienced all of the reverse incentives, but they have quickly become successful, because they maintain a separate culture. The negative power of the ghetto culture all but guarantees that any attempt to solve the problems of the underclass in the ghettos won't work—the culture is too strong by now. Any solution that does work, whatever it does about welfare and unemployment, will also have to get people physically away from the ghettos.

ONE OF THE LARGEST MIGRATIONS in history created the urban black ghettos. Almost all black southerners who came north arrived essentially penniless, and almost all settled initially in all-black, all-poor areas. Most of the migrants made it. The prevailing theories about why a substantial minority spectacularly did not make it cannot account for the relative success of most blacks who moved north. Answering the question of how and why some of the migrants got out of the ghettos and some did not, I thought, might be one of the keys to the mystery of the underclass. So I got to know a group of friends in Chicago who had come from one town in Mississippi—Canton, population 12,000, fifteen miles north of Jackson.

Between 1910 and 1920 the first wave of 572,000 blacks moved from the South to the North, almost always to cities. In the twenties 913,000 left; in the thirties 473,000; in the forties 1.7 million, 18 percent of the black population of the South; in the fifties 1.5 million; in the sixties 1.4 million. The number of blacks who moved north, about 6.5 million, is greater than the number of Italians or Irish or Jews or Poles who moved to this country during their great migrations. Today there are 1.2 million black Chicagoans. A reasonable estimate of the number who are in the underclass would be somewhere between 200,000, roughly the total population of all the low-income housing projects, including men who aren't official residents, and 420,000, the number of black Chicagoans on welfare. Even the highest estimate is only a third of the current black population, which does not include the approximately 230,000 blacks in Chicago suburbs.

The experience in Chicago of the majority of blacks who migrated, then, has not been one of defeat and failure. A much more typical story would be that of Mildred Nichols, one of the group I met from Canton. I met Nichols at a restaurant called Soul Queen, on the far South Side, near a neighborhood called Pill Hill (black doctors live there). We talked in the bar, where the waitress who served our drinks was wearing a gold paper crown.

Nichols graduated from Cameron Street High School, in Canton, on May 28, 1955, and arrived in Chicago on June 5. She moved in with an aunt and uncle she had never met and began looking for a job. She took a test to be an order-filler at the big Montgomery Ward catalogue store but was told that she had failed. She was convinced that she had really passed and was being tricked, so she told the woman who had administered the test that she would be back in the afternoon to retake it, and back again every day until she passed. She got the job, stayed there until after the Christmas rush, and then began working as a waitress on the midnight-to-8 A.M. shift at a restaurant in the heart of the ghetto.

The themes that Mildred Nichols emphasized to me during our conversation were pride and success. Today she works in the office at a nursing home called Bethune Plaza, also in the heart of the ghetto. She has been with the same company for ten years. Of her five siblings, all younger, a sister has a master's degree and teaches school, one brother is an attorney in Jackson, married to a nurse, the next brother is a businessman in Canton, the next is a graduate of Northwestern Law School, and the youngest sister is a pharmacist.

I asked her what their secret was. She said, "It might have been that we had a two-parent family. My father had a fourth-grade education, and my mother had eighth grade—we were middle-class. We lived in town. My father taught us that you have to be a strong person to survive. Willpower! Nothing, nobody is better than you. Nobody. Welfare? No! Jesus! No! Because I simply could not be bought. Never! Never! Catholic schools for my kids. No truancy. I told them, 'Give me two years of college. You must!' My son has no police record. My daughter didn't have her first child till she was twenty-five. I never did domestic work, darling. Never! I've always had office jobs."

What about the people who had failed in Chicago? What was the difference? "They had low self-esteem. They didn't have the drive you need in Chicago. You see, this city is Jaws—One, Two, Three, and Four. They didn't want to!"

In Mildred Nichols's view, the people on welfare were primarily children of sharecroppers from what southern blacks call "the rural"—the farming areas outside of town. "The persons who aren't able to deal with this society," she said, "are the ones from the deep-rural part of the South that had to drop out of school to pick cotton. They had no one to teach them. They still live that life-style of the rural South up here."

What was striking about this answer was how foreign Nichols found the commonly held idea that a poor black underclass has emerged over the past twenty years, starting with the flowering of the Great Society programs. The main characteristics of the underclass—poverty, crime, poor education, dependency, and teenage out-of-wedlock childbearing—were nothing new to her. She and her friends, and white people in Canton, too, had seen them all their lives.

Canton was established in 1834, as the trading center and seat of government for Madison County, Mississippi. It seems warranted to say that slavery was the town's central and defining institution. From the beginning blacks outnumbered whites by three to one (the ratio did not drop significantly until after the Second World War), and the whites' economic status and comfort and safety depended on keeping the blacks subjugated.

Through the mid-twentieth century Madison County was settled into a system of segregation and sharecropping. I found no real disagreement between blacks and whites about the particulars: All but a handful of blacks, fewer than a hundred, were denied the right to vote, by means of a poll tax and a "literacy test," in which the registrar of voters would pick at random a section of the Mississippi constitution and ask black would-be voters to read it aloud and then deliver an interpretation. There were separate black and white schools in Canton, and in the countryside blacks went to one-room schoolhouses with no new books, heat, electricity, or running water. In April and May, and then again in September and October, many blacks, especially in the country, had to leave school to work in the cotton fields, so even a decent junior high school education was a great rarity among rural blacks.

In the country some blacks owned small farms but most were employees or, more likely, tenants. They would live on big farms in unpainted two- and three-room wooden shacks, with no plumbing or heat. Families were big, in part because the more hands there were to go out in the fields the more money the family would make. The sharecropper kept anywhere from half to four-fifths of the proceeds from his cash crops, which he received from the landowner in a settling-up at the end of the year. The sharecropper could never come out ahead. He had to borrow from the white man he worked for all year long, in order to feed his family and buy his implements, feed, and fertilizer. In bad years he would still be behind after the settling-up, sometimes so far behind that he would have to leave in a hurry; in good years, after all the deductions had been made, he would somehow be only a few dollars ahead. The result, fully intended, was an ethic of dependency. Sharecroppers had no money and practically no education, and they counted on the landowner to provide for them—which he did, meagerly. On Saturday afternoon the sharecroppers would travel into town on foot or by mule, on Sunday they'd go to church, and on Monday they'd be back in the fields.

The idea that black Cantonians began moving to Chicago in droves during the Second World War in order to escape segregation is appealing but not really true. They moved to escape poverty and in most cases the dignity of making a decent living was far more gratifying at first than the dignity of having equal rights under the law. There is nothing comparable in American life today to the amount of financial gain southern blacks could realize instantly by moving less than a thousand miles away, to another part of the same country, and getting the kind of unskilled jobs—laborer, sales clerk—that were unavailable to them in Canton.

At the time of the migration to the North the sharecroppers in Mississippi were moving off the land, because they were being replaced in the fields by machines. Heavy tractors and cotton-picking machines became common equipment on farms in the fifties; by 1960 what was once the work of fifty field hands could be done by only three or four. Typically, the sharecroppers were simply dismissed; white farmers in Canton who had dozens of people living on their property have no idea where they are today. Deserted sharecropper cabins are a common sight in the country outside Canton, spectral presences falling down at the edges of open fields.

The similarities between sharecropping and welfare are eerie: dependency on "the man"; more money for having more children; little value placed on education; no home ownership; an informal attitude toward marriage and childbearing. I met several Cantonians who had done well and whose parents had been sharecroppers, but in every case they came from a two-parent family and at some time during their childhood their parents had scraped together enough money to buy a farm of their own and stop sharecropping. In contrast, everybody I met in the Robert Taylor Homes who was a migrant from the South had been in a sharecropper family right up to the move to Chicago. Others in the Chicago underclass have their roots in the southern small-town black lower class.

Mildred Nichols told me, "Most people on welfare here, they were on welfare there, in a sense, because they were sharecroppers. There they were working hard for nothing, now they're not working for nothing. They have been mentally programmed that Mister Charlie's going to take care of them."

THE MIGRATION TO THE NORTH transferred the black societies of Canton and a hundred towns like it, with all their complexities and problems, to Chicago. After that several factors combined to turn the small underclass that came up from the South into the large and separate culture that it is today. In the city—away from the family, religious, and social structure of small-town life back home—all the migrants experienced a loosening of the constraints on their behavior (a process that should be familiar to readers not only of black writers like Richard Wright and Malcolm X but also of Balzac and Dreiser). This was made more pronounced because blacks who moved to Chicago from the South were funneled into a ghetto that was strikingly crowded, walled off from the rest of society, and different from what its residents had known before. The greater prosperity of blacks in the North, however, meant that there was a strong leadership in the ghettos working to counteract the forces of social entropy. But then the working black population made its rapid exodus from the ghettos, leaving the underclass disastrously cut off from the rest of the world.

The black illegitimacy rate has risen dramatically over the past twenty years, but the problem did not begin with the Great Society programs. Every first-hand observer of black society in this country has mentioned it in connection with both rural and ghetto life. E. Franklin Frazier, in his classic work *The Negro Family in the United States* (1939), attributed most black out-of-wedlock childbirths to southern migrants just arrived in the North. Sometimes, he said, migrants became pregnant because of "the absence of family traditions and community controls," and sometimes it was simply "the persistence in the urban environment of folkways"—namely, the lack of a legal marriage ceremony—"that were relatively harmless in the rural community."

Drake and Cayton, in *Black Metropolis*, said that the black lower class in Chicago in the forties "not only tolerates illegitimacy, but actually seems almost indifferent toward it." Daniel Patrick Moynihan's 1965 report, "The Negro Family," put the 1963 rate at 23.6 percent nationally and as high as 49 percent in some parts of Harlem. I suspect that all these rates are skewed to the low side, because of the practice, common through the mid-sixties, of black women in the rural South and northern ghettos saying they were married when they were really just living with someone.

I mention these figures in order to dispute the notion that either welfare or unemployment is the overarching reason for the explosion in the black illegitimacy rate. During the Reagan years, as the welfare rolls have shrunk, the illegitimacy rate has gone up. Today, in fact, many more black women have children out of wedlock than go on welfare. As for black unemployment, whereas there is some statistical match between it and illegitimacy, the match is far from perfect. The Moynihan report, after factoring out blacks in the South, concluded that black unemployment rates had been double the white rates continuously since the early thirties, but the illegitimacy rate had not taken off until the 1950s.

The point is not to deny that either welfare or unemployment is a factor in rising illegitimacy—both plainly are. But there is a third factor: the rapid urbanization of most blacks, followed by the isolation of the black lower class in the cities. High illegitimacy has always been much more closely identified with blacks than with all poor people or all unemployed people or all immigrants. It is a peculiarity of black culture, and within that of the black lower class, and within that, of isolation. . . . If, from the late sixties through the early eighties, the black urban lower class became significantly more isolated than it ever had been before, wouldn't that help explain what happened?

In Chicago and other northern cities there was a direct link between the magnitude of the black migration from the South and the degree of residential segregation imposed by whites. In 1898 only 11 percent of black Chicagoans lived in neighborhoods more than 75 percent black. In 1900 thirty-three of Chicago's thirty-five wards were at least 0.5 percent black. As soon as the flow of migrants became significant, white hostility toward blacks surged, growing partly from pure prejudice, partly from fear of the importation of the social ills created by Jim Crow, partly from intense competition in the labor market. It is a pattern of long standing, reminiscent even of Mississippi in the mid-nineteenth century: a primal white antipathy toward the black masses, which always leads to the creation of iron restrictions on where blacks can live and work.

In the late forties, with southern blacks again pouring into the city and racial tensions rising (there were riots when black veterans tried to move into temporary housing in white neighborhoods), Chicago, like many cities, began building many public-housing projects. At the time, integrated public housing was one of the great liberal causes, and it was also a constant, long-standing political demand of blacks. In the liberal dream, housing projects would be filled by a racially integrated, clean-living, well-educated working class. Ward politicians with white constituents to keep happy were adamantly opposed to integration, though, and in 1949 the state legislature passed a law that boxed out the liberals by requiring that the Chicago City Council approve all public-housing sites. This virtually ensured that projects would be segregated. . . . The private housing market was, by unwritten law, strictly segregated in most places. By 1970 Chicago was the most residentially segregated city in America.

What happened in Chicago is an especially dramatic version of what happened all over the country: just as the number of new, poor, migrant blacks in the cities reached its all-time peak, the country decided to mount a real attack on segregation in housing and employment, and otherwise to help those blacks capable of moving closer to the mainstream of American society to do so. The result is evident in the census data, as we have already seen: there has been another major migration of blacks over the past twenty years, out of the ghettos. Even more pronounced than the social and economic deterioration of the ghettos between 1970 and 1980 is their depopulation. This isn't happening just in Chicago. The South Bronx lost 37 percent of its population between 1970 and 1980. More than 100,000 black Chicagoans moved to the suburbs in the seventies; 224,000 blacks moved from Washington, D.C., to its suburbs, 124,000 from Atlanta to its suburbs. These are unusually high numbers for neighborhood population loss, and the comparable numbers today would be even higher.

There's no mystery to why so many people left the ghettos. They wanted to feel safe on the streets, to send their children to better schools, and to live in more pleasant surroundings; in particular, riots drove many people away. Probably everyone who could leave did. Many businesses and churches (except for tiny "storefront" churches, which often are unaffiliated with any organized religion) left with them. What was unusual about the migration of the black working population out of the ghettos, compared with that of other immigrant groups, is that it was for many years delayed and then suddenly made possible by race-specific government policies. That's why it happened so fast. One reason that the numbers for unemployment and poverty and female-headed families in the ghettos have gone up so much is that nearly everyone who was employed and married moved away (also, the fertility rate of black married women has dropped substantially, which is a sign of assimilation into the middle class). Very quickly, around 1970, the ghettos went from being exclusively black to being exclusively black lower-class, and there was no countervailing force to the venerable, but always carefully contained, disorganized side of the ghetto culture. No wonder it flourished in the seventies. The "losing ground" phenomenon, in which black ghettos paradoxically became worse during the time of the War on Poverty, can be explained partly by the abrupt disappearance of all traces of bourgeois life in the ghettos and the complete social breakdown that resulted.

GODS AND MONSTERS

Thoreau

RALPH WALDO EMERSON ‖ 1862

*This rich and powerful portrait of Henry David Thoreau by his friend,
mentor, and occasional rival Ralph Waldo Emerson (1803–1882) can be
seen as a prototype of the modern profile—a biographical sketch that
evenhandedly embraces both the strengths and the weaknesses of its subject. It also ranks with the greatest obituaries in American literature. Delivered as a eulogy at Thoreau's funeral, in May 1862, and published in
The Atlantic three months later, "Thoreau" puts on full display the
wealth of impressions that Emerson, by then internationally famous as
an essayist, poet, and lecturer, had gathered over the course of a twenty-
five-year relationship with the reclusive naturalist. It was, to say the
least, an improbable pairing: when the men were introduced, in 1837,
Thoreau was only twenty years old, an impoverished, eccentric, painfully
shy Harvard senior; Emerson, fourteen years older, was gregarious, moneyed, and, as the author of a just-published, book-length essay, Nature, a
gathering force in American letters. Yet whatever differences separated
the two were bridged by their shared affinity for the core ideas of transcendentalism—a near-religious reverence for nature and a belief in the
sanctity of individual conscience.*

*It was on Emerson's property just outside the town of Concord,
Massachusetts, that Thoreau built the one-room cabin (with the help of
an Emerson-advanced loan) in which he lived in solitude for precisely
two years, two months, and two days—a sojourn of self-discovery
that evolved into his most iconic work, Walden. In return, Emerson
got to enjoy the company of an indefatigable younger man, whose
insight, eloquence, and biting wit he found intoxicating and whose
uncompromising life choices embodied the Emersonian ideal of self-
reliance. Nevertheless, their long friendship was not without its problems.
Thoreau deplored what he regarded as Emerson's unhealthy preoccupation with fame and bridled under the stiflingly long shadow cast by his
mentor; for his part, Emerson, a man of social aspirations and epicurean
tastes, grew weary of Thoreau's implacable nonconformity and contempt
for worldly pleasures. When, in 1862, Thoreau died of tuberculosis, at the
age of forty-four, Emerson got to have the last word on their tumultuous
relationship, composing this heart-wrenching reminiscence (the last major piece of writing he would produce) that bespeaks both his admiration
and vexation. His Thoreau is harsh and frigid, possessed of an imperious*

manner that is "chilling to the social affections." But he is also brave and honorable, a man "incapable of any profanation, by act or by thought." All of these virtues and failings are contained in the Thoreau that posterity has come to celebrate. In the ringing words of Emerson, "No truer American existed than Thoreau."

Henry David Thoreau was the last male descendant of a French ancestor who came to this country from the Isle of Guernsey. His character exhibited occasional traits drawn from this blood in singular combination with a very strong Saxon genius.

He was born in Concord, Massachusetts, on the 12th of July, 1817. He was graduated at Harvard College in 1837, but without any literary distinction. An iconoclast in literature, he seldom thanked colleges for their service to him, holding them in small esteem, whilst yet his debt to them was important. After leaving the University, he joined his brother in teaching a private school, which he soon renounced. His father was a manufacturer of lead-pencils, and Henry applied himself for a time to this craft, believing he could make a better pencil that was then in use. After completing his experiments, he exhibited his work to chemists and artists in Boston, and having obtained their certificates to its excellence and to its quality with the best London manufacturer, he returned home contented. His friends congratulated him that he had now opened his way to fortune. But he replied, that he should never make another pencil. "Why should I? I would not do again what I have done once." He resumed his endless walks and miscellaneous studies, making every day some new acquaintance with Nature, though as yet never speaking of zoology or botany, since, though very studious of natural facts, he was incurious of technical and textual science.

At this time, a strong, healthy youth, fresh from college, while all his companions were choosing their profession, or eager to begin some lucrative employment, it was inevitable that his thoughts should be exercised on the same conditions, and it required rare decision to refuse all the accustomed paths, and keep his solitary freedom at the cost of disappointing the natural expectations of his family and friends: all the more difficult that he had a perfect probity, was exact in securing his own independence, and in holding every man to the like duty. But Thoreau never faltered. He was a born protestant. He declined to give up his large ambition of knowledge and action for any narrow craft or profession, aiming at a much more comprehensive calling, the art of living well. If he slighted and defied the opinions of others, it was only that he was more intent to reconcile his practice with his own belief. Never idle or self-indulgent, he preferred, when he wanted money, earning it by some piece of manual labor agreeable to him, as building a boat or a fence, planting, grafting, surveying, or other short work, to any long engagement. With his hardy habits and few wants, his skill in wood-craft, and his powerful arithmetic, he was very competent to live in any part of the world.

He was bred to no profession; he never married; he lived alone; he never went to church; he never voted; he refused to pay a tax to the State; he ate no flesh, he drank no wine, he never knew the use of tobacco; and, though a naturalist, he used neither trap nor gun. He chose, wisely, no doubt, for himself, to be the bachelor of thought and Nature. He had no talent for wealth, and knew how to be poor without the least hint of squalor or inelegance. Perhaps he fell into his way of living without fore-casting it much, but approved it with later wisdom. "I am often reminded," he wrote in his journal, "that, if I had bestowed on me the wealth of Croe-sus, my aims must be still the same, and my means essentially the same." He had no temptations to fight against,—no appetites, no passions, no taste for elegant trifles. A fine house, dress, the manners and talk of highly cultivated people were all thrown away on him. He much preferred a good Indian, and considered these refinements as impediments to conversation, wishing to meet his companion on the simplest terms. He declined invita-tions to dinner-parties, because there each was in every one's way, and he could not meet the individuals to any purpose. "They make their pride," he said, "in making their dinner cost much; I make my pride in making my dinner cost little."

There was somewhat military in his nature not to be subdued, always manly and able, but rarely tender, as if he did not feel himself except in op-position. He wanted a fallacy to expose, a blunder to pillory, I may say re-quired a little sense of victory, a roll of the drum, to call his powers into full exercise. It cost him nothing to say No; indeed, he found it much easier than to say Yes. It seemed as if his first instinct on hearing a proposition was to controvert it, so impatient was he of the limitations of our daily thought. This habit, of course, is a little chilling to the social affections; and though the companion would in the end acquit him of any malice or un-truth, yet it mars conversation. Hence, no equal companion stood in affec-tionate relations with one so pure and guileless. "I love Henry," said one of his friends, "but I cannot like him; and as for taking his arm, I should as soon think of taking the arm of an elm-tree."

He was a speaker and actor of the truth,—born such,—and was ever running into dramatic situations from this cause. In any circumstance, it interested all bystanders to know what part Henry would take, and what he would say; and he did not disappoint expectation, but used an original judgment on each emergency. In 1845 he built himself a small framed house on the shores of Walden Pond, and lived there two years alone, a life of labor and study. This action was quite native and fit for him. No one who knew him would tax him with affection. He was more unlike his neighbors in his thought than in his action. As soon as he had exhausted the advantages of that solitude, he abandoned it. In 1847, not approving some uses to which the public expenditure was applied, he refused to pay his town tax, and was put in jail. A friend paid the tax for him, and he was released. The like annoyance was threatened the next year. But, as his friends paid the tax, notwithstanding his protest, I believe he ceased to resist. No opposition or ridicule had any weight with him. He coldly and fully stated his opinion without affecting to believe that it was the opinion of the company. It was of no consequence, if every one present held the opposite opinion. On one occasion he went to the University Library to procure some books. The librarian refused to lend them. Mr. Thoreau repaired to the President, who stated to him the rules and usages, which permitted the loan of books to resident graduates, to Lyceum who were alumni, and to some other resident within a circle of ten miles radius from the College. Mr. Thoreau explained to the President that the railroad had destroyed the old scale of distances,—that the library was useless, yes, and President and College useless, on the terms of his rules,—that the one benefit he owed to the College was its library,—that, at this moment, not only his want of books was imperative, but he wanted a large number of books, and assured him that he, Thoreau, and not the librarian, was the proper custodian of these. In short, the President found the petitioner so formidable, and the rules getting to look so ridiculous, that he ended by giving him a privilege which in his hands proved unlimited thereafter.

No truer American existed than Thoreau. His preference of his country and condition was genuine, and his aversation from English and European manners and tastes almost reached contempt. He listened impatiently to news or *bon mots* gleaned from London circles; and though he tried to be civil, these anecdotes fatigued him. The men were all imitating each other, and on a small mould. Why can they not live as far apart as possible, and each be a man by himself? What he sought was the most energetic nature; and he wished to go to Oregon, not to London. "In every part of Great Britain," he wrote in his diary, "are discovered traces of the Romans, their funereal urns, their camps, their roads, their dwellings. But New England, at least, is not based on any Roman ruins. We have not to lay the foundations of our houses on the ashes of a former civilization."

But, idealist as he was, standing for abolition of slavery, abolition of tariffs, almost for abolition of government, it is needless to say he found himself not only unrepresented in actual politics, but almost equally opposed to every class of reformers. Yet he paid the tribute of his uniform respect to the Anti-Slavery Party. One man, whose personal acquaintance he had formed, he honored with exceptional regard. Before the first friendly word had been spoken for Captain John Brown, after the arrest, he sent notices to most houses in Concord, that he would speak in a public hall on the condition and character of John Brown, on Sunday evening, and invited all people to come. The Republican Committee, the Abolitionist Committee, sent him word that it was premature and not advisable. He replied,—"I did not send to you for advice, but to announce that I am to speak." The hall was filled at an early hour by people of all parties, and his earnest eulogy of the hero was heard by all respectfully, by many with a sympathy that surprised themselves.

It was said of Plotinus that he was ashamed of his body, and 'tis very likely he had good reason for it,—that his body was a bad servant, and he had not skill in dealing with the material world, as happens often to men of abstract intellect. But Mr. Thoreau was equipped with a most adapted and serviceable body. He was of short stature, firmly built, of light complexion, with strong, serious blue eyes, and a grave aspect,—his face covered in the late years with a becoming beard. His senses were acute, his frame well-knit and hardy, his hands strong and skillful in the use of tools. And there was a wonderful fitness of body and mind. He could pace sixteen rods more accurately than another man could measure them with rod and chain. He could find his path in the woods at night, he said, better by his feet than his eyes. He could estimate and measure of a tree very well by his eyes; he could estimate the weight of a calf or a pig, like a dealer. From a box containing a bushel or more of loose pencils, he could take up with his hands fast enough just a dozen pencils at every grasp. He was a good swimmer, runner, skater, boatman, and would probably outwalk most countrymen in a day's journey. And the relation of body to mind was still finer than we have indicated. He said he wanted every stride his legs made. The length of his walk uniformly made the length of his writing. If shut up in the house, he did not write at all.

He lived for the day, not cumbered and mortified by his memory. If he brought you yesterday a new proposition, he would bring you to-day another not less revolutionary. A very industrious man, and setting, like all highly organized men, a high value on his time, he seemed the only man of leisure in town, always ready for any excursion that promised well, or for conversation prolonged into late hours. His trenchant sense was never stopped by his rules of daily prudence, but was always up to the new occasion. He said,—"You can sleep near the railroad, and never be disturbed: Nature knows very well what sounds are worth attending to, and has made up her mind not to hear the railroad-whistle. But things respect the devout mind, and a mental ecstasy was never interrupted." He noted, what repeatedly befell him, that, after receiving from a distance a rare plant, he would presently find the same in his own haunts. And those pieces of luck which happen only to good players happened to him. One day, walking with a stranger, who inquired where Indian arrow-heads could be found, he replied, "Everywhere," and, stooping forward, picked one on the instant from the ground. At Mount Washington, in Tuckerman's Ravine, Thoreau had a bad fall, and sprained his foot. As he was in the act of getting up from his fall, he saw for the first time the leaves of the *Arnica mollis*.

His robust common sense, armed with stout hands, keen perceptions, and strong will, cannot yet account for the superiority which shone in his simple and hidden life. I must add the cardinal fact, that there was an excellent wisdom in him, proper to a rare class of men, which showed him the material world as a means and symbol. This discovery, which sometimes yields to poets a certain casual and interrupted light, serving for the ornament of their writing, was in him an unsleeping insight; and whatever faults or obstructions of temperament might cloud it, he was not disobedient to the heavenly vision. In his youth, he said, one day, "The other world is all my art; my pencils will draw no other; my jack-knife will cut nothing else; I do not use it as a means." This was the muse and genius that ruled his opinions, conversation, studies, work, and course of life. This made him a searching judge of men. At first glance he measured his companion, and, though insensible to some fine traits of culture, could very well report his weight and calibre. And this made the impression of genius which his conversation often gave.

He understood the matter in hand at a glance, and saw the limitations and poverty of those he talked with, so that nothing seemed concealed from such terrible eyes. I have repeatedly known young men of sensibility converted in a moment to the belief that this was the man they were in search of, the man of men, who could tell them all they should do. His own dealing with them was never affectionate, but superior, didactic, scorning their petty ways,—very slowly conceding, or not conceding at all, the promise of his society at their houses, or even at his own. "Would he not walk with them?" "He did not know. There was nothing so important to him as his walk; he had no walks to throw away on company."

Mr. Thoreau dedicated his genius with such entire love to the fields, hills, and waters of his native town, that he made them known and interesting to all reading Americans, and to people over the sea. The river on whose banks he was born and died he knew from its springs to its confluence with the Merrimack. He had made summer and winter observations on it for many years, and at every hour of the day and the night. The result of the recent survey of the Water Commissioners appointed by the State of Massachusetts he had reached by his private experiments, several years earlier. Every fact which occurs in the bed, on the banks, or in the air over it; the fishes, and their spawning and nests, their manners, their food; the shad-flies which fill the air on a certain evening once a year, and which are snapped at by the fishes so ravenously that many of these die of repletion; the conical heaps of small stones on the river-shallows, one of which heaps will sometimes overfill a cart,—these heaps the huge nests of small fishes; the birds which frequent the stream, heron, duck, sheldrake, loon, osprey; the snake, musk-rat, otter, woodchuck, and fox, on the banks; the turtle, frog, hyla, and cricket, which make the banks vocal,—were all known to him, and, as it were, townsmen and fellow-creatures; so that he felt an absurdity or violence in any narrative of one of these by itself apart, and still more of its dimensions on an inch-rule, or in the exhibition of its skeleton, or the specimen of a squirrel or a bird in brandy. He liked to speak of the manners of the river, as itself a lawful creature, yet with exactness, and always to an observed fact. As he knew the river, so the ponds in this region.

Under his arm he carried an old music-book to press plants; in his pocket, his diary and pencil, a spy-glass for birds, microscope, jack-knife, and twine. He wore straw hat, stout shoes, strong gray trousers, to brave shrub-oaks and smilax, and to climb a tree for a hawk's or a squirrel's nest. He waded into the pool for the water-plants, and his strong legs were no insignificant part of his armor. His power of observation seemed to indicate additional senses. He saw as with microscope, heard as with car-trumpet, and his memory was a photographic register of all he saw and heard. And yet none knew better than he that it is not the fact that imports, but the impression or effect of the fact on your mind. Every fact lay in glory in his mind, a type of the order and beauty of the whole.

[One] weapon with which he conquered all obstacles in science was patience. He knew how to sit immovable, a part of the rock he rested on, until the bird, the reptile, the fish, which had retired from him, should come back, and resume its habits, nay, moved by curiosity, should come to him and watch him. . . . Snakes coiled round his leg; the fishes swam into his hand, and he took them out of the water; he pulled the woodchuck out of its hole by the tail, and took the foxes under his protection from the hunters. Our naturalist had perfect magnanimity; he had no secrets; he would carry you to the heron's haunt, or even to his most prized botanical swamp,—possibly knowing that you could never find it again, yet willing to take his risks. No college ever offered him a diploma, or a professor's chair; no academy made him its corresponding secretary, its discoverer, or even its member. Perhaps these learned bodies feared the satire of his presence. Yet so much knowledge of Nature's secret and genius few others possessed, none in a more large and religious synthesis. He grew to be revered and admired by his townsmen, who had at first known him only as an oddity.

His poetry might be bad or good; he no doubt wanted a lyric facility and technical skill; but he had the source of poetry in his spiritual perception. He was a good reader and critic, and his judgment on poetry was to the ground of it. He could not be deceived as to the presence or absence of the poetic element in any composition, and his thirst for this made him negligent and perhaps scornful of superficial graces. . . . His own verses are often rude and defective. The gold does not yet run pure, is drossy and crude. The thyme and marjoram are not yet honey. But if he want lyric fineness and technical merits, if he have not the poetic temperament, he never lacks the causal thought, showing that his genius was better than his talent. He knew the worth of the Imagination for the uplifting and consolation of human life, and liked to throw every thought into a symbol. The fact you tell is of no value, but only the impression. For this reason his presence was poetic, [and it] always piqued the curiosity to know more deeply the secrets of his mind. He had many reserves, an unwillingness to exhibit to profane eyes what was still sacred in his own, and knew well how to throw a poetic veil over his experience. All readers of "Walden" will remember his mythical record of his disappointments:

"I long ago lost a hound, a bay horse, and a turtle-dove, and am still on their trail. Many are the travellers I have spoken concerning them, describing their tracks, and what calls they answered to. I have met one or two who had heard the hound, and the tramp of the horse, and even seen the dove disappear behind a cloud; and they seemed as anxious to recover them as if they had lost them themselves."

Whilst he used in his writings a certain petulance of remark in reference to churches or churchmen, he was a person of a rare, tender, and absolute religion, a person incapable of any profanation, by act or by thought. Of course, the same isolation which belonged to his original thinking and living detached him from the social religious forms. This is neither to be censured nor regretted. Aristotle long ago explained it, when he said, "One who surpasses his fellow-citizen in virtue is no longer a part of the city. Their law is nor for him, since he is a law to himself."

Thoreau was sincerity itself, and might fortify the convictions of prophets in the ethical laws by his holy living. It was an affirmative experience which refused to be set aside. A truth-speaker he, capable of the most deep and strict conversation; a physician to the wounds of any soul; a friend, knowing not only the secret of friendship, but almost worshipped by those few persons who resorted to him as their confessor and prophet, and knew the deep value of his mind and great heart. He thought that without religion or devotion of some kind nothing great was ever accomplished; and he thought that the bigoted sectarian had better bear this in mind.

His virtues, of course, sometimes ran into extremes. It was easy to trace to the inexorable demand in all for exact truth that austerity which made this willing hermit more solitary even than he wished. Himself of a perfect probity, he required not less of others. He had a disgust at crime, and no worldly success could cover it. He detected paltering as readily in dignified and prosperous persons as in beggars, and with equal scorn. Such dangerous frankness was in his dealing that his admirers called him "that terrible Thoreau," as if he spoke when silent, and was still present when he had departed. I think the severity of his ideal interfered to deprive him of a healthy sufficiency of human society.

Had his genius been only contemplative, he had been fitted to his life, but with his energy and practical ability he seemed born for great enterprise and for command; and I so much regret the loss of his rare powers of action, that I cannot help counting it a fault in him that he had no ambition. Wanting this, instead of engineering for all America, he was the captain of a huckleberry party. Pounding beans is good to the end of pounding empires one of these days; but if, at the end of years, it is still only beans!

But these foibles, real or apparent, were fast vanishing in the incessant growth of a spirit so robust and wise, and which effaced its defeats with new triumphs. His study of Nature was a perpetual ornament to him, and inspired his friends with curiosity to see the world through his eyes, and to hear his adventures. They possessed every kind of interest.

The country knows not yet, or in the least part, how great a son it has lost. It seems an injury that he should leave in the midst his broken task, which none else can finish,—a kind of indignity to so noble a soul, that it should depart out of Nature before yet he has been really shown to his peers for what he is. But he, at least, is content. His soul was made for the noblest society; he had in a short life exhausted the capabilities of this world; wherever there is knowledge, wherever there is virtue, wherever there is beauty, he will find a home.

No figure in American history has preoccupied The Atlantic *quite so much as Abraham Lincoln. Over the course of 150 years, Lincoln has been the subject of no fewer than sixty articles, and his name has appeared in the table of contents in every one of the magazine's fifteen decades, often in several years of a decade. This enduring fascination with America's sixteenth president has taken many forms: personal reminiscence, historical reassessment, political endorsement, literary analysis, book review, hagiographic poem, even a speculative essay on how the Great Emancipator might have remedied the national rupture over abortion. Alas, that same interest in all things Lincoln once beguiled the magazine into a truly embarrassing episode. In 1928, a San Diego woman named Wilma Frances Minor offered the editors of* The Atlantic *a trove of documents that appeared to authenticate a torrid romance between Lincoln and Ann Routledge, a young woman he had met in 1831, when, as a young lawyer, he first arrived in New Salem, Illinois. After engaging two eminent authorities, Ida Tarbell and Carl Sandburg, to vet the documents, and obtaining their confidence-inspiring imprimaturs, the editors rushed into print with a trio of articles entitled "Lincoln the Lover." In short order, Lincoln experts from around the country began to detect glaring factual errors, and the documents were exposed as forgeries. Today the "Minor Affair" can be found alongside the "Hitler Diaries" and Clifford Irving's "interviews" with Howard Hughes in the pantheon of twentieth-century journalistic hoaxes. Yet even this fiasco failed to dampen the magazine's enthusiasm for Lincoln. In 1992,* The Atlantic *published "The Words That Remade America"* (see p. 517), *Garry Wills's landmark reappraisal of the Gettysburg Address. And in 2005, the magazine published two major articles on Lincoln back to back—the first a lengthy cover story on his struggles with what some now believe was clinical depression, and the second a prepublication report on the historian Doris Kearns Goodwin's ten-year quest to capture him in her book* Team of Rivals: The Political Genius of Abraham Lincoln. *Although admittedly emblems of a continuing obsession, these pieces also reflect the natural kinship between a president and a publication whose values were forged in the crucible of the nation's most troubled time.*

The Place of Abraham Lincoln in History

GEORGE BANCROFT || 1865

On April 25, 1865, eleven days after John Wilkes Booth fired the shot that twisted the course of American history, the body of Abraham Lincoln arrived in New York City—a major stop on a cross-country funeral procession that reversed the president's life journey from Springfield, Illinois, to the White House. Among the grief-besotted crowd, 160,000 strong, that surged around Lincoln's casket that day was the prominent historian and statesman George Bancroft (1800–1891), who had been asked to deliver a eulogy for the fallen president. To many of the mourners, Bancroft might have seemed an odd choice for the job. His curriculum vitae was impressive enough: as a historian, he had already produced eight of the ten volumes that would comprise his History of the United States, *the monumental project that would earn him the title "Father of American History"; as a government official, he had already served as both secretary of the navy and minister to Great Britain. But Bancroft had been no admirer of Lincoln's. A lifelong Democrat who had worked in the administration of James K. Polk, he had been a caustic critic of the sixteenth president's political skills. "We have a president without brains and a cabinet whose personal views outweigh patriotism," Bancroft wrote in a letter to his wife in 1861. Yet as the Civil War unfolded and the fortunes of the North began to look up, the president's star rose dramatically in the eyes of the historian. By June of 1865, when Bancroft wrote this stirring tribute for* The Atlantic, *he had come full circle, seeing Lincoln as a noble instrument of the popular will—a simple, average American who, "held fast by the hand of the people," freed the oppressed and thus saved the Union.*

The funeral procession of the late President of the United States has passed through the land from Washington to his final resting-place in the heart of the Prairies. Along the line of more than fifteen hundred miles his remains were borne, as it were, through continued lines of the people; and the number of mourners and the sincerity and unanimity of grief were such as never before attended the obsequies of a human being; so that the terrible catastrophe of his end hardly struck more awe than the majestic sorrow of the people. The thought of the individual was effaced; and men's minds were drawn to the station which he filled, to his public career, to the principles he represented, to his martyrdom.

There was at first impatience at the escape of his murderer, mixed with contempt for the wretch who was guilty of the crime; and there was relief in the consideration, that one whose personal insignificance was in such a contrast with the greatness of his crime had met with a sudden and ignoble death. No one stopped to remark on the personal qualities of Abraham Lincoln, except to wonder that his gentleness of nature had not saved him from the designs of assassins. It was thought then, and the event is still so recent it is thought now, that the analysis and graphic portraiture of his personal character and habits should be deferred to less excited times; as yet the attempt would wear the aspect of cruel indifference or levity, inconsistent with the sanctity of the occasion. Men ask one another only, Why has the President been struck down, and why do the people mourn? We think we pay the best tribute to his memory and the most fitting respect to his name, if we ask after the relation in which he stands to the history of his country and his fellow-men.

James Buchanan, who took the Presidential chair in 1857, had no traditional party against him; he owed his nomination to confidence in his moderation and supposed love of Union. He might have united the whole North and secured a good part of the South. Constitutionally timid, on taking the oath of office, he betrayed his own weakness, and foreshadowed the forthcoming decision of the Supreme Court. Under the wing of the Executive, Chief-Justice Taney* gave his famed disquisition. The delivery of that opinion was an act of revolution. The truth of history was scorned; the voice of passion was put forward as the rule of law; doctrines were laid down which, if they are just, give a full sanction to the rebellion which ensued. The country was stung to the quick by the reckless conduct of a body which it needed to trust, and which now was leading the way to the overthrow of the Constitution and the dismemberment of the Republic.

At the same time, Buchanan, in selecting the members of his cabinet, chose four of the seven from among those who were prepared to sacrifice the country to the interests of Slavery. . . . Cannon and muskets and military stores were sent in numbers where they could most surely fall into the hands of the coming rebellion; troops of the United States were placed un-

---

*In 1857, Supreme Court chief justice Roger Brooke Taney (1777–1864) wrote the majority opinion in the case of *Dred Scott v. Sanford*—ruling that blacks were not citizens of the United States and that Congress had no right to prohibit slavery in the territories.

der disloyal officers and put out of the way; the navy was scattered abroad. And then, that nothing might be wanting to increase the agony of the country, an attempt to force the institution of Slavery on the people of Kansas, that refused it, received the encouragement and aid of Buchanan.

The position of Abraham Lincoln, on the day of his inauguration, was apparently one of helpless debility. A bark canoe in a tempest on mid-ocean seemed hardly less safe. The vital tradition of the country on Slavery no longer had its adequate expression in either of the two great political parties, and the Supreme Court had uprooted the old landmarks and guides. The men who had chosen him President did not constitute a con-solidated party, and did not profess to represent either of the historic par-ties which had been engaged in the struggles of three quarters of a century. They were a heterogeneous body of men, of the most various political at-tachments in former years, and on many questions of economy of the most discordant opinions. Scarcely knowing each other, they did not form a nu-merical majority of the whole country, were in a minority in each branch of Congress except from the willful absence of members, and they could not be sure of their own continuance as an organized body. They did not know their own position, and were startled by the consequences of their success.

The new President himself was, according to his own description, a man of defective education, a lawyer by profession, knowing nothing of administration beyond having been master of a very small post-office, knowing nothing of war but as a captain of volunteers in a raid against an Indian chief; repeatedly a member of the Illinois Legislature, once a mem-ber of Congress. He spoke with ease and clearness, but not with eloquence. He wrote concisely and to the point, but was unskilled in the use of the pen. He had no accurate knowledge of the public defences of the country, no exact conception of its foreign relations, no comprehensive perception of his duties. The qualities of his nature were not suited to hardy action. His temper was soft and gentle and yielding; reluctant to refuse anything that presented itself to him as an act of kindness; loving to please and will-ing to confide; not trained to confine acts of good-will within the stern limits of duty. He was of the temperament called melancholic, scarcely concealed by an exterior of lightness of humor,—having a deep and fixed seriousness, jesting lips, and wanness of heart. And this man was sum-moned to stand up directly against a power with which Henry Clay had never directly grappled, before which Webster at last had quailed, which no President had offended and yet successfully administered the Government, to which each great political party had made concessions, to which in various measures of compromise the country had repeatedly capitulated, and with which he must now venture a struggle for the life or death of the nation.

The credit of the country had not fully recovered from the shock it had treacherously received in the former administration. A part of the navy-yards were intrusted to incompetent agents or enemies. The social spirit of the city of Washington was against him, and spies and enemies abounded in the circles of fashion. Every executive department swarmed with men of treasonable inclinations, so that it was uncertain where to rest for support. The army officers had been trained in unsound political principles. The chief of staff of the highest of the general officers, wearing the mask of loyalty, was a traitor at heart. The country was ungenerous towards the negro, who in truth was not in the least to blame,—was impatient that such a strife should have grown out of his condition, and wished that he were far away. On the side of prompt decision the advantage was with the Rebels; the President sought how to avoid war without compromising his duty; and the Rebels, who knew their own purpose, won incalculable advantages by the start which they thus gained. The country stood aghast, and would not believe in the full extent of the conspiracy to shatter it in pieces; men were uncertain if there would be a great uprising of the people. The President and his cabinet were in the midst of an enemy's country and in personal danger, and at one time their connections with the North and West were cut off; and that very moment was chosen by the trusted chief of staff of the Lieutenant-General to go over to the enemy. Every one remembers how this state of suspense was terminated by the uprising of a people who now showed strength and virtues which they were hardly conscious of possessing.

In some respects Abraham Lincoln was peculiarly fitted for his task, in connection with the movement of his countrymen. He was of the North-west; and this time it was the Mississippi River, the needed outlet for the wealth of the Northwest, that did its part in asserting the necessity of Union. He was one of the mass of the people; he represented them, because he was of them; and the mass of the people, the class that lives and thrives by self-imposed labor, felt that the work which was to be done was a work of their own: the assertion of equality against the pride of oligarchy; of free labor against the lordship over slaves; of the great industrial people against all the expiring aristocracies of which any remnants had tided down from the Middle Age. He was of a religious turn of mind, without superstition; and the unbroken faith of the mass was like his own. As he went along through his difficult journey, sounding his way, he held fast by the hand of the people, and "tracked its footsteps with even feet." "His pulse's beat twinned with their pulses." He committed faults; but the people were resolutely generous, magnanimous, and forgiving; and he in his turn was willing to take instructions from their wisdom.

The measure by which Abraham Lincoln takes his place, not in American history only, but in universal history, is his Proclamation of January 1, 1863, emancipating all slaves within the insurgent States. It was, indeed, a military necessity, and it decided the result of the war. It took from the public enemy one or two millions of bondmen, and placed between one and two hundred thousand brave and gallant troops in arms on the side of the Union. A great deal has been said in time past of the wonderful results of the toil of the enslaved negro in the creation of wealth by the culture of cotton; and now it is in part to the aid of the negro in freedom that the country owes its success in its movement of regeneration,—that the world of mankind owes the continuance of the United States as the example of a Republic. The death of President Lincoln sets the seal to that Proclamation, which must be maintained. It cannot but be maintained. It is the only rod that can safely carry off the thunderbolt. He came to it perhaps reluctantly; he was brought to adopt it, as it were, against his will, but compelled by inevitable necessity. He disclaimed all praise for the act, saying reverently, after it had succeeded, "The nation's condition God alone can claim."

Ode to Lincoln

JAMES RUSSELL LOWELL ‖ 1865

Of the many luminaries who came forward to sing the praises of Abraham Lincoln after his assassination, none was more qualified to do so than James Russell Lowell, the first editor-in-chief of The Atlantic. *As early as 1860, Lowell had used the magazine as a pulpit from which to rally readers around the Republican candidate (see "The Election in November," p. 3), and throughout the Civil War his impassioned essays, in* The Atlantic *and other publications, displayed such an acute understanding of Lincoln's policies that the president himself once felt compelled to send a letter of appreciation. The following lines, written the summer after the assassination, express Lowell's profound anguish over the loss of a leader he considered a national hero. Although contemporary critics have occasionally dismissed Lowell's poetry as didactic and self-consciously literary, this "Ode" (which is part of a much longer poem composed in honor of Harvard graduates killed in battle) drew kudos from readers no less distinguished than Ralph Waldo Emerson and Henry James, who thought it pulsated with "the great historic throb" of the tragic war.*

Such was he, our Martyr-Chief,
Whom late the Nation he had led,
With ashes on her head,
Wept with the passion of an angry grief:
Forgive me, if from present things I turn
To speak what in my heart will beat and burn,
And hang my wreath on his world-honored urn.
Nature, they say, doth dote,
And cannot make a man
Save on some worn-out plan,
Repeating us by rote:
For him her Old-World moulds aside she threw,
And, choosing sweet clay from the breast
Of the unexhausted West,
With stuff untainted shaped a hero new,
Wise, stedfast in the strength of God, and true.
How beautiful to see

Once more a shepherd of mankind indeed,
Who loved his charge, but never loved to lead;
One whose meek flock the people joyed to be,
Not lured by any cheat of birth,
But by his clear-grained human worth,
And brave old wisdom of sincerity!
They knew that outward grace is dust;
They could not choose but trust
In that sure-footed mind's unfaltering skill,
And supple-tempered will
That bent like perfect steel to spring again and thrust.
Nothing of Europe here,
Or, then, of Europe fronting mornward still,
Ere any names of Serf and Peer
Could Nature's equal scheme deface;
Here was a type of the true elder race,
And one of Plutarch's men talked with us face to face.
I praise him not; it were too late;
And some innative weakness there must be
In him who condescends to victory
Such as the Present gives, and cannot wait,
Safe in himself as in a fate.
So always firmly he:
He knew to bide his time,
And can his fame abide,
Still patient in his simple faith sublime,
Till the wise years decide.
Great captains, with their guns and drums,
Disturb our judgment for the hour,
But at last silence comes;
These are all gone, and, standing like a tower,
Our children shall behold his fame,
The kindly-earnest, brave, foreseeing man,
Sagacious, patient, dreading praise, not blame,
New birth of our new soil, the first American.

The Natural

ISAIAH BERLIN ‖ 1955

> At the height of World War II, the British Foreign Office dispatched Isa-
> iah Berlin (1909–1997), the celebrated Oxford political philosopher and
> historian of ideas, to Washington, D.C., on a special assignment. Berlin's
> mandate was to compile reports, for the edification of British prime min-
> ister Winston Churchill, on the state of wartime America, or at least the
> prevailing moods of official Washington. The author of such canonical
> essays as "The Hedgehog and the Fox" (1953) and "Two Concepts of Lib-
> erty" (1958), Berlin fulfilled his charge with characteristic thoroughness
> and brio, forming close intellectual bonds with the likes of Supreme
> Court justice Felix Frankfurter, the journalist Walter Lippmann, and the
> foreign policy guru George Kennan (all Atlantic contributors). But much
> to his disappointment, as he notes at the start of this elegant encomium,
> Berlin never got to meet his hero, Franklin Delano Roosevelt. Berlin, a
> subscriber to the Great Man theory of history, was convinced that from
> time to time extraordinarily talented leaders emerge from the pack, and
> that, by sheer force of personality and character, they have the power to
> shape events. This interplay between history and character was central to
> Berlin's worldview, and Roosevelt was his shining exemplar. Although
> Berlin also wrote a well-regarded essay on his former boss, Winston
> Churchill, for The Atlantic, it is this rousing assessment of Roosevelt
> that best exhibits his gift for portraiture.

I never met Roosevelt, and although I spent more than three years in
Washington during the war, I never even saw him. I regret this, for it seems
to me that to see and, in particular, to hear the voice of someone who has
occupied one's imagination for many years, must modify one's impression
in some way, and make it more concrete and three dimensional. However,
I never did see him, and I heard him only over the radio. Consequently,
I must try to convey my impression without the benefit of personal acquaintance, and without, I ought to add, any expert knowledge of American history or international relations. Nor am I competent to speak of
Mr. Roosevelt's domestic or foreign policies, nor of their larger political or
economic effects. I shall try to give only a personal impression of the general impact of his personality on my generation.

The most insistent propaganda in [the 1930s] declared that humanitarianism and liberalism and democratic forces were played out, and that the choice now lay between two bleak extremes, Communism and Fascism—the red or the black. To those who were not carried away by this patter the only light in the darkness was the administration of Mr. Roosevelt and the New Deal in the United States. At a time of weakness and mounting despair in the democratic world, Mr. Roosevelt radiated confidence and strength. He was the leader of the democratic world, and even today upon him alone, of all the statesmen of the thirties, no cloud has rested—neither on him nor on the New Deal, which to European eyes still looks a bright chapter in the history of mankind. It was true that his great social experiment was conducted with an isolationist disregard of the outside world, but it was psychologically intelligible that America, which had come into being in reaction against the follies and evils of a Europe perpetually distraught by religious or national struggles, should try to seek salvation undisturbed by the currents of European life, particularly at a moment when Europe seemed about to collapse into a totalitarian nightmare. Mr. Roosevelt was therefore forgiven by those who found the European situation tragic for pursuing no particular foreign policy—indeed for trying to do, if not without any foreign policy at all, at any rate with a minimum of relationship with the outside world; for that was to some degree part of the American political tradition.

HIS INTERNAL POLICY WAS PLAINLY ANIMATED by a humanitarian purpose. After the unbridled individualism of the twenties which had led to economic collapse and widespread misery, he was seeking to establish new rules of social justice. He was trying to do this without forcing his country into some doctrinaire strait jacket, whether of socialism or state capitalism or the kind of new social organization which the Fascist régimes flaunted as the New Order. Social discontent was high in the United States; faith in businessmen as saviors of society had evaporated overnight after the famous Wall Street crash, and Mr. Roosevelt was providing a vast safety valve for pent-up bitterness and indignation, and trying to prevent revolution and construct a régime which should establish greater economic equality, social justice and happiness, above all, human happiness—ideals which were in the best tradition of American life—without altering the basis of freedom and democracy in his country.

This was being done by what, to unsympathetic critics, seemed a haphazard collection of amateurs, college professors, journalists, personal friends, freelancers of one kind or another, intellectuals, ideologists—what are nowadays called eggheads—whose very appearance and methods of conducting business or constructing policies irritated the servants of old established government institutions in Washington and tidy-minded conservatives everywhere. Yet it was clear that the very amateurishness of these men, the fact that they were allowed to talk to their hearts' content, to experiment, to indulge in a vast amount of trial and error, that relations were personal and not institutional, bred its own vitality and enthusiasm.

Washington was doubtless full of quarrels, resignations, palace intrigues, perpetual warfare between individuals and groups of individuals, parties, cliques, personal supporters of this or that great captain, which must have maddened sober and responsible officials used to the slower tempo and more normal patterns of administration. As for bankers and businessmen, the feelings of many of them were past describing; but at this period they were little regarded, since they were considered to have discredited themselves too deeply, and indeed forever.

Over this vast, seething chaos presided a handsome, charming, gay, intelligent, delightful, very audacious man, Mr. Franklin Delano Roosevelt. He was accused of many weaknesses. He had betrayed his class; he was ignorant, unscrupulous, irresponsible. He was ruthless in playing with the lives and careers of individuals. He was surrounded by adventurers, slick opportunists, intriguers. He made conflicting promises, cynically and brazenly, to individuals and groups and representatives of foreign nations. He made up, with his vast irresistible public charm and his astonishing high spirits, for a lack of virtues considered more important in the leader of the most powerful democracy in the world: the virtues of application, industry, responsibility.

All this was said and some of it may indeed have been just. What attracted his followers were countervailing qualities of a rare and inspiring order. He was large-hearted and possessed wide political horizons, imaginative sweep, understanding of the time in which he lived and of the direction of the great new forces at work in the twentieth century—technological, racial, imperialist, anti-imperialist. He was in favor of life and movement, the promotion of the most generous possible fulfillment of the largest possible number of human wishes, and not in favor of caution and retrenchment and sitting still. Above all, he was absolutely fearless.

He was one of the few statesmen in the twentieth or any other century who seemed to have no fear at all of the future. He believed in his own strength and ability to manage, and to succeed, whatever happened. He believed in the capacity and loyalty of his lieutenants, so that he looked upon the future with a calm eye, as if to say, "Let it come, whatever it may be, it will all be grist to our great mill. We shall turn it all to benefit." It was this, perhaps, more than any other quality, which drew men of very different outlooks to him. In a despondent world which appeared divided between wicked and fatally efficient fanatics marching to destroy, and bewildered populations on the run, unenthusiastic martyrs in a cause they could not define, he believed in his own ability, so long as he was in control, to stem the terrible tide.

He had all the character and energy and skill of the dictators, and he was on our side. He was, in his opinions and public actions, every inch a democrat. All the political and personal and public criticism of him might be true; all the personal defects which his enemies and some of his friends attributed to him might be real; yet as a public figure he was unique. As the skies of Europe grew darker, in particular after war broke out, he seemed to the poor and the unhappy in Europe a kind of benevolent demigod who alone could and would save them in the end. His moral authority, the degree of confidence which he inspired outside his own country—far more beyond America's frontiers than within them at all times—has no parallel. Perhaps President Wilson in the early days after the end of the First World War, when he drove in triumph through the streets of London and Paris, may have inspired some such feeling; but it disappeared quickly and left behind it a terrible feeling of disenchantment. It was plain even to his enemies that President Roosevelt would not be broken as President Wilson had been. For to his prestige and to his personality he added a degree of political skill—indeed virtuosity—which no American before him had ever possessed. His chance of realizing his wishes was plainly greater; his followers would be less likely to reap bitter disappointment.

Indeed he was very different from Wilson. Indeed they represent two contrasting types of statesmen, in each of which, occasionally, men of compelling stature appear. The first kind of statesman is essentially a man of single principle and fanatical vision. Possessed by his own bright, coherent dream, he usually understands neither people nor events. He has no doubts or hesitations, and by concentration of will power, by directness and strength, is able to ignore a great deal of what goes on outside him. His very blindness and stubborn self-absorption, in certain situations, enables him to bend events and men to his own fixed pattern. His strength lies in the fact that weak and vacillating human beings, themselves too insecure or confused to be capable of deciding between alternatives, find relief and peace and strength in submitting to the authority of a single leader of superhuman size to whom all issues are clear, and who marches toward his goal looking neither to right nor to left, buoyed up by the violent vision within him.

Such men differ widely in moral and intellectual quality, and, like forces of nature, do both good and harm in the world. To this type belong Garibaldi, Trotsky, Parnell, De Gaulle, perhaps Lenin too—the distinction I am drawing is not a moral one, not one of value but one of type. There are great benefactors, like Wilson, as well as fearful evildoers, like Hitler, within this category.

The other kind of effective statesman is a naturally political being, as the simple hero is often explicitly anti-political and comes to rescue men, at least ostensibly, from the subtleties and frauds of political life. The second type of politician possesses antennae of the greatest possible delicacy, which convey to him, in ways difficult or impossible to analyze, the perpetually changing contours of events and feelings and human activities around him. He is gifted with a peculiar political sense fed on a capacity to take in minute impressions, to integrate a vast multitude of small, evanescent, unseizable detail, such as artists possess in relation to their material. Statesmen of this type know what to do and when to do it, if they are to achieve their ends; which themselves are usually not born within some private world of inner thought or introverted feeling, but represent the crystallization of what a large number of their fellow citizens are thinking in some dim, inarticulate, but nevertheless persistent fashion. In virtue of this capacity to judge their material very much as a sculptor knows what can be carved out of wood and what out of marble, and how and when, they resemble doctors who have a natural gift for healing which does not directly depend upon (though it could not exist without) that knowledge of scientific anatomy which can only be learned by observation or experiment or from the experience of others.

This instinctive, or at any rate incommunicable, knowledge of where to look for what one needs, the power of divining where the treasure lies, is something common to many types of genius, to scientists and mathematicians no less than to businessmen and administrators and politicians. Such men, when they are statesmen, are acutely aware of the direction in which the thoughts and feelings of human beings are flowing, of where life presses on them most heavily; and they convey to these human beings a sense of understanding their inner needs, of responding to their own deepest impulses—above all, of being alone capable of organizing the world along lines for which the masses are instinctively groping.

To this type of statesmen belong Bismarck and Abraham Lincoln, Lloyd George and Thomas Masaryk, perhaps to some extent Gladstone, and to a minor degree Walpole. Roosevelt was a magnificent virtuoso of this type, and he was the most benevolent as well as the greatest master of his craft in modern times. He really did desire a better life for mankind. The great majorities which he obtained in the elections in the United States during his four terms in office, despite the mounting hostility of the press and perpetual prophecies on its part that he had gone too far and would fail to be re-elected, were ultimately due to an obscure feeling on the part of the majority of the citizens of the United States that he was on their side, that he wished them well, and that he would do something for them. And this feeling gradually spread over the entire civilized world. He became a legendary hero—they themselves did not know quite why—to the indigent and the oppressed far beyond the confines of the English-speaking world.

AS I SAID BEFORE, he was, by some of his opponents, accused of betraying his class; and so he had. When a man who retains the manners, style of life, the emotional texture and the charm of the old order, of some free aristocratic upbringing, revolts against his milieu and adopts the ideas and aspiration of the new, socially *révolté* class—and adopts them not from motives of expediency but out of genuine moral conviction, or from love of life—inability to remain on the side of what seems to him narrow, corrupt, mean, restrictive—the result is fascinating and moving. This is what makes the figures of such men as Condorcet or Charles James Fox, or some of the Russian, Italian, and Polish revolutionaries in the nineteenth century, so attractive; for all we know, this may have been the secret also of Moses or Pericles or Julius Caesar. It was this gentlemanly quality, together with the fact that they felt him to be deeply committed to their side in the struggle and in favor of their way of life, as well as his open and fearless lack of neutrality in the war against the Nazis and Fascists, that endeared him so deeply to the British people during the war years.

I remember well in London, in November, 1940, how excited most people were about the result of the presidential election in the United States. In theory they need not have worried. Mr. [Wendell] Willkie, the Republican candidate, had expressed himself forcibly and sincerely as a supporter of the democracies. Yet it was absurd to say that the people of Britain were neutral in their feelings vis-à-vis the two candidates. They felt in their bones that Mr. Roosevelt was their lifelong friend, that he hated the Nazis as deeply as they did, that he wanted democracy and civilization, in the sense in which they believed in it, to prevail, that he knew what he wanted, and that his goal resembled their own ideals more than it did those of all his opponents. They felt that his heart was in the right place, and they did not, therefore, if they gave it a thought, care whether his political appointments were made under the influence of bosses, or for personal reasons, or thoughtlessly; whether his economic doctrines were heretical; whether he had a sufficiently scrupulous regard for the views of the Senate or the House of Representatives, or the prescriptions of the United States Constitution, or the opinions of the Supreme Court. These matters were very remote from them. They knew that he would, to the extent of his enormous energy and ability, see them through.

There is probably no such thing as long-lived mass hypnotism; the masses know what it is that they like, what genuinely appeals to them. What most Germans thought Hitler to be, Hitler, in fact, largely was; and what free men in Europe and in America and in Asia and in Africa and in Australia, and wherever else the rudiments of free political thought stirred at all—what all these felt Roosevelt to be, he, in fact, was. He was the greatest leader of democracy, the greatest champion of social progress, in the twentieth century.

His enemies accused him of plotting to get America into the war. I am not competent to discuss this controversial issue, but it seems to me that the evidence for it is lacking. I think that when he promised to keep America at peace he meant to try as hard as he could to do so, compatibly with helping to promote the victory of the democracies. He must at one period have thought that he could win the war without entering it, and so, at the end of it, be in the unique position, hitherto achieved by no one, of being the arbiter of the world's fate, without needing to placate those bitter forces which involvement in a war inevitably brings about, and which are an obstacle to reason and humanity in the making of the peace.

No doubt he trusted too often in his own magical power of improvisation. Doubtless he made many political mistakes, some of them difficult to remedy. Some say he was disastrously wrong about Stalin and his intentions and the nature of the Soviet state; others, with equal justice, point to his coolness to the Free French movement, his cavalier intentions with regard to the Supreme Court in the United States, his errors about a good many other issues. He irritated his staunchest supporters and most faithful servants because he did not tell them what he was doing; his government was highly personal and it maddened tidy-minded officials and humiliated those who thought that his policy should be conducted in consultation with and through them. His anti-imperialism at times (in Yalta, for example) assumed gaily irresponsible forms. He vastly oversimplified many issues. He overestimated his own capacity to build a new world by the sole use of his own prodigious powers of manipulation in the course of breezily informal dealings with other statesmen on a purely personal basis. All this sometimes exasperated his allies, but when these last bethought them of who most of his ill-wishers were in the United States and in the world outside, and what their motives were, their own respect, affection, and loyalty tended to return. No man made more public enemies, yet no man had a right to take greater pride in the quality and the motives of some of those enemies. He could justly call himself the friend of the people, and although his opponents accused him of being a demagogue, this charge seems to me unjust. He did not sacrifice fundamental political principles to a desire to retain power; he did not whip up evil passions merely in order to avenge himself upon those whom he disliked or wished to crush, or because it was an atmosphere in which he found it convenient to operate. He saw to it that his administration was in the van of public opinion and drew it on instead of being dragged by it. He made the majority of his fellow citizens prouder to be Americans than they had been before. He raised their status in their own eyes, and in those of the rest of the world. It was an extraordinary transformation of an individual. Perhaps it was largely brought about by the collapse of his health in the early twenties, and his marvelous triumph over his disabilities. For he began life as a well-born, polite, agreeable, debonair, not particularly gifted young man, something of a prig, liked but not greatly admired by his contemporaries at Groton and at Harvard, a competent Assistant Secretary of the Navy in the First World War; in short, he seemed embarked on the routine career of an American patrician with moderate political ambitions. His illness and the support and encouragement and political qualities of his wife—whose greatness of character and goodness of heart history will duly record—seemed to transfigure his public personality into the strong and beneficent champion who became the father of his people, in an altogether unique fashion.

He was more than this: it is not too much to say that he altered the fundamental concept of government and its obligations to the governed. In this respect Lloyd George was no more than a forerunner. The welfare state, so much denounced, has obviously come to stay: the direct moral responsibility for minimum standards of living and social services which it took for granted, are today accepted almost without a murmur by the most conservative politicians in the Western democracies. The Republican Party in 1952 made no effort to upset the basic principles—which seemed utopian in the twenties—of Mr. Roosevelt's social legislation.

But Mr. Roosevelt's greatest service to mankind (after ensuring victory against the enemies of freedom) consists in the fact that he showed that it is possible to be politically effective and yet benevolent and civilized: that the fierce left and right wing propaganda of the thirties, according to which the conquest and retention of political power is not compatible with human qualities, but necessarily demands from those who pursue it seriously the sacrifice of their lives upon the altar of some ruthless ideology, or the systematic practice of despotism—this propaganda, which filled the art and talk of the day, was simply untrue. Mr. Roosevelt's example strengthened democracy everywhere—that is to say, the view that the promotion of social justice and individual liberty does not necessarily mean the end of all efficient government; that power and order are not identical with a strait jacket of doctrine, whether economic or political; that it is possible to reconcile individual liberty and a loose texture of society with the indispensable minimum of organization and authority. And in this belief lies what Mr. Roosevelt's greatest predecessor once described as the last best hope on earth.

Stalin's Chuckle

IAN FRAZIER || 1995

The brutal reign of Joseph Stalin has inspired a large body of serious and damnatory work, from Robert Conquest's The Great Terror *to Robert Service's* Stalin *to Anne Applebaum's Pulitzer Prize–winning* Gulag: A History. *Yet rarely has the Soviet dictator been more memorably portrayed—or deliciously skewered—than in this comic gem by Ian Frazier (1951–   ). A longtime contributor to* The Atlantic *and a staff writer for* The New Yorker, *Frazier is the author of a half dozen idiosyncratic, highly regarded books, three of which chronicle life in the heart of the heart of the country* (Great Plains, Family, On the Rez). *But he is equally admired for his talents as a humor writer, especially among fellow humor writers. Frazier's comedic premises, in such collections as* Dating Your Mom *and* Coyote v. Acme, *often originate with a quotation he has stumbled on and revolve around a wildly incongruous juxtaposition. In "Stalin's Chuckle," the springboard quotation is an innocent aside found buried within the memoir of a Soviet military commander, and the incongruity comes from the odd-coupling of Soviet totalitarian terror and American stand-up comedy.*

Seldom did anyone see Stalin laugh.

When he did, it was more like a chuckle, as though to himself.

—G. ZHUKOV, MARSHALL OF THE SOVIET UNION:
REMINISCENCES AND REFLECTIONS

IRWIN C. BROWN, *TV and Radio Entertainers' Retirement Home*

Stalin's dacha, his summer place or whatever—now, that was a hard room. I worked it just the one time when I was on my world tour in the fifties. No stage or nothin', only a little, like, conference table with a lectern. I pushed the lectern aside, didn't need that for my act. They offered me some herring, but herring dries my pipes. I just started right in. They was all sittin' there, right in the front row. Matter of fact, it was the only row, these big high-backed chairs: Beria, Krushchev, Poskrebyshev, Litvinov, Molotov. Stalin sat on the aisle. Kept his hat on. I thought I saw the moustache go up when I did my "Go get yourself your *own* white man!" It just sort of went up, oh, 'bout a quarter inch. That room was quiet, man. I could see Beria holdin' it in, face turnin' purple. And Molotov was makin' these little chokin' sounds, kinda snortin' out the nose every once in a while. But if Joe don't laugh, don't *nobody* laugh.

FREDDIE DRAKE, *Friars Club*

I worked ten days at the old Flamingo in Las Vegas and then flew straight to Moscow. A. N. Poskrebyshev, the personal secretary, booked me. They put me up in a God-awful hotel, hot and cold running soot. At eleven at night some guy called for me and took me to the private apartment in the Kremlin where Stalin stayed when he couldn't get home. A lot of guys were sitting around with cigars and wine. It was a smoker, basically. I took one look and told myself, "Freddie, tonight you work blue." I used material so adult it would've gotten me kicked off American TV for life. Stalin was tanked but he didn't show it. I did the Shorty's joke, I did "Run, Harold, Run!," I did "Death of Chi-Chi"—nothing. I ended with my killer, really hit the punch line hard: "So the plumber says, 'I can save your wife, Mr. Schonstein—*but I'm afraid it's too late for the rabbi!'*" Stalin wanted to laugh, I know that. He did laugh, sort of, in that there was possibly a slightly redder color in his face. He gave off a strong feeling as if he might have been laughing. But did he *laugh* laugh? Not per se, no.

A. N. POSKREBYSHEV, *Palace of Party Members, Moscow*

I remember he used to play Allan Sherman's "Hello Muddah, Hello Fadduh!" over and over again on the phonograph. This story-song of the young boy's letter home from summer camp made him helpless with laughing. Sometimes his moustache would rise perhaps half a centimeter. As his personal secretary, I had the job of replacing the needle at the beginning of each recording after it had reached the end. He especially liked the song "God Rest You, Gary Mandelbaum," and sometimes you would think he was almost humming along. Many other so-called novelty songs from America had a similarly strong effect on him. He often spoke of his desire to meet the man who wrote the song "I'm My Own Grandpaw."

KAYLA T., *Los Angeles*

As a humor therapist, I immediately got the sense that all these men at the Kremlin were very stiff and rigid, and that uninhibited laughter might break up the rigidity—as it so often does. So I had the idea of getting everybody on the floor for a game of Ha. Now, in

Ha what you do is you lie on the floor on your back, and somebody lies on his back perpendicular to you and rests his head on your stomach, and so on across the floor in sort of a herringbone pattern, and then the first person says "Ha," and the second person says "Ha, ha," and the third person is supposed to say "Ha, ha, ha," and so on. And the way your head bobs up and down on the other person's stomach when he says "Ha," it generally has everybody laughing hysterically by the time you get to three "Ha"s. I laid them out carefully—Mr. Molotov, Mr. Beria, Mr. Malenkov, and the others, with Mr. Stalin at the end. I told them all to relax and take deep breaths. Then Mr. Molotov said "Ha." Mr. Beria, suppressing giggles, continued with "Ha, ha." Mr. Malenkov strained to control his dignity as he added his "Ha, ha, ha." Mr. Krushchev's attempt at "Ha, ha, ha, ha" became an uncontrollable fit of belly laughs, which violently bounced Mr. Mikoyan's head, causing him to laugh until he wept, which in turn set off Mr. Yagoda. In a minute the whole line was howling with nonstop laughter—all except Mr. Stalin. His head bounced and bounced on his neighbor's stomach, but his expression didn't change. He stood, excused himself, and walked over to the men's room. He closed the door and slid the bolt. Gradually his colleagues on the floor began to calm down, and one by one they sat up. Soon we all fell completely silent. From the men's room we heard a faint sound. I am of the belief that what we heard was Mr. Stalin chuckling as though to himself.

A. N. POSKREBYSHEV

Booking comedy acts added greatly to my secretarial responsibilities, and I often neglected it in favor of more-regular tasks. Comrade Stalin noticed this, imprisoned my wife, Bronislava, and then asked me to obtain at all costs a performance by a Mexican comedian. Through our embassy in Mexico City, I got in touch with ex-Comrade Trotsky, who was living there at the time. As it happened, Trotsky knew the Mexican comedy circuit well and had even contributed a few gags to some of its leading members. So in a manner of speaking certain comedians owed Trotsky a favor, and here was a perfect opportunity to make use of it. I was delighted with all these developments and did not conceal my pleasure from Comrade Stalin. At the mention of Comrade Trotsky's name, however, Comrade Stalin grew agitated and began to chuckle, as though to himself. Still chuckling, he insisted that I telephone immediately to Comrade Beria at his flat and summon him. When Beria arrived, Stalin rushed to the door, answered it, chuckled again, and screamed at Beria for his slowness. Chuckling very loudly as though to himself, he pushed Beria before him into the inner office and slammed the door. Soon after this he told me he would prefer to be entertained only by comedians from cold countries. "A Finn, for example, is always funny," he advised.

Though others may disagree, I have always maintained that Comrade Stalin knew funny. Hidden among his many attributes was a sure comedic sense. "You must never forget," he exhorted me, "a comic is one who says things *funny*, while a comedian is one who says funny *things*. Both of these phases, however, must be passed through on the way to the third and final phase: good stand-up. When we as a society attain really good stand-up, every evening will be open mike and the state as we know it will wither away. For jokes, we will require new ones appropriate to our modern times, and on modern themes—airplane food, for example, that syphilitic abomination! Or how about the vapid and syphilitic listings of television programs published in the newspapers? Such a form, if used in proper satiric style, could be most effective. A master of stand-up should possess a full repertoire of funny voices—Negro, sports announcer, and robot, to name only a few. Draw your comedy from daily life if you wish to reach the true audience: the people. Enough of the syphilitic vaudevillians' noise! The modern comedian will instead find his subject at airports, in the behavior of overbearing shop clerks, and in the differences between one's own city and Los Angeles. Let us develop a scientific system for the production of trenchant comedy riffs, using as our models the best comedians of the past. Let our youngsters who wish to perform stand-up devote hours, years, to the watching of films of these masters. The true comic is the revolutionary, sticking swords in the stuffed shirts of the bourgeoisie. Let the comedy revolution never end, let it fill entire television channels, let it grow until everything is thoroughly funny!"

Eventually Comrade Stalin began to question my own sense of humor, and I was dismissed from his service. My wife, Bronislava, remained in prison until she was shot, I believe. Toward the end, the splendid theories of comedy Comrade Stalin had developed were under attack. Saddened as I was by his treatment of my wife and me, I did not lose faith in the soundness of these theories. Properly applied, they could have provided uproarious material on an international scale for years to come. The noise resembling a chuckle that we delighted to hear from Comrade Stalin's lips could have spread to every land. But, unfortunately for the cause of world humor, such a result was not to be.

The Path to Power

ROBERT A. CARO || 1981

When Robert A. Caro (1935–   ) embarked, more than three decades ago, on his multivolume opus The Years of Lyndon Johnson, he was venturing into a crowded field: almost two dozen full-blown biographies of LBJ had already been published. Yet none of the previous efforts, despite undeniable virtues, had approached their outsized subject with the sweep, the ambition, or the sheer narrative drive that Caro was determined to bring to the job. In the 1960s, as an investigative reporter for Newsday, Caro had set his sights on a lofty literary goal: he wanted to write big-topic biography and, as he recalled in a 1999 interview with the novelist Kurt Vonnegut, to redefine the genre as "a means of illuminating the times and the great forces that shape the times" and to dig down to "the reality of power, its true essence." For his first book, the Pulitzer Prize–winning biography The Power Broker (1974), Caro conducted more than five hundred interviews and scrutinized tens of thousands of pages of government documents to produce his scathing portrait of Robert Moses, the autocratic transportation and urban-planning czar who did more to change the physiognomy of the New York metropolitan area than all of its elected representatives put together. But with Caro's next subject, Lyndon Baines Johnson, the challenges would be even greater. In order to chronicle LBJ's early life, from his hardscrabble Texas upbringing to his first failed bid, in 1941, to reach the Senate, Caro spent seven years tracking down virtually everyone who had known Johnson, navigating the immense repository of archives at the Johnson Library in Austin, and even living for months at a time in the remote, rugged Hill Country where Johnson grew up.

Although the resulting book, The Path to Power (1982), was impugned by several critics for being overlong and polemical, it was hailed by many more as a landmark in American nonfiction, the first installment of what the Los Angeles Times called "the political biography of our time." It was also, at almost nine hundred pages, a book that The Atlantic, with its history of opening up vast tracts of space for ground-breaking work, was ideally suited to introduce to the world. William Whitworth, the magazine's eleventh editor-in-chief (1981–2000), had made a name for himself, while an editor at The New Yorker, by transforming long and sometimes unwieldy manuscripts into compelling, stand-alone magazine articles. (The Power Broker, Whitworth remem-

bers, arrived on his desk "in a huge box.") At The Atlantic, Whitworth
plunged headlong into The Path to Power, *carving out five substantial
magazine pieces to run over the course of the next thirteen months. The
following excerpt, which serves as the introduction both to the magazine
series and (in slightly different form) to the book, encapsulates Caro's
Johnson—a preternaturally manipulative, monstrously power-seeking,
endlessly complex political giant of the twentieth century who, as the
principal author of both the Great Society and the Vietnam War,
presided over one of the most momentous periods in American history.*

Two of the men lying on the blanket that day in the autumn of 1940 were
rich. The third was poor—so poor that he had only recently bought the
first suit he had ever owned that fit correctly—and desperately anxious not
to be: thirty-two-year-old Congressman Lyndon B. Johnson had recently
been pleading with one of the men, George Brown, to find him a business
in which he could make a little money. So when Brown, relaxing in the
still-warm October sun at the luxurious Greenbrier Hotel in the mountains of West Virginia, heard the other man on the blanket, Charles Marsh,
make his offer to Lyndon Johnson, he felt sure he knew what the answer
would be.

Brown wasn't surprised by the offer. Marsh, a tall, imperious man of
fifty-three, whose profile and arrogance reminded friends of a Roman emperor, was addicted to the grandiose gesture, particularly toward young
men in whom he took a paternal interest. Only recently, Marsh, pleased
with a reporter's work, had told him he deserved a "tip"—and had there-
upon given him a newspaper company. Some years earlier, his sympathies
having been engaged by the story of Sid Richardson, a young oil wildcatter
reduced by a series of dry wells to pawning his hunting rifle for room and
board, Marsh had, in return for a share of future profits (profits he believed
would never materialize), agreed to guarantee bank loans to enable the
young man to continue drilling. And Marsh's feelings toward Johnson,
whose control of his congressional district had been cemented by the enthusiastic support of Marsh's powerful Austin, Texas, newspaper, were
particularly warm. "Charles loved Lyndon like a son," Brown says.

Brown wasn't even surprised by the size of the offer. A rich man himself by most standards, he knew how far from rich he was by Marsh's. The
newspaper Marsh had so casually given away was only one of a dozen he
owned; and he held—and collected interest on—the notes of a dozen
more. In Austin alone, his possessions included the city's biggest newspa-

per, much of the stock in its biggest bank, all of the stock in its streetcar franchise, and vast tracts of its most valuable real estate. And newspapers, banks, streetcars, and real estate were just minor items on Marsh's balance sheet, for his partnership with Richardson was not his only venture in the fabulous oil fields of West Texas; forests of derricks pumped black gold out of the earth for his sole account. So Brown listened with interest but not astonishment when Marsh said he no longer got along with Richardson and he had one inflexible rule: if he didn't like a partner, he got out of the partnership. This partnership, he said, hadn't cost him a dime, anyway—he had obtained his share in Richardson's wells just by guaranteeing those bank loans years before. He would sell his share to Johnson at a low price, he said, and, Brown recalls, he said, using a characteristic phrase: "I'll sell it to you in a way you can buy it." There was only one way for a young man without resources, and that was the way Marsh was proposing: as Brown listened, Marsh offered to let the young congressman buy his share in the Richardson enterprises without a down payment. "He told Lyndon he could pay for it out of his profits each year," Brown explains. The share was probably not worth a million dollars, says Brown, who had seen the partnership's balance sheets—but it was worth "close to" a million, "certainly three quarters of a million." Marsh was offering to make Lyndon Johnson rich, without Johnson's investing even a dollar of his own.

But if George Brown wasn't surprised by the offer, he was surprised by the response it received. Johnson, polite, ingratiating, and deferential as he always was with the older man, thanked Marsh. But, polite, ingratiating, and deferential as he was, he was also, Brown recalls, quite firm. He would like to think the offer over, he said, but he felt almost certain he was going to have to decline. I can't be an oilman, he said. If the public knew I had oil interests, it would kill me politically.

All that week, Lyndon Johnson considered the offer—in a setting that emphasized what he would be giving up if he declined it: the Greenbrier, with its immense, colonnaded Main House rearing up, gleaming white, in the midst of 6,500 acres of lush, manicured lawns and serene gardens; its vast, marble-floored ballroom, in which guests danced under cut-glass chandeliers; its Spring House, surmounted by a bronze Hebe, cupbearer to the gods, around which, every afternoon, cold champagne was served at canopied tables; its arcade lined with expensive shops; its fleet of limousines, which brought arriving guests from the nearby station, at which their private railroad cars were lined up in a long row; its battalions of green-liveried servants, was, as *Holiday* magazine put it, "opulent America at its richest"—the distillation of all that was available in the United States to the wealthy, and not to others. As the three men lay every morning on their blanket, which had been spread on a slope in front of their accommodations—a row of white cottages, set away from the main building for privacy, which were the resort's most expensive—the mountain slopes before them were turning, day by day, into the glorious shades of an Allegheny autumn, like a show presented for their private enjoyment. Day after day, Johnson discussed the offer with Brown, telling him details of his life he had often told him before: about the terrible poverty of his youth, about his struggle to go to college, and about the fact that, after three years in Congress, three years, moreover, in which he had accumulated, thanks to President Roosevelt's friendship, far more than three years' worth of power, he still had nothing—not a thousand dollars, he said—in the bank. Again and again, he told Brown about his fear (a fear that, Brown believed, tormented him) of ending up like his father, who had also been an elected official—six times elected to the Texas State Legislature—but had died penniless. He talked repeatedly about his realization that a seat in Congress, with its inadequate salary and no pension, was not a hedge against that fate; so many times since he had come to Washington, he said, he had seen former congressmen, men who had once sat in the great chamber as he was sitting now, working in poorly paid or humiliating jobs. Again and again, he harked back to one particular incident he could not get out of his mind: while riding an elevator in the Capitol one day, he had struck up a conversation with the elevator operator, who had said that *he* had once been a congressman too. He didn't want to end up an elevator operator, he said. Accepting Marsh's offer would free him from such fears forever, he knew. But, again and again, Johnson would return to the statement he had made when Marsh had first made the offer: It would kill me politically.

George Brown had been working closely with Johnson for three years; Johnson's initial nomination to Congress, in 1937, had, in fact, been the result of an immensely complicated transaction with a very simple central point: the firm in which Brown and his brother, Herman, were the principals—Brown & Root, Inc.—was building a dam near Austin under an arrangement with the federal government that was of dubious legality, and needed a congressman who could get the arrangement legalized. Johnson had succeeded in doing so, and the Browns had made a million dollars from the new federal contract. Ever since, Johnson had been trying to make them more, an effort that had recently been climaxed by the award to Brown & Root of the contract for a gigantic naval base at Corpus Christi; this contract would make the Browns not one million but many. Having worked with Johnson so long, Brown felt he knew the young congressman and understood how anxious he was to obtain money. He had a feeling, moreover, that this anxiety was intensifying, a feeling nurtured not only by the increased intensity of Johnson's pleas that Brown find him a business of his own but by a story circulating among Johnson's intimates. Several months before, Johnson had introduced two men to each other at an Austin party, and one had later bought a piece of Austin real estate from the other. The seller, a local businessman, had been astonished when the congressman approached him one evening and asked for a "finder's fee" for the role he had played in the transaction. Telling Johnson that he hadn't played any role beyond the social introduction, he had refused to give him a fee, and had considered the matter closed; the transaction, he recalls, was small, and the finder's fee would not have amounted to "more than a thousand dollars, if that." When, therefore, he opened the front door of his home at 6:30 the next morning to pick up the newspaper that had been dropped on his lawn, he was astonished to see his congressman sitting on the curb, waiting to ask him again for the money. And when he again explained to him that he wasn't entitled to a fee, he recalls, "Lyndon started— well, really, to beg me for it—and when I refused, I thought he was going to cry." Brown, knowing how anxious Johnson had been for a thousand dollars, was surprised to hear him hesitate over three quarters of a million.

He was surprised also by the reason Johnson had advanced for his hesitation. *It would kill me politically*—what "politically" was Johnson talking about? Until that week at the Greenbrier, Brown had thought he had measured Johnson's political ambition—had considered the measuring simple, in fact, for Johnson talked so incessantly about what he wanted out of politics. He was always saying that he wanted to stay in Congress until a Senate seat opened up, and then run for the Senate. Well, his congressional district was absolutely safe. Being an oilman couldn't hurt him there. And when he ran for the Senate, he would be running in Texas, and being an oilman wouldn't hurt him in Texas. For what office, then, would Johnson be "killed" by being an oilman?

Only when he asked himself that question, George Brown recalls— only during that week at the Greenbrier—did he finally realize, after three years of intimate association with Lyndon Johnson, what Johnson really wanted.

And only when, at the end of that week, Johnson firmly refused Marsh's offer did Brown realize how much Johnson wanted it.

GEORGE BROWN, WHO HAD THOUGHT he knew Lyndon Johnson so well, realized during that week at the Greenbrier that he didn't know him at all.

Their lives would be entwined for thirty more years: as Brown & Root became, with Johnson's help, an industrial colossus, one of the largest construction companies—and shipbuilding companies and oil-equipment companies—in the world, holder of Johnson-arranged government contracts and receiver of Johnson-arranged government favors amounting to billions of dollars, suave George Brown and his fierce brother Herman became the principal financiers of Johnson's rise to national power. But at the end of those thirty years—on the day Lyndon Johnson died—George Brown still felt that to some extent he didn't really know Lyndon Johnson at all.

No one knew him. Enlisting all his energy and all his cunning in a life-long attempt—the details of which are in themselves a remarkable story—to obscure the facts of his personal life, his rise to power, and his use of power, he succeeded so well that no one saw him whole: not his wife, who, contrary to the carefully contrived legend, was until the last decade of his life kept largely in the dark about his political and financial activities; not his mother, who had a mother's unique understanding of his complex personality but who saw her son infrequently after he reached manhood; not his "intimates," for no intimate was permitted to see more than a fraction of the man or his maneuvers; not the citizenry of the nation he led as President, the citizenry that gave him his full term as its leader by what was then the greatest voting majority in history. No one. He rose to the leadership of the nation's Senate, held the leadership for five years, and during those years exercised more power in the Senate than any other man in the nation's history—enough so that he was called, during those years, "the second most powerful man in Washington"—and was the subject of a thousand newspaper and magazine articles, and no one knew him. He came to the presidency and remained in it for five years, during which he was perhaps the most powerful man on earth, and, despite newspapers and magazines and television, still no one knew him. In a nation whose Constitution provided, in the words of an earlier President, Abraham Lincoln, that "no one man should hold the power of bringing the nation into war," this one man brought the nation into war—escalating a limited involvement into a war that drained its treasurehouses, and soaked up the blood of hundreds of thousands of its young men; into a war that not only cost it more money than World War II but also lasted longer; into a war abroad that caused civil disobedience verging on civil insurrection at home—and the nation did not know that man. He attempted to make that nation a Great Society—with education acts, and civil-rights acts, and antipoverty acts, and Model Cities acts, and a hundred other laws that constituted the most sweeping attempt at social reform since the New Deal—and the nation did not know the man who was doing that, either. If, during the long evolution from a "constitutional" to an "imperial" presidency, there was a single administration in which the balance tipped decisively from one to the other, it was the presidency of Lyndon Johnson. It was during his presidency also that there began the widespread mistrust of the President that was symbolized by the phrase, coined during his administration, "credibility gap." Both these developments, which were to affect the nation's history profoundly, were to a considerable extent a function of the personality of the man—but the nation did not know the man.

THIS LACK OF KNOWLEDGE WAS NOT DUE to lack of curiosity. Indeed, during Lyndon Johnson's presidency, there was in Washington what one columnist termed an "obsession" with his personality. ("Under Kennedy," a columnist's wife said, the main topic of Washington dinner-table conversation was ideas; "now it is Lyndon Johnson's personality.") Rather, the lack of knowledge was due to an aspect of that personality with which Washington had become familiar: Lyndon Johnson's preoccupation with and talent for secrecy. This talent was striking even in his youth, and in the concealment of his own life story the President had outdone himself. His years at college are one illustration—one among very many—of his efforts at concealment, and of their success. While still an undergraduate at Southwest Texas State Teachers College, in San Marcos, he arranged to have excised (literally cut out) from hundreds of copies of the college yearbook certain pages that gave clues to his years there (luckily for history, some copies escaped the scissors). Issues of the college newspaper that chronicle certain crucial episodes in his college career are missing from the college library. A ruthless use thereafter of political power in San Marcos made faculty members and classmates reluctant to discuss those aspects of his career.

As a result, although twenty-one previous biographies have been written about Lyndon Johnson, not one has mentioned certain facts about his college years that should at least be considered in assessing his character and personality: that, for example, Lyndon Johnson, who won a seat in the United States Senate in a stolen election in 1948, stole his first election in 1930, to give himself a seat on his college's senior council. No previous biography has mentioned that if he stole one election at college, he won another by the use, against a young woman guilty of a single, insignificant indiscretion, of what his lieutenants call "blackmail"; that a score of political tricks on the same moral level earned him a reputation on campus as a man who was not "straight," not honest; that he was, in fact, so deeply and widely mistrusted at college that his nickname, the nickname he bore during all his years at college, the nickname by which he was identified in the college yearbook, was "Bull" (for "Bullshit") Johnson. (The yearbook, in terms far harsher than those employed about any other student, also mentions his "sophistry," and calls him "a master of the gentle art of spoofing the general public.") Most significant, perhaps, no biography has mentioned that the dislike and mistrust extended beyond politics: no biography of Lyndon Johnson, who as President was accused of lying to the American people, has mentioned that some of his fellow students (who used his nickname to his face: "Hiya, Bull"; "Howya doin', Bull?") believed not only that he lied to them—lied to them constantly, lied about big matters and small, lied so incessantly that he was, in a widely used phrase, "the biggest liar on campus"—but also that some psychological element *impelled* him to lie, made him, in one classmate's words, "a man who just could not tell the truth."

BUT IF IN SAN MARCOS HE WAS REGARDED with mistrust, in another little town in Texas, during these same years, Lyndon Johnson was regarded as "a blessing, a blessing from a clear sky."

The town was Cotulla, a tiny, predominantly Mexican community of tin-roofed shacks broiling under the fierce sun on the vast, desolate plains of the South Texas brush country. Having been forced to drop out of college for lack of funds, Johnson spent a year there teaching in the town's Mexican school.

He got the job because no one else would take it, and Cotulla had never had a teacher like him. No teacher had ever cared if the Mexican children learned anything or not; this teacher cared. He battled the school board to get them equipment so that they could play games at recess like the white kids, and insisted that they, too, have baseball games and track meets with other schools. And he taught—taught with a furious energy, coming to school very early and staying very late, inspiring his thirty-two pupils with the promise that if they learned, success would surely be theirs, spanking them if they didn't do their homework. His pupils didn't resent the spanking, because they felt that the emotion behind it was concern for their future—and they were right; for the rest of his life, Lyndon Johnson would remember lying in his room before daylight and hearing motors, and realizing that his pupils wouldn't be in school that day because they were being "hauled off in a truck to a beet patch or a cotton patch" to earn a few dollars instead. And he didn't teach only children. The school's Mexican janitor didn't speak English; Johnson bought him a textbook and tutored him on the steps of the school with endless patience as the loafers across the street sat laughing at them. Hints of the Great Society as well as of the credibility gap can be found in Lyndon Johnson's youth.

Before San Marcos and Cotulla was Johnson City, a town in the Texas Hill Country, one of the most remote and impoverished areas in the United States. In Johnson City, a town so isolated its inhabitants felt it was an island surrounded by an ocean of empty land, Lyndon Johnson spent a childhood in which he was held in contempt, not so much because of his personality (although the determination to manipulate and dominate was already vividly apparent, and aroused resentment) but because he was a member of a despised family. He spent a childhood in which, often, the only food in his house was the food that neighbors brought out of charity, a childhood in which he had to wonder, from month to month, if the mortgage payments would be met and his family would still have a home to live in; a childhood in which the parents of the girl he wanted to marry refused him permission to date her because he was "a Johnson," and as he stood in the courthouse square with his cousins in the evenings, he had to watch her drive around with another man. Before San Marcos and Cotulla, also, was California. Trying to escape a life of brutally hard physical labor wresting a living from an infertile soil, Lyndon Johnson ran away to California to become a lawyer, but the attempt came to nothing, and he found himself back in Johnson City working on a road-building gang, in effect working in harness with a mule, the two of them forcing a scoop through the rocky Hill Country soil. He emerged from his childhood—broke out of Johnson City—desperate for respect and security, so desperate that for the rest of his life all considerations fell before the demands of ambition.

HIS PURSUIT OF WEALTH WAS ONE EXAMPLE.

If at the Greenbrier Johnson subordinated his desire for money to his desire to become President of the United States, he found, not long thereafter, a way to reconcile the two ambitions—and in years to come he found a dozen ways: twenty-three years after he had lain poor on the Greenbrier blanket, he entered the Oval Office the richest man ever to occupy it. By the time he assumed the presidency, *Life* magazine estimated his fortune at $14 million; Johnson's representatives protested publicly that that estimate was far too high; privately, some now admit that it was far too low.

Attainment of the presidency did not slake his thirst for money. Upon assuming the office, he announced that he was immediately placing all his business affairs in a "blind trust," of whose activities, he said, he would not even be informed. In truth, however, the establishment of the trust was virtually simultaneous with the installation in the Oval Office of private telephone lines to certain Texas attorneys associated with the administration of the trust—and over those lines, during the entire five years of his presidency, Johnson personally directed his business affairs, down to the most minute details, not infrequently working on those affairs, according to some of his attorneys, for several hours a day. Johnson's business could be conducted even during affairs of state. For example, during a visit to the Johnson Ranch by German Chancellor Ludwig Erhard, the President sat behind closed doors browbeating a group of businessmen in connection with a television option agreement—an agreement he had won through his behind-the-scenes influence over the Austin City Council, which he had earlier manipulated like a ward boss. In his direction of his business affairs, he did not hesitate to use the power of the presidency itself, and to use it with utter ruthlessness. And during his presidency, Lyndon Johnson piled atop the millions of dollars he had already made millions more.

More significant than the dollar total of Lyndon Johnson's fortune were the methods he employed to accumulate it—for a detailed examination of such methods is an instructive lesson in the means by which, in twentieth-century America, a position of public power can be used to accumulate private wealth. But although dedicated investigative journalists produced from time to time scattered articles detailing one or another episode in that accumulation, these episodes were never pulled together to show an overall pattern, in part because of Johnson's talent for secrecy; for example, the telephone setup was arranged so that those business-related calls would not be handled by a White House operator or appear in White House telephone logs. The one aspect of his accumulation of wealth that was explored in any depth at all was the Johnson radio and television interests, which were in his wife's name. There existed a vague public awareness that Johnson had somehow employed political pressure to force the Federal Communications Commission to grant concessions to his small Austin radio station and to the Austin television station that he later added to it. There were jokes—bitter in Austin, knowing in Washington—about the fact that for fifteen years the capital of Texas had to make do with a single television channel. But the extent of the pressure and of the concessions was seldom detailed; little public understanding existed of the fact that the FCC not only created the Johnson broadcasting monopoly and protected it against incursion but steadily expanded its sphere until it was a radio-television empire that, far from being limited to Austin, or even to Texas, eventually spread over cities in three states. This empire, which had grown from a radio station that the Johnsons bought on Christmas Day of 1942 for $17,500, was by the time he entered the presidency worth $7 million—and was producing profits of $10,000 a week.

The growth of the radio-television empire was, in fact, one of the less sordid episodes in the story of his accumulation of wealth. Never explored in sufficient detail was the economic fate of those men who, owning their own television stations (or banks, or ranches), tried to compete with Lyndon Johnson, or simply to hold on, against his wishes, to their property—men who were broken financially on the wheel of his power. And Lyndon Johnson left the presidency, and lived out his life, and died, with the American people still ignorant not only of the dimensions of his greed but of its intensity.

IF, HOWEVER, JOHNSON THREW HIMSELF into the pursuit of wealth with a furious, frenzied, almost desperate energy, that energy characterized his work in other areas, as well.

His election to Congress came when he was only twenty-eight years old, but as a result of it the land in which he had been raised was transformed. When he went to Congress, in 1937, the Hill Country had only recently obtained its first paved roads, and had not yet obtained electricity; its families worked their impoverished farms by the same methods by which they had been worked a hundred years before. If he went to Congress to get a dam built and make its backers rich, before he left Congress he got a half-dozen dams built—and he also succeeded, in the face of difficulties almost unimaginable to residents of more highly developed areas, in using the dams to provide electricity to the lonely ranches of the Hill Country. When he realized that he had to teach the people of the Hill Country how to use electricity—that it meant more than just light bulbs hanging from the ceiling—he taught them to use it, and he taught them soil conservation and crop rotation, and other methods of easing a harsh round of life that had gone uneased since the first settlers came to that country, in 1836. During his first years as a congressman, he obtained for his congressional district, a district in which county budgets were figured in tens of thousands of dollars, $70 million—for the biggest rural electrification cooperative in the United States, for roads, for schools, for federally insured mortgages to save his people's farms, for federal loans to help his people's children go to college. Johnson's effort to bring the people of his region into the twentieth century is as much the bright side of democracy as other aspects of his career are the dark side of democracy.

THE STORY OF LYNDON JOHNSON'S RISE to political power sheds light on economic forces that had immense impact on the nation.

Two incidents are particularly significant in this story. One occurred in 1944, the other in 1948. In the 1944 incident, President Franklin D. Roosevelt, after a conference in the Oval Office with Johnson and the President's viceroy for Texas—a shrewd, silent country lawyer named Alvin J. Wirtz, who was Johnson's political godfather—personally intervened with the Internal Revenue Service to quash an investigation into Brown & Root's financing of the career of the young congressman who would one day sit in Roosevelt's chair. In the 1948 incident, President Harry Truman was whistlestopping through Texas. Aboard his campaign train were the local dignitaries who could be expected to be aboard—among them the governor of Texas and two of the state's congressmen, House Speaker Sam Rayburn and Lyndon Johnson—and one whose presence was entirely unexpected: George Parr, the "Duke of Duval." Parr, who ruled sunbaked, cracked-clay Duval County and a half-dozen others stretching down to the Mexican border with gangs of armed *pistoleros*, wanted certain assurances from the President himself in connection with his gift to Lyndon Johnson of the votes that had elected him to the Senate and placed him finally on the path to the presidency. The notorious Parr was not the type of figure a President would want on a train ridden by the national press corps, but Johnson and Rayburn had insisted that Truman see Parr, and the border-county dictator was not only on the President's train but in the President's compartment, closeted with him in private conference—and receiving the assurances he wanted.

Both these incidents occurred because of a President's realization of the importance, in an era in which money increasingly was becoming the basic fuel of politics, of coming to terms with new economic forces. Minor though they are, therefore, they are convenient benchmarks of the rise of these forces. The impact on America's politics, its governmental institutions, its foreign and domestic policy, of these new economic forces that surged out of the Southwest in the middle of the twentieth century has not been adequately explored by historians. America has had its great books on the robber barons of the nineteenth century and on the impact on the nation of the economic forces they represented. The great books on the robber barons of the twentieth century—the oil and sulfur and gas and defense barons of the Southwest—have yet to be written. And they should be written. As the robber barons of the last century looted the nation's land of its wealth—its coal and coke, its oil and ore, its iron, its forests—and used part of that wealth to ensure that the government would not force them to return more than a pittance of their loot to the nation's people, so the robber barons of this century have drained the earth of the Southwest of its riches and have used those riches to armor themselves against government.

Lyndon Johnson was not the architect of this control, but he was its embodiment and its instrument—its most effective instrument. It was these new economic forces—the oil, gas, sulfur, defense, space, and other new industries of the Southwest—that raised him to power and, once he was in power, helped him to extend it. For years, men came into Lyndon Johnson's office and handed him envelopes stuffed with cash. They didn't stop coming even when the office in which he sat was the office of the Vice President of the United States. Fifty thousand dollars (in hundred-dollar bills in sealed envelopes) was what one lobbyist—for *one* oil company—testified that he brought to Johnson's office during his term as Vice President. They placed at his disposal sums of money whose dimensions were revolutionary in politics, and he used it to bend other politicians to his will. From the day, before the 1940 election, on which, still a young, unknown congressman from a remote region of Texas, he went to President Roosevelt and asked for a political role with national power—and told the President that he would bring with him to the national campaign, to be dispensed to Democratic congressional candidates, huge donations from Charles Marsh and George Brown (and from their friends, the newly rich Texas oilmen)—he played an increasingly prominent role in the financing of the careers of other legislators. Congressmen and senators worried about money to ensure their return to Capitol Hill learned that all the money they needed was available from Texas—from Texas and from the new industrial order of the Southwest, of which Texas was the heart—and that Lyndon Johnson, more than any other single figure, controlled it. This money was the basic source of his power on Capitol Hill. Lyndon Johnson was described as a legislative genius, a reader of men, a leader of men—thousands of articles described how he could grasp men's lapels, peer into their eyes, and talk them around, of how he could create consensus out of disparity. Lyndon Johnson *was* a legislative genius, a reader of men, and a leader of men, but his genius would have had far less impact without the money to back it up, without the knowledge on the part of the legislator being approached that the man grasping his lapel had the power to help his political career or—by aiding his opponent, instead—to end it. The "Johnson Treatment"—his blend of threats and pleading, of curses and cajolery—became a staple of the national political folklore. But these picturesque elements of the Johnson Treatment were only tassels on the bludgeon of power.

Tales of the Tyrant

MARK BOWDEN ‖ 2002

*For months after this cover story was assigned, it was affectionately re-
ferred to around the offices of* The Atlantic *as "The Sex Life of Saddam
Hussein." But that moniker belied the project's serious objective, which
was to provide readers not just with a detailed picture of Saddam's daily
life, from the moment he woke up in the morning till the moment he
went to bed at night, but also with a plumb line into the depths of
his psyche. As a high-profile player on the world stage for many years,
Saddam had inspired innumerable articles and books—the emphasis
almost always on his tribal past, his opulent lifestyle, and his murderous
regime—but rarely had the Iraqi dictator been written about on this
level of intimacy. For this ambitious task, the magazine's editors turned
to Mark Bowden (1951–   ), the author of the international bestseller*
Black Hawk Down *(1999) and a former reporter for the* Philadelphia
Inquirer *with a talent for the narrative-driven profile. Unable to gain
an audience with Saddam himself (his request, sent through the Iraqi
consulate in New York, was ignored), Bowden tracked down and interviewed Iraqi exiles, foes and former allies of Saddam alike, in cities as far
flung as Rome and Detroit. This intensive reporting informs "Tales of the
Tyrant," an article that, in its steady accretion of personal, often mundane details ("He enjoys movies, particularly those involving intrigue,
assassination, and conspiracy—*The Day of the Jackal, The Conversation, Enemy of the State*"), is at once demonizing and surprisingly hu-
manizing. In Bowden's impressionistic portrait, Saddam is not, as he is
often depicted, a cartoon monster but a deformed man—hopelessly cor-
rupted by his own vainglory and pathetically constrained by his own
power. "One might think the most powerful man has the most choices,
but in reality he has the fewest," writes Bowden, who shortly after the
publication of this article became an* Atlantic *national correspondent.
"Too much depends on his every move.... Power gradually shuts the
tyrant off from the world."*

The tyrant must steal sleep. He must vary the locations and times. He
never sleeps in his palaces. He moves from secret bed to secret bed. Sleep
and a fixed routine are among the few luxuries denied him. It is too dangerous to be predictable, and whenever he shuts his eyes, the nation drifts.

His iron grip slackens. Plots congeal in the shadows. For those hours he must trust someone, and nothing is more dangerous to the tyrant than trust.

Saddam Hussein, the Anointed One, Glorious Leader, Direct Descendant of the Prophet, President of Iraq, Chairman of its Revolutionary Command Council, field marshal of its armies, doctor of its laws, and Great Uncle to all its peoples, rises at about three in the morning. He sleeps only four or five hours a night. When he rises, he swims. All his palaces and homes have pools. Water is a symbol of wealth and power in a desert country like Iraq, and Saddam splashes it everywhere—fountains and pools, indoor streams and waterfalls. It is a theme in all his buildings. His pools are tended scrupulously and tested hourly, more to keep the temperature and the chlorine and pH levels comfortable than to detect some poison that might attack him through his pores, eyes, mouth, nose, ears, penis, or anus—although that worry is always there too.

He has a bad back, a slipped disk, and swimming helps. It also keeps him trim and fit. This satisfies his vanity, which is epic, but fitness is critical for other reasons. He is now sixty-five, an old man, but because his power is grounded in fear, not affection, he cannot be seen to age. The tyrant cannot afford to become stooped, frail, and gray. Weakness invites challenge, coup d'état. One can imagine Saddam urging himself through a fixed number of laps each morning, pushing to exceed the number he swam the previous year, as if time could be undone by effort and will. Death is an enemy he cannot defeat—only, perhaps, delay. So he works. He also dissembles. He dyes his gray hair black and avoids using his reading glasses in public. When he is to give a speech, his aides print it out in huge letters, just a few lines per page. Because his back problem forces him to walk with a slight limp, he avoids being seen or filmed walking more than a few steps.

He is long-limbed, with big, strong hands. In Iraq the size of a man still matters, and Saddam is impressive. At six feet two he towers over his shorter, plumper aides. He lacks natural grace but has acquired a certain elegance of manner, the way a country boy learns to match the right tie with the right suit. His weight fluctuates between about 210 and 220 pounds, but in his custom-tailored suits the girth isn't always easy to see. His paunch shows when he takes off his suit coat. Those who watch him carefully know he has a tendency to lose weight in times of crisis and to gain it rapidly when things are going well.

Fresh food is flown in for him twice a week—lobster, shrimp, and fish, lots of lean meat, plenty of dairy products. The shipments are sent first to his nuclear scientists, who x-ray them and test them for radiation and poison. The food is then prepared for him by European-trained chefs, who work under the supervision of al Himaya, Saddam's personal bodyguards. Each of his more than twenty palaces is fully staffed, and three meals a day are cooked for him at every one; security demands that palaces from which he is absent perform an elaborate pantomime each day, as if he were in residence. Saddam tries to regulate his diet, allotting servings and portions the way he counts out the laps in his pools. For a big man he usually eats little, picking at his meals, often leaving half the food on his plate. Sometimes he eats dinner at restaurants in Baghdad, and when he does, his security staff invades the kitchen, demanding that the pots and pans, dishware, and utensils be well scrubbed, but otherwise interfering little. Saddam appreciates the culinary arts. He prefers fish to meat, and eats a lot of fresh fruits and vegetables. He likes wine with his meals, though he is hardly an oenophile; his wine of choice is Mateus rosé. But even though he indulges only in moderation, he is careful not to let anyone outside his most trusted circle of family and aides see him drinking. Alcohol is forbidden by Islam, and in public Saddam is a dutiful son of the faith.

He has a tattoo on his right hand, three dark-blue dots in a line near the wrist. These are given to village children when they are only five or six years old, a sign of their rural, tribal roots. Girls are often marked on their chins, forehead, or cheeks (as was Saddam's mother). For those who, like Saddam, move to the cities and come up in life, the tattoos are a sign of humble origin, and some later have them removed, or fade them with bleach until they almost disappear. Saddam's have faded, but apparently just from age; although he claims descent from the prophet Muhammad, he has never disguised his humble birth.

The President-for-life spends long hours every day in his office—whichever office he and his security minders select. He meets with his ministers and generals, solicits their opinions, and keeps his own counsel. He steals short naps during the day. He will abruptly leave a meeting, shut himself off in a side room, and return refreshed a half hour later. Those who meet with the President have no such luxury. They must stay awake and alert at all times. In 1986, during the Iran-Iraq war, Saddam caught Lieutenant General Aladin al-Janabi dozing during a meeting. He stripped the general of his rank and threw him out of the army. It was years before al-Janabi was able to win back his position and favor.

Saddam's desk is always immaculate. Reports from his various department heads are stacked neatly, each a detailed accounting of recent accomplishments and spending topped by an executive summary. Usually he reads only the summaries, but he selects some reports for closer examination. No one knows which will be chosen for scrutiny. If the details of the full report tell a story different from the summary, or if Saddam is confused, he will summon the department head. At these meetings Saddam is always polite and calm. He rarely raises his voice. He enjoys showing off a mastery of every aspect of his realm, from crop rotation to nuclear fission. But these meetings can be terrifying when he uses them to cajole, upbraid, or interrogate his subordinates. Often he arranges a surprise visit to some lower-level office or laboratory or factory—although, given the security preparations necessary, word of his visits outraces his arrival. Much of what he sees from his offices and on his "surprise" inspections is doctored and full of lies. Saddam has been fed unrealistic information for so long that his expectations are now also uniformly unrealistic. His bureaucrats scheme mightily to maintain the illusions. So Saddam usually sees only what those around him want him to see, which is, by definition, what he wants to see. A stupid man in this position would believe he had created a perfect world. But Saddam is not stupid. He knows he is being deceived, and he complains about it.

He reads voraciously—on subjects from physics to romance—and has broad interests. He has a particular passion for Arabic history and military history. He likes books about great men, and he admires Winston Churchill, whose famous political career is matched by his prodigious literary output. Saddam has literary aspirations himself. He employs ghostwriters to keep up a ceaseless flow of speeches, articles, and books of history and philosophy; his oeuvre includes fiction as well. In recent years he appears to have written and published two romantic fables, *Zabibah and the King* and *The Fortified Castle*; a third, as-yet-untitled work of fiction is due out soon. Before publishing the books Saddam distributes them quietly to professional writers in Iraq for comments and suggestions. No one dares to be candid—the writing is said to be woefully amateurish, marred by a stern pedantic strain—but everyone tries to be helpful, sending him gentle suggestions for minor improvements. The first two novels were published under a rough Arabic equivalent of "Anonymous" that translates as "Written by He Who Wrote It," but the new book may bear Saddam's name.

Saddam likes to watch TV, monitoring the Iraqi stations he controls and also CNN, Sky, al Jazeera, and the BBC. He enjoys movies, particularly those involving intrigue, assassination, and conspiracy—*The Day of the Jackal, The Conversation, Enemy of the State*. Because he has not traveled extensively, such movies inform his ideas about the world and feed his inclination to believe broad conspiracy theories. To him the world is a puzzle that only fools accept at face value. He also appreciates movies with more literary themes. Two of his favorites are the *Godfather* series and *The Old Man and the Sea.*

Saddam has been advised by his doctors to walk at least two hours a day. He rarely manages that much time, but he breaks up his days with strolls. He used to take these walks in public, swooping down with his entourage on neighborhoods in Baghdad, his bodyguards clearing sidewalks and streets as the tyrant passed. Anyone who approached him unsolicited was beaten nearly to death. But now it is too dangerous to walk in public— and the limp must not be seen. So Saddam makes no more unscripted public appearances. He limps freely behind the high walls and patrolled fences of his vast estates. Often he walks with a gun, hunting deer or rabbit in his private preserves. He is an excellent shot.

Saddam has been married for nearly forty years. His wife, Sajida, is his first cousin on his mother's side and the daughter of Khairallah Tulfah, Saddam's uncle and first political mentor. Sajida has borne him two sons and three daughters, and remains loyal to him, but he has long had relationships with other women. Stories circulate about his nightly selecting young virgins for his bed, like the Sultan Shahryar in *The Thousand and One Nights,* about his having fathered a child with a longtime mistress, and even about his having killed one young woman after a kinky tryst. It is hard to sort the truth from the lies. So many people, in and out of Iraq, hate Saddam that any disgraceful or embarrassing rumor is likely to be embraced, believed, repeated, and written down in the Western press as truth. Those who know him best scoff at the wildest of these tales.

Saddam is a loner by nature, and power increases isolation. A young man without power or money is completely free. He has nothing, but he also has everything. He can travel, he can drift. He can make new acquaintances every day, and try to soak up the infinite variety of life. He can seduce and be seduced, start an enterprise and abandon it, join an army or flee a nation, fight to preserve an existing system or plot a revolution. He can reinvent himself daily, according to the discoveries he makes about the world and himself. But if he prospers through the choices he makes, if he acquires a wife, children, wealth, land, and power, his options gradually and inevitably diminish. Responsibility and commitment limit his moves. One might think that the most powerful man has the most choices, but in reality he has the fewest. Too much depends on his every move. The tyrant's choices are the narrowest of all. His life—the nation!—hangs in the balance. He can no longer drift or explore, join or flee. He cannot reinvent himself, because so many others depend on him—and he, in turn, must depend on so many others. He stops learning, because he is walled in by fortresses and palaces, by generals and ministers who rarely dare to tell him what he doesn't wish to hear. Power gradually shuts the tyrant off from the world. Everything comes to him second or third hand. He is deceived daily. He becomes ignorant of his land, his people, even his own family. He exists, finally, only to preserve his wealth and power, to build his legacy. Survival becomes his one overriding passion. So he regulates his diet, tests his food for poison, exercises behind well-patrolled walls, trusts no one, and tries to control everything.

SADDAM'S RISE THROUGH THE RANKS may have been slow and deceitful, but when he moved to seize power, he did so very openly. He had been serving as vice-chairman of the Revolutionary Command Council, and as Vice President of Iraq, and he planned to step formally into the top positions. Some of the party leadership, including men who had been close to Saddam for years, had other ideas. Rather than just hand him the reins, they had begun advocating a party election. So Saddam took action. He staged his ascendancy like theater.

On July 18, 1979, he invited all the members of the Revolutionary Command Council and hundreds of other party leaders to a conference hall in Baghdad. He had a video camera running in the back of the hall to record the event for posterity. Wearing his military uniform, he walked slowly to the lectern and stood behind two microphones, gesturing with a big cigar. His body and broad face seemed weighted down with sadness. There had been a betrayal, he said. A Syrian plot. There were traitors among them. Then Saddam took a seat, and Muhyi Abd al-Hussein Mashhadi, the secretary-general of the Command Council, appeared from behind a curtain to confess his own involvement in the putsch. He had been secretly arrested and tortured days before; now he spilled out dates, times, and places where the plotters had met. Then he started naming names. As he fingered members of the audience one by one, armed guards grabbed the accused and escorted them from the hall. When one man shouted that he was innocent, Saddam shouted back, "*Itla! Itla!*"—"Get out! Get out!" (Weeks later, after secret trials, Saddam had the mouths of the accused taped shut so that they could utter no troublesome last words before their firing squads.) When all of the sixty "traitors" had been removed, Saddam again took the podium and wiped tears from his eyes as he repeated the names of those who had betrayed him. Some in the audience, too, were crying— perhaps out of fear. This chilling performance had the desired effect.

Everyone in the hall now understood exactly how things would work in Iraq from that day forward. The audience rose and began clapping, first in small groups and finally as one. The session ended with cheers and laughter. The remaining "leaders"—about 300 in all—left the hall shaken, grateful to have avoided the fate of their colleagues, and certain that one man now controlled the destiny of their entire nation. Videotapes of the purge were circulated throughout the country.

It was what the world would come to see as classic Saddam. He tends to commit his crimes in public, cloaking them in patriotism and in effect turning his witnesses into accomplices. The purge that day reportedly resulted in the executions of a third of the Command Council. (Mashhadi's performance didn't spare him; he, too, was executed.) During the next few weeks scores of other "traitors" were shot, including government officials, military officers, and people turned in by ordinary citizens who responded to a hotline phone number broadcast on Iraqi TV. Some Council members say that Saddam ordered members of the party's inner circle to participate in this bloodbath.

While he served as vice-chairman, from 1968 to 1979, the party's goals had seemed to be Saddam's own. That was a relatively good period for Iraq, thanks to Saddam's blunt effectiveness as an administrator. He orchestrated a draconian nationwide literacy project. Reading programs were set up in every city and village, and failure to attend was punishable by three years in jail. Men, women, and children attended these compulsory classes, and hundreds of thousands of illiterate Iraqis learned to read. UNESCO gave Saddam an award. There were also ambitious drives to build schools, roads, public housing, and hospitals. Iraq created one of the best public-health systems in the Middle East. There was admiration in the West during those years, for Saddam's accomplishments if not for his methods. After the Islamic fundamentalist revolution in Iran, and the seizure of the U.S. embassy in Tehran in 1979, Saddam seemed to be the best hope for secular modernization in the region.

Today all these programs are a distant memory. Within two years of his seizing full power, Saddam's ambitions turned to conquest, and his defeats have ruined the nation. His old party allies in exile now see his support for the social-welfare programs as an elaborate deception. The broad ambitions for the Iraqi people were the party's, they say. As long as he needed the party, Saddam made its programs his own. But his single, overriding goal throughout was to establish his own rule.

"In the beginning the Baath Party was made up of the intellectual elite of our generation," says Hamed al-Jubouri, a former Command Council member who now lives in London. "There were many professors, physicians, economists, and historians—really the nation's elite. Saddam was charming and impressive. He appeared to be totally different from what we learned he was afterward. He took all of us in. We supported him because he seemed uniquely capable of controlling a difficult country like Iraq, a difficult people like our people. We wondered about him. How could such a young man, born in the countryside north of Baghdad, become such a capable leader? He seemed both intellectual and practical. But he was hiding his real self. For years he did this, building his power quietly, charming everyone, hiding his true instincts. He has a great ability to hide his intentions; it may be his greatest skill. I remember his son Uday said one time, 'My father's right shirt pocket doesn't know what is in his left shirt pocket.'"

What does Saddam want? By all accounts, he is not interested in money. This is not the case with other members of his family. His wife, Sajida, is known to have gone on million-dollar shopping sprees in New York and London, back in the days of Saddam's good relations with the West. Uday drives expensive cars and wears custom-tailored suits of his own design. Saddam himself isn't a hedonist; he lives a well-regulated, somewhat abstemious existence. He seems far more interested in fame than in money, desiring above all to be admired, remembered, and revered. A nineteen-volume official biography is mandatory reading for Iraqi government officials, and Saddam has also commissioned a six-hour film about his life, called *The Long Days*, which was edited by Terence Young, best known for directing three James Bond films. Saddam told his official biographer that he isn't interested in what people think of him today, only in what they will think of him in five hundred years. The root of Saddam's bloody, single-minded pursuit of power appears to be simple vanity.

But what extremes of vanity compel a man to jail or execute all who criticize or oppose him? To erect giant statues of himself to adorn the public spaces of his country? To commission romantic portraits, some of them twenty feet high, portraying the nation's Great Uncle as a desert horseman, a wheat-cutting peasant, or a construction worker carrying bags of cement? To have the nation's television, radio, film, and print devoted to celebrating his every word and deed? Can ego alone explain such displays? Might it be the opposite? What colossal insecurity and self-loathing would demand such compensation?

The sheer scale of the tyrant's deeds mocks psychoanalysis. What begins with ego and ambition becomes a political movement. Saddam embodies first the party and then the nation. Others conspire in this process in order to further their own ambitions, selfless as well as selfish. Then the tyrant turns on them. His cult of self becomes more than a political strategy. Repetition of his image in heroic or paternal poses, repetition of his name, his slogans, his virtues, and his accomplishments, seeks to make his power seem inevitable, unchallengeable. Finally he is praised not out of affection or admiration but out of obligation. One *must* praise him.

EACH TIME SADDAM HAS ESCAPED DEATH—when he survived, with a minor wound to his leg, a failed attempt in 1959 to assassinate Iraqi President Abd al-Karim Qasim; when he avoided the ultimate punishment in 1964 for his part in a failed Baath Party uprising; when he survived being trapped behind Iranian lines in the Iran-Iraq war; when he survived attempted coups d'état; when he survived America's smart-bombing campaign against Baghdad, in 1991; when he survived the nationwide revolt after the Gulf War—it has strengthened his conviction that his path is divinely inspired and that greatness is his destiny. Because his world view is essentially tribal and patriarchal, destiny means blood. So he has ordered genealogists to construct a plausible family tree linking him to Fatima, the daughter of the prophet Muhammad. Saddam sees the prophet less as the bearer of divine revelation than as a political precursor—a great leader who unified the Arab peoples and inspired a flowering of Arab power and culture. The concocted link of bloodlines to Muhammad is symbolized by a 600-page hand-lettered copy of the Koran that was written with Saddam's own blood, which he donated a pint at a time over three years. It is now on display in a Baghdad museum.

If Saddam has a religion, it is a belief in the superiority of Arab history and culture, a tradition that he is convinced will rise up again and rattle the world. His imperial view of the grandeur that was Arabia is romantic, replete with fanciful visions of great palaces and wise and powerful sultans and caliphs. His notion of history has nothing to do with progress, with the advance of knowledge, with the evolution of individual rights and liberties, with any of the things that matter most to Western civilization. It has to do simply with power. To Saddam, the present global domination by the West, particularly the United States, is just a phase. America is infidel and inferior. It lacks the rich ancient heritage of Iraq and other Arab states. Its place at the summit of the world powers is just a historical quirk, an aberration, a consequence of its having acquired technological advantages. It cannot endure.

In a speech this past January 17, the eleventh anniversary of the start of the Gulf War, Saddam explained, "The Americans have not yet established a civilization, in the deep and comprehensive sense we give to civilization. What they have established is a metropolis of force. . . . Some people, perhaps including Arabs and plenty of Muslims and more than these in the wide world . . . considered the ascent of the U.S. to the summit as the last scene in the world picture, after which there will be no more summits and no one will try to ascend and sit comfortably there. They considered it the end of the world as they hoped for, or as their scared souls suggested it to them."

Arabia, which Saddam sees as the wellspring of civilization, will one day own that summit again. When that day comes, whether in his lifetime or a century or even five centuries hence, his name will rank with those of the great men in history. Saddam sees himself as an established member of the pantheon of great men—conquerors, prophets, kings and presidents, scholars, poets, scientists. It doesn't matter if he understands their contributions and ideas. It matters only that they are the ones history has remembered and honored for their accomplishments.

American Everyman

WALTER KIRN || 2004

With the possible exception of J. P. Morgan, Warren Buffett is the most successful investor in United States history. Through his company, Berkshire Hathaway, Buffett has turned tens of thousands of working stiffs into multimillionaires and himself into the second-wealthiest man in the world (after Bill Gates), with a net worth of $52 billion and counting. But as the critic and novelist Walter Kirn (1962–   ) points out in this fresh and distinctively angled reappreciation of the so-called Oracle of Omaha, Buffett ought to be prized as a cultural icon as much as a financial one. For Kirn, the author of Up in the Air *(2001) and other acclaimed, offbeat novels, Buffett's second great talent, rarely if ever commented on despite all the media attention, is verbal. His speeches and public utterances, a mix of one-liners, unconventional folk wisdom, and plainspoken truths, hark back to Mark Twain, Will Rogers, and other legendary American communicators—many of them, like Buffett, sons of the heartland. In "American Everyman," Kirn, who grew up in rural Minnesota, not far geographically or psychically from Berkshire's Nebraska headquarters, explores Buffett's mastery of the American idiom via a close reading of the financier's literary oeuvre—as represented by the much-anticipated letters to shareholders Buffett contributes to the company's annual reports. Poring over twenty years' worth of the wit and wisdom of Warren Buffett with the punctiliousness of a Dead Sea Scroll scholar, Kirn discovers, barely concealed behind an opening scrim of formulaic businessman's prose, "a conscious, sophisticated performer, the inventor and caretaker of a rare persona that has no equivalent in American business."*

On a Sunday afternoon in May of last year Warren Buffett, America's second richest man and, some feel, the greatest investor in its history, was meeting the press in an Omaha hotel when a dark-suited man—a bodyguard, apparently—hustled up onto the platform where Buffett was seated and whispered into his ear. The multibillionaire listened without expression while the man in the seat beside him, Charlie Munger, the vice-chairman of their company, Berkshire Hathaway, stared ahead through a pair of horn-rimmed glasses whose lenses weren't merely thick but virtually spherical, like a pair of crystal Ping-Pong balls. Buffett and Munger are quite a duo, with the conversational timing and style of a vaudeville comedy team—Buffett dry and jovial and extroverted, and Munger even drier but blunt and mordant. For an hour or so, until this interruption, the two—both native Nebraskans—had been answering questions on everything from corporate-governance scandals to the likelihood that a major act of terrorism would bankrupt the insurance industry. It's their gift to be able to talk about such subjects so plainly, incisively, and honestly that the reporters had been laughing the whole time.

Now, though, it seemed that something dire was happening. The bodyguard looked concerned—a little panicky, even. When the guard left the platform, Buffett looked up and spoke. The hotel, he informed us, was advising everyone to take shelter immediately in a windowless safe room located in the center of the building: tornadoes had been sighted in western Omaha, and radar indicated that they were headed this way.

For his part, however, he intended to keep on taking questions until no one had anything more to ask or the whole building blew away. He sipped from a can of Cherry Coke and exchanged a look with his straight man Munger, whose myopic self-containment seemed impregnable. Moments later sirens started to wail. A few reporters scuttled out, but most of them took up Buffett's stoic challenge to ignore the warnings and carry on.

The reporters who had done their research knew that this was how Buffett always operates—not only in the face of violent winds but in the face of turbulent markets. He sits tight. He keeps his head while others are losing theirs, and then he moves in, if he wishes, and buys those heads (meaning large blocks of stock or entire companies) at an advantageous price. And then he keeps them. He rolls them into Berkshire Hathaway's almost comically diverse portfolio (the company's wholly owned properties, to list just a few, include a chocolate-candy retailer, an underwear manufacturer, a furniture store, a chain of ice-cream restaurants, a maker of cowboy boots, and an insurance firm that insures insurance firms) and watches his wealth, and that of his shareholders, grow and grow. He watches it grow while the fortunes of other investors—more-excitable types with more-fashionable holdings, which they tend to think about selling the moment they buy them—rise and fall and gyrate and go sideways and eventually, in all too many cases, are ground down between the twin millstones of fear and greed.

The weekend of that stormy Sunday was dedicated to celebrating Buffett's success, or what the business writer Robert Hagstrom has called "the Warren Buffett way"—as though there were some sort of wizardry behind what may be the most thoroughly explained investment method in recent history. Every May, Buffett, Munger, and attending shareholders, whom the two like to refer to as "our partners," gather for Berkshire Hathaway's annual meeting: two hectic days of capitalist frolicking, featuring exhibition Scrabble games, hot-dog feeds, and shareholders-only sales at Borsheim's Jewelers and the Nebraska Furniture Mart, two of the company's retail properties. Though Buffett's personal thrift is the stuff of legend (he still lives in the fairly modest house that he bought in the 1950s), he isn't shy about encouraging shareholders to break out their credit cards for diamonds and carpets. At the end of the weekend he totals the receipts and makes the figures public.

The annual meeting's main event, which took place on a Saturday in 2003, is a freewheeling question-and-answer session with Buffett and Munger, held in a cavernous downtown sports arena. Among the thousands of adoring fans are scores of millionaires who owe their net worth to Berkshire's lofty stock price, which hit a three-year low on March 10, 2000, on the same day the NASDAQ reached its all-time high, and then reversed course while the NASDAQ sank and sank. In the 1990s highfliers derided Buffett for sitting out the run-up in high-tech and dot-com stocks (he once famously said that he simply "didn't understand" them), but this contrarian feat provided sweet vindication.

Buffett is a conscious, sophisticated performer, the inventor and caretaker of a rare persona that has no equivalent in American business. Not since Samuel Goldwyn, perhaps, has a tycoon functioned in the culture as both a first-class entertainer and the embodiment of his industry. Buffett's Will Rogers folksiness and Mark Twain wit ("Never ask the barber if you need a haircut"; "Price is what you give; value is what you get"; "Predicting rain doesn't count; building arks does") aren't merely colorful secondary traits but stylized expressions of his very being. They represent more than that, in fact. Buffett's attitudes and mannerisms now stand for American capitalism itself—or at least for its more positive aspects. He is what's good about the free market, in human form—akin to what Joe DiMaggio was to baseball. Bill Gates may be richer, and Donald Trump (the anti-Buffett) flashier, but compared with Buffett they're mere character actors. The role of the straight-shooting leading man, trusted by all, belongs to Buffett alone.

And yet, the popular business media have for some time now been missing the big story when it comes to the country's second richest man. Buffett's fortune—and the oft-told tale of how he made it and continues to add to it—has become the least interesting thing about him. It's Buffett the symbol that matters now, Buffett the folk hero, Buffett the communicator. As a successful investor, he merely moved markets; but as the charismatic, reassuring, quotable prototype of the honest capitalist (a sort of J. P. Morgan with a moral sense), he's capable of influencing elections, galvanizing rock-concert-size crowds, and in general defining how we Americans feel about the system that underlies our wealth.

THERE IS A LINE of self-made, iconoclastic, pragmatic, larger-than-life American Everymen that begins in the popular mind with Benjamin Franklin, and runs through Mark Twain, Will Rogers, and Harry Truman, but also shows up in such far-flung characters as Walt Whitman, Henry Ford, and Ernest Hemingway. They are the fresh-air paragons of democratic self-invention—the anti-phonies who tell it like it is and, with their grassroots words and ways, rebuke the pretentious sophistication of Europeanized elites. Even when they hold liberal political views, they sometimes come off as reactionary cornballs, because of the way they extend our native mythology of salty, slightly cranky individualism.

Warren Buffett, as much as anyone else alive right now, belongs to this indispensable tradition of truth-telling Americans so square and forthright that they end up seeming subversive. His "true" identity—the stuff about him that can be discovered by interviewing his family and associates or digging through his garbage—doesn't really matter, finally, compared with the reputation he has created, and which the public has chosen to embrace, even idolize. This outward self is a literary artifact. It's a *book*, not a life. It cries out to be *read*.

The best way to start reading Warren Buffett is to gather up ten or twenty years' worth of his annual letters to Berkshire Hathaway shareholders (these "Chairman's letters" make up the bulk of the company's annual reports, and copies are available on the Internet), which may be the only documents of their type whose prose is worth poring over even for those who have no stake in the appended balance sheets. Buffett's choice of such a dreary medium as the primary showcase for his thoughts has always sent a message in itself. While the Trumps and Iacoccas of the world prefer to present themselves in garish books with jackets featuring large color photos of their own faces, Buffett, the legendary midwestern cheapskate with a knack for discovering hidden value in cookware clubs (The Pampered Chef) and encyclopedia publishers (World Book), has reclaimed a form of junk mail for his collected works.

"Fear is the foe of the faddist," he wrote in the 1994 report, "but the friend of the fundamentalist." This is the soul of the Buffett program: Stay cool. Exploit the follies of the crowd. It's the oldest investment advice there is, but Buffett has personalized it over the years by showing a certain contempt for the financial markets themselves, which he likes to portray as dens of waste and vanity rather than basically efficient systems for allotting capital. It's one of the reasons he's adored: he treats his shareholders as fellow members of a morally solid, wised-up in crowd surrounded by ethically wayward crazy people. It's us against them, the sane versus the mad, the prudent versus the greedy, and it's our right, perhaps even our duty, to grab the money from their trembling, sweaty hands.

To be both an overlord and an underdog, an opportunist and a populist, is quite a trick, but Buffett manages to pull it off by implying that contemporary capitalism has fallen into a self-indulgent decadence that requires a puritan resistance movement led by the likes of Berkshire and its subsidiaries, whose CEOs he loves to praise as exemplars of uncorrupted, old-school enterprise. Bracing stories of Buffett's clear-eyed managers stand in contrast to his chronic warnings about the dangerous softheadedness of almost everyone else. "Nothing sedates rationality like large doses of effortless money," he observed in the 2000 report, in an essay on the difference between investment and speculation. With the S&P 500 down almost 10 percent for the year, after a prolonged bull run that Buffett had been mocked for missing out on, and with Berkshire showing a 6.5 percent gain, the time had come for the old man to gloat. His 1999 letter had predicted an imminent comeuppance for the markets, and payback had arrived as if on schedule. He shamed everyone involved, but especially the promoters of hyped-up tech stocks, whom he accused first of running a con game and then of suffering from a disease. "It was as if some virus, racing wildly among investment professionals as well as amateurs, induced hallucinations," he wrote.

Mental illness is one of Buffett's pet metaphors. (Indeed, his fixation on it makes one wonder if losing his own mind is his deepest fear.) Again and again in his letters he compares—by implication, at least—his own stability with the manic-depression displayed by Wall Street, which Buffett and his mentor Benjamin Graham, of Columbia University—the author of *The Intelligent Investor*, the classic primer on value-based stock picking—have famously personified as the flighty "Mr. Market." According to this conceit, investing success is a matter not of intelligence, social position, or inside information but of simple common sense and psychological self-control—an encouraging message for the average person, and perhaps the best reason for Buffett's popularity with the aspiring middle class. Suppressing emotion is the key to wealth, he preaches; the dull and steadfast will inherit the earth from the fancy and neurotic.

Not many people have Bill Gates's IQ, Donald Trump's brazenness, or Tom Cruise's looks, but almost anyone—with a bit of discipline—can have Warren Buffett's temperament. That, at least, is the promise he holds out: unlike most tycoons, he can be imitated, because he's just like the rest of us, only more so.

BEHIND THE SCENES

Chiefly About War Matters
by a Peaceable Man

NATHANIEL HAWTHORNE || 1862

From the first cannon fire, Nathaniel Hawthorne (1804–1864) was wracked by ambivalence about the Civil War. As a Northerner, Massachusetts born and bred, Hawthorne was naturally drawn to the Union cause, but he expressed grave doubts as to what, precisely, the war was about: Abolition? Preservation of the Union? Sovereignty of federal over states' rights? "We seem to have little, or, at least, a very misty idea of what we are fighting for," he complained in a 1861 letter to an English correspondent. In March 1862, Hawthorne was presented with an unusual opportunity to clear up his confusion. Invited by a U.S. naval official and old Bowdoin College friend to observe the war firsthand, Hawthorne, despite developing health problems, set out on a four-hundred-mile journey from his home in Concord, Massachusetts, to heavily fortified Washington, D.C.

Four months later, The Atlantic *published a thirteen-thousand-word chronicle of his trip that bears many of the earmarks of classic nineteenth-century narrative nonfiction—but with a late-twentieth-century twist. Like Charles Dickens's* American Notes *(1842) and Mark Twain's* The Innocents Abroad *(1869), "Chiefly About War Matters by a Peaceable Man" is a discursive, self-referential account of a writer's journey into alien terrain, that, with novelistic verisimilitude, conveys the sights, sounds, and smells of his picaresque adventures (including an early look at the painter Emanuel Leutze's famous mural "Westward the Course of Empire Takes Its Way," which still graces the U.S. Capitol). "Chiefly About War Matters" also features a pair of noteworthy tics: a frequently bilious tone and a satirical device intended to make that tone both more barbed and more palatable. Certain that* The Atlantic's *readers would not tolerate his most acid observations, Hawthorne preemptively excised several paragraphs from his original manuscript but marked the deletions with a series of footnotes written in the voice of a meddling, censorious editor. With the help of this innovative call and response (which predates the footnote pyrotechnics of David Foster Wallace by 130 years), the famously dyspeptic Hawthorne was able to lampoon not only slaveholding Southerners, bloodthirsty generals, and colorless Washingtonians, but* The Atlantic *itself, which to his mind was becoming politically predictable and parochial.*

He was also able to poke fun at the magazine's second editor-in-chief, James T. Fields, a close friend and the copublisher of his most distinguished novels, The Scarlet Letter *(1850) and* The House of the Seven Gables *(1851). When Hawthorne's article arrived at the magazine's offices, despite its largely admiring treatment of Lincoln, Fields had strenuously objected to a section that depicted the president as ungainly and uncouth. The writer agreed to remove the offending pages (which have been reinstated below) but insisted on inserting a prickly textual aside. Hawthorne would go to his grave only two years later, still harboring questions about the Civil War. But as far as the Lincoln episode was concerned, he would always have the last word. "What a terrible thing it is," he wrote in a letter to Fields, "to try to let off a little truth into this miserable humbug of a world!"*

There is no remoteness of life and thought, no hermetically sealed seclusion, except, possibly, that of the grave, into which the disturbing influences of this war do not penetrate. Of course, the general heart-quake of the country long ago knocked at my cottage-door, and compelled me, reluctantly, to suspend the contemplation of certain fantasies, to which, according to my harmless custom, I was endeavoring to give a sufficiently life-like aspect to admit of their figuring in a romance. As I make no pretensions to state-craft or soldiership, and could promote the common weal neither by valor nor counsel, it seemed, at first, a pity that I should be debarred from such unsubstantial business as I had contrived for myself, since nothing more genuine was to be substituted for it. But I magnanimously considered that there is a kind of treason in insulating one's self from the universal fear and sorrow, and thinking one's idle thought in the dread time of civil war; and could a man be so cold and hard-hearted, he would better deserve to be sent to Fort Warren than many who have found their way thither on the score of violent, but misdirected sympathies. I remembered the touching rebuke administered by King Charles to that rural squire the echo of whose hunting-horn came to the poor monarch's ear on the morning before a battle, where the sovereignty and constitution of England were set to be at stake. So I gave myself up to reading newspapers and listening to the click of the telegraph, like other people; until, after a great many months of such pastime, it grew so abominably irksome that I determined to look a little more closely at matters with my own eyes.

Accordingly we set out—a friend and myself—towards Washington, while it was still the long, dreary January of our Northern year, though March in name; nor were we unwilling to clip a little margin off the five months' winter, during which there is nothing genial in New England save the fireside. It was a clear, frosty morning, when we started. The sun shone brightly on snow-covered hills in the neighborhood of Boston, and burnished the surface of frozen ponds; and the wintry weather kept along with us while we trundled through Worcester and Springfield, and all those old, familiar towns, and through the village-cities of Connecticut. In New York the streets were afloat with liquid mud and slosh. Over New Jersey there was still a thin covering of snow, with the face of Nature visible through the rents in her white shroud, though with little or no symptom of reviving life. But when we reached Philadelphia, the air was mild and balmy; there was but a patch or two of dingy winter here and there, and the bare, brown fields about the city were ready to be green. We had met the Spring halfway, in her slow progress from the South; and if we kept onward at the same pace, and could get through the Rebel lines, we should soon come to fresh grass, fruit-blossoms, green peas, strawberries, and all such delights of early summer.

On our way, we heard many rumors of the war, but saw few signs of it. The people were staid and decorous, according to their ordinary fashion; and business seemed about as brisk as usual,—though, I suppose, it was considerably diverted from its customary channels into warlike ones. In the cities, especially in New York, there was a rather prominent display of military goods at the shop-windows,—such as swords with gilded scabbards and trappings, epaulets, carabines, revolvers, and sometimes a great iron cannon at the edge of the pavement, as if Mars had dropped one of his pocket pistols there, while hurrying to the field. As railway companions, we had now and then a volunteer in his French-gray greatcoat, returning from furlough, or a new-made officer in his new-made uniform, which was perhaps all of the military character that he had about him,— but proud of his eagle buttons, and likely enough to do them honor before the gilt should be wholly dimmed. The country, in short, so far as bustle and movement went, was more quiet than in ordinary times, because so large a proportion of its restless elements had been drawn towards the seat of conflict. But the air was full of a vague disturbance. To me, at least, it seemed so, emerging from such a solitude as has been hinted at, and the more impressible by rumors and indefinable presentiments, since I had not lived, like other men, in an atmosphere of continual talk about the war. A battle was momentarily expected on the Potomac; for, though our army was still on the hither side of the river, all of us were looking towards the mysterious and terrible Manassas, with the idea that somewhere in its neighborhood lay a ghastly battlefield, yet to be fought, but foredoomed of old to be bloodier than the one where we had reaped such shame. Of all haunted places, methinks such a destined field should be thickest thronged with ugly phantoms, ominous of mischief through ages beforehand.

Beyond Philadelphia there was a much greater abundance of military people. Between Baltimore and Washington a guard seemed to hold every station along the railroad; and frequently, on the hillsides, we saw a collection of weather-beaten tents, the peaks of which, blackened with smoke, indicated that they had been made comfortable by stove heat throughout the winter. At several commanding positions we saw fortifications, with the muzzles of cannon protruding from the ramparts, the slopes of which were made of the yellow earth of that region, and still unsodded; whereas, till these troublous times, there have been no forts but what were grass grown with the lapse of at least a lifetime of peace. Our stopping-places were thronged with soldiers, some of whom came through the cars, asking for newspapers that contained accounts of the battle between the Merrimack and Monitor, which had been fought the day before. A railway-train met us, conveying a regiment out of Washington to some unknown point; and reaching the capital, we filed out of the station between lines of soldiers, with shouldered muskets, putting us in mind of similar spectacles at the gates of European cities. It was not without sorrow that we saw the free circulation of the nation's life-blood (at the very heart, moreover) clogged with such strictures as these, which have caused chronic diseases in almost all countries save our own. Will the time ever come again, in America, when we may live half a score of years without once seeing the likeness of a soldier, except it be in the festal march of a company on its summer tour? Not in this generation, I fear, nor in the next, nor till the Millennium; and even that blessed epoch, as the prophecies seem to intimate, will advance to the sound of the trumpet.

One terrible idea occurs in reference to this matter. Even supposing the war should end to-morrow, and the army melt into the mass of the population within the year, what an incalculable preponderance will there be of military titles and pretensions for at least half a century to come! Every country-neighborhood will have its general or two, its three or four colonels, half a dozen majors, and captains without end,—besides non-commissioned officers and privates, more than the recruiting offices ever knew of,—all with their campaign stories, which will become the staple of fireside-talk forevermore. Military merit, or rather, since that is not so readily estimated, military notoriety, will be the measure of all claims to civil distinction. One bullet-headed general will succeed another in the Presidential chair; and veterans will hold the offices at home and abroad, and sit in Congress and the State legislatures, and fill all the avenues of public life. And yet I do not speak of this deprecatingly, since, very likely, it may substitute something more genuine, instead of the many shams on which men have heretofore founded their claims to public regard; but it behooves civilians to consider their wretched prospects in the future, and assume the military button before it is too late.

We were not in time to see Washington as a camp. On the very day of our arrival sixty thousand men had crossed the Potomac on their march towards Manassas; and almost with their first step into the Virginia mud, the phantasmagory of a countless host and impregnable ramparts, before which they had so long remained quiescent, dissolved quite away. It was as if General McClellan had thrust his sword into a gigantic enemy, and beholding him suddenly collapsed, had discovered to himself and the world that he had merely punctured an enormously swollen bladder. There are instances of a similar character in old romances, where great armies are long kept at bay by the arts of necromancers, who build airy towers and battlements, and muster warriors of terrible aspect, and thus feign a defense of seeming impregnability, until some bolder champion of the besiegers dashes forward to try an encounter with the foremost male and finds himself melt away in the death grapple. With such heroic adventures let the march upon Manassas be hereafter reckoned. The whole business, though connected with the destinies of a nation, takes inevitably a tinge of the ludicrous. The vast preparation of men and warlike material—the majestic patience and docility with which the people waited through those weary and dreary months,—the martial skill, courage, and caution with which our movement was ultimately made,—and, at last, the tremendous shock with which we were brought suddenly up against nothing at all! The Southerners show little sense of humor nowadays, but I think they must have meant to provoke a laugh at our expense, when they planted those Quaker guns. At all events, no other Rebel artillery has played upon us with such overwhelming effect.

The troops being gone, we had the better leisure and opportunity to look into other matters. It is natural enough to suppose that the center and heart of Washington is the Capitol; and certainly, in its outward aspect, the world has not many statelier or more beautiful edifices, nor any, I should suppose, more skillfully adapted to legislative purposes, and to all accompanying needs. But, etc., etc.*

We found one man, however, at the Capitol who was satisfactorily adequate to the business which brought him thither. In quest of him, we went through halls, galleries, and corridors, and ascended a noble staircase, balustraded with a dark and beautifully variegated marble from Tennessee, the richness of which is quite a sufficient cause for objecting to the secession of that State. At last we came to a barrier of pine boards, built right across the stairs. Knocking at a rough, temporary door, we thrust a card beneath; and in a minute or two it was opened by a person in his shirt-sleeves, a middle-aged figure, neither tall nor short, of Teutonic build and aspect, with an ample beard of ruddy tinge and chestnut hair. He looked at us, in the first place, with keen and somewhat guarded eyes, as if it were not his practice to vouchsafe any great warmth of greeting, except upon sure ground of observation. Soon, however, his look grew kindly and genial (not that it had ever been in the least degree repulsive, but only reserved), and Leutze allowed us to gaze at the cartoon of his great fresco, and talked about it unaffectedly, as only a man of true genius can speak of his own works. Meanwhile the noble design spoke for itself upon the wall. A sketch in color, which we saw afterwards, helped us to form some distant and flickering notion of what the picture will be, a few months hence, when these bare outlines, already so rich in thought and suggestiveness, shall glow with a fire of their own,—a fire which, I truly believe, will consume every other pictorial decoration of the Capitol, or, at least, will compel us to banish those stiff and respectable productions to some less conspicuous gallery. The work will be emphatically original and American, embracing the characteristics that neither art nor literature have yet dealt with, and producing new forms of artistic beauty from the natural features of the Rocky-Mountain region, which Leutze seems to have studied broadly and minutely. The garb of the hunters and wanderers of those deserts, too, under his free and natural management, is shown as the most picturesque of costumes. But it would be doing this admirable painter no kind office to overlay his picture with any more of my colorless and uncertain words; so I shall merely add that it looked full of energy, hope, progress, irrepressible movement onward, all represented in a momentary pause of triumph; and

---

* We omit several paragraphs here, in which the author speaks of some prominent Members of Congress with a freedom that seems to have been not unkindly meant, but might be liable to misconstruction. As he admits that he never listened to an important debate, we can hardly recognize his qualification to estimate these gentlemen, in their legislative and oratorical capacities.

it was most cheering to feel its good augury at this dismal time, when our country might seem to have arrived at such a deadly stand-still.

It was absolute comfort, indeed, to find Leutze so quietly busy at this great national work, which is destined to glow for centuries on the walls of the Capitol, if that edifice shall stand, or must share its fate, if treason shall succeed in subverting it with the Union which it represents. It was delightful to see him so calmly elaborating his design, while other men doubted and feared, or hoped treacherously, and whispered to one another that the nation would exist only a little longer, or that, if a remnant still held together, its center and seat of government would be far northward and westward of Washington. But the artist keeps right on, firm of heart and hand, drawing his outlines with an unwavering pencil, beautifying and idealizing our rude, material life, and thus manifesting that we have an indefeasible claim to a more enduring national existence. In honest truth, what with the hope-inspiring influence of the design, and what with Leutze's undisturbed evolvement of it, I was exceedingly encouraged, and allowed these cheerful auguries to weigh against a sinister omen that was pointed out to me in another part of the Capitol. The freestone walls of the central edifice are pervaded with great cracks, and threaten to come thundering down, under the immense weight of the iron dome,—an appropriate catastrophe enough, if it should occur on the day when we drop the Southern stars out of our flag.

Everybody seems to be at Washington, and yet there is a singular dearth of imperatively noticeable people there. I question whether there are half a dozen individuals, in all kinds of eminence, at whom a stranger, wearied with the contact of a hundred moderate celebrities, would turn round to snatch a second glance. Secretary [of State William] Seward, to be sure,—a pale, large-nosed, elderly man, of moderate stature, with a decided originality of gait and aspect, and a cigar in his mouth,—etc., etc.*

Of course, there was one other personage, in the class of statesman, whom I should have been truly mortified to leave Washington without seeing; since (temporarily, at least, and by force of circumstances) he was the man of men. But a private grief had built up a barrier about him, impeding the customary free intercourse of Americans with their chief magistrate; so that I might have come away without a glimpse of his very remarkable physiognomy, save for a semi-official opportunity of which I

---

* We are again compelled to interfere with out friend's license of personal description and criticism. Even Cabinet Ministers (to whom the next few pages of the article were devoted) have their private immunities, which ought to be conscientiously observed,—unless, indeed, the writer chanced to have some very piquant motives for violating them.

was glad to take advantage. The fact is, we were invited to annex ourselves, as supernumeraries, to a deputation that was about to wait upon the President, from a Massachusetts whip-factory, with a present of a splendid whip.

Our immediate party consisted only of four or five, but we were joined by several other persons, who seemed to have been lounging about the precincts of the White House, under the spacious porch or within the hall, and who swarmed in with us to take the chances of a presentation. Nine o'clock had been appointed as the time for receiving the deputation, and we were punctual to the moment but not so the President, who sent us word that he was eating his breakfast, and would come as soon as he could. His appetite, we were glad to think, must have been a pretty fair one; for we waited about half an hour in one of his antechambers, and then were ushered into a reception-room, in one corner of which sat the Secretaries of War and of the Treasury, expecting, like ourselves, the termination of the Presidential breakfast. During this interval there were several new additions to our group, one or two of whom were in a working-garb, so that we formed a very miscellaneous collection of people, mostly unknown to each other, and without any common sponsor, but all with an equal right to look our head-servant in the face.

By-and-by there was a little stir on the staircase and in the passage-way, and in lounged a tall, loose-jointed figure, of an exaggerated Yankee port and demeanor, whom (as being about the homeliest man I ever saw, yet by no means repulsive or disagreeable) it was impossible not to recognize as Uncle Abe.

Unquestionably, Western man though he be, and Kentuckian by birth, President Lincoln is the essential representative of all Yankees, and the veritable specimen, physically, of what the world seems determined to regard as our characteristic qualities. It is the strangest and yet the fittest thing in the jumble of human vicissitudes, that he, out of so many millions, unlooked for, unselected by any intelligible process that could be based upon his genuine qualities, unknown to those who chose him, and unsuspected of what endowments may adapt him for his tremendous responsibility, should have found the way open for him to fling his lank personality into the chair of state,—where, I presume, it was his first impulse to throw his legs on the council-table, and tell the Cabinet Ministers a story. There is no describing his lengthy awkwardness, nor the uncouthness of his movement, and yet it seemed as if I had been in the habit of seeing him daily, and had shaken hands with him a thousand times in some village street; so true was he to the aspect of the pattern American, though with a certain extravagance which, possibly, I exaggerated still further by the delighted eagerness with which I took it in. If put to guess his calling and livelihood, I should have taken him for a country schoolmaster as soon as anything else. He was dressed in a rusty black frock-coat and pantaloons, unbrushed, and worn so faithfully that the suit had adapted itself to the curves and angularities of his figure, and had grown to be an outer skin of the man. He had shabby slippers on his feet. His hair was black, still unmixed with gray, stiff, somewhat bushy, and had apparently been acquainted with neither brush nor comb that morning, after the disarrangement of the pillow; and as to a night-cap, Uncle Abe probably knows nothing of such effeminacies. His complexion is dark and sallow, betokening, I fear, an insalubrious atmosphere around the White House; he has thick black eyebrows and an impending brow; his nose is large, and the lines about his mouth are very strongly defined.

The whole physiognomy is as coarse a one as you would meet anywhere in the length and breadth of the States; but, withal, it is redeemed, illuminated, softened, and brightened by a kindly though serious look out of his eyes, and an expression of homely sagacity, that seems weighted with rich results of village experience. A great deal of native sense; no bookish cultivation, no refinement; honest at heart, and thoroughly so, and yet, in some sort, sly,—at least, endowed with a sort of tact and wisdom that are akin to craft, and would impel him, I think, to take an antagonist in flank rather than to make a bull-run at him right in front. But, on the whole, I like this sallow, queer, sagacious visage, with the homely human sympathies that warmed it; and, for my small share in the matter, would as lief have Uncle Abe for a ruler as any man whom it would have been practicable to put in his place.

Immediately on his entrance the President accosted our member of Congress, who had us in charge, and, with a comical twist of his face, made some jocular remark about the length of his breakfast. He then greeted us all round, not waiting for an introduction, but shaking and squeezing everybody's hand with the utmost cordiality, whether the individual's name was announced to him or not. His manner towards us was wholly without pretence, but yet had a kind of natural dignity, quite sufficient to keep the forwardest of us from clapping him on the shoulder and asking him for a story. A mutual acquaintance being established, our leader took the whip out of its case, and began to read the address of presentation. The whip was an exceedingly long one, its handle wrought in ivory (by some artist in the Massachusetts State Prison, I believe), and ornamented with a medallion of the President, and other equally beautiful devices; and along its whole length there was a succession of golden bands and ferrules. The address was shorter than the whip, but equally well made, consisting chiefly of an explanatory description of these artistic designs, and closing with a hint that the gift was a suggestive and emblematic one, and that the President would recognize the use to which such an instrument should be put.

This suggestion gave Uncle Abe rather a delicate task in his reply, because, slight as the matter seemed, it apparently called for some declaration, or intimation, or faint foreshadowing of policy in reference to the conduct of the war, and the final treatment of the Rebels. But the President's Yankee aptness and not-to-be-caughtness stood him in good stead, and he jerked or wiggled himself out of the dilemma with an uncouth dexterity that was entirely in character; although, without his gesticulation of eye and mouth,—and especially the flourish of the whip, with which he imagined himself touching up a pair of fat horses,—I doubt whether his words would be worth recording, even if I could remember them. The gist of the reply was, that he accepted the whip as an emblem of peace, not punishment; and, this great affair over, we retired out of the presence in high good-humor, only regretting that we could not have seen the President sit down and fold up his legs (which is said to be a most extraordinary spectacle), or have heard him tell one of those delectable stories for which he is so celebrated. A good many of them are afloat upon the common talk of Washington, and are certainly the aptest, pithiest, and funniest little things imaginable; though, to be sure, they smack of the frontier freedom, and would not always bear repetition in a drawing-room, or on the immaculate page of *The Atlantic*.

Good Heavens! What liberties I have been taking with one of the potentates of the earth, and the man on whose conduct more important consequences depend than on that of any other historical personage of the century! But with whom is an American citizen entitled to take a liberty, if not with his own chief magistrate? However, lest the above allusions to President Lincoln's little peculiarities (already well known to the country and to the world) should be misinterpreted, I deem it proper to say a word or two, in regard to him, of unfeigned respect and measurable confidence. He is evidently a man of keen faculties, and, what is still more to the purpose, of powerful character. As to his integrity, the people have that intuition of it which is never deceived. Before he actually entered upon his great office, and for a considerable time afterwards, there is no reason to suppose that he adequately estimated the gigantic task about to be imposed on him, or, at least, had any distinct idea how it was to be managed;

and I presume there may have been more than one veteran politician who proposed to himself to take the power out of President Lincoln's hands into his own, leaving our honest friend only the public responsibility for the good or ill success of the career. The extremely imperfect development of his statesmanly qualities, at that period, may have justified such designs. But the President is teachable by events, and has now spent a year in a very arduous course of education; he has a flexible mind, capable of much expansion, and convertible towards far loftier studies and activities than those of his early life; and if he came to Washington a backwoods humorist, he has already transformed himself into as good a statesman (to speak moderately) as his prime minister.

Death of a Pig

E. B. WHITE || 1948

The year 1938 was a watershed in the history of the personal essay. That was when E. B. White (1899–1985) decided to give up his staff position at The New Yorker, *where he had been for more than a decade the principal writer of the weekly's unsigned opening column, "Notes and Comment," and to retreat to his saltwater farm in North Brooklin, Maine. There White, who had long chafed under the burden of the anonymous "we" then associated with "Notes and Comment," began to write the first-person, meticulously observed narratives about rural life that would deliver him from editorial bondage and establish him as one of the great American prose stylists. As he wrote in the introduction to his collection* One Man's Meat *(1942), "The first-person singular is the only grammatical implement I can use without cutting myself." In his classic book-length ode to Manhattan,* Here Is New York *(1949), White wrote as perceptively about city life as anyone has before or since. But he was clearly most at home on his forty-acre farm, where he devoted his pastoral energies to administering a burgeoning animal kingdom, and his literary ones to, as he modestly put it, "writing of the small things of the day, the trivial matters of the heart, the inconsequential but near things of this living." Out of these fecund Maine years came one of White's masterpieces, "Death of a Pig," which he wrote for* The Atlantic's *ninetieth-anniversary issue at the request of its editor-in-chief, Edward Weeks, who had long coveted the* New Yorker *star. "Death of a Pig," which foreshadowed White's children's classic* Charlotte's Web *(1952), is the tragicomic account of his futile attempts to nurse an ailing hog, originally scheduled for the slaughter, back to life. As the hollow-eyed animal slips away— and "the pig's imbalance becomes the man's, vicariously, and life seems insecure, displaced, transitory"—White's elegant, understated narrative voice creates as powerful a chronicle of dying and loss as any in American literature.*

I spent several days and nights in mid-September with an ailing pig and I feel driven to account for this stretch of time, more particularly since the pig died at last, and I lived, and things might easily have gone the other way round and none left to do the accounting. Even now, so close to the event, I cannot recall the hours sharply and am not ready to say whether death came on the third night or the fourth night. This uncertainty afflicts me with a sense of personal deterioration; if I were in decent health I would know how many nights I had sat up with a pig.

The scheme of buying a spring pig in blossom time, feeding it through summer and fall, and butchering it when the solid cold weather arrives, is a familiar scheme to me and follows an antique pattern. It is a tragedy enacted on most farms with perfect fidelity to the original script. The murder, being premeditated, is in the first degree but is quick and skillful, and the smoked bacon and ham provide a ceremonial ending whose fitness is seldom questioned.

Once in a while something slips—one of the actors goes up in his lines and the whole performance stumbles and halts. My pig simply failed to show up for a meal. The alarm spread rapidly. The classic outline of the tragedy was lost. I found myself cast suddenly in the role of pig's friend and physician—a farcical character with an enema bag for a prop. I had a presentiment, the very first afternoon, that the play would never regain its balance and that my sympathies were now wholly with the pig. This was slapstick—the sort of dramatic treatment which instantly appealed to my old dachshund, Fred, who joined the vigil, held the bag, and, when all was over, presided at the interment. When we slid the body into the grave, we both were shaken to the core. The loss we felt was not the loss of ham but the loss of pig. He had evidently become precious to me, not that he represented a distant nourishment in a hungry time, but that he had suffered in a suffering world. But I'm running ahead of my story and shall have to go back.

My pigpen is at the bottom of an old orchard below the house. The pigs I have raised have lived in a faded building which once was an icehouse. There is a pleasant yard to move about in, shaded by an apple tree which overhangs the low rail fence. A pig couldn't ask for anything better—or none has, at any rate. The sawdust in the icehouse makes a comfortable bottom in which to root, and a warm bed. This sawdust, however, came under suspicion when the pig took sick. One of my neighbors said he thought the pig would have done better on new ground—the same principle that applies in planting potatoes. He said there might be something unhealthy about that sawdust, that he never thought well of sawdust.

It was about four o'clock in the afternoon when I first noticed that there was something wrong with the pig. He failed to appear at the trough for his supper, and when a pig (or a child) refuses supper a chill wave of fear runs through any household, or ice household. After examining my pig, who was stretched out in the sawdust inside the building, I went to the phone and cranked it four times. Mr. Henderson answered. "What's good for a sick pig?" I asked. (There is never any identification needed on a country phone; the person on the other end knows who is talking by the sound of the voice and by the character of the question.)

"I don't know, I never had a sick pig," said Mr. Henderson, "but I can find out quick enough. You hang up and I'll call Irving."

Mr. Henderson was back on the line again in five minutes. "Irving says roll him over on his back and give him two ounces of castor oil or sweet oil, and if that doesn't do the trick give him an injection of soapy water. He says he's sure the pig's plugged up, and even if he's wrong it can't do any harm."

I thanked Mr. Henderson. I didn't go right down to the pig, though. I sank into a chair and sat still for a few minutes to think about my troubles, and then I got up and went to the barn, catching up on some odds and ends that needed tending to. Unconsciously I held off, for an hour, the deed by which I would officially recognize the collapse of the performance of raising a pig; I wanted no interruption in the regularity of feeding, the steadiness of growth, the even succession of days. I wanted no interruption, wanted no oil, no deviation. I just wanted to keep on raising a pig, full meal after full meal, spring into summer into fall. I didn't even know whether there were two ounces of castor oil on the place.

SHORTLY AFTER FIVE O'CLOCK I remembered that we had been invited out to dinner that night and realized that if I were to dose a pig there was no time to lose. The dinner date seemed a familiar conflict: I move in a desultory society and often a week or two will roll by without my going to anybody's house to dinner or anyone's coming to mine, but when an occasion does arise, and I am summoned, something usually turns up (an hour or two in advance) to make all human intercourse seem vastly inappropriate. I have come to believe that there is in hostesses a special power of divination, and that they deliberately arrange dinners to coincide with pig failure or some other sort of failure. At any rate, it was after five o'clock and I knew I could put off no longer the evil hour.

When my son and I arrived at the pigyard, armed with a small bottle of castor oil and a length of clothesline, the pig had emerged from his house and was standing in the middle of his yard, listlessly. He gave us a slim greeting. I could see that he felt uncomfortable and uncertain. I had brought the clothesline thinking I'd have to tie him (the pig weighed more than a hundred pounds) but we never used it. My son reached down, grabbed both front legs, upset him quickly, and when he opened his mouth to scream I turned the oil into his throat—a pink, corrugated area I had never seen before. I had just time to read the label while the neck of the bottle was in his mouth. It said Puretest. The screams, slightly muffled by oil, were pitched in the hysterically high range of pig sound, as though torture were being carried out, but they didn't last long: it was all over rather suddenly, and, his legs released, the pig righted himself.

In the upset position the corners of his mouth had been turned down, giving him a frowning expression. Back on his feet again, he regained the set smile that a pig wears even in sickness. He stood his ground, sucking slightly at the residue of oil; a few drops leaked out of his lips while his wicked eyes, shaded by their coy little lashes, turned on me in disgust and hatred. I scratched him gently with oily fingers and he remained quiet, as though trying to recall the satisfaction of being scratched when in health, and seeming to rehearse in his mind the indignity to which he had just been subjected. I noticed, as I stood there, four or five small dark spots on his back near the tail end, reddish brown in color, each about the size of a housefly. I could not make out what they were. They did not look troublesome but at the same time they did not look like mere surface bruises or chafe marks. Rather they seemed blemishes of internal origin. His stiff white bristles almost completely hid them and I had to part the bristles with my fingers to get a good look.

Several hours later, a few minutes before midnight, having dined well and at someone else's expense, I returned to the pighouse with a flashlight. The patient was asleep. Kneeling, I felt his ears (as you might put your hand on the forehead of a child) and they seemed cool, and then with the light made a careful examination of the yard and the house for sign that the oil had worked. I found none and went to bed.

We had been having an unseasonable spell of weather—hot, close days, with the fog shutting in every night, scaling for a few hours in midday, then creeping back again at dark, drifting in first over the trees on the point, then suddenly blowing across the fields, blotting out the world and taking possession of houses, men, and animals. Everyone kept hoping for a break, but the break failed to come. Next day was another hot one. I visited the pig before breakfast and tried to tempt him with a little milk in his trough. He just stared at it, while I made a sucking sound through my teeth to remind him of past pleasures of the feast. With very small, timid pigs, weanlings, this ruse is often quite successful and will encourage them to eat; but with a large, sick pig the ruse is senseless and the sound I made must have made him feel, if anything, more miserable. He not only did not crave food, he felt a positive revulsion to it. I found a place under the apple tree where he had vomited in the night.

At this point, although a depression had settled over me, I didn't suppose that I was going to lose my pig. From the lustiness of a healthy pig a man derives a feeling of personal lustiness; the stuff that goes into the trough and is received with such enthusiasm is an earnest of some later feast of his own, and when this suddenly comes to an end and the food lies stale and untouched, souring in the sun, the pig's imbalance becomes the man's, vicariously, and life seems insecure, displaced, transitory.

AS MY OWN SPIRITS DECLINED, along with the pig's, the spirits of my vile old dachshund rose. The frequency of our trips down the footpath through the orchard to the pigyard delighted him, although he suffers greatly from arthritis, moves with difficulty, and would be bedridden if he could find anyone willing to serve him meals on a tray.

He never missed a chance to visit the pig with me, and he made many professional calls on his own. You could see him down there at all hours, his white face parting the grass along the fence as he wobbled and stumbled about, his stethoscope dangling—a happy quack, writing his villainous prescriptions and grinning his corrosive grin. When the enema bag appeared, and the bucket of warm suds, his happiness was complete, and he managed to squeeze his enormous body between the two lowest rails of the yard and then assumed full charge of the irrigation. Once, when I lowered the bag to check the flow, he reached in and hurriedly drank a few mouthfuls of the suds to test their potency. I have noticed that Fred will feverishly consume any substance that is associated with trouble—the bitter flavor is to his liking. When the bag was above reach, he concentrated on the pig and was everywhere at once, a tower of strength and inconvenience. The pig, curiously enough, stood rather quietly through this colonic carnival, and the enema, though ineffective, was not as difficult as I had anticipated.

I discovered, though, that once having given a pig an enema there is no turning back, no chance of resuming one of life's more stereotyped roles. The pig's lot and mine were inextricably bound now, as though the rubber tube were the silver cord. From then until the time of his death I held the pig steadily in the bowl of my mind; the task of trying to deliver him from his misery became a strong obsession. His suffering soon became the embodiment of all earthly wretchedness. Along toward the end of the afternoon, defeated in physicking, I phoned the veterinary twenty miles away and placed the case formally in his hands. He was full of questions, and when I casually mentioned the dark spots on the pig's back, his voice changed its tone.

"I don't want to scare you," he said, "but when there are spots, erysipelas has to be considered."

Together we considered erysipelas, with frequent interruptions from the telephone operator, who wasn't sure the connection had been established.

"If a pig has erysipelas can he give it to a person?" I asked.

"Yes, he can," replied the vet.

"Have they answered?" asked the operator.

"Yes, they have," I said. Then I addressed the vet again. "You better come over here and examine this pig right away."

"I can't come myself," said the vet, "but McDonald can come this evening if that's all right. Mac knows more about pigs than I do anyway. You needn't worry too much about the spots. To indicate erysipelas they would have to be deep hemorrhagic infarcts."

"Deep hemorrhagic what?" I asked.

"Infarcts," said the vet.

"Have they answered?" asked the operator.

"Well," I said, "I don't know what you'd call these spots, except they're about the size of a housefly. If the pig has erysipelas I guess I have it, too, by this time, because we've been very close lately."

"McDonald will be over," said the vet.

I hung up. My throat felt dry and I went to the cupboard and got a bottle of whiskey. Deep hemorrhagic infarcts—the phrase began fastening its hooks in my head. I had assumed that there could be nothing much wrong with a pig during the months it was being groomed for murder; my confidence in the essential health and endurance of pigs had been strong and deep, particularly in the health of pigs that belonged to me and that were part of my proud scheme. The awakening had been violent and I minded it all the more because I knew that what could be true of my pig could be true also of the rest of my tidy world. I tried to put this distasteful idea from me but it kept recurring. I took a short drink of the whiskey and then, although I wanted to go down to the yard and look for fresh signs, I was scared to. I was certain I had erysipelas.

It was long after dark and the supper dishes had been put away when a car drove in and McDonald got out. He had a girl with him. I could just make her out in the darkness—she seemed young and pretty. "This is Miss Wyman," he said. "We've been having a picnic supper on the shore, that's why I'm late."

McDonald stood in the driveway and stripped off his jacket, then his shirt. His stocky arms and capable hands showed up in my flashlight's gleam as I helped him find his coverall and get zipped up. The rear seat of his car contained an astonishing amount of paraphernalia, which he soon overhauled, selecting a chain, a syringe, a bottle of oil, a rubber tube, and some other things I couldn't identify. Miss Wyman said she'd go along with us and see the pig. I led the way down the warm slope of the orchard, my light picking out the path for them, and we all three climbed the fence, entered the pighouse, and squatted by the pig while McDonald took a rectal reading. My flashlight picked up the glitter of an engagement ring on the girl's hand.

"No elevation," said McDonald, twisting the thermometer in the light. "You needn't worry about erysipelas." He ran his hand slowly over the pig's stomach and at one point the pig cried out in pain.

"Poor piggledy-wiggledy!" said Miss Wyman.

The treatment I had been giving the pig for two days was then repeated, somewhat more expertly, by the doctor, Miss Wyman and I handing him things as he needed them—holding the chain that he had looped around the pig's upper jaw, holding the syringe, holding the bottle stopper, the end of the tube, all of us working in darkness and in comfort, working with the instinctive teamwork induced by emergency conditions, the pig unprotesting, the house shadowy, protecting, intimate. I went to bed tired but with a feeling of relief that I had turned over part of the responsibility of the case to a licensed doctor. I was beginning to think, though, that the pig was not going to live.

HE DIED TWENTY-FOUR HOURS LATER, or it might have been forty-eight— there is a blur in time here, and I may have lost or picked up a day in the telling and the pig one in the dying. At intervals during the last day I took cool fresh water down to him and at such times as he found the strength to get to his feet he would stand with head in the pail and snuffle his snout around. He drank a few sips but no more; yet it seemed to comfort him to dip his nose in water and bobble it about, sucking in and blowing out through his teeth. Much of the time, now, he lay indoors half buried in sawdust. Once, near the last, while I was attending him I saw him try to make a bed for himself but he lacked the strength, and when he set his snout into the dust he was unable to plow even the little furrow he needed to lie down in.

He came out of the house to die. When I went down, before going to bed, he lay stretched in the yard a few feet from the door. I knelt, saw that he was dead, and left him there: his face had a mild look, expressive neither of deep peace nor of deep suffering, although I think he had suffered a good deal. I went back up to the house and to bed and cried internally—deep hemorrhagic intears. I didn't wake till nearly eight the next morning, and when I looked out the open window the grave was already being dug, down beyond the dump under a wild apple. I could hear the spade strike against the small rocks that blocked the way. Never send to know for whom the grave is dug, I said to myself, it's dug for thee. Fred, I well knew, was supervising the work of digging, so I ate breakfast slowly.

It was a Saturday morning. The thicket in which I found the grave-diggers at work was dark and warm, the sky overcast. Here, among alders and young hackmatacks, at the foot of the apple tree, Howard had dug a beautiful hole, five feet long, three feet wide, three feet deep. He was standing in it, removing the last spadefuls of earth while Fred patrolled the brink in simple but impressive circles, disturbing the loose earth of the mound so that it trickled back in. There had been no rain in weeks and the soil, even three feet down, was dry and powdery. As I stood and stared, an enormous earthworm which had been partially exposed by the spade at the bottom dug itself deeper and made a slow withdrawal, seeking even remoter moistures at even lonelier depths. And just as Howard stepped out and rested his spade against the tree and lit a cigarette, a small green apple separated itself from a branch overhead and fell into the hole. Everything about this last scene seemed overwritten—the dismal sky, the shabby woods, the imminence of rain, the worm (legendary bedfellow of the dead), the apple (conventional garnish of a pig).

But even so, there was a directness and dispatch about animal burial, I thought, that made it a more decent affair than human burial: there was no stopover in the undertaker's foul parlor, no wreath nor spray; and when we hitched a line to the pig's hind legs and dragged him swiftly from his yard, throwing our weight into the harness and leaving a wake of crushed grass and smoothed rubble over the dump, ours was a businesslike procession, with Fred, the dishonorable pallbearer, staggering along in the rear, his perverse bereavement showing in every seam in his face; and the post-mortem performed handily and swiftly—right at the edge of the grave, so that the inwards which had caused the pig's death preceded him into the ground and he lay at last resting squarely on the cause of his own undoing.

I threw in the first shovelful, and then we worked rapidly and without talk, until the job was complete. I picked up the rope, made it fast to Fred's collar (he is a notorious ghoul), and we all three filed back up the path to the house, Fred bringing up the rear and holding back every inch of the way, feigning unusual stiffness. I noticed that although he weighed far less than the pig, he was harder to drag, being possessed of the vital spark.

The news of the death of my pig traveled fast and far, and I received many expressions of sympathy from friends and neighbors, for no one took the event lightly and the premature expiration of a pig is, I soon discovered, a departure which the community marks solemnly on its calendar, a sorrow in which it feels fully involved. I have written this account in penitence and in grief, as a man who failed to raise his pig, and to explain my deviation from the classic course of so many raised pigs. The grave in the woods is unmarked, but Fred can direct the mourner to it unerringly and with immense good will, and I know he and I shall often revisit it, singly and together, in seasons of reflection and despair, on flagless memorial days of our own choosing.

Flying Upside Down

TRACY KIDDER || 1981

The "process piece" now occupies hallowed ground in narrative nonfiction writing. But at the time that The Atlantic *published this first of a two-part installment from* The Soul of a New Machine *(1981), by Tracy Kidder (1945–   ), the technique of penetrating a sharply circumscribed world in order to show readers how things really operate there was almost unheard of. It's hard to overstate the impact of Kidder's backstage account of a cadre of overcaffeinated computer wizards working around the clock to design and build a state-of-the-art minicomputer. To gather material for his story, Kidder, a frequent contributor to* The Atlantic *for a decade, gained unfettered access to his subjects and camped out, virtually day and night for almost a year, in a top-secret basement computer lab of the Data General Corporation, in Westborough, Massachusetts. He took notes on everything he saw and heard, monitoring the triumphs and setbacks as well as the rising tensions among the young engineers, as they bent and, occasionally, broke under the weight of their almost impossible deadlines. In finely honed, deceptively casual prose, Kidder tells the story of a great race, building his central narrative around a series of taut, cinematic scenes. The quiet authority of the writing, the thoroughness of the reporting, and the fluid handling of the complex technology all helped make* The Soul of a New Machine *a bestseller, conferring on its author not only the Pulitzer Prize and the National Book Award but the mantle of role model for a younger generation of narrative nonfiction practitioners, among them Jonathan Harr, Alex Kotlowitz, and Ted Conover. Over the course of a half dozen books and many other articles for* The Atlantic, *Kidder would continue to test the boundaries of narrative journalism on such diverse subjects as the construction of a family home (*House, *1985) and an idealist physician's one-man quest to bring modern medicine to the Third World (*Mountains Beyond Mountains, *2003). But he is still best known for his cutting-edge chronicle of the daredevil computer engineers—what* Wired *magazine, looking back at the accomplishment twenty years later, called "the original nerd epic."*

One holiday morning in 1978, Tom West traveled to a city that was situated, he would later say guardedly, "somewhere in America." He entered a building as though he belonged there, strolled down a hallway, and let himself quietly into a windowless room. Just inside the door, he stopped.

The floor was torn up; a shallow trench filled with fat power cables traversed it. Along the far wall, at the end of the trench, enclosed in three large, cream-colored steel cabinets, stood a VAX 11/780, the most important of a new class of computers called "32-bit superminis." To West's surprise, one of the cabinets was open and a man with tools was standing in front of it. A technician, still installing the machine, West figured.

Although West's designs weren't illegal, they were sly, and he had no intention of embarrassing the friend who had told him he could visit this room. If the technician had asked West to identify himself, West wouldn't have lied and he wouldn't have answered the question, either. But the moment went by. The technician didn't inquire. West stood around and watched him work, and in a little while the technician packed up his tools and left.

Then West closed the door and walked back across the room to the computer, which was now all but fully assembled. He began to take it apart.

West was the leader of a team of computer engineers at a company called Data General. The machine that he was disassembling was produced by a rival firm, Digital Equipment Corporation, or DEC. A VAX and a modest amount of adjunctive equipment sold for something like $200,000, and as West liked to say, DEC was beginning to sell VAXes "like jellybeans." West had traveled to this room to find out for himself just how good this computer was, compared with the one that his team was building.

West spent the morning removing the VAX's twenty-seven printed circuit boards. He'd take one out, study it, make a few notes, and then put it back. These boards were flat plates, each about the size of a shirt cardboard. In regular columns across their surfaces lay small rectangular boxes. Each of these boxes enclosed an integrated circuit, or "chip"; if bared and examined under a microscope, the chips would look like mazes—imagine the wiring diagram of an office building inscribed on a fingernail. It's possible to get inside the chips, inside the littlest boxes inside the boxes that constitute the central works of a modern computer, and, bringing back the details, to create a functionally equivalent copy of a machine. "Reverse engineering" is the name for that art, and it takes time and equipment. West called such engineering "knock-off copy work." He had a simpler purpose. He was not going to imitate VAX; he just wanted to size it up.

Looking into the VAX, West felt that he saw a diagram of DEC's corporate organization. He found the VAX "too complicated." He did not like, for instance, the system by which various parts of the machine communicated with each other; for his taste, there was too much protocol involved. The machine expressed DEC's cautious, bureaucratic style. West was pleased with this idea.

His hands in the machine, West was also studying and counting parts; many of the chips had numbers on their housings that were like names familiar to him. When he was all done, he added everything up and decided that it probably cost $22,500 to manufacture the essential hardware of a VAX. He left the machine exactly as he had found it.

"I'd been living in fear of VAX for a year," West said one evening afterward, while driving along Route 495 in central Massachusetts. "I wasn't really into G-2. VAX was in the public domain, and I wanted to see how bad the damage was. I think I got a high when I looked at it and saw how complex and expensive it was. It made me feel good about some of the decisions we've made."

West was forty but looked younger. He was thin and had a long narrow face and a mane of brown hair that spilled over the back of his collar. These days he went to work in freshly laundered blue jeans or pressed khakis, in leather moccasins, and in solid-colored long-sleeved shirts, with the sleeves rolled up in precise folds, like the pages of a letter, well above his bony elbows. He expostulated with his hands. When dismissing someone or some idea or both, he made a fist and then exploded it, fingers splaying wide. The gesture was well known to those engineers who worked for him. Long index fingers inserted under either side of the bridge of his glasses signified thought, and when accompanied by a long *"Ummmmmmmmmh"* warned that some emphatic statement was near. Indeed, West made few statements that were not emphatic. Seen at the wheel of his shiny red Saab, he made a picture of impatience. His jaw was set; he had a forward lean. Sometimes he briefly wore a mysterious smile. He was a man on a mission.

"With VAX, DEC was trying to minimize the risk," West said, as he swerved around another car. "We're trying to maximize the win. . . ."

IN THE EARLY 1960S, several companies began to manufacture computers that were much less powerful but also much smaller and cheaper than the machines then in existence. These new devices were called minicomputers. By 1978, the increasingly imprecise term "minicomputer company" could be applied to about fifty corporations. Minicomputer sales had grown from about $1.5 million worth of shipments in 1968 to about $3.5 billion in 1978, and most interested parties believed that the business would continue to grow by about 30 percent a year.

DEC was one of the first minicomputer companies, and it was the largest corporation in this segment of the computer industry: the IBM of minis. In 1968, three young computer engineers who left DEC and a salesman from another company founded Data General. Minicomputer companies were known for playing rough; Data General had acquired a reputation as one of the roughest of them all. "The Darth Vader of the computer industry" was the way one trade journalist described the company. Meanwhile, Data General thrived. It made good computers inexpensively and it managed its business adroitly. By 1978, Data General was taking in about half a billion dollars a year. It was only ten years old, and its name had just been added to the list of the nation's 500 largest industrial corporations. Moreover, for most of its history Data General had maintained the highest profit margins in the computer industry, after IBM.

Making computers is a risky enterprise. Young, successful computer companies often get into serious trouble, largely because success in their business means rapid, stressful growth. Data General grew by more than 30 percent a year for a decade, and all the while the technology of computers was changing.

At some computer companies, it has fallen mainly to engineers, working below decks, as it were, to make the first decisions about new products. Data General was such a company, and one often heard that its president, Edson deCastro, himself a very successful computer engineer, liked "self-starters." By 1978, though the company's balance sheet had never looked better, it was becoming apparent that Data General had need of initiative from its engineers. Into the world of the minicomputer had come a new kind of machine—the 32-bit supermini. DEC's VAX was the best-known example of such a machine, and several other of Data General's rivals had also produced superminis. Data General, meanwhile, had yet to offer one of its own. "A disaster," Tom West said of this situation.

The most important characteristic of the 32-bit mini was its system of storage. Storage in a computer resembles a telephone system, in the sense that every piece of information in storage is assigned a unique number, so that it can be readily found. If the standard length of a phone number is seven digits, then enough unique numbers can be generated to serve the needs of New York City; but if a three-digit area code is added, every telephone customer in America can have a unique number. The 32-bit supermini was a computer with an area code. Since the advent of Data General, most minis had been "16-bit" machines. The standard length of the numbers that such a machine assigns to items in its storage is 16 bits, 16 binary digits. A 16-bit machine can directly generate only about 65,000 unique numbers for its storage system. A 32-bit machine, however, can directly generate some 4.3 *billion* different numbers.

All interested parties agreed that the demand for superminis would be huge; the market might be worth several billion dollars by the 1980s, some said. If Data General failed to produce a 32-bit machine or something equivalent, it could expect to lose some old customers, and, perhaps more important, it would forfeit one of the next decade's best opportunities for gaining new business. The company could not now be the first to enter this new market, but that was all right; sometimes it was better not to be first. However, Data General had to field a suitable machine fairly soon, because customers get married to computer companies in intricate ways, and once they've married elsewhere they're often gone for good. Time was running out, Tom West maintained. "We're gonna get schmeared if we don't react to VAX," he said.

DATA GENERAL'S HEADQUARTERS STAND near the intersection of two super-highways some thirty miles west of Boston. It is a low-lying brick building with TV cameras mounted on the corners of its roof, and all in all looks like a fort. Its official name is Building 14 A/B. Inside, it is essentially divided into an upstairs and a downstairs. The executives work upstairs. The lower level of Building 14, subterranean in front and at ground level in back, is another country. It belongs mainly to engineers.

West led the way down into this region one evening in the late fall of 1978, through confusing corridors and past mysterious doors that were locked up and bearing signs that read "RESTRICTED AREA." Then the hallways ended, and all around, under fluorescent light, lay fields of cubicles without doors. Their walls stood too low for privacy. Most contained a desk with a computer terminal on it. In many, there was a green houseplant. Green plants poked their heads, like periscopes, above the cubicles' walls. "The great statement," said West, gesturing at the foliage and smiling faintly. "It's basically a cattle yard."

By day, the basement held a homogeneous-looking throng, made up largely of young white males wearing jeans and corduroys and hiking boots; few wore neckties, but neat grooming was the rule. Now and then a visitor might catch a glimpse of a fellow with wild hair, dressed in Army-surplus clothes, but such figures were rare.

West's team specialized in the design and development of the hardware of new computers. It was only one of several such teams at Data General, and it was not the largest or, in the fall of 1978, the most prestigious. It was named the Eclipse Group, after the current generation of 16-bit Data General computers. The Eclipse Group, which numbered about thirty then, occupied a portion of a field of cubicles and a few narrow, windowless offices, one of which belonged to West. No sign announced that this was the group's territory. At night, it did seem that more lamps burned on in the Eclipse Group's offices and cubicles than in many other parts of the basement. At some moments during the day, the area had the atmosphere of a commuter train, and at others it reminded one of a college library on the eve of exams: silent and intent youngsters leafing through thick documents and peering into the screens of computer terminals. Conversation, especially the speech of the senior engineers, contained words and phrases such as these: a *canard* was anything false, usually a wrongheaded notion entertained by some other engineering group or other company; things could be done in ways that created *no muss, no fuss*, that were *quick and dirty*, that were *clean. Fundamentals* were the source of all right thinking, and weighty sentences often began with the adverb *fundamentally*, while *realistically* prefaced many flights of fancy. There was talk of *wars, shootouts, hired guns*, and people who *shot from the hip*. The *win* was the object of all this sport, and *the big win* was something that could be achieved by *maximizing* the lesser one. From the vocabulary alone, one could have guessed that West had been there and that these engineers were up to something special.

In fact, they were building their own 32-bit supermini, a machine that West fervently hoped would be a worthy rival to DEC's VAX and maybe the basis for Data General's ascent in the Fortune 500. Oddly, though, West and some of the senior engineers on his team expressed the paradoxical feeling that they were building a machine absolutely essential to the company but were doing it largely on their own. "I think we're doing it in spite of Data General," said one of West's lieutenants in the middle of the project.

Setting up intramural competition among various parts of a company is an old strategy of management. Many firms in the computer industry, most notably IBM, have used it; they deliberately establish internal competition, partly on the theory that it's a useful prelude to competition with other companies. At Data General, such internal struggle had the name "competition for resources." An engineering team such as the Eclipse Group sometimes had to vie with other engineering groups for the right to produce a new computer. A year or so before, some members of the Eclipse Group had found themselves in such a competition, against a much larger team of Data General engineers, situated in North Carolina. The Eclipse Group had been competing with the team in North Carolina essentially for the right to produce Data General's supermini, what West would later call "the answer to VAX." The Eclipse Group's project had been scrapped. There had been an intramural competition for resources, and the Eclipse Group had lost. But West had decided not to abide by the decision. He had launched the Eclipse Group on another big project, one that would rival North Carolina's. Doing so had taken him some months. It had also required that he pursue some indirect measures.

West had believed that whatever its other virtues, the machine that the company engineers in North Carolina were building did not represent a timely solution to the problem that DEC's VAX posed for Data General. West also wanted to save the Eclipse Group and himself from the fate of working only on small projects. So he had borrowed ideas from anyone who had some to share, and by the very early spring of 1978 he had settled on a new plan. The Eclipse Group would build a schizophrenic computer, one that would work as both a 16-bit Eclipse and a 32-bit supermini. The proposed machine was nicknamed "Eagle."

The production of software, the programs that tell computers what to do, costs customers time and money and sometimes entails awful administrative problems. Eagle would protect old customers' substantial investments in 16-bit Eclipse software and would offer prospective buyers at least the possibility of savings in software development. At the same time, this machine would fulfill Data General's need for a computer with enlarged "logical address space." And West thought that the front office was likely to let the Eclipse Group build this computer, if it was presented correctly.

"You gotta distinguish between the internal promotion to the actual workers and the promoting we did to other parts of the company," West later explained. "Outside the group, I tried to low-key the thing. I tried to dull the impression that this was a competing project with North Carolina. I tried to sell it externally as not much of a threat. I was selling insurance; this would be there if something went wrong in North Carolina. It was just gonna be a fast, Eclipse-like machine. This was the only way it was gonna live. We had to get the resources quietly, without creating a big brouhaha."

And so, when he proposed the idea to people outside his group, West made Eagle appear to be a modest project, and he got permission to go ahead. But when he proselytized engineers who might help build this machine, it was clear that West's intentions weren't modest at all.

From the point of view of a purist ("technology bigot" is the usual term), Eagle in its vague outlines looked messy. Indeed, some engineers called the plan "a kludge," computer jargon for any ill-conceived thing. West varied his pitch to suit his audience. His general remarks ran as follows: Eagle might not look it from the outside, but in fact it was going to be a new, a fast, a "sexy" machine. It would be software-compatible with 16-bit Eclipses, not because it was going to be just another Eclipse, but because that feature would make it a "big win" commercially. They were going to build Eagle in record time, working "flat out by definition," because the company needed this machine desperately. And when they succeeded and Eagle went out the door with their names on it, as West put it, and started selling like jellybeans, then they would all be heroes.

Once in a while West and some members of his staff asked themselves whether the company's president, deCastro, might not have orchestrated everything, including their feeling that they were on their own. Whatever its origin, though, that feeling was evidently invigorating. "Anytime you do anything on the sly, it's always more interesting than if you do it up front," one of West's lieutenants remarked. West said, wearing his wry smile, "We're building what I thought we could get away with."

BY THE SPRING OF 1978, West had gathered a cadre of fairly experienced engineers. But to build Eagle, it was soon clear, more engineers were needed.

West conferred with an old colleague named Carl Alsing. Alsing was in his mid-thirties, a veteran, and a practitioner of an abstruse but essential craft called microcoding. He was soft-spoken. He had a mischievous air and—in all matters, it seemed—an aversion to the blunt approach. Alsing had joined the Eagle project without any coaxing, and was the only one of West's three lieutenants to do so. West regarded Alsing as one of the few people around Building 14 in whom he could confide, and for his part, Alsing, who was something of a watcher—a moviegoer—was fascinated by West, especially at the onset of the project.

"We need more bodies, Alsing," West said that spring. "Shall we hire kids?"

A famous computer engineer had remarked that he liked to hire inexperienced engineers fresh from college, because they did not usually know what was supposed to be impossible. West had heard the remark. He liked the sound of it. He figured, too, that "kids" would be relatively inexpensive to hire. Moreover, this could be another way of disguising his true intentions: who would imagine that a bunch of recruits could build an important new computer? To Alsing, the idea was vintage West. It looked risky and compelling. Alsing became the Eclipse Group's chief recruiter.

West and Alsing agreed that they would have to hire the very best of that year's college graduates, even though, they told each other, they might be hiring their own replacements, their own "assassins." That was all very well, but the demand for young computer engineers far exceeded the supply. What enticement could the Eclipse Group offer that companies such as IBM could not? Clearly, it had to be the Eagle project itself. It was thought to be a fine thing in the fraternity of hardware engineers to be a builder of new computers—in the local idiom, it was the "sexy" job—and, Alsing knew, most big companies just didn't offer recruits the opportunity to be such a person right away. So they had what West called "a high-energy story."

But the new recruits were going to be asked to work at a feverish pace almost at once, and they'd have no time to learn the true meaning of the Eclipse Group's mysterious rite of initiation, which was known as "signing up." In the Eclipse Group, when you signed up, you agreed to do whatever was necessary for success and to forsake time with family, hobbies, and friends—if you had any of those left, and you might not, if you had signed up for too many projects before. In effect, a person who signed up declared, "I want to do this job and I'll give it my heart and soul." Formal declarations weren't called for. A simple "Yeah, I'll do that" could constitute signing up. But only veterans knew what such a statement might entail.

The Eclipse Group solicited applications. One candidate listed "family life" as his main avocation. Alsing and another of West's lieutenants were skeptical when they saw that entry. Not that they wanted to exclude family men, being such men themselves. But Alsing thought: "He seems to be saying he doesn't want to sign up." The other lieutenant pondered the application. "I don't think he'd be happy here," he said to himself.

Any likely-looking candidate was invited to Building 14, and the elders of the group would interview the young man; it was usually a young man, for female engineers specializing in the hardware of computers were still quite scarce. If the recruit was a potential microcoder, his interview with Alsing was crucial. And a successful interview with Alsing constituted signing up.

Alsing would ask the young engineer, "What do you want to do?"

If the recruit seemed to say, "Well, I'm just out of grad school and I'm not really sure," then Alsing would usually find a polite way to abbreviate the conversation. But if the recruit said, for instance, "I'm really interested in computer design," then Alsing would press on. The ideal interview would proceed in this fashion:

"What interests you about computer design?"

"I want to build one," says the recruit.

"What makes you think you can build a new computer?"

"Hey," says the recruit, "no offense, but I've used some of the machines you guys have built. I think I can do a better job."

"Well, we're building this machine that's way out in front in technology," says Alsing. "We're gonna design all new hardware and tools. Do you like the sound of that?"

"Oh, yeah," says the recruit.

"It's gonna be tough," says Alsing. "If we hired you, you'd be working with a bunch of cynics and egotists and it'd be hard to keep up with them."

"That doesn't scare me," says the recruit.

"There's a lot of fast people in this group," Alsing goes on. "It's gonna be a real hard job with a lot of long hours. And I mean *long* hours."

"No," says the recruit. "That's what I want to do, get in on the ground floor of a new architecture. I want to do a big machine. I want to be where the action is."

"Well," says Alsing, pulling a long face. "We can only let in the best of this year's graduates. We've already let in some awfully fast people. We'll have to let you know."

"We tell him that we only let in the best—then we let him in," Alsing said, after it was all done. "I don't know. It was kind of like recruiting for a suicide mission. You're gonna die, but you're gonna die in glory."

SOME OF THE YOUNG ENGINEERS were assigned to work on microcode; they were called, and called themselves, "the Microkids." Those who went to work on the hardware, the actual circuitry, were known as "the Hardy Boys." This was the first real job for most of them. For some, at least, it was a strange beginning. Eager to make a good impression, and thinking it was the proper thing to do, one of the Hardy Boys set out, when he arrived, to meet his new team's leader. He went into West's office, extended his hand, and said, "Hi, I'm Dave." He would never forget that experience. "West just sat there and stared at me. After a few seconds I decided I'd better get out of there."

One newcomer was astonished at the way the team was being managed. Hardy Boys and Microkids were making deals, saying to each other, in effect, "I'll do this function in microcode if you'll do this one in hardware." He was a little older than the other newcomers and had some experience in computer design, and he had never seen it done this way. "There's no grand design," he said. "People are just reaching out in the dark, touching hands." He was having some problems with his own part of the design and he felt sure that he could solve them properly if the managers would simply give him time. But they kept saying there was no time. No one seemed to be in control. Nothing was ever explained. The team's leader rarely even said hello to his troops. Make a mistake, however, and the managers came at you from all sides.

"The whole management structure . . ." said this young engineer. "Anyone in Harvard Business School would have barfed."

If West had heard that remark, he might have taken it as a compliment. Carl Alsing had often heard West use the phrase "flying upside down." The inspiration for it evidently came from a friend of West's who used to do that very thing in his airplane. By the term, West seemed to mean the assumption of large risks, and the ways in which he applied it left Alsing in no doubt that flying upside down was supposed to be a desirable activity, the very stuff of a vigorous life.

The Crash of EgyptAir 990

WILLIAM LANGEWIESCHE || 2001

On September 10, 2001, the staff of The Atlantic *was in the final stages of closing the magazine's November cover story, a wide-ranging survey of the many bizarre religions constantly popping up around the globe. The next morning, New York City and Washington, D.C., came under attack, and the magazine's editors found themselves in desperate need of a cover more appropriate to the darkened geopolitical landscape. Into the breach stepped William Langewiesche (1955–), a national correspondent for* The Atlantic *and a writer with an unsurpassed gift for dramatizing disaster. For months, Langewiesche had been researching and reporting a story with eerie echoes of 9/11: In 1999, an EgyptAir passenger jet, bound from New York to Cairo, had plunged, without warning, into the Atlantic Ocean off Nantucket, killing all 217 people on board. Langewiesche had amassed a battery of evidence to support the theory—strongly advanced by the American officials investigating the crash, bitterly denied by the Egyptian officials attempting to obstruct that investigation—that the tragedy had been precipitated by the plane's suicidal copilot, Gameel al-Batouti. Yet at the time the Twin Towers fell, Langewiesche was still in the early stages of writing the article. Working under intense deadline pressure, the writer produced an immaculate ten-thousand-word first draft in three days, and "The Crash of EgyptAir 990" went on to win the National Magazine Award for reporting.*

Langewiesche would later remark in an interview that he had come to view the crash as a lens through which to explore the fraught political relationship between the United States and Egypt. But it is safe to say that what resounded most with readers in the terrifying wake of 9/11 was his reenactment of the crash itself. In a classic example of reportorial reconstruction, Langewiesche weaves together the decisive details from radar logs, black-box transcripts, and investigator interviews to produce a narrative of such realism, suspense, and emotional firepower that it is hard to believe he was not on board the ill-fated plane. In part, this achievement can be explained by a line from the writer's résumé: before he became a journalist, Langewiesche, who now writes for Vanity Fair, *worked for more than a decade as a professional pilot, flying cargo planes, air ambulances, and corporate jets. For his EgyptAir article, Langewiesche even spent time at Boeing operating the controls of a specially outfitted 767 flight simulator, experiencing what must have been,*

in his words, a "strange and dreamlike period for the pilots, hurtling
through the night with no chance of awakening."

I remember first hearing about the accident early in the morning after the
airplane went down. It was October 31, 1999, Halloween morning. I was in
my office when a fellow pilot, a former flying companion, phoned with the
news: It was EgyptAir Flight 990, a giant twin-engine Boeing 767 on the
way from New York to Cairo, with 217 people aboard. It had taken off from
Kennedy Airport in the middle of the night, climbed to 33,000 feet, and
flown normally for half an hour before mysteriously plummeting into the
Atlantic Ocean sixty miles south of Nantucket. Rumor had it that the crew
had said nothing to air-traffic control, that the flight had simply dropped
off the New York radar screens. Soon afterward an outbound Air France
flight had swung over the area, and had reported no fires in sight—only a
dim and empty ocean far below. It was remotely possible that Flight 990
was still in the air somewhere, diverting toward a safe landing. But sometime around daybreak a Merchant Marine training ship spotted debris
floating on the waves—aluminum scraps, cushions and clothing, some human remains. The midshipmen on board gagged from the stench of jet
fuel—a planeload of unburned kerosene rising from shattered tanks on the
ocean floor, about 250 feet below. By the time rescue ships and helicopters
arrived, it was obvious that there would be no survivors. I remember reacting to the news with regret for the dead, followed by a thought for the complexity of the investigation that now lay ahead. This accident had the
markings of a tough case. The problem was not so much the scale of the
carnage—a terrible consequence of the 767's size—but, rather, the still-
sketchy profile of the upset that preceded it, this bewildering fall out of the
sky on a calm night, without explanation, during an utterly uncritical
phase of the flight.

I don't fly the 767, or any other airliner. In fact, I no longer fly for a living. But I know through long experience with flight that such machines are
usually docile, and that steering them does not require the steady nerves
and quick reflexes that passengers may imagine. Indeed, as we saw on September 11, steering them may not even require much in the way of
training—the merest student-pilot level is probably enough. It's not hard
to understand why. Airplanes at their core are very simple devices—
winged things that belong in the air. They are designed to be flyable, and
they are. Specifically, the 767 has ordinary mechanical and hydraulic flight
controls that provide the pilot with smooth and conventional responses; it

is normally operated on autopilot, but can easily be flown by hand; if you remove your hands from the controls entirely, the airplane sails on as before, until it perhaps wanders a bit, dips a wing, and starts into a gentle descent; if you pull the nose up or push it down (within reason) and then fold your arms, the airplane returns unassisted to steady flight; if you idle the engines, or shut them off entirely, the airplane becomes a rather well-behaved glider. It has excellent forward visibility, through big windshields. It has a minimalist cockpit that may look complicated to the untrained eye but is a masterpiece of clean design. It can easily be managed by the standard two-person crew, or even by one pilot alone. The biggest problem in flying the airplane on a routine basis is boredom. Settled into the deep sky at 33,000 feet, above the weather and far from any obstacle, the 767 simply makes very few demands.

Not that it's idiot-proof, or necessarily always benign. As with any fast and heavy airplane, operating a 767 safely even under ordinary circumstances requires anticipation, mental clarity, and a practical understanding of the various systems. Furthermore, when circumstances are *not* ordinary—for example, during an engine failure just after takeoff or an encounter with unexpected wind shear during an approach to landing—a wilder side to the airplane's personality suddenly emerges. Maintaining control then requires firm action and sometimes a strong arm. There's nothing surprising about this: all airplanes misbehave on occasion, and have to be disciplined. "Kicking the dog," I called it in the ornery old cargo crates I flew when I was in college—it was a regular part of survival. In the cockpits of modern jets it is rarely necessary. Nonetheless, when trouble occurs in a machine as massive and aerodynamically slick as the 767, if it is not quickly suppressed the consequences can blossom out of control. During a full-blown upset like that experienced by the Egyptian crew, the airplane may dive so far past its tested limits that it exceeds the very scale of known engineering data—falling off the graphs as well as out of the sky. Afterward the profile can possibly be reconstructed mathematically by aerodynamicists and their like, but it cannot be even approximated by pilots in flight if they expect to come home alive.

I got a feel for the 767's dangerous side last summer, after following the accident's trail from Washington, D.C., to Cairo to the airplane's birthplace, in Seattle, where Boeing engineers let me fly a specially rigged 767 simulator through a series of relevant upsets and recoveries along with some sobering replays of Flight 990's final moments. These simulations had been flown by investigators more than a year before and had been reported on in detail in the publicly released files. Boeing's argument was not that the 767 is a flawless design but, more narrowly, that none of the imaginable failures of its flight-control systems could explain the known facts of this accident.

But that's getting ahead of the story. Back on October 31, 1999, with the first news of the crash, it was hard to imagine any form of pilot error that could have condemned the airplane to such a sustained and precipitous dive. What switch could the crew have thrown, what lever? Nothing came to mind. And why had they perished so silently, without a single distress call on the radio? A total electrical failure was very unlikely, and would not explain the loss of control. A fire would have given them time to talk. One thing was certain: the pilots were either extremely busy or incapacitated from the start. Of course there was always the possibility of a terrorist attack—a simple if frightening solution. But otherwise something had gone terribly wrong with the airplane itself, and that could be just as bad. There are more than 800 Boeing 767s in the world's airline fleet, and they account for more transatlantic flights than all other airplanes combined. They are also very similar in design to the smaller and equally numerous Boeing 757s. So there was plenty of reason for alarm.

ONE OF THE WORLD'S REALLY IMPORTANT DIVIDES lies between nations that react well to accidents and nations that do not. This is as true for a confined and technical event like the crash of a single flight as it is for political or military disasters. The first requirement is a matter of national will, and never a sure thing: it is the intention to get the story right, wherever the blame may lie. The second requirement follows immediately upon the first, and is probably easier to achieve: it is the need for people in the aftermath to maintain even tempers and open minds. The path they follow may not be simple, but it can provide for at least the possibility of effective resolutions.

In the case of EgyptAir Flight 990 the only information available at first was external. The airplane had arrived in New York late on a flight from Los Angeles, and had paused to refuel, take on passengers, and swap crews. Because of the scheduled duration of the flight to Cairo, two cockpit crews had been assigned to the ocean crossing—an "active crew," including the aircraft commander, to handle the first and last hours of the flight; and a "cruise crew," whose role was essentially to monitor the autopilot during the long, sleepy mid-Atlantic stretch. Just before midnight these four pilots rode out to the airport on a shuttle bus from Manhattan's Pennsylvania Hotel, a large establishment where EgyptAir retained rooms for the use of its personnel. The pilots had been there for several days and, as usual, were well rested. Also in the bus was one of the most senior of EgyptAir's captains, the company's chief 767 pilot, who was not scheduled to fly but would be "deadheading" home to Cairo. An EgyptAir dispatcher rode out on the bus with them, and subsequently reported that the crew members looked and sounded normal. At the airport he gave them a standard briefing and an update on the New York surface weather, which was stagnant under a low, thin overcast, with light winds and thickening haze.

Flight 990 pushed back from the gate and taxied toward the active runway at 1:12 A.M. Because there was little other traffic at the airport, communications with the control tower were noticeably relaxed. At 1:20 Flight 990 lifted off. It topped the clouds at 1,000 feet and turned out over the ocean toward a half moon rising above the horizon. The airplane was identified and tracked by air-traffic-control radar as it climbed through the various New York departure sectors and entered the larger airspace belonging to the en-route controllers of New York Center; its transponder target and data block moved steadily across the controllers' computer-generated displays, and its radio transmissions sounded perhaps a little awkward, but routine. At 1:44 it leveled off at the assigned 33,000 feet.

The en-route controller working the flight was a woman named Ann Brennan, a private pilot with eight years on the job. She had the swagger of a good controller, a real pro. Later she characterized the air traffic that night as slow, which it was—during the critical hour she had handled only three other flights. The offshore military-exercise zones, known as warning areas, were inactive. The sky was sleeping.

At 1:47 Brennan said, "EgyptAir Nine-ninety, change to my frequency one-two-five-point-niner-two."

EgyptAir acknowledged the request with a friendly "Good day," and after a pause checked in on the new frequency: "New York, EgyptAir Nine-nine-zero heavy, good morning."

Brennan answered, "EgyptAir Nine-ninety, roger."

That was the last exchange. Brennan noticed that the flight still had about fifteen minutes to go before leaving her sector. Wearing her headset, she stood up and walked six feet away to sort some paperwork. A few minutes later she approved a request by Washington Center to steer an Air France 747 through a corner of her airspace. She chatted for a while with her supervisor, a man named Ray Redhead. In total she spent maybe six minutes away from her station, a reasonable interval on such a night. It was just unlucky that while her back was turned Flight 990 went down.

A computer captured what she would have seen—a strangely abstract death no more dramatic than a video game. About two minutes after the final radio call, at 1:49:53 in the morning, the radar swept across EgyptAir's transponder at 33,000 feet. Afterward, at successive twelve-second intervals, the radar read 31,500, 25,400, and 18,300 feet—a descent rate so great that the air-traffic-control computers interpreted the information as false, and showed "XXXX" for the altitude on Brennan's display. With the next sweep the radar lost the transponder entirely, and picked up only an unenhanced "primary" blip, a return from the airplane's metal mass. The surprise is that the radar continued to receive such returns (which show only location, and not altitude) for nearly another minute and a half, indicating that the dive must have dramatically slowed or stopped, and that the 767 remained airborne, however tenuously, during that interval. A minute and a half is a long time. As the Boeing simulations later showed, it must have been a strange and dreamlike period for the pilots, hurtling through the night with no chance of awakening.

When radar contact was lost, the display for EgyptAir 990 began to "coast," indicating that the computers could no longer find a correlation between the stored flight plan and the radar view of the sky. When Brennan noticed, she stayed cool. She said, "EgyptAir Nine-ninety, radar contact lost, recycle transponder, squawk one-seven-one-two." EgyptAir did not answer, so she tried again at unhurried intervals over the following ten minutes. She advised Ray Redhead of the problem, and he passed the word along. She called an air-defense radar facility, and other air-traffic-control centers as far away as Canada, to see if by any chance someone was in contact with the flight. She asked a Lufthansa crew to try transmitting to EgyptAir from up high. Eventually she brought in Air France for the overflight. The prognosis was of course increasingly grim, but she maintained her professional calm. She continued to handle normal operations in her sector while simultaneously setting the search-and-rescue forces in motion. Half an hour into the process, when a controller at Boston Center called and asked, "Any luck with the EgyptAir?" she answered simply, "No."

AMONG THE DEAD WERE 100 Americans, eighty-nine Egyptians (including thirty-three army officers), twenty-two Canadians, and a few people of other nationalities. As the news of the disaster spread, hundreds of frantic friends and relatives gathered at the airports in Los Angeles, New York, and Cairo. EgyptAir officials struggled to meet people's needs—which were largely, of course, for the sort of information that no one yet had. Most of the bodies remained in and around the wreckage at the bottom of the sea. Decisions now had to be made, and fast, about the recovery operation and the related problem of an investigation. Because the airplane had crashed in international waters, Egypt had the right to lead the show. Realistically, though, it did not have the resources to salvage a heavy airplane in waters 250 feet deep and 5,000 miles away.

The solution was obvious, and it came in the form of a call to the White House from Egyptian President Hosni Mubarak, an experienced military pilot with close ties to EgyptAir, requesting that the investigation be taken over by the U.S. government. The White House in turn called Jim Hall, the chairman of the National Transportation Safety Board, an investigative agency with a merited reputation for competence. Hall, a Tennessee lawyer and friend of the Gores, had in the aftermath of the TWA Flight 800 explosion parlayed his position into one of considerable visibility. The Egyptians produced a letter formally signing over the investigation to the United States, an option accorded under international convention, which would place them in a greatly diminished role (as "accredited representatives") but would also save them trouble and money. Mubarak is said to have regretted the move ever since.

In retrospect it seems inevitable that the two sides would have trouble getting along. The NTSB is a puritanical construct, a small federal agency without regulatory power whose sole purpose is to investigate accidents and issue safety recommendations that might add to the public discourse. Established in 1967 as an "independent" unit of the Washington bureaucracy, and shielded by design from the political currents of that city, the agency represents the most progressive American thinking on the role and character of good government. On call twenty-four hours a day, with technical teams ready to travel at a moment's notice, it operates on an annual baseline budget of merely $62 million or so, and employs only about 420 people, most of whom work at the headquarters on four floors of Washington's bright and modern Loews L'Enfant Plaza Hotel. In part because the NTSB seems so lean, and in part because by its very definition it advocates for the "right" causes, it receives almost universally positive press coverage. The NTSB is technocratic. It is clean. It is Government Lite.

EgyptAir, in contrast, is Government Heavy—a state-owned airline with about 600 pilots and a mixed fleet of about forty Boeings and Airbuses that serves more than eighty destinations worldwide and employs 22,000 people. It operates out of dusty Stalinist-style office buildings at the Cairo airport, under the supervision of the Ministry of Transport, from which it is often practically indistinguishable. It is probably a safe airline, but passengers dislike it for its delays and shoddy service. They call it Air Misère, probably a play on the airline's former name, Misr Air ("Misr" is Arabic for "Egypt"). It has been treated as a fiefdom for years by Mubarak's old and unassailable air-force friends, and particularly by the company's chairman, a man named Mohamed Fahim Rayan, who fights off all attempts at reform or privatization. This is hardly a secret. In parliamentary testimony six months before the crash of Flight 990, Rayan said, "My market is like a water pond which I developed over the years. It is quite unreasonable for alien people to come and seek to catch fish in my pond." His critics answer that the pond is stagnant and stinks of corruption—but this, too, is nothing new. The greatest pyramids in Egypt are made not of stone but of people: they are the vast bureaucracies that constitute society's core, and they function not necessarily to get the "job" done but to reward the personal loyalty of those at the bottom to those at the top. Once you understand that, much of the rest begins to make sense. The bureaucracies serve mostly to shelter their workers and give them something like a decent life. They also help to define Cairo. It is a great capital city, as worldly as Washington, D.C., and culturally very far away.

An official delegation traveled from Cairo to the United States and ended up staying for more than a year. It was led by two EgyptAir pilots, Mohsen al-Missiry, an experienced accident investigator on temporary assignment to the Egyptian Civil Aviation Authority for this case, and Shaker Kelada, who had retired from active flying to become a flight-operations manager and eventually vice-president for safety and quality assurance. These men were smart and tough, and managed a team primarily of EgyptAir engineers, many of whom were very sharp.

The U.S. Navy was given the job of salvage, and it in turn hired a contractor named Oceaneering, which arrived with a ship and grapples and remote-controlled submarines. The debris was plotted by sonar, and found to lie in two clusters: the small "west field," which included the left engine; and, 1,200 feet beyond it in the direction of flight, the "east field," where most of the airplane lay. From what was known of the radar profile and from the tight concentration of the debris, it began to seem unlikely that an in-flight explosion was to blame. The NTSB said nothing. Nine days after the accident the flight-data recorder—the "black box" that records flight and systems data—was retrieved and sent to the NTSB laboratory in Washington. The NTSB stated tersely that there was preliminary evidence that the initial dive may have been a "controlled descent." Five days later, on Sunday, November 14, a senior official at the Egyptian Transportation Ministry—an air-force general and a former EgyptAir pilot—held a news conference in Cairo and, with Rayan at his side, announced that the evidence from the flight-data recorder had been inconclusive but the dive could be explained only by a bomb in the cockpit or in the lavatory directly behind it. It was an odd assertion to make, but of little importance, because the second black box, the cockpit voice recorder, had been salvaged the night before and was sent on Sunday to the NTSB. The tape was cleaned and processed, and a small group that included a translator (who was not Egyptian) gathered in a listening room at L'Enfant Plaza to hear it through.

LISTENING TO COCKPIT RECORDINGS is a tough and voyeuristic duty, restricted to the principal investigators and people with specific knowledge of the airplane or the pilots, who might help to prepare an accurate transcript. Experienced investigators grow accustomed to the job, but I talked to several who had heard the EgyptAir tape, and they admitted that they had been taken aback. Black boxes are such pitiless, unblinking devices. When the information they contained from Flight 990 was combined with the radar profile and the first, sketchy information on the crew, this was the story it seemed to tell:

The flight lasted thirty-one minutes. During the departure from New York it was captained, as required, by the aircraft commander, a portly senior pilot named Ahmad al-Habashi, fifty-seven, who had flown thirty-six years for the airline. Habashi of course sat in the left seat. In the right seat was the most junior member of the crew, a thirty-six-year-old co-pilot who was progressing well in his career and looking forward to getting married. Before takeoff the co-pilot advised the flight attendants by saying, in Arabic, "In the name of God, the merciful, the compassionate. Cabin crew takeoff position." This was not unusual.

After takeoff the autopilot did the flying. Habashi and the co-pilot kept watch, talked to air-traffic control, and gossiped about their work. The cockpit door was unlocked, which was fairly standard on EgyptAir flights. Various flight attendants came in and left; for a while the chief pilot, the man who was deadheading back to Cairo, stopped by the cockpit to chat. Then, twenty minutes into the flight, the "cruise" co-pilot, Gameel al-Batouti, arrived. Batouti was a big, friendly guy with a reputation for telling jokes and enjoying life. Three months short of sixty, and mandatory retirement, he was unusually old for a co-pilot. He had joined the airline in his mid-forties, after a career as a flight instructor for the air force, and had rejected several opportunities for command. His lack of ambition was odd but not unheard of: his English was poor and might have given him trouble on the necessary exams; moreover, as the company's senior 767 co-pilot, he made adequate money and had his pick of long-distance flights. Now he used his seniority to urge the junior co-pilot to cede the right seat ahead of the scheduled crew change. When the junior man resisted, Batouti said, "You mean you're not going to get up? You will get up. Go and get some rest and come back." The junior co-pilot stayed in his seat a bit longer and then left the cockpit. Batouti took the seat and buckled in.

Batouti was married and had five children. Four of them were grown and doing well. His fifth child was a girl, age ten, who was sick with lupus but responding to treatment that he had arranged for her to receive in Los Angeles. Batouti had a nice house in Cairo. He had a vacation house on the beach. He did not drink heavily. He was moderately religious. He had his retirement planned. He had acquired an automobile tire in New Jersey the day before, and was bringing it home in the cargo hold. He had also picked up some free samples of Viagra, to distribute as gifts.

Captain Habashi was more religious, and was known to pray sometimes in the cockpit. He and Batouti were old friends. Using Batouti's nickname, he said, in Arabic, "How are you, Jimmy?" They groused to each other about the chief pilot and about a clique of young and arrogant "kids," junior EgyptAir pilots who were likewise catching a ride back to the Cairo base. One of those pilots came into the cockpit dressed in street clothes. Habashi said, "What's with you? Why did you get all dressed in red like that?" Presumably the man then left. Batouti had a meal. A female flight attendant came in and offered more. Batouti said pleasantly, "No, thank you, it was marvelous." She took his tray.

At 1:47 A.M. the last calls came in from air-traffic control, from Ann Brennan, far off in the night at her display. Captain Habashi handled the calls. He said, "New York, EgyptAir Nine-nine-zero heavy, good morning," and she answered with her final "EgyptAir Nine-ninety, roger."

At 1:48 Batouti found the junior co-pilot's pen and handed it across to Habashi. He said, "Look, here's the new first officer's pen. Give it to him, please. God spare you." He added, "To make sure it doesn't get lost."

Habashi said, "Excuse me, Jimmy, while I take a quick trip to the toilet." He ran his electric seat back with a whir. There was the sound of the cockpit door moving.

Batouti said, "Go ahead, please."

Habashi said, "Before it gets crowded. While they are eating. And I'll be back to you."

Again the cockpit door moved. There was a *clunk*. There was a *clink*. It seems that Batouti was now alone in the cockpit. The 767 was at 33,000 feet, cruising peacefully eastward at .79 Mach.

At 1:48:30 a strange, wordlike sound was uttered, three syllables with emphasis on the second, perhaps more English than Arabic, and variously heard on the tape as "control it," "hydraulic," or something unintelligible.

The NTSB ran extensive speech and sound-spectrum studies on it, and was never able to assign it conclusively to Batouti or to anyone else. But what is clear is that Batouti then softly said, "*Tawakkalt ala Allah,*" which proved difficult to translate, and was at first rendered incorrectly, but essentially means "I rely on God." An electric seat whirred. The autopilot disengaged, and the airplane sailed on as before for another four seconds. Again Batouti said, "I rely on God." Then two things happened almost simultaneously, according to the flight-data recorder: the throttles in the cockpit moved back fast to minimum idle, and a second later, back at the tail, the airplane's massive elevators (the pitch-control surfaces) dropped to a three-degrees-down position. When the elevators drop, the tail goes up; and when the tail goes up, the nose points down. Apparently Batouti had chopped the power and pushed the control yoke forward.

The effect was dramatic. The airplane began to dive steeply, dropping its nose so quickly that the environment inside plunged to nearly zero gs, the weightless condition of space. Six times in quick succession Batouti repeated, "I rely on God." His tone was calm. There was a loud thump. As the nose continued to pitch downward, the airplane went into the negative-g range, nudging loose objects against the ceiling. The elevators moved even farther down. Batouti said, "I rely on God."

Somehow, in the midst of this, now sixteen seconds into the dive, Captain Habashi made his way back from the toilet. He yelled, "What's happening? What's happening?"

Batouti said, "I rely on God."

The wind outside was roaring. The airplane was dropping through 30,800 feet, and accelerating beyond its maximum operating speed of .86 Mach. In the cockpit the altimeters were spinning like cartoon clocks. Warning horns were sounding, warning lights were flashing—low oil pressure on the left engine, and then on the right. The master alarm went off, a loud high-to-low warble.

For the last time Batouti said, "I rely on God."

Again Habashi shouted, "What's happening?" By then he must have reached the left control yoke. The negative gs ended as he countered the pitch-over, slowing the rate at which the nose was dropping. But the 767 was still angled down steeply, 40 degrees below the horizon, and it was accelerating. The rate of descent hit 39,000 feet a minute.

"What's happening, Gameel? What's happening?"

Habashi was clearly pulling very hard on his control yoke, trying desperately to raise the nose. Even so, thirty seconds into the dive, at 22,200 feet, the airplane hit the speed of sound, at which it was certainly not meant to fly. Many things happened in quick succession in the cockpit. Batouti reached over and shut off the fuel, killing both engines. Habashi screamed, "What is this? What is this? Did you shut the engines?" The throttles were pushed full forward—for no obvious reason, since the engines were dead. The speed-brake handle was then pulled, deploying drag devices on the wings.

At the same time, there was an unusual occurrence back at the tail: the right-side and left-side elevators, which normally move together to control the airplane's pitch, began to "split," or move in opposite directions. Specifically: the elevator on the right remained down, while the left-side elevator moved up to a healthy recovery position. That this could happen at all was the result of a design feature meant to allow either pilot to overpower a mechanical jam and control the airplane with only one elevator. The details are complex, but the essence in this case seemed to be that the right elevator was being pushed down by Batouti while the left elevator was being pulled up by the captain. The NTSB concluded that a "force fight" had broken out in the cockpit.

Words were failing Habashi. He yelled, "Get away in the engines!" And then, incredulously, ". . . shut the engines!"

Batouti said calmly, "It's shut."

Habashi did not have time to make sense of the happenings. He probably did not have time to get into his seat and slide it forward. He must have been standing in the cockpit, leaning over the seatback and hauling on the controls. The commotion was horrendous. He was reacting instinctively as a pilot, yelling, "Pull!" and then, "Pull with me! Pull with me! Pull with me!"

It was the last instant captured by the on-board flight recorders. The elevators were split, with the one on the right side, Batouti's side, still pushed into a nose-down position. The ailerons on both wings had assumed a strange upswept position, normally never seen on an airplane. The 767 was at 16,416 feet, doing 527 miles an hour, and pulling a moderately heavy 2.4 gs, indicating that the nose, though still below the horizon, was rising fast, and that Habashi's efforts on the left side were having an effect. A belated recovery was under way. At that point, because the engines had been cut, all nonessential electrical devices were lost, blacking out not only the recorders, which rely on primary power, but also most of the instrument displays and lights. The pilots were left to the darkness of the sky, whether to work together or to fight. I've often wondered what happened between those two men during the 114 seconds that remained of their lives. We'll never know. Radar reconstruction showed that the 767 recovered from the dive at 16,000 feet and, like a great wounded glider, soared steeply back to 24,000 feet, turned to the southeast while beginning to break apart, and shed its useless left engine and some of its skin before giving up for good and diving to its death at high speed.

STATES OF WAR

Paul Revere's Ride

HENRY WADSWORTH LONGFELLOW || 1861

By the time of The Atlantic's *founding, Henry Wadsworth Longfellow (1807–1882) had already established himself, both at home and abroad, as far and away the most popular American poet of the era. His book-length narrative poems,* Evangeline *(1847) and* The Song of Hiawatha *(1855), had sold in the then lofty tens of thousands, and his talismanic images of village blacksmiths pounding away under spreading chestnut trees and of Indian chiefs encamping by the shores of Gitche Gumee had become ingrained in the American idiom. Born in Portland, Maine, and educated at Bowdoin College, where one of his classmates was Nathaniel Hawthorne, Longfellow was also a gifted linguist who had mastered twelve languages and earned an appointment to Harvard before he was thirty. Owing to these formidable talents, Longfellow became, during* The Atlantic's *early years, virtually the house bard, contributing more than fifty poems on an array of subjects, from the death of Hawthorne to the celestial escapades of a medieval rabbi, in addition to excerpts from his celebrated translation of Dante's* Divine Comedy.

Among the earliest and most famous of Longfellow's Atlantic poems was "Paul Revere's Ride," a galloping ode to the heroic exploits of the Revolutionary War patriot that would ensure both subject and author a permanent place in the affections of their countrymen. The poem, which Longfellow planned from the outset to feature in Tales of a Wayside Inn *(1863), another of his ambitious efforts to mythologize American history through a series of verse narratives, was forged in the heat of the political moment. Only a few months later, a Confederate Army attack on Fort Sumter would ignite the Civil War, and Longfellow's rousing dramatization of Revere's midnight ride in "the hour of darkness and peril and need" was calculated to serve as an unspoken rallying cry for the abolitionist cause and the preservation of the Union. Yet what makes the work so memorable—and, as generations of American schoolchildren can attest, so ripe for memorization—has less to do with political purpose than with technical prowess: taut pacing, evocative phrasing, rhythmic drive, and oratorical command. Although critics and historians have periodically taken Longfellow to task for his stagy depiction of events and his hagiographic treatment of Revere, there is no disputing the poem's emblematic power as a patriotic anthem and as a perennial touchstone of American valor.*

Listen, my children, and you shall hear
Of the midnight ride of Paul Revere,
On the eighteenth of April, in Seventy-Five:
Hardly a man is now alive
Who remembers that famous day and year.

He said to his friend,—"If the British march
By land or sea from the town to-night,
Hang a lantern aloft in the belfry-arch
Of the North-Church-tower, as a signal-light,—
One if by land, and two if by sea;
And I on the opposite shore will be,
Ready to ride and spread the alarm
Through every Middlesex village and farm,
For the country-folk to be up and to arm."

Then he said good-night, and with muffled oar
Silently rowed to the Charlestown shore,
Just as the moon rose over the bay,
Where swinging wide at her moorings lay
The Somersett, British man-of-war:
A phantom ship, with each mast and spar
Across the moon, like a prison-bar,
And a huge, black hulk, that was magnified
By its own reflection in the tide.

Meanwhile, his friend, through alley and street
Wanders and watches with eager ears,
Till in the silence around him he hears
The muster of men at the barrack-door,
The sound of arms, and the tramp of feet,
And the measured tread of the grenadiers
Marching down to their boats on the shore.

Then he climbed to the tower of the church,
Up the wooden stairs, with stealthy tread,
To the belfry-chamber overhead,
And startled the pigeons from their perch
On the sombre rafters, that round him made
Masses and moving shapes of shade,—

Up the light ladder, slender and tall,
To the highest window in the wall,
Where he paused to listen and look down
A moment on the roofs of the town,
And the moonlight flowing over all.

Beneath, in the churchyard, lay the dead
In their night-encampment on the hill,
Wrapped in silence so deep and still,
That he could hear, like a sentinel's tread,
The watchful night-wind, as it went
Creeping along from tent to tent,
And seeming to whisper, "All is well!"
A moment only he feels the spell
Of the place and the hour, the secret dread
Of the lonely belfry and the dead;
For suddenly all his thoughts are bent
On a shadowy something far away,
Where the river widens to meet the bay,—
A line of black, that bends and floats
On the rising tide, like a bridge of boats.

Meanwhile, impatient to mount and ride,
Booted and spurred, with a heavy stride,
On the opposite shore walked Paul Revere
Now he patted his horse's side,
Now gazed on the landscape far and near,
Then impetuous stamped the earth,
And turned and tightened his saddle-girth;
But mostly he watched with eager search
The belfry-tower of the old North Church,
As it rose above the graves on the hill,
Lonely, and spectral, and sombre, and still.

And lo! as he looks, on the belfry's height,
A glimmer, and then a gleam of light!
He springs to the saddle, the bridle he turns,
But lingers and gazes, till full on his sight
A second lamp in the belfry burns!

A hurry of hoofs in a village-street,
A shape in the moonlight, a bulk in the dark,
And beneath from the pebbles, in passing, a spark
Struck out by a steed that flies fearless and fleet:
That was all! And yet, through the gloom and the light,
The fate of a nation was riding that night;
And the spark struck out by that steed, in his flight,
Kindled the land into flame with its heat.

It was twelve by the village-clock,
When he crossed the bridge into Medford town.
He heard the crowing of the cock,
And the barking of the farmer's dog,
And felt the damp of the river-fog,
That rises when the sun goes down.

It was one by the village-clock,
When he rode into Lexington.
He saw the gilded weathercock
Swim in the moonlight as he passed,
And the meeting-house windows, blank and bare,
Gaze at him with a spectral glare,
As if they already stood aghast
At the bloody work they would look upon.

It was two by the village-clock,
When he came to the bridge in Concord town.
He heard the bleating of the flock,
And the twitter of birds among the trees,
And felt the breath of the morning-breeze
Blowing over the meadows brown.
And one was safe and asleep in his bed
Who at the bridge would be first to fall,
Who that day would be lying dead,
Pierced by a British musket-ball.

You know the rest. In the books you have read
How the British regulars fired and fled,—
How the farmers gave them ball for ball,
From behind each fence and farmyard-wall,

Chasing the red-coats down the lane,
Then crossing the fields to emerge again
Under the trees at the turn of the road,
And only pausing to fire and load.

So through the night rode Paul Revere;
And so through the night went his cry of alarm
To every Middlesex village and farm,—
A cry of defiance, and not of fear,—
A voice in the darkness, a knock at the door,
And a word that shall echo forevermore!
For, borne on the night-wind of the Past,
Through all our history, to the last,
In the hour of darkness and peril and need,
The people will waken and listen to hear
The hurrying hoof-beat of that steed,
And the midnight-message of Paul Revere.

The Psychological Roots of War

WILLIAM JAMES || 1904

On February 4, 1899, William James (1842–1910) wept for the first time
in years. By his own account, what brought James to tears that day was
the dramatic news that American forces had become embroiled in fierce
fighting against republican soldiers in the Philippines. For James, one of
the towering intellects of American history, as well as for a number of
other leading thinkers of the time, the United States' annexation and
occupation of the Philippines following the Spanish-American War of
1898 marked a disastrous turning point in the country's national life—
signaling the end not only of a 125-year age of innocence but of the very
idea of America as a reigning symbol of freedom, democracy, and magnanimity in a stubbornly belligerent world. "The stars and stripes . . .
are now a lying rag, pure and simple," an embittered James wrote in a
letter to a friend. But James's anguish over American expansionism
quickly morphed into action. He became a frequent critic of American
foreign policy and a key member of the American Anti-Imperialist
League, an activist organization whose ranks included such prominent
figures as Mark Twain, Andrew Carnegie, and former president Grover
Cleveland.

But perhaps the most characteristically Jamesian response to his
political concerns was a decision to devote himself to a vigorous philosophical inquiry into the role that the human psyche plays in the perva-
siveness of warfare. "The Psychological Roots of War," one of eight
articles that James published in The Atlantic over a twenty-four-year
span, elegantly attempts to explain the elemental appeal of military conflict in human affairs. This concise essay, which originally appeared in
the magazine under the title "Remarks at the Peace Banquet," was first
delivered as the keynote address at the Thirteenth Universal Peace Congress, in Boston, and it offers an unsparing appraisal of the magnitude
and intractability of the problem: Human beings, according to James,
are innately militaristic, ineluctably drawn to "the thrills and excitements" of waging war. Because "our permanent enemy is the noted bellicosity of human nature," he writes, those who seek to advance the cause
of pacifism confront an almost insurmountable challenge. In a bold and
prodigious body of writings on philosophy, religion, and psychology,
James would give new meaning to the term "polymath," but he appears
to flounder at the conclusion of this essay, when he proposes a series of

*woolly suggestions for turning the terrible tide of war. (He would develop
these thoughts more fully and persuasively six years later in one of his
most famous essays, "The Moral Equivalent of War.") But this 1904 At-*
lantic *article remains invaluable not only for its lacerating vision of the
nature of man but also for its prophetic presentiment of the most war-
torn century in human history.*

I am only a philosopher, and there is only one thing that a philosopher
can be relied on to do. You know that the function of statistics has been in-
geniously described as being the refutation of other statistics. Well, a
philosopher can always contradict other philosophers. In ancient times
philosophers defined man as the rational animal; and philosophers since
then have always found much more to say about the rational than about
the animal part of the definition. But looked at candidly, reason bears
about the same proportion to the rest of human nature that we in this hall
bear to the rest of America, Europe, Asia, Africa, and Polynesia. Reason is
one of the very feeblest of Nature's forces, if you take it at any one spot and
moment. It is only in the very long run that its effects become perceptible.
Reason assumes to settle things by weighing them against one another
without prejudice, partiality, or excitement; but what affairs in the concrete
are settled by is and always will be just prejudices, partialities, cupidities,
and excitements. Appealing to reason as we do, we are in a sort of a forlorn
hope situation, like a small sand-bank in the midst of a hungry sea ready
to wash it out of existence. But sand-banks grow when the conditions favor; and weak as reason is, it has the unique advantage over its antagonists
that its activity never lets up and that it presses always in one direction,
while men's prejudices vary, their passions ebb and flow, and their excitements are intermittent. Our sand-bank, I absolutely believe, is bound to
grow,—bit by bit it will get dyked and breakwatered. But sitting as we do
in this warm room, with music and lights and the flowing bowl and smiling faces, it is easy to get too sanguine about our task, and since I am called
to speak, I feel as if it might not be out of place to say a word about the
strength of our enemy.

Our permanent enemy is the noted bellicosity of human nature. Man,
biologically considered, and whatever else he may be in the bargain, is simply the most formidable of all beasts of prey, and, indeed, the only one that
preys systematically on its own species. We are once for all adapted to the
military *status.* A millennium of peace would not breed the fighting disposition out of our bone and marrow, and a function so ingrained and vital

will never consent to die without resistance, and will always find impassioned apologists and idealizers.

Not only men born to be soldiers, but non-combatants by trade and nature, historians in their studies, and clergymen in their pulpits, have been war's idealizers. They have talked of war as of God's court of justice. And, indeed, if we think how many things beside the frontiers of states the wars of history have decided, we must feel some respectful awe, in spite of all the horrors. Our actual civilization, good and bad alike, has had past war for its determining condition. Great-mindedness among the tribes of men has always meant the will to prevail, and all the more so if prevailing included slaughtering and being slaughtered. Rome, Paris, England, Brandenburg, Piedmont—soon, let us hope, Japan—along with their arms have made their traits of character and habits of thought prevail among their conquered neighbors. The blessings we actually enjoy, such as they are, have grown up in the shadow of the wars of antiquity. The various ideals were backed by fighting wills, and where neither would give way, the God of battles had to be the arbiter. A shallow view, this, truly; for who can say what might have prevailed if man had ever been a reasoning and not a fighting animal? Like dead men, dead causes tell no tales, and the ideals that went under in the past, along with all the tribes that represented them, find to-day no recorder, no explainer, no defender.

But apart from theoretic defenders, and apart from every soldierly individual straining at the leash, and clamoring for opportunity, war has an omnipotent support in the form of our imagination. Man lives *by* habits, indeed, but what he lives *for* is thrills and excitements. The only relief from Habit's tediousness is periodical excitement. From time immemorial wars have been, especially for non-combatants, the supremely thrilling excitement. Heavy and dragging at its end, at its outset every war means an explosion of imaginative energy. The dams of routine burst, and boundless prospects open. The remotest spectators share the fascination. With that awful struggle now in progress on the confines of the world, there is not a man in this room, I suppose, who doesn't buy both an evening and a morning paper, and first of all pounce on the war column.

A deadly listlessness would come over most men's imagination of the future if they could seriously be brought to believe that never again *in saecula saeculorum* would a war trouble human history. In such a stagnant summer afternoon of a world, where would be the zest or interest?

This is the constitution of human nature which we have to work against. The plain truth is that people *want* war. They want it anyhow; for itself; and apart from each and every possible consequence. It is the final bouquet of life's fireworks. The born soldiers want it hot and actual. The non-combatants want it in the background, and always as an open possibility, to feed imagination on and keep excitement going. Its clerical and historical defenders fool themselves when they talk as they do about it. What moves them is not the blessings it has won for us, but a vague religious exaltation. War, they feel, is human nature at its uttermost. We are here to do our uttermost. It is a sacrament. Society would rot, they think, without the mystical blood-payment.

We do ill, I fancy, to talk much of universal peace or of a general disarmament. We must go in for preventive medicine, not for radical cure. We must cheat our foe, politically circumvent his action, not try to change his nature. In one respect war is like love, though in no other. Both leave us intervals of rest; and in the intervals life goes on perfectly well without them, though the imagination still dallies with their possibility. Equally insane when once aroused and under headway, whether they shall be aroused or not depends on accidental circumstances. How are old maids and old bachelors made? Not by deliberate vows of celibacy, but by sliding on from year to year with no sufficient matrimonial provocation. So of the nations with their wars. Let the general possibility of war be left open, in Heaven's name, for the imagination to dally with. Let the soldiers dream of killing, as the old maids dream of marrying. But organize in every conceivable way the practical machinery for making each successive chance of war abortive. Put peacemen in power; educate the editors and statesmen to responsibility. . . . Seize every pretext, however small, for arbitration methods, and multiply the precedents; foster rival excitements and invent new outlets for heroic energy; and from one generation to another, the chances are that irritations will grow less acute and states of strain less dangerous among the nations. Armies and navies will continue, of course, and will fire the minds of populations with their potentialities of greatness. But their officers will find that somehow or other, with no deliberate intention on any one's part, each successive "incident" has managed to evaporate and to lead nowhere, and that the thought of what might have been remains their only consolation.

The last weak runnings of the war spirit will be "punitive expeditions." A country that turns its arms only against uncivilized foes is, I think, wrongly taunted as degenerate. Of course it has ceased to be heroic in the old grand style. But I verily believe that this is because it now sees something better. It has a conscience. It knows that between civilized countries a war is a crime against civilization. It will still perpetrate peccadillos, to be sure. But it is afraid, afraid in the good sense of the word, to engage in absolute crimes against civilization.

Atomic War or Peace

ALBERT EINSTEIN ‖ 1947

Despite the conventional wisdom that his famous equation, $E = mc^2$, had opened the conceptual door to the nuclear age, Albert Einstein (1879–1955) tended to downplay his significance in the development of nuclear weapons. "I do not consider myself the father of the release of atomic energy," Einstein declared in an interview in November 1945, several months after the bombing of Hiroshima and Nagasaki that ended the Second World War. "My part in it was quite indirect." Nonetheless, it was Einstein's signature on an all-important letter to Franklin Delano Roosevelt in 1939, urging the president to pursue an atomic weapons program in response to Germany's own bomb-building efforts, that provided the impetus for the Manhattan Project. The great physicist would live to regret his lobbying: "Had I known that the Germans would not succeed in developing an atomic bomb," he told Newsweek in 1947, "I would have done nothing."

Thus, a certain measure of guilt may have been at work in Einstein's fervent postwar campaign to educate the public about the dangers of nuclear war, which found its most eloquent expression in the essay that follows. Speaking out at a moment when the United States still enjoyed a nuclear monopoly (the Soviets were two years away from detonating their first bomb), Einstein limns the bleak consequences of global conflict in the nuclear age, which would, he writes, "bring destruction on a scale never before held possible and even now hardly conceived." The best way to avoid this horrific prospect, he argues, is for the nations of the world to place their militaries under the control of a much-strengthened United Nations—a "partial world government," charged with providing security to the entire globe. A lifelong pacifist, Einstein would live to see his high hopes dashed by a force whose power he acknowledges in this essay: the reluctance of any nation, and particularly the Soviet Union, to surrender its sovereignty and state secrets for the good of mankind. But half a century later, his call for a world at peace—in which nuclear war is avoided through cooperation and conciliation, rather than through mutually assured destruction and a balance of terror—endures as a vision of a road not taken.

Since the completion of the first atomic bomb nothing has been accomplished to make the world more safe from war, while much has been done to increase the destructiveness of war. I am not able to speak from any firsthand knowledge about the development of the atomic bomb, since I do not work in this field. But enough has been said by those who do to indicate that the bomb has been made more effective. Certainly the possibility can be envisaged of building a bomb of far greater size, capable of producing destruction over a larger area. It also is credible that an extensive use could be made of radioactivated gases which would spread over a wide region, causing heavy loss of life without damage to buildings.

I do not believe it is necessary to go on beyond these possibilities to contemplate a vast extension of bacteriological warfare. I am skeptical that this form presents dangers comparable with those of atomic warfare. Nor do I take into account a danger of starting a chain reaction of a scope great enough to destroy part or all of this planet. I dismiss this on the ground that if it could happen from a man-made atomic explosion it would already have happened from the action of the cosmic rays which are continually reaching the earth's surface.

But it is not necessary to imagine the earth being destroyed like a nova by a stellar explosion to understand vividly the growing scope of atomic war and to recognize that unless another war is prevented it is likely to bring destruction on a scale never before held possible and even now hardly conceived, and that little civilization would survive it.

In the first two years of the atomic era another phenomenon is to be noted. The public, having been warned of the horrible nature of atomic warfare, has done nothing about it, and to a large extent has dismissed the warning from its consciousness. A danger that cannot be averted had perhaps better be forgotten; or a danger against which every possible precaution has been taken also had probably better be forgotten. That is, if the United States had dispersed its industries and decentralized its cities, it might be reasonable for people to forget the peril they face.

I should say parenthetically that it is well that this country has not taken these precautions, for to have done so would make atomic war still more probable, since it would convince the rest of the world that we are resigned to it and are preparing for it. But nothing has been done to avert war, while much has been done to make atomic war more horrible; so there is no excuse for ignoring the danger.

I say that nothing has been done to avert war since the completion of the atomic bomb, despite the proposal for supranational control of atomic energy put forward by the United States in the United Nations. This country has made only a conditional proposal, and on conditions which the Soviet Union is now determined not to accept. This makes it possible to blame the failure on the Russians.

But in blaming the Russians the Americans should not ignore the fact that they themselves have not voluntarily renounced the use of the bomb as an ordinary weapon in the time before the achievement of supranational control, or if supranational control is not achieved. Thus they have fed the fear of other countries that they consider the bomb a legitimate part of their arsenal so long as other countries decline to accept their terms for supranational control.

Americans may be convinced of their determination not to launch an aggressive or preventive war. So they may believe it is superfluous to announce publicly that they will not a second time be the first to use the atomic bomb. But this country has been solemnly invited to renounce the use of the bomb—that is, to outlaw it—and has declined to do so unless its terms for supranational control are accepted.

I believe this policy is a mistake. I see a certain military gain from not renouncing the use of the bomb in that this may be deemed to restrain another country from starting a war in which the United States might use it. But what is gained in one way is lost in another. For an understanding over the supranational control of atomic energy has been made more remote. That may be no military drawback so long as the United States has the exclusive use of the bomb. But the moment another country is able to make it in substantial quantities, the United States loses greatly through the absence of an international agreement, because of the vulnerability of its concentrated industries and its highly developed urban life.

In refusing to outlaw the bomb while having the monopoly of it, this country suffers in another respect, in that it fails to return publicly to the ethical standards of warfare formally accepted previous to the last war. It should not be forgotten that the atomic bomb was made in this country as a preventive measure; it was to head off its use by the Germans, if they discovered it. The bombing of civilian centers was initiated by the Germans and adopted by the Japanese. To it the Allies responded in kind—as it turned out, with greater effectiveness—and they were morally justified in doing so. But now, without any provocation, and without the justification of reprisal or retaliation, a refusal to outlaw the use of the bomb save in reprisal is making a political purpose of its possession; this is hardly pardonable.

I am not saying that the United States should not manufacture and stockpile the bomb, for I believe that it must do so; it must be able to deter another nation from making an atomic attack when it also has the bomb. But deterrence should be the only purpose of the stockpile of bombs. In the same way I believe that the United Nations should have the atomic bomb when it is supplied with its own armed forces and weapons. But it too should have the bomb for the sole purpose of deterring an aggressor or rebellious nations from making an atomic attack. It should not use the atomic bomb on its own initiative any more than the United States or any other power should do so. To keep a stockpile of atomic bombs without promising not to initiate its use is exploiting the possession of bombs for political ends. It may be that the United States hopes in this way to frighten the Soviet Union into accepting supranational control of atomic energy. But the creation of fear only heightens antagonism and increases the danger of war. I am of the opinion that this policy has detracted from the very real virtue in the offer of supranational control of atomic energy.

We have emerged from a war in which we had to accept the degradingly low ethical standards of the enemy. But instead of feeling liberated from his standards, and set free to restore the sanctity of human life and the safety of noncombatants, we are in effect making the low standards of the enemy in the last war our own for the present. Thus we are starting toward another war degraded by our own choice.

It may be that the public is not fully aware that in another war atomic bombs will be available in large quantities. It may measure the dangers in the terms of the bombs exploded before the end of the last war. The public also may not appreciate that, in relation to the damage inflicted, atomic bombs already have become the most economical form of destruction that can be used on the offensive. In another war the bombs will be plentiful and they will be comparatively cheap. Unless there is a determination not to use them that is stronger than can be noted today among American political and military leaders, and on the part of the public itself, atomic warfare will be hard to avoid. Unless Americans come to recognize that they are not stronger in the world because they have the bomb, but weaker because of their vulnerability to atomic attack, they are not likely to conduct their relations with Russia in a spirit that furthers the arrival at an understanding.

BUT I DO NOT SUGGEST that the American failure to outlaw the use of the bomb except in retaliation is the only cause of the absence of an agreement with the Soviet Union over atomic control. The Russians have made it clear that they will do everything in their power to prevent a supranational regime from coming into existence. They not only reject it in the range of atomic energy: they reject it sharply on principle, and thus have spurned in advance any overture to join a limited world government.

Mr. Gromyko has rightly said that the essence of the American atomic proposal is that national sovereignty is not compatible with the atomic era. He declares that the Soviet Union cannot accept this thesis. The reasons he gives are obscure, for they quite obviously are pretexts. But what seems to be true is that the Soviet leaders believe they cannot preserve the social structure of the Soviet state in a supranational regime. The Soviet government is determined to maintain its present social structure, and the leaders of Russia, who hold their great power through the nature of that structure, will spare no effort to prevent a supranational regime from coming into existence, to control atomic energy or anything else.

The Russians may be partly right about the difficulty of retaining their present social structure in a supranational regime, though in time they may be brought to see that this is a far lesser loss than remaining isolated from a world of law. But at present they appear to be guided by their fears, and one must admit that the United States has made ample contributions to these fears, not only as to atomic energy but in many other respects. Indeed this country has conducted its Russian policy as though it were convinced that fear is the greatest of all diplomatic instruments.

That the Russians are striving to prevent the formation of a supranational security system is no reason why the rest of the world should not work to create one. It has been pointed out that the Russians have a way of resisting with all their arts what they do not wish to have happen; but once it happens, they can be flexible and accommodate themselves to it. So it would be well for the United States and other powers not to permit the Russians to veto an attempt to create supranational security. They can proceed with some hope that once the Russians see they cannot prevent such a regime they may join it.

So far the United States has shown no interest in preserving the security of the Soviet Union. It has been interested in its own security, which is characteristic of the competition which marks the conflict for power between sovereign states. But one cannot know in advance what would be the effect on Russian fears if the American people forced their leaders to pursue a policy of substituting law for the present anarchy of international relations. In a world of law, Russian security would be equal to our own, and for the American people to espouse this wholeheartedly, something that should be possible under the workings of democracy, might work a kind of miracle in Russian thinking.

At present the Russians have no evidence to convince them that the American people are not contentedly supporting a policy of military preparedness which they regard as a policy of deliberate intimidation. If they had evidences of a passionate desire by Americans to preserve peace in the one way it can be maintained, by a supranational regime of law, this would upset Russian calculations about the peril to Russian security in current trends of American thought. Not until a genuine, convincing offer is made to the Soviet Union, backed by an aroused American public, will one be entitled to say what the Russian response would be.

It may be that the first response would be to reject the world of law. But if from that moment it began to be clear to the Russians that such a world was coming into existence without them, and that their own security was being increased, their ideas necessarily would change.

I am in favor of inviting the Russians to join a world government authorized to provide security, and if they are unwilling to join, to proceed to establish supranational security without them. Let me admit quickly that I see great peril in such a course. If it is adopted it must be done in a way to make it utterly clear that the new regime is not a combination of power against Russia. It must be a combination that by its composite nature will greatly reduce the chances of war. It will be more diverse in its interests than any single state, thus less likely to resort to aggressive or preventive war. It will be larger, hence stronger than any single nation. It will be geographically much more extensive, and thus more difficult to defeat by military means. It will be dedicated to supranational security, and thus escape the emphasis on national supremacy which is so strong a factor in war.

If a supranational regime is set up without Russia, its service to peace will depend on the skill and sincerity with which it is done. Emphasis should always be apparent on the desire to have Russia take part. It must be clear to Russia, and no less so to the nations comprising the organization, that no penalty is incurred or implied because a nation declines to join. If the Russians do not join at the outset, they must be sure of a welcome when they do decide to join. Those who create the organization must understand that they are building with the final objective of obtaining Russian adherence.

These are abstractions, and it is not easy to outline the specific lines a partial world government must follow to induce the Russians to join. But two conditions are clear to me: the new organization must have no military secrets; and the Russians must be free to have observers at every session of the organization, where its new laws are drafted, discussed, and adopted, and where its policies are decided. That would destroy the great factory of secrecy where so many of the world's suspicions are manufactured.

It may affront the military-minded person to suggest a regime that does not maintain any military secrets. He has been taught to believe that secrets thus divulged would enable a war-minded nation to seek to conquer the earth. (As to the so-called secret of the atomic bomb, I am assuming the Russians will have this through their own efforts within a short time.) I grant there is a risk in not maintaining military secrets. If a sufficient number of nations have pooled their strength they can take this risk, for their security will be greatly increased. And it can be done with greater assurance because of the decrease of fear, suspicion, and distrust that will result. The tensions of the increasing likelihood of war in a world based on sovereignty would be replaced by the relaxation of the growing confidence in peace. In time this might so allure the Russian people that their leaders would mellow in their attitude toward the West.

MEMBERSHIP IN A SUPRANATIONAL SECURITY SYSTEM should not, in my opinion, be based on any arbitrary democratic standards. The one requirement from all should be that the representatives to supranational organizations—assembly and council—must be elected by the people in each member country through a secret ballot. These representatives must represent the people rather than any government—which would enhance the pacific nature of the organization.

To require that other democratic criteria be met is, I believe, inadvisable. Democratic institutions and standards are the result of historic developments to an extent not always appreciated in the lands which enjoy them. Setting arbitrary standards sharpens the ideological differences between the Western and Soviet systems.

But it is not the ideological differences which now are pushing the world in the direction of war. Indeed, if all the Western nations were to adopt socialism, while maintaining their national sovereignty, it is quite likely that the conflict for power between East and West would continue. The passion expressed over the economic systems of the present seems to me quite irrational. Whether the economic life of America should be dominated by relatively few individuals, as it is, or these individuals should be controlled by the state may be important, but it is not important enough to justify all the feelings that are stirred up over it.

I should wish to see all the nations forming the supranational state pool all their military forces, keeping for themselves only local police. Then

I should like to see these forces commingled and distributed as were the regiments of the former Austro-Hungarian Empire. There it was appreciated that the men and officers of one region would serve the purposes of empire better by not being stationed exclusively in their own provinces, subject to local and racial pulls.

I should like to see the authority of the supranational regime restricted altogether to the field of security. Whether this would be possible I am not sure. Experience may point to the desirability of adding some authority over economic matters, since under modern conditions these are capable of causing national upsets that have in them the seeds of violent conflict. But I should prefer to see the function of the organization altogether limited to the tasks of security. I also should like to see this regime established through the strengthening of the United Nations, so as not to sacrifice continuity in the search for peace.

I do not hide from myself the great difficulties of establishing a world government, either beginning without Russia or with Russia. I am aware of the risks. Since I should not wish it to be permissible for any country that has joined the supranational organization to secede, one of these risks is possible civil war. But I also believe that world government is certain to come in time, and that the question is how much it is to be permitted to cost. It will come, I believe, even if there is another world war, though after such a war, if it is won, it would be world government established by the victor, resting on the victor's military power, and thus to be maintained permanently only through the permanent militarization of the human race.

But I also believe it can come through agreement and through the force of persuasion alone, hence at low cost. But if it is to come in this way it will not be enough to appeal to reason. One strength of the communist system of the East is that it has some of the character of a religion and inspires the emotions of a religion. Unless the cause of peace based on law gathers behind it the force and zeal of a religion, it hardly can hope to succeed. Those to whom the moral teaching of the human race is entrusted surely have a great duty and a great opportunity. The atomic scientists, I think, have become convinced that they cannot arouse the American people to the truths of the atomic era by logic alone. There must be added that deep power of emotion which is a basic ingredient of religion. It is to be hoped that not only the churches but the schools, the colleges, and the leading organs of opinion will acquit themselves well of their unique responsibility in this regard.

"The Good War"

STUDS TERKEL || 1984

Of the many wars that the United States has waged over the course of its history, none holds a more honored place in the national memory than World War II. Unlike a couple of our more recent international conflicts—undeclared, unresolved, and highly divisive—the Second World War, with its clear-cut provocation, its well-defined enemy, and its unambiguous outcome, continues to evoke in many Americans powerful feelings of national unity, moral certitude, and patriotic pride. For the fortieth anniversary of the invasion of Normandy, in 1984—a pinnacle of national fixation on World War II—Studs Terkel (1912–) set out to lift the veil of myth and hype that enshrouds the American experience of the war with an ambitious oral history he called "The Good War." Mustering a battalion's worth of eclectic voices and points of view—men and women, combatants and noncombatants, high-ranking officers and low-ranking grunts—Terkel delivers a portrait of the war years that is remarkable for its complexity, psychological texture, and absence of cliché. In a brief author's note, the legendary Chicago-based writer, historian, and radio host had this to say about his title: "Quotation marks have been added, not as a matter of caprice or editorial comment but simply because the adjective 'good' mated to the noun 'war' is so incongruous."

Among Terkel's interview subjects, the one whose dramatic monologue most compellingly captures this incongruity is E. R. "Sledgehammer" Sledge, a Marine Corps veteran of the Pacific theater. In the excerpt below, Sledge describes in plainspoken language the transformation he saw in himself, as well as in his fellow marines, from reluctant warrior ("I don't like violence") to efficient killing machine ("After a while, the veneer of civilization wore pretty thin"). At the time of the book's publication, Terkel had already produced a half dozen oral histories, most notably Hard Times *(1970), a chronicle of the Great Depression, and* Working *(1974), in which Americans from every walk of life talked with unusual candor about their jobs. But it was "The Good War," which became a bestseller and went on to win a Pulitzer Prize for general nonfiction, that firmly established him as America's preeminent oral historian. "Studs Terkel is more than a writer," observed the economist and historian John Kenneth Galbraith, himself one of the sparkling interviewees of* "The Good War." "*He is a national resource. . . . Studs gets to the deeper heart of our history and our national life.*"

Half hidden in the hilly greenery toward the end of a winding country road is the house he helped build. It is on the campus of the University of Montevallo, a forty-five-minute drive from Birmingham, Alabama.

It is his remarkable memoir, *With the Old Breed at Peleliu and Okinawa*, published by Presidio Press in 1981, that led me to him.

Small-boned, slim, gentle in demeanor, he is a professor of biology at the university. "My main interest is ornithology. I've been a bird watcher since I was a kid in Mobile. Do you see irony in that? Interested in birds, nature, a combat Marine in the front lines? People think of bird watchers as not macho."

There was nothing macho about the war at all. We were a bunch of scared kids who had to do a job. People tell me I don't act like an ex-Marine. How is an ex-Marine supposed to act? They have some Hollywood stereotype in mind. No, I don't look like John Wayne. We were in it to get it over with so we could go back home and do what we wanted to do with our lives.

I was nineteen. A replacement in June of 1944. Eighty percent of the division in the Guadalcanal campaign was less than twenty-one years of age. We were much younger than the general Army units.

To me, there were two different wars. There was the war of the guy on the front lines. You don't come off until you are wounded or killed. Or, if lucky, relieved. Then there was the support personnel. In the Pacific, for every rifleman on the front lines there were nineteen people in the back. Their view of the war was different than mine. The man up front puts his life on the line day after day after day to the point of utter hopelessness.

The only thing that kept you going was your faith in your buddies. It wasn't just a case of friendship. I never heard of self-inflicted wounds out there. Fellows from other services said they saw this in Europe. Oh, there were plenty of times when I wished I had a million-dollar wound [laughs softly]. Like maybe shooting a toe off. What was worse than death was the indignation of your buddies. You couldn't let 'em down. It was stronger than flag and country.

With the Japanese the battle was all night long. Infiltrating the lines, slipping up, and throwing in grenades. Or running in with a bayonet or saber. They were active all night. Your buddy would try to get a little cat-nap and you'd stay on watch. Then you'd switch off. It went on day in and day out. A matter of simple survival. The only way you could get it over with was to kill them before they killed you. The war I knew was totally savage.

The Japanese fought by a code they thought was right: *bushido*. The code of the warrior: no surrender. You don't really comprehend it until you get out there and fight people who are faced with an absolutely hopeless situation and will not give up. If you tried to help one of the Japanese, he'd usually detonate a grenade and kill himself as well as you. To be captured was a disgrace. To us, it was impossible too; we knew what happened in Bataan.

Toward the end of the Okinawa campaign we found this emaciated Japanese in the bunk of what may have been a field hospital. We were on a patrol. There had been torrential rains for two weeks. The foxholes were filled with water. The Jap didn't have but a G-string on him. About ninety pounds. Pitiful. This buddy of mine picked him up and carried him out. Laid him out in the mud. There was no other place to put him.

We were sitting on our helmets waiting for the medical corpsman to check him out. He was very docile. We figured he couldn't get up. Suddenly he pulled a Japanese grenade out of his G-string. He jerked the pin out and hit it on his fist to pop open the cap. He was gonna make hamburger of me and my buddy and himself. I yelled, "Look out!" So my buddy said, "You son of a bitch, if that's how you feel about it . . ." He pulled out his forty-five and shot him right between the eyes.

This is what we were up against. I don't like violence, but there are times when you can't help it. I don't like to watch television shows with vi-olence in them. I hate to see anything afraid. But I was afraid so much, day after day, that I got tired of being scared. I've seen guys go through three campaigns and get killed on Okinawa on the last day. You knew all you had was that particular moment you were living.

You developed an attitude of no mercy because they had no mercy on us. It was a no-quarter, savage kind of thing. At Peleliu it was the first time I was close enough to see one of their faces. This Jap had been hit. One of my buddies was field-stripping him for souvenirs. I must admit it really bothered me. The guys dragging him around like a carcass. I was just hor-rified. This guy had been a human being. It didn't take me long to overcome that feeling. A lot of my buddies hit, the fatigue, the stress. After a while, the veneer of civilization wore pretty thin.

I've seen guys shoot Japanese wounded when it really was not necessary, and knock gold teeth out of their mouths. Most of them had gold teeth. I remember one time at Peleliu, I thought I'd collect gold teeth. One of my buddies carried a bunch of 'em in a sock. What you did is you took your Ka-Bar, a fighting knife [he displays a seven-inch knife]. We all had one because they'd creep into your foxhole at night. We were on Half Moon Hill, in Okinawa, about ten days. It happened every night.

The way you extracted gold teeth was by putting the tip of the blade on the tooth of the dead Japanese—I've seen guys do it to wounded ones—and hit the hilt of the knife to knock the tooth loose. How could American boys do this? If you're reduced to savagery by a situation, anything's possible. When Lindbergh made a trip to the Philippines, he was horrified at the way American GIs talked about the Japanese. It was so savage. We *were* savages.

When I leaned to make the extraction, as the troops used to say, this Navy corpsman, Doc Caswell, God bless his soul, said, "Sledgehammer, what are you doing?" I says, "Doc, I'm gonna get me some gold teeth." He said, very softly, "You don't want to do that." I said, "All the other guys are doing it." He says, "What would your folks think?" I said, "Gosh, my dad is a medical doctor back in Mobile; he might think it's interesting." He said, "Well, you might get germs." I said, "I hadn't thought of that, Doc." In retrospect I realized Ken Caswell wasn't worried about germs. He just didn't want me to take another step toward abandoning all concepts of decency.

I saw this Jap machine gunner squatting on the ground. One of our Browning-automatic-rifle men had killed him. Took the top of his skull off. It rained all that night. This Jap gunner didn't fall over for some reason. He was just sitting upright in front of the machine gun. His arms were down at his side. His eyes were wide open. It had rained all night and the rain had collected inside of his skull. We were just sitting around on our helmets, waiting to be relieved. I noticed this buddy of mine just flipping chunks of coral into the skull, about three feet away. Every time he'd get one in there, it'd splash. It reminded me of a child throwing pebbles into a puddle. It was so unreal. There was nothing malicious in his action. This was just a mild-mannered kid who was now a twentieth-century savage.

We had broken through the Japanese lines at Okinawa. I had a Thompson submachine gun and went in to check this little grass-thatched hut. An old woman was sitting just inside the door. She held out her hand. There was an hourglass figure tattooed on it to show she was Okinawan. She said, "No Nipponese." She opened her kimono and pointed to this terrible wound in her lower abdomen. You could see gangrene had set in. She didn't have a chance to survive and was obviously in great pain. She probably had caught it in an exchange of artillery fire or an air strike.

She very gently reached around, got the muzzle of my tommy gun, and moved it around to her forehead. She motioned with her other hand for me to pull the trigger. I jerked it away and called the medical corpsman. "There's an old gook woman, got a bad wound." This is what we called the natives in the Pacific. "Hey, Doc, can you do anything?"

He put a dressing on it and called someone in the rear to evacuate the old woman. We started moving out when we heard a rifle shot ring out. The corpsman and I went into a crouch. "That was an M-1, wasn't it?" We knew it was an American rifle. We looked back toward the hut and thought maybe there was a sniper in there and the old woman was acting as a front for him.

Well, here comes one of the guys in the company, walking out, checking the safety on his rifle. I said, "Was there a Nip in that hut?" He said, "Naw, it was just an old gook woman. She wanted to be put out of her misery and join her ancestors, I guess. So I obliged her."

I just blew my top. "You son of a bitch. They didn't send us out here to kill old women." He started all these excuses. By that time a sergeant came over and we told him. We moved on. I don't know what was ever done about it. He was a nice guy, like the boy next door. He wasn't just a hotheaded crazy kid. He wanted to join the best. Why one individual would act differently from another, I'll never know.

We had all become hardened. We were out there, human beings, the most highly developed form of life on earth, fighting each other like wild animals. We were under constant mortar fire. Our wounded had to be carried two miles through the mud. The dead couldn't be removed. Dead Japs all around. We'd throw mud over 'em and shells would come, blow it off, and blow them apart. The maggots were in the mud like in some corruption or compost pile.

We all had different kinds of mania. To me, the most horrible thing was to be under shellfire. You're absolutely helpless. The damn thing comes in like a freight train and there's a terrific crash. The ground shakes, and all this shrapnel ripping through the air.

I remember one afternoon on Half Moon Hill. The foxhole next to me had two boys in it. The next one to that had three. It was fairly quiet. We heard the shell come screeching over. They were firing it at us like a rifle.

The shell passed no more than a foot over my head. Two foxholes down, a guy was sitting on his helmet drinking C-ration hot chocolate. It exploded in his foxhole. I saw this guy, Bill Leyden, go straight up in the air. The other two kids fell over backwards. Dead, of course. The two in the hole next to me were killed instantly.

Leyden was the only one who survived. Would you believe he gets only partial disability, for shrapnel wounds? His record says nothing about concussion. He has seizures regularly. He was blown up in the air! If you don't call that concussion . . . The corpsmen were too busy saving lives to fill out records.

Another kid got his leg blown off. He had been a lumberjack, about twenty-one. He was always telling me how good spruce Christmas trees smelled. He said, "Sledgehammer, you think I'm gonna lose my leg?" If you don't think that just tore my guts out . . . My God, there was his field shoe on the stretcher with this stump of his ankle sticking out. The stretcher bearers just looked at each other and covered him with his poncho. He was dead.

It was raining like hell. We were knee-deep in mud. And I thought, What in the hell are we doing on this nasty stinking muddy ridge? What is this all about? You know what I mean? Wasted lives on a muddy slope.

People talk about Iwo Jima as the most glorious amphibious operation in history. I've had Iwo veterans tell me it was more similar to Peleliu than any other battle they read about. What in the hell was glorious about it?

What Is It About?

THOMAS POWERS || 1984

As the Cold War dragged on, it was only natural for Americans to assume that their dangerous standoff with the Soviet Union had become a
permanent feature of their national life. After almost four decades of incessant diplomatic wrangling, Third World proxy conflicts, and nuclear
saber rattling, few people on either side could explain why the Cold War
was still casting such a large and deadly shadow. Not long after taking
over as The Atlantic's editor-in-chief, in 1981, William Whitworth began
to ponder the possibility of an ambitious cover story about the astonishing staying power of the Cold War, the longest and most costly noncom-
bat military operation in United States history. How had the superpower
showdown, with all its annihilative potential, managed to outlive not
only its original architects but also its original provocation—the
post–World War II division of Europe? Could the persistence of the Cold
War be attributable to anything more than force of habit?

 To examine these critical questions, Whitworth called on the services
of Thomas Powers, an Atlantic contributing editor and a widely respected investigative journalist with a special brief in national security
and intelligence issues. Powers had already won a Pulitzer Prize for national reporting, in 1971, for a series of articles he wrote for United Press
International chronicling the short, violent life of the Weatherman terrorist Diana Oughton and had also published, to great acclaim, The
Man Who Kept the Secrets (1979), a biography of the longtime CIA director Richard Helms. For his Cold War article, Powers probed the forces
that had propelled previous major wars and traveled extensively on both
sides of the Iron Curtain to ask leading experts a question that was stunning in its simplicity: What is it about? In one of the article's most surprising revelations, it is the Soviets, far more than the Americans, who
express a desire to reconfigure the fundamental calculus of mutually assured destruction. Their words betray fear, fatigue, and a discernible
lack of will to continue the crushingly expensive arms race—a harbinger
of the collapse of the Soviet Union seven years later. But even so, of the
nearly one hundred experts Powers interviews, not one, he writes,
"showed anything more than a polite interest in the [central] question."
They preferred instead to talk about more practical matters, such as recent developments in military technology and diplomatic strategy. "It is
process that absorbs the managers and publicists of the Cold War," Pow-

ers observes sadly. "Not words but the Great Game itself, not why we act but what we do."

In May of 1983, I spent a week with two dozen Russians at a conference in Minneapolis. In July, I talked at length with another fifteen or twenty during a two-week stay in Moscow. They were all, in their different ways, much concerned by the danger of war between the United States and the Soviet Union. Many things worried them—the motives behind the Reagan Administration's program to build new strategic weapons, such as the MX missile (the "Peacekeeper") and the B-1 bomber, the fearful expense of trying to keep up, the failure of SALT, the apparent impasse of the Euromissile talks in Geneva, the prospect of accurate new American Pershing II missiles in Germany, barely six minutes away from the western suburbs of Moscow. But I certainly never heard anything like doubt that the missiles would work if fired. On this point they required no reassurance.

Russians claim America still has a technological edge, but being behind in the arms race is not what frightens the ones I talked to. They have been behind before. It is war that frightens them—not the chance of losing, but war itself. They have absorbed the bad news. I can only suppose this is a result of the Second World War, in which so many Russians died. Twenty million is, of course, a round number. I have been told that its source was Stalin himself, who wanted to emphasize Russian suffering but did not dare reveal the true figure—said to be even higher—lest it reflect on his leadership. If you ask a Russian whether anyone in his own family was killed during the war, you will generally get a list for an answer.

One of the people I met in Moscow was the physicist M. A. Markov, a leader of the Soviet Academy of Sciences and the chairman of the Soviet Pugwash group, which has been meeting with scientists from the United States and other countries since 1957. Markov is seventy-five and in frail health. When he travels, his daughter, a physician, goes with him. His movements are tremulous and uncertain. He speaks in a wavering voice, but with great passion and urgency. In 1955, he showed up in London, quite unexpectedly, for a conference organized by Bertrand Russell on the danger posed by nuclear weapons. Russell and Albert Einstein had issued a declaration, which became the founding document of the Pugwash movement. Markov quoted from the document as if its language were sacred. "It is the most important declaration that exists in the world today," he said. "It was signed by Communists and non-Communists alike. What kind of wisdom signed this declaration? The danger is for all people. The declaration said, 'Remember your humanity, and forget all other things.' It contains the widest possible platform—'Man, whose continued existence is in doubt . . . !' " It would be impossible to exaggerate the passion with which Markov spoke. He stressed the gravity of each word: " 'Man, whose continued existence is in doubt.' " How could you say more than that? Who could remain unmoved by such a danger?

Markov does not share with other Russians the anxiety that American technical abilities will allow the United States to race ahead. "The development of the first bomb shows that if something will be done in the U.S.A., very soon it will be done in our country, too," he said. "As a rule, my point of view is that the arms race is like a piece of iron. If you heat one end of it, very soon the other end will be the same temperature. That's a law of thermodynamics. You may be first, but after a while there will be equality again—but at a very high temperature. It is impossible to violate equality."

Markov is haunted by the possibility of a nuclear war. Sometimes he imagines—he knows the idea is scientifically unfounded—that Mars is a dead planet because its atmosphere was destroyed by a nuclear war. "I do not exclude such a possibility on our planet," he said. He makes no effort to spin scenarios of events that might lead to hostilities. The world is too unpredictable for that. "I once had a long discussion about this with Paul Doty [an American biochemist, also active in Pugwash] in a London restaurant," he said. "I told him the most serious historical events were unpredictable. It was very difficult to predict that in Germany—with such strong Socialist and Communist parties—Hitler could arise. It was hard to predict that his first move would be toward the West, instead of the East. It was not easy to predict that Japan's first move would be toward the U.S., not the USSR. It was hard to predict there would be such a dramatic change in relations between Russia and China."

In this world, things happen. "There is a Russian proverb: Even an unloaded gun will fire sooner or later." Markov told a story to illustrate the point. "When I was very young—about fifteen [in 1923]—I spent my vacation in Siberia with my family. I had a gun to shoot ducks, and one morning I had it with me at breakfast. I was sure my gun was unloaded. My sister sat on one side of me, the samovar was on the table here, and across the table was a cossack. My sister said, 'I know that gun is unloaded, but I don't like to see that dark hole pointed at me.' The cossack said, 'I'm a soldier; I don't mind, you can point it at me.' So I pointed it at the cossack. The gun went off. It had been loaded with solid shot, for wolves, and the bullet passed right through that cossack's hair, right down the middle. At the time

I was afraid only of what my father would say. But now it's what almost happened that I feel so strongly."

IN MINNEAPOLIS LAST MAY, the Russian delegation to the conference I attended, which was jointly sponsored by the Institute for Policy Studies and two Russian groups, the Soviet-American Friendship Committee and the Institute of the U.S.A. and Canada, had a firm agenda: they wanted to talk about arms control, . . . and how to get détente going again.

If there was a single dominant theme to Russian remarks at the conference, it was Euromissiles—the Pershing II and cruise missiles that NATO planned to deploy in the absence of a Geneva agreement. "Inevitably there would be a heightened tension," said Vikenty Matve'ev, a columnist for *Izvestia*, the official government paper. "Of course, the sky would not fall, but the ground may shake. We might have to break off the Geneva talks, because these talks sometimes give a false illusion." (Earlier, at lunch, Matve'ev told me, "In this world it's not easy to be an optimist. I have lived long enough, I don't care about myself—but my children . . .") Another journalist, Fyodor Burlatsky, was even more pessimistic. Deployment would bring "a really dramatic situation in Europe," he said. "It seems to me we are underestimating this situation. I don't want to draw a parallel between then [the Cuban missile crisis, in October of 1962] and now, but . . ."

For the Russians the Euromissiles—the merest handful of new warheads (572), compared with the thousands already deployed on both sides—were nevertheless a direct, almost a pugnacious, threat to the Soviet Union: a symbol of the breakdown of arms-control efforts; even an omen of war. Genrikh Trofimenko, an arms-control expert from the Institute of the U.S.A. and Canada, pointed out that negotiating to limit strategic arms, instead of to get rid of them altogether, was an American idea. In the 1950s, the Soviets had argued for general and complete disarmament. "Now the situation is reversed," he said. "The ideologues are in the White House and the pragmatists are in Moscow." Mikhail Milshtein, a retired army general who works for the institute, pressed the same point: "It took almost ten years to reach a second [SALT] agreement, and it takes only one election to repudiate everything. Speaking frankly, my personal opinion—the situation is very gloomy. It seems to me we are moving toward an irreversible stage of the arms race."

So it went. The Russians had come to discuss new weapons. The Americans were first with the bomb, first with a workable thermonuclear weapon, first with the long-range bomber, first with an effective inter-continental-missile fleet, first with hardened missile silos, first with missile-firing submarines, first with multiple warheads that could be inde-pendently targeted. Every new system increased the danger. The Soviets had always managed to keep up; they would continue to keep up. In their view there was only one sensible alternative—to parse the problem, isolate each dangerous element, and then hedge, limit, and ultimately reduce the weaponry step by step.

In Washington, in certain intelligence circles, there are analysts who keep close track of the Russians who troop about the world to conferences like this. Of course that's the line, these analysts say, but what they're really trying to do is to lock in their current strategic advantages. Georgi Arbatov [the head of the Institute of the U.S.A. and Canada, who did not attend the conference], Trofimenko, Milshtein—these guys are just salesmen.

These analysts have their arguments. They are technical in nature. The Soviets have their counterarguments. The subtleties of parity cannot be settled one, two, three. But in Minneapolis there was no mistaking what was on the Russians' minds. They were plainly worried by and obviously eager to avoid the expensive new round of weaponry symbolized by the Euromissiles.

In the midst of the discussion, one of the American delegates, W. H. Ferry, a consultant to foundations who has been writing about the dangers of the arms race for twenty years, took the floor to make a short statement. I believe I am reporting it whole: "I raise the question here of what this is all about. What issue could possibly warrant the use of nuclear weapons? Are they issues of territory, or human rights? What is it that justifies this confrontation?"

This was followed by a long moment of silence. Perhaps no one could believe Ferry had concluded so soon. No one made any attempt to answer his question. It was never referred to again, by Russians or Americans. It elicited no interest whatsoever.

MICHAEL HOWARD IS A DISTINGUISHED BRITISH MILITARY HISTORIAN and the Regius Professor of Modern History at Oxford University. Many of his articles and scholarly papers have discussed war as a thing, a phenomenon, "a continuing activity within human society," something men do. This is a neglected subject. The shelves of libraries groan with the histories of par-ticular wars, battles, and even individual military units. When the authors are writing from personal experience, they sometimes pause to reflect on the deeper meaning of war, the awful gap between the reasons and the thing itself. The reasons are often trivial, the thing itself a matter of fear, pain, and death.

The First World War revealed the awful gap to millions of young men in Europe, including many scores of thousands who had been expensively educated at the great universities of Britain, France, and Germany. Before the war, it had been popularly supposed that Europe was too civilized, too closely intertwined economically, and too sensible ever to fight another general war on the Napoleonic scale. A few writers—notably Sir Norman Angell, in Britain, and the Polish banker Ivan Bliokh—even argued that war was impossible. Modern weaponry was simply too destructive for men to endure. In *The Future of War,* a mammoth six-volume work published in Russian in the 1890s, Bliokh described in detail the terrors of the modern battlefield, swept by machine-gun fire and racked by high-explosive artillery shells. A big war would bring millions of men into the field, he predicted. Rates of fire would force them to dig in. It would be a war of trenches. The advantages of the defense would preclude decisive attacks. A war of attrition would follow—in effect, the siege of whole nations. In the end, deaths in the millions, financial ruin, and famine would settle the matter. The defeated would not lose, in the traditional sense, but collapse. Regimes would be swept away in the revolutions that followed. In *The Fate of the Earth,* published two years ago, Jonathan Schell took an approach similar to Bliokh's. Both simply described the horrors we could expect, given the facts. When Bliokh said war was "impossible"—a term he insisted on with journalists—he meant not that it couldn't happen but that the survival of nations would be at risk if it did. Schell, reflecting the strides of science since, goes a step further and says that now civilization, and perhaps even human life itself, is at risk.

Bliokh's vision was unique in its breadth and prophetic accuracy, but a few military men also got an inkling of what was to come from the bloodletting horrors of the American Civil War and the Prussian use of modern breech-loading artillery in the Franco-Prussian War of 1870–1871 (the subject of one of Michael Howard's books). But the Franco-Prussian War ended too quickly for the bad news to sink in. The Russo-Japanese War of 1904–1905, involving heavy casualties and trench warfare, was too far away. The military observers who saw what happened were mostly of field grade, and the duffers on the general staffs at home did not listen. Thus, only a few prescient military men understood what science, industry, and railroads were doing to the scale of war in the decades before 1914. One of them was Helmuth von Moltke the elder, an architect of the modern German army, who wrote in 1890:

If the war which has hung over our heads, like the sword of Damocles, for more than ten years past, ever breaks out, its duration and end cannot be foreseen. The greatest powers of Europe, armed as never before, will then stand face to face. No one power can be shattered in one or two campaigns so completely as to confess itself beaten, and conclude peace on hard terms. It may be a Seven Years' war; it may be a Thirty Years' war—woe to him who first sets fire to Europe. . . .

Such premonitions were fully borne out by the horrors of trench warfare on the Western Front between 1914 and 1918. The dead numbered in the millions. Of course men had died in war before, but not like this— blown to bits, buried in collapsing bunkers, drowned in mud, machine-gunned as they tried to make their way through thickets of barbed wire and then left to die of their wounds in no-man's-land. On the first day of the Battle of the Somme, in 1916, the British suffered 60,000 casualties— 20,000 of them deaths. The brief official communiqué called the opening of the Somme a success. It was duly printed in British newspapers, followed by page upon page of the names of the killed and the wounded.

The Somme lasted from July into November. Some 1,300,000 soldiers were killed or wounded on both sides. The advance gained seven miles of shattered ground at its deepest point, but left the German front intact. When the British writer Martin Middlebrook, decades later, interviewed survivors for his book *First Day on the Somme* (published in 1972), he found that many of them still dreamed about what they had been through. Another writer, Paul Fussell, argued, in *The Great War and Modern Memory* (1975), that the First World War permanently darkened the collective mind of Western man, replacing the confidence of the nineteenth century with a foreboding sense of fragility, helplessness, and doom. When enthusiasts of aerial bombing began to write, in the 1920s and 1930s, one of their arguments for strategic attack on cities and factories deep within enemy territory was the chance it offered to avoid another great bloodletting by troops on the ground. The devastation of London, Coventry, Hamburg, Dresden, Berlin, Hiroshima, and Nagasaki duly followed. The significant change at Hiroshima was that one plane, with one bomb, accomplished what it had taken a thousand planes to do before.

The flood of memoirs that followed the First World War broached the awful disparity between the reasons for the war and the war itself. What was it about? How did it start? Why was it allowed to continue? What did it settle? The war bled a generation white, destroyed three of the four dynasties that had ruled in 1914—the Hapsburgs in Austria-Hungary, the Hohenzollerns in Germany, the Romanovs in Russia—and ended in a vindictive peace, which only set the stage for a new war in 1939. The origins of the war have recently been revived as a subject for scholarly study, for a simple and practical reason: the world of 1914 bears a certain disturbing resemblance to our own. Then, as now, the Great Powers were heavily armed. Two alliances confronted each other. An upstart power—Germany—was demanding an equal role on the world stage. Britain was frightened by Germany's construction of big modern battleships. Why did Berlin need this "luxury fleet," if not to challenge British supremacy on the seas? British Conservatives insisted that new dreadnoughts must be built to deter the Germans, and damn the expense. In 1908 they campaigned for the ships on the slogan "We want eight and we won't wait!" Crises were frequent; demands were routinely backed up by military gestures implying a threat of war. The Great Powers confronted each other in peripheral arenas—the Balkans then, the Middle East now. When Bismarck was asked what he thought would set off the next big European war, he said, "Some damned foolishness in the Balkans." But perhaps the most disturbing contemporary parallel is the confidence that all this long preparation for war meant nothing; there would be no war. For twenty or thirty years the optimists were right. Until 1914, the diplomats always managed to settle things before armies were mobilized and shots were fired.

Why did they fail in 1914? In a recent essay, Michael Howard confessed that he has lately begun to rethink the whole subject of the origins of the First World War. He said that he used to assume that an event so large must have had causes to match—deep undercurrents of social change and irreconcilable differences between nations, pushing events into a kind of inevitable, fatal slide that no mere statesman could hope to brake. But now Howard is not so sure. Maybe it was simple, after all—the result of bungling. Maybe Lloyd George, the British prime minister during the last half of the war, was right when he said "We all muddled into war." We might call this the tinderbox theory of the causes of wars: The problem is not sources of conflict, things nations might be expected to fight *about*, but simply the readiness for war itself. Military strength on one side inevitably arouses fear in the other, which strives to catch up. The first grows alarmed in turn. In such a world it does not take something large to start a war but something small, something unexpected—an assassination in a provincial town like Sarajevo, say—something that might be considered, perhaps for purely tactical reasons, to require a determined response. After that, one thing can lead to another. The armies of Europe did not have to mobilize in the summer of 1914. They just did.

You can see the appeal here to a scholar interested in our own day. Clausewitz says that war is the continuation of policy by other means. It is supposed to make sense. But the outbreak of war in 1914 made no sense. Nothing was at stake that could reasonably be said to justify war on a continental scale. Even statesmen at the time admitted as much. But Europe was ready for war. Once the Great Powers began to mobilize, they could not stop. The statesmen of our own day insist that there will be no great war between Russia and the United States so long as war doesn't make sense. Nuclear weapons make it impossible—but impossible, alas, in Bliokh's sense, which is to say, suicidal.

THE STUDY OF WAR is generally neglected for the study of military history, which is concerned with how wars are won, not why they take place. Even a long human life holds room for only one or two big wars. The fact that they are hard to stop, once begun, obscures the fact that they are usually a long time in coming. Before the outbreak of the Peloponnesian War, in the fifth century B.C., the Athenian leader Pericles warned his fellow citizens that in war chance rules, that no one can predict how things will turn out, that even the rosiest prospects may be dashed by unforeseen events. Statesmen understand this point. They thrive as long as war only threatens, and are cautious about war itself, especially big, decisive wars against strong opponents. These are generally slow to develop and are preceded by such extended episodes of quarreling, alliance-making, and tentative skirmishing—all more or less obscured by secrecy—that just untangling the true sequence of events can absorb a historian's whole career. The consequences of such wars can be so vast—possibly including the disappearance of peoples and the eclipse of empires—that the historian's eye is held fast by the awful spectacle immediately before him. The horrors and the relative infrequency of big wars encourage attention to the particular. Thus historians traditionally have been inclined to ask not why we have wars but why we had this one, and then why we had that one. The answers generally stick to the sequence of events, as if there were no such thing as war itself, war as a thing, war as a form of common social behavior, something men in groups habitually and characteristically do.

Perhaps this is inevitable. So much rides on the details. If the First World War had been postponed ten years, a different generation would have died. Rupert Brooke might have spent a long life writing bucolic poetry, and W. H. Auden might have died in his place. The generals of 1914, with their muttonchops and walrus moustaches, would have been mostly in the obscurity of retirement by 1924. The development of aircraft and armored fighting vehicles might have avoided the carnage of static trench warfare. Liberal Western tendencies might have secured a firmer hold in Russia, forestalling the Bolshevik Revolution. Another decade of German submarine-building might have been enough to let Germany starve out Britain when war came. Defeat might have cost the Windsors their throne, and left the Kaiser on his. Who can say? That the potential differences are of such dramatic moment—especially when the war in question is still in the future—tends to narrow the focus of all concerned, leaders and ordinary citizens alike, to the dangers of the day. From the point of view of God it may be immaterial whether war happens now or next year, whether it kills this man or that, whether the side that dictates the peace appears in a gray uniform or a brown. But for men these are the urgent questions, with the result that they study their wars the same way they fight them—one at a time.

This approach begs an important question. Explaining wars by retelling their histories is like trying to explain the phenomenon of divorce by recounting who said what to whom, in every separate instance, through years of quarrelsome marriages. War and the preparation for war are such an integral part of history—the great constant in all times and places—that they may be presumed to constitute one of the great determining characteristics of the human animal. We have a nature; the tabula is not quite rasa. We live in cities, marry in pairs, and make war against our neighbors. In 1971, J. David Singer, of the University of Michigan, published a study of international wars during the 150 years from 1816 to 1965. He found that there were 6.2 wars in the average decade; that especially intense episodes of violence occurred every twenty years or so; that Europe was the most war-prone part of the world, followed by the Middle East; and that 29 million soldiers had died fighting in the ninety-three wars that took place during the century and a half he studied. Who can mistake a pattern so pronounced? Somewhere in those statistics lurks war as an endemic thing, the sort of war that the British historian Arnold Toynbee once said could be identified as "the proximate cause of the breakdown of every civilization which is known for certain to have broken down."

Toynbee never attempted to say precisely what war is. That would be a tremendous intellectual undertaking, demanding a Darwin, a Marx, or a Freud. But Toynbee's long study of history—he lived to be eighty-six, and wrote till the end—convinced him that the explanation for cataclysmic wars could not be found in the details of who said what to whom and when. He was suffering from chronic dysentery when the First World War began, and so escaped the fate of about half his schoolmates. He was a distinguished sage when Hitler attacked Poland in 1939. He did not watch these wars from lonely academic eminence but was active in establishment circles. He attended the peace conferences in Paris in 1919 and 1946. Twice in his life he was certain there would never again be another big European war—at the beginning of 1914, and at the end of 1918. This confidence could not survive another great war. The onset of the Cold War convinced him that the pattern was still incomplete. In 1950 he wrote:

> . . . The most ominous thing about these wars is that they were not isolated or unprecedented calamities. They were two wars in a series; and, when we envisage the whole series in a synoptic view, we discover that this is not only a series but a progression. In our recent Western history war has been following war in an ascending order of intensity; and to-day it is already apparent that the War of 1939–45 was not the climax of this crescendo movement.

Toynbee's gloom was not unusual in the late 1940s and early 1950s. There was a wide gap between the observers outside of government, horrified by the implications of atomic weapons, and the statesmen inside, who had to reorganize the world. Einstein might have said that atomic weapons "changed everything," but statesmen did not agree. The Allies of 1945 were already deeply suspicious of one another. As early as 1943, an American general in Sicily remarked to the British bombing expert Solly Zuckerman, "Zuck, when we've finished with Germany we'll still want you when we take on the Russians. Don't forget." At war's end, the United States went on producing fissionable material for nuclear weapons, and Britain, France, and Russia all raced to catch up. In 1946, Truman quietly but explicitly threatened to attack Russia with atomic weapons if it did not withdraw its troops from northern Iran, and Stalin complied. By 1948, talk of war was general. The speed with which a war-wracked world chose up sides for a new contest was bewildering. Polemicists on each side leaped forward to explain why the other was to blame, and subsequently historians—in the West, at least—have filled in the details. In my own view, a good case can be made that Stalin's absorption of Eastern Europe, beginning with Poland, virtually guaranteed enmity with the West, but I doubt that scholarly arguments of that kind really explain very much. The history helps, but it is like a medical history that recounts the onset and progress of a disease without explaining what the disease is. These events happened too quickly, almost automatically, like the exchange of partners in a dance, as if a Great Power can be expected, by its very nature, to cast about restlessly for the next-greatest, and then to direct at it questions of a type certain to promote hostility. Why did the United States go on building nuclear weapons? Why didn't Russia disband its army? Why did the United States cut off lend-lease aid to Russia on a moment's notice, in 1945, turning its ships around in mid-ocean? Why did Russia impose client regimes on Eastern Europe? Both sides' official answers to these questions have been patently disingenuous. Both sides were afraid, not of what the other side did but because they could do nothing about it—short of war. The essence of the situation, when all the details have been argued to a fare-thee-well, is an elemental fact: in 1945, the United States and the Soviet Union were big, were autonomous, and had a capacity to injure each other. This confrontation had been waiting to happen.

TALKING ABOUT WAR WITH RUSSIANS in Russia is a curiously unsettling experience. Russians have had a hard life since the expulsion from Eden; history never lets up on them. The miseries suffered by ordinary people in the nineteenth century are well documented. In the First World War, the slaughter was so immense that the soldiers finally threw down their guns, climbed out of the trenches, and set out to walk home. The revolutions of 1917 were followed by a civil war of unparalleled ferocity, in which prisoners, hostages, and ordinary citizens were routinely shot and whole provinces were devastated. Scarcely had the White generals been defeated when Lenin died, Stalin took over, and the ensuing forced collectivization of peasant landholdings resulted in famines, which killed millions. Stalinist terror killed millions more. Hitler killed further millions. Ordinary Russians know all about this terrible history, but the only episode they can talk about freely is the Second World War. This they do. I know of only one other country where everybody seems to have so many horrors to relate—Israel. Doubting the Russians' sincerity when they talk of the pain of war strikes me as willful and perverse.

Unlike Americans, Russians fear that war is really possible. Ordinary citizens encountered by chance in the street invariably bring up the subject. There must never be another war, they say as one. Why can't we be allies again, the way we were in the war against Hitler? They seem genuinely puzzled. I heard many Russians say they felt it would come to war in the end. I have never heard an American say this. I heard many Russians cite Chekhov's famous principle of dramaturgy: If there is a gun on the wall in the first act, it will fire in the third. I have never heard an American official or professional defense analyst speak in such fatalistic tones.

The Russians I spoke to feel pushed and crowded. The Soviet Union has proven it is a power in the world; why can't America accept this, and deal with it as an equal? The Russians draw quick, rough maps of the Eurasian heartland, with bold "X"s marking the vast ring of American military bases surrounding the Soviet Union from Japan to Norway. Most of them insist that current American strategic programs are all aimed at building first-strike capability. Why else would the United States be committed to building the MX—a super-accurate weapon that is vulnerable and must therefore be fired first if it is to be fired at all? they ask. Why is the United States planning to deploy Pershing II missiles in Europe—also super-accurate weapons—only six minutes away from the Soviet missiles and command centers in western Russia? Why is the United States building super-accurate missiles for the new Trident submarines? The Americans write about limited nuclear war and selective strikes against hard, well-protected military targets. They write about "decapitating" the Soviet Union with nuclear attacks on the institutions that run the country and on the civil-defense shelters where Soviet leaders plan to take refuge. Are the Soviets to brush all this aside as just talk?

Russians insist that they will maintain parity now that they have finally achieved it. "Don't judge Russian missiles by your TV set," one said after I had told him that the set in my hotel room didn't work. "Some things we can do," he said. Some American experts think super-sophisticated new weapons systems may offer a genuine strategic edge; many doubt it. But none doubt that we can build some pretty fancy hardware if we decide to. Russians say they can, but with an air of determination, of sheer assertion, that sounded to me, after a while, uncertain. I think they're afraid that the Americans are going to spring a surprise—something so advanced, so magically versatile, so big and expensive, that the Soviet Union will suddenly find itself pushed back to 1950, trying to hide its weakness behind a curtain of secrecy. In Moscow, this self-doubt makes perfect sense. The city is clean and orderly, but decrepit and run-down. Clouds of oil smoke pour from the rattletrap cars, buses, and trucks. In GUM, the big department store on Red Square, the shoppers are crowded twenty deep around the counters. The imported radios and hi-fis sold only in foreign-currency shops cost a fortune. Everything has an archaic air, as if the Soviet Union were still struggling to do 1950 right. Russians see this clumsy backwardness too. Some take a perverse pride in it, as if it reflected a purity of spirit in contrast to the sybaritic materialism of the West. But more of them frankly admire the West. Despite all its sins, the West is advanced. So I was not surprised by the note of fear at the prospect of a new round of the arms race in the one field where Russians are weakest. Harold Brown, Carter's secretary of defense, once said, "Our technology is what will save us." The Russians fear that he is right. They fear that we might use a strategic advantage to push them around, or even to attack out of the blue. To an American, these Russian fears are especially unsettling. They are all based on what we write and do. I found myself trying to explain these things away as politics and idle theorizing, but the Russians, though polite, did not appear to be convinced.

IN WASHINGTON, a small but currently influential circle believes that the Soviet Union is an empire of the nineteenth-century variety, the world's last; that its power rests on a frail economic base; and that it may already be in decline. Russia has no allies of importance; its clients in Eastern Europe hate its guts; it can sell nothing but arms and raw materials. No other country shows the slightest interest in Soviet "culture" or imitates Russia in anything whatever except the techniques of domestic coercion. Its scholars do not count for much even in the field of Marxist studies. The noted Soviet analyst Seweryn Bialer has said that if Russia did not possess nuclear weapons it would not even be classed as a major power.

Starting from these premises, some analysts believe that the Soviet Union can be forced into economic collapse, and thence into eclipse, by a combination of expensive arms-building and economic warfare. Reagan's former national security adviser, William Clark, once described the Soviet regime as an "evil and bizarre episode" in human history. The implications of the word episode can hardly be taken lightly in Moscow. When I saw Arbatov, he bitterly criticized the American "strategic" approach, as it is sometimes called. Despite its many critics in the United States, the strategic approach is nevertheless "taken seriously here," he said. "These troglodytic sentiments can be found even among the top people in your government. They seem to feel 'Maybe now at last the moment has come when we can do away with them [that is, the Soviets], or undermine them completely.' It explains this attempt to impose on us a much more costly arms race, to try to ruin us economically."

Other Russians addressed this question as well. The strategic approach seemed to baffle and to anger them in equal measure, and their comments all had a similar drift, as if to say, You're trying to destroy us—literally break up our state and change our whole government. You admit you're trying to destroy us. And you claim you are committed to peace? If that is peace, what is war?

There is no question that this policy can poison relations, but can it work? The basic weakness of the strategic approach is the obvious one: it is transparently hostile, it precludes accommodation, it encourages arms-building, and the closer it comes to working, the greater the chance of war through fear and desperation.

In the opening pages of *The Peloponnesian War*, Thucydides offered a conventional account of the causes of the war that broke out in 431 B.C.—a typically muddled chain of action and reaction—but added that in his opinion the real cause was much simpler: it was Spartan fear of growing Athenian power. This fear had first been aroused forty-eight years earlier, at the end of the Greek allies' victorious war against the Persians, in 479 B.C., when Athens began to rebuild its city walls and decided to retain its wartime navy, the most powerful military force in Greece. These two facts poisoned the well, and the allies became rivals. Causes do not come much more basic than that.

This is one of the patterns of history: a city or nation rises to power, absorbs or threatens to absorb its neighbors, and finally collapses when it has aroused the fear of more enemies than it can handle. Spain in the sixteenth century, France in the early nineteenth, and Germany in the twentieth are notable examples. All three came close to establishing hegemony over Europe. All three were successfully opposed by Britain, in the last instance with the aid of the United States. Britain's policy had always been the simple one of seeking to prevent the domination of Europe by any single power. But the two wars with Germany destroyed Britain as a world power and the United States took its place in the defense of Europe. Did Stalin dream of conquering the whole of the Continent? No one can say; Stalin kept his plans to himself. But what he did was enough. He imposed Soviet control over Eastern Europe, redrew its boundaries to his liking, and guaranteed the fact of possession with Russian armies.

The United States and Russia are both Great Powers of the traditional kind. Both have expanded rapidly, over the past two centuries, at the expense of weak neighbors; both are blessed with abundant natural resources; both draw their power from huge populations and economies; both are convinced that the destiny of the world is in their hands; and both are showing signs of the awful financial strain of sustaining a global conflict. For both sides the focus is Europe, where Russian and American armies face each other across the line established by the calamities of the

Second World War. There the Americans are far from home but have friendly allies. The Russians are closer to home but must keep an eye on hostile clients. The question at the heart of the Cold War—the thing it is most nearly "about"—is which of these two armies will go home first. It is hard to imagine a confrontation with fewer exits.

The problem now is that the closing stages of the traditional pattern always involve great wars, but we—Russia and the West alike—cannot hope to gain from a great war. In the past, when somebody lost, somebody won. Now, nuclear weapons make that unlikely. The side closest to losing retains the power to drag down its rival with it. Many people grasped this point right away in 1945, when atomic weapons destroyed Hiroshima and Nagasaki—but, for the most part, national leaders did not. They thought we were smart enough to conduct a Great Power conflict without sliding into war. They still think so. As a result, we behave as Great Powers have always behaved—raising armies, seeking advantage, and supporting our demands with threats of war when conflict comes to crisis. The only difference now is that we tell ourselves it will never come to war in the end. It will just go on indefinitely.

In one of his essays, E. P. Thompson wrote, "If we ask the partisans of either side what the Cold War is now about, they regard us with the glazed eyes of addicts." I have found this to be true. Over the past year I have asked perhaps a hundred people—Russians and Americans alike—what it is about. Of course, this is a hard question. I did not expect anyone to sort the whole matter out in an afternoon. But I had in mind a story, possibly apocryphal, I once read about the composer Stravinsky. He had written a new piece with a difficult violin passage. After it had been in rehearsal for several weeks, the solo violinist came to Stravinsky and said he was sorry, he had tried his best, the passage was too difficult, no violinist could play it. Stravinsky said, "I understand that. What I am after is the sound of someone trying to play it." I asked my question in that spirit.

But none of the people I approached showed anything more than a polite interest in the question. No one offered the sort of ready answer that suggested he had been thinking about it. No one found it easy to propose the name of someone who might actually have been thinking about it. Their eyes were not exactly glazed, but they were certainly blank. I had figured that the Russians, at least, would be quick to propose a dialectical interpretation. They were not. The few who alluded vaguely to history said all that was behind us now. The responses, after an awkward moment, were pretty much the same: *That's a very interesting question; we ought to concentrate more on that, I agree, yes, but the really pressing matter now is the question of the Euromissiles*—or something else of the kind. It was questions about hardware that interested them, or the details of negotiating positions, or the dangers posed to the fundamentals of deterrence by new weapons technology, or the rights and wrongs of the Soviet use of Cuban proxies in Angola and Ethiopia, or the slippage of Soviet control in Eastern Europe, or the motives behind the counterforce revolution in American military thinking. It is process that absorbs the managers and publicists of the Cold War—not words but the Great Game itself, not why we act but what we do. Things can go so terribly wrong tomorrow that it is hard to concentrate on anything but the awful dilemma of what to do today.

Thompson wrote in the essay quoted above, "What is the Cold War now about? It is about itself." I think Thompson is right, with one qualification: the Cold War has always been about itself. It's about what happened last week, and what we hope—or fear—will happen next week. The military power of the two sides is in constant flux. Today's allies may falter tomorrow. Each side feels that defeat on its periphery is a threat to its center. Both sides are incapable of explaining why things have to be this way, but act as if fate offered no alternative. When we ask what this great struggle is about we betray our own helplessness. The answers are just words. For nearly forty years we have talked and talked without mitigating the danger that we will fight in the end. No single issue divides us, nothing we can settle through negotiation and compromise. It is only propagandists who insist that the history of the Cold War explains it. The problem at its heart is an elemental one. It is our nature that makes us draw lines in the earth and grimace when anyone approaches in strange garb, not some legalistic litany of rights threatened or violated. The Cold War has a new name, but follows an old pattern. Among the things we seek or fear from this conflict there is not one on a scale even close to the scale of the war we are preparing to fight with each other. We are trapped in a tightening spiral of fear and hostility. We don't know why we have got into this situation, we don't know how to get out of it, and we have not found the humility to admit we don't know. In desperation, we simply try to manage our enmity from day to day. When Germany fell in 1945, only two Great Powers remained in the world—Russia and the United States. Only the United States has the power to threaten Russia. We fear each other. We wish each other ill. All the rest is detail.

CONTROVERSIES

For the Union Dead

ROBERT LOWELL || 1960

*In early 1960, the city fathers of Boston dispatched a small battalion of
bulldozers to the Boston Common—that stately swath of urban greenery
that once served as Ralph Waldo Emerson's family cow pasture—to
make way for a massive underground parking garage. The "urban development" project stirred no small anguish in the poet Robert Lowell
(1917–1976), who had a complex relationship with Boston and its history.
Lowell was himself the scion of one of the city's most eminent Brahmin
clans: his forebears included the celebrated Imagist poet Amy Lowell, the
longtime Harvard president A. Lawrence Lowell, and The Atlantic's first
editor, James Russell Lowell. If, during the course of Robert Lowell's troubled life, his bloodline proved to be as much a burden as a blessing, his
efforts to come to grips with his native city's freighted past were equally
vexed. A manic-depressive who was often institutionalized, Lowell
poured all of his deep-seated ambivalence over ancestral privilege and
egalitarian aspiration into "For the Union Dead," a brooding threnody
that remains virtually unrivaled in American poetry as an expression
of public conscience.*

*Much of the poem's power resides in its sense of occasion. Lowell,
who had won a National Book Award the previous year for* Life Studies,
*his breakthrough collection of confessional poems, had been commis-
sioned to compose and recite a new poem to keynote the Boston Arts Festival, which was scheduled to be held in June of 1960 in the city's Public
Garden, adjoining the Boston Common. Whatever the culture grandees
of Boston were expecting, "For the Union Dead" turned out to be a far cry
from a conventional commemorative poem. In taking as his focal point
the famous bas-relief sculpture by Augustus Saint-Gaudens that is dedicated to a fallen all-black Union regiment and that stands at the edge of
the Common (and next to the site of the transgressing parking garage),
Lowell was in essence reconnoitering his own heritage. He was born a
stone's throw away in the Beacon Hill home of his grandfather Winslow,
and the Common had been his playground. Robert Gould Shaw, the white
colonel who led the 54th Regiment of Negro Infantry and who had been
buried with his men in a mass grave in Charleston, South Carolina, was a
member of the Lowell family by marriage. But while the poem celebrates
Lowell's kinsman Shaw, it also bitterly alludes to a letter that Shaw's own
father had written expressing satisfaction that his son would not be*

returned to Boston for interment but instead would lie with his "niggers."
With its tumbling montage of images setting Boston's past at odds with its
present and its aggrieved survey of the city's crumbling heritage, "For the
Union Dead" delivers up a fierce indictment of the city's tortured racial
history and the manner in which the 54th Regiment's heroic sacrifice had
been betrayed by the "savage servility" of commercial exploitation. As
The Atlantic's longtime poetry editor Peter Davison observed in a column
on the magazine's website in 2001: "Everything in Lowell's nature com-
bined to compose this powerful poem, which seems to many readers the
most sublime he ever wrote, the poem most completely suited to his talent,
his voice, and his vision of America."

"RELINQUUNT OMNIA SERVARE REM PUBLICAM."

The old South Boston Aquarium stands
in a Sahara of snow now. Its broken windows are boarded.
The bronze weathervane cod has lost half its scales.
The airy tanks are dry.

Once my nose crawled like a snail on the glass;
my hand tingled
to burst the bubbles,
drifting from the noses of the cowed, compliant fish.

My hand draws back. I often sigh still
for the dark downward and vegetating kingdom
of the fish and reptile. One morning last March,
I pressed against the new barbed and galvanized

fence on the Boston Common. Behind their cage,
yellow dinosaur steam shovels were grunting
as they cropped up tons of mush and grass
to gouge their underworld garage.

Parking lots luxuriate like civic
sand piles in the heart of Boston.
A girdle of orange, Puritan-pumpkin-colored girders
braces the tingling Statehouse, shaking

over the excavations, as it faces Colonel Shaw
and his bell-cheeked Negro infantry
on St. Gaudens' shaking Civil War relief,
propped by a plank splint against the garage's earthquake.

Two months after marching through Boston,
half the regiment was dead;
at the dedication,
William James could almost hear the bronze Negroes breathe.

The monument sticks like a fishbone
in the city's throat.
Its colonel is as lean
as a compass needle.

He has an angry wrenlike vigilance,
a greyhound's gentle tautness;
he seems to wince at pleasure
and suffocate for privacy.

He is out of bounds. He rejoices in man's lovely,
peculiar power to choose life and die—
when he leads his black soldiers to death,
he cannot bend his back.

On a thousand small-town New England greens,
the old white churches hold their air
of sparse, sincere rebellion; frayed flags
quilt the graveyards of the Grand Army of the Republic.

The stone statues of the abstract Union Soldier
grow slimmer and younger each year—
wasp-waisted, they doze over muskets,
and muse through their sideburns.

Shaw's father wanted no monument
except the ditch,
where his son's body was thrown
and lost with his "niggers."

The ditch is nearer.
There are no statues for the last war here;
on Boylston Street, a commercial photograph
showed Hiroshima boiling

over a Mosler Safe, "the Rock of Ages,"
that survived the blast. Space is nearer.
When I crouch to my television set,
the drained faces of Negro school children rise like balloons.

Colonel Shaw
is riding on his bubble,
he waits
for the blesséd break.

The Aquarium is gone. Everywhere,
giant finned cars nose forward like fish;
a savage servility
slides by on grease.

Mr. Sammler's Planet

SAUL BELLOW || 1969

*The recipient of three National Book Awards, a Pulitzer Prize, and a No-
bel Prize for literature, Saul Bellow (1915–2005) was one of the most honored novelists of the twentieth century. And yet throughout his illustrious
career as a writer and a professor at the University of Chicago, Bellow
found himself with surprising frequency at the center of political
firestorms—often, as he himself was first to acknowledge, of his own
making. A Trotskyist as a young man, Bellow veered sharply to the right
in response to the upheavals of the 1960s, becoming well known, in both
his novels and public statements, for his pointed and sometimes inflam-
matory criticisms of the changes that were reshaping American culture,
higher education, and race relations. Asked in a 1988 interview for his
opinions of multiculturalism and non-Western literature then ascendant
on college campuses, Bellow posed a famous question—"Who is the Tol-
stoy of the Zulus? The Proust of the Papuans? I'd be glad to read him"—
that, for all its arch cleverness, sounded to some like a racial put-down.*

*But perhaps the biggest controversy that the Chicago-bred novelist
ever set off originated in the pages of* The Atlantic, *in late 1969, when
the magazine serialized in two parts his then-forthcoming novel* Mr.
Sammler's Planet. *At issue was Bellow's depiction of a black pickpocket,
a physically imposing, magnificently dressed African American male in
his thirties who is spotted by the novel's title character, Artur Sammler,
ritually and adroitly preying upon bus riders on the Upper West Side
of Manhattan. Sammler is a classic Bellow protagonist, a Polish-born,
Oxford-educated intellectual and a Holocaust survivor, struggling
through his twilight years in the theatrical squalor of New York City,
and he becomes obsessed with the charismatic criminal, whom he variously describes as an "elegant brute," a "great black beast," and "a
puma." So fascinated is Sammler that he even seeks the black man out
on city buses to watch him work. In the climactic scene that ends the excerpt below, the pickpocket, realizing that he is under surveillance, turns
the tables on Sammler and follows the septuagenarian home, accosting
him in the vestibule of his apartment building and wordlessly baring his
penis for Sammler's contemplation—and for Bellow's memorably
graphic description.*

*For years after the novel's publication, accusations of racial stereo-
typing and outright racism rained down on Bellow, and even such ad-*

mirers of his work as the critic Joseph Epstein maintained that Mr. Sammler's Planet *seemed designed "to offend whole categories of the reading public as well as most of the people who write about books." But other critics and readers rose to Bellow's defense, contending that the novelist had himself been victimized by an early upwelling of political correctness and that he had properly exercised the prerogatives of fiction to present the menacing character of urban life in New York City as experienced by at least some of those who lived there.*

Shortly after dawn, or what would have been dawn in a normal sky, Mr. Artur Sammler with his bushy eye took in the books and papers of his West Side bedroom and suspected strongly that they were the wrong books, the wrong papers. In a way it did not matter much to a man of seventy plus, and at leisure.

He thought, since he had no job to wake up to, that he might give sleep a second chance to resolve certain difficulties imaginatively for him, and pulled up the disconnected electric blanket with its internal sinews and lumps. The satin binding was nice to the fingertips. He was still drowsy, but not really inclined to sleep. Time to be conscious.

He had only one good eye. The left distinguished only light and shade. But the good eye was dark-bright, full of observation through the overhanging hair of the brows as in some breeds of dog. For his height he had a small face. The combination made him conspicuous.

His conspicuousness was on his mind; it worried him. For several days, Mr. Sammler returning on the customary bus late afternoons from the 42nd Street Library had been watching a pickpocket at work. The man got on at Columbus Circle. The job, the crime, was done by 72nd Street. Mr. Sammler if he had not been a tall straphanger would not with his one good eye have seen these things happening. But now he wondered whether he had not drawn too close, whether he had also been seen seeing. He wore smoked glasses, at all times protecting his vision, but he couldn't be taken for a blind man. He didn't have the white cane, only a rolled umbrella, British-style. Moreover, he didn't have the look of blindness. The pickpocket himself wore dark shades. He was a powerful Negro in a camel's-hair coat, dressed with extraordinary elegance, as if by Mr. Fish of London, or Turnbull and Asser of Jermyn Street. (Mr. Sammler knew his England.) The Negro's perfect circles of gentian violet banded with lovely gold turned toward Sammler, but the face showed the effrontery of a big animal. Sammler was not timid, but he had had as much trouble in life as he wanted. A good deal of this, waiting for assimilation, would never be accommodated. He suspected the criminal was aware that a tall old white man passing as blind had observed, had seen, the minutest details of his crimes. Staring down. As if watching open-heart surgery. And though he dissembled, deciding not to turn aside when the thief looked at him, his elderly, his compact, civilized face colored strongly, the short hairs bristled, the lips and gums were stinging. He felt a constriction, a clutch of sickness at the base of the skull, where the nerves, muscles, blood vessels were tightly interlaced. The breath of wartime Poland passing over the damaged tissues—that nerve-spaghetti, as he thought of it.

Buses were bearable, subways were killing. Must he give up the bus? He had not minded his own business as a man of seventy in New York should do. It was always Mr. Sammler's problem that he didn't know his proper age, didn't appreciate his situation, unprotected here by position, by privileges of remotion made possible by an income of fifty thousand dollars in New York—club membership, taxis, doormen, guarded approaches. For him it was the buses, or the grinding subway, lunch at the Automat. No cause for grave complaint, but his years as an "Englishman," two decades in London as correspondent for Warsaw papers and journals, had left him with attitudes not especially useful to a refugee in Manhattan. He had developed expressions suited to an Oxford Common Room; he had the face of a British Museum reader. Sammler as a schoolboy in Cracow before World War I fell in love with England. Most of that nonsense had been knocked out of him. He had reconsidered the whole question of Anglophilia with numerous cases of Salvador de Madariagas, Mario Prazes, André Maurois, and Colonel Brambles. He knew the phenomenon. Still, confronted by the elegant brute in the bus he had seen picking a purse— the purse still hung open—he adopted an English tone. A dry, a neat, a prim face declared that one had not crossed anyone's boundary; one was satisfied with one's own business. But under the high armpits Mr. Sammler was intensely hot, wet; hanging on his strap, sealed in by bodies, taking their weight and laying his own on them as the fat tires went around the giant curve on 72nd Street with a growl of flabby power.

He didn't in fact appear to know his age, or at what point of life he stood. You could see that in his way of walking. On the streets, he was tense, quick, erratically light and reckless, the elderly hair stirring on the back of his head. Crossing, he lifted the rolled umbrella high and pointed to show cars, buses, speeding trucks, and cabs bearing down on him the way he intended to go. They might run him down, but he could not help his style of striding blind.

With the pickpocket we were in an adjoining region of recklessness. He knew the man was working the Riverside bus. He had seen him picking purses, and he had reported it to the police. The police were not greatly interested in the report. It had made Sammler feel like a fool to go immediately to a phone booth on Riverside Drive. Of course the phone was smashed. Most outdoor telephones were smashed, crippled. They were urinals, also. New York was getting worse than Naples or Salonika. It was like an Asian, an African, city from this standpoint. The opulent sections of the city were not immune. You opened a jeweled door into degradation, from hypercivilized Byzantine luxury straight into the state of nature, the barbarous world of color erupting from beneath. It might well be barbarous on either side of the jeweled door. Sexually, for example. The thing evidently, as Mr. Sammler was beginning to grasp, consisted in obtaining the privileges, and the free ways of barbarism, under the protection of civilized order, property rights, refined technological organization, and so on.

In the bus he had been seeing well enough. He saw a crime committed. He reported it to the cops. They were not greatly shaken. He might then have stayed away from that particular bus, but instead he tried hard to repeat the experience. He went to Columbus Circle and hung about until he saw his man again. Four fascinating times he had watched the thing done, the crime, the first afternoon staring down at the masculine hand that came from behind lifting the clasp and tipping the pocketbook lightly to make it fall open. Sammler saw a polished Negro forefinger, turning aside a plastic folder with social security or credit cards, emery sticks, a lipstick capsule, coral paper tissues, nipping open the catch of a change purse, and there lay the green of money. Still at the same rate, the fingers took out the dollars. Then with the touch of a doctor on a patient's belly moved back the slope leather, turned the gilded scallop catch. Sammler, feeling his head small, shrunk with strain, the teeth tensed, still was looking at the picked patent-leather bag on the woman's hip, finding that he was irritated with her. That she felt nothing. What an idiot! Going around with some kind of stupid mold in her skull. Zero instincts, no grasp of New York. While the man turned from her broad-shouldered in the camel's-hair coat. The dark glasses, the original design by Christian Dior, a powerful throat banded by a tab collar and a cherry silk necktie spouting out. Under the African nose, a cropped mustache. Ever so slightly inclining toward him Sammler believed he could smell French perfume from the breast of the camel's-hair coat. Had the man then noticed him? Had he perhaps followed him home? Of this Sammler was not sure.

He didn't give a damn for the glamour, the style, the art of criminals.

They were no social heroes to him. He had had some talks on this very matter with one of his younger cousins once or twice removed, Angela Gruner, the daughter of Dr. Arnold Gruner in New Rochelle, who had brought him over to the States in 1947, digging him out of the DP camp in Salzburg. Because Arnold (Elya) Gruner had Old World family feelings. And studying the lists of refugees in the Yiddish papers, he had found the names Artur and Shula Sammler. Angela, who was in Sammler's neighborhood several times a week because her psychiatrist was just around the corner, often stopped in for a visit. She was one of those handsome, passionate, rich girls who were always an important social and human category. A bad education. In literature, mostly French. At Sarah Lawrence College. And Mr. Sammler had to try hard to remember the Balzac he had read in Cracow in 1913. Vautrin the escaped criminal. From the hulks. *Trompe la mort*. No, he didn't have much use for the romance of the outlaw. Angela sent money to defense funds for black murderers and rapists. That was her business, of course.

However, Mr. Sammler had to admit that once he had seen the pickpocket at work he wanted very much to see the thing again. He didn't know why. It was a powerful event, and illicitly—that is, against his own stable principles—he craved a repetition. One detail of old readings he recalled without effort—the moment in *Crime and Punishment* at which Raskolnikov brought down the ax on the bare head of the old woman, her thin gray-streaked grease-smeared hair, the rat's-tail braid fastened by a broken horn comb on her neck. That is to say that horror, crime, murder did vivify all the phenomena, the most ordinary details, of experience. In evil as in art there was illumination. It was, of course, like the tale by Charles Lamb, burning down a house to roast a pig. Was a general conflagration necessary? All you needed was a controlled fire in the right place. Still, to ask everyone to refrain from setting fires until the thing could be done in the right place, in a higher manner, was possibly too much. And while Sammler, getting off the bus, intended to phone the police, he nevertheless received from the crime the benefit of an enlarged vision. The air was bright—late afternoon daylight saving time. The world, Riverside Drive, was wickedly lighted up. Wicked because the clear light made all objects so explicit, and this explicitness taunted Mr. Minutely-Observant Artur Sammler. All metaphysicians please note. Here is how it is. You will never see more clearly. And what do you make of it? This phone booth has a metal floor; smooth-hinged the folding green doors, but the floor is smarting with dry urine, the plastic telephone instrument is smashed, and a stump is hanging at the end of the cord.

Not in three blocks did he find a phone he could safely put a dime into, and so he went home. In his lobby the building management had set up a television screen so the doorman could watch for criminals. But the doorman was always off somewhere. The buzzing rectangle of electronic radiance was vacant. Underfoot was the respectable carpet, brown as gravy. The inner gate of the elevator, supple brass diamonds folding, grimy and gleaming. Sammler went into the apartment and sat on the sofa in the foyer, which Margotte had covered with large squares of Woolworth bandanas, tied at the corners and pinned to the old cushions. He dialed the police and said, "I want to report a crime."

"What kind of crime?"

"A pickpocket."

"Just a minute, I'll connect you."

There was a long buzz. A voice toneless with indifference or fatigue said, "Yes."

Mr. Sammler in his foreign Polish Oxonian English tried to be as compressed, direct, and factual as possible. To save time. To avoid complicated interrogation, needless detail.

"I wish to report a pickpocket on the Riverside bus."

"OK."

"Sir?"

"OK. I said OK, report."

"A Negro, about six feet tall, about two hundred pounds, about thirty-five years old, very good looking, very well dressed."

"OK."

"I thought I should call in."

"OK."

"Are you going to do anything?"

"We're supposed to, aren't we? What's your name?"

"Artur Sammler."

"All right, Art. Where do you live?"

"Dear sir, I will tell you, but I am asking what you intend to do about this man."

"What do you think we should do?"

"Arrest him."

"We have to catch him first."

"You should put a man on the bus."

"We haven't got a man to put on the bus. There are lots of buses, Art, and not enough men. Lots of conventions, banquets, and so on we have to cover, Art, VIP's and brass. There are lots of ladies shopping at Lord & Taylor's, Bonwit's, and Saks', leaving purses on chairs while they go to feel the goods."

"I understand. You don't have the personnel, and there are priorities, political pressures. But I could point out the man.' "

"Some other time."

"You don't want him pointed out?"

"Sure, but we have a waiting list."

"I have to get on *your* list?"

"That's right, Abe."

"Artur."

"Arthur."

Tensely sitting forward in bright lamplight, Artur Sammler like a motorcyclist who has been struck in the forehead by a pebble from the road, trivially stung, smiled with long lips. America (he was speaking to himself)! Advertised throughout the universe as the most normal of all nations.

"Let me make sure I understand you, officer—mister detective. This man is going to rob more people, but you aren't going to do anything about it. Is that right?"

It was right—confirmed by silence, though no ordinary silence. Mr. Sammler said, "Good-bye, sir."

After this, when Sammler should have shunned the bus, he rode it oftener than ever. The thief had a regular route, and he dressed for the ride, for his work. Always gorgeously garbed. Mr. Sammler was struck once, but not astonished, to see that he wore a single gold earring. This was too much to keep to himself, and for the first time he then mentioned to Margotte, his niece and landlady, to Shula, his daughter, that this handsome, this striking, arrogant pickpocket, this African prince or great black beast was seeking whom he might devour between Columbus Circle and Verdi Square.

MR. SAMMLER, WITH BITTER ANGRY MIND, held the top rail of his jammed bus, riding downtown, a short journey. He certainly had not thought of his black pickpocket. Him he connected with Columbus Circle. He always went uptown, not down. But at the rear, in his camel's-hair coat, filling up a corner with his huge body, he was standing. Sammler against strong internal resistance saw him. He resisted because at this swaying difficult moment he had no wish to see him. Inside, Sammler felt an immediate descent; his heart sinking. As sure as fate, as a law of nature, a stone falling, a gas rising. He knew the thief did not ride the bus for transportation. To

meet a woman, to go home—however he diverted himself—he unquestionably took cabs. He could afford them. But now Mr. Sammler was looking down at his shoulder, the tallest man in the bus, except for the thief
himself. He saw that in the long rear seat he had cornered someone. Powerfully bent, the wide back concealed the victim from the other passengers.
Only Sammler because of his height could see. Nothing to be grateful to
height or vision for. The cornered man was old, was weak; poor eyes, watering with terror; white lashes, red lids, and a seamucus blue, his eyes; the
mouth open, with false teeth dropping from the upper gums. Coat and
jacket were open also, the shirt pulled forward like detached green wall-
paper, and the lining of the jacket ragged. The thief tugged his clothes like
a doctor with a clinic patient. Pushing aside tie and scarf, he took out the
wallet. His own homburg he then eased back (an animal movement, simply) slightly from his forehead, furrowed but not with anxiety. The wallet
was long—leatherette, plastic. Open, it yielded a few dollar bills. There
were cards. The thief put them in his palm. Read them with a tilted head.
Let them drop. Examined a green federal-looking check, probably social
security. Mr. Sammler in his goggles was troubled in focusing. Too much
adrenalin was passing with light, thin, frightening rapidity through his
heart. He himself was not frightened, but his heart seemed to record fear,
it had a seizure. He recognized it—knew what name to apply: tachycardia.
Breathing was hard. He wondered whether he might not faint away.
Whether worse might not happen. The check the black man put into his
own pocket. Snapshots like the cards fell from his fingers. Finished, he then
dropped the wallet back into the gray torn lining, flipped back the old
man's muffler. In ironic calm, thumb and forefinger took the knot of the
necktie and yanked it approximately, but only approximately, into place. It
was at this moment that, in a quick turn of the head, he saw Mr. Sammler.
Mr. Sammler seen seeing was still in rapid currents with his heart. Like an
escaping creature racing away from him. His throat ached, up to the root
of his tongue. There was a pang in the bad eye. But he had some presence
of mind. Gripping the overhead chrome rail, he stooped forward as if to
see what street was coming up. 96th. In other words, he avoided a gaze that
might be held, or any interlocking of looks. He acknowledged nothing, and
now began to work his way toward the rear exit, gently urgent, stooping
downward. He reached, found the cord, pulled, made it to the step,
squeezed through the door, and stood on the sidewalk holding the umbrella by the fabric, at the button.

The tachycardia now running itself out, he was able to walk, though
not at the usual rate. His stratagem was to cross Riverside Drive and enter

the first building, as if he lived there. He had beaten the pickpocket to the door. Maybe effrontery would dismiss him as too negligible to pursue. The man did not seem to feel threatened by anyone. Took the slackness, the cowardice of the world for granted. Sammler, with effort, opened a big glass black-grilled door and found himself in an empty lobby. Avoiding the elevator he located the staircase, trudged the first flight and sat down on the landing. A few minutes of rest, and he recovered his oxygen level, although something within felt attenuated. Simply thinned out. Before returning to the street (there was no rear exit) he took the umbrella inside the coat, hooking it in the armhole and belting it up, more or less securely. He also made an effort to change the shape of his hat, punching it out. He went past West End to Broadway, entering the first hamburger joint, sitting in the rear and ordering tea. He drank to the bottom, to the tannic taste, squeezing the sopping bag and asking the counterman for more water, feeling parched. Through the window his thief did not appear. By now Sammler's greatest need was for his bed. But he knew something about lying low. He had learned in Poland, in the war, in forests, cellars, passageways, cemeteries. Things he had passed through once which had abolished a certain margin or leeway ordinarily taken for granted. Taking for granted that one will not be shot stepping into the street, or clubbed to death as one stoops to relieve oneself, or hunted in an alley like a rat. This civil margin once removed, Mr. Sammler would never trust the restoration totally. He had had little occasion to practice the arts of hiding and escaping in New York. But now, although his bones ached for the bed and his skull was famished for the pillow, he sat at the counter with his tea. He could not use buses anymore. From now on it was the subway. The subway was an abomination.

But Mr. Sammler had not shaken the pickpocket. The man obviously could move fast. He might have forced his way out of the bus in midblock and sprinted back, heavy but swift in homburg and camel's-hair coat. Much more likely, the thief had observed him earlier, had once before shadowed him, had followed him home. Yes, that must have been the case. For when Mr. Sammler entered the lobby of his building the man came up behind him quickly, and not simply behind but pressing him bodily, belly to back. He did not lift his hands to Sammler but pushed. There was no building employee. The doormen, also running the elevator, spent much of their time in the cellar.

"What is the matter? What do you want?" said Mr. Sammler.

He was never to hear the black man's voice. He no more spoke than a puma would. What he did was to force Sammler into a corner beside the long blackish carved table, a sort of Renaissance piece, a thing which added to the lobby-melancholy, by the buckling canvas of the old wall, by the red-eyed lights of the brass double fixture. There the man held Sammler against the wall with his forearm. The umbrella fell to the floor with a sharp crack of the ferrule on the tile. It was ignored. The pickpocket unbuttoned himself. Sammler heard the zipper descend. Then the smoked glasses were removed from Sammler's face and dropped on the table. He was directed, silently, to look downward. The black man had opened his fly and taken out his penis. It was displayed to Sammler with the great oval testicles, a large tan and purple uncircumcised thing—a tube, a snake; metallic hairs bristled at the thick base and the tip curled beyond the supporting, demonstrating hand, suggesting the fleshy mobility of an elephant's trunk, though the skin was somewhat iridescent rather than thick or rough. Over the forearm and fist that held him Sammler was required to gaze at this organ. No compulsion would have been necessary. He would in any case have looked.

The interval was long. The man's expression was not directly menacing but oddly, serenely masterful. The thing was shown with mystifying certitude. Lordliness. Then it was returned to the trousers. "*Quod Erat Demonstrandum.*" Sammler was released. The fly was closed, the coat buttoned, the marvelous streaming silk salmon necktie smoothed with a powerful hand on the powerful chest. The black eyes with a light of super candor moved softly, concluding the session, the lesson, the warning, the encounter, the transmission. He picked up Sammler's dark glasses and returned them to his nose. He then unfolded and mounted his own, circular, of gentian violet gently banded with the lovely Dior gold. Then he departed.

Among the Believers

V. S. NAIPAUL || 1981

Few twentieth-century writers have inspired so much fractious debate as the journalist, novelist, and Nobel laureate V. S. Naipaul (1932–   ). Alternately hailed as a gimlet-eyed chronicler of the dislocations of postcolonial life and reviled for betraying his own heritage by telling westerners what they want to hear about the failings of the Third World, Naipaul has traveled the globe for nearly five decades for his thirty-two novels and nonfiction books—producing unsentimental and sometimes scathing portrayals of societies in flux and trauma, notably in Africa (A Bend in the River, *1979), in the Caribbean (*The Middle Passage, *1962), and in India (*India: A Wounded Civilization, *1977), the country that his family left more than a century ago.*

But none of Naipaul's books has generated such polar extremes of admiration and condemnation as Among the Believers, *an account of his seven-month journey to the heart of the Islamic world. Watching the Iranian hostage crisis unfold on television in the fall of 1979, Naipaul decided to visit Iran, as well as three other Muslim countries—Pakistan, Malaysia, and Indonesia—to catalog the changes that rising Islamic fundamentalism had wrought. The book, a collection of vignettes, character sketches, and geopolitical observations, instantly established its author as one of contemporary Islam's fiercest critics and turned him into an international lighting rod. One British reviewer characterized* Among the Believers *as Naipaul's "magnificently disdainful journey through Islam," while Edward Said—who in his book* Orientalism *(1978) sought to discredit western attempts to capture the zeitgeist of eastern civilization—accused the author of displaying "a kind of half-stated but finally unexamined reverence for the colonial order."*

In the excerpt below, drawn from the section of Naipaul's book that describes postrevolutionary Iran, the writer evokes a country intoxicated by an incongruous mix of the ancient and the modern: it is a place where the Ayatollah Khomeini and Karl Marx jostle for space on the bookshelves and where leaders promise to launch their assaults on modernity with state-of-the-art fighter jets. More than a quarter of a century later, Naipaul's depictions of political Islam's allures and contradictions have outlasted the barbs of his detractors, and his portraits of cultures seeking political salvation through religious absolutism feel as up to the minute as the latest headlines from the Middle East.

Tehran, since the revolution, couldn't be said to be a city at work; but people had cars, and the idle city—so many projects abandoned, so many unmoving cranes on the tops of unfinished buildings—could give an impression of desperate busyness.

The desperation was suggested by the way the Iranians drove. They drove like people to whom the motorcar was new. They drove as they walked; and a stream of Tehran traffic, jumpy with individual stops and swerves, with no clear lanes, was like a jostling pavement crowd. This manner of driving didn't go with any special Tehran luck. The door or fender of every other car was bashed in, or bashed in and mended. An item in a local paper (blaming the Shah for not having given the city a more modern road system) had said that traffic accidents were the greatest single cause of deaths in Tehran; two thousand people were killed or injured every month.

We came to an intersection. And there I lost [my interpreter] Behzad. I was waiting for the traffic to stop. But Behzad didn't wait with me. He simply began to cross, dealing with each approaching car in turn, now stopping, now hurrying, now altering the angle of his path, and, like a man crossing a forest gorge by a slender fallen tree trunk, never looking back. He did so only when he got to the other side. He waved me over, but I couldn't move. Traffic lights had failed higher up, and the cars didn't stop.

He understood my helplessness. He came back through the traffic to me, and then—like a moorhen leading its chick across the swift current of a stream—he led me through dangers that at every moment seemed about to sweep me away. He led me by the hand; and, just as the moorhen places herself a little downstream from the chick, breaking the force of the current, which would otherwise sweep the little thing away forever, so Behzad kept me in his lee, walking a little ahead of me and a little to one side, so that he would have been hit first.

And when we were across the road he said, "You must always give your hand to me."

It was, in effect, what I had already begun to do. Without Behzad, without the access to the language that he gave me, I had been like a half-blind man in Tehran. And it had been especially frustrating to be without the language in these streets, scrawled and counter-scrawled with aerosol slogans in many colors in the flowing Persian script, and plastered with revolutionary posters and cartoons with an emphasis on blood. Now, with Behzad, the walls spoke; many other things took on meaning; and the city changed.

Behzad had at first seemed neutral in his comments, and I had thought that this was part of his correctness, his wish not to go beyond his function as a translator. But Behzad was neutral because he was confused. He was a revolutionary and he welcomed the overthrow of the Shah; but the religious revolution that had come to Iran was not the revolution that Behzad wanted. Behzad was without religious faith.

How had that happened? How, in a country like Iran, and growing up in a provincial town, had he learned to do without religion? It was simple, Behzad said. He hadn't been instructed in the faith by his parents; he hadn't been sent to the mosque. Islam was a complicated religion. It wasn't philosophical or speculative. It was a revealed religion, with a Prophet and a complete set of rules. To believe, it was necessary to know a lot about the Arabian origins of the religion, and to take this knowledge to heart.

Islam in Iran was even more complicated. It was a divergence from the main belief; and this divergence had its roots in the political-racial dispute about the succession to the Prophet, who died in 632 A.D. Islam, almost from the start, had been an imperialism as well as a religion, with an early history remarkably like a speeded-up version of the history of Rome, developing from city state to peninsular overlord to empire, with corresponding stresses at every stage. The Iranian divergence had become doctrinal, and there had been divergences within the divergence. Iranians recognized a special line of succession to the Prophet. But a group loyal to the fourth man in this Iranian line, the fourth Imam, had hived off; another group had their own ideas about the seventh. Only one Imam, the eighth (poisoned, like the fourth), was buried in Iran; and his tomb, in Mashhad, not far from the Russian border, was an object of pilgrimage.

"A lot of those people were killed or poisoned," Behzad said, as though explaining his lack of belief.

Islam in Iran, Shia Islam, was an intricate business. To keep alive ancient animosities, to hold on to the idea of personal revenge even after a thousand years, to have a special list of heroes and martyrs and villains, it was necessary to be instructed. And Behzad hadn't been instructed; he had simply stayed away. He had, if anything, been instructed in disbelief by his father, who was a communist. It was of the poor rather than of the saints that Behzad's father had spoken. The memory that Behzad preserved with special piety was of the first day his father had spoken to him about poverty—his own poverty, and the poverty of others.

ON THE PAVEMENT outside the Turkish embassy two turbanned, sunburned medicine men sat with their display of different-colored powders, roots, and minerals. I had seen other medicine men in Tehran and had thought of them as Iranian equivalents of the homeopathic medicine men of India. But the names these Iranians were invoking as medical authorities—as Behzad told me, after listening to their sales talk to a peasant group—were Avicenna, Galen, and "Hippocrat."

Avicenna! To me only a name, someone from the European Middle Ages: it had never occurred to me that he was a Persian. In this dusty pavement medical stock was a reminder of the Arab glory of a thousand years before, when the Arab faith mingled with Persia, India, and the remnant of the classical world it had overrun, and Moslem civilization was the central civilization of the West.

Behzad was less awed than I was. He didn't care for that Moslem past; and he didn't believe in pavement medicines. He didn't care for the Shah's architecture, either: the antique Persian motifs of the Central Bank of Iran, and the Aryan, pre-Islamic past that it proclaimed. To Behzad that stress on the antiquity of Persia and the antiquity of the monarchy was only part of the Shah's vainglory.

He looked at the bank, at the bronze and the marble, and said without passion, "That means nothing to me."

We turned once more, as we walked, to the revolution. There were two posters I had seen in many parts of the city. They were of the same size, done in the same style, and clearly made a pair. One showed a small peasant group working in a field, using a barrow or a plough—it wasn't clear which, from the drawing. The other showed, in silhouette, a crowd raising rifles and machine guns as if in salute. They were like the posters of a people's revolution: an awakened, victorious people, a new dignity of labor. But what was the Persian legend at the top?

Behzad translated: " 'Twelfth Imam, we are waiting for you.' "

"What does that mean?"

"It means they are waiting for the Twelfth Imam."

The Twelfth Imam was the last of the Iranian line of succession to the Prophet. That line had ended over eleven hundred years ago. But the Twelfth Imam hadn't died; he survived somewhere, waiting to return to earth. And his people were waiting for him; the Iranian revolution was an offering to him.

Behzad couldn't help me more; he couldn't help me understand that ecstasy. He could only lay out the facts. Behzad was without belief, but he was surrounded by belief and he could understand its emotional charge. For him it was enough to say—as he did say, without satirical intention—that the Twelfth Imam was the Twelfth Imam.

Later on my Islamic journey, as difficult facts of history and genealogy became more familiar, became more than facts, became readily comprehended articles of faith, I was to begin to understand a little of Moslem passion. But when Behzad translated the legend of those revolutionary posters for me I was at a loss.

It wasn't of this hidden messiah that Iranians had written on the walls of London and other foreign cities before the revolution. They had written—in English—about democracy; about torture by the Shah's secret police; about the "fascism" of the Shah. "Down with fascist Shah": that was the slogan that recurred.

I hadn't followed Iranian affairs closely; but it seemed to me, going only by the graffiti of Iranians abroad, that religion had come late to Iranian protest. It was only when the revolution had started that I understood that it had a religious leader, who had been in exile for many years. The Ayatollah Khomeini, I felt, had been revealed slowly. As the revolution developed, his sanctity and authority appeared to grow and at the end were seen to have been absolute all along.

Fully disclosed, the Ayatollah had turned out to be nothing less than the interpreter, for Iranians, of God's will. By his emergence he annulled, or made trivial, all previous protests about the "fascism" of the Shah. And he accepted his role.

And it was as the interpreter of God's will, the final judge of what was Islamic and what was not Islamic, that Khomeini ruled Iran. Some days after I arrived in Tehran, this was what he said on the radio: "I must tell you that during the previous dictatorial regime strikes and sit-ins pleased God. But now, when the government is a Moslem and a national one, the enemy is busy plotting against us. And therefore staging strikes and sit-ins is religiously forbidden because they are against the principles of Islam."

This was familiar to me, and intellectually manageable, even after a few days in Tehran: the special authority of the man who ruled both as political head and as voice of God. But the idea of the revolution as something more, as an offering to the Twelfth Imam, the man who had vanished in 873 A.D. and remained "in occultation," was harder to seize. And the mimicry of the revolutionary motifs of the late twentieth century—the posters that appeared to celebrate peasants and urban guerrillas, the Che Guevara outfits of the Revolutionary Guards—made it more unsettling.

Behzad translated; the walls spoke; Tehran felt strange. And North Tehran—an expensive piece of Europe expensively set down in the sand and rock of the hills, the creation of the Shah and the large middle class that had been brought into being by the uncreated wealth of oil—felt like a fantasy. There were skyscrapers, international hotels, shops displaying expensive goods with international brand names; but this great city had been grafted onto South Tehran. South Tehran was the community out of which the North had too quickly evolved. And South Tehran, obedient to the will of God and the Twelfth Imam, had laid it low.

MOSLEMS WERE PART of the small Indian community of Trinidad, which was the community into which I was born; and it could be said that I had known Moslems all my life. But I knew little of their religion. My own background was Hindu, and I grew up with the knowledge that Moslems, though ancestrally of India and therefore like ourselves in many ways, were different. I was never instructed in the religious details, and perhaps no one in my family really knew. The difference between Hindus and Moslems was more a matter of group feeling, and mysterious: the animosities our Hindu and Moslem grandfathers had brought from India had softened into a kind of folk wisdom about the unreliability and treachery of the other side.

I was without religious faith myself. I barely understood the rituals and ceremonies I grew up with. In Trinidad, with its many races, my Hinduism was really an attachment to my family and its ways, an attachment to my own difference; and I imagined that among Moslems and others there were similar attachments and privacies.

What I knew about Islam was what was known to everyone on the outside. They had a Prophet and a Book; they believed in one God and disliked images; they had an idea of heaven and hell—always a difficult idea for me. Islam, going by what I saw of it from the outside, was less metaphysical and more direct than Hinduism. In this religion of fear and reward, oddly compounded with war and worldly grief, there was much that reminded me of Christianity—more visible and "official" in Trinidad; and it was possible for me to feel that I knew about it. Its doctrine, or what I thought was its doctrine, didn't attract me. It didn't seem worth inquiring into; and over the years, in spite of travel, I had added little to the knowledge gathered in my Trinidad childhood. The glories of this religion were in the remote past; it had generated nothing like a Renaissance. Moslem countries, where not colonized, were despotisms; and nearly all, before oil, were poor.

The idea of traveling to certain Moslem countries had come to me the previous winter, during the Iranian revolution. I was in Connecticut, and on some evenings I watched the television news. As interesting to me as the events in Iran were the Iranians in the United States who were interviewed on some of the programs.

There was a man in a tweed jacket who spoke the pure language of Marxism, but was more complicated than his language suggested. He was a bit of a dandy, and proud of his ability to handle the jargon he had picked up; he was like a man displaying an idiomatic command of a foreign language. He was proud of his Iranian revolution—it gave him glamour. But at the same time he understood that the religious side of the revolution would appear less than glamorous to his audience; and so he was trying—with the help of his tweed acket, his idiomatic language, his manner—to present himself as sophisticated as any man who watched, and sophisticated in the same way.

Another evening, on another program, an Iranian woman came on with her head covered to tell us that Islam protected women and gave them dignity. Fourteen hundred years ago in Arabia, she said, girl children were buried alive; it was Islam that put a stop to that. Well, we didn't all live in Arabia (not even the woman with the covered head); and many things had happened since the sixth century. Did women—especially someone as fierce as the woman addressing us—still need the special protection that Islam gave them? Did they need the veil? Did they need to be banned from public life and from appearing on television?

These were the questions that occurred to me. But the interviewer, who asked people prepared questions every day, didn't dally. He passed on to his next question, which was about the kind of Islamic state that the woman wanted to see in Iran. Was it something like Saudi Arabia she had in mind? Fierce enough already, she flared up at that; and with her chador-encircled face she looked like an angry nun, full of reprimand. It was a mistake many people made, she said; but Saudi Arabia was not an Islamic state. And it seemed that she was saying that Saudi Arabia was an acknowledged barbarism, and that the Islamic state of Iran was going to be quite different. (It was only in Iran that I understood the point the woman with the chador had made about Saudi Arabia. It was a sectarian point and might have been thought too involved for a television audience: the Arabians and the Persians belong to different sects, have different lines of succession to the Prophet, and there is historical bad blood between them.)

IN AUGUST OF 1979, six months after the overthrow of the Shah, the news from Iran was still of executions. The official Iranian news agency kept count, and regularly gave a new grand total. The most recent executions had been of prostitutes and brothel-managers; the Islamic revolution had taken that wicked turn. The Ayatollah Khomeini was reported to have outlawed music. And Islamic rules about women were being enforced again. Mixed bathing had been banned; Revolutionary Guards watched the beaches at the Caspian Sea resorts and separated the sexes.

After all that I had heard about the Shah's big ideas for his country, the airport building at Tehran was a disappointment. The arrival hall was like a big shed. Blank rectangular patches edged with reddish dust—ghost pictures in ghostly frames—showed where, no doubt, there had been photographs of the Shah and his family or his monuments. Revolutionary leaflets and caricatures were taped down on walls and pillars; and—also taped down: sticky paper and handwritten notices giving a curious informality to great events—there were colored photographs of the Ayatollah Khomeini, as hard-eyed and sensual and unreliable and roguish-looking as any enemy might have portrayed him.

The colors of the city were as dusty and pale as they had appeared from the air. Dust blew about the road, coated the trees, dimmed the colors of cars. Bricks and plaster were the color of dust; unfinished buildings looked abandoned and crumbling; and walls, like abstracts of the time, were scribbled over in the Persian script and stenciled with portraits of Khomeini.

The pavements were broken. Many shop signs were broken or had lost some of their raised letters. Dust and grime were so general, and on illuminated signs looked so much like the effect of smoke, that buildings that had been burned out in old fires did not immediately catch the eye. Building work seemed to have been suspended; rubble heaps and gravel heaps looked old, settled.

In the pavement kiosks there were magazines of the revolution. The cover of one had a composite photograph of the Shah as a bathing beauty: the head of the Shah attached to the body of a woman in a bikini—but the bikini had been brushed over with a broad stroke of black, not to offend modesty. In another caricature the Shah, jacketed, his tie slackened, sat on a lavatory seat with his trousers down, and with a tommy gun in his hand. A suitcase beside him was labeled To Israel and Bahama; an open canvas bag showed a bottle of whiskey and a copy of *Time* magazine.

Young men in tight, open-necked shirts dawdled on the broken pavements. They were handsome men of a clear racial type, small, broad-shouldered, narrow-waisted. They were working men of peasant antecedents, and there was some little air of vanity and danger about them that afternoon: they must have been keyed up by the communal Friday prayers. In their clothes, and especially their shirts, there was that touch of flashiness that—going by what I had seen in India—I associated with people who had just emerged from traditional ways and now possessed the idea that, in clothes as in other things, they could choose for themselves.

The afternoon cars and motorcycles went by, driven in the Iranian way. I saw two collisions. One shop had changed its name. It was now "Our Fried Chicken," no longer the chicken of Kentucky, and the figure of the southern colonel had been fudged into something quite meaningless (except to those who remembered the colonel). Revolutionary Guards, young men with guns, soon ceased to be surprising.

BEHZAD AND I WENT to Qom by car. Qom had a famous shrine, the tomb of the sister of the eighth Shia Imam; for a thousand years it had been a place of pilgrimage. It also had a number of theological schools. Khomeini had taught and lectured at Qom; and on his return to Iran after the fall of the Shah he had made Qom his headquarters. He was surrounded there by ayatollahs, people of distinction in their own right, and it was one of these attendant figures, Ayatollah Khalkhalli, whom I was hoping to see.

Khomeini received and preached and blessed; Khalkhalli hanged. He was Khomeini's hanging judge. It was Khalkhalli who had conducted many of those swift Islamic trials that had ended in executions, with official before-and-after photographs: men shown before they were killed, and then shown dead, naked on the sliding mortuary slabs.

Khalkhalli had recently been giving interviews, emphasizing his activities as judge, and a story in Tehran was that he had fallen out of favor and was trying through these interviews to keep his reputation alive. He told the *Tehran Times* that he had "probably" sentenced four hundred people to death in Tehran: "On some nights, he said, bodies of 30 or more people would be sent out in trucks from the prison. He claimed he had also signed the death warrants of a large number of people in Khuzistan Province." Khuzistan was the Arab province in the southwest, where the oil was.

He told another paper that there had been a plot—worked out in the South Korean Embassy—to rescue Hoveyda, the Shah's prime minister, and other important people from the Tehran jail. As soon as he, Khalkhalli, had heard of this plot he had decided—to deal a blow to the CIA and Zionism—to bring forward the cases. "I reviewed all their cases in one night and had them face the firing squad." He told the *Tehran Times* how Hoveyda had died. The first bullet hit Hoveyda in the neck; it didn't kill him. Hoveyda was then ordered by his executioner—a priest—to hold his head up; the second bullet hit him in the head and killed him.

"Would this man see me?" I had asked an agency correspondent, when we were talking about Khalkhalli.

"He would love to see you."

And Behzad thought it could be arranged. Behzad said he would telephone Khalkhalli's secretary when we got to Qom.

The telephone, the secretary: the modern apparatus seemed strange. But Khalkhalli saw himself as a man of the age. "He said" (this was from the *Tehran Times*) "the religious leaders were trying to enforce the rule of the Holy Prophet Mohammed in Iran. During the days of the Prophet swords were used to fight, now they have been replaced by Phantom aircraft." Phantoms: not American, not the products of a foreign science, but as international as swords, part of the stock of the great world bazaar, and rendered Islamic by purchase.

I had imagined that Qom, a holy city, would be built on hills: it would be full of cliff walls and shadows and narrow lanes cut into the rock, with cells or caves where pious men meditated. It was set flat in the desert, and the approach to it was like the approach to any other desert town: shacks, gas stations. The road grew neater; shacks gave way to houses. A garden bloomed on a traffic roundabout—Persian gardens have this abrupt, enclosed, oasis-like quality. A dome gleamed in the distance between minarets. It was the dome of the famous shrine.

Behzad said, "That dome is made of gold."

It had been gilded in the last century. But the city we began to enter had been enriched by oil; and it seemed like a reconstructed bazaar city, characterless except for the gold dome and its minarets.

Behzad said, "How shall I introduce you? Correspondent? Khalkhalli likes correspondents."

"That isn't how I want to talk to him, though. I really just want to chat with him. I want to understand how he became what he is."

KHALKHALLI'S HOUSE WAS THE LAST in a dead end, a newish road with young trees on the pavement. It was near sunset; the desert sky was full of color. There were men with guns about, and we stopped a house or two away. Behzad went and talked to somebody and then called me. The house was new, of concrete, not big, and it was set back from the pavement, with a little paved area in front.

In the veranda, or gallery, we were given a body search by a short, thickly built young man in a tight blue jersey, who ran or slapped rough hands down our legs; and then we went into a small carpeted room. There were about six or eight people there, among them an African couple, sitting erect and still on the floor. The man wore a dark-gray suit and was hard to place; but from the costume of the woman I judged them to be Somalis, people from the northeastern horn of Africa.

I wasn't expecting this crowd—in fact, a little court. I was hoping for a more intimate conversation with a man who, I thought, had fallen from power and might be feeling neglected.

A hanging judge, a figure of revolutionary terror, dealing out Islamic justice to young and old, men and women: but the bearded little fellow, about five feet tall, who, preceded by a reverential petitioner, presently came out of an inner room—and was the man himself—was plump and jolly, with eyes merry behind his glasses.

He moved with stiff little steps. He was fair-skinned, with a white skull-cap, no turban or clerical cloak or gown; and he looked a bit of a mess, with a crumpled, long-tailed tunic or shirt, brown-striped, covering a couple of cotton garments at the top and hanging out over slack white trousers.

This disorder of clothes in one who might have assumed the high clerical style was perhaps something Khalkhalli cultivated or was known for: the Iranians in the room began to smile as soon as he appeared. The African man fixed glittering eyes of awe on him, and Khalkhalli was tender with him, giving him an individual greeting. After tenderness with the African, Khalkhalli was rough with Behzad and me. The change in his manner was abrupt, willful, a piece of acting: it was the clown wishing to show his other side. It didn't disturb me; it told me that having me in the room, another stranger who had come from far, was flattering to him.

He said, "I am busy. I have no time for interviews. Why didn't you telephone?"

Behzad said, "We telephoned twice."

Khalkhalli didn't reply. He took another petitioner to the inner room with him.

Behzad said, "He's making up his mind."

But I knew that he had already made up his mind, that the idea of the interview was too much for him to resist. When he came out—and before he led someone else in to his room—he said, with the same unconvincing roughness, "Write out your questions."

It was another piece of picked-up style, but it was hard for me. I had been hoping to get him to talk about his life; I would have liked to enter his mind, to see the world as he saw it. I had been hoping for conversation. I couldn't say what questions I wanted to put to him until he had begun to talk. But I had to do as he asked: the Iranians and the Africans were waiting to see me carry out his instructions. How could I get this hanging judge to show a little more than his official side? How could I get this half-clown, with his medieval learning, to illuminate his passion?

I could think of nothing extraordinary; I decided to be direct. On a sheet of hotel paper, which I had brought with me, I wrote: Where were you born? What made you decide to take up religious studies? What did your father do? Where did you study? Where did you first preach? How did you become an ayatollah? What was your happiest day?

He was pleased, when he finally came out, to see Behzad with the list of questions, and he sat cross-legged in front of us. Our knees almost touched. He answered simply at first. He was born in Azerbaijan. His father was a very religious man. His father was a farmer.

I asked, "Did you help your father?"

"I was a shepherd when I was a boy." And then he began to clown. Raising his voice, making a gesture, he said, "Right now I know how to cut off a sheep's head." And the Iranians in the room—including some of his bodyguards—rocked with laughter. "I did every kind of job. Even selling. I know everything."

But how did the shepherd boy become a mullah?

"I studied for thirty-five years."

That was all. He could be prodded into no narrative, no story of struggle or rise. He had simply lived; experience wasn't something he had reflected on. And, vain as he was ("I am very clever, very intelligent"), the questions about his past didn't interest him. He wanted more to talk about his present power, or his closeness to power; and that was what, ignoring the remainder of the written questions, he began to do.

He said, "I was taught by Ayatollah Khomeini, you know. And I was the teacher of the son of Ayatollah Khomeini." He thumped me on the shoulder and added archly, to the amusement of the Iranians, "So I cannot say I am very close to Ayatollah Khomeini."

His mouth opened wide, stayed open, and soon he appeared to be choking with laughter, showing me his gums, his tongue, his gullet. When he recovered he said, with a short, swift wave of his right hand, "The mullahs are going to rule now. We are going to have ten thousand years of the Islamic Republic. The Marxists will go on with their Lenin. We will go on in the way of Khomeini."

He went silent. Crossing his legs neatly below him, fixing me with his eyes, becoming grave, appearing to look up at me through his glasses, he said, in the silence he had created, "I killed Hoveyda, you know."

The straightness of his face was part of the joke for the Iranians. They—squatting on the carpet—threw themselves about with laughter.

It was what was closest to him, his work as revolutionary judge. He had given many interviews about his sentencing of the Shah's prime minister; and he wanted to tell the story again.

I said, "You killed him yourself?"

Behzad said, "No, he only gave the order. Hoveyda was killed by the son of a famous ayatollah."

"But I have the gun," Khalkhalli said, as though it was the next best thing.

Again the Iranians rolled about the carpet with laughter. And even the African, never taking his glittering eyes off Khalkhalli, began to smile.

Behzad said, "A Revolutionary Guard gave him the gun."

I said, "Do you have it on you?"

Khalkhalli said, "I have it in the next room."

So at the end he had forced me, in that room full of laughter, to be his straight man.

It was fast-breaking time now, no time to dally, time for all visitors to leave, except the Africans. For some minutes young men had been placing food on the veranda floor. Khalkhalli, dismissing us, appeared to forget us. Even before we had put our shoes on and got to the gate, he and the African couple were sitting down to dinner. It was a big dinner; the clown ate seriously.

And at last our driver could eat, and Behzad could repeat the sacramental moment of food-sharing with him. We drove back to the center of the town, near the shrine, and they ate in the cafe where we had waited earlier in the afternoon, in a smell of cooking mutton.

They ate rice, mutton, and flat Persian bread. It was all that the cafe offered. I left them together, bought some nuts and dried fruit from a stall, and walked along the river, among families camping and eating on the river embankment in the dark. Across the road from the embankment electric lights shone on melons and other fruit in stalls: a refreshing night scene, after the glare and colorlessness of the day.

When I was walking back to the cafe, and was on the other side of the river, I passed an illuminated shoe shop.

It had a big color photograph of Khomeini. I stopped to consider his unreliable face again: the creased forehead, the eyebrows, the hard eyes, the sensual lips. In the light of the shop I looked at the handful of nuts and kishmish raisins I was about to put in my mouth. It contained a thumbtack. Without that pause in front of Khomeini's picture, I would have done damage to my mouth in ways I preferred not to think of; and my unbeliever's day in Khomeini's holy city of Qom would have ended with a nasty surprise.

Dan Quayle Was Right

BARBARA DAFOE WHITEHEAD || 1993

In May of 1992, in the thick of a presidential campaign, then vice president Dan Quayle decided to go on the attack—against a television character. In a speech on family values and moral decay delivered in the wake of the Rodney King riots in Los Angeles, Quayle told a California audience: "It doesn't help matters when primetime TV has Murphy Brown [a fictional newswoman played by Candice Bergen] . . . mocking the importance of fathers, by bearing a child alone, and calling it just another 'lifestyle choice.' " The reaction was swift and merciless—outrage from feminists, ridicule from late-night television hosts, and near-unanimous agreement that the "Murphy Brown speech" constituted a new milestone in Quayle's long litany of public embarrassments.

But there was only one problem, as the sociologist Barbara Dafoe Whitehead (1944–　) argued a year later in this much-discussed essay: Dan Quayle was actually right. According to Whitehead, the codirector of the National Marriage Project at Rutgers University and one of the nation's leading experts on the American family, Quayle was right to assert that children of divorce, as well as those who are born out of wedlock, tend to lead more troubled lives than children who grow up in traditional two-parent households; Quayle was right to insist upon a connection between the growing incidence of absent-father families and the epidemic of crime, drug abuse, and unemployment roiling America's underclass; and Quayle was right to put an important subject on the table that had for so long appeared inimical to rational discussion.

Dating back to the mid-1960s—when Daniel Patrick Moynihan, then an assistant secretary of labor, was bitterly denounced as a racist for warning, in a report called "The Negro Family: The Case for National Action," that the increasing prevalence of single-mother families threatened African American advancement—there had been a clear pattern: anyone who called attention to the negative consequences of the decline of the two-parent family could expect to catch hell for appearing to be picking on, as Whitehead puts it, "struggling single mothers and their children." Meanwhile, the rate of out-of-wedlock births kept rising: when Moynihan sounded the alarm of a "crisis" in the black family, in 1965, 25 percent of African American births were to unwed mothers; by 1990, the black illegitimacy rate had climbed to 57 percent, and the white rate had edged toward 20 percent. Although divorce and illegitimacy may provide

short-term benefits to adults, observes Whitehead, they are ultimately
harmful not only to children but to the social fabric.

Whitehead's potent cover story—the issue in which it appeared was
the second highest selling in Atlantic *history—helped provoke a pro-*
found shift in the national debate on the state of the family. Within a
year, Bill Clinton would use his State of the Union address to proclaim
that "we cannot renew our country when, within a decade, more than
half of our children will be born into families where there is no mar-
riage," and efforts to combat illegitimacy have been a feature of an-
tipoverty programs ever since (albeit with limited success). Even Murphy
Brown herself eventually joined the pro-Quayle chorus: asked about the
former vice president's famous rebuke in an interview in 2002, Candice
Bergen allowed that "[it] was a perfectly intelligent speech about fathers
not being dispensable and nobody agreed with that more than I did."

Divorce and out-of-wedlock childbirth are transforming the lives of
American children. In the postwar generation more than 80 percent of
children grew up in a family with two biological parents who were married
to each other. By 1980 only 50 percent could expect to spend their entire
childhood in an intact family. If current trends continue, less than half of
all children born today will live continuously with their own mother and
father throughout childhood. Most American children will spend several
years in a single-mother family. Some will eventually live in stepparent
families, but because stepfamilies are more likely to break up than intact
(by which I mean two-biological-parent) families, an increasing number of
children will experience family breakup two or even three times during
childhood.

According to a growing body of social-scientific evidence, children in
families disrupted by divorce and out-of-wedlock birth do worse than children in intact families on several measures of well-being. Children in
single-parent families are six times as likely to be poor. They are also likely
to stay poor longer. Twenty-two percent of children in one-parent families
will experience poverty during childhood for seven years or more, as compared with only two percent of children in two-parent families. A 1988 survey by the National Center for Health Statistics found that children in
single-parent families are two to three times as likely as children in two-
parent families to have emotional and behavioral problems. They are also
more likely to drop out of high school, to get pregnant as teenagers, to
abuse drugs, and to be in trouble with the law. Compared with children in

intact families, children from disrupted families are at a much higher risk for physical or sexual abuse.

Contrary to popular belief, many children do not "bounce back" after divorce or remarriage. Difficulties that are associated with family breakup often persist into adulthood. Children who grow up in single-parent or stepparent families are less successful as adults, particularly in the two domains of life—love and work—that are most essential to happiness. Needless to say, not all children experience such negative effects. However, research shows that many children from disrupted families have a harder time achieving intimacy in a relationship, forming a stable marriage, or even holding a steady job.

Despite this growing body of evidence, it is nearly impossible to discuss changes in family structure without provoking angry protest. Many people see the discussion as no more than an attack on struggling single mothers and their children: Why blame single mothers when they are doing the very best they can? After all, the decision to end a marriage or a relationship is wrenching, and few parents are indifferent to the painful burden this decision imposes on their children. Many take the perilous step toward single parenthood as a last resort, after their best efforts to hold a marriage together have failed. Consequently, it can seem particularly cruel and unfeeling to remind parents of the hardships their children might suffer as a result of family breakup. Other people believe that the dramatic changes in family structure, though regrettable, are impossible to reverse. Family breakup is an inevitable feature of American life, and anyone who thinks otherwise is indulging in nostalgia or trying to turn back the clock. Since these new family forms are here to stay, the reasoning goes, we must accord respect to single parents, not criticize them. Typical is the view expressed by a Brooklyn woman in a recent letter to *The New York Times*: "Let's stop moralizing or blaming single parents and unwed mothers, and give them the respect they have earned and the support they deserve."

Such views are not to be dismissed. Indeed, they help to explain why family structure is such an explosive issue for Americans. The debate about it is not simply about the social-scientific evidence, although that is surely an important part of the discussion. It is also a debate over deeply held and often conflicting values. How do we begin to reconcile our long-standing belief in equality and diversity with an impressive body of evidence that suggests that not all family structures produce equal outcomes for children? How can we square traditional notions of public support for dependent women and children with a belief in women's right to pursue autonomy and independence in childbearing and child-rearing? How do we uphold the freedom of adults to pursue individual happiness in their private relationships and at the same time respond to the needs of children for stability, security, and permanence in their family lives? What do we do when the interests of adults and children conflict? These are the difficult issues at stake in the debate over family structure.

In the past these issues have turned out to be too difficult and too politically risky for debate. In the mid-1960s Daniel Patrick Moynihan, then an assistant secretary of labor, was denounced as a racist for calling attention to the relationship between the prevalence of black single-mother families and the lower socioeconomic standing of black children. For nearly twenty years the policy and research communities backed away from the entire issue. In 1980 the Carter Administration convened a historic White House Conference on Families, designed to address the growing problems of children and families in America. The result was a prolonged, publicly subsidized quarrel over the definition of family. No President since has tried to hold a national family conference. Last year, at a time when the rate of out-of-wedlock births had reached a historic high, Vice President Dan Quayle was ridiculed for criticizing Murphy Brown. In short, every time the issue of family structure has been raised, the response has been first controversy, then retreat, and finally silence.

Yet it is also risky to ignore the issue of changing family structure. In recent years the problems associated with family disruption have grown. Overall child well-being has declined, despite a decrease in the number of children per family, an increase in the educational level of parents, and historically high levels of public spending. After dropping in the 1960s and 1970s, the proportion of children in poverty has increased dramatically, from 15 percent in 1970 to 20 percent in 1990, while the percentage of adult Americans in poverty has remained roughly constant. The teen suicide rate has more than tripled. Juvenile crime has increased and become more violent. School performance has continued to decline. There are no signs that these trends are about to reverse themselves.

If we fail to come to terms with the relationship between family structure and declining child well-being, then it will be increasingly difficult to improve children's life prospects, no matter how many new programs the federal government funds. Nor will we be able to make progress in bettering school performance or reducing crime or improving the quality of the nation's future work force—all domestic problems closely connected to family breakup. Worse, we may contribute to the problem by pursuing policies that actually increase family instability and breakup.

ACROSS TIME AND ACROSS CULTURES, family disruption has been regarded as an event that threatens a child's well-being and even survival. This view is rooted in a fundamental biological fact: unlike the young of almost any other species, the human child is born in an abjectly helpless and immature state. Years of nurture and protection are needed before the child can achieve physical independence. Similarly, it takes years of interaction with at least one but ideally two or more adults for a child to develop into a socially competent adult. Children raised in virtual isolation from human beings, though physically intact, display few recognizably human behaviors. The social arrangement that has proved most successful in ensuring the physical survival and promoting the social development of the child is the family unit of the biological mother and father. Consequently, any event that permanently denies a child the presence and protection of a parent jeopardizes the life of the child.

The classic form of family disruption is the death of a parent. Throughout history this has been one of the risks of childhood. Mothers frequently died in childbirth, and it was not unusual for both parents to die before the child was grown. As recently as the early decades of this century children commonly suffered the death of at least one parent. Almost a quarter of the children born in this country in 1900 lost one parent by the time they were fifteen years old. Many of these children lived with their widowed parent, often in a household with other close relatives. Others grew up in orphanages and foster homes.

The meaning of parental death, as it has been transmitted over time and faithfully recorded in world literature and lore, is unambiguous and essentially unchanging. It is universally regarded as an untimely and tragic event. Death permanently severs the parent-child bond, disrupting forever one of the child's earliest and deepest human attachments. It also deprives a child of the presence and protection of an adult who has a biological stake in, as well as an emotional commitment to, the child's survival and well-being. In short, the death of a parent is the most extreme and severe loss a child can suffer.

It has taken thousands upon thousands of years to reduce the threat of parental death. Not until the middle of the twentieth century did parental death cease to be a commonplace event for children in the United States. By then advances in medicine had dramatically reduced mortality rates for men and women.

At the same time, other forms of family disruption—separation, divorce, out-of-wedlock birth—were held in check by powerful religious, so-

cial, and legal sanctions. Divorce was widely regarded both as a deviant behavior, especially threatening to mothers and children, and as a personal
lapse: "Divorce is the public acknowledgment of failure," a 1940s sociology
textbook noted. Out-of-wedlock birth was stigmatized, and stigmatization
is a powerful means of regulating behavior, as any smoker or overeater will
testify. Sanctions against nonmarital childbirth discouraged behavior that
hurt children and exacted compensatory behavior that helped them. Shotgun marriages and adoption, two common responses to nonmarital birth,
carried a strong message about the risks of premarital sex and created an
intact family for the child.

Consequently, children did not have to worry much about losing a
parent through divorce or never having had one because of nonmarital
birth. After a surge in divorces following the Second World War, the rate
leveled off. Only 11 percent of children born in the 1950s would by the time
they turned eighteen see their parents separate or divorce. Out-of-wedlock
childbirth barely figured as a cause of family disruption. In the 1950s and
early 1960s, five percent of the nation's births were out of wedlock. Blacks
were more likely than whites to bear children outside marriage, but the
majority of black children born in the twenty years after the Second World
War were born to married couples. The rate of family disruption reached
a historic low point during those years.

A new standard of family security and stability was established in postwar America. For the first time in history the vast majority of the nation's
children could expect to live with married biological parents throughout
childhood. Children might still suffer other forms of adversity—poverty,
racial discrimination, lack of educational opportunity—but only a few
would be deprived of the nurture and protection of a mother and a father.
No longer did children have to be haunted by the classic fears vividly
dramatized in folklore and fable—that their parents would die, that they
would have to live with a stepparent and stepsiblings, or that they would be
abandoned. These were the years when the nation confidently boarded up
orphanages and closed foundling hospitals, certain that such institutions
would never again be needed. In movie theaters across the country parents
and children could watch the drama of parental separation and death in
the great Disney classics, secure in the knowledge that such nightmare visions as the death of Bambi's mother and the wrenching separation of
Dumbo from his mother were only make believe.

In the 1960s the rate of family disruption suddenly began to rise. After
inching up over the course of a century, the divorce rate soared. Throughout the 1950s and early 1960s the divorce rate held steady at fewer than ten

divorces a year per 1,000 married couples. Then, beginning in about 1965, the rate increased sharply, peaking at twenty-three divorces per 1,000 marriages by 1979. (In 1974 divorce passed death as the leading cause of family breakup.) The rate has leveled off at about twenty-one divorces per 1,000 marriages—the figure for 1991. The out-of-wedlock birth rate also jumped. It went from five percent in 1960 to 27 percent in 1990. In 1990 close to 57 percent of births among black mothers were nonmarital, and about 17 percent among white mothers. Altogether, about one out of every four women who had a child in 1990 was not married. With rates of divorce and nonmarital birth so high, family disruption is at its peak. Never before have so many children experienced family breakup caused by events other than death. Each year a million children go through divorce or separation and almost as many more are born out of wedlock.

Half of all marriages now end in divorce. Following divorce, many people enter new relationships. Some begin living together. Nearly half of all cohabiting couples have children in the household. Fifteen percent have new children together. Many cohabiting couples eventually get married. However, both cohabiting and remarried couples are more likely to break up than couples in first marriages. Even social scientists find it hard to keep pace with the complexity and velocity of such patterns. In the revised edition (1992) of his book *Marriage, Divorce, Remarriage*, the sociologist Andrew Cherlin ruefully comments: "If there were a truth-in-labeling law for books, the title of this edition should be something long and unwieldy like *Cohabitation, Marriage, Divorce, More Cohabitation, and Probably Remarriage.*"

Under such conditions growing up can be a turbulent experience. In many single-parent families children must come to terms with the parent's love life and romantic partners. Some children live with cohabiting couples, either their own unmarried parents or a biological parent and a live-in partner. Some children born to cohabiting parents see their parents break up. Others see their parents marry, but 56 percent of them (as compared with 31 percent of the children born to married parents) later see their parents' marriages fall apart. All told, about three quarters of children born to cohabiting couples will live in a single-parent home at least briefly. One of every four children growing up in the 1990s will eventually enter a stepfamily. According to one survey, nearly half of all children in stepparent families will see their parents divorce again by the time they reach their late teens. Since 80 percent of divorced fathers remarry, things get even more complicated when the romantic or marital history of the noncustodial parent, usually the father, is taken into account. Consequently, as it affects a significant number of children, family disruption is best under-stood not as a single event but as a string of disruptive events: separation, divorce, life in a single-parent family, life with a parent and live-in lover, the remarriage of one or both parents, life in one stepparent family com-bined with visits to another stepparent family, the breakup of one or both stepparent families. And so on. This is one reason why public schools have a hard time knowing whom to call in an emergency.

Given its dramatic impact on children's lives, one might reasonably ex-pect that this historic level of family disruption would be viewed with alarm, even regarded as a national crisis. Yet this has not been the case. In recent years some people have argued that these trends pose a serious threat to children and to the nation as a whole, but they are dismissed as declinists, pessimists, or nostalgists, unwilling or unable to accept the new facts of life. The dominant view is that the changes in family structure are, on balance, positive.

There are several reasons why this is so, but the fundamental reason is that at some point in the 1970s Americans changed their minds about the meaning of these disruptive behaviors. What had once been regarded as hostile to children's best interests was now considered essential to adults' happiness. In the 1950s most Americans believed that parents should stay in an unhappy marriage for the sake of the children. By the mid-1970s a majority of Americans rejected that view. At about the same time, the long-standing taboo against out-of-wedlock childbirth also collapsed. By the mid-1970s three fourths of Americans said that it was not morally wrong for a woman to have a child outside marriage.

Over the past two and a half decades Americans have been conducting what is tantamount to a vast natural experiment in family life. The results of the experiment are coming in, and they are clear. Adults have benefited from the changes in family life in important ways, but the same cannot be said for children. Indeed, this is the first generation in the nation's history to do worse psychologically, socially, and economically than its parents. Most poignantly, in survey after survey the children of broken families confess deep longings for an intact family.

Nonetheless, [this cultural shift] is not an irresistible undertow that will carry away the family. It is more like a swift current, against which it is possible to swim. People learn; societies can change, particularly when it becomes apparent that certain behaviors damage the social ecology, threaten the public order, and impose new burdens on core institutions. Whether Americans will act to overcome the legacy of family disruption is a crucial but as yet unanswered question.

CAPITALISM AND ITS DISCONTENTS

Story of a Great Monopoly

HENRY DEMAREST LLOYD || 1881

"Story of a Great Monopoly," by Henry Demarest Lloyd (1847–1903), is among the most influential articles that The Atlantic *has ever published and a landmark in the annals of journalism. Many historians view Lloyd's report, a scathing indictment of John D. Rockefeller's Standard Oil Company, as the earliest example of progressive muckraking; it was certainly the first serious exposé of a corporate monopoly to appear in a national magazine. Lloyd was a wealthy lawyer turned financial journalist whom the press had dubbed "the Millionaire Socialist," and his detailed revelations of price fixing, intimidation, and collusion between Standard Oil and the railroads caused a sensation. (The issue in which they appeared sold out seven printings.) His characterization of the oil company as an "octopus," according to one historian, "stuck to Standard . . . like the barnacles on the hulls of a tanker." The exposé not only changed American perceptions of big business but also created an indignant climate of opinion that eventually led to major legislative crackdowns on monopolies, including the Interstate Commerce Act of 1887 and the Sherman Antitrust Act of 1890. It also earned Lloyd a place at the head of a long line of muckrakers, from Ida Tarbell to Upton Sinclair to Ralph Nader—and the undying enmity of one John D. Rockefeller.*

Kerosene has become, by its cheapness, the people's light the world over. In the United States we used 220,000,000 gallons of petroleum last year. It has come into such demand abroad that our exports of it increased from 79,458,888 gallons in 1868, to 417,648,544 in 1879. It goes all over Europe, and to the far East. After articles of food, this country has but one export, cotton, more valuable than petroleum. [In] the cities as well as the country, petroleum is the general illuminator. We use more kerosene lamps than Bibles.

Very few of the forty millions of people in the United States who burn kerosene know that its production, manufacture, and export, its price at home and abroad, have been controlled for years by a single corporation,—the Standard Oil Company. This company began in a partnership, in the early years of the civil war, between Samuel Andrews and John Rockefeller in Cleveland. Rockefeller had been a bookkeeper in some interior town in Ohio, and had afterwards made a few thousand dollars by keeping a flour store in Cleveland. Andrews had been a day laborer in refineries, and so poor that his wife took in sewing. He found a way of refining by which more kerosene could be got out of a barrel of petroleum than by any other method, and set up for himself a ten-barrel still in Cleveland, by which he cleared $500 in six months. Andrews' still and Rockefeller's savings have grown into the Standard Oil Company. It has a capital, nominally $3,500,000, but really much more, on which it divides among its stockholders every year millions of dollars of profits.

The Standard produces only one fiftieth or sixtieth of our petroleum, but dictates the price of all, and refines nine tenths. Circulars are issued at intervals by which the price of oil is fixed for all the cities of the country, except New York, where a little competition survives. There is not to-day a merchant in Chicago, or in any other city in the New England, Western, or Southern States, dealing in kerosene, whose prices are not fixed for him by the Standard. This corporation has driven into bankruptcy, or out of business, or into union with itself, all the petroleum refineries of the country except five in New York, and a few of little consequence in Western Pennsylvania. Nobody knows how many millions Rockefeller is worth. Current gossip among his business acquaintances in Cleveland puts his income last year at a figure second only, if second at all, to that of [the railroad magnate William Henry] Vanderbilt. His partner, Samuel Andrews, the poor English day laborer, retired years ago with millions.

Their great business capacity would have insured the managers of the Standard success, but the means by which they achieved monopoly was by conspiracy with the railroads. Mr. Simon Sterne, counsel for the merchants of New York in the New York investigation, declared that the relations of the railroads to the Standard exhibited "the most shameless perversion of the duties of a common carrier to private ends that has taken place in the history of the world." The Standard killed its rivals, in brief, by getting the great trunk lines to refuse to give them transportation. Commodore Vanderbilt [William Henry's father, Cornelius] is reported to have said that there was but one man—Rockefeller—who could dictate to him. Whether or not Vanderbilt said it, Rockefeller did it. The Standard has done everything with the Pennsylvania legislature, except refine it.

Vanderbilt signed an agreement, March 25, 1872, that "all agreements for the transportation of oil after this date shall be upon a basis of perfect equality," and ever since has given the Standard special rates and privileges. He has paid it back in rebates millions of dollars, which have enabled it to crush out all competitors. . . . So closely had the Standard octopus gripped itself about Mr. Vanderbilt that even at the outside rates its competitors could not get transportation from him. He allowed the Standard to become the owner of all the oil cars run over his road, and of all his terminal facilities for oil. Hundreds and thousands of men have been ruined by these acts of the Standard and the railroads; whole communities have been rendered desperate.

Its genius for monopoly has given the Standard control of more than the product of oil and its manufacture. Wholesale merchants in all the cities of the country, except New York, have to buy and sell at the prices it makes. Merchants who buy oil of the Standard are not allowed to sell to dealers who buy of its few competitors. Some who have done so have been warned not to repeat the offense, and have been informed that, if they did so, the Standard, though under contract to supply them with oil, would cut them off, and would fight any suit they might bring through all the courts without regard to expense. These oil producers and refiners whom the Standard was robbing with and without forms of law fought with every weapon they could command. The struggle has been going on continuously for nine years. All that men could do who were fighting for self-preservation was done. They caused to be introduced into Congress the first original bill to regulate railroads in interstate commerce. The outrages done by the roads and the Standard were proved before an investigating committee of Congress, but Congress did nothing. America has the proud satisfaction of having furnished the world with the greatest, wisest, and meanest monopoly known to history.

The time has come to face the fact that the forces of capital and industry have outgrown the forces of our government. The corporation and the trades-union have forgotten that they are the creatures of the state. Our strong men are engaged in a headlong fight for fortune, power, precedence, success. Americans as they are, they ride over the people like Juggernaut to gain their ends. The moralists have preached to them since the world began, and have failed. The common people, the nation, must take them in hand. The people can be successful only when they are right. When monopolies succeed, the people fail; when a rich criminal escapes justice, the people are punished; when a legislature is bribed, the people are cheated. There is nobody richer than Vanderbilt except the body of citizens; no corporation more powerful than the transcontinental railroad except the corporate sovereign at Washington. The nation is the engine of the people. They must use it for their industrial life, as they used it in 1861 for their political life. The States have failed. The United States must succeed, or the people will perish.

Have You Ever Tried to Sell a Diamond?

EDWARD JAY EPSTEIN || 1982

For more than 125 years, De Beers Consolidated Mines, Ltd., has reigned supreme over the glittering world of diamonds. By any measure, the multinational behemoth, headquartered in Johannesburg, South Africa, has led a charmed corporate life, and it continues to generate more than $6 billion in annual revenues despite some relatively recent challenges to its global hegemony. These have included the rise of competing mining operations in Siberia, Australia, and Canada; a nettlesome antitrust lawsuit filed by the U.S. Justice Department in 1994 (and settled in 2004); and a well-publicized, United Nations–led campaign, launched in the 1990s, to ban the sale of so-called "blood diamonds"—gems that are harvested in war-ravaged African countries and then used to bankroll internecine fighting there. But it was the disclosures of this rigorously reported exposé by the longtime investigative journalist Edward Jay Epstein (1935–   ) that seem to have inflicted the first significant cracks in the De Beers corporate image. With a historian's reach and a detective's eye for the telltale clue, Epstein reconstructs in elaborate detail the backstage machinations and brilliant, multibillion-dollar marketing campaign that enabled De Beers not only to create what the writer calls "the most successful cartel arrangement in the annals of modern commerce" but also to transform essentially valueless, pebble-like crystals of carbon into "universally recognized tokens of wealth, power, and romance."

Epstein, an author well known for his dogged inquiries into Cold War espionage (Deception: The Invisible War Between the KGB and the CIA, *1989) and Hollywood financial skullduggery* (The Big Picture, *2005), stumbled upon this extraordinary tale of mass manipulation in the late 1970s, while on a routine reporting assignment for a now-defunct magazine on the processes by which diamonds are mined, cut, polished, and sold. He soon became far more intrigued by the scent of monopolistic business practices he was picking up on and abandoned the original article to devote himself full-time to researching and writing* The Rise and Fall of Diamonds: The Shattering of a Brilliant Illusion *(1982), from which this* Atlantic *article was drawn. As a result of the publication of "Have You Ever Tried to Sell a Diamond?" twenty-five years ago, the diamond industry has faced an escalation of unwelcome scrutiny in at least a half dozen books and countless newspaper and magazine articles. Meanwhile, to the surprise of many, including Epstein, his groundbreak-*

ing magazine article has come to enjoy a remarkable new life on the Internet, where it has been one of the most requested pieces on The Atlantic's *website since it was posted there seven years ago. But the diamond exposé cost the magazine dearly. Upon its publication in 1982, De Beers pulled its six-figure-a-year advertising campaign ("A Diamond Is Forever") from* The Atlantic's *pages, never to return.*

The diamond invention—the creation of the idea that diamonds are rare and valuable, and are essential signs of esteem—is a relatively recent development in the history of the diamond trade. Until the late nineteenth century, diamonds were found only in a few riverbeds in India and in the jungles of Brazil, and the entire world production of gem diamonds amounted to a few pounds a year. In 1870, however, huge diamond mines were discovered near the Orange River, in South Africa, where diamonds were soon being scooped out by the ton. Suddenly, the market was deluged with diamonds. The British financiers who had organized the South African mines quickly realized that their investment was endangered; diamonds had little intrinsic value—and their price depended almost entirely on their scarcity. The financiers feared that when new mines were developed in South Africa, diamonds would become at best only semiprecious gems.

The major investors in the diamond mines realized that they had no alternative but to merge their interests into a single entity that would be powerful enough to control production and perpetuate the illusion of scarcity of diamonds. The instrument they created, in 1888, was called De Beers Consolidated Mines, Ltd., incorporated in South Africa. As De Beers took control of all aspects of the world diamond trade, it assumed many forms. In London, it operated under the innocuous name of the Diamond Trading Company. In Israel, it was known as "The Syndicate." In Europe, it was called the "C.S.O."—initials referring to the Central Selling Organization, which was an arm of the Diamond Trading Company. And in black Africa, it disguised its South African origins under subsidiaries with names like Diamond Development Corporation and Mining Services, Inc. At its height—for most of this century—it not only either directly owned or controlled all the diamond mines in southern Africa but also owned diamond-trading companies in England, Portugal, Israel, Belgium, Holland, and Switzerland.

De Beers proved to be the most successful cartel arrangement in the annals of modern commerce. While other commodities, such as gold, silver, copper, rubber, and grains, fluctuated wildly in response to economic conditions, diamonds have continued, with few exceptions, to advance upward in price every year since the Depression. Indeed, the cartel seemed so superbly in control of prices—and unassailable—that, in the late 1970s, even speculators began buying diamonds as a guard against the vagaries of inflation and recession.

The diamond invention is far more than a monopoly for fixing diamond prices; it is a mechanism for converting tiny crystals of carbon into universally recognized tokens of wealth, power, and romance. To achieve this goal, De Beers had to control demand as well as supply. Both women and men had to be made to perceive diamonds not as marketable precious stones but as an inseparable part of courtship and married life. To stabilize the market, De Beers had to endow these stones with a sentiment that would inhibit the public from ever reselling them. The illusion had to be created that diamonds were forever—"forever" in the sense that they should never be resold.

In September of 1938, Harry Oppenheimer, son of the founder of De Beers and then twenty-nine, traveled from Johannesburg to New York City, to meet with Gerold M. Lauck, the president of N. W. Ayer, a leading advertising agency in the United States. Lauck and N. W. Ayer had been recommended to Oppenheimer by the Morgan Bank, which had helped his father consolidate the De Beers financial empire. His bankers were concerned about the price of diamonds, which had declined worldwide.

In Europe, where diamond prices had collapsed during the Depression, there seemed little possibility of restoring public confidence in diamonds. In Germany, Austria, Italy, and Spain, the notion of giving a diamond ring to commemorate an engagement had never taken hold. In England and France, diamonds were still presumed to be jewels for aristocrats rather than the masses. Furthermore, Europe was on the verge of war, and there seemed little possibility of expanding diamond sales. This left the United States as the only real market for De Beers's diamonds. In fact, in 1938 some three quarters of all the cartel's diamonds were sold for engagement rings in the United States. Most of these stones, however, were smaller and of poorer quality than those bought in Europe, and had an average price of $80 apiece. Oppenheimer and the bankers believed that an advertising campaign could persuade Americans to buy more expensive diamonds.

Oppenheimer suggested to Lauck that his agency prepare a plan for creating a new image for diamonds among Americans. He assured Lauck that De Beers had not called on any other American advertising agency with this proposal, and that if the plan met with his father's approval, N. W. Ayer would be the exclusive agents for the placement of newspaper and radio advertisements in the United States. Oppenheimer agreed to underwrite the costs of the research necessary for developing the campaign. Lauck instantly accepted the offer.

In their subsequent investigation of the American diamond market, the staff of N. W. Ayer found that since the end of World War I, in 1919, the total amount of diamonds sold in America, measured in carats, had declined by 50 percent; at the same time, the quality of diamonds, measured in dollar value, had declined by nearly 100 percent. An Ayer memo concluded that the depressed state of the market for diamonds was "the result of the economy, changes in social attitudes and the promotion of competitive luxuries."

Although it could do little about the state of the economy, N. W. Ayer suggested that through a well-orchestrated advertising and public-relations campaign it could have a significant impact on the "social attitudes" of the public at large and thereby channel American spending toward larger and more expensive diamonds instead of "competitive luxuries." Specifically, the Ayer study stressed the need to strengthen the association in the public's mind of diamonds with romance. Since "young men buy over 90% of all engagement rings," it would be crucial to inculcate in them the idea that diamonds were a gift of love: the larger and finer the diamond, the greater the expression of love. Similarly, young women had to be encouraged to view diamonds as an integral part of any romantic courtship.

Since the Ayer plan to romanticize diamonds required subtly altering the public's picture of the way a man courts—and wins—a woman, the advertising agency strongly suggested exploiting the relatively new medium of motion pictures. Movie idols, the paragons of romance for the mass audience, would be given diamonds to use as their symbols of indestructible love. In addition, the agency suggested offering stories and society photographs to selected magazines and newspapers which would reinforce the link between diamonds and romance. Stories would stress the size of diamonds that celebrities presented to their loved ones, and photographs would conspicuously show the glittering stone on the hand of a well-known woman. Fashion designers would talk on radio programs about the "trend towards diamonds" that Ayer planned to start. The Ayer plan also envisioned using the British royal family to help foster the romantic allure of diamonds. An Ayer memo said, "Since Great Britain has such an important interest in the diamond industry, the royal couple could be of tremendous assistance to this British industry by wearing diamonds rather than other jewels." Queen Elizabeth later went on a well-publicized trip to several South African diamond mines, and she accepted a diamond from Oppenheimer.

In addition to putting these plans into action, N. W. Ayer placed a series of lush four-color advertisements in magazines that were presumed to mold elite opinion, featuring reproductions of famous paintings by such artists as Picasso, Derain, Dali, and Dufy. The advertisements were intended to convey the idea that diamonds, like paintings, were unique works of art.

BY 1941, THE ADVERTISING AGENCY REPORTED to its client that it had already achieved impressive results in its campaign. The sale of diamonds had increased by 55 percent in the United States since 1938, reversing the previous downward trend in retail sales. N. W. Ayer noted also that its campaign had required "the conception of a new form of advertising which has been widely imitated ever since. There was no direct sale to be made. There was no brand name to be impressed on the public mind. There was simply an idea—the eternal emotional value surrounding the diamond." It further claimed that "a new type of art was devised . . . and a new color, diamond blue, was created and used in these campaigns. . . ."

In its 1947 strategic plan, the advertising agency strongly emphasized a psychological approach. "We are dealing with a problem in mass psychology. We seek to . . . strengthen the tradition of the diamond engagement ring—to make it a psychological necessity capable of competing successfully at the retail level with utility goods and services. . . ." It defined as its target audience "some 70 million people 15 years and over whose opinion we hope to influence in support of our objectives." N. W. Ayer outlined a subtle program that included arranging for lecturers to visit high schools across the country. "All of these lectures revolve around the diamond engagement ring, and are reaching thousands of girls in their assemblies, classes and informal meetings in our leading educational institutions," the agency explained in a memorandum to De Beers. The agency had organized, in 1946, a weekly service called "Hollywood Personalities," which provided 125 leading newspapers with descriptions of the diamonds worn by movie stars. And it continued its efforts to encourage news coverage of celebrities displaying diamond rings as symbols of romantic involvement. In 1947, the agency commissioned a series of portraits of "engaged socialites." The idea was to create prestigious "role models" for the poorer middle-class wage-earners. The advertising agency explained, in its 1948 strategy paper, "We spread the word of diamonds worn by stars of screen and stage, by wives and daughters of political leaders, by any woman who can make the grocer's wife and the mechanic's sweetheart say 'I wish I had what she has.' "

De Beers needed a slogan for diamonds that expressed both the theme of romance and legitimacy. An N. W. Ayer copywriter came up with the caption "A Diamond Is Forever," which was scrawled on the bottom of a picture of two young lovers on a honeymoon. Even though diamonds can in fact be shattered, chipped, discolored, or incinerated to ash, the concept of eternity perfectly captured the magical qualities that the advertising agency wanted to attribute to diamonds. Within a year, "A Diamond Is Forever" became the official motto of De Beers.

N. W. Ayer was always searching for new ways to influence American public opinion. Not only did it organize a service to "release to the women's pages [of daily newspapers] all the fresh material that we can find or create about the engagement ring" but it set about exploiting the relatively new medium of television by arranging for actresses and other celebrities to wear diamonds when they appeared before the camera. It also established a "Diamond Information Center" that placed a stamp of quasi-authority on the flood of "historical" data and "news" it released. "We work hard to keep ourselves known throughout the publishing world as the source of information on diamonds," N. W. Ayer commented in a memorandum to De Beers, and added: "Because we have done it successfully, we have opportunities to help with articles originated by others."

N. W. Ayer proposed to apply to the diamond market Thorstein Veblen's idea, stated in *The Theory of the Leisure Class*, that Americans were motivated in their purchases not by utility but by "conspicuous consumption." "The substantial diamond gift can be made a more widely sought symbol of personal and family success—an expression of socio-economic achievement," N. W. Ayer said in a report. To exploit this desire for conspicuous display, the agency specifically recommended, "Promote the diamond as one material object which can reflect, in a very personal way, a man's . . . success in life." Since this campaign would be addressed to upwardly mobile men, the advertisements ideally "should have the aroma of tweed, old leather and polished wood which is characteristic of a good club."

Toward the end of the 1950s, N. W. Ayer reported to De Beers that twenty years of advertisements and publicity had had a pronounced effect on the American psyche. "Since 1939 an entirely new generation of young people have grown to marriageable age," it said. "To this new generation a diamond ring is considered a necessity to engagements by virtually everyone." The message had been so successfully impressed on the minds of this generation that those who could not afford to buy a diamond at the time of their marriage would "defer the purchase" rather than forgo it.

THE CAMPAIGN TO INTERNATIONALIZE THE DIAMOND INVENTION began in earnest in the mid-1960s. The prime targets were Japan, Germany, and Brazil. Since N. W. Ayer was primarily an American advertising agency, De Beers brought in the J. Walter Thompson agency, which had especially strong advertising subsidiaries in the target countries, to place most of its international advertising. Within ten years, De Beers succeeded beyond even its most optimistic expectations, creating a billion-dollar-a-year diamond market in Japan, where matrimonial custom had survived feudal revolutions, world wars, industrialization, and even the American occupation.

In America, which remained the most important market for most of De Beers's diamonds, N. W. Ayer recognized the need to create a new demand for diamonds among long-married couples. "Candies come, flowers come, furs come," but such ephemeral gifts fail to satisfy a woman's psychological craving for "a renewal of the romance," N. W. Ayer said in a report. An advertising campaign could instill the idea that the gift of a second diamond, in the later years of marriage, would be accepted as a sign of "ever-growing love." In 1962, N. W. Ayer asked for authorization to "begin the long-term process of setting the diamond aside as the only appropriate gift for those later-in-life occasions where sentiment is to be expressed." De Beers immediately approved the campaign.

By 1979, N. W. Ayer had helped De Beers expand its sales of diamonds in the United States to more than $2.1 billion, at the wholesale level, compared with a mere $23 million in 1939. In forty years, the value of its sales had increased nearly a hundredfold. The expenditure on advertisements, which began at a level of only $200,000 a year and gradually increased to $10 million, seemed a brilliant investment.

Except for those few stones that have been destroyed, every diamond that has been found and cut into a jewel still exists today and is literally in the public's hands. Some hundred million women wear diamonds, while millions of others keep them in safe-deposit boxes or strongboxes as family heirlooms. It is conservatively estimated that the public holds more than 500 million carats of gem diamonds, which is more than fifty times the number of gem diamonds produced by the diamond cartel in any given year. Since the quantity of diamonds needed for engagement rings and other jewelry each year is satisfied by the production from the world's mines, this half-billion-carat supply of diamonds must be prevented from ever being put on the market. The moment a significant portion of the public begins selling diamonds from this inventory, the price of diamonds cannot be sustained. For the diamond invention to survive, the public must be inhibited from ever parting with its diamonds.

In developing a strategy for De Beers in 1953, N. W. Ayer said: "In our opinion old diamonds are in 'safe hands' only when widely dispersed and held by individuals as cherished possessions valued far above their market price." As far as De Beers and N. W. Ayer were concerned, "safe hands" belonged to those women psychologically conditioned never to sell their diamonds. This conditioning could not be attained solely by placing advertisements in magazines. The diamond-holding public, which includes people who inherit diamonds, had to remain convinced that diamonds retained their monetary value. If it saw price fluctuations in the diamond market and attempted to dispose of diamonds to take advantage of changing prices, the retail market would become chaotic. It was therefore essential that De Beers maintain at least the illusion of price stability.

In the 1971 De Beers annual report, Harry Oppenheimer explained the unique situation of diamonds in the following terms: "A degree of control is necessary for the well-being of the industry, not because production is excessive or demand is falling, but simply because wide fluctuations in price, which have, rightly or wrongly, been accepted as normal in the case of most raw materials, would be destructive of public confidence in the case of a pure luxury such as gem diamonds, of which large stocks are held in the form of jewelry by the general public." During the periods when production from the mines temporarily exceeds the consumption of diamonds—the balance is determined mainly by the number of impending marriages in the United States and Japan—the cartel can preserve the illusion of price stability by either cutting back the distribution of diamonds at its London "sights," where, ten times a year, it allots the world's supply of diamonds to about 300 hand-chosen dealers, called "sight-holders," or by itself buying back diamonds at the wholesale level. The underlying assumption is that as long as the general public never sees the price of diamonds fall, it will not become nervous and begin selling its diamonds. If this huge inventory should ever reach the market, even De Beers and all the Oppenheimer resources could not prevent the price of diamonds from plummeting.

Selling individual diamonds at a profit, even those held over long periods of time, can be surprisingly difficult. For example, in 1970 the London-based consumer magazine *Money Which?* decided to test diamonds as a decade-long investment. It bought two gem-quality diamonds, weighing approximately one-half carat apiece, from one of London's most reputable diamond dealers, for £400 (then worth about a thousand dollars). For nearly nine years, it kept these two diamonds sealed in an envelope in its vault. During this same period, Great Britain experienced inflation that ran as high as 25 percent a year. For the diamonds to have kept pace with inflation, they would have had to increase in value at least 300 percent, making them worth some £1,400 pounds by 1978. But when the magazine's editor, Dave Watts, tried to sell the diamonds in 1978, he found that neither jewelry stores nor wholesale dealers in London's Hatton Garden district would pay anywhere near that price for the diamonds. Most of the stores refused to pay any cash for them; the highest bid Watts received was £500, which amounted to a profit of only £100 in over eight years, or less than 3 percent at a compound rate of interest. If the bid were calculated in 1970 pounds, it would amount to only £167. Dave Watts summed up the magazine's experiment by saying, "As an 8-year investment the diamonds that we bought have proved to be very poor." The problem was that the buyer, not the seller, determined the price.

The magazine conducted another experiment to determine the extent to which larger diamonds appreciate in value over a one-year period. In 1970, it bought a 1.42-carat diamond for £745. In 1971, the highest offer it received for the same gem was £568. Rather than sell it at such an enormous loss, Watts decided to extend the experiment until 1974, when he again made the rounds of the jewelers in Hatton Garden to have it appraised. During this tour of the diamond district, Watts found that the diamond had mysteriously shrunk in weight to 1.04 carats. One of the jewelers had apparently switched diamonds during the appraisal. In that same year, Watts, undaunted, bought another diamond, this one 1.4 carats, from a reputable London dealer. He paid £2,595. A week later, he decided to sell it. The maximum offer he received was £1,000.

In 1976, the Dutch Consumer Association also tried to test the price appreciation of diamonds by buying a perfect diamond of over one carat in Amsterdam, holding it for eight months, and then offering it for sale to the twenty leading dealers in Amsterdam. Nineteen refused to buy it, and the twentieth dealer offered only a fraction of the purchase price.

Selling diamonds can also be an extraordinarily frustrating experience for private individuals. In 1978, for example, a wealthy woman in New York City decided to sell back a diamond ring she had bought from Tiffany two years earlier for $100,000 and use the proceeds toward a necklace of matched pearls that she fancied. She had read about the "diamond boom" in news magazines and hoped that she might make a profit on the diamond. Instead, the sales executive explained, with what she said seemed to be a touch of embarrassment, that Tiffany had "a strict policy against repurchasing diamonds." He assured her, however, that the diamond was extremely valuable, and suggested another Fifth Avenue jewelry store. The woman went from one leading jeweler to another, attempting to sell her diamond. One store offered to swap it for another jewel, and two other jewelers offered to accept the diamond "on consignment" and pay her a percentage of what they sold it for, but none of the half-dozen jewelers she visited offered her cash for her $100,000 diamond. She finally gave up and kept the diamond.

Retail jewelers, especially the prestigious Fifth Avenue stores, prefer not to buy back diamonds from customers, because the offer they would make would most likely be considered ridiculously low. The "keystone," or markup, on a diamond and its setting may range from 100 to 200 percent, depending on the policy of the store; if it bought diamonds back from customers, it would have to buy them back at wholesale prices. Most jewelers would prefer not to make a customer an offer that might be deemed insulting and also might undercut the widely held notion that diamonds go up in value. Moreover, since retailers generally receive their diamonds from wholesalers on consignment, and need not pay for them until they are sold, they would not readily risk their own cash to buy diamonds from customers. Rather than offer customers a fraction of what they paid for diamonds, retail jewelers almost invariably recommend to their clients firms that specialize in buying diamonds "retail."

The firm perhaps most frequently recommended by New York jewelry shops is Empire Diamonds Corporation, which is situated on the sixty-sixth floor of the Empire State Building, in midtown Manhattan. Empire's reception room, which resembles a doctor's office, is usually crowded with elderly women who sit nervously in plastic chairs waiting for their names to be called. One by one, they are ushered into a small examining room, where an appraiser scrutinizes their diamonds and makes them a cash offer. "We usually can't pay more than a maximum of 90 percent of the current wholesale price," says Jack Brod, president of Empire Diamonds. "In most cases we have to pay less, since the setting has to be discarded, and we have to leave a margin for error in our evaluation—especially if the diamond is mounted in a setting." Empire removes the diamonds from the settings, which are sold as scrap, and resells them to wholesalers. Because of the steep markup on diamonds, individuals who buy retail and in effect sell wholesale often suffer enormous losses. For example, Brod estimates that a half-carat diamond ring, which might cost $2,000 at a retail jewelry store, could be sold for only $600 at Empire.

While those who attempt to sell diamonds often experience disappointment at the low price they are offered, stories in gossip columns suggest that diamonds are resold at enormous profits. This is because the column items are not about the typical diamond ring that a woman desperately attempts to peddle to small stores and diamond-buying services like Empire but about truly extraordinary diamonds that movie stars sell, or claim to sell, in a publicity-charged atmosphere. The legend created around the so-called "Elizabeth Taylor" diamond is a case in point. This pear-shaped diamond, which weighed 69.42 carats after it had been cut and polished, was the fifty-sixth largest diamond in the world and one of the few large-cut diamonds in private hands. Except that it was a diamond, it had little in common with the millions of small stones that are mass-marketed each year in engagement rings and other jewelry.

"There's going to come a day when all those doctors, lawyers, and other fools who bought diamonds over the phone take them out of their strongboxes, or wherever, and try to sell them," one dealer predicted last year. Another gave a gloomy picture of what would happen if this accumulation of diamonds were suddenly sold by speculators. "Investment diamonds are bought for $30,000 a carat, not because any woman wants to wear them on her finger but because the investor believes they will be worth $50,000 a carat. He may borrow heavily to leverage his investment. When the price begins to decline, everyone will try to sell their diamonds at once. In the end, of course, there will be no buyers for diamonds at $30,000 a carat or even $15,000. At this point, there will be a stampede to sell investment diamonds, and the newspapers will begin writing stories about the great diamond crash. Investment diamonds constitute, of course, only a small fraction of the diamonds held by the public, but when women begin reading about a diamond crash, they will take their diamonds to retail jewelers to be appraised and find out that they are worth less than they paid for them. At that point, people will realize that diamonds are not forever, and jewelers will be flooded with customers trying to sell, not buy, diamonds. That will be the end of the diamond business."

On the Liquidation of the Mustang Ranch by the Internal Revenue Service

X. J. KENNEDY || 1991

The Atlantic *has published its fair share of occasional and topical verse over the years, but one can only wonder what Emerson and Longfellow would have made of this mordant ditty on the decline and fall of a storied Nevada bordello. Founded in the badlands outside of Reno by former cabdriver and ex-con Joseph Conforte and his wife, Sally, in 1967, the Mustang Ranch was granted a license as the first legal brothel in Nevada by Storey County in 1971, paving the way for several other counties in the state to sanction regulated prostitution. Even during the enterprise's boom times, however, the seamy side of its business operations kept local prosecutors busy. The Confortes were in and out of court battling tax evasion and racketeering charges, and in September 1990 the IRS seized the property in an attempt to recoup $13 million in back taxes. Two months later, following Chapter 11 bankruptcy proceedings, the IRS liquidated the company's holdings and auctioned off a gaudy array of Mustang Ranch memorabilia. The press naturally had a field day covering the spectacle, but it was left to the New Jersey–born and –bred satirical poet X. J. Kennedy (1929–   ), the author of such admired collections as* Nude Descending a Staircase *(1961), to commemorate the occasion with epigrammatic aplomb, slyly casting his eulogy in the form of an elegant yet hardboiled Petrarchan sonnet. Longfellow might have blanched, but somewhere Catullus was smiling.*

This poor old spread, its waterholes turned dust,
    Its paying herd stampeded, lies here slain.
    On Reno's rock-shanked hills frustrated rain
Refuses to descend. Spangles of rust
Bestride the bar where hands no longer shake
    Quick daiquiris to blur the fear of AIDS,
    Net stockings dangle hollow, grand parades
Kick off no more. A hibernating snake

Lies not more still. Beneath the auctioneer's
   Gavel fall crates of condoms, lingerie,
   The sign from the mirrored orgy chamber: FIRE
EXIT, the kindly tank of oxygen
   Whose sweet breath could that reveler inspire
To flare, who might have smoldered in dismay.

Why McDonald's Fries Taste So Good

ERIC SCHLOSSER || 2001

The United States, according to surveys, is a country where the Golden Arches of McDonald's are as pervasive and universally identifiable as the crucifix—where the company's mascot, Ronald McDonald, is a celebrity on the order of Santa Claus. The transformations wrought by the explosive growth of the fast-food industry, since its seedbed beginnings in the postwar car culture of Southern California, have been monumental both in scale and in scope, and few developments of the last half century have had a comparable influence on American life. The commercial juggernaut that is McDonald's, Burger King, KFC, Domino's Pizza, and the other fast-food leviathans has radically changed not only the American diet but also the American family, the American landscape, the American economy, American agriculture, and American popular culture. It has also radically changed the American waistline, contributing to an obesity epidemic that has remodeled the average American into the most overweight person on the planet.

"The impact of McDonald's on how we live today is hard to overstate," observes Eric Schlosser (1959–　) in an introduction to Fast Food Nation *(2001), his landmark chronicle of the rise of—and fallout from—the fast-food industry. The book, which has sold more than one million copies worldwide and earned its author comparisons with the muckraker Upton Sinclair, the environmentalist Rachel Carson, and even his own literary hero and Princeton writing teacher, John McPhee, artfully mixes scene setting, investigative reporting, historical research, and cultural analysis to impart fresh perspective on some of our most familiar institutions. It is a strategy that Schlosser has used to great effect since he made his magazine debut in* The Atlantic, *in 1993. His memorable articles for the magazine—including "Reefer Madness," an investigation of the draconian prison sentences being handed down for marijuana possession (which won a National Magazine Award for reporting in 1995), and his heart-wrenching cover story "A Grief Like No Other," which examined the plight of the families of murder victims—have showcased an unusual talent for harnessing the techniques of narrative nonfiction to serious social issues. In "Why McDonald's Fries Taste So Good," one of the most eye-opening and talked-about sections of* Fast Food Nation, *Schlosser takes readers deep into the heart of a top-secret, futuristic New Jersey laboratory, where an elite band of "flavorists" engineers the chemical*

*compounds needed to resuscitate highly processed foods with flavor,
aroma, and color. Even as simple a concoction as a Burger King strawberry milk shake, Schlosser discloses, contains forty-eight separate
chemicals—and not a single strawberry.*

The french fry was "almost sacrosanct to me," Ray Kroc, one of the
founders of McDonald's, wrote in his autobiography, "its preparation a ritual to be followed religiously." During the chain's early years french fries
were made from scratch every day. Russet Burbank potatoes were peeled,
cut into shoestrings, and fried in McDonald's kitchens. As the chain expanded nationwide, in the mid-1960s, it sought to cut labor costs, reduce
the number of suppliers, and ensure that its fries tasted the same at every
restaurant. McDonald's began switching to frozen french fries in 1966—
and few customers noticed the difference. Nevertheless, the change had a
profound effect on the nation's agriculture and diet. A familiar food had
been transformed into a highly processed industrial commodity. McDonald's fries now come from huge manufacturing plants that can peel, slice,
cook, and freeze two million pounds of potatoes a day. The rapid expansion of McDonald's and the popularity of its low-cost, mass-produced fries
changed the way Americans eat. In 1960 Americans consumed an average
of about eighty-one pounds of fresh potatoes and four pounds of frozen
french fries. In 2000 they consumed an average of about fifty pounds of
fresh potatoes and thirty pounds of frozen fries. Today McDonald's is the
largest buyer of potatoes in the United States.

The taste of McDonald's french fries played a crucial role in the chain's
success—fries are much more profitable than hamburgers—and was long
praised by customers, competitors, and even food critics. James Beard
loved McDonald's fries. Their distinctive taste does not stem from the kind
of potatoes that McDonald's buys, the technology that processes them, or
the restaurant equipment that fries them: other chains use Russet Bur-
banks, buy their french fries from the same large processing companies,
and have similar fryers in their restaurant kitchens. The taste of a french fry
is largely determined by the cooking oil. For decades McDonald's cooked
its french fries in a mixture of about seven percent cottonseed oil and 93
percent beef tallow. The mixture gave the fries their unique flavor—and
more saturated beef fat per ounce than a McDonald's hamburger.

In 1990, amid a barrage of criticism over the amount of cholesterol in
its fries, McDonald's switched to pure vegetable oil. This presented the
company with a challenge: how to make fries that subtly taste like beef

without cooking them in beef tallow. A look at the ingredients in McDonald's french fries suggests how the problem was solved. Toward the end of the list is a seemingly innocuous yet oddly mysterious phrase: "natural flavor." That ingredient helps to explain not only why the fries taste so good but also why most fast food—indeed, most of the food Americans eat today—tastes the way it does.

Open your refrigerator, your freezer, your kitchen cupboards, and look at the labels on your food. You'll find "natural flavor" or "artificial flavor" in just about every list of ingredients. The similarities between these two broad categories are far more significant than the differences. Both are man-made additives that give most processed food most of its taste. People usually buy a food item the first time because of its packaging or appearance. Taste usually determines whether they buy it again. About 90 percent of the money that Americans now spend on food goes to buy processed food. The canning, freezing, and dehydrating techniques used in processing destroy most of food's flavor—and so a vast industry has arisen in the United States to make processed foods palatable. Without this flavor industry today's fast food would not exist. The names of the leading American fast-food chains and their best-selling menu items have become embedded in our popular culture and famous worldwide. But few people can name the companies that manufacture fast food's taste.

The flavor industry is highly secretive. Its leading companies will not divulge the precise formulas of flavor compounds or the identities of clients. The secrecy is deemed essential for protecting the reputations of beloved brands. The fast-food chains, understandably, would like the public to believe that the flavors of the food they sell somehow originate in their restaurant kitchens, not in distant factories run by other firms. A McDonald's french fry is one of countless foods whose flavor is just a component in a complex manufacturing process. The look and the taste of what we eat now are frequently deceiving—by design.

THE NEW JERSEY TURNPIKE RUNS through the heart of the flavor industry, an industrial corridor dotted with refineries and chemical plants. International Flavors & Fragrances (IFF), the world's largest flavor company, has a manufacturing facility off Exit 8A in Dayton, New Jersey; Givaudan, the world's second-largest flavor company, has a plant in East Hanover. Haarman & Reimer, the largest German flavor company, has a plant in Teterboro, as does Takasago, the largest Japanese flavor company. Flavor Dynamics has a plant in South Plainfield; Frutarom is in North Bergen; Elan Chemical is in Newark. Dozens of companies manufacture flavors in the corridor between Teaneck and South Brunswick. Altogether the area produces about two thirds of the flavor additives sold in the United States.

The IFF plant in Dayton is a huge pale-blue building with a modern office complex attached to the front. It sits in an industrial park, not far from a BASF plastics factory, a Jolly French Toast factory, and a plant that manufactures Liz Claiborne cosmetics. Dozens of tractor-trailers were parked at the IFF loading dock the afternoon I visited, and a thin cloud of steam floated from a roof vent. Before entering the plant, I signed a nondisclosure form, promising not to reveal the brand names that contain IFF flavors. The place reminded me of Willy Wonka's chocolate factory. Wonderful smells drifted through the hallways, men and women in neat white lab coats cheerfully went about their work, and hundreds of little glass bottles sat on laboratory tables and shelves. The bottles contained powerful but fragile flavor chemicals, shielded from light by brown glass and round white caps shut tight. The long chemical names on the little white labels were as mystifying to me as medieval Latin. These odd-sounding things would be mixed and poured and turned into new substances, like magic potions.

I was not invited into the manufacturing areas of the IFF plant, where, it was thought, I might discover trade secrets. Instead I toured various laboratories and pilot kitchens, where the flavors of well-established brands are tested or adjusted, and where whole new flavors are created. IFF's snack-and-savory lab is responsible for the flavors of potato chips, corn chips, breads, crackers, breakfast cereals, and pet food. The confectionery lab devises flavors for ice cream, cookies, candies, toothpastes, mouthwashes, and antacids. Everywhere I looked, I saw famous, widely advertised products sitting on laboratory desks and tables. The beverage lab was full of brightly colored liquids in clear bottles. It comes up with flavors for popular soft drinks, sports drinks, bottled teas, and wine coolers, for all-natural juice drinks, organic soy drinks, beers, and malt liquors. In one pilot kitchen I saw a dapper food technologist, a middle-aged man with an elegant tie beneath his crisp lab coat, carefully preparing a batch of cookies with white frosting and pink-and-white sprinkles. In another pilot kitchen I saw a pizza oven, a grill, a milk-shake machine, and a french fryer identical to those I'd seen at innumerable fast-food restaurants.

In addition to being the world's largest flavor company, IFF manufactures the smells of six of the ten best-selling fine perfumes in the United States, including Estée Lauder's Beautiful, Clinique's Happy, Lancôme's Trésor, and Calvin Klein's Eternity. It also makes the smells of household products such as deodorant, dishwashing detergent, bath soap, shampoo, furniture polish, and floor wax. All these aromas are made through essentially the same process: the manipulation of volatile chemicals. The basic science behind the scent of your shaving cream is the same as that governing the flavor of your TV dinner.

SCIENTISTS NOW BELIEVE that human beings acquired the sense of taste as a way to avoid being poisoned. Edible plants generally taste sweet, harmful ones bitter. The taste buds on our tongues can detect the presence of half a dozen or so basic tastes, including sweet, sour, bitter, salty, astringent, and umami, a taste discovered by Japanese researchers—a rich and full sense of deliciousness triggered by amino acids in foods such as meat, shellfish, mushrooms, potatoes, and seaweed. Taste buds offer a limited means of detection, however, compared with the human olfactory system, which can perceive thousands of different chemical aromas. Indeed, "flavor" is primarily the smell of gases being released by the chemicals you've just put in your mouth. The aroma of a food can be responsible for as much as 90 percent of its taste.

The acting of drinking, sucking, or chewing on a substance releases its volatile gases. They flow out of your mouth and up your nostrils, or up the passageway in the back of your mouth, to a thin layer of nerve cells called the olfactory epithelium, located at the base of your nose, right between your eyes. Your brain combines the complex smell signals from your olfactory epithelium with the simple taste signals from your tongue, assigns a flavor to what's in your mouth, and decides if it's something you want to eat.

A person's food preferences, like his or her personality, are formed during the first years of life, through a process of socialization. Babies innately prefer sweet tastes and reject bitter ones; toddlers can learn to enjoy hot and spicy food, bland health food, or fast food, depending on what the people around them eat. The human sense of smell is still not fully understood. It is greatly affected by psychological factors and expectations. The mind focuses intently on some of the aromas that surround us and filters out the overwhelming majority. People can grow accustomed to bad smells or good smells; they stop noticing what once seemed overpowering. Aroma and memory are somehow inextricably linked. A smell can suddenly evoke a long-forgotten moment. The flavors of childhood foods seem to leave an indelible mark, and adults often return to them, without always knowing why. These "comfort foods" become a source of pleasure and reassurance—a fact that fast-food chains use to their advantage. Childhood memories of Happy Meals, which come with french fries, can translate into frequent adult visits to McDonald's. On average, Americans now eat about four servings of french fries every week.

THE HUMAN CRAVING for flavor has been a largely unacknowledged and unexamined force in history. For millennia royal empires have been built, unexplored lands traversed, and great religions and philosophies forever changed by the spice trade. In 1492 Christopher Columbus set sail to find seasoning. Today the influence of flavor in the world marketplace is no less decisive. The rise and fall of corporate empires—of soft-drink companies, snack-food companies, and fast-food chains—is often determined by how their products taste.

The flavor industry emerged in the mid-nineteenth century, as processed foods began to be manufactured on a large scale. Recognizing the need for flavor additives, early food processors turned to perfume companies that had long experience working with essential oils and volatile aromas. The great perfume houses of England, France, and the Netherlands produced many of the first flavor compounds. In the early part of the twentieth century Germany took the technological lead in flavor production, owing to its powerful chemical industry. Legend has it that a German scientist discovered methyl anthranilate, one of the first artificial flavors, by accident when mixing chemicals in his laboratory. Suddenly the lab was filled with the sweet smell of grapes. Methyl anthranilate later became the chief flavor compound in grape Kool-Aid. After World War II much of the perfume industry shifted from Europe to the United States, settling in New York City near the garment district and the fashion houses. The flavor industry came with it, later moving to New Jersey for greater plant capacity. Man-made flavor additives were used mostly in baked goods, candies, and sodas until the 1950s, when sales of processed food began to soar. The invention of gas chromatographs and mass spectrometers—machines capable of detecting volatile gases at low levels—vastly increased the number of flavors that could be synthesized. By the mid-1960s flavor companies were churning out compounds to supply the taste of Pop Tarts, Bac-Os, Tab, Tang, Filet-O-Fish sandwiches, and literally thousands of other new foods.

The American flavor industry now has annual revenues of about $1.4 billion. Approximately 10,000 new processed-food products are introduced every year in the United States. Almost all of them require flavor additives. And about nine out of ten of these products fail. The latest flavor innovations and corporate realignments are heralded in publications such as *Chemical Market Reporter*, *Food Chemical News*, *Food Engineering*, and *Food Product Design*. The progress of IFF has mirrored that of the flavor industry as a whole. IFF was formed in 1958, through the merger of two small companies. Its annual revenues have grown almost fifteenfold since the early 1970s, and it currently has manufacturing facilities in twenty countries.

TODAY'S SOPHISTICATED SPECTROMETERS, gas chromatographs, and headspace-vapor analyzers provide a detailed map of a food's flavor components, detecting chemical aromas present in amounts as low as one part per billion. The human nose, however, is even more sensitive. A nose can detect aromas present in quantities of a few parts per trillion—an amount equivalent to 0.000000000003 percent. Complex aromas, such as those of coffee and roasted meat, are composed of volatile gases from nearly a thousand different chemicals. The smell of a strawberry arises from the interaction of about 350 chemicals that are present in minute amounts. The quality that people seek most of all in a food—flavor—is usually present in a quantity too infinitesimal to be measured in traditional culinary terms such as ounces or teaspoons. The chemical that provides the dominant flavor of bell pepper can be tasted in amounts as low as 0.02 parts per billion; one drop is sufficient to add flavor to five average-size swimming pools. The flavor additive usually comes next to last in a processed food's list of ingredients and often costs less than its packaging. Soft drinks contain a larger proportion of flavor additives than most products. The flavor in a twelve-ounce can of Coke costs about half a cent.

The color additives in processed foods are usually present in even smaller amounts than the flavor compounds. Many of New Jersey's flavor companies also manufacture these color additives, which are used to make processed foods look fresh and appealing. Food coloring serves many of the same decorative purposes as lipstick, eye shadow, mascara—and is often made from the same pigments. Titanium dioxide, for example, has proved to be an especially versatile mineral. It gives many processed candies, frostings, and icings their bright white color; it is a common ingredient in women's cosmetics; and it is the pigment used in many white oil paints and house paints. At Burger King, Wendy's, and McDonald's coloring agents have been added to many of the soft drinks, salad dressings, cookies, condiments, chicken dishes, and sandwich buns.

Studies have found that the color of a food can greatly affect how its taste is perceived. Brightly colored foods frequently seem to taste better than bland-looking foods, even when the flavor compounds are identical. Foods that somehow look off-color often seem to have off tastes. For thousands of years human beings have relied on visual cues to help determine what is edible. The color of fruit suggests whether it is ripe, the color of meat whether it is rancid. Flavor researchers sometimes use colored lights to modify the influence of visual cues during taste tests. During one experiment in the early 1970s people were served an oddly tinted meal of steak and french fries that appeared normal beneath colored lights. Everyone thought the meal tasted fine until the lighting was changed. Once it became apparent that the steak was actually blue and the fries were green, some people became ill.

The federal Food and Drug Administration does not require companies to disclose the ingredients of their color or flavor additives so long as all the chemicals in them are considered by the agency to be GRAS ("generally recognized as safe"). This enables companies to maintain the secrecy of their formulas. It also hides the fact that flavor compounds often contain more ingredients than the foods to which they give taste. The phrase "artificial strawberry flavor" gives little hint of the chemical wizardry and manufacturing skill that can make a highly processed food taste like strawberries.

A typical artificial strawberry flavor, like the kind found in a Burger King strawberry milk shake, contains the following ingredients: amyl acetate, amyl butyrate, amyl valerate, anethol, anisyl formate, benzyl acetate, benzyl isobutyrate, butyric acid, cinnamyl isobutyrate, cinnamyl valerate, cognac essential oil, diacetyl, dipropyl ketone, ethyl acetate, ethyl amyl ketone, ethyl butyrate, ethyl cinnamate, ethyl heptanoate, ethyl heptylate, ethyl lactate, ethyl methylphenylglycidate, ethyl nitrate, ethyl propionate, ethyl valerate, heliotropin, hydroxyphenyl-2-butanone (10 percent solution in alcohol), α-ionone, isobutyl anthranilate, isobutyl butyrate, lemon essential oil, maltol, 4-methylacetophenone, methyl anthranilate, methyl benzoate, methyl cinnamate, methyl heptine carbonate, methyl napthyl ketone, methyl salicylate, mint essential oil, neroli essential oil, nerolin, neryl isobutyrate, orris butter, phenethyl alcohol, rose, rum ether, γ-undecalactone, vanillin, and solvent.

Although flavors usually arise from a mixture of many different volatile chemicals, often a single compound supplies the dominant aroma. Smelled alone, that chemical provides an unmistakable sense of the food. Ethyl-2-methyl butyrate, for example, smells just like an apple. Many of today's highly processed foods offer a blank palette: whatever chemicals are added to them will give them specific tastes. Adding methyl-2-pyridyl ketone makes something taste like popcorn. Adding ethyl-3-hydroxy butanoate makes it taste like marshmallow. The possibilities are almost limitless. Without affecting appearance or nutritional value, processed foods could be made with aroma chemicals such as hexanol (the smell of freshly cut grass) or 3-methyl butanoic acid (the smell of body odor).

The 1960s were the heyday of artificial flavors in the United States. The synthetic versions of flavor compounds were not subtle, but they did not have to be, given the nature of most processed food. For the past twenty years food processors have tried hard to use only "natural flavors" in their products. According to the FDA, these must be derived entirely from natural sources—from herbs, spices, fruits, vegetables, beef, chicken, yeast, bark, roots, and so forth. Consumers prefer to see natural flavors on a label, out of a belief that they are more healthful. Distinctions between artificial and natural flavors can be arbitrary and somewhat absurd, based more on how the flavor has been made than on what it actually contains.

"A natural flavor," says Terry Acree, a professor of food science at Cornell University, "is a flavor that's been derived with an out-of-date technology." Natural flavors and artificial flavors sometimes contain exactly the same chemicals, produced through different methods. Amyl acetate, for example, provides the dominant note of banana flavor. When it is distilled from bananas with a solvent, amyl acetate is a natural flavor. When it is produced by mixing vinegar with amyl alcohol and adding sulfuric acid as a catalyst, amyl acetate is an artificial flavor. Either way it smells and tastes the same. "Natural flavor" is now listed among the ingredients of everything from Health Valley Blueberry Granola Bars to Taco Bell Hot Taco Sauce.

A natural flavor is not necessarily more healthful or purer than an artificial one. When almond flavor—benzaldehyde—is derived from natural sources, such as peach and apricot pits, it contains traces of hydrogen cyanide, a deadly poison. Benzaldehyde derived by mixing oil of clove and amyl acetate does not contain any cyanide. Nevertheless, it is legally considered an artificial flavor and sells at a much lower price. Natural and artificial flavors are now manufactured at the same chemical plants, places that few people would associate with Mother Nature.

THE SMALL AND ELITE GROUP OF SCIENTISTS who create most of the flavor in most of the food now consumed in the United States are called "flavorists." They draw on a number of disciplines in their work: biology, psychology, physiology, and organic chemistry. A flavorist is a chemist with a trained nose and a poetic sensibility. Flavors are created by blending scores of different chemicals in tiny amounts—a process governed by scientific principles but demanding a fair amount of art. In an age when delicate aromas and microwave ovens do not easily co-exist, the job of the flavorist is to conjure illusions about processed food and, in the word of one flavor company's literature, to ensure "consumer likeability." The flavorists with whom I spoke were discreet, in keeping with the dictates of their trade. They were also charming, cosmopolitan, and ironic. They not only enjoyed fine wine but could identify the chemicals that give each grape its unique aroma. One flavorist compared his work to composing music. A well-made flavor compound will have a "top note" that is often followed by a "dry-down" and a "leveling-off," with different chemicals responsible for each stage. The taste of a food can be radically altered by minute changes in the flavoring combination. "A little odor goes a long way," one flavorist told me.

In order to give a processed food a taste that consumers will find appealing, a flavorist must always consider the food's "mouthfeel"—the unique combination of textures and chemical interactions that affect how the flavor is perceived. Mouthfeel can be adjusted through the use of various fats, gums, starches, emulsifiers, and stabilizers. The aroma chemicals in a food can be precisely analyzed, but the elements that make up mouthfeel are much harder to measure. How does one quantify a pretzel's hardness, a french fry's crispness? Food technologists are now conducting basic research in rheology, the branch of physics that examines the flow and deformation of materials. A number of companies sell sophisticated devices that attempt to measure mouthfeel. The TA.XT2i Texture Analyzer, produced by the Texture Technologies Corporation, of Scarsdale, New York, performs calculations based on data derived from as many as 250 separate probes. It is essentially a mechanical mouth. It gauges the most-important rheological properties of a food—bounce, creep, breaking point, density, crunchiness, chewiness, gumminess, lumpiness, rubberiness, springiness, slipperiness, smoothness, softness, wetness, juiciness, spreadability, springback, and tackiness.

Some of the most important advances in flavor manufacturing are now occurring in the field of biotechnology. Complex flavors are being made using enzyme reactions, fermentation, and fungal and tissue cultures. All the flavors created by these methods—including the ones being synthesized by fungi—are considered natural flavors by the FDA. The new enzyme-based processes are responsible for extremely true-to-life dairy flavors. One company now offers not just butter flavor but also fresh creamy butter, cheesy butter, milky butter, savory melted butter, and superconcentrated butter flavor, in liquid and powder form. The development of new fermentation techniques, along with new techniques for heating mixtures of sugar and amino acids, have led to the creation of much more realistic meat flavors.

The McDonald's Corporation most likely drew on these advances when it eliminated beef tallow from its french fries. The company will not reveal the exact origin of the natural flavor added to its fries. In response to inquiries from *Vegetarian Journal*, however, McDonald's did acknowledge that its fries derive some of their characteristic flavor from "an animal source." Beef is the probable source, although other meats cannot be ruled out. In France, for example, fries are sometimes cooked in duck fat or horse tallow.

Other popular fast foods derive their flavor from unexpected ingredients. McDonald's Chicken McNuggets contain beef extracts, as does Wendy's Grilled Chicken Sandwich. Burger King's BK Broiler Chicken Breast Patty contains "natural smoke flavor." A firm called Red Arrow Products specializes in smoke flavor, which is added to barbecue sauces, snack foods, and processed meats. Red Arrow manufactures natural smoke flavor by charring sawdust and capturing the aroma chemicals released into the air. The smoke is captured in water and then bottled, so that other companies can sell food that seems to have been cooked over a fire.

The Vegetarian Legal Action Network recently petitioned the FDA to issue new labeling requirements for foods that contain natural flavors. The group wants food processors to list the basic origins of their flavors on their labels. At the moment vegetarians often have no way of knowing whether a flavor additive contains beef, pork, poultry, or shellfish. One of the most widely used color additives—whose presence is often hidden by the phrase "color added"—violates a number of religious dietary restrictions, may cause allergic reactions in susceptible people, and comes from an unusual source. Cochineal extract (also known as carmine or carminic acid) is made from the desiccated bodies of female *Dactylopius coccus Costa*, a small insect harvested mainly in Peru and the Canary Islands. The bug feeds on red cactus berries, and color from the berries accumulates in the females and their unhatched larvae. The insects are collected, dried, and ground into a pigment. It takes about 70,000 of them to produce a pound of carmine, which is used to make processed foods look pink, red, or purple. Dannon strawberry yogurt gets its color from carmine, and so do many frozen fruit bars, candies, and fruit fillings, and Ocean Spray pink-grapefruit juice drink.

IN A MEETING AT IFF, Brian Grainger let me sample some of the company's flavors. It was an unusual taste test—there was no food to taste. Grainger is a senior flavorist at IFF, a soft-spoken chemist with graying hair, an English accent, and a fondness for understatement. He could easily be mistaken for a British diplomat or the owner of a West End brasserie with two Michelin stars. Like many in the flavor industry, he has an Old World, old-fashioned sensibility. When I suggested that IFF's policy of secrecy and discretion was out of step with our mass-marketing, brand-conscious, self-promoting age, and that the company should put its own logo on the countless products that bear its flavors, instead of allowing other companies to enjoy the consumer loyalty and affection inspired by those flavors, Grainger politely disagreed, assuring me that such a thing would never be done. In the absence of public credit or acclaim, the small and secretive fraternity of flavor chemists praise one another's work. By analyzing the flavor formula in a product, Grainger can often tell which of his counterparts at a rival firm devised it. Whenever he walks down a supermarket aisle, he takes a quiet pleasure in seeing the well-known foods that contain his flavors.

Grainger had brought a dozen small glass bottles from the lab. After he opened each bottle, I dipped a fragrance-testing filter into it—a long white strip of paper designed to absorb aroma chemicals without producing off notes. Before placing each strip of paper in front of my nose, I closed my eyes. Then I inhaled deeply, and one food after another was conjured from the glass bottles. Grainger's most remarkable creation took me by surprise. After closing my eyes, I suddenly smelled a grilled hamburger. The aroma was uncanny, almost miraculous—as if someone in the room were flipping burgers on a hot grill. But when I opened my eyes, I saw just a narrow strip of white paper and a flavorist with a grin.

THE NATURAL WORLD

Walking

HENRY DAVID THOREAU ‖ 1862

The marriage of Henry David Thoreau (1817–1862) and The Atlantic
Monthly *got off to a miserable start. From even before the first issue,
James Russell Lowell was keen to have Thoreau's writing in the magazine, despite the fact that the editor-in-chief privately viewed the eccentric writer and naturalist as a megalomaniac and self-promoter. By the
summer of 1858, thanks to the intercession of Emerson, their mutual
friend, Lowell had landed his first Thoreau, a transcendentalist take on
life in the Maine woods called "Chesuncook," which he decided to publish as a three-part essay. At the last moment, however, Lowell deleted a
sentence that he considered theologically tendentious, even though the
author had insisted it should be retained. When Thoreau discovered the
gap in the published text, he angrily cut all ties with the magazine and
dashed off a letter accusing Lowell of "mean and cowardly" behavior. "I
do not expect anybody to adopt my opinions," he wrote, "but I do expect
that when they ask for them to print, they will print them, or obtain my
consent to their alteration or omission."*

*It was not until four years later, after the editorial baton had passed
to the more diplomatically inclined James T. Fields, that the damage was
repaired. Underlying this rapprochement was a grim reality: Thoreau,
who had been sickly his entire life, was suffering from terminal tuberculosis, and* The Atlantic *provided a durable literary outlet that could
transmit to future generations the voluminous notes, journal entries, and
lecture transcripts he had accumulated over the years. At Fields's request,
Thoreau began, in February of 1862, to rework his material into a series
of seven essays.*

*"Walking," the first to be published, is the most celebrated of the
group and, in the opinion of many Thoreau scholars, the author's quintessential essay. Adapted from a favorite lecture that Thoreau had first
given at the Lyceum in Concord, Massachusetts, eleven years before,
"Walking" is arguably the author's most fervent declaration of faith in
the moral primacy of the natural world. The essay begins as a simple
paean to the glories of the impromptu, open-ended stroll, but, like its
narrator, it exuberantly meanders—from physical to mental to spiritual
journey—eventually rejecting all claims of human society in favor of
solitary communion with life in the wild. A century and a half later,
Thoreau's utopian vision of nature's redemptive power continues to*

speak to millions around the world and is a bellwether for the modern environmental movement. Tragically, Thoreau did not live to see "Walking" into print. By the time the essay appeared in The Atlantic, *in June 1862, he had been dead a month. But it is worth noting that he departed this world with the same spirit of adventure that he celebrates here, calling out from his deathbed: "Here comes good sailing."*

I wish to speak a word for Nature, for absolute freedom and wildness, as contrasted with a freedom and culture merely civil—to regard man as an inhabitant, or a part and parcel of Nature, rather than a member of society. I wish to make an extreme statement, if so I may make an emphatic one, for there are enough champions of civilization: the minister and the school committee and every one of you will take care of that.

I HAVE MET with but one or two persons in the course of my life who understood the art of Walking, that is, of taking walks—who had a genius, so to speak, for *sauntering*, which word is beautifully derived "from idle people who roved about the country, in the Middle Ages, and asked charity, under pretense of going *à la Sainte Terre*," to the Holy Land, till the children exclaimed, "There goes a *Sainte-Terrer*," a Saunterer, a Holy-Lander. They who never go to the Holy Land in their walks, as they pretend, are indeed mere idlers and vagabonds; but they who do go there are saunterers in the good sense, such as I mean. Some, however, would derive the word from *sans terre*, without land or a home, which, therefore, in the good sense, will mean, having no particular home, but equally at home everywhere. For this is the secret of successful sauntering. He who sits still in a house all the time may be the greatest vagrant of all; but the saunterer, in the good sense, is no more vagrant than the meandering river, which is all the while sedulously seeking the shortest course to the sea. But I prefer the first, which, indeed, is the most probable derivation. For every walk is a sort of crusade, preached by some Peter the Hermit in us, to go forth and reconquer this Holy Land from the hands of the Infidels.

It is true, we are but faint-hearted crusaders, even the walkers, nowadays, who undertake no persevering, never-ending enterprises. Our expeditions are but tours, and come round again at evening to the old hearthside from which we set out. Half the walk is but retracing our steps. We should go forth on the shortest walk, perchance, in the spirit of undying adventure, never to return, prepared to send back our embalmed hearts only as relics to our desolate kingdoms. If you are ready to leave father and mother, and brother and sister, and wife and child and friends, and never see them again—if you have paid your debts, and made your will, and settled all your affairs, and are a free man—then you are ready for a walk.

To come down to my own experience, my companion and I, for I sometimes have a companion, take pleasure in fancying ourselves knights of a new, or rather an old, order—not Equestrians or Chevaliers, not Ritters or Riders, but Walkers, a still more ancient and honorable class, I trust. The chivalric and heroic spirit which once belonged to the Rider seems now to reside in, or perchance to have subsided into, the Walker—not the Knight, but Walker, Errant. He is a sort of fourth estate, outside of Church and State and People.

We have felt that we almost alone hereabouts practiced this noble art; though, to tell the truth, at least if their own assertions are to be received, most of my townsmen would fain walk sometimes, as I do, but they cannot. No wealth can buy the requisite leisure, freedom, and independence which are the capital in this profession. It comes only by the grace of God. It requires a direct dispensation from Heaven to become a walker. You must be born into the family of the Walkers. *Ambulator nascitur, non fit.* Some of my townsmen, it is true, can remember and have described to me some walks which they took ten years ago, in which they were so blessed as to lose themselves for half an hour in the woods; but I know very well that they have confined themselves to the highway ever since, whatever pretensions they may make to belong to this select class. No doubt they were elevated for a moment as by the reminiscence of a previous state of existence, when even they were foresters and outlaws.

I think that I cannot preserve my health and spirits, unless I spend four hours a day at least—and it is commonly more than that—sauntering through the woods and over the hills and fields, absolutely free from all worldly engagements. You may safely say, A penny for your thoughts, or a thousand pounds. When sometimes I am reminded that the mechanics and shopkeepers stay in their shops not only all the forenoon, but all the afternoon too, sitting with crossed legs, so many of them—as if the legs were made to sit upon, and not to stand or walk upon—I think that they deserve some credit for not having all committed suicide long ago. I, who cannot stay in my chamber for a single day without acquiring some rust, and when sometimes I have stolen forth for a walk at the eleventh hour, or four o'clock in the afternoon, too late to redeem the day, when the shades of night were already beginning to be mingled with the daylight, have felt as if I had committed some sin to be atoned for—I confess that I am astonished at the power of endurance, to say nothing of the moral insensibility, of my neighbors who confine themselves to shops and offices the whole day for weeks and months, aye, and years almost together. I know not what manner of stuff they are of, sitting there now at three o'clock in the afternoon, as if it were three o'clock in the morning. Bonaparte may talk of the three-o'clock-in-the-morning courage, but it is nothing to the courage which can sit down cheerfully at this hour in the afternoon over against one's self whom you have known all the morning, to starve out a garrison to whom you are bound by such strong ties of sympathy. I wonder that about this time, or say between four and five o'clock in the afternoon, too late for the morning papers and too early for the evening ones, there is not a general explosion heard up and down the street, scattering a legion of antiquated and house-bred notions and whims to the four winds for an airing—and so the evil cure itself.

No doubt temperament, and, above all, age, have a good deal to do with it. As a man grows older, his ability to sit still and follow indoor occupations increases. He grows vespertinal in his habits as the evening of life approaches, till at last he comes forth only just before sundown, and gets all the walk that he requires in half an hour.

But the walking of which I speak has nothing in it akin to taking exercise, as it is called, as the sick take medicine at stated hours—as the swinging of dumbbells or chairs; but is itself the enterprise and adventure of the day. If you would get exercise, go in search of the springs of life. Think of a man's swinging dumbbells for his health, when those springs are bubbling up in far-off pastures unsought by him!

Moreover, you must walk like a camel, which is said to be the only beast which ruminates when walking. When a traveler asked Wordsworth's servant to show him her master's study, she answered, "Here is his library, but his study is out of doors."

When we walk, we naturally go to the fields and woods: what would become of us, if we walked only in a garden or a mall? I am alarmed when it happens that I have walked a mile into the woods bodily, without getting there in spirit. In my afternoon walk I would fain forget all my morning occupations and my obligations to society. But it sometimes happens that I cannot easily shake off the village. The thought of some work will run in my head and I am not where my body is—I am out of my senses. In my walks I would fain return to my senses. What business have I in the woods, if I am thinking of something out of the woods? I suspect myself, and cannot help a shudder when I find myself implicated in what are called good works—for this may sometimes happen.

My vicinity affords many good walks; and though for so many years I have walked almost every day, and sometimes for several days together, I have not yet exhausted them. An absolutely new prospect is a great happiness, and I can still get this any afternoon. Two or three hours' walking will carry me to as strange a country as I expect ever to see. A single farmhouse which I had not seen before is sometimes as good as the dominions of the King of Dahomey. There is in fact a sort of harmony discoverable between the capabilities of the landscape within a circle of ten miles' radius, or the limits of an afternoon walk, and the threescore years and ten of human life. It will never become quite familiar to you.

I can easily walk ten, fifteen, twenty, any number of miles, commencing at my own door, without going by any house, without crossing a road except where the fox and the mink do: first along by the river, and then the brook, and then the meadow and the woodside. There are square miles in my vicinity which have no inhabitant. From many a hill I can see civilization and the abodes of man afar. The farmers and their works are scarcely more obvious than woodchucks and their burrows. Man and his affairs, church and state and school, trade and commerce, and manufactures and agriculture, even politics, the most alarming of them all—I am pleased to see how little space they occupy in the landscape.

At present, in this vicinity, the best part of the land is not private property; the landscape is not owned, and the walker enjoys comparative freedom. But possibly the day will come when it will be partitioned off into so-called pleasure-grounds, in which a few will take a narrow and exclusive pleasure only—when fences shall be multiplied, and man-traps and other engines invented to confine men to the public road, and walking over the surface of God's earth shall be construed to mean trespassing on some gentleman's grounds. To enjoy a thing exclusively is commonly to exclude yourself from the true enjoyment of it. Let us improve our opportunities, then, before the evil days come.

WHAT IS IT THAT MAKES IT so hard sometimes to determine whither we will walk? I believe that there is a subtle magnetism in Nature, which, if we unconsciously yield to it, will direct us aright. It is not indifferent to us which way we walk. There is a right way; but we are very liable from heedlessness and stupidity to take the wrong one. We would fain take that walk, never yet taken by us through this actual world, which is perfectly symbolical of the path which we love to travel in the interior and ideal world; and sometimes, no doubt, we find it difficult to choose our direction, because it does not yet exist distinctly in our idea.

When I go out of the house for a walk, uncertain as yet whither I will bend my steps, and submit myself to my instinct to decide for me, I find, strange and whimsical as it may seem, that I finally and inevitably settle southwest, toward some particular wood or meadow or deserted pasture or hill in that direction. My needle is slow to settle, varies a few degrees, and does not always point due southwest, it is true, and it has good authority for this variation, but it always settles between west and south-southwest. The future lies that way to me, and the earth seems more unexhausted and richer on that side. Eastward I go only by force; but westward I go free. Thither no business leads me. It is hard for me to believe that I shall find fair landscapes or sufficient wildness and freedom behind the eastern horizon. I am not excited by the prospect of a walk thither; but I believe that the forest which I see in the western horizon stretches uninterruptedly toward the setting sun, and there are no towns nor cities in it of enough consequence to disturb me. Let me live where I will, on this side is the city, on that the wilderness, and ever I am leaving the city more and more, and withdrawing into the wilderness. I should not lay so much stress on this fact, if I did not believe that something like this is the prevailing tendency of my countrymen. I must walk toward Oregon, and not toward Europe. And that way the nation is moving, and I may say that mankind progress from east to west.

We go eastward to realize history and study the works of art and literature, retracing the steps of the race; we go westward as into the future, with a spirit of enterprise and adventure. The Atlantic is a Lethean stream, in our passage over which we have had an opportunity to forget the Old World and its institutions. If we do not succeed this time, there is perhaps one more chance for the race left before it arrives on the banks of the Styx; and that is in the Lethe of the Pacific, which is three times as wide.

Every sunset which I witness inspires me with the desire to go to a West as distant and as fair as that into which the sun goes down. He appears to migrate westward daily, and tempt us to follow him. He is the Great Western Pioneer whom the nations follow. We dream all night of those mountain-ridges in the horizon, though they may be of vapor only, which were last gilded by his rays. The island of Atlantis, and the islands and gardens of the Hesperides, a sort of terrestrial paradise, appear to have been the Great West of the ancients, enveloped in mystery and poetry. Who has not seen in imagination, when looking into the sunset sky, the gardens of the Hesperides, and the foundation of all those fables?

Where on the globe can there be found an area of equal extent with that occupied by the bulk of our States, so fertile and so rich and varied in its productions, and at the same time so habitable by the European, as this is? Michaux, who knew but part of them, says that "the species of large trees are much more numerous in North America than in Europe; in the United States there are more than one hundred and forty species that exceed thirty feet in height; in France there are but thirty that attain this size." Later botanists more than confirm his observations. Humboldt came to America to realize his youthful dreams of a tropical vegetation, and he beheld it in its greatest perfection in the primitive forests of the Amazon, the most gigantic wilderness on the earth, which he has so eloquently described.

Sir Francis Head, an English traveler and a Governor-General of Canada, tells us that "in both the northern and southern hemispheres of the New World, Nature has not only outlined her works on a larger scale, but has painted the whole picture with brighter and more costly colors than she used in delineating and in beautifying the Old World. . . . The heavens of America appear infinitely higher, the sky is bluer, the air is fresher, the cold is intenser, the moon looks larger, the stars are brighter, the thunder is louder, the lightning is vivider, the wind is stronger, the rain is heavier, the mountains are higher, the rivers longer, the forests bigger, the plains broader."

These are encouraging testimonies. If the moon looks larger here than in Europe, probably the sun looks larger also. If the heavens of America appear infinitely higher, and the stars brighter, I trust that these facts are symbolical of the height to which the philosophy and poetry and religion of her inhabitants may one day soar. At length, perchance, the immaterial heaven will appear as much higher to the American mind, and the intimations that star it as much brighter. For I believe that climate does thus react on man—as there is something in the mountain air that feeds the spirit and inspires. Will not man grow to greater perfection intellectually as well as physically under these influences? Or is it unimportant how many foggy days there are in his life? I trust that we shall be more imaginative, that our thoughts will be clearer, fresher, and more ethereal, as our sky—our understanding more comprehensive and broader, like our plains—our intellect generally on a grander scale, like our thunder and lightning, our rivers and mountains and forests—and our hearts shall even correspond in breadth and depth and grandeur to our inland seas. Perchance there will appear to the traveler something, he knows not what, of *laeta* and *glabra*, of joyous and serene, in our very faces. Else to what end does the world go on, and why was America discovered?

THE WEST OF WHICH I SPEAK is but another name for the Wild; and what I have been preparing to say is, that in Wildness is the preservation of the World. Every tree sends its fibers forth in search of the Wild. The cities import it at any price. Men plow and sail for it. From the forest and wilderness come the tonics and barks which brace mankind. Our ancestors were savages. The story of Romulus and Remus being suckled by a wolf is not a meaningless fable. The founders of every state which has risen to eminence have drawn their nourishment and vigor from a similar wild source. It was because the children of the Empire were not suckled by the wolf that they were conquered and displaced by the children of the northern forests who were.

I believe in the forest, and in the meadow, and in the night in which the corn grows. We require an infusion of hemlock, spruce or arbor vitae in our tea. There is a difference between eating and drinking for strength and from mere gluttony. Life consists with wildness. The most alive is the wildest. Not yet subdued to man, its presence refreshes him. One who pressed forward incessantly and never rested from his labors, who grew fast and made infinite demands on life, would always find himself in a new country or wilderness, and surrounded by the raw material of life. He would be climbing over the prostrate stems of primitive forest-trees.

Hope and the future for me are not in lawns and cultivated fields, not in towns and cities, but in the impervious and quaking swamps. When, formerly, I have analyzed my partiality for some farm which I had contemplated purchasing, I have frequently found that I was attracted solely by a few square rods of impermeable and unfathomable bog—a natural sink in one corner of it. That was the jewel which dazzled me. I derive more of my subsistence from the swamps which surround my native town than from the cultivated gardens in the village. There are no richer parterres to my eyes than the dense beds of dwarf andromeda (*Cassandra calyculata*) which cover these tender places on the earth's surface. I often think that I should like to have my house front on this mass of dull red bushes, omitting other flower plots and borders, transplanted spruce and trim box, even graveled walks—to have this fertile spot under my windows, not a few imported barrowfuls of soil only to cover the sand which was thrown out in digging the cellar. Why not put my house, my parlor, behind this plot, instead of behind that meager assemblage of curiosities, that poor apology for a Nature and Art, which I call my front yard? It is an effort to clear up and make a decent appearance when the carpenter and mason have departed, though done as much for the passer-by as the dweller within. The most tasteful front-yard fence was never an agreeable object of study to me; the most elaborate ornaments, acorn tops, or what not, soon wearied and disgusted me. Bring your sills up to the very edge of the swamp, then (though it may not be the best place for a dry cellar), so that there be no access on that side to citizens. Front yards are not made to walk in, but, at most, through, and you could go in the back way.

Yes, though you may think me perverse, if it were proposed to me to dwell in the neighborhood of the most beautiful garden that ever human art contrived, or else of a Dismal Swamp, I should certainly decide for the swamp. How vain, then, have been all your labors, citizens, for me!

When I would recreate myself, I seek the darkest wood, the thickest and most interminable and, to the citizen, most dismal, swamp. I enter a swamp as a sacred place, a *sanctum sanctorum*. There is the strength, the marrow, of Nature. The wildwood covers the virgin mould, and the same soil is good for men and for trees. A man's health requires as many acres of meadow to his prospect as his farm does loads of muck. There are the strong meats on which he feeds. A town is saved, not more by the righteous men in it than by the woods and swamps that surround it. A township where one primitive forest waves above while another primitive forest rots below—such a town is fitted to raise not only corn and potatoes, but poets and philosophers for the coming ages. In such a soil grew Homer and Confucius and the rest, and out of such a wilderness comes the Reformer eating locusts and wild honey.

The civilized nations—Greece, Rome, England—have been sustained by the primitive forests which anciently rotted where they stand. They survive as long as the soil is not exhausted. Alas for human culture! little is to be expected of a nation, when the vegetable mould is exhausted, and it is compelled to make manure of the bones of its fathers. There the poet sustains himself merely by his own superfluous fat, and the philosopher comes down on his marrow-bones.

It is said to be the task of the American "to work the virgin soil," and that "agriculture here already assumes proportions unknown everywhere else." I think that the farmer displaces the Indian even because he redeems the meadow, and so makes himself stronger and in some respects more natural. I was surveying for a man the other day a single straight line one hundred and thirty-two rods long, through a swamp at whose entrance might have been written the words which Dante read over the entrance to the infernal regions, "Leave all hope, ye that enter"—that is, of ever getting out again; where at one time I saw my employer actually up to his neck and swimming for his life in his property, though it was still winter. He had another similar swamp which I could not survey at all, because it was completely under water, and nevertheless, with regard to a third swamp, which I did survey from a distance, he remarked to me, true to his instincts, that he would not part with it for any consideration, on account of the mud which it contained. And that man intends to put a girdling ditch round the whole in the course of forty months, and so redeem it by the magic of his spade.

The weapons with which we have gained our most important victories, which should be handed down as heirlooms from father to son, are not the sword and the lance, but the bushwhack, the turf-cutter, the spade, and the bog hoe, rusted with the blood of many a meadow, and begrimed with the dust of many a hard-fought field.

In literature it is only the wild that attracts us. Dullness is but another name for tameness. It is the uncivilized free and wild thinking in *Hamlet* and the *Iliad*, in all the scriptures and mythologies, not learned in the schools, that delights us. As the wild duck is more swift and beautiful than the tame, so is the wild—the mallard—thought, which 'mid falling dews wings its way above the fens. A truly good book is something as natural, and as unexpectedly and unaccountably fair and perfect, as a wild-flower discovered on the prairies of the West or in the jungles of the East. Genius is a light which makes the darkness visible, like the lightning's flash, which perchance shatters the temple of knowledge itself—and not a taper lighted at the hearthstone of the race, which pales before the light of common day.

Where is the literature which gives expression to Nature? He would be a poet who could impress the winds and streams into his service, to speak for him; who nailed words to their primitive senses, as farmers drive down stakes in the spring, which the frost has heaved; who derived his words as often as he used them—transplanted them to his page with earth adhering to their roots; whose words were so true and fresh and natural that they would appear to expand like the buds at the approach of spring, though they lay half smothered between two musty leaves in a library—aye, to bloom and bear fruit there, after their kind, annually, for the faithful reader, in sympathy with surrounding Nature.

I do not know of any poetry to quote which adequately expresses this yearning for the Wild. Approached from this side, the best poetry is tame. I do not know where to find in any literature, ancient or modern, any account which contents me of that Nature with which even I am acquainted. You will perceive that I demand something which no Augustan nor Elizabethan age, which no *culture*, in short, can give. Mythology comes nearer to it than anything. How much more fertile a Nature, at least, has Grecian mythology its root in than English literature! Mythology is the crop which the Old World bore before its soil was exhausted, before the fancy and imagination were affected with blight; and which it still bears, wherever its pristine vigor is unabated.

The West is preparing to add its fables to those of the East. The valleys of the Ganges, the Nile, and the Rhine having yielded their crop, it remains to be seen what the valleys of the Amazon, the Plate, the Orinoco, the St. Lawrence, and the Mississippi will produce. Perchance, when, in the course of ages, American liberty has become a fiction of the past—as it is to some extent a fiction of the present—the poets of the world will be inspired by American mythology.

In short, all good things are wild and free. There is something in a strain of music, whether produced by an instrument or by the human voice—take the sound of a bugle in a summer night, for instance—which by its wildness, to speak without satire, reminds me of the cries emitted by wild beasts in their native forests. It is so much of their wildness as I can understand. Give me for my friends and neighbors wild men, not tame ones. The wildness of the savage is but a faint symbol of the awful ferity with which good men and lovers meet.

I love even to see the domestic animals reassert their native rights—any evidence that they have not wholly lost their original wild habits and vigor; as when my neighbor's cow breaks out of her pasture early in the spring and boldly swims the river, a cold, gray tide, twenty-five or thirty rods wide, swollen by the melted snow. It is the buffalo crossing the Mississippi. This exploit confers some dignity on the herd in my eyes—already dignified. The seeds of instinct are preserved under the thick hides of cattle and horses, like seeds in the bowels of the earth, an indefinite period.

WHILE ALMOST ALL MEN feel an attraction drawing them to society, few are attracted strongly to Nature. In their reaction to Nature men appear to me for the most part, notwithstanding their arts, lower than the animals. It is not often a beautiful relation, as in the case of the animals. How little appreciation of the beauty of the land-scape there is among us! We have to be told that the Greeks called the world κόσμος, Beauty, or Order, but we do not see clearly why they did so, and we esteem it at best only a curious philological fact.

For my part, I feel that with regard to Nature I live a sort of border life, on the confines of a world into which I make occasional and transient forays only, and my patriotism and allegiance to the state into whose territories I seem to retreat are those of a moss-trooper. Unto a life which I call natural I would gladly follow even a will-o'-the-wisp through bogs and sloughs unimaginable, but no moon nor firefly has shown me the causeway to it. Nature is a personality so vast and universal that we have never seen one of her features. The walker in the familiar fields which stretch around my native town sometimes finds himself in another land than is described in their owners' deeds, as it were in some faraway field on the confines of the actual Concord, where her jurisdiction ceases, and the idea which the word Concord suggests ceases to be suggested. These farms which I have myself surveyed, these bounds which I have set up, appear dimly still as through a mist; but they have no chemistry to fix them; they fade from the surface of the glass, and the picture which the painter painted stands out dimly from beneath. The world with which we are commonly acquainted leaves no trace, and it will have no anniversary.

I took a walk on Spaulding's Farm the other afternoon. I saw the setting sun lighting up the opposite side of a stately pine wood. Its golden rays straggled into the aisles of the wood as into some noble hall. I was impressed as if some ancient and altogether admirable and shining family had settled there in that part of the land called Concord, unknown to me—to whom the sun was servant—who had not gone into society in the village—who had not been called on. I saw their park, their pleasure-ground, beyond through the wood, in Spaulding's cranberry-meadow. The pines furnished them with gables as they grew. Their house was not obvious to vision; the trees grew through it. I do not know whether I heard the sounds of a suppressed hilarity or not. They seemed to recline on the sunbeams. They have sons and daughters. They are quite well. The farmer's cart-path, which leads directly through their hall, does not in the least put them out, as the muddy bottom of a pool is sometimes seen through the reflected skies. They never heard of Spaulding, and do not know that he is their neighbor—notwithstanding I heard him whistle as he drove his team through the house. Nothing can equal the serenity of their lives. Their coat-of-arms is simply a lichen. I saw it painted on the pines and oaks. Their attics were in the tops of the trees. They are of no politics. There was no noise of labor. I did not perceive that they were weaving or spinning. Yet I did detect, when the wind lulled and hearing was done away, the finest imaginable sweet musical hum—as of a distant hive in May—which perchance was the sound of their thinking. They had no idle thoughts, and no one without could see their work, for their industry was not as in knots and excrescences embayed.

But I find it difficult to remember them. They fade irrevocably out of my mind even now while I speak, and endeavor to recall them and recollect myself. It is only after a long and serious effort to recollect my best thoughts that I become again aware of their cohabitancy. If it were not for such families as this, I think I should move out of Concord.

WE HUG THE EARTH—how rarely we mount! Methinks we might elevate ourselves a little more. We might climb a tree, at least. I found my account in climbing a tree once. It was a tall white pine, on the top of a hill; and though I got well pitched, I was well paid for it, for I discovered new mountains in the horizon which I had never seen before—so much more of the earth and the heavens. I might have walked about the foot of the tree for threescore years and ten, and yet I certainly should never have seen them. But, above all, I discovered around me—it was near the end of June—on the ends of the topmost branches only, a few minute and delicate red cone-like blossoms, the fertile flower of the white pine looking heavenward. I carried straightway to the village the topmost spire, and showed it to stranger jurymen who walked the streets—for it was court week—and to farmers and lumber-dealers and woodchoppers and hunters, and not one had ever seen the like before, but they wondered as at a star dropped down. Tell of ancient architects finishing their works on the tops of columns as perfectly as on the lower and more visible parts! Nature has from the first expanded the minute blossoms of the forest only toward the heavens, above men's heads and unobserved by them. We see only the flowers that are under our feet in the meadows. The pines have developed their delicate blossoms on the highest twigs of the wood every summer for ages, as well over the heads of Nature's red children as of her white ones; yet scarcely a farmer or hunter in the land has ever seen them.

ABOVE ALL, WE CANNOT AFFORD not to live in the present. He is blessed over all mortals who loses no moment of the passing life in remembering the past. Unless our philosophy hears the cock crow in every barnyard within our horizon, it is belated. That sound commonly reminds us that we are growing rusty and antique in our employments and habits of thought. His philosophy comes down to a more recent time than ours. There is something suggested by it that is a newer testament—the gospel according to this moment. He has not fallen astern; he has got up early and kept up early, and to be where he is is to be in season, in the foremost rank of time. It is an expression of the health and soundness of Nature, a brag for all the world—healthiness as of a spring burst forth, a new fountain of the Muses, to celebrate this last instant of time.

WE HAD A REMARKABLE SUNSET one day last November. I was walking in a meadow, the source of a small brook, when the sun at last, just before setting, after a cold, gray day, reached a clear stratum in the horizon, and the softest, brightest morning sunlight fell on the dry grass and on the stems of the trees in the opposite horizon and on the leaves of the shrub oaks on the hillside, while our shadows stretched long over the meadow eastward, as if we were the only motes in its beams. It was such a light as we could not have imagined a moment before, and the air also was so warm and serene that nothing was wanting to make a paradise of that meadow. When we reflected that this was not a solitary phenomenon, never to happen again, but that it would happen forever and ever, an infinite number of evenings, and cheer and reassure the latest child that walked there, it was more glorious still.

The sun sets on some retired meadow, where no house is visible, with all the glory and splendor that it lavishes on cities, and perchance as it has never set before—where there is but a solitary marsh hawk to have his wings gilded by it, or only a musquash looks out from his cabin, and there is some little black-veined brook in the midst of the marsh, just beginning to meander, winding slowly round a decaying stump. We walked in so pure and bright a light, gilding the withered grass and leaves, so softly and serenely bright, I thought I had never bathed in such a golden flood, without a ripple or a murmur to it. The west side of every wood and rising ground gleamed like the boundary of Elysium, and the sun on our backs seemed like a gentle herdsman driving us home at evening.

So we saunter toward the Holy Land, till one day the sun shall shine more brightly than ever he has done, shall perchance shine into our minds and hearts, and light up our whole lives with a great awakening light, as warm and serene and golden as on a bankside in autumn.

"Birches," "The Road Not Taken," and "The Sound of Trees"

ROBERT FROST ‖ 1915

With his four Pulitzer Prizes, countless honorary degrees, and legions of
avid readers who otherwise had little or no use for poetry, Robert Frost
(1874–1963) was without question the most lionized and beloved American poet of his time (see "Poetry and Power" by John F. Kennedy, p. 609).
Yet the man who would earn lasting renown as the archetypal Yankee
farmer-poet was actually born and raised in San Francisco, and his early
efforts to publish verse met with little success. It was only after Frost
moved to England with his young family, in 1912, when he was already
thirty-eight, that his shapely poems on rural New England landscapes
and folkways began to win public favor, aided in large measure by the
energetic support of the expatriate poet and critic Ezra Pound. American
recognition did not come Frost's way until early 1915, when he returned
to his native country and was greeted by the unexpected news that a recently published U.S. edition of his second collection, North of Boston,
was making a significant splash.

Among those clamoring for his work was The Atlantic's editor-in-
chief Ellery Sedgwick, who some years earlier had turned down several
poems Frost had submitted to the magazine with a curt reply that the
struggling poet had taken for a snub. Sedgwick was eager to make
amends. He had recently received a letter from the noted English editor
and critic Edward Garnett hailing Frost as the most uniquely American
poet since Walt Whitman, and a meeting was arranged at the magazine's
offices overlooking the Boston Common. The three poems Sedgwick acquired that day appeared in The Atlantic's August 1915 issue, under the
heading "A Group of Poems by Robert Frost," and were accompanied by
Garnett's testamentary essay "A New American Poet." They were the
first poems Frost published in America after returning from abroad
and would come to be regarded as prime specimens of his fully ripened
talents.

Pound's patronage notwithstanding, Frost's work, as evidenced by
the poems that follow, has little in common with the resolutely dissonant
and often recondite free verse of Pound, T. S. Eliot, and other illustrious
American modernists. What this famous trio of bucolic poems does show
is Frost's ardent sense of place, his intimate and accessible voice, his gift

for endowing rustic experience with mythic power, and his sometimes
underappreciated range of feeling and playful turn of mind. Although
he would go on to publish twenty-eight more poems in The Atlantic—*a*
total exceeded only by his industrious New England forerunner, Henry
Wadsworth Longfellow—it is these debut selections that best exemplify
Frost's core conception of how poetry weaves its spell. As he writes in his
trenchant manifesto, "The Figure a Poem Makes": "It begins in delight,
it inclines to the impulse, it assumes direction with the first line laid
down, it runs a course of lucky events, and ends in a clarification of
life—not necessarily a great clarification, such as sects and cults are
founded on, but a momentary stay against confusion."

BIRCHES

When I see birches bend to left and right
Across the lines of straighter darker trees,
I like to think some boy's been swinging them.
But swinging doesn't bend them down to stay.
Ice-storms do that. Often you must have seen them
Loaded with ice a sunny winter morning
After a rain. They click upon themselves
As the breeze rises, and turn many-colored
As the stir cracks and crazes their enamel.
Soon the sun's warmth makes them shed crystal shells
Shattering and avalanching on the snow-crust—
Such heaps of broken glass to sweep away
You'd think the inner dome of heaven had fallen.
They are dragged to the withered bracken by the load
And they seem not to break; though once they are bowed
So low for long they never right themselves:
You may see their trunks arching in the woods
Years afterwards, trailing their leaves on the ground
Like girls on hands and knees that throw their hair
Before them over their heads to dry in the sun.
But I was going to say when truth broke in
With all her matter-of-fact about the ice storm,
(Now am I free to be poetical?)
I should prefer to have some boy bend them
As he went out and in to fetch the cows—
Some boy too far from town to learn baseball,

Whose only play was what he found himself,
Summer or winter, and could play alone.
One by one he subdued his father's trees
By riding them down over and over again
Until he took the stiffness out of them
And not one but hung limp, not one was left
For him to conquer. He learned all there was
To learn about not launching out too soon
And so not carrying the tree away
Clear to the ground. He always kept his poise
To the top branches, climbing carefully
With the same pains you use to fill a cup
Up to the brim, and even above the brim.
Then he flung outward, feet first, with a swish,
Kicking his way down through the air to the ground.
So was I once myself a swinger of birches.
And so I dream of going back to be.
It's when I'm weary of considerations,
And life is too much like a pathless wood
Where your face burns and tickles with the cobwebs
Broken across it, and one eye is weeping
From a twig's having lashed across it open.
I'd like to get away from earth awhile
And then come back to it and begin over.
May no fate willfully misunderstand me
And half grant what I wish and snatch me away
Not to return. Earth's the right place for love:
I don't know where it's likely to go better.
I'd like to go by climbing a birch tree,
And climb black branches up a snow-white trunk
Toward heaven, till the tree could bear no more,
But dipped its top and set me down again.
That would be good both going and coming back.
One could do worse than be a swinger of birches.

THE ROAD NOT TAKEN

Two roads diverged in a yellow wood,
And sorry I could not travel both
And be one traveler, long I stood

And looked down one as far as I could
To where it bent in the undergrowth;

Then took the other, as just as fair,
And having perhaps the better claim
Because it was grassy and wanted wear,
Though as for that the passing there
Had worn them really about the same,

And both that morning equally lay
In leaves no step had trodden black.
Oh, I marked the first for another day!
Yet knowing how way leads on to way
I doubted if I should ever come back.

I shall be telling this with a sigh
Somewhere ages and ages hence:
Two roads diverged in a wood, and I,
I took the one less traveled by,
And that has made all the difference.

The Sound of Trees

I wonder about the trees:
Why do we wish to bear
Forever the noise of these
More than another noise
So close to our dwelling place?
We suffer them by the day
Till we lose all measure of pace
And fixity in our joys,
And acquire a listening air.
They are that that talks of going
But never gets away;
And that talks no less for knowing,
As it grows wiser and older,
That now it means to stay.
My feet tug at the floor
And my head sways to my shoulder
Sometimes when I watch trees sway

From the window or the door.
I shall set forth for somewhere,
I shall make the reckless choice,
Some day when they are in voice
And tossing so as to scare
The white clouds over them on.
I shall have less to say,
But I shall be gone.

Teaching a Stone to Talk

ANNIE DILLARD ‖ 1981

In a prefatory author's note to her renowned 1982 book of essays, Teaching a Stone to Talk, *Annie Dillard (1945–) addresses her readers on what they are about to encounter with a characteristic combination of forthrightness and humility. "This is not a collection of occasional pieces, such as a writer brings out to supplement her real work," Dillard writes. "Instead this is my real work, such as it is." This caveat much too modestly conveys Dillard's commitment to the narrative-nonfiction form, which in her dexterous hands becomes a consummate vehicle for the observation and celebration of the natural world. Dillard, who started out as a poet, began to dedicate herself to nonfiction with the publication of her first prose book,* Pilgrim at Tinker Creek *(1974), a rapturous nonfiction account of a single year spent wandering, watching, and ruminating in the Roanoke Valley of Virginia. That book won the then twenty-nine-year-old author a Pulitzer Prize, a wide following, and comparisons to one of her intellectual forebears, Henry David Thoreau. Indeed, Dillard's literary kinship with Thoreau seems almost embedded in her genetic code: she is married to one of the most respected Thoreau biographers, Robert D. Richardson, Jr., and with her naturalist's nose for the decisive physical detail, her scholar's passion for forging historical connection, and her mystic's hunger for epiphany, she is, among living writers, the one most prominently carrying on and reinventing the great American tradition of nineteenth-century transcendentalism. Many of Dillard's considerable gifts are on display in this compact title essay from* Teaching a Stone to Talk. *The essay ostensibly concerns an eccentric young man's attempt to coax human speech from an ordinary gray cobblestone. But this simple story soon evolves into an elaborate meditation on the beauty and mystery of nature's silence, and a powerful appeal to readers to make our all-too-brief time on earth an occasion for metaphysical wonder.*

The island where I live is peopled with cranks like myself. In a cedar-shake shack on a cliff is a man in his thirties who lives alone with a stone he is trying to teach to talk.

Wisecracks on this topic abound, as you might expect, but they are made, as it were, perfunctorily, and mostly by the young. For in fact, almost everyone here respects what Larry is doing, as do I, which is why I am protecting his (or her) privacy, and confusing for you the details. It could be, for instance, a pinch of sand he is teaching to talk, or a prolonged northerly, or any one of a number of waves. But it is, I assure you, a stone. It is—for I have seen it—a palm-sized, oval beach cobble whose dark gray is cut by a band of white which runs around and, presumably, through it; such stones we call "wishing stones," for reasons obscure but not, I think, unimaginable.

He keeps it on a shelf. Usually the stone lies protected by a square of untanned leather, like a canary asleep under its cloth. Larry removes the cover for the stone's lessons, or, more accurately, I should say for the ritual or rituals they perform together several times a day.

No one knows what goes on at these sessions, least of all myself, for I know Larry but slightly, and that owing only to a mix-up in our mail. I assume that, like any other meaningful effort, the ritual involves sacrifice, the suppression of self-consciousness, and a certain precise tilt of the will, so that the will becomes transparent and hollow, a channel for the work. I wish him well. It is a noble work, and beats, from any angle, selling shoes.

Reports differ on precisely what he expects or wants the stone to say. I do not think he expects the stone to speak as we do, and describe for us its long life and many, or few, sensations. I think instead that he is trying to teach it to say a single word, such as "cup," or "uncle." For this purpose he has not, as some have seriously suggested, carved the stone a little mouth, or furnished it in any way with a pocket of air which it might then expel. Rather—and I think he is wise in this—he plans to initiate his son, who is now an infant and living with Larry's estranged wife, into the work, so that it may continue and bear fruit after his death.

NATURE'S SILENCE IS ITS ONE REMARK, and every flake of world is a chip off that old mute and immutable block. The Chinese say that we live in the world of the ten thousand things. Each of the ten thousand cries out to us precisely nothing.

God used to rage at the Israelites for frequenting sacred groves. I wish I could find one. Martin Buber says, "The crisis of all primitive mankind comes with the discovery of that which is fundamentally not-holy, the a-sacramental, which withstands the methods, and which has no 'hour,' a province which steadily enlarges itself." Now we are no longer primitive; now the whole world seems not-holy. We have drained the light from the boughs in the sacred grove and snuffed it in the high places and along the banks of sacred streams. We as a people have moved from pantheism to panatheism. Silence is not our heritage but our destiny; we live where we want to live.

The soul may ask God for anything, and never fail. You may ask God for his presence, or for wisdom, and receive each at his hands. Or you may ask God, in the words of the shopkeeper's little gag sign, that he not go away mad, but just go away. Once, in Israel, an extended family of nomads did that. They heard God's speech and found it too loud. The wilderness generation was at Sinai; it witnessed there the thick darkness where God was: "And all the people saw the thunderings, and the lightnings, and the noise of the trumpet, and the mountain smoking." It scared them witless. Then they asked Moses to beg God, please, never to speak to them directly again. "Let not God speak with us, lest we die." Moses took the message. And God, pitying their fear, agreed. And he added to Moses, "Go say to them, *Get into your tents again.*"

IT IS DIFFICULT to undo our own damage, and to recall to our presence that which we have asked to leave. It is hard to desecrate a grove and change your mind. The very holy mountains are keeping mum. We doused the burning bush and cannot rekindle it; we are lighting matches in vain under every green tree. Did the wind once cry, and the hills shout forth praise? Now speech has perished from among the lifeless things of earth, and living things say very little to very few. Birds may crank out sweet gibberish and monkeys howl; horses neigh and pigs say, as you recall, oink oink. But so do cobbles rumble when a wave recedes, and thunders break the air in lightning storms. I call these noises silence. It could be that wherever there is motion there is noise, as when a whale breeches and smacks the water—and wherever there is stillness there is the still small voice, God's speaking from the whirlwind, nature's old song and dance, the show we drove from town. At any rate, now it is all we can do, and among our best efforts, to try to teach a given human language, English, to chimpanzees.

In the forties an American psychologist and his wife tried to teach a chimp actually to speak. At the end of three years the creature could pronounce, in a hoarse whisper, the words "mama," "papa," and "cup." After another three years of training she could whisper, with difficulty, still only "mama," "papa," and "cup." The more recent successes at teaching chimpanzees American Sign Language are well known. Just the other day a chimp told us, if we can believe that we truly share a vocabulary, that she had been sad in the morning. I'm sorry we asked.

What have we been doing all these centuries but trying to call God back to the mountain, or, failing that, raise a peep out of anything that isn't us? What is the difference between a cathedral and a physics lab? Are they not both saying Hello? We spy on whales and on interstellar radio objects; we starve ourselves and pray till we're blue.

I HAVE BEEN READING comparative cosmology. At this time most cosmologists favor the picture of the evolving universe described by Lamaître and Gamow. But I prefer a suggestion made years ago by Paul Valéry. He set forth the notion that the universe might be "head-shaped." To what is the head listening, what does it see, of what does it think? Or is the universe and all it contains a snippet of mind?

The mountains are great stone bells; they clang together like nuns. Who shushed the stars? A thousand million galaxies are easily seen in the Palomar reflector; collisions between and among them do, of course, occur. But these collisions are very long and silent slides. Billions of stars sift among each other untouched, too distant even to be moved, heedless as always, hushed. The sea pronounces something, over and over, in a hoarse whisper; I can't quite make it out. But God knows I've tried.

At a certain point you say to the woods, to the sea, to the mountains, the world, Now I am ready. Now I will stop and be wholly attentive. You empty yourself and wait, listening. After a time you hear it: there is nothing there. There is nothing but those things only, those created objects, discrete, growing or holding, or swaying, being rained on or raining, held, flooding or ebbing, standing, or spread. You feel the world's word as a tension, a hum, a single chorused note everywhere the same. This is it: this hum is the silence. Nature does utter a peep—just this one. The birds and insects, the meadows and swamps and rivers and stones and mountains and clouds: they all do it; they all don't do it. There is a vibrancy to the silence, a suppression, as if something were gagging the world. But you wait, you give your life's length to listening, and nothing happens. The ice rolls up, the ice rolls back, and still the single note obtains. The tension, or lack of it, is intolerable. The silence is not actually suppression; instead, it is all there is.

WE ARE HERE TO WITNESS. There is nothing else to do with those mute materials we do not need. Until Larry teaches his stone to talk, until God changes his mind, or until the pagan gods slip back to their hilltop groves, all we can do with the whole inhuman array is watch it. We can stage our own act on the planet—build our cities on its plains, dam its rivers, plant its topsoils—but our meaningful activity scarcely covers the terrain. We don't use the songbirds, for instance. We don't eat many of them; we can't befriend them; we can't persuade them to eat more mosquitoes or plant fewer weed seeds. We can only witness them—whoever they are. If we weren't here, they would be songbirds falling in the forest. If we weren't here, material events such as the passage of the seasons would lack even the meager meanings we are able to muster for them. The show would play to an empty house, as do all those stars that fall in the daytime. That is why I take walks: to keep an eye on things. And that is why I went to the Galapagos Islands.

ALL OF THIS BECOMES ESPECIALLY CLEAR on the Galapagos Islands. The Galapagos Islands blew up out of the ocean, some plants blew in on them, some animals drifted aboard and evolved weird forms—and there they all are. The Galapagos are a kind of metaphysics laboratory, almost wholly uncluttered by human culture or history. Whatever happens on those bare volcanic rocks happens in full view, whether anyone is watching or not.

What happens there is this, and precious little it is: clouds come and go as well as the round of similar seasons; a pig eats a tortoise or doesn't eat a tortoise; Pacific waves fall up and slide back; a lichen expands; night follows day; an albatross dies and dries on a cliff; a cool current upwells from the ocean floor; fishes multiply, flies swarm, stars rise and fall, and diving birds dive. The news, in other words, breaks on the beaches. And taking it all in are the trees. The palo santo trees crowd the hillsides like any outdoor audience; they face the lagoons, the lava lowlands, and the shores.

I have some experience of these palo santo trees. They interest me as emblems of the muteness of the human stance in relation to all that is not human. I see us all as palo santo trees, holy sticks, together watching everything that we watch, and growing in silence.

In the Galapagos, I didn't notice the palo santo trees for a long time. Like everyone else, I specialized in sea lions. My shipmates and I liked the sea lions, and envied their lives. Their joy seemed conscious. They were engaged in full-time play. They were all either fat or dead. By day they played in the shallows, alone or together, greeting each other and us with great noises of joy, or they took a turn offshore and body-surfed in the breakers, exultant. By night on the sand they lay in each other's flippers and slept. My shipmates joked, often, that when they "came back," they would just as soon do it all over again as sea lions. I concurred. The sea lion game looked unbeatable.

But, a year and a half later, I returned to those unpeopled islands. In the interval my attachment to them had shifted, and my memories of them had altered, the way memories do, like particolored pebbles rolled back and forth over a grating, so that after a time those hard bright ones, the ones you thought you would never lose, have vanished, passed through the grating, and only a few big, unexpected ones remain, no longer unnoticed but now selected out for some meaning, large or unknown.

Such were the palo santo trees. Before, I had never given them a thought. They were just miles of half-dead trees on the red lava sea cliffs of some deserted islands. They were only a name in a notebook: "Palo santo—those strange white trees." Look at the sea lions! Look at the flightless cormorants, the penguins, the iguanas, the sunsets! But after eighteen months the wonderful cormorants, penguins, iguanas, sunsets, and even the sea lions had dropped from my holey heart. I returned to the Galapagos to see the palo santo trees.

They are thin, pale, wispy trees. You walk among them on the lowland deserts, where they grow beside the prickly pear. You see them from the water on the steeps that face the sea, hundreds together small and thin and spread, and so much more pale than their red soils that any black-and-white print of them looks like a negative. Their stands look like blasted orchards. At every season they all seem newly dead, pale and bare as birches drowned in a beaver pond—for at every season they look leafless, paralyzed, mute. But, in fact, you can see during the rainy months a few meager deciduous leaves here and there on their brittle twigs. And hundreds of lichens always grow on their bark in overlapping explosions which barely enlarge in the course of the decade, lichens pink and orange, lavender, yellow, and green. The palo santo trees bear the lichens effortlessly, unconsciously, the way they bear everything. Their multitudes, transparent as line drawings, crowd the cliffsides like whirling dancers, like empty groves, and look out over the cliff-wrecked breakers toward more unpeopled islands, with their freakish lizards and birds, toward the grieving lagoons and the bays where the sea lions wander, and beyond to the clamoring seas.

Now I no longer concur with my shipmates' joke; I no longer wanted to "come back" as a sea lion. For I thought, and I still think, that if I came back to life in the sunlight where everything changes, I would like to come back as a palo santo tree, one of thousands on a cliffside on those godforsaken islands, where a million events occur among the witless, where a splash of rain may drop on a yellow iguana the size of a dachshund, and ten minutes later the iguana may blink. I would like to come back as a palo santo tree on the weather side of an island, so that I could be, myself, a perfect witness, and look, mute, and wave my arms.

THE SILENCE IS ALL THERE IS. It is the alpha and the omega. It is God's brooding over the face of the waters; it is the blended note of the ten thousand things, the whine of wings. You take a step in the right direction to pray to this silence, and even to address the prayer to "World." Distinctions blur. Quit your tents. Pray without ceasing.

The Wellfleet Whale

STANLEY KUNITZ ‖ 1981

One day late in the summer of 1968, the Pulitzer Prize–winning poet Stanley Kunitz (1905–2006) spotted a magnificent finback whale cavorting through the water near his home on Cape Cod, Massachusetts. During the night, the whale ran aground on the rocky sands, and Kunitz, along with a growing crowd of onlookers, stood vigil as the marooned creature fought for its life. "Finally, on the next morning, while I was about one foot away from it, it opened its eyes and stared at me," Kunitz recalled in an 1981 interview with the New York Times. *"There was an act of recognition. Then it gave a great groan and died." So moved was Kunitz that he scribbled some thoughts for a future poem in his notebook, but it would be thirteen long years before those thoughts crystallized into one of his most admired poems, "The Wellfleet Whale." As Kunitz told the* Times: *"For all those years I thought of it as a possibility for a poem I had to write, but the narrative element was difficult to master." Kunitz continued to produce exceptional work late into his nineties, but his early poems, published in the volumes* Intellectual Things *(1930) and* Passport to War *(1944), are also formidable—cerebral and oracular, reverberating with the echoes of Blake and the English metaphysical poets. By the 1950s, his work had taken on the spare colloquial tenor of numinous reflection on which his reputation rests. ("I want poems that don't tell secrets but are full of them," he told another interviewer.) "The Wellfleet Whale" epitomizes Kunitz's penchant for portraying elemental nature with plainspoken immediacy and revelatory urgency. As for the lengthy gap between idea and execution, Kunitz was philosophical: "Often that's the way things happen with poems. They simmer and simmer, and then they make the right connections, and suddenly they're alive and thrashing. But it doesn't usually take thirteen years."*

1.

You have your language too,
  an eerie medley of clicks
    and hoots and trills,
location-notes and love calls,
  whistles and grunts. Occasionally,
    it's like furniture being smashed,

or the creaking of a mossy door,
    sounds that all melt into a liquid
        song with endless variations,
as if to compensate
    for the vast loneliness of the sea.
        Sometimes a disembodied voice
breaks in, as if from distant reefs,
    and it's as much as one can bear
        to listen to its long mournful cry,
a sorrow without name, both more
    and less than human. It drags
        across the ear like a record
running down.

2.
No wind. No waves. No clouds.
    Only the whisper of the tide,
        as it withdrew, stroking the shore,
a lazy drift of gulls overhead,
    and tiny points of light
        bubbling in the channel.
It was the tag-end of summer.
    From the harbor's mouth
        you coasted into sight,
flashing news of your advent,
    the crescent of your dorsal fin
        clipping the diamonded surface.
We cheered at the sign of your greatness
    when the black barrel of your head
        erupted, ramming the water,
and you flowered for us
    in the jet of your spouting.

3.
All afternoon you swam
    tirelessly round the bay,
        with such an easy motion,
the slightest downbeat of your tail,
    an almost imperceptible
        undulation of your flippers,

you seemed like something poured,
    not driven; you seemed
        to marry grace with power.
And when you bounded into air,
    slapping your flukes,
        we thrilled to look upon
pure energy incarnate
    as nobility of form.
        You seemed to ask of us
not sympathy, or love,
    or understanding,
        but awe and wonder.

That night we watched you
    swimming in the moon.
        Your back was molten silver.
We guessed your silent passage
    by the phosphorescence in your wake.
        At dawn we found you stranded on the rocks.

4.
There came a boy and a man
    and yet other men running, and two
        schoolgirls in yellow halters
and a housewife bedecked
    with curlers, and whole families in beach
        buggies with assorted yelping dogs.
The tide was almost out.
    We could walk around you,
        as you heaved deeper into the shoal,
crushed by your own weight,
    collapsing into yourself,
        your flippers and your flukes
quivering, your blowhole
    spasmodically bubbling, roaring.
        In the pit of your gaping mouth
you bared your fringework of baleen,
    a thicket of horned bristles.
        When the Curator of Mammals
arrived from Boston

to take samples of your blood
    you were already oozing from below.
Somebody had carved his initials
    in your flank. Hunters of souvenirs
      had peeled off strips of your skin,
a membrane thin as paper.
    You were blistered and cracked by the sun.
    The gulls had been pecking at you.
The sound you made was a hoarse and fitful bleating.

What drew us to the magnet of your dying?
    You made a bond between us,
      the keepers of the nightfall watch,
who gathered in a ring around you,
    boozing in the bonfire light.
      Toward dawn we shared with you
your hour of desolation,
    the huge lingering passion
      of your unearthly outcry,
as you swung your blind head
    toward us and laboriously opened
      a bloodshot, glistening eye,
in which we swam with terror and recognition.

5.
Voyager, chief of the pelagic world,
    you brought with you the myth
      of another country, dimly remembered,
where flying reptiles
    lumbered over the steaming marshes
      and trumpeting thunder lizards
wallowed in the reeds.
    While empires rose and fell on land,
      your nation breasted the open main,
rocked in the consoling rhythm
    of the tides. Which ancestor first plunged
      head-down through zones of colored twilight
to scour the bottom of the dark?
    You ranged the North Atlantic track
      from Port-of-Spain to Baffin Bay,

edging between the ice-floes
    through the fat of summer,
        lob-tailing, breaching, sounding,
grazing in the pastures of the sea
    on krill-rich orange plankton
        crackling with life.
You prowled down the continental shelf,
    guided by the sun and stars
        and the taste of alluvial silt
on your way southward
    to the warm lagoons,
        the tropic of desire,
where the lovers lie belly to belly
    in the rub and nuzzle of their sporting;
        and you turned, like a god in exile,
out of your wide primeval element,
    delivered to the mercy of time.
        Master of the whale-roads,
let the white wings of the gulls
    spread out their cover.
        You have become like us,
disgraced and mortal.

CROWD PLEASERS

Three Days to See

HELEN KELLER || 1933

Four decades after her death, Helen Keller (1880–1968), the celebrated author, lecturer, and champion of the disabled, remains an American icon—admired, even revered, not only in this country but throughout the world. Stricken with a debilitating illness (believed to have been either scarlet fever or meningitis) at the age of nineteen months, Keller survived the ordeal but was left permanently unable to see or hear. When she was nearly seven and, by her own later account, "a wild, unruly child," her parents sought a consultation with the director of the Perkins School for the Blind, in Boston, after coming across a story in Charles Dickens's American Notes *of how a young blind-and-deaf girl named Laura Bridgman had been successfully educated there some fifty years earlier. The school arranged for Anne Sullivan, a visually impaired Perkins valedictorian who had learned tactile sign language from Bridgman herself, to live with the Kellers, at their home in Tuscumbia, Alabama, and to serve as Helen's governess and tutor.*

The uplifting saga of how the young Keller learned to read and write through the devoted ministrations of Sullivan first come to light in Keller's memoir of her early years, The Story of My Life *(1902), which was published shortly before she graduated magna cum laude from Radcliffe College as the first blind-and-deaf person in America to earn a college degree, and which is still in print in more than fifty languages. But it was William Gibson's play* The Miracle Worker, *which began its two-year run on Broadway in 1959, and the movie version that followed, in 1962, that indelibly etched the tale into the public consciousness. As dramatized by Gibson, what began as a fierce contest of wills soon blossomed into a model teacher–pupil relationship. After a breakthrough in which Sullivan traced the letters spelling out "water" on her charge's palm while holding her other hand under a garden pump, Keller rapidly learned to communicate with the outside world and to read English—as well as German, French, Latin, and Greek—in braille. Sullivan remained her inseparable companion and helpmate through Keller's flourishing career as a much-in-demand public speaker, organizer, and fund-raiser; during the 1920s they even appeared together on the vaudeville circuit, demonstrating their communication techniques to great popular acclaim.*

By the time "Three Days to See" appeared in The Atlantic, *Keller*

*was already a major cultural figure, internationally renowned for her in-
fluential advocacy of such social causes as women's suffrage, the trade
union movement, and, of course, the treatment of the blind and the deaf.
In this essay, however, she hews to the homiletic form of reflection that
was the trademark of her personal writing, musing about how she would
fill her hours if she could regain her sight for three fleeting days. Describing the crowded events of her "imagined miracle" in avid detail—visits
to the American Museum of Natural History and the Metropolitan
Museum of Art, an evening at the theater, and a long walk through the
streets of Manhattan—she reveals what her first sighted thrill would
be: to drink in the shining countenance of her beloved mentor, Annie
Sullivan.*

All of us have read thrilling stories in which the hero had only a limited
and specified time to live. Sometimes it was as long as a year; sometimes as
short as twenty-four hours. But always we were interested in discovering
just how the doomed man chose to spend his last days or his last hours. I
speak, of course, of free men who have a choice, not condemned criminals
whose sphere of activities is strictly delimited.

Such stories set us thinking, wondering what we should do under similar circumstances. What events, what experiences, what associations, should
we crowd into those last hours as mortal beings? What happiness should we
find in reviewing the past, what regrets?

Sometimes I have thought it would be an excellent rule to live each day
as if we should die tomorrow. Such an attitude would emphasize sharply
the values of life. We should live each day with a gentleness, a vigor, and a
keenness of appreciation which are often lost when time stretches before
us in the constant panorama of more days and months and years to come.
There are those, of course, who would adopt the epicurean motto of "Eat,
drink, and be merry," but most people would be chastened by the certainty
of impending death.

In stories, the doomed hero is usually saved at the last minute by some
stroke of fortune, but almost always his sense of values is changed. He becomes more appreciative of the meaning of life and its permanent spiritual
values. It has often been noted that those who live, or have lived, in the
shadow of death bring a mellow sweetness to everything they do.

Most of us, however, take life for granted. We know that one day we
must die, but usually we picture that day as far in the future. When we are
in buoyant health, death is all but unimaginable. We seldom think of it.

The days stretch out in an endless vista. So we go about our petty tasks, hardly aware of our listless attitude toward life.

The same lethargy, I am afraid, characterizes the use of all our faculties and senses. Only the deaf appreciate hearing, only the blind realize the manifold blessings that lie in sight. Particularly does this observation apply to those who have lost sight and hearing in adult life. But those who have never suffered impairment of sight or hearing seldom make the fullest use of these blessed faculties. Their eyes and ears take in all sights and sounds hazily, without concentration and with little appreciation. It is the same old story of not being grateful for what we have until we lose it, of not being conscious of health until we are ill.

I have often thought it would be a blessing if each human being were stricken blind and deaf for a few days at some time during his early adult life. Darkness would make him more appreciative of sight; silence would teach him the joys of sound.

Now and then I have tested my seeing friends to discover what they see. Recently I was visited by a very good friend who had just returned from a long walk in the woods, and I asked her what she had observed. "Nothing in particular," she replied. I might have been incredulous had I not been accustomed to such responses, for long ago I became convinced that the seeing see little.

How was it possible, I asked myself, to walk for an hour through the woods and see nothing worthy of note? I who cannot see find hundreds of things to interest me through mere touch. I feel the delicate symmetry of a leaf. I pass my hands lovingly about the smooth skin of a silver birch, or the rough, shaggy bark of a pine. In spring I touch the branches of trees hopefully in search of a bud, the first sign of awakening Nature after her winter's sleep. I feel the delightful, velvety texture of a flower, and discover its remarkable convolutions; and something of the miracle of Nature is revealed to me. Occasionally, if I am very fortunate, I place my hand gently on a small tree and feel the happy quiver of a bird in full song. I am delighted to have the cool waters of a brook rush through my open fingers. To me a lush carpet of pine needles or spongy grass is more welcome than the most luxurious Persian rug. To me the pageant of seasons is a thrilling and unending drama, the action of which streams through my finger tips.

At times my heart cries out with longing to see all these things. If I can get so much pleasure from mere touch, how much more beauty must be revealed by sight. Yet, those who have eyes apparently see little. The panorama of color and action which fills the world is taken for granted. It is human, perhaps, to appreciate little that which we have and to long for that which we have not, but it is a great pity that in the world of light the gift of sight is used only as a mere convenience rather than as a means of adding fullness to life.

If I were the president of a university I should establish a compulsory course in "How to Use Your Eyes." The professor would try to show his pupils how they could add joy to their lives by really seeing what passes unnoticed before them. He would try to awake their dormant and sluggish faculties.

PERHAPS I CAN BEST ILLUSTRATE by imagining what I should most like to see if I were given the use of my eyes, say, for just three days. And while I am imagining, suppose you, too, set your mind to work on the problem of how you would use your own eyes if you had only three more days to see. If with the oncoming darkness of the third night you knew that the sun would never rise for you again, how would you spend those three precious intervening days? What would you most want to let your gaze rest upon?

I, naturally, should want most to see the things which have become dear to me through my years of darkness. You, too, would want to let your eyes rest long on the things that have become dear to you so that you could take the memory of them with you into the night that loomed before you.

If, by some miracle, I were granted three seeing days, to be followed by a relapse into darkness, I should divide the period into three parts.

On the first day, I should want to see the people whose kindness and gentleness and companionship have made my life worth living. First I should like to gaze long upon the face of my dear teacher, Mrs. Anne Sullivan Macy, who came to me when I was a child and opened the outer world to me. I should want not merely to see the outline of her face, so that I could cherish it in my memory, but to study that face and find in it the living evidence of the sympathetic tenderness and patience with which she accomplished the difficult task of my education. I should like to see in her eyes that strength of character which has enabled her to stand firm in the face of difficulties, and that compassion for all humanity which she has revealed to me so often.

I do not know what it is to see into the heart of a friend through that "window of the soul," the eye. I can only "see" through my finger tips the outline of a face. I can detect laughter, sorrow, and many other obvious emotions. I know my friends from the feel of their faces. But I cannot really picture their personalities by touch. I know their personalities, of course, through other means, through the thoughts they express to me, through whatever of their actions are revealed to me. But I am denied that deeper understanding of them which I am sure would come through sight of them, through watching their reactions to various expressed thoughts and circumstances, through noting the immediate and fleeting reactions of their eyes and countenance.

Friends who are near to me I know well, because through the months and years they reveal themselves to me in all their phases; but of casual friends I have only an incomplete impression, an impression gained from a handclasp, from spoken words which I take from their lips with my finger tips, or which they tap into the palm of my hand.

How much easier, how much more satisfying it is for you who can see to grasp quickly the essential qualities of another person by watching the subtleties of expression, the quiver of a muscle, the flutter of a hand. But does it ever occur to you to use your sight to see into the inner nature of a friend or acquaintance? Do not most of you seeing people grasp casually the outward features of a face and let it go at that?

For instance, can you describe accurately the faces of five good friends? Some of you can, but many cannot. As an experiment, I have questioned husbands of long standing about the color of their wives' eyes, and often they express embarrassed confusion and admit that they do not know. And, incidentally, it is a chronic complaint of wives that their husbands do not notice new dresses, new hats, and changes in household arrangements.

The eyes of seeing persons soon become accustomed to the routine of their surroundings, and they actually see only the startling and spectacular. But even in viewing the most spectacular sights the eyes are lazy. Court records reveal every day how inaccurately "eyewitnesses" see. A given event will be "seen" in several different ways by as many witnesses. Some see more than others, but few see everything that is within the range of their vision.

Oh, the things that I should see if I had the power of sight for just three days!

The first day would be a busy one. I should call to me all my dear friends and look long into their faces, imprinting upon my mind the outward evidences of the beauty that is within them. I should let my eyes rest, too, on the face of a baby, so that I could catch a vision of the eager, innocent beauty which precedes the individual's consciousness of the conflicts which life develops.

And I should like to look into the loyal, trusting eyes of my dogs—the grave, canny little Scottie, Darkie, and the stalwart, understanding Great Dane, Helga, whose warm, tender, and playful friendships are so comforting to me.

On that busy first day I should also view the small simple things of my home. I want to see the warm colors in the rugs under my feet, the pictures on the walls, the intimate trifles that transform a house into home. My eyes would rest respectfully on the books in raised type which I have read, but they would be more eagerly interested in the printed books which seeing people can read, for during the long night of my life the books I have read and those which have been read to me have built themselves into a great shining lighthouse, revealing to me the deepest channels of human life and the human spirit.

In the afternoon of that first seeing day, I should take a long walk in the woods and intoxicate my eyes on the beauties of the world of Nature, trying desperately to absorb in a few hours the vast splendor which is constantly unfolding itself to those who can see. On the way home from my woodland jaunt my path would lie near a farm so that I might see the patient horses ploughing in the field (perhaps I should see only a tractor!) and the serene content of men living close to the soil. And I should pray for the glory of a colorful sunset.

When dusk had fallen, I should experience the double delight of being able to see by artificial light, which the genius of man has created to extend the power of his sight when Nature decrees darkness.

In the night of that first day of sight, I should not be able to sleep, so full would be my mind of the memories of the day.

THE NEXT DAY—the second day of sight—I should arise with the dawn and see the thrilling miracle by which night is transformed into day. I should behold with awe the magnificent panorama of light with which the sun awakens the sleeping earth.

This day I should devote to a hasty glimpse of the world, past and present. I should want to see the pageant of man's progress, the kaleidoscope of the ages. How can so much be compressed into one day? Through the museums, of course. Often I have visited the New York Museum of Natural History to touch with my hands many of the objects there exhibited, but I have longed to see with my eyes the condensed history of the earth and its inhabitants displayed there—animals and the races of men pictured in their native environment; gigantic carcasses of dinosaurs and mastodons which roamed the earth long before man appeared, with his tiny stature and powerful brain, to conquer the animal kingdom; realistic presentations of the processes of evolution in animals, in man, and in the implements which man has used to fashion for himself a secure home on this planet; and a thousand and one other aspects of natural history.

I wonder how many readers of this article have viewed this panorama of the face of living things as pictured in that inspiring museum. Many, of course, have not had the opportunity, but I am sure that many who *have* had the opportunity have not made use of it. There, indeed, is a place to use your eyes. You who see can spend many fruitful days there, but I, with my imaginary three days of sight, could only take a hasty glimpse, and pass on.

My next stop would be the Metropolitan Museum of Art, for just as the Museum of Natural History reveals the material aspects of the world, so does the Metropolitan show the myriad facets of the human spirit. Throughout the history of humanity the urge to artistic expression has been almost as powerful as the urge for food, shelter, and procreation. And here, in the vast chambers of the Metropolitan Museum, is unfolded before me the spirit of Egypt, Greece, and Rome, as expressed in their art. I know well through my hands the sculptured gods and goddesses of the ancient Nile land. I have felt copies of Parthenon friezes, and I have sensed the rhythmic beauty of charging Athenian warriors. Apollos and Venuses and the Winged Victory of Samothrace are friends of my finger tips. The gnarled, bearded features of Homer are dear to me, for he, too, knew blindness.

My hands have lingered upon the living marble of Roman sculpture as well as that of later generations. I have passed my hands over a plaster cast of Michelangelo's inspiring and heroic Moses; I have sensed the power of Rodin; I have been awed by the devoted spirit of Gothic wood carving. These arts which can be touched have meaning for me, but even they were meant to be seen rather than felt, and I can only guess at the beauty which remains hidden from me. I can admire the simple lines of a Greek vase, but its figured decorations are lost to me.

So on this, my second day of sight, I should try to probe into the soul of man through his art. The things I knew through touch I should now see. More splendid still, the whole magnificent world of painting would be opened to me, from the Italian Primitives, with their serene religious devotion, to the Moderns, with their feverish visions. I should look deep into the canvases of Raphael, Leonardo da Vinci, Titian, Rembrandt. I should want to feast my eyes upon the warm colors of Veronese, study the mysteries of El Greco, catch a new vision of Nature from Corot. Oh, there is so much rich meaning and beauty in the art of the ages for you who have eyes to see!

Upon my short visit to this temple of art I should not be able to review a fraction of that great world of art which is open to you. I should be able to get only a superficial impression. Artists tell me that for a deep and true appreciation of art one must educate the eye. One must learn through experience to weigh the merits of line, of composition, of form and color. If I had eyes, how happily would I embark upon so fascinating a study! Yet I am told that, to many of you who have eyes to see, the world of art is a dark night, unexplored and unilluminated.

It would be with extreme reluctance that I should leave the Metropolitan Museum, which contains the key to beauty—a beauty so neglected. Seeing persons, however, do not need a Metropolitan to find this key to beauty. The same key lies waiting in smaller museums, and in books on the shelves of even small libraries. But naturally, in my limited time of imaginary sight, I should choose the place where the key unlocks the greatest treasures in the shortest time.

The evening of my second day of sight I should spend at a theatre or at the movies. Even now I often attend theatrical performances of all sorts, but the action of the play must be spelled into my hand by a companion. But how I should like to see with my own eyes the fascinating figure of Hamlet, or the gusty Falstaff amid colorful Elizabethan trappings! How I should like to follow each movement of the graceful Hamlet, each strut of the hearty Falstaff! And since I could see only one play, I should be confronted by a many-horned dilemma, for there are scores of plays I should want to see. You who have eyes can see any you like. How many of you, I wonder, when you gaze at a play, a movie, or any spectacle, realize and give thanks for the miracle of sight which enables you to enjoy its color, grace, and movement?

I cannot enjoy the beauty of rhythmic movement except in a sphere restricted to the touch of my hands. I can vision only dimly the grace of a Pavlowa, although I know something of the delight of rhythm, for often I can sense the beat of music as it vibrates through the floor. I can well imagine that cadenced motion must be one of the most pleasing sights in the world. I have been able to gather something of this by tracing with my fingers the lines in sculptured marble; if this static grace can be so lovely, how much more acute must be the thrill of seeing grace in motion.

One of my dearest memories is of the time when Joseph Jefferson allowed me to touch his face and hands as he went through some of the gestures and speeches of his beloved Rip Van Winkle. I was able to catch thus a meagre glimpse of the world of drama, and I shall never forget the delight of that moment. But, oh, how much I must miss, and how much pleasure you seeing ones can derive from watching and hearing the interplay of speech and movement in the unfolding of a dramatic performance! If I could see only one play, I should know how to picture in my mind the action of a hundred plays which I have read or had transferred to me through the medium of the manual alphabet.

So, through the evening of my second imaginary day of sight, the great figures of dramatic literature would crowd sleep from my eyes.

THE FOLLOWING MORNING, I should again greet the dawn, anxious to discover new delights, for I am sure that, for those who have eyes which really see, the dawn of each day must be a perpetually new revelation of beauty.

This, according to the terms of my imagined miracle, is to be my third and last day of sight. I shall have no time to waste in regrets or longings; there is too much to see. The first day I devoted to my friends, animate and inanimate. The second revealed to me the history of man and Nature. Today I shall spend in the workaday world of the present, amid the haunts of men going about the business of life. And where can one find so many activities and conditions of men as in New York? So the city becomes my destination.

I start from my home in the quiet little suburb of Forest Hills, Long Island. Here, surrounded by green lawns, trees, and flowers, are neat little houses, happy with the voices and movements of wives and children, havens of peaceful rest for men who toil in the city. I drive across the lacy structure of steel which spans the East River, and I get a new and startling vision of the power and ingenuity of the mind of man. Busy boats chug and scurry about the river—racy speed boats, stolid, snorting tugs. If I had long days of sight ahead, I should spend many of them watching the delightful activity upon the river.

I look ahead, and before me rise the fantastic towers of New York, a city that seems to have stepped from the pages of a fairy story. What an awe-inspiring sight, these glittering spires, these vast banks of stone and steel—structures such as the gods might build for themselves! This animated picture is a part of the lives of millions of people every day. How many, I wonder, give it so much as a second glance? Very few, I fear. Their eyes are blind to this magnificent sight because it is so familiar to them.

I hurry to the top of one of those gigantic structures, the Empire State Building, for there, a short time ago, I "saw" the city below through the eyes of my secretary. I am anxious to compare my fancy with reality. I am sure I should not be disappointed in the panorama spread out before me, for to me it would be a vision of another world.

Now I begin my rounds of the city. First, I stand at a busy corner, merely looking at people, trying by sight of them to understand something of their lives. I see smiles, and I am happy. I see serious determination, and I am proud. I see suffering, and I am compassionate.

I stroll down Fifth Avenue. I throw my eyes out of focus, so that I see no particular object but only a seething kaleidoscope of color. I am certain that the colors of women's dresses moving in a throng must be a gorgeous spectacle of which I should never tire. But perhaps if I had sight I should be like most other women—too interested in styles and the cut of individual dresses to give much attention to the splendor of color in the mass. And I am convinced, too, that I should become an inveterate window shopper, for it must be a delight to the eye to view the myriad articles of beauty on display.

From Fifth Avenue I make a tour of the city—to Park Avenue, to the slums, to factories, to parks where children play. I take a stay-at-home trip abroad by visiting the foreign quarters. Always my eyes are open wide to all the sights of both happiness and misery so that I may probe deep and add to my understanding of how people work and live. My heart is full of the images of people and things. My eye passes lightly over no single trifle; it strives to touch and hold closely each thing its gaze rests upon. Some sights are pleasant, filling the heart with happiness; but some are miserably pathetic. To these latter I do not shut my eyes, for they, too, are part of life. To close the eye on them is to close the heart and mind.

My third day of sight is drawing to an end. Perhaps there are many serious pursuits to which I should devote the few remaining hours, but I am afraid that on the evening of that last day I should again run away to the theatre, to a hilariously funny play, so that I might appreciate the overtones of comedy in the human spirit.

At midnight my temporary respite from blindness would cease, and permanent night would close in on me again. Naturally in those three short days I should not have seen all I wanted to see. Only when darkness had again descended upon me should I realize how much I had left unseen. But my mind would be so crowded with glorious memories that I should have little time for regrets. Thereafter the touch of every object would bring a glowing memory of how that object looked.

Perhaps this short outline of how I should spend three days of sight does not agree with the programme you would set for yourself if you knew that you were about to be stricken blind. I am, however, sure that if you actually faced that fate your eyes would open to things you had never seen before, storing up memories for the long night ahead. You would use your eyes as never before. Everything you saw would become dear to you. Your eyes would touch and embrace every object that came within your range of vision. Then, at last, you would really see, and a new world of beauty would open itself before you.

I who am blind can give one hint to those who see—one admonition to those who would make full use of the gift of sight: Use your eyes as if tomorrow you would be stricken blind. And the same method can be applied to the other senses. Hear the music of voices, the song of a bird, the mighty strains of an orchestra, as if you would be stricken deaf tomorrow. Touch each object you want to touch as if tomorrow your tactile sense would fail. Smell the perfume of flowers, taste with relish each morsel, as if tomorrow you could never smell and taste again. Make the most of every sense; glory in all the facets of pleasure and beauty which the world reveals to you through the several means of contact which Nature provides. But of all the senses, I am sure that sight must be the most delightful.

The Blow That Hurts

GENE TUNNEY ‖ 1939

The heavyweight boxing champion of the world from 1926 to 1928, James Joseph Tunney (1897–1978) retired with a sparkling professional record, marred by only a single defeat. The son of a longshoreman who grew up in the then working-class neighborhood of Greenwich Village, in New York City, Tunney (who preferred to be called by his nickname "Gene") was a rare species in the boxing world: handsome, articulate, bookish, and abstemious. His brief reign atop the sport's glamour division was highlighted by two upset victories over Jack Dempsey, the fabled "Man-assa Mauler" who had dominated the heavyweight ranks for the previous seven years. Tunney was a cerebral fighter who relied on ring science and defensive skills to compensate for lack of speed and punching power—a style that displeased some fight fans but made him a perfect foil for Dempsey's ferocious aggression. In their first meeting, in September 1926, before a record crowd of 120,000 in Sesquicentennial Park, in Philadelphia, Tunney handily won the ten-round bout on points and left the dethroned champ so battered that it prompted Dempsey's legendary dressing-room quip to his wife (recycled some fifty years later by President Ronald Reagan, after surviving a 1981 assassination attempt): "Honey, I forgot to duck." The Tunney–Dempsey rematch the following year, at Soldiers Field in Chicago, holds a special place in American sporting lore as the famous "Long Count Fight." Trailing on points in the seventh round, Dempsey floored Tunney with a thunderous left hook but was slow to honor an Illinois boxing rule requiring fighters to retreat to a neutral corner after scoring a knockdown. Taking full advantage of an extra seven seconds to recover, Tunney wobbled to his feet, managed to hold the charging Dempsey at bay, and went on to retain his title in a unanimous ten-round decision.

Following his retirement from the ring, Tunney successfully pursued a career in business in New York City, married a steel heiress, and fathered four children, one of whom, John V. Tunney, represented the state of California in the United States Senate. But of all Gene Tunney's accomplishments, none was a source of greater personal pride than his writing. An autodidact who never went to college, he was an omnivorous reader, given to quoting Shakespeare soliloquies, and was rarely seen without a book under his arm, even in training camp. (Before the first Dempsey fight, he took heat from his manager for spending too much time leafing through the Rubaiyat of Omar Khayyam.*) Tunney's literary output included two memoirs—*A Man Must Fight *(1932) and* Arms for Living *(1941)—and numerous magazine articles, many of them dealing with the psychology of sports and all distinguished by a writerly voice of such uncommon grace, intelligence, and wit that it earned accolades from the likes of Ernest Hemingway and George Bernard Shaw. In "The Blow That Hurts," Tunney explores a double paradox: why boxers who brutalize each other during a match often become lifelong friends and why the punishment fighters suffer inside the ring pales by comparison with the punishment they suffer outside of it.*

A punch in the nose might seem to be an intensely personal thing—much more so, for example, than pushing the queen's rook's pawn on a board of checkered squares. Yet I have been astonished to hear of enmities and feuds in the game of chess, that epitome of abstract combat. The queen's rook's pawn seems to have occasioned a surprising lot of rancor and fury. I find it difficult to understand, but then I have been merely a boxer, a devotee of one of the most noted of all physical-contest sports.

Some years ago a great international chess tournament was staged in New York, with an imposing array of the grand masters of the game. Newspaper files will reveal that this tournament made the front pages in a spectacular way, though chess is hardly of headline popularity. The tournament was ornamented by the presence not only of Capablanca, then at the height of his genius, but also of Dr. Emanuel Lasker, the venerated adept who for so many years was the champion. Dr. Lasker had a peculiarity—he loved strong black cigars and smoked them always. Other grand masters charged that when they played him he would blow clouds of acrid and noxious smoke across the board and into their faces, thereby disconcerting them and throwing them off their game. Foul play, they roared. This state of affairs was only exacerbated by the popularity and honored regard that the almost legendary chess master enjoyed in New York. His admirers, knowing his love for strong black cigars, sent him many gifts of them—the strongest and the blackest. In consequence, the Doctor had an abundance of acrid and noxious smoke to blow into the faces of his opponents. The more deeply he became absorbed in profound combinations at the chessboard, the harder he would puff away and the more wrathfully other chess masters would protest to the officials. As for the merits of the case, I surely am not one to adjudicate at this late day, but I'd suppose that where there's smoke there's fire—or at any rate some heat.

By way of contrast, take prize fighting. Few human beings have fought each other more savagely or more often than Harry Greb and I. We punched and cut and bruised each other in a series of bouts, five of them. In the first Greb gave me a ferocious beating, closed both eyes, broke my nose, chipped my teeth, and cut my lips to pieces. He did everything but knock me out. In our last fight I beat him about as badly, so badly that he was helpless in the latter rounds. He seemed like a dead-game fighter, wanting to be spared the indignity of being knocked out. Pain meant nothing—he didn't want the folks back home to read of his being knocked out. From the beginning of our first to the end of our last bout, Greb and I went through the ferocious gamut of giving and taking, hitting and being hit. We were always the best of friends; never any ill will or anger. You see, we were not chess players.

Harry was bitter about one fight, our fourth. I won the decision, and this enraged him. He was sure he had beaten me, felt to the depths of his soul that he was the victor. It was one of those newspaper-decision affairs of the period, sports writers giving the verdict in their stories. Cleveland was the place; and Regis Walsh of the *Pittsburgh Post*, one of Greb's best friends, in his newspaper story the day after the fight gave the decision to me, putting my photo on the front page with the caption "Too Much for Our Boy." Greb never spoke to him again. They were enemies ever after. All the bitterness the battle had stirred in Greb was directed, not against me, not against the antagonist who had been in there hitting him, but against his newspaper friend who had merely tapped a few keys on a typewriter. He didn't resent the physical pain of being murdered, he resented losing—losing unjustly, as he thought.

It isn't the physical pain that hurts so much, it's the blow to one's vanity. But what is vanity? What are we most proud of? A whole lot of things, among which physical prowess in a fight is by no means the most important. Intellectual pride, as any theologian will tell you, is the most damning; and the vanity of artists is famous in the literature of history and comedy alike. As a boxer I should say that it's in the realm of the intellectual and artistic that a blow is the most painful, where feelings are hurt the most. For example, I think the man I hit the hardest in my whole boxing career was onetime heavyweight champion of Europe, Erminio Spalla, but I never hurt Spalla's feelings. Yet I might have—I'm sure I could have turned him into a rancorous enemy, but he remains an excellent friend. I knocked him out in a bout at the Polo Grounds back in 1924. He was no boxing master; he was crude, but he could hit. I didn't want him to lay that powerful right of his on my chin—it might be uncomfortable, and so it was when it eventually landed. After being hit I boxed him carefully, waiting for a decisive opening, and then hit him with every ounce of strength I had. I knocked him out with what I imagine was the hardest blow I ever struck. But, as I have remarked, I never hurt his feelings.

One day last fall I was having dinner in New York at Christ Cella's place of unceremonious hospitality, and heard a couple of Italian waiters chattering about Spalla. He had been Italy's pride, and my presence made them recall him. But they were by no means talking about boxing—their topic was opera, the newest operatic star in Italy. They were discussing what they had read in their Mulberry Street newspaper—that prize fighter Spalla, former champion of Italy and all Europe, had just made a resounding success in his debut at La Scala in Milan singing "Amonasro" in Verdi's *Aïda*. This did not surprise me a bit, because the very point on which I remembered I had never hurt Spalla's feelings was his singing.

Several years before I fought him, he and I had trained together with other boxers in the same quarters in New Jersey—and he was always singing. He told me he was studying baritone, and when we were not sparring in training bouts he was caroling operatic arias. He had a rich and beautiful voice, and I used to ask him to sing for me, which he did with a lusty good will—*Pagliacci,* and *Trovatore.* After we fought and the knockout brought Spalla's pugilistic career to an end, he went back to Italy. Later on he wrote to me, and told me that with the money he had earned in the prize ring he was pursuing his studies for an operatic career. I suspect he was grateful because that hardest punch I ever hit finished him in pugilism. We corresponded on and off, and he kept me informed how he was getting along with the arias and the high notes. Then came a letter in which he told me that he was soon to make his debut at La Scala—which he did with first-rate success.

Just a few days ago I had a letter from my old prize-ring antagonist. It's worth quoting: "Dear Gene: Following the hostiliti between America and Italy in the cinema world I was urgently called by the La Scalla Film Company to play the role in many of their films. And so to quote the old proverb—'It is an ill wind that blows, etc. etc.' I am enclosing my autographed fotograph, and I trust you will send me yours, as I always want to see you in the best of health. My wife has had another son and so I am the father of five. And how is your family progressing?" Quite nicely, Erminio, quite nicely.

What I am sure of is this—if, instead of hitting Spalla so hard, I had made a disparaging comment about his singing, he would have hated me. Remarks about faulty production, vibrato, and flatting on the top notes—

that's the sort of thing which creates those embittered vendettas in opera companies. I liked Spalla's singing, but even if I hadn't I should never have told him so. I would have punched him in the nose instead, for I don't like to make enemies.

Among people who have no contact with the boxing tradition of the English-speaking world, a blow in the face is a deadly insult—while a wound with a sword may be taken with equanimity. Our boxing tradition has ameliorated the innate combativeness of man, has taken much of the homicide out of fight and physical clash. The fistic exchange has become conventionalized. It's not good sportsmanship to resent with abiding rancor a punch in a fight. So a prize fight, being the epitome of the boxing tradition, is decidedly impersonal—a thing of abstraction.

I recall a scene the morning after my first fight with Jack Dempsey as one of the strangest I ever experienced. It had me disconcerted, as well as considerably embarrassed.

After that bout in the rain in Philadelphia it seemed to me proper to go and pay my respects to Jack. He had been severely punished, and must feel pretty blue after losing the championship. The next afternoon I went to his hotel. He had a suite of rooms, and when I got there Jack was in an inside bedroom. In the outer room were gathered the Dempsey entourage of manager, handlers, trainers, and disappointed followers. They greeted me with an instant bristling of hostility. I was the focus of scowls and angry, sullen glances. Gene Normile was in tears. Jerry the Greek came to me, shook his fist, and mumbled coarsely, "You can't licka the 'Chump,' you can't licka the 'Chump.'" Jack Dempsey always inspired loyalty, and this was it. They bitterly resented my defeating him.

I had the nervous feeling of being in the camp of the enemy, surrounded by smouldering hatred. I had only one impulse—to get in there to Jack. I found him sitting on a bed, and then I realized how badly he had been battered in that downpour the night before. He put out his hand, and said, "Hello, Gene." It was as if we were visiting casually, in the course of commonplace acquaintance. Before that Jack and I had never been friends particularly. In fact, I think he rather resented me as a challenger. But after we had fought and I had defeated him for the championship—Jack was the only friend I had in the camp of the enemy.

Of all the sports, it is my opinion that boxing, though the most physically injurious, is the most impersonal. I indulge in golf, tennis, squash rackets, and shooting, and can conscientiously say that my resentment in defeat in any of them is far greater than anything I ever felt or experienced in a long career of boxing. There is a subconscious mutuality of respect engendered by the give-and-take of the prize fight that has a certain spiritual quality to it which leaves no room for rancor, resentment, or jealousy. It is true that prize fighting seems sheerly physical and elemental, but what other sport or art has as little bitterness or envy among its devotees? Could the answer be that the more elemental we become in sport and art, the closer to the spiritual we get?

Blue Highways

WILLIAM LEAST HEAT-MOON || 1982

Having lost both his wife of eleven years and his teaching job at the University of Missouri over the course of one very long day, William Trogdon (1940–) resorted to a time-honored American stratagem for dealing with personal crisis: he hit the road. Humbly provisioned with a few primitive cooking tools, the last of his savings, and a battered Ford Econoline van he had nicknamed "Ghost Dancing," Trogdon, then thirty-eight, set out from his home, in Columbia, Missouri, for his own anti–Grand Tour of the United States. His only game plan was to steer clear of the anesthetizing interstates and to stick to the country's meandering network of two-lane back roads—the so-called "blue highways" that derive their name from the color in which they appear on maps.

*The 1982 book that grew out of Trogdon's circular, fourteen-thousand-mile odyssey—*Blue Highways: A Journey into America—*transformed him from an out-of-work academic to a bestselling author, writing under the pen name William Least Heat-Moon. Still delighting readers a quarter of a century later with its limpid depictions of American landscapes, its jaunty sketches of one-street towns with bizarre names, and its gently satirical observations of human nature,* Blue Highways *is now permanently ensconced in the pantheon of American road literature, alongside such kinetic classics as Jack Kerouac's* On the Road *(1957),* John Steinbeck's Travels with Charley *(1962), and Tom Wolfe's* The Electric Kool-Aid Acid Test *(1968).*

The adaptation of Blue Highways *that appeared as* The Atlantic's *September 1982 cover story marked a milestone of a different kind for the magazine—the continuation of a long-standing commitment to publishing top-flight travel writing. That tradition stretches back to Henry David Thoreau's "Chesuncook" (1859) and Mark Twain's "Old Times on the Mississippi" (1875) and encompasses more recent work that has helped shape the modern era of the form, most notably Rebecca West's Balkan epic,* Black Lamb and Grey Falcon *(1941). Least Heat-Moon, who is of mixed Osage and English heritage, followed the success of* Blue Highways *with* PrairyErth *(1991), a meditation upon the history and geography of a small county in Kansas, and* River-Horse *(1999), another first-person account of a cross-country trip, this time entirely by small boat. But he is still best known and loved for* Blue Highways *and for putting his own special stamp on one of the great themes of American life—self-reinvention.*

The idea came to me on February 17, a day of canceled expectations: the day I learned my job teaching English was finished because of declining enrollment at the college, the day I called my wife, from whom I'd been separated for nine months, to give her the news; the day she let slip about her "friend"—Rick or Dick or Chick. Something like that. I decided that a man who couldn't make things go right could at least go. He could quit trying to get out of the way of life. Chuck routine. Live the real jeopardy of circumstance.

The result: on March 19, the last night of winter, I lay awake in a tangled bed and doubted the wisdom of just walking out on things; I doubted the whole plan that would begin at daybreak—to set out on a long (equivalent to half the circumference of the earth), circular trip over the back roads of the United States. Following a circle would give a purpose—to come around again—where taking a straight line would not. And I was going to do it by living out of the back end of a truck.

The vernal equinox came on gray and quiet, a curiously still morning neither winter nor spring, as if the cycle had paused. Because things go their own way, my daybreak departure turned into a morning departure, then to an afternoon departure. Finally, I climbed into the van, rolled down the window, looked a last time at the rented apartment.

I drove into the street, around the corner, through the intersection, over the bridge onto the highway. I was heading toward those little towns that get on the map—if they get on at all—only because some cartographer has a blank space to fill: Remote, Oregon; Simplicity, Virginia; New Freedom, Pennsylvania; New Hope, Tennessee; Why, Arizona; Whynot, Mississippi; Igo, California (just down the road from Ono), here I come.

MY FATHER CALLS HIMSELF HEAT MOON, my elder brother Little Heat Moon. I, coming last, am therefore Least. It has been a long lesson of a name to learn. To the Siouan peoples, the Moon of Heat is the seventh month, a time also known as the Blood Moon because, I think, of its dusky midsummer color. I have other names: Buck, once a slur—never mind the predominant Anglo features. Also Bill Trogdon. The Christian names come from a grandfather eight generations back, one William Trogdon, an immigrant Lancashireman living in North Carolina, who was killed by the Tories for providing food to rebel patriots and thereby got his name in volume four of *Makers of America*. Yet to the red way of thinking, a man who makes peace with the new by destroying the old is not to be honored. So I hear.

My wife, a woman of striking mixed-blood features, came from the Cherokee. Our battles, my Cherokee and I, we called the "Indian wars."

I named my truck Ghost Dancing, a heavy-handed symbol alluding to ceremonies of the 1890s in which the Plains Indians, wearing cloth shirts they believed rendered them indestructible, danced for the return of warriors, bison, and the fervor of the old life that would sweep away the new. Ghost dances, desperate resurrection rituals, were the dying battles of people whose last defense was delusion—about all that remained to them in their futility.

A final detail: On the morning of my departure, I had seen thirty-eight Blood Moons, an age that carries its own madness and futility. With a nearly desperate sense of isolation and a growing suspicion that I lived in an alien land, I took to the open road in search of places where change did not mean ruin and where time and men and deeds connected.

THE TUMULT OF ST. LOUIS BEHIND, the Illinois superwide quiet but for the rain, I turned south onto State 4, a shortcut to I-64. After that, the 42,500 miles of straight and wide could lead to hell for all I cared; I was going to stay on the 3 million miles of bent and narrow rural American two-lane, the roads that used to be shown in blue on highway maps to distinguish them from the main routes, in red.

Driving through the washed land in my small, self-propelled box—a "wheel estate," a mechanic had called it—I felt clean and almost disentangled. I had what I needed for now, much of it stowed under the wooden bunk:

1 sleeping bag and blanket;
1 Coleman cooler (empty but for a can of chopped liver a friend had given me so there would always be something to eat);
1 Rubbermaid basin and a plastic gallon jug (the sink);
1 Sears Roebuck portable toilet;
1 Optimus 8R white gas cookstove (hardly bigger than a can of beans);
1 knapsack of utensils, a pot, a skillet;
1 U.S. Navy seabag of clothes;
1 tool kit;
1 satchel full of notebooks, pens, road atlas, and a microcassette recorder;

2 Nikon F2 35mm cameras and five lenses;

2 vade mecums: Whitman's *Leaves of Grass* and Neihardt's *Black Elk Speaks.*

In my billfold were four gasoline credit cards and twenty-six dollars. Hidden under the dash were the remnants of my savings account: $428.

Ghost Dancing, a 1975 half-ton Econoline (the smallest van Ford makes), rode self-contained but not self-containing. So I hoped. It had two worn rear tires and an ominous knocking in the water pump. I had converted the van from a clangy tin box into a six-by-ten place at once a bedroom, kitchen, bathroom, parlor. Everything simple and light-weight: no crushed velvet upholstery, no wine racks, no built-in television. It came equipped with power nothing and drove like what it was—a truck. Your basic plumber's model.

THERE IS ONE ALMOST INFALLIBLE WAY to find honest food at just prices in blue-highway America: count the wall calendars in a café.

No calendar: Same as an interstate pit stop.

One calendar: Preprocessed food assembled in New Jersey.

Two calendars: Only if fish trophies are present.

Three calendars: Can't miss on the farmboy breakfasts.

Four calendars: Try the "ho-made" pie, too.

Five calendars: Keep it under your hat, or they'll franchise.

One time I found a six-calendar café in the Ozarks which served fried chicken, peach pie, and chocolate malts that left me searching for another one ever since. I've never seen a seven-calendar place. But old-time travelers—roadmen in a day when cars had running boards and lunchroom windows said AIR COOLED in blue letters with icicles dripping from the tops—those travelers have told me the golden legends of seven-calendar cafés.

To the rider of back roads, nothing shows the tone, the voice of a small town more quickly than the breakfast grill or the five-thirty tavern. Much of what the people do and believe and share is evident there. The City Café in Gainesboro, Tennessee, had three calendars that I could see from the walk. Inside were no interstate refugees with full bladders and empty tanks, no wild-eyed children just released from the glassy cell of a station wagon back seat, no long-haul truckers talking in CB numbers. There were only townspeople wearing overalls, or catalogue-order suits with five and dime ties, or uniforms. That is, there were farmers and mill hands, bank clerks, the dry-goods merchant, a policeman, and the chiropractor's receptionist. Because it was Saturday, there were also mothers and children.

I ordered my standard on-the-road breakfast: two eggs up, hash browns, tomato juice. The waitress, whose pale, almost translucent skin shifted hue in the gray light like a thin slice of mother-of-pearl, brought the food. Next to the eggs was a biscuit with a little yellow Smiley button stuck in it. She said, "You from the North?"

"I guess I am." A Missourian gets used to southerners thinking him a Yankee, a northerner considering him a cracker, a westerner sneering at his effete easternness, and an easterner taking him for a cowhand.

"So whata you doin' in the mountains?"

"Talking to people. Taking some pictures. Looking, mostly."

"Lookin' for what?"

"A three-calendar café that serves Smiley buttons on the biscuits."

"You needed a smile. Tell me really."

"I don't know. Actually, I'm looking for some jam to put on this biscuit, now you've brought one."

She came back with grape jelly. In a land of quince jelly, apple butter, apricot jam, blueberry preserves, pear conserves, and lemon marmalade, you always get grape jelly.

"Whata you lookin' for?"

Like anyone else, I'm embarrassed to eat in front of a watcher, particularly if I'm getting interviewed. "Why don't you have a cup of coffee?"

"Cain't right now. You gonna tell me?"

"I don't know how to describe it to you. Call it harmony."

She waited for something more. "Is that it?"

Someone called her to the kitchen. I had managed almost to finish by the time she came back. She sat on the edge of the booth. "I started out in life not likin' anything but then it grew on me. Maybe that'll happen to you." She watched me spread the jelly. "Saw your van." She watched me eat the biscuit. "You sleep in there?" I told her I did. "I'd love to do that, but I'd be scared spitless."

"I don't mind being scared spitless. Sometimes."

"I'd love to take off cross-country. I like to look at different license plates. But I'd take a dog. You carry a dog?"

"No dogs, no cats, no budgie birds. It's a one-man campaign to show Americans a person can travel alone, without a pet."

"Cain't travel without a dog!"

"I like to do things the hard way."

IN THE LAND OF "CO-COLA" it was hot and dry. Along Route 72, I tried not to look for a spring; I knew I wouldn't find one, but I kept looking. The Savannah River, dammed to an unnatural wideness, lay below, wet and cool. I'd come into Georgia. The sun seemed to press on the roadway, and inside the truck hot light bounced off chrome, flickering like a torch.

Sunset arrived west of Oglesby, and the air cooled. I hadn't eaten since morning. A road sign:

SWAMP GUINEA'S FISH LODGE
ALL YOU CAN EAT!

An arrow pointed down a country road. I would gorge myself. A record would be set. They'd ask me to leave. An embarrassment to all.

The road through the orange earth of north Georgia passed an old, three-story house with a thin black child hanging out of every window, like an illustration for "The Old Woman Who Lived in a Shoe," and on into hills and finally to Swamp Guinea's, a conglomerate of plywood and two-by-fours laid over with the smell of damp pine woods.

Inside, wherever an oddity or a natural phenomenon could hang, one hung: stuffed rump of a deer, snowshoe, flintlock, hornet's nest. The place looked as if a Boy Scout troop had decorated it. Thirty or so people, black and white, sat around tables that almost foundered under piled platters of food. I took a seat by the reproduction of a seventeenth-century woodcut depicting some Rabelaisian banquet at the groaning board.

The diners were mostly Oglethorpe County red-dirt farmers. In Georgia tones they talked about their husbandry in terms of rain and nitrogen and hope. An immense woman with a glossy picture of a hooked bass leaping on the front of her shirt said, "I'm gonna be sick from how much I've ate."

I was watching everyone else and didn't see the waitress standing quietly by. Her voice was deep and soft, like water moving in a cavern. I ordered the $4.50 special. In a few minutes she wheeled up a cart and began off-loading dinner: ham and eggs, fried catfish, fried perch fingerlings, fried shrimp, chunks of barbecued beef, fried chicken, French fries, hush puppies, a broad bowl of coleslaw, another of lemon, a quart of iced tea, and an entire loaf of factory-wrapped white bread. The table was covered.

"Call me if y'all want any more." She wasn't joking.

I quenched the thirst and then—slowly—went to the eating. I had to stand to reach plates across the table, but I intended to do the supper in. It was all southern-fried and good, except for the southern-style sweetened iced tea, and I even took care of a quart of that. As I ate, making up for meals lost, the Old Woman's house flashed before me, lightning in darkness. I had no moral right to eat so much. But I did.

The loaf of bread lay unopened when I finally abandoned the meal. At the register, I paid a man who looked as if he'd been chipped out of Georgia chert. The Swamp Guinea. I asked about the name. He spoke of himself in the third person, like the Wizard of Oz. "The Swamp Guinea only tells regulars."

"I'd be one, Mr. Guinea, if I didn't live in Missouri."

"Y'all from the North? Here, I got somethin' for you."

He went to the office and returned with a 45-rpm record. "It's my daughter singin'. A little promotion we did. Take it along." Later, I heard a throaty North Georgia voice let go a down-home, lyric rendering of Swamp Guinea's menu:

> "That's all you can eat
> For a dollar fifty
> Hey! The barbecue's nifty!"

And so on through the fried chicken and potatoes.

As I left, the Swamp Guinea, a former antique dealer whose name was Rudell Burroughs, said, "The nickname don't mean anything. Just made it up. Tried to figure a good one so we can franchise someday."

The frogs, high and low, shrilled and bellowed from the trees and ponds. It was cool going into Athens, a city suffering from a nasty case of the sprawls. On the University of Georgia campus, I tried to walk down Swamp Guinea's supper; everywhere couples were entwined like moonflower vines, each waiting for the blossom that opens only once.

WHAT DOES THE TRAVELER DO at night in a strange town when he wants conversation? In the United States, there's usually a single choice—a tavern.

The Oil City Bar, in Shelby, Montana, was north of the railroad tracks, near the spot where the Great Northern accidentally founded Shelby in 1891 by dumping off an old boxcar. From it the town grew, and the antecedents still showed.

One of the authors of the Montana Federal Writers' Project describes Shelby in the 1890s as the sort of town that producers of western movies have ever since been trying to reproduce in papier-mâché. . . . The town playboys were featured in the Police Gazette after holding up an opera troupe passing through on a railroad train. . . . They shot out the engine headlight, the car windows, and the red signal lights, and forced the conductor to execute a clog dance.

I was out looking around to see how the old Wild West was doing when I came across the Oil City Bar. Although the night had turned cold and gusty, only the screen door was closed; the wooden one stood open so men in down vests wouldn't overheat. A shattered pool cue lay in the corner, and to one side was a small room lighted only by the blue-neon flicker of a beer sign—the kind of light you could go mad in. Left of the ten-point buck trophy and above the gallon jars of pickled pigs' feet and hard-boiled eggs hung a big lithograph of a well-formed woman, shotgun in hand. She was duck hunting. Other than her rubber boots, she wore not a stitch.

A man somewhat taller than the barstool and dressed in yellow from shoulders to cowboy boots drank with assembly-line regularity. He leered wobbly-eyed at the huntress, tried to speak, but blew a bubble instead.

I blame what was about to happen to him on the traditional design of the American bar: a straight counter facing a mirrored wall, which forces the customer to stare at himself or put a crick in his neck looking at someone else. The English build their bars in circles or horseshoes or right angles—anything to get another face in your line of sight. Their bars, as a result, are more sociable. The American stares into his own face, or at bottles of golden liquors, or at whatever hangs above the bar; conversation declines and drinking increases. If the picture above the bar is a nude—as is common in old western bars—you have an iconography for creating unfulfilled desire: the reality of a man's own six o'clock face below the dream of perfect flesh.

I turned away from the huntress to watch a pool game. There was a loud *flump* beside me. Knees to his chest, the man in yellow lay dead drunk on the floor. He looked like a cheese curl. His friend said, "Chuckie's one good little drinker."

A woman of sharp face, pretty ten years ago, kept watching me. She had managed to pack her hips into what she hoped was a pair of mean jeans; a cigarette was never out of her mouth, and, after every deep draw, her exhalations were smokeless. She was trying for trouble, but I minded my own business. More or less. The man with her, Lonnie, walked up to me. He looked as if he were made out of whipcord. "Like that lady?" he said.

"What lady is that?"

"One you been staring at."

"Without my glasses, I can't distinguish a man from a woman." That was a lie.

"The lady said you were distinguishing her pretty good."

Some fading face trying to make herself the center of men's anger, proving she could still push men to their limits.

"Couldn't recognize her from here if I did know her."

He pressed up close. Trouble coming. "Don't tell me," he said. "Happens all the time. She thinks men stare at her."

"Look. No offense, but I've no interest in the woman."

"I can see it, and she can see it, and that's the trouble. But let's talk."

It was an act he had been coerced into. He was faking it. He called for two beers and set one in front of me. "Take it," he said. "When I sit down, I'm going to tell her you apologized for staring but you just thought she was one hell of a fox. Don't make a liar out of me."

He walked off. That was the silliest row I never got into.

I went to the restroom. When I came out, Lonnie was standing at the bar and the woman had gone to sit with three other women. She didn't buy it, I thought.

"Trouble?" I said.

"Forget it. She works with those broads. Castrating bitches every one."

There was a commotion that got loud and moved outside to the windy street. Two men from Mountain Bell, the phone company, were going to fight. They came at each other; locked outstretched arms, and pushed, circling slowly as if turned by the prairie wind. They tired and revolved more slowly, but neither let go or fell down. A police car drove up and honked. The fighters went to the squad car, both leaning on the window to listen. After a while, they slumped off in opposite directions, and that was the end of it.

Lonnie and I watched from the bar. After it was over, he said, "Jack Dempsey had a real fight here."

"A fight in this very bar?"

"Not a bar fight—heavyweight boxing. Shelby built a grandstand for it. Forty thousand seats. Seven thousand people showed up. Town almost went bust."

The woman came over to Lonnie and said, "Let's go." She was mad. I left soon after, walking out into the streets of the new Wild West.

AT THE HIGH-LINE TOWN of Culbertson, I turned north toward treeless Plentywood, Montana, then went east again, down forsaken blue Highway 5, a road virtually on the forty-ninth parallel, which is the Canadian border in North Dakota. In a small flourish of hills, the last I was to see for hundreds of miles, on an upthrust lump sat a cube of concrete with an Air Force radar antenna sweeping the long horizon for untoward blips. A Martello tower of the twentieth century. Below the installation, in the Ice Age land, lay a fine, clear lake. Fingerlings whisked the marsh weed, coots twittered on the surface, and at bankside a muskrat munched greens. It seemed as if I were standing between two worlds. But they were one: a few permutations of life going on about themselves, each thing trying to continue its way.

East of Fortuna, North Dakota, just eight miles south of Saskatchewan, the high-moraine wheat fields took up the whole landscape. There was nothing else, except piles of stones like Viking burial mounds at the verges of tracts and big rock-pickers running steely fingers through the glacial soil to glean stone that freezes had heaved to the surface; behind the machines, the fields looked vacuumed. At a filling station, a man who had long farmed the moraine said the great ice sheets had gone away only to get more rock. "They'll be back. They always come back. What's to stop them?"

The country gave up the glacial hills and flattened to perfection. The road went on, on, on. Straight and straight. Ahead and behind, it ran through me like an arrow. North Dakota up here was a curveless place—not just roads but land, people too, and the flight of birds. Things were angular: fenceposts against the sky, the line of a jaw, the ways of mind, the lay of crops.

The highway, oh, the highway. No place, in theory, is boring of itself. Boredom lies only with the traveler's limited perception and his failure to explore deeply enough. After a while, I found my perception limited. The Great Plains, showing so many miles in an immodest exposure of itself, wearied my eyes; the openness was overdrawn.

You'd think anything giving variety to the near blankness would be prized, yet when a Pleistocene pond got in the way, the road cut right through it, never yielding its straightness to nature. If you fired a rifle down the highway, a mile or so east you'd find the spent slug in the middle of the blacktop.

Here the earth, as if to prove its immensity, empties itself. Gertrude Stein said: "In the United States there is more space where nobody is than where anybody is. This is what makes America what it is."

Lake Wobegon Days

GARRISON KEILLOR || 1985

On assignment in 1973 to write an article for The New Yorker *about the Grand Ole Opry, Garrison Keillor (1942–) seized upon an inspired idea: to create a show that would conjure up the Golden Age of Radio. It would be a weekly variety program—a medley of comedy skits, playful monologues, and musical interludes—to be performed before a live audience every Saturday night back home in his native Minnesota, and broadcast on one of the local public radio stations there. On July 6 of the following year,* A Prairie Home Companion *went on the air for the first time, with Keillor as head writer and militantly laid-back master of ceremonies, sporting a baritone voice so soothing it suggested an oboe on Quaaludes. What began, in Keillor's words, "as something funny to do with my friends" evolved in less than a decade into a national institution, which today attracts a listening audience of more than four million a week across six hundred stations in the United States.*

The format of A Prairie Home Companion *has varied little over the years, providing its legion of loyalists with a dependable diet of parody commercial spots, country music, and sketch material punctuated by the occasional oversized sound effect. But the signature moment of the show—and its most enduringly popular feature—is the "News from Lake Wobegon," a twenty-minute monologue delivered, often extemporaneously, by Keillor, who chronicles the latest happenings in a mythical hamlet in central Minnesota that bears more than a passing resemblance to his own hometown of Anoka, just outside of Minneapolis.*

Keillor's radio reports on Lake Wobegon began with the very first show, but it was not until the publication of his collection of tales, Lake Wobegon Days *(1985), that his vision of the imaginary town became fully realized. In this excerpt from a section of the book that appeared originally in* The Atlantic, *we meet a gaggle of God-fearing inhabitants: the gas-pumping mayor, the showbiz preacher, the eavesdropping telephone operator, and a group of Norwegian bachelor farmers with bottled-up eccentricities and muted dreams.*

Since the hugely successful publication of Lake Wobegon Days, *Keillor has gone on to produce another twelve books and has continued to contribute stories regularly to* The Atlantic. *But the humorist's relationship with the magazine was not always a happy one. In 1966, as a young aspiring writer, he interviewed for a job as an Atlantic intern—*

and failed to make the grade. Keillor later recalled the rejection with a Wobegonian mix of barely concealed pride and unabashed self-mockery: "I think they could tell I was somebody who had just changed in a public restroom. I had a hangdog look about me. I looked a little stiff, too, because I had to keep my hand on my leg where I had spilled some Orange Julius two days before."

The town of Lake Wobegon, Minnesota, lies on the shore against Adams Hill, looking east across the blue-green water to the dark woods. From the south the highway aims for the lake, bends hard left by the magnificent concrete Grecian grain silos, and eases over a leg of the hill past the SLOW CHILDREN sign, bringing the traveler in on Main Street toward the town's one traffic light, which is almost always green. A few elms shade the street. Along the ragged dirt path between asphalt and grass a child walks to Ralph's Pretty Good Grocery, kicking an asphalt chunk ahead of him, which after four blocks he is now mesmerized by, to which he is completely dedicated. At Bunsen Motors the sidewalk begins. A breeze off the lake brings a sweet air of mud and rotting wood, a slight fishy smell, the sweetness of old grease, a sharp whiff of gasoline, fresh tires, spring dust, and, from across the street, the faint essence of tuna hot dish at the Chatterbox Cafe. A stout figure in green coveralls disappears inside. The boy kicks the chunk at the curb once, twice, then lofts it over the curb and sidewalk, across the concrete to the island of the Pure Oil pumps. He jumps three times on the Bunsen bell hose, making three dings back in the dark garage. The mayor of Lake Wobegon, Clint Bunsen, peers out from the deep pit, under a black Ford pickup. His brother, Clarence, wiping the showroom glass (BUNSEN MOTORS—FORD—NEW & USED—SALES & SERVICE) with an old blue shirt, knocks on the window. The showroom is empty. The boy follows the chunk a few doors north to Ralph's window, which displays two old cardboard placards, one of a cow, one of a pig, each labeled with the names of cuts. An old man sits on a bench, white hair as fine as spun glass poking out under his green feed cap, his grizzled chin on his skinny chest, dozing, the sun at three o'clock now reaching under the faded brown canvas awning up to his belt. He is not Ralph. Ralph is the thin man in the white apron who has stepped out the back door of the store, away from the meat counter, to get a breath of fresh, meatless air. He stands on a rickety porch that looks across the lake, a stone's throw away. The beach there is stony; the sandy beach is two blocks to the north. A girl, perhaps one of his, stands on the diving dock, plugs her nose, and executes a perfect cannonball, and he hears the dull *thunsh*. A quarter mile away a silver boat sits off the weeds in Sunfish Bay. A man in a bright blue jacket waves his pole; the line is hooked on weeds. The sun makes a trail of shimmering lights across the water. It would make quite a picture if you had the right lens, which no-body in this town has got.

The lake is 678.2 acres, a little more than a section, fed by cold springs and drained from the southeast by a creek, the Lake Wobegon River, which flows to the Sauk, which joins the Mississippi. In 1836 an Italian count waded up the creek, towing his canoe, and camped on the lakeshore, where he imagined for a moment that he was the hero who had found the true headwaters of the Mississippi. Then something about the place made him decide he was wrong. He was right—we're not the headwaters—but what made him jump to that conclusion? What has made so many others look at us and think, *It doesn't start here*?

The woods are red oak, maples, some spruce and pine, birch, alder, and thick brush except where cows have been put, which is like a park. The mu-nicipal boundaries take in quite a bit of pasture and cropland, including wheat, corn, oats, and alfalfa, and also the homes of some nine hundred souls, most of them small white frame houses sitting forward on their lots and boasting large, tidy vegetable gardens and modest lawns, many featur-ing cast-iron deer, small windmills, clothespoles and clotheslines, various plaster animals such as squirrels and lambs and small elephants, white-painted rocks at the end of the driveway, a nice bed of petunias planted within a white tire, and some with a shrine in the rock garden, the Blessed Virgin standing, demure, her eyes averted, arms slightly extended, above the peonies and marigolds. In the garden behind the nunnery next door to Our Lady of Perpetual Responsibility she stands on a brick pedestal and her eyes meet yours with an expression of deep sympathy for the sufferings of the world, including this little town.

It is a quiet town, where much of the day you could stand in the mid-dle of Main Street and not be in anyone's way—not forever, but for as long as a person would want to stand in the middle of the street. It's a wide street; the early Yankee promoters thought they would need it wide to han-dle the crush of traffic. The double white stripe is for show, as are the two parking meters. Two was all they could afford. They meant to buy more meters with the revenue, but nobody puts nickels in them because parking nearby is free. Parking is diagonal.

Merchants call it downtown, other people say "up town"—two words, as in "I'm going up town to get me some socks."

Most men wear their belts low here, there being so many outstanding bellies, some big enough to have names of their own and be formally introduced. Those men don't suck them in or hide them in loose shirts. They let them hang free, they pat them, they stroke them as they stand around and talk. How could a man be so vain as to ignore this old friend who's been with him at the great moments of his life?

The buildings are quite proud in their false fronts, trying to be everything that two stories can be and a little bit more. The first stories have newer fronts, of aluminum and fake marble and stucco and fiber-glass stonework, meant to make them modern. A child might have cut them off a cornflakes box and fastened them with two tabs, A and B. They go well with the ladies leaving the Chatterbox Cafe from their tuna-sandwich lunch: three old ladies with wispy white hair, in sensible black shoes and long print dresses with the waist up under the bosom, and the fourth in a deep purple pantsuit and purple pumps, wearing a jet-black wig. She, too, is seventy but looks like a thirty-four-year-old who has led a very hard life. She is Carl Krebsbach's mother, Myrtle, who they say enjoys two pink daiquiris every Friday night and between the first and the second hums "Tiptoe Through the Tulips" and does a turn that won her first prize in a Knights of Columbus talent show in 1936 at the Alhambra Ballroom. It burned to the ground in 1955. "Myrtle has natural talent, you know," people have always said, according to her. "She had a chance to go on to Minneapolis." Perhaps she is still considering the offer.

Her husband, Florian, pulls his '66 Chevy into a space between two pickups in front of the Clinic. To look at his car you'd think it was 1966 now, not 1985; it's so new, especially the back seat, which looks as if nobody ever sat there unless they were gift-wrapped. He is coming to see Dr. DeHaven about stomach pains that he thinks could be cancer, which he believes he has a tendency toward. Still, though he may be dying, he takes a minute to get a clean rag out of the trunk, soak it with gasoline, lift the hood, and wipe off the engine. He says she runs cooler when she's clean, and it's better if you don't let the dirt get baked on. Nineteen years old, she has only 42,000 miles on her, as he will tell you if you admire how new she looks. "Got her in '66. Just 42,000 miles on her." It's odd, maybe, that a man should be so proud of not having gone far, but not in this town. Under his Trojan Seed Corn cap, pulled down tight on his head, is the face of a boy, and when he talks his voice breaks, as if he hasn't talked enough to get over adolescence completely. Time hardly exists for Florian, who has lived one place all his life, and when he looks at this street and when he sees his wife, he sees them brand-new, like this car. Later, driving the four blocks home at about trolling speed, having forgotten the indignity of a rectal examination, he will notice a slight rhythmic imperfection when the car idles, which he will spend an hour happily correcting.

LAKE WOBEGON, WHATEVER ITS FAULTS, is not dreary. Back for a visit one August, I crossed Main Street toward Ralph's and stopped, hearing a sound from childhood in the distance. The faint mutter of ancient combines. Norwegian bachelor farmers combining in their antique McCormacks, the old six-footers. New combines cut a twenty-foot swath, but these guys aren't interested in getting done sooner; it would only mean a longer wait until bedtime. I stood and listened. My eyes got blurry. Of course, thanks to hay fever, wheat has always put me in an emotional state, and then the clatter brings back memories of old days of glory in the field, when I was a boy among giants. My uncle lifted me up and put me on the seat so I could ride alongside him. The harness jingled on Brownie and Pete and Queenie and Scout, and we bumped along in the racket, row by row. Now all the giants are gone; everyone's about my size or smaller. Few people could lift me up, and I don't know that I'm even interested. It's sad to be so old. I postponed it as long as I could, but when I weep at the sound of a combine, I know I'm there. A young man wouldn't have the background for it.

IN A TOWN WHERE EVERYONE was either Lutheran or Catholic, our family was not and never had been. We were Sanctified Brethren, a sect so tiny that nobody but us and God knew about it, so when kids asked what I was, I just said Protestant. It was too much to explain, like having six toes. You would rather keep your shoes on.

Grandpa Cotton was once tempted toward Lutheranism by a preacher who gave a rousing sermon on grace that Grandpa heard as a young man while taking Aunt Esther's dog home who had chased a Model T across town. He sat down on the church steps and listened to the voice boom out the open windows until he made up his mind to go in and unite with the truth, but he took one look from the vestibule and left. "He was dressed up like the Pope of Rome," said Grandpa, "and the altar and the paintings and the gold candlesticks—my gosh, it was just a big show. And he was reading the whole darn thing off a page, like an actor."

Jesus said, "Where two or three are gathered together in my name, there I am in the midst of them," and the Brethren believed that was enough. We met in Uncle Al and Aunt Flo's bare living room, with plain folding chairs arranged facing in toward the middle. No clergyman in a black smock. No organ or piano, for that would make one person too prominent. No upholstery—it would lead to complacence. No picture of Jesus—He was in our Hearts. The faithful sat down at the appointed hour and waited for the Spirit to move one of them to speak or to pray or to give out a hymn from our Little Flock hymnal. No musical notation, for music must come from the heart and not off a page. We sang the texts to a tune that fit the meter of the many tunes we all knew. The idea of reading a prayer was sacrilege to us—"If a man can't remember what he wants to say to God, let him sit down and think a little harder," Grandpa said.

"There's the Lord's Prayer," said Aunt Esther meekly. We were sitting on the porch after Sunday dinner. Esther and Harvey were visiting from Minneapolis and had attended Lake Wobegon Lutheran, she having turned Lutheran when she married him, a subject that was never brought up in our family.

"You call that prayer? Sitting and reciting like a bunch of school-children?"

Harvey cleared his throat and turned to me and smiled. "Speaking of school, how are you doing?" he asked.

There was a lovely silence in the Brethren assembled on Sunday morning as we waited for the Spirit. Either the Spirit was moving someone to speak who was taking his sweet time or else the Spirit was playing a wonderful joke on us and letting us sit, or perhaps silence was the point of it. We sat listening to rain on the roof, distant traffic, a radio playing from across the street, kids whizzing by on bikes, dogs barking, as we waited for the spirit to inspire us. It was like sitting on the porch with your family, when nobody feels that they have to make talk. So quiet in church. Minutes drifted by in silence that was sweet to us. The old Regulator clock ticked, the rain stopped, and the room changed light as the sun broke through—shafts of brilliant sun through the windows and motes of dust falling through it—the smell of clean clothes and floor wax and wine and the fresh bread of Aunt Flo, which was Christ's body given for us. Jesus in our midst, who loved us. So peaceful; and we loved each other, too. I thought perhaps the Spirit was leading me to say that, but I was just a boy, and children were supposed to keep still.

And my affections were not pure. They were tainted with a sneaking admiration of Catholics—Catholic Christmas, Easter, the Living Rosary, and the Blessing of the Animals, all magnificent. Everything we did was plain, but they were regal—especially the Feast Day of Saint Francis, which they did right out in the open, a feast for the eyes. Cows, horses, some pets, right on the church lawn. The turmoil, animals bellowing and barking and clucking and a cat scheming how to escape and suddenly leaping out of the girl's arms who was holding on tight, the cat dashing through the crowd, dogs straining at the leash, and the ocarina band of third graders playing a song, and the great calm of the sisters, and the flags, and the Knights of Columbus decked out in their handsome black suits—the whole thing was gorgeous. I stared at it until my eyes almost fell out, and then I wished it would go on much longer.

"Christians," my Uncle Al used to say, "do not go in for show," referring to the Catholics. We were sanctified by the blood of the Lord, therefore we were saints, like Saint Francis, but we didn't go in for feasts or ceremonies, involving animals or not. We went in for sitting, all nineteen of us, in Uncle Al and Aunt Flo's living room on Sunday morning and having a plain meeting and singing hymns in our poor thin voices, while not far away the Catholics were whooping it up. I wasn't allowed inside Our Lady, of course, but if the Blessing of the Animals on the Feast Day of Saint Francis was any indication, Lord, I didn't know but what they had elephants in there and acrobats. I sat in our little group and envied them for the splendor and gorgeousness, as we tried to sing without even so much as a harmonica to give us the pitch. Hymns, Uncle Al said, didn't have to be sung perfect, because God looks on the heart, and if you are In The Spirit, then all praise is good.

[ONE] SUNDAY WE DROVE TO ST. CLOUD for dinner and traipsed into a restaurant that a friend of Dad's had recommended, Phil's House of Good Food. The waitress pushed two tables together and we sat down and studied the menu. My mother blanched at the prices. A chicken dinner went for $2.50, the roast beef for $3.75. "It's a nice place," Dad said, multiplying the five of us times $2.50. "I'm not so hungry, I guess," he said. "Maybe I'll just have soup." We weren't restaurantgoers—"Why pay good money for food you could make better at home?" was Mother's philosophy—so we weren't at all sure about restaurant customs. For example, could a person who had been seated in a restaurant simply get up and walk out? Would it be proper? *Would it be legal?*

The waitress came and stood by Dad. "Can I get you something from the bar?" she said. Dad blushed a deep red. The question seemed to imply that he looked like a drinker.

"No," he whispered, as if he were turning down her offer to take off her clothes and dance on the table.

Then another waitress brought a tray of glasses to a table of four couples next to us. "Martini," she said, setting the drink down, "whiskey sour, whiskey sour, Manhattan, whiskey sour, gin and tonic, martini, whiskey sour."

"Ma'am? Something from the bar?" Mother looked at her in disbelief.

Suddenly the room changed for us. Our waitress looked hardened, rough, cheap; across the room a woman laughed obscenely, "Haw, haw, haw"; the man with her lit a cigarette and blew a cloud of smoke; a swearword drifted out from the kitchen like a whiff of urine; even the soft lighting seemed suggestive, diabolical. To be seen in such a place on the Lord's Day—*what had we done?*

"Ed," my mother said, rising.

"We can't stay. I'm sorry," Dad told the waitress. We all got up and put on our coats. Everyone in the restaurant had a good long look at us. A bald little man in a filthy white shirt emerged from the kitchen, wiping his hands. "Folks? Something wrong?" he said.

"We're in the wrong place," Mother told him. Mother always told the truth, or something close to it.

"This is *humiliating*," I said on the sidewalk. "I feel like a *leper* or something. Why do we always have to make such a big production out of everything? Why can't we be like regular people?"

She put her hand on my shoulder. "Be not conformed to this world," she said. I knew the rest by heart: ". . . but be ye transformed by the renewing of your mind, that ye may prove what is that good and acceptable and perfect will of God."

"Where we gonna eat?" Phyllis asked.

"We'll find someplace reasonable," said Mother, and we walked six blocks across the river and found a lunch counter and ate sloppy joes (called Maid-Rites) for fifteen cents apiece. They did not agree with us, and we were aware of them all afternoon through prayer meeting and Young People's.

MY GRANDFATHER WAS THE LEADING LIGHT of the Lake Wobegon Rural Telephone Cooperative, its first president, the man who signed up investors and walked the fencerows and dug holes for the posts. The first ones stood about eight feet tall, the wire hung on a bent nail. They had telephones in town long before, of course—the Ingqvist twins, who lived for innovation, had the first, a line to their mother's, in 1894—but it took my grandfather to convince the good country people that the phone was more than a toy. He was a tall, handsome, godly man, and so admired that when the preacher at his funeral chose the text "For all have sinned and come short of the glory of God," his neighbors considered it an insult. One cold day his chimney caught on fire and his house burned to the ground, and as he stood raking the coals in the cellar, he thought about telephones. He was not a man to take suffering as God's judgment if a remedy was close at hand. In 1921 he rebuilt the house (without a fireplace), organized the phone company, and drew up a contract between the township and the Lake Wobegon volunteer fire brigade. In the same year he bought a Model T, his first car, and gave an acre of pasture for a township cemetery.

The rural co-op merged with the town company in 1933, and a pupil in Grandpa's Sunday-school class who worshipped the ground he walked on has been running it from her pantry since 1942—Elizabeth, who was my Sunday-school teacher for many years. When she was a child, Grandpa took her along when he walked the phone line in the spring, checking for loose or leaning posts and also watching for hummingbirds and picking purple lilac blossoms and a toad or two. "He never went anywhere without a child in tow," she says. "He had seven of his own, but if those weren't available, he'd shop around until he found another. He might be driving to town for a bag of nails he wanted for roofing, but he still needed that child to ride with him—he'd come pull you out of school if he had to."

The pantry off her kitchen holds the old switchboard, still in good condition, and also the steel cabinet with the switching equipment that took over from it when they went to dial telephones in 1960, but she keeps on top of things just the same. If someone doesn't answer their phone by the fifth ring, she does, and usually she knows where they went and when they're expected, so many customers don't bother dialing in-town calls, they just dial o and she puts them through. If you do reach her instead of your party—say, your mother—she may clue you in on things your mom would never tell you, about your mom's bad back, a little fall on the steps the week before, or the approach of Mother's Day, or the fact that when you were born you were shown off like you were the Prince of Wales. A few customers accuse Elizabeth of listening in and claim they know the click that means she's there, but it isn't a click, it's an echoey sound, as if you and your party had moved into a bigger room. It's a wonder that she keeps track of us so faithfully, what with her age and arthritis and her great weight. She suffers from a glandular condition and is pushing three hundred pounds. Nowadays five rings is as quick as she can make it to the phone, even from her kitchen table.

When I talk to her, I don't always hear an old fat lady; sometimes I hear the girl who walked the line with Grandpa in the spring of '21. I am a person she bawls out on a regular basis, and when I call home and the phone rings and rings, I brace myself for her "Yes?" and "Oh. It's you" and "I don't know if I care to talk to you or not" and then the lecture. I have disappointed my friend so many times. I live far away, but news of my sins travels fast and she always finds out. She found out when I flunked out of college. And then when I got a divorce—the worst, in her book, and for almost a year afterward she cried on the phone when I called. Many times she has told me, "I just thank God that your grandfather is dead and not around to see you now." And yet, if I ask her about him, she is always ready to change the subject, a sort of forgiveness. I simply say, "Is it true that you used to go with him when he walked the phone line?" and she says, "You *know* I did. Heavens. I've told you that a hundred times," but she's willing to tell it once more, and then it's spring, the sweet song of the rosebreasted grosbeak drifts from the wood tinged with green across the young alfalfa, the bumblebees buzz, the toads sing in the ditch, my tall handsome grandfather with the sharp blue eyes and brush moustache ambles along the bank above the road looking for the first rhubarb, the little girl scrambling to keep up.

"To me, there wasn't a thing he didn't know. Every flower, every tree. Every living thing, he just cared about it all and he expected you to care, and so of course you did. He talked to you like you were smart and would want to know these things, what bird that is and, here, this is a jack-in-the-pulpit and—the *names* of things, that everything has a name. That isn't a 'bush' over there, those are *chokecherries*, birds eat them, we make jelly from them. I don't think that man was ever bored in his life unless he was sick in bed. After my father died of diphtheria, when I was five years old, I always looked on him as my father, and I used to stay up to his house with your aunts and uncles when my mother would go to Iowa to see her relatives, and once I remember—it was January and *bitter* cold—he woke up all us children in the middle of the night and told us to get dressed. Well, we did. We didn't ask any questions, we just got bundled up, and he led us out through the yard and up the path into the woods, eight children—your Aunt Flo was only four, I believe, and I helped carry her—*in the dark*, no lantern, mind you, just the moon, the coldest night of the year, and none of us was a bit afraid, because he was there. Not even when we came to the edge of the trees and looked up and there on the top of the hill was a wolf. He sat on the snowbank and looked at us. He was pure silver. He didn't move a muscle. In the moonlight he looked like a ghost. Your grandpa knelt down and put his arms around us and said, 'I want you to take a good look and remember this, because you may never see it again.' So we looked good. I can still remember it like I'm looking at it right now. I can see that wolf and I can feel his arm around me.'"

When I talk to her, I often feel I'm talking to my grandfather, who died before I was born, and I try not to hold back the truth, even when the news is so bad it almost breaks her heart. There is some dignity to this, though the truth is not easy. When her nephew Wesley was replacing some shingles on her roof, he put his foot on the main phone trunk line to steady himself and snapped it off and then figured if he didn't mention it, just tied the line to the gutter, maybe no one would notice, maybe it would get better on its own. So the phones were out for five hours, and when Bud found the break, Wesley said, "Oh, yeah, I saw that—I was sort of wondering what it was."

When I look at the lines I've busted, I don't sort of wonder about them, I know what I did, I know they didn't fall off the side of the house because they were tired. Still, it's not easy to say what you've done and not write up a better version.

I CAN SEE HOW I could write a bold account of myself as a passionate man who rose from humble beginnings to cut a wide swath in the world, whose crimes along the way might be written off to extravagance and love and art, and could even almost believe some of it myself on certain days after the sun went down if I'd had a snort or two and was in Los Angeles and it was February and I was twenty-four, but I find a truer account in the *Herald-Star*, where it says:

> Mr. Gary Keillor visited at the home of Al and Florence Crandall on Monday and after lunch returned to St. Paul where he is currently employed in the radio show business. Mr. Lew Powell also visited, who recently celebrated his ninety-third birthday and is enjoying excellent health. Almost twelve quarts of string beans were picked and some strawberries. Lunch was fried chicken with gravy and creamed peas.

The newspaper's correspondent on the scene was Aunt Flo herself, and the careful reader can see that she still dotes on her wayward nephew, pointing out his gainful and glamorous employment and suggesting that he is no slouch on a bean row either, giving a little plug for family longevity, and complimenting the guests with a good lunch. Aunt Flo does not make her famous fried chicken for any old shirttail relative who comes in off the road.

It's my first appearance in the paper in several years, and though it leaves out so much that one might want to add, about travels, awards, publications, it leaves out even more that one is glad not to see, about pride, gluttony, lust, and leaves me feeling better about home journalism. The story is accurate, as I read it, and everything is there: the sun beating down on us in the beanfield, the elderly gent sampling the berry crop, the goodness of creamed peas and of poultry allowed a free and happy life and then rolled in flour and pan-fried, the goodness of Uncle Al, who said, "You remind me so much of your grandfather." He was referring not to my life or character but to a similarity of mustache. A small compliment, and it pleased me for days afterward, and I read as much into it as I possibly could.

The Last Resort

CULLEN MURPHY || 1992

On the fifth floor of the converted loft building that served as The Atlantic Monthly's *last headquarters in Boston, there stood an imposing old bank of six-foot-high metal filing cabinets. For the most part, these cabinets had a strictly utilitarian purpose: to centralize the magazine's monthly flow of manuscripts and galleys and to safeguard legally sensitive fact-checking documents. But for many of* The Atlantic's *three dozen staff members, there was an aura of mystery and amused wonder about those faded pieces of office furniture, for they also happened to warehouse the voluminous and wildly eclectic research files of Cullen Murphy (1952–), the magazine's managing editor from 1985 to 2002 and, from 2002 to 2005, its de facto editor-in-chief. A chronic saver of journalistic and scholarly string, Murphy kept his files filled to overflowing with clippings, tear sheets, and scraps of recondite information that perfectly reflected the amplitude of his enthusiasms and erudition. A search of his archives might have typically unearthed not just an impressive collection of bits and pieces from the* New York Times, *the* Washington Post, *and the* Economist, *but also a vast array of curios, such as the Centers for Disease Control's weekly report "Morbidity and Mortality," a British historian's article entitled "Pulling Teeth in Eighteenth-Century Paris," and a story from the* National Enquirer *bearing the headline* PREACHER EXPLODES DURING SERMON: THE MOST BIZARRE CASE OF SPONTANEOUS COMBUSTION EVER!

Yet it would be a mistake to dismiss Murphy's voracious research operation as simply the fetishistic foraging of a compulsive collector. The stockpiling had a nobler aim: each factoid, random quote, and stray snippet of data became potential fodder, even a potential launch pad, for the idiosyncratic, delicately droll column that Murphy penned for The Atlantic *for two decades. Beginning around the time of his arrival in the mid-1980s and appearing, for the last six years of his tenure, under the rubric "Innocent Bystander," Murphy's columns constituted a regular tongue-in-cheek exercise in connecting the micro to the macro. From month to month, he assayed the cultural significance of such diverse developments as the changing contents of the school lunch box, the movement afoot to eliminate the penny, the growing wave of nostalgia in America for all things medieval, and the not-altogether-successful efforts of Enron managers to destroy incriminating evidence. Often the columns proposed a highly satisfying comedic solution to a knotty present-day problem. In "The Last Resort," Murphy, who is now the editor-at-large of Vanity Fair, wonders what the world ought to do about its oversupply of deposed dictators—and offers a mischievously novel remedy.*

When Erich Honecker, seventy-nine, the former East German Communist leader, was spirited out of Germany in March of last year and smuggled into the Soviet Union, he may have believed that his troubles were over. In Germany, Honecker was facing manslaughter charges in connection with a standing "shoot-to-kill" order he issued many years ago, under which East German border guards were authorized to kill East Germans trying to flee to the West. Seeing Honecker's predicament, the Soviet Union, which had long been a friend to East Germany, did the fraternal thing. It took Honecker in.

And then, abruptly, the Soviet Union ceased to exist. Honecker suddenly found himself under the jurisdiction of the newly independent Russian Federation, which last December responded favorably to a request by Germany, Russia's banker, for Honecker's extradition. Honecker fled to the Chilean embassy—the ambassador was an old friend—and began casting about for a country where he could settle permanently (provided that he could get safe passage out of Russia). Honecker and his wife, Margot, eventually came to realize that the countries willing to give them permanent asylum were only three: Chile, North Korea, and Cuba.

This is but the most recent episode in a long-running series in which discarded rulers of oppressive states have sought to grope their way to a globally sanctioned limbo. It is a sorry spectacle whenever it occurs, and deeply bothersome for somewhat contradictory reasons. First, on the level of principle, the fact that leaders on the lam manage to find safe haven at all means that they have eluded the clutches of justice. Second, as pragmatic observers have frequently pointed out, the fact that finding safe haven can prove difficult or impossible sometimes keeps autocrats clinging to their jobs longer than they otherwise might. Beyond those considerations is the fact that these people and their families seldom just go away. The Marcoses, the Duvaliers, the Amins, the Somozas—they make news for the rest of their lives, often while living in galling comfort and continuing to involve themselves unhelpfully in events back home.

This state of affairs is untidy, unsatisfying, and inefficient, and each frenzied new departure of an odious head of government prompts editorialists to throw up their hands and wonder if there must not be some better way. A few years ago, at a time when Panama's recent ruler, Manuel Noriega, was clinging desperately to sanctuary in the local Vatican embassy, *The Economist* suggested that perhaps the solution was to put people like Noriega and Romania's Nicolae Ceausescu "all together in a remote spot" where they could pass their days comfortably under United Nations supervision. This idea owes much to Viscount Castlereagh, who in 1815 oversaw Napoleon's successful dispatch to the island of Saint Helena, in the South Atlantic, and it has always had much to recommend it. But no concrete steps in that direction have yet been taken, perhaps for lack of firm answers to some fundamental questions. Where in the modern world, precisely, should that "remote spot" be? Should we not try to strike a balance between pragmatism and justice: offering refuge with the one hand, yes, but exacting retribution with the other? And if so, by what means can this be accomplished?

HAPPILY, THE ANSWER TO THE FIRST of these questions may have just come, inadvertently, from Fidel Castro, who has reason of late to be thinking about such things. According to an article by Benito Alonso Artigas in a recent issue of the Cuban émigré newspaper *Diario Las Américas*, which was brought to my attention by a friend, "The criminals Fidel and Raúl Castro Ruz have tried to rent, buy, or receive a grant of the Island of Socotra, in the Indian Ocean." The intention, apparently, is to secure a place of asylum in the event that life in Havana becomes untenable. Socotra is a windswept island of temperate clime that lies in shark-infested waters midway between the Horn of Africa and the Arabian Peninsula. It is mountainous, has only a small airstrip to which there are no scheduled flights, and is inaccessible to shipping during the monsoon season. It is sparsely inhabited—cattle outnumber people—and is known in the region mostly for its superior ghee, which is a kind of clarified butter. Socotra is owned by Yemen, and if Yemen is seriously interested in selling, the new Secretary-General of the United Nations, Boutros Boutros Ghali, should as one of his first official acts arrange for the UN to outbid Cuba, acquire the island, and turn part of it into a permanent homeland for deposed or weary despots. It could perhaps be known as The Last Resort.

Here is the lure: Tyrants could check in at The Last Resort at any time in their careers, and could bring with them as much money as they wished, no questions asked. Their persons and their fortunes would be off limits to law-enforcement agencies. The accommodations at their disposal, for which they would pay a high monthly rent, would be luxurious, and the management would make available various basic services, including a modern hospital and modern communications. Neither journalists nor tourists would be permitted on the island. The United Nations would widely publicize all these features of life on Socotra, and would guarantee the world community's acquiescence (however grudging) in the basic arrangement. All in all, Socotra would probably be seen by many of its potential guests as an attractive proposition—the option of first choice in the event of job-threatening hostilities at home.

So much for the enticements. It remains to be noted that certain features of life on Socotra—the fine print, as it were—would not be widely publicized. Indeed, many of these features would become apparent only as time unfolded. To begin with, having arrived on Socotra, the former heads of government would never be allowed to leave. (Accompanying staff and family members, on the other hand, would be free to leave, even encouraged to do so—but never permitted to return.) There is also the matter of the help. None of the natives currently living on Socotra can offer quite the right background for employment at The Last Resort, except maybe in the ghee shop, so labor would have to be imported. Because Socotra would be a United Nations operation, it would make sense to award various functions to selected member states. This could be done by bearing in mind the old joke about which nationalities will be doing what in heaven and in hell. The medical-care system, for example, might appropriately be run by the Russians, and the telephone system by the Irish (though the Mexicans could be asked to make the wake-up calls). All the servants at The Last Resort should be French. Complaints could be handled by bureaucrats seconded from Italian government ministries. The lifeguards would be Mongolian, the sommeliers Iranian, the meter maids from Singapore. Robert J. Lurtsema would control the public-address system.

It would be natural to have the English run the kitchens, but responsibility for the cooking might in fact be handled a little differently. One promising suggestion is that each newly arrived fugitive would get to have his cooks prepare all the meals at The Last Resort until the next fugitive arrived. Thus, if Mengistu Haile Mariam were to show up, the cuisine would suddenly become Ethiopian. Some time later, with the arrival of, say, Jerry Rawlings, it would become Ghanaian. The advent of the occasional alleged anthropophagite, like Jean-Bédel Bokassa, would be a culinary event. If nothing else, such a regime in the kitchen would ensure rapt attention on Socotra to news of the latest coup. The English could be compensated for the loss of the menu by being given charge of the staff's trade union.

There would have to be a bank. In one of his books, *The Getaway*, the novelist Jim Thompson imagined a bank owned by a man known as El Rey, who operates a community in Mexico where criminals in hiding can safely run to ground with their assets.

> The bank makes no loans, of course. Who would it make them to? So the only available source of revenue is interest, paid by the depositor rather than to him. On balances of one hundred thousand dollars or more, the rate is six percent; but on lesser sums it rises sharply, reaching a murderous twenty-five percent on amounts of fifty thousand and under.

Thompson's novel was published in 1958, and the dollar amounts will thus seem quaint. But the overall way of doing business would be appropriate for the Bank of Socotra. All profits would accrue to the UN High Commissioner for Refugees.

As long as the guests at The Last Resort had money, they could spend as much of it as they pleased on imports, through a UN facility to be established in Hadibu, Socotra's one harbor, and operated jointly by Lebanese accountants and the Port Authority of New York and New Jersey. However, one friend suggests the following stipulation: the money could be spent only on items native to or manufactured in a guest's country of origin. The stipulation would apply to everything: furniture, electronics, clothing, art, literature, television programs. One result would be a much-needed influx of capital from Socotra into some very poor economies. Guests on Socotra would also no doubt start praying fervently for the rapid modernization of their native lands.

What would happen when one or more residents of The Last Resort ran out of money, as the procedures of the Bank of Socotra virtually guarantee? Obviously, these people would have to find work. The local economy has little to offer, save for the job of tending the island's 20,000 distinctive humpless kine. Perhaps a pattern would evolve whereby impoverished longtime residents would become the indentured servants of still-wealthy recent arrivals. Thus, for example, Idi Amin might wind up in the employ of a newly arrived Saddam Hussein—his cooks, after all, would be needing an extra sous chef or two for a while—who in turn might one day labor in the service of a Mobutu Sese Seko or, God forbid, a Hafez al-Assad. Upon a guest's death, any funds remaining in his account would revert to the United Nations.

TO BE SURE, SEVERAL OPERATIONAL MATTERS concerning The Last Resort remain to be worked out. The day-to-day social dynamics of the establishment would almost certainly be problematic, deriving as they must from its peculiar demographics. There would be feuds, a black market, occasional bloodshed. The world, perhaps, can live with all that. On the whole, the advantages of the proposed arrangement, or some variant on it, seem clear. There is no reason, moreover, why its benefits could not one day be extended to cover international terrorists and rapacious multinational executives. And tinkering will surely introduce further refinements. Did I mention that the lingua franca of The Last Resort would be Sanskrit? That is the language from which the name Socotra derives. It means "island abode of bliss."

Lamentations of the Father

IAN FRAZIER || 1997

To research his 1994 book Family, *a personal history of his Protestant forebears in the American Midwest, Ian Frazier (1951–) steeped himself in the literature of his ancestral faith, studying not only the Old and New Testaments but also nineteenth-century frontier sermons and theological commentaries on the state of Christian grace. In the process, the author and humorist worked up a special enthusiasm for* Leviticus, *which he still believes is "the funniest book in the Bible." What appealed most to Frazier's comic sensibilities was* Leviticus's *predilection for laying down labyrinthine dietary regulations for the Israelites to follow (Example: "All teeming winged creatures that go on four legs shall be vermin to you, except those which have legs jointed above their feet for leaping on the ground")—all divinely directed ("I am the Lord Thy God"). At the time of Frazier's immersion in biblical lore and laws, he and his wife were also raising two children, Cora and Thomas, who had entered a tempestuous stage of behavioral development, particularly at the kitchen table. Over the course of countless interrupted meals and many frustrated attempts to restore order, Frazier came to realize that his incessant paternal law-giving ("Eat your vegetables before you have any dessert!") and his justifications for those laws ("Because I'm your father!") bore a striking resemblance to those promulgated in the Old Testament. Indeed, after being driven around the bend one too many times by the unremitting disobedience of his dependents, he began to feel a certain empathy with the Lord.*

The upshot of these associations is a comedic tour de force—a pitch-perfect application of the fire-and-brimstone injunctions of the Pentateuch to the mundane travails of middle-class parenting—and, by any measure, one of the most popular pieces that The Atlantic *has ever published. Frazier's short essay, which originally appeared under the title "Laws Concerning Food and Drink; Household Principles; Lamentations of the Father," caused such a sensation that the author had no end of difficulty trying to protect its copyright. In the months after the piece ran in* The Atlantic, *"Lamentations of the Father," as it became more succinctly known, circulated ceaselessly in e-mails and around the Internet, always without permission and often without attribution. One newspaper,* The Fort Worth Star-Telegram, *published a version that had been stripped of its byline, truncated, and renamed "Thus Mom Spake." (Frazier, who still writes on a typewriter and refuses to own a cell phone or use e-mail ["not even at gunpoint"], learned of these appropriations through phone calls from friends and colleagues.) The humorist himself has since taken the lead in getting the piece out to the widest possible readership. He has read it aloud before a live audience on Garrison Keillor's* A Prairie Home Companion, *authorized its publication as a compact, illustrated gift book, and will showcase it as the title piece of his third collection of humor, which will be published in the spring of 2008.*

Of the beasts of the field, and of the fishes of the sea, and of all foods that are acceptable in my sight you may eat, but not in the living room. Of the hoofed animals, broiled or ground into burgers, you may eat, but not in the living room. Of the cloven-hoofed animal, plain or with cheese, you may eat, but not in the living room. Of the cereal grains, of the corn and of the wheat and of the oats, and of all the cereals that are of bright color and un-known provenance you may eat, but not in the living room. Of the quies-cently frozen dessert and of all frozen after-meal treats you may eat, but absolutely not in the living room. Of the juices and other beverages, yes, even of those in sippy-cups, you may drink, but not in the living room, nei-ther may you carry such therein. Indeed, when you reach the place where the living room carpet begins, of any food or beverage there you may not eat, neither may you drink.

But if you are sick, and are lying down and watching something, then may you eat in the living room.

LAWS WHEN AT TABLE

And if you are seated in your high chair, or in a chair such as a greater per-son might use, keep your legs and feet below you as they were. Neither raise up your knees, nor place your feet upon the table, for that is an abomina-tion to me. Yes, even when you have an interesting bandage to show, your feet upon the table are an abomination, and worthy of rebuke. Drink your milk as it is given you, neither use on it any utensils, nor fork, nor knife, nor spoon, for that is not what they are for; if you will dip your blocks in the milk, and lick it off, you will be sent away. When you have drunk, let the empty cup then remain upon the table, and do not bite it upon its edge and by your teeth hold it to your face in order to make noises in it sound-ing like a duck; for you will be sent away.

When you chew your food, keep your mouth closed until you have swallowed, and do not open it to show your brother or your sister what is within; I say to you, do not do so, even if your brother or your sister has done the same to you. Eat your food only; do not eat that which is not food; neither seize the table between your jaws, nor use the raiment of the table to wipe your lips. I say again to you, do not touch it, but leave it as it is. And though your stick of carrot does indeed resemble a marker, draw not with it upon the table, even in pretend, for we do not do that, that is why. And though the pieces of broccoli are very like small trees, do not stand them upright to make a forest, because we do not do that, that is why. Sit just as I have told you, and do not lean to one side or the other, nor slide down until you are nearly slid away. Heed me; for if you sit like that, your hair will go into the syrup. And now behold, even as I have said, it has come to pass.

Laws Pertaining to Dessert

For we judge between the plate that is unclean and the plate that is clean, saying first, if the plate is clean, then you shall have dessert. But of the unclean plate, the laws are these: If you have eaten most of your meat, and two bites of your peas with each bite consisting of not less than three peas each, or in total six peas, eaten where I can see, and you have also eaten enough of your potatoes to fill two forks, both forkfuls eaten where I can see, then you shall have dessert. But if you eat a lesser number of peas, and yet you eat the potatoes, still you shall not have dessert; and if you eat the peas, yet leave the potatoes uneaten, you shall not have dessert, no, not even a small portion thereof. And if you try to deceive by moving the potatoes or peas around with a fork, that it may appear you have eaten what you have not, you will fall into iniquity. And I will know, and you shall have no dessert.

On Screaming

Do not scream; for it is as if you scream all the time. If you are given a plate on which two foods you do not wish to touch each other are touching each other, your voice rises up even to the ceiling, while you point to the offense with the finger of your right hand; but I say to you, scream not, only remonstrate gently with the server, that the server may correct the fault. Likewise if you receive a portion of fish from which every piece of herbal seasoning has not been scraped off, and the herbal seasoning is loathsome to you, and steeped in vileness, again I say, refrain from screaming. Though the vileness overwhelm you, and cause you a faint unto death, make not that sound from within your throat, neither cover your face, nor press your fingers to your nose. For even now I have made the fish as it should be; behold, I eat of it myself, yet do not die.

Concerning Face and Hands

Cast your countenance upward to the light, and lift your eyes to the hills, that I may more easily wash you off. For the stains are upon you; even to the very back of your head, there is rice thereon. And in the breast pocket of your garment, and upon the tie of your shoe, rice and other fragments are distributed in a manner wonderful to see. Only hold yourself still; hold still, I say. Give each finger in its turn for my examination thereof, and also each thumb. Lo, how iniquitous they appear. What I do is as it must be; and you shall not go hence until I have done.

Various Other Laws, Statutes, and Ordinances

Bite not, lest you be cast into quiet time. Neither drink of your own bath water, nor of bath water of any kind; nor rub your feet on bread, even if it be in the package; nor rub yourself against cars, nor against any building; nor eat sand.

Leave the cat alone, for what has the cat done, that you should so afflict it with tape? And hum not that humming in your nose as I read, nor stand between the light and the book. Indeed, you will drive me to madness. Nor forget what I said about the tape.

Complaints and Lamentations

O my children, you are disobedient. For when I tell you what you must do, you argue and dispute hotly even to the littlest detail; and when I do not accede, you cry out, and hit and kick. Yes, and even sometimes do you spit, and shout "stupid-head" and other blasphemies, and hit and kick the wall and the molding thereof when you are sent to the corner. And though the law teaches that no one shall be sent to the corner for more minutes than he has years of age, yet I would leave you there all day, so mighty am I in anger. But upon being sent to the corner you ask straightaway, "Can I come out?" and I reply, "No, you may not come out." And again you ask, and again I give the same reply. But when you ask again a third time, then you may come out.

Hear me, O my children, for the bills they kill me. I pay and pay again, even to the twelfth time in a year, and yet again they mount higher than before. For our health, that we may be covered, I give six hundred and twenty talents twelve times in a year; but even this covers not the fifteen hundred deductible for each member of the family within a calendar year. And yet for ordinary visits we still are not covered, nor for many medicines, nor for the teeth within our mouths. Guess not at what rage is in my mind, for surely you cannot know.

For I will come to you at the first of the month and at the fifteenth of the month with the bills and a great whining and moan. And when the month of taxes comes, I will decry the wrong and unfairness of it, and mourn with wine and ashtrays, and rend my receipts. And you shall remember that I am that I am: before, after, and until you are twenty-one. Hear me then, and avoid me in my wrath, O children of me.

THE AMERICAN IDEA

The Words That Remade America

GARRY WILLS || 1992

On July 1, 1863, the forces of the Union general George G. Meade and of the Confederate general Robert E. Lee squared off across a twenty-five-square-mile swath of rolling hills in southeastern Pennsylvania for what would be the bloodiest and most famous encounter of the Civil War. By the time the Battle of Gettysburg came to an end, after three consecutive days of fierce and unrelenting combat, Lee's rebel army was broken and in retreat, and tens of thousands of dead and wounded soldiers from both sides blanketed the killing fields, the corpses rotting in the summer heat.

"The Words That Remade America," by the prolific journalist, historian, and critic Garry Wills (1934–), is the remarkable account—part historical investigation, part literary exegesis—of how President Abraham Lincoln transformed this scene of apocalyptic horror into one of the defining moments in United States history. Lincoln was able to work this magic, marvels Wills, by virtue of a single speech that was so disarmingly modest in scope and devoid of pretension that it consisted of a mere ten sentences (a total of 272 words) and took only about three minutes to deliver. "The power of words has rarely been given a more compelling demonstration," writes Wills.

Countering claims that Lincoln, while en route to the November 19 ceremony consecrating Gettysburg as a national cemetery, had hurriedly scrawled his remarks on the back of an envelope, Wills contends that, in fact, the president had been thinking about the speech for months; he had discerned an urgent need to make a bold and uplifting statement to the American people on the subject of the war—to explain its larger significance, to justify its enormous costs, and to demonstrate that the future of American democracy was at stake. For Wills, Lincoln's great achievement at Gettysburg that day was nothing less than reinventing the Constitution, repairing its fatal flaw—a tacit acceptance of slavery—by infusing the document with the aggressively egalitarian precepts of the Declaration of Independence. "The crowd departed with a new thing in its ideological luggage, the new Constitution Lincoln had substituted for the one they had brought there with them," Wills writes in his essay, adapted by The Atlantic *from his book* Lincoln at Gettysburg *(1992), which later won the Pulitzer Prize for general nonfiction. "They walked off from those curving graves on the hillside, under a changed sky, into a different America."*

In the aftermath of the Battle of Gettysburg, both sides, leaving fifty thousand dead or wounded or missing behind them, had reason to maintain a large pattern of pretense—Lee pretending that he was not taking back to the South a broken cause, Meade that he would not let the broken pieces fall through his fingers. It would have been hard to predict that Gettysburg, out of all this muddle, these missed chances, all the senseless deaths, would become a symbol of national purpose, pride, and ideals. Abraham Lincoln transformed the ugly reality into something rich and strange—and he did it with 272 words. The power of words has rarely been given a more compelling demonstration.

The residents of Gettysburg had little reason to be satisfied with the war machine that had churned up their lives. General George Gordon Meade may have pursued General Robert E. Lee in slow motion, but he wired headquarters that "I cannot delay to pick up the debris of the battlefield." That debris was mainly a matter of rotting horseflesh and manflesh—thousands of fermenting bodies, with gas-distended bellies, deliquescing in the July heat. For hygienic reasons, the five thousand horses and mules had to be consumed by fire, trading the smell of decaying flesh for that of burning flesh. Human bodies were scattered over, or (barely) under, the ground. Suffocating teams of Union soldiers, Confederate prisoners, and dragooned civilians slid the bodies beneath a minimal covering as fast as possible—crudely posting the names of the Union dead with sketchy information on boards, not stopping to figure out what units the Confederate bodies had belonged to. It was work to be done hugger-mugger or not at all, fighting clustered bluebottle flies black on the earth, shoveling and retching by turns.

The whole area of Gettysburg—a town of only twenty-five hundred inhabitants—was one makeshift burial ground, fetid and steaming. Andrew Curtin, the Republican governor of Pennsylvania, was facing a difficult reelection campaign. He must placate local feeling, deal with other states diplomatically, and raise the funds to cope with corpses that could go on killing by means of fouled streams or contaminating exhumations.

Curtin made the thirty-two-year-old David Wills, a Gettysburg lawyer, his agent on the scene. Wills (who is no relation to the author) had studied law with Gettysburg's most prominent former citizen, Thaddeus Stevens, the radical Republican now representing Lancaster in Congress. Wills was a civic leader, and he owned the largest house on the town square. He put an end to land speculation for the burial ground and formed an interstate commission to collect funds for the cleansing of Gettysburg's bloodied fields. The states were to be assessed according to their representation in Congress. To charge them by the actual number of each state's dead would have been a time-consuming and complicated process, waiting on identification of each corpse, on the division of costs for those who could not be identified, and on the fixing of per-body rates for exhumation, identification, and reinterment.

Wills put up for bids the contract to rebury the bodies; out of thirty-four bids, the high one was eight dollars per corpse and the winning one was $1.59. The federal government was asked to ship in the thousands of caskets needed, courtesy of the War Department. All other costs were handled by the interstate commission. Wills took title to seventeen acres for the new cemetery in the name of Pennsylvania.

Wills meant to dedicate the ground that would hold the corpses even before they were moved. He felt the need for artful words to sweeten the poisoned air of Gettysburg. He asked the principal wordsmiths of his time to join this effort—Longfellow, Whittier, Bryant. All three poets, each for his own reason, found their muse unbiddable. But Wills was not terribly disappointed. The normal purgative for such occasions was a large-scale, solemn act of oratory, a kind of performance art that had great power over audiences in the middle of the nineteenth century. Some later accounts would emphasize the length of the main speech at the Gettysburg dedication, as if that were an ordeal or an imposition on the audience. But a talk of several hours was customary and expected then—much like the length and pacing of a modern rock concert. The crowds that heard Lincoln debate Stephen Douglas in 1858, through three-hour engagements, were delighted to hear Daniel Webster and other orators of the day recite carefully composed paragraphs for two hours at the least.

The champion at such declamatory occasions, after the death of Daniel Webster, was Webster's friend Edward Everett. Everett was that rare thing, a scholar and an Ivy League diplomat who could hold mass audiences in thrall. His voice, diction, and gestures were successfully dramatic, and he habitually performed his well-crafted text, no matter how long, from memory. Everett was the inevitable choice for Wills, the indispensable component in the scheme for the cemetery's consecration. Battlefields were something of a specialty with Everett—he had augmented the fame of Lexington and Concord and Bunker Hill by his oratory at those Revolutionary sites. Simply to have him speak at Gettysburg would add this field to the sacred roll of names from the Founders' battles.

Everett was invited, on September 23, to appear October 23. That would leave all of November for filling the graves. But a month was not sufficient time for Everett to make his customary preparation for a major speech. He did careful research on the battles he was commemorating—a task made difficult in this case by the fact that official accounts of the engagement were just appearing. Everett would have to make his own inquiries. He could not be ready before November 19. Wills seized on that earliest moment, though it broke with the reburial schedule that had been laid out to follow on the October dedication. He decided to move up the reburial, beginning it in October and hoping to finish by November 19.

The careful negotiations with Everett form a contrast, more surprising to us than to contemporaries, with the casual invitation to President Lincoln, issued some time later as part of a general call for the federal Cabinet and other celebrities to join in what was essentially a ceremony of the participating states.

No insult was intended. Federal responsibility for or participation in state activities was not assumed then. And Lincoln took no offense. Though specifically invited to deliver only "a few appropriate remarks" to open the cemetery, he meant to use this opportunity. The partly mythical victory of Gettysburg was an element of his Administration's war propaganda. (There were, even then, few enough victories to boast of.) Beyond that, he was working to unite the rival Republican factions of Governor Curtin and Simon Cameron, Edwin Stanton's predecessor as Secretary of War. He knew that most of the state governors would be attending or sending important aides—his own bodyguard, Ward Lamon, who was acting as chief marshal organizing the affair, would have alerted him to the scale the event had assumed, with a tremendous crowd expected. This was a classic situation for political fence-mending and intelligence-gathering. Lincoln would take with him aides who would circulate and bring back their findings; Lamon himself had a cluster of friends in Pennsylvania politics, including some close to Curtin, who had been infuriated when Lincoln overrode his opposition to Cameron's Cabinet appointment.

Lincoln also knew the power of his rhetoric to define war aims. He was seeking occasions to use his words outside the normal round of proclamations and reports to Congress. His determination not only to be present but to speak is seen in the way he overrode staff scheduling for the trip to Gettysburg. Stanton had arranged for a 6:00 A.M. train to take him the hundred and twenty rail miles to the noontime affair. But Lincoln was familiar enough by now with military movement to appreciate what Clausewitz called "friction" in the disposal of forces—the margin for error that must always be built into planning. Lamon would have informed Lincoln about the potential for muddle on the nineteenth. State delegations, civic organizations, military bands and units, were planning to come by train and road, bringing at least ten thousand people to a town with poor resources for feeding and sheltering crowds (especially if the weather turned bad). So Lincoln countermanded Stanton's plan:

> I do not like this arrangement. I do not wish to so go that by the slightest accident we fail entirely, and, at the best, the whole to be a mere breathless running of the gauntlet. . . .

If Lincoln had not changed the schedule, he would very likely not have given his talk. Even on the day before, his trip to Gettysburg took six hours, with transfers in Baltimore and at Hanover Junction. Governor Curtin, starting from Harrisburg (thirty miles away) with six other governors as his guests, was embarrassed by breakdowns and delays that made them miss dinner at David Wills's house. They had gathered at 2:00 P.M., started at five, and arrived at eleven. Senator Alexander Ramsey, of Minnesota, was stranded, at 4:00 A.M. on the day of delivery, in Hanover Junction, with "no means of getting up to Gettysburg." Lincoln kept his resolution to leave a day early even when he realized that his wife was hysterical over one son's illness soon after the death of another son. The President had important business in Gettysburg.

FOR A MAN SO DETERMINED TO GET THERE, Lincoln seems—in familiar accounts—to have been rather cavalier about preparing what he would say in Gettysburg. The silly but persistent myth is that he jotted his brief remarks on the back of an envelope. (Many details of the day are in fact still disputed, and no definitive account exists.) Better-attested reports have him considering them on the way to a photographer's shop in Washington, writing them on a piece of cardboard as the train took him on the hundred-and-twenty-mile trip, penciling them in David Wills's house on the night before the dedication, writing them in that house on the morning of the day he had to deliver them, and even composing them in his head as Everett spoke, before Lincoln rose to follow him.

These recollections, recorded at various times after the speech had been given and won fame, reflect two concerns on the part of those speaking them. They reveal an understandable pride in participation at the historic occasion. It was not enough for those who treasured their day at Gettysburg to have heard Lincoln speak—a privilege they shared with ten to twenty thousand other people, and an experience that lasted no more than three minutes. They wanted to be intimate with the gestation of that extraordinary speech, watching the pen or pencil move under the inspiration of the moment.

That is the other emphasis in these accounts—that it was a product of the moment, struck off as Lincoln moved under destiny's guidance. Inspiration was shed on him in the presence of others. The contrast with Everett's long labors of preparation is always implied. Research, learning, the student's lamp—none of these were needed by Lincoln, whose unsummoned muse was prompting him, a democratic muse unacquainted with the library. Lightning struck, and each of our informants (or their sources) was there when it struck.

The trouble with these accounts is that the lightning strikes too often, as if it could not get the work done on its first attempt. It hits Lincoln on the train, in his room, at night, in the morning. If inspiration was treating him this way, he should have been short-circuited, not inspired, by the time he spoke.

These mythical accounts are badly out of character for Lincoln, who composed his speeches thoughtfully. His law partner, William Herndon, having observed Lincoln's careful preparation of cases, recorded that he was a slow writer, who liked to sort out his points and tighten his logic and his phrasing. That is the process vouched for in every other case of Lincoln's memorable public statements. It is impossible to imagine him leaving his Gettysburg speech to the last moment. He knew he would be busy on the train and at the site—important political guests were with him from his departure, and more joined him at Baltimore, full of talk about the war, elections, and policy. In Gettysburg he would be entertained at David Wills's house, with Everett and other important guests. State delegations would want a word with him. He hoped for a quick tour of the battle site (a hope fulfilled early on the nineteenth). He could not count on any time for the concentration he required when weighing his words.

In fact, at least two people testified that the speech was mainly composed in Washington, before Lincoln left for Gettysburg—though these reports, like all later ones describing this speech's composition, are themselves suspect. Lamon claimed that a day or two before the dedication Lincoln read him substantially the text that was delivered. But Lamon's remarks are notoriously imaginative, and he was busy in Gettysburg from November 13 to 16. He made a swift trip back to Washington on the sixteenth to collect his marshals and instruct them before departing again the next morning. His testimony here, as elsewhere, does not have much weight.

Noah Brooks, Lincoln's journalist friend, claimed that he talked with

Lincoln on November 15, when Lincoln told him he had written his speech "over, two or three times"—but Brooks also said that Lincoln had with him galleys of Everett's speech, which had been set in type for later printing by the Boston *Journal*. In fact the Everett speech was not set until November 14, and then by the Boston *Daily Advertiser*. It is unlikely that a copy could have reached Lincoln so early.

LINCOLN'S TRAIN ARRIVED toward dusk in Gettysburg. There were still coffins stacked at the station for completing the reburials. Lamon, Wills, and Everett met Lincoln and escorted him the two blocks to the Wills home, where dinner was waiting, along with almost two dozen other distinguished guests. Lincoln's black servant, William Slade, took his luggage to the second-story room where he would stay that night, which looked out on the square.

Everett was already in residence at the Wills house, and Governor Curtin's late arrival led Wills to suggest that the two men share a bed. The governor thought he could find another house to receive him, though lodgings were so overcrowded that Everett said in his diary that "the fear of having the Executive of Pennsylvania tumbled in upon me kept me awake until one." Everett's daughter was sleeping with two other women, and the bed broke under their weight. William Saunders, the cemetery's designer, who would have an honored place on the platform the next day, could find no bed and had to sleep sitting up in a crowded parlor.

It is likely that Everett, who had the galleys of his speech with him, showed them to Lincoln that night. Noah Brooks, who mistook the *time* when Everett showed Lincoln his speech, probably gave the right *reason*— so that Lincoln would not be embarrassed by any inadvertent correspondences or unintended differences.

Lincoln greeted Curtin after his late arrival, and was otherwise interrupted during the night. Bands and serenades were going through the crowded square under his window. One group asked him to speak, and the newspaper reported his words:

> I appear before you, fellow-citizens, merely to thank you for this compliment. The inference is a very fair one that you would hear me for a little while at least, were I to commence to make a speech. I do not appear before you for the purpose of doing so, and for several substantial reasons. The most substantial of these is that I have no speech to make. [Laughter.] In my position it is somewhat important that I should not say any foolish things. [A voice: If you can help it.]

It very often happens that the only way to help it is to say nothing at all. [Laughter.] Believing that is my present condition this evening, I must beg of you to excuse me from addressing you further.

This displays Lincoln's normal reluctance to improvise words as President. Lincoln's secretary John Hay, watching the scene from the crowd, noted in his diary: "The President appeared at the door and said half a dozen words meaning nothing & went in."

Early in the morning Lincoln took a carriage ride to the battle sites. Later, Ward Lamon and his specially uniformed marshals assigned horses to the various dignitaries (carriages would have clogged the site too much). Although the march was less than a mile, Lamon had brought thirty horses into town, and Wills had supplied a hundred, to honor the officials present.

Lincoln sat his horse gracefully (to the surprise of some), and looked meditative during the long wait while marshals tried to coax into line important people more concerned about their dignity than the President was about his. Lincoln was wearing a mourning band on his hat for his dead son. He also wore white gauntlets, which made his large hands on the reins dramatic by contrast with his otherwise black attire.

Everett had gone out earlier, by carriage, to prepare himself in the special tent he had asked for near the platform. At sixty-nine, he had kidney trouble and needed to relieve himself just before and after the three-hour ceremony. (He had put his problem so delicately that his hosts did not realize that he meant to be left alone in the tent; but he finally coaxed them out.) Everett mounted the platform at the last moment, after most of the others had arrived.

Those on the raised platform were hemmed in close by standing crowds. When it had become clear that the numbers might approach twenty thousand, the platform had been set at some distance from the burial operations. Only a third of the expected bodies had been buried, and those under fresh mounds. Other graves had been readied for the bodies, which arrived in irregular order (some from this state, some from that), making it impossible to complete one section at a time. The whole burial site was incomplete. Marshals tried to keep the milling thousands out of the work in progress.

Everett, as usual, had neatly placed his thick text on a little table before him—and then ostentatiously refused to look at it. He was able to indicate with gestures the sites of the battle's progress, visible from where he stood. He excoriated the rebels for their atrocities, implicitly justifying the fact that some Confederate skeletons were still unburied, lying in the clefts of Devil's Den under rocks and autumn leaves. Two days earlier Everett had been shown around the field, and places were pointed out where the bodies lay. His speech, for good or ill, would pick its way through the carnage.

As a former Secretary of State, Everett had many sources, in and outside government, for the information he had gathered so diligently. Lincoln no doubt watched closely how the audience responded to passages that absolved Meade of blame for letting Lee escape. The setting of the battle in a larger logic of campaigns had an immediacy for those on the scene which we cannot recover. Everett's familiarity with the details was flattering to the local audience, which nonetheless had things to learn from this shapely presentation of the whole three days' action. This was like a modern "docudrama" on television, telling the story of recent events on the basis of investigative reporting. We badly misread the evidence if we think Everett failed to work his customary magic. The best witnesses on the scene—Lincoln's personal secretaries, John Hay and John Nicolay, with their professional interest in good prose and good theater—praised Everett at the time and ever after. He received more attention in their biography's chapter on Gettysburg than did their own boss.

When Lincoln rose, it was with a sheet or two, from which he read. Lincoln's three minutes would ever after be obsessively contrasted with Everett's two hours in accounts of this day. It is even claimed that Lincoln disconcerted the crowd with his abrupt performance, so that people did not know how to respond ("Was that *all*?"). Myth tells of a poor photographer making leisurely arrangements to take Lincoln's picture, expecting him to be standing for some time. But it is useful to look at the relevant part of the program:

Music. *by Birgfield's Band.*
Prayer. *by Rev. T. H. Stockton, D.D.*
Music. *by the Marine Band.*
ORATION. *by Hon. Edward Everett.*
Music. *Hymn composed by B. B. French.*
DEDICATORY REMARKS BY THE PRESIDENT OF THE UNITED STATES.
Dirge. *sung by Choir selected for the occasion.*
Benediction. *by Rev. H. L. Baugher, D.D.*

There was only one "oration" announced or desired here. Though we call Lincoln's text *the* Gettysburg Address, that title clearly belongs to Everett. Lincoln's contribution, labeled "remarks," was intended to make the dedication formal (somewhat like ribbon-cutting at modern openings). Lincoln was not expected to speak at length, any more than Rev. T. H. Stockton was (though Stockton's prayer *is* four times the length of the President's remarks). A contrast of length with Everett's talk raises a false issue. Lincoln's text *is* startlingly brief for what it accomplished, but that would be equally true if Everett had spoken for a shorter time or had not spoken at all.

Nonetheless, the contrast was strong. Everett's voice was sweet and expertly modulated; Lincoln's was high to the point of shrillness, and his Kentucky accent offended some eastern sensibilities. But Lincoln derived an advantage from his high tenor voice—carrying power. If there is agreement on any one aspect of Lincoln's delivery, at Gettysburg or elsewhere, it is on his audibility. Modern impersonators of Lincoln, such as Walter Huston, Raymond Massey, Henry Fonda, and the various actors who give voice to Disneyland animations of the President, bring him before us as a baritone, which is considered a more manly or heroic voice—though both the Roosevelt Presidents of our century were tenors. What should not be forgotten is that Lincoln was himself an actor, an expert raconteur and mimic, and one who spent hours reading speeches out of Shakespeare to any willing (or sometimes unwilling) audience. He knew a good deal about rhythmic delivery and meaningful inflection. John Hay, who had submitted to many of those Shakespeare readings, gave high marks to his boss's performance at Gettysburg. He put in his diary at the time that "the President, in a fine, free way, with more grace than is his wont, said his half dozen words of consecration." Lincoln's text was polished, his delivery emphatic; he was interrupted by applause five times. Read in a slow, clear way to the farthest listeners, the speech would take about three minutes. It is quite true the audience did not take in all that happened in that short time—we are still trying to weigh the consequences of Lincoln's amazing performance. But the myth that Lincoln was disappointed in the result—that he told the unreliable Lamon that his speech, like a bad plow, "won't scour"—has no basis. He had done what he wanted to do, and Hay shared the pride his superior took in an important occasion put to good use.

AT THE LEAST, Lincoln had far surpassed David Wills's hope for words to disinfect the air of Gettysburg. His speech hovers far above the carnage. He lifts the battle to a level of abstraction that purges it of grosser matter—even "earth" is mentioned only as the thing from which the tested form of government shall not perish. The nightmare realities have been etherealized in the crucible of his language.

Lincoln was here to clear the infected atmosphere of American history itself, tainted with official sins and inherited guilt. He would cleanse the Constitution—not as William Lloyd Garrison had, by burning an instrument that countenanced slavery. He altered the document from within, by appeal from its letter to the spirit, subtly changing the recalcitrant stuff of that legal compromise, bringing it to its own indictment. By implicitly doing this, he performed one of the most daring acts of open-air sleight of hand ever witnessed by the unsuspecting. Everyone in that vast throng of thousands was having his or her intellectual pocket picked. The crowd departed with a new thing in its ideological luggage, the new Constitution Lincoln had substituted for the one they had brought there with them. They walked off from those curving graves on the hillside, under a changed sky, into a different America. Lincoln had revolutionized the Revolution, giving people a new past to live with that would change their future indefinitely.

Some people, looking on from a distance, saw that a giant (if benign) swindle had been performed. The Chicago *Times* quoted the letter of the Constitution to Lincoln—noting its lack of reference to equality, its tolerance of slavery—and said that Lincoln was betraying the instrument he was on oath to defend, traducing the men who died for the letter of that fundamental law:

> It was to uphold this constitution, and the Union created by it, that our officers and soldiers gave their lives at Gettysburg. How dared he, then, standing on their graves, misstate the cause for which they died, and libel the statesmen who founded the government? They were men possessing too much self-respect to declare that negroes were their equals, or were entitled to equal privileges.

Heirs to this outrage still attack Lincoln for subverting the Constitution at Gettysburg—suicidally frank conservatives like M. E. Bradford and the late Willmoore Kendall. But most conservatives are understandably unwilling to challenge a statement now so hallowed, so literally sacrosanct, as Lincoln's clever assault on the constitutional past. They would rather hope or pretend, with some literary critics, that Lincoln's emotionally moving address had no discernible intellectual content, that, in the words of the literary critic James Hurt, "the sequence of ideas is commonplace to the point of banality, the ordinary coin of funereal oratory."

People like Kendall and the Chicago *Times* editors might have wished this were true, but they knew better. They recognized the audacity of

Lincoln's undertaking. Kendall rightly says that Lincoln undertook a new founding of the nation, to correct things felt to be imperfect in the Founders' own achievement:

> Abraham Lincoln and, in considerable degree, the authors of the post-civil-war amendments, attempted a new act of founding, involving concretely a startling new interpretation of that principle of the founders which declares that "All men are created equal."

Edwin Meese and other "original intent" conservatives also want to go back before the Civil War amendments (particularly the Fourteenth) to the original Founders. Their job would be comparatively easy if they did not have to work against the values created by the Gettysburg Address. Its deceptively simple-sounding phrases appeal to Americans in ways that Lincoln had perfected in his debates over the Constitution during the 1850s. During that time Lincoln found the language, the imagery, the myths, that are given their best and briefest embodiment at Gettysburg. In order to penetrate the mystery of his "refounding," we must study all the elements of that stunning verbal coup. Without Lincoln's knowing it himself, all his prior literary, intellectual, and political labors had prepared him for the intellectual revolution contained in those 272 words.

LINCOLN'S SPEECH IS BRIEF, one might argue, because it is silent on so much that one would expect to hear about. The Gettysburg Address does not mention Gettysburg. Or slavery. Or—more surprising—the Union. (Certainly not the South.) The other major message of 1863, the Emancipation Proclamation, is not mentioned, much less defended or vindicated. The "great task" mentioned in the address is not emancipation but the preservation of self-government. We assume today that self-government includes self-rule by blacks as well as whites; but at the time of his appearance at Gettysburg, Lincoln was not advocating even eventual suffrage for African-Americans. The Gettysburg Address, for all its artistry and eloquence, does not directly address the prickliest issues of its historical moment.

Lincoln was accused during his lifetime of clever evasions and key silences. He was especially indirect and hard to interpret on the subject of slavery. That puzzled his contemporaries, and has infuriated some later students of his attitude. Theodore Parker, the Boston preacher who was the idol of Lincoln's law partner, William Herndon, found Lincoln more clever than principled in his 1858 Senate race, when he debated Stephen Douglas. Parker initially supported William Seward for President in 1860, because he found Seward more forthright than Lincoln in his opposition to slavery. But Seward probably lost the Republican nomination *because* of that forthrightness. Lincoln was more cautious and circuitous. The reasons for his reserve before his nomination are clear enough—though that still leaves the omissions of the Gettysburg Address to be explained.

Lincoln's political base, the state of Illinois, runs down to a point (Cairo) farther south than all of what became West Virginia, and farther south than most of Kentucky and Virginia. The "Negrophobia" of Illinois led it to vote overwhelmingly in 1848, just ten years before the Lincoln-Douglas debates, to amend the state constitution so as to deny freed blacks all right of entry to the state. The average vote of the state was 79 percent for exclusion, though southern and some central counties were probably more than 90 percent for it. Lincoln knew the racial geography of his own state well, and calibrated what he had to say about slavery according to his audience.

Lincoln knew it was useless to promote the abolitionist position in Illinois. He wanted to establish some common ground to hold together the elements of his fledgling Republican Party. Even as a lawyer, Herndon said, he concentrated so fiercely on the main point to be established ("the nub") that he would concede almost any ancillary matter. Lincoln's accommodation to the prejudice of his time did not imply any agreement with the points he found it useless to dispute. One sees his attitude in the disarming concession he made to Horace Greeley, in order to get to the nub of their disagreement:

> I have just read yours of the 19th addressed to myself through the New-York Tribune. If there be in it any statements, or assumptions of fact, which I may know to be erroneous, I do not, now and here, controvert them. If there be in it any inferences which I may believe to be falsely drawn, I do not, now and here, argue against them. If there be perceptible in it an impatient and dictatorial tone, I waive it in deference to an old friend, whose heart I have always supposed to be right.

Obviously, Lincoln did not agree with the aspersions that Greeley had cast, but this was not a matter he could usefully pursue "now and here." In the same way, Lincoln preferred agnosticism about blacks' intellectual inferiority to whites, and went along with the desire to keep them socially inferior. As George Fredrickson points out, agnosticism rather than *certainty* about blacks' intellectual disability was the liberal position of that time, and there was nothing Lincoln or anyone else could do about social mixing. Lincoln refused to let the matter of political equality get tangled up with such emotional and (for the time) unresolvable issues. What, for him, was the nub, the realizable minimum—which would be hard enough to establish in the first place?

At the very least, it was wrong to treat human beings as property. Lincoln reduced the slaveholders' position to absurdity by spelling out its consequences:

> If it is a sacred right for the people of Nebraska to take and hold slaves there, it is equally their sacred right to buy them where they can buy them cheapest; and that undoubtedly will be on the coast of Africa . . . [where a slavetrader] buys them at the rate of about a red cotton handkerchief a head. This is very cheap.

Why do people not take advantage of this bargain? Because they will be hanged like pirates if they try. Yet if slaves are just one form of property like any other,

> it is a great abridgement of the sacred right of self-government to hang men for engaging in this profitable trade!

Not only had the federal government, following international sentiment, outlawed the slave trade, but the domestic slave barterer was held in low esteem, even in the South:

> You do not recognize him as a friend, or even as an honest man. Your children must not play with his. . . . Now why is this? You do not so treat the man who deals in corn, cattle or tobacco.

And what kind of *property* is "set free"? People do not "free" houses or their manufactures to fend for themselves. But there were almost half a million freed blacks in Lincoln's America:

> How comes this vast amount of property to be running about without owners? We do not see free horses or free cattle running at large.

Lincoln said that in 1854, three years before Chief Justice Roger Taney declared, in the Dred Scott case, that slaves were movable property like any other chattel goods. The absurd had become law. No wonder Lincoln felt he had to fight for even minimal recognition of human rights.

If the black man owns himself and is not another person's property, then he has rights in the product of his labor:

> I agree with Judge Douglas [the Negro] is not my equal in many respects—certainly not in color, perhaps not in moral or intellectual endowment. But in the right to eat the bread, without leave of anybody else, which his own hand earns, *he is my equal and the equal of Judge Douglas, and the equal of every living man.*

Lincoln, as often, was using a Bible text, and one with a sting in it. The *curse* of mankind in general, that "in the sweat of thy face shalt thou eat bread" (Genesis 3:19), is, at the least, a *right* for blacks.

Lincoln tried to use one prejudice against another. There was in Americans a prejudgment in favor of anything biblical. There was also antimonarchical bias. Lincoln put the text about eating the bread of one's own sweat in an American context of antimonarchism.

> That is the issue that will continue in this country when these poor tongues of Judge Douglas and myself shall be silent. It is the eternal struggle between these two principles—right and wrong— throughout the world. They are the two principles that have stood face to face from the beginning of time; and will ever continue to struggle. The one is the common right of humanity and the other the divine right of kings. It is the same principle in whatever shape it develops itself. It is the same spirit that says, "You work and toil and earn bread, and I'll eat it." [Loud applause.] No matter in what shape it comes, whether from the mouth of a king who seeks to bestride the people of his own nation and live by the fruit of their labor, or from one race of men as an apology for enslaving another race, it is the same tyrannical principle.

In at least these two ways, then, slavery is wrong. One cannot own human beings, and one should not be in the position of a king over human beings.

Lincoln knew how to sneak around the frontal defenses of prejudice and find a back way into agreement with bigots. This explains, at the level of tactics, the usefulness to Lincoln of the Declaration of Independence. That revered document was antimonarchical in the common perception, and on that score unchallengeable. But because it indicted King George III in terms of the equality of men, the Declaration committed Americans to claims even more at odds with slavery than with kingship—since kings do not necessarily claim to own their subjects. Put the claims of the Declaration as mildly as possible, and they still cannot be reconciled with slavery:

> I, as well as Judge Douglas, am in favor of the race to which I belong having the [politically and socially] superior position. I have never said anything to the contrary, but I hold that notwithstanding all this, there is no reason in the world why the negro is not entitled to all the natural rights enumerated in the Declaration of Independence, the right to life, liberty and the pursuit of happiness. [Loud cheers.] I hold that he is as much entitled to these as the white man.

LINCOLN'S SPEECH AT GETTYSBURG WORKED several revolutions, beginning with one in literary style. Everett's talk was given at the last point in history when such a performance could be appreciated without reservation. It was made obsolete within a half hour of the time when it was spoken. Lincoln's remarks anticipated the shift to vernacular rhythms which Mark Twain would complete twenty years later. Hemingway claimed that all modern American novels are the offspring of *Huckleberry Finn*. It is no greater exaggeration to say that all modern political prose descends from the Gettysburg Address.

The address looks less mysterious than it should to those who believe there is such a thing as "natural speech." All speech is unnatural. It is artificial. Believers in "artless" or "plain" speech think that rhetoric is added to some prior natural thing, like cosmetics added to the unadorned face. But human faces are born, like kitten faces. Words are not born in that way. Human babies, unlike kittens, later produce an artifact called language, and they largely speak in jingles, symbols, tales, and myths during the early stages of their talk. Plain speech is a later development, in whole cultures as in individuals. Simple prose depends on a complex epistemology—it depends on concepts like "objective fact." Language reverses the logic of horticulture: here the blossoms come first, and *they* produce the branches.

Lincoln, like most writers of great prose, began by writing bad poetry. Early experiments with words are almost always stilted, formal, tentative. Economy of words, grip, precision come later (if at all). A Gettysburg Address does not precede rhetoric but burns its way through the lesser toward the greater eloquence, by long discipline. Lincoln not only exemplifies this process but studied it, in himself and others. He was a student of the word.

Lincoln's early experiences with language have an exuberance that is almost comic in its playing with contrivances. His showy 1838 speech to the Young Men's Lyceum is now usually studied to support or refute Edmund Wilson's claim that it contains oedipal feelings. But its most obvious feature is the attempt to describe a complex situation in neatly balanced structures (emphasized here by division into rhetorical units).

> *Their's was the task*
> *(and nobly they performed it)*
>   *to possess themselves,*
>   *and through themselves, us,*
>   *of this goodly land;*
> *and to uprear upon its hills*
>   *and its valleys,*
>   *a political edifice of liberty*
>   *and equal rights;*
> *'tis ours only,*
>   *to transmit these,*
>   *the former, unprofaned by the foot of an*
>   *invader;*
>   *the latter, undecayed by the lapse of time,*
>   *and untorn by usurpation—*
>   *to the latest generation that fate shall permit*
>   *the world to know.*

This is too labored to be clear. One has to look a second time to be sure that "the former" refers to "this goodly land" and "the latter" to "a political edifice." But the exercise is limbering Lincoln up for subtler uses of such balance and antithesis. The parenthetic enriching of a first phrase is something he would use in his later prose to give it depth (I have added all but the first set of parentheses):

> *Their's was the task*
>   *(and nobly they performed it)*
> *to possess themselves*

> *(and through themselves, us)*
>   *of this goodly land*

It is the pattern of

> *The world will little note*
>   *(nor long remember)*
>   *what we say here*

And, from the Second Inaugural Address, of

> *Fondly do we hope*
>   *(fervently do we pray)*
>   *that this mighty scourge of war*
>   *may speedily pass away*

And, also from the Second Inaugural,

> *. . . with firmness in the right*
>   *(as God gives us to see the right)*
>   *let us strive on to finish*
>   *the work we are in*

To end after complex melodic pairings with a strong row of monosyllables was an effect he especially liked. Not only "the world to know" and "what we say here" and "the work we are in" in the examples above but also, from the 1861 Farewell Address at Springfield, Illinois, in

> *Trusting in Him,*
>   *who can go with me,*
>   *and remain with you*
>   *and be every where for good,*
> *let us confidently hope*
>   *that all will yet be well.*

And in this, from the Second Inaugural,

> *Both parties deprecated war;*
>   *but one of them would* make war
>   *rather than let the nation survive;*

and the other would accept *war*
rather than let it perish.
And the war came.

And, in the 1862 message to Congress,

In giving *freedom to the slave,*
we assure *freedom to the free—*
honorable alike in what we give,
and what we preserve.
We shall nobly save,
or meanly lose,
the last best hope of earth.

The closing of the sentence above from Lincoln's early Lyceum speech ("to the latest generation") gives a premonition of famous statements to come.

The fiery trial through which we pass,
will light us down,
(in honor or dishonor)
to the latest generation.

Those words to Congress in 1862 were themselves forecast in Lincoln's Peoria address of 1854.

If we do this,
we shall not only have saved the Union;
but we shall have so saved it,
as to make, and to keep it,
forever worthy of the saving.
We shall have so saved it,
that the succeeding millions
of free happy people,
the world over,
shall rise up,
and call us blessed, to the latest generations.

It would be wrong to think that Lincoln moved toward the plain style of the Gettysburg Address just by writing shorter, simpler sentences. Actually, that address ends with a very long sentence—eighty-two words, almost a third of the whole talk's length. So does the Second Inaugural Address, Lincoln's second most famous piece of eloquence: its final sentence runs to seventy-five words. Because of his early experiments, Lincoln's prose acquired a flexibility of structure, a rhythmic pacing, a variation in length of words and phrases and clauses and sentences, that make his sentences move "naturally," for all their density and scope. We get inside his verbal workshop when we see how he recast the suggested conclusion to his First Inaugural given him by William Seward. Every sentence is improved, in rhythm, emphasis, or clarity:

Seward	Lincoln
I close.	I am loth to close.
We are not, we must not be aliens or enemies, but fellow-countrymen and brethren.	We are not enemies, but friends. We must not be enemies.
Although passion has strained our bonds of affection too hardly, they must not, I am sure they will not, be broken.	Though passion may have strained, it must not break our bonds of affection.
The mystic chords which, proceeding from so many battle-fields and so many patriot graves, pass through all the hearts and all the hearths in this broad continent of ours, will yet harmonize in their ancient music when breathed upon by the guardian angel of the nation.	The mystic chords of memory stretching from every battle-field, and patriot grave, to every living heart and hearthstone, all over this broad land, will yet swell the chorus of the Union, when again touched, as surely they will be, by the better angels of our nature.

Lincoln's lingering monosyllables in the first sentence seem to cling to the occasion, not wanting to break off the communication on which the last hopes of union depend. He simplified the next sentence using two terms ("enemies," "friends") where Seward had used two *pairs* ("aliens" and "enemies," "fellow-countrymen" and "brethren"), but Lincoln repeated "enemies" in the urgent words "We must not be enemies." The next sentence was also simplified, to play off against the long, complex image of the concluding sentence. The "chords of memory" are not musical sounds. Lincoln spelled "chord" and "cord" indiscriminately; they are the same etymologically. He used the geometric term "chord" for a line across a circle's arc. On the other hand, he spelled the word "cord" (in an 1858 speech) when calling the Declaration of Independence an electrical wire sending messages to American hearts: "the electric cord in that Declaration that links the hearts of patriotic and liberty loving men together."

Seward knew that the chord to be breathed on was a string (of a harp or lute, though his "chords proceeding from graves" is grotesque). Lincoln stretched the cords between graves and living hearts, as in his earlier image of the Declaration. Seward also got ethereal when he talked of harmonies that come from breathing on the chords. Lincoln was more believable (and understandable) when he had the better angels of our nature touch the cords to swell the chorus of union. Finally, Seward made an odd picture to get his jingle of chords passing through "hearts and hearths." Lincoln stretched the chords from graves to hearts and hearthstones. He got rid of the crude rhyme by making a chiastic (a-b-b-a) cluster of "living heart and hearthstone"; the vital heart is contrasted with the inert hearth-stuff. Seward's clumsy image of stringing together these two different items has disappeared. Lincoln gave to Seward's fustian a pointedness of imagery, a euphony and interplay of short and long sentences and phrases, that lift the conclusion almost to the level of his own best prose.

The spare quality of Lincoln's prose did not come naturally but was worked at. Lincoln not only read aloud, to think his way into sounds, but also wrote as a way of ordering his thought. He had a keenness for analytical exercises. He was proud of the mastery he achieved over Euclid's Elements, which awed Herndon and others. He loved the study of grammar, which some think the most arid of subjects. Some claimed to remember his gift for spelling, a view that our manuscripts disprove. Spelling as he had to learn it (separate from etymology) is more arbitrary than logical. It was the logical side of language—the principles of order as these reflect patterns of thought or the external world—that appealed to him.

He was also, Herndon tells us, laboriously precise in his choice of words. He would have agreed with Mark Twain that the difference between the right word and the nearly right one is that between lightning and a lightning bug. He said, debating Douglas, that his foe confused a similarity of words with a similarity of things—as one might equate a horse chestnut with a chestnut horse.

As a speaker, Lincoln grasped Twain's later insight: "Few sinners are saved after the first twenty minutes of a sermon." The trick, of course, was not simply to be brief but to say a great deal in the fewest words. Lincoln justly boasted of his Second Inaugural's seven hundred words, "Lots of wisdom in that document, I suspect." The same is even truer of the Gettysburg Address, which uses fewer than half that number of words.

The unwillingness to waste words shows up in the address's telegraphic quality—the omission of coupling words, a technique rhetoricians call asyndeton. Triple phrases sound as to a drumbeat, with no "and" or "but" to slow their insistency:

we are engaged . . .
We are met . . .
We have come . . .

we can not dedicate . . .
we can not consecrate . . .
we can not hallow . . .

that from these honored dead . . .
that we here highly resolve . . .
that this nation, under God . . .

government of the people,
by the people,
for the people . . .

Despite the suggestive images of birth, testing, and rebirth, the speech is surprisingly bare of ornament. The language itself is made strenuous, its musculature easily traced, so that even the grammar becomes a form of rhetoric. By repeating the antecedent as often as possible, instead of referring to it indirectly by pronouns like "it" and "they," or by backward referential words like "former" and "latter," Lincoln interlocks his sentences, making of them a constantly self-referential system. This linking up by explicit repetition amounts to a kind of hook-and-eye method for joining the parts of his address. The rhetorical devices are almost invisible, since they use no figurative language. (I highlight them typographically here.)

Four score and seven years ago our fathers brought forth on this continent, *a new nation, conceived* in Liberty, *and dedicated* to the proposition that all men are created equal.

Now we are engaged in A GREAT CIVIL WAR, testing whether *that nation,* or any nation *so conceived and so dedicated,* can long endure.

We are met on a great BATTLE-FIELD of THAT WAR.

We have come to *dedicate* a portion of THAT FIELD, as a final resting place for those who here gave their lives that *that nation* might live. It is altogether fitting and proper that we should do this.

But, in a larger sense, we can not *dedicate*—we can not *consecrate*—we can not hallow—this ground.

The brave men, living and dead, **who struggled here,** have *consecrated* it, far above our poor power to add or detract. The world will little note, nor long remember what we say here, but it can never forget what they did here.

It is for us the living, rather, to be *dedicated* here to the unfinished work which they **who fought here** have thus far so nobly advanced. It is rather for us to be here *dedicated* to the great task remaining before us—that from THESE HONORED DEAD we take increased devotion to that cause for which they gave the last full measure of devotion—

that we here highly resolve that THESE DEAD shall not have died in vain—that this nation, under God, shall have a new birth of freedom—and that government of the people, by the people, for the people, shall not perish from the earth.

Each of the paragraphs printed separately here is bound to the preceding and the following by some resumptive element. Only the first and last paragraphs do not (because they cannot) have this two-way connection to their setting. Not all of the "pointer" phrases replace grammatical antecedents in the technical sense. But Lincoln makes them perform analogous work. The nation is declared to be "dedicated" before the term is given further uses for individuals present at the ceremony, who repeat (as it were) the national consecration. The compactness of the themes is emphasized by this reliance on a few words in different contexts.

A similar linking process is performed, almost subliminally, by the repeated pinning of statements to *this* field, *these* dead, who died *here,* for *that* kind of nation. The reverential touching, over and over, of the charged moment and place leads Lincoln to use "here" eight times in the short text, the adjectival "that" five times, and "this" four times. The spare vocabulary is not impoverishing, because of the subtly interfused constructions, in which the classicist Charles Smiley identified "two antitheses, five cases of anaphora, eight instances of balanced phrases and clauses, thirteen alliterations." "Plain speech" was never less artless. Lincoln forged a new lean language to humanize and redeem the first modern war.

This was the perfect medium for changing the way most Americans thought about the nation's founding. Lincoln did not argue law or history, as Daniel Webster had. He *made* history. He came not to present a theory but to impose a symbol, one tested in experience and appealing to national values, expressing emotional urgency in calm abstractions. He came to change the world, to effect an intellectual revolution. No other words could have done it. The miracle is that these words did. In his brief time before the crowd at Gettysburg he wove a spell that has not yet been broken—he called up a new nation out of the blood and trauma.

JAMES MCPHERSON HAS DESCRIBED LINCOLN as a revolutionary in terms of the economic and other physical changes he effected, whether intentionally or not—a valid point that McPherson discusses sensibly. But Lincoln was a revolutionary in another sense as well—the one Willmoore Kendall denounced him for: he not only presented the Declaration of Independence in a new light, as a matter of founding law, but put its central proposition, equality, in a newly favored position as a principle of the Constitution (whereas, as the Chicago *Times* noticed, the Constitution never uses the word). What had been mere theory in the writings of James Wilson, Joseph Story, and Daniel Webster—that the nation preceded the states, in time and importance—now became a lived reality of the American tradition. The results of this were seen almost at once. Up to the Civil War "the United States" was invariably a plural noun: "The United States are a free country." After Gettysburg it became a singular: "The United States is a free country." This was a result of the whole mode of thinking that Lincoln expressed in his acts as well as his words, making union not a mystical hope but a constitutional reality. When, at the end of the address, he referred to government "of the people, by the people, for the people," he was not, like Theodore Parker, just praising popular government as a Transcendentalist's ideal. Rather, like Webster, he was saying that America was *a* people accepting as its great assignment what was addressed in the Declaration. This people was "conceived" in 1776, was "brought forth" as an entity whose birth was datable ("four score and seven years" before) and placeable ("on this continent"), and was capable of receiving a "new birth of freedom."

Thus Abraham Lincoln changed the way people thought about the

Constitution. For a states'-rights advocate like Willmoore Kendall, for an "original intent" advocate like Edwin Meese, the politics of the United States has all been misdirected since that time. The Fourteenth Amendment was, in their view, ultimately bootlegged into the Bill of Rights. But as soon as it was ratified, the Amendment began doing harm, in the eyes of strict constructionists.

As Robert Bork put it:

> Unlike the [Fourteenth Amendment's] other two clauses, [the due-process clause] quickly displayed the same capacity to accommodate judicial constitution-making which Taney had found in the fifth amendment's version.

Bork, too, thinks that equality as a national commitment has been sneaked into the Constitution. There can be little doubt about the principal culprit. As Kendall put it, Lincoln's use of the phrase from the Declaration about all men being equal is an attempt "to wrench from it a single proposition and make that our supreme commitment."

> We should not allow [Lincoln]—not at least without some probing inquiry—to "steal" the game, that is, to accept his interpretation of the Declaration, its place in our history, and its meaning as "true," "correct," and "binding."

But, as Kendall himself admitted, the professors, the textbooks, the politicians, the press, *have* overwhelmingly accepted Lincoln's vision. The Gettysburg Address has become an authoritative expression of the American spirit—as authoritative as the Declaration itself, and perhaps even more influential, since it determines how we read the Declaration. For most people now, the Declaration means what Lincoln told us it means, as he did to correct the Constitution without overthrowing it. It is this correction of the spirit, this intellectual revolution, that makes attempts to go back beyond Lincoln to some earlier version so feckless. The proponents of states' rights may have arguments to advance, but they have lost their force, in the courts as well as in the popular mind. By accepting the Gettysburg Address, and its concept of a single people dedicated to a proposition, we have been changed. Because of it, we live in a different America.

American Civilization

RALPH WALDO EMERSON || 1862

*Compared with the others in his close-knit community of radical
thinkers, Ralph Waldo Emerson (1803–1882) came conspicuously late to
the cause of abolition. The source of his tardiness, apart from a commonly held assumption (even among Northerners) of Anglo-Saxon superiority, was a deep-rooted antipathy to political activism. The celebrated
apostle of self-reliance strongly believed that partisan enterprises threatened intellectual autonomy, and for years he remained aloof from politics on philosophical grounds. After one foray through what he called
"the philanthropic mud," in 1838, Emerson vowed, "I will let the republic
alone until the republic comes to me." It soon did. The notorious Fugitive
Slave Law of 1850, which compelled officials above the Mason–Dixon
Line to capture and return escaped slaves, outraged Emerson, as it did
many Northerners, and drove him firmly into the antislavery camp. In
the years that followed, he delivered dozens of lectures advocating an immediate end to slavery and, later, he supported the enlistment of blacks
in the Union Army.*

*In "American Civilization," presented first as a lecture at the Smith-
sonian Institution in Washington, D.C., in January 1862, and published
in* The Atlantic *four months later, Emerson makes a characteristically
high-minded argument for emancipation of the slaves, casting it as a
necessary moral action for Americans to take not only for themselves but
for all mankind. His clarion call had an ultimate target: Abraham Lincoln, whose early halting moves to free the slaves win Emerson's praise at
the end of "American Civilization," even as he urges the president to act
more speedily. There is some dispute among historians over whether Lincoln was actually in the Smithsonian audience that night. Regardless,
two days later Emerson got an even better chance to influence Lincoln,
thanks to a White House meeting arranged by Massachusetts senator
Charles Sumner. Emerson and Lincoln hit it off so well that after their
conversation, the philosopher began to extol the president's cautious
sense of timing. Eight months later, to Emerson's unalloyed joy, Lincoln
issued the Emancipation Proclamation.*

At this moment in America the aspects of political society absorb attention. In every house, from Canada to the Gulf, the children ask the serious

father,—"What is the news of the war today? and when will there be better times?" The boys have no new clothes, no gifts, no journeys; the girls must go without new bonnets; boys and girls find their education, this year, less liberal and complete. All the little hopes that heretofore made the year pleasant are deferred. The state of the country fills us with anxiety and stern duties. We have attempted to hold together two states of civilization: a higher state, where labor and the tenure of land and the right of suffrage are democratical; and a lower state, in which the old military tenure of prisoners or slaves, and of power and land in a few hands, makes an oligarchy: we have attempted to hold these two states of society under one law. But the rude and early state of society does not work well with the later, nay, works badly, and has poisoned politics, public morals, and social intercourse in the Republic, now for many years.

The times put this question,—Why cannot the best civilization be extended over the whole country, since the disorder of the less civilized portion menaces the existence of the country? Is this secular progress we have described, this evolution of man to the highest powers, only to give him sensibility, and not to bring duties with it? Is he not to make his knowledge practical? to stand and to withstand? Is not civilization heroic also? Is it not for action? has it not a will? . . . America is another word for Opportunity. Our whole history appears like a last effort of the Divine Providence in behalf of the human race; and a literal slavish following of precedents, as by a justice of the peace, is not for those who at this hour lead the destinies of this people. The evil you contend with has taken alarming proportions, and you still content yourself with parrying the blows it aims, but, as if enchanted, abstain from striking at the cause.

In this national crisis, it is not argument that we want, but that rare courage which dares commit itself to a principle, believing that Nature is its ally, and will create the instruments it requires, and more than make good any petty and injurious profit which it may disturb. There never was such a combination as this of ours, and the rules to meet it are not set down in any history. We want men of original perception and original action, who can open their eyes wider than to a nationality, namely, to considerations of benefit to the human race, can act in the interest of civilization. Government must not be a parish clerk, a justice of the peace. It has, of necessity, in any crisis of the State, the absolute powers of a Dictator. The existing Administration is entitled to the utmost candor. It is to be thanked for its angelic virtue, compared with any executive experiences with which we have been familiar. But the times will not allow us to indulge in compliment. I wish I saw in the people that inspiration which, if Government would not obey the same, it would leave the Government behind, and create on the moment the means and executors it wanted. Better the war should more dangerously threaten us,—should threaten fracture in what is still whole, and punish us with burned capitals and slaughtered regiments, and so exasperate the people to energy, exasperate our nationality. There are Scriptures written invisibly on men's hearts, whose letters do not come out until they are enraged. They can be read by war-fires, and by eyes in the last peril.

We cannot but remember that there have been days in American history, when, if the Free States had done their duty, Slavery had been blocked by an immovable barrier, and our recent calamities forever precluded. The Free States yielded, and every compromise was surrender, and invited new demands. Here again is a new occasion which Heaven offers to sense and virtue. It looks as if we held the fate of the fairest possession of mankind in our hands, to be saved by our firmness or to be lost by hesitation.

Emancipation is the demand of civilization. That is a principle; everything else is an intrigue. This is a progressive policy;—puts the whole people in healthy, productive, amiable position,—puts every man in the South in just and natural relations with every man in the North, laborer with laborer.

The war is welcome to the Southerner: a chivalrous sport to him, like hunting, and suits his semi-civilized condition. On the climbing scale of progress, he is just up to war, and has never appeared to such advantage as in the last twelve-month. It does not suit us. We are advanced some ages on the war-state,—to trade, art, and general cultivation. His laborer works for him at home, so that he loses no labor by the war. All our soldiers are laborers; so that the South, with its inferior numbers, is almost on a footing in effective war-population with the North. Again, as long as we fight without any affirmative step taken by the Government, any word intimating forfeiture in the rebel States of their old privileges under the law, they and we fight on the same side, for Slavery.

But one weapon we hold which is sure. Congress can, by edict, as a part of the military defense which it is the duty of Congress to provide, abolish slavery, and pay for such slaves as we ought to pay for. Then the slaves near our armies will come to us: those in the interior will know in a week what their rights are, and will, where opportunity offers, prepare to take them. Instantly, the armies that now confront you must run home to protect their estates, and must stay there, and your enemies will disappear.

There can be no safety until this step is taken. We fancy that the endless debate, emphasized by the crime and by the cannons of this war, has brought the Free States to some conviction that it can never go well with us whilst this mischief of Slavery remains in our politics, and that by concert or by might we must put an end to it. But we have too much experience of the futility of an easy reliance on the momentary good dispositions of the public. There does exist, perhaps, a popular will that the Union shall not be broken,—that our trade, and therefore our laws, must have the whole breadth of the continent, and from Canada to the Gulf. But, since this is the rooted belief and will of the people, so much the more are they in danger, when impatient of defeats, or impatient of taxes, to go with a rush for some peace, and what kind of peace shall at that moment be easiest attained: they will make concessions for it,—will give up the slaves; and the whole torment of the past half century will come back to be endured anew. . . . [Slavery] cannot live but by injustice, and it will be unjust and violent to the end of the world.

The power of Emancipation is this, that it alters the atomic social constitution of the Southern people. Now their interest is in keeping out white labor; then, when they must pay wages, their interest will be to let it in, to get the best labor, and, if they fear their blacks, to invite Irish, German, and American laborers. Thus, whilst Slavery makes and keeps disunion, Emancipation removes the whole objection to union. Emancipation at one stroke elevates the poor white of the South, and identifies his interest with that of the Northern laborer.

Now, in the name of all that is simple and generous, why should not this great right be done? Why should not America be capable of a second stroke for the well-being of the human race, as eighty or ninety years ago she was for the first? an affirmative step in the interests of human civility, urged on her, too, not by any romance of sentiment, but by her own extreme perils? It is very certain that the statesman who shall break through the cobwebs of doubt, fear, and petty cavil that lie in the way, will be greeted by the unanimous thanks of mankind.

The end of all political struggle is to establish morality as the basis of all legislation. It is not free institutions, 'tis not a republic, 'tis not a democracy, that is the end,—no, but only the means. Morality is the object of government. We want a state of things in which crime shall not pay. This is the consolation on which we rest in the darkness of the future and the afflictions of today, that the government of the world is moral, and does forever destroy what is not.

President Lincoln has proposed to Congress that the Government shall cooperate with any State that shall enact a gradual abolishment of Slavery. In the recent series of national successes, this Message is the best. It marks the happiest day in the political year. The American Executive ranges itself for the first time on the side of freedom. If Congress has been backward, the President has advanced. This state-paper is the more interesting that it appears to be the President's individual act, done under a strong sense of duty. He speaks his own thought in his own style. All thanks and honor to the Head of the State! The Message has been received throughout the country with praise, and, we doubt not, with more pleasure than has been spoken. If Congress accords with the President, it is not yet too late to begin the emancipation; but we think it will always be too late to make it gradual. All experience agrees that it should be immediate. More and better than the President has spoken shall, perhaps, the effect of this Message be,—but, we are sure, not more or better than he hoped in his heart, when, thoughtful of all the complexities of his position, he penned these cautious words.

Bardic Symbols

WALT WHITMAN || 1860

A great nation must have great poets, Ralph Waldo Emerson decreed in his 1844 essay "The Poet." Walt Whitman (1819–1892), although then just a neophyte dabbler in verse, was quick to see himself as both the embodiment and the guardian of that vision, and he would dedicate the better part of his life to composing, embellishing, and endlessly revising his monumental tribute to American democracy, Leaves of Grass.

After working on and off for years as a newspaperman and printer in Brooklyn, New York, Whitman self-published, in 1855, the first edition of Leaves of Grass *as a collection of twelve poems. At first, the book was a commercial flop, and Whitman's efforts to free himself from English poetry's formal conventions of meter and rhyme met with outright hostility among the critics—with one notable exception. Emerson, that era's make-or-break literary arbiter, had received a gift copy of* Leaves of Grass, *courtesy of its author, and had sent a now-legendary note back to Whitman hailing the work as "the most extraordinary piece of wit and wisdom that America has yet contributed."*

Yet despite this heady accolade, Whitman suffered agonizing self-doubt in the early stages of his epic project, as "Bardic Symbols," the first of two poems that he would publish in The Atlantic, *suggests. Now known by its melancholy revised title, "As I Ebb'd with the Ocean of Life," the poem, which would be incorporated into the third edition of* Leaves of Grass *later that year, is a brooding lamentation on the hardships of self-knowledge and self-expression, shot through with stark images of spiritual bewilderment and artistic futility; it was written during a grim time in Whitman's life—after he had quit his position as an editorial writer at the* Brooklyn Times *and before he had begun to find firm footing in the literary establishment. But by the time* The Atlantic *published its second Whitman poem, an extended canticle called "Proud Music of the Sea Storm," in 1869, his fortunes had changed dramatically: a biographical pamphlet by the journalist William Douglas O'Connor had championed him as America's "Good Gray Poet," and* Leaves of Grass *was winning plaudits both in America and Europe. For the next two decades, Whitman would continue to expand and amend his magnum opus, striving to forge an oracular poetry to match the sprawling, multifarious, improvisational character of the nation that was his great subject, and becoming, in his own words, "An American bard at last!"*

I.

Elemental drifts!

Oh, I wish I could impress others as you and the waves have just been impressing me!

II.

As I ebbed with an ebb of the ocean of life,

As I wended the shores I know,

As I walked where the sea-ripples wash you, Paumanok,

Where they rustle up, hoarse and sibilant,

Where the fierce old mother endlessly cries for her castaways,

I, musing, late in the autumn day, gazing off southward,

Alone, held by the eternal self of me that threatens to get the better of me and stifle me,

Was seized by the spirit that trails in the lines underfoot,

In the ruin, the sediment, that stands for all the water and all the land of the globe.

III.

Fascinated, my eyes, reverting from the south, dropped, to follow those slender windrows,

Chaff, straw, splinters of wood, weeds, and the sea-gluten,

Scum, scales from shining rocks, leaves of salt-lettuce, left by the tide.

IV.

Miles walking, the sound of breaking waves the other side of me,

Paumanok, there and then as I thought the old thought of likenesses,

These you presented to me, you fish-shaped island,

As I wended the shores I know,

As I walked with that eternal self of me, seeking types.

V.

As I wend the shores I know not,

As I listen to the dirge, the voices of men and women wrecked,

As I inhale the impalpable breezes that set in upon me,

As the ocean so mysterious rolls toward me closer and closer,

At once I find, the least thing that belongs to me, or that I see or touch,
    I know not;
I, too, but signify a little washed-up drift,—a few sands and dead leaves
    to gather,
Gather, and merge myself as part of the leaves and drift.

VI.

Oh, baffled, lost,
Bent to the very earth, here preceding what follows,
Terrified with myself that I have dared to open my mouth,
Aware now, that, amid all the blab whose echoes recoil upon me, I have
    not once had the least idea who or what I am,
But that before all my insolent poems the real me still stands untouched,
    untold, altogether unreached,
Withdrawn far, mocking me with mock-congratulatory signs and bows,
With peals of distant ironical laughter at every word I have written or
    shall write,
Striking me with insults, till I fall helpless upon the sand!

VII.

Oh, I think I have not understood anything,—not a single object,—and
    that no man ever can!

VIII.

I think Nature here, in sight of the sea, is taking advantage of me to
    oppress me,
Because I was assuming so much,
And because I have dared to open my mouth to sing at all.

IX.

You oceans both! You tangible land! Nature!
Be not too stern with me,—I submit,—I close with you,—
These little shreds shall, indeed, stand for all.

X.

You friable shore, with trails of debris!
You fish-shaped island! I take what is underfoot:
What is yours is mine, my father!

XI.

I, too, Paumanok,

I, too, have bubbled up, floated the measureless float, and been washed
on your shores.

XII.

I, too, am but a trail of drift and debris,—

I, too, leave little wrecks upon you, you fish-shaped island!

XIII.

I throw myself upon your breast, my father!

I cling to you so that you cannot unloose me,—

I hold you so firm, till you answer me something.

XIV.

Kiss me, my father!

Touch me with your lips, as I touch those I love!

Breathe to me, while I hold you close, the secret of the wondrous
murmuring I envy!

For fear I shall become crazed, if I cannot emulate it, and utter myself as
well as it.

XV.

Sea-raff! Torn leaves!

Oh, I sing, some day, what you have certainly said to me!

XVI.

Ebb, ocean of life! (the flow will return,)—

Cease not your moaning, you fierce old mother!

Endlessly cry for your castaways! Yet fear not, deny not me,—

Rustle not up so hoarse and angry against my feet, as I touch you, or
gather from you.

XVII.

I mean tenderly by you,—

I gather for myself, and for this phantom, looking down where we lead,
and following me and mine.

XVIII.

Me and mine!
We, loose windrows, little corpses,
Froth, snowy white, and bubbles,
Tufts of straw, sands, fragments,
Buoyed hither from many moods, one contradicting another,
From the storm, the long calm, the darkness, the swell,
Musing, pondering, a breath, a briny tear, a dab of liquid or soil,
Up just as much out of fathomless workings fermented and thrown,
A limp blossom or two, torn, just as much over waves floating, drifted at
    random,
Just as much for us that sobbing dirge of Nature,
Just as much, whence we come, that blare of the cloud-trumpets,—
We, capricious, brought hither, we know not whence, spread out before
    you,—you, up there, walking or sitting,
Whoever you are,—we, too, lie in drifts at your feet.

The Duties of Privilege

THEODORE ROOSEVELT || 1894

*Not long after his graduation from Harvard, Theodore Roosevelt
(1858–1919) began openly to criticize the university for what he saw as a
failure to inspire its students with a proper sense of civic obligation. As
he recalled in* An Autobiography *(1913): "There was almost no teaching
of the need for collective action, and of the fact that in addition to, not as
a substitute for, individual responsibility, there is a collective responsibility." For a man of Roosevelt's lineage, it was an unusual lament. Like
many of his Harvard classmates, he himself was the scion of a moneyed
family—the Roosevelts had been prominent in New York society since
the seventeenth century—and he was a thoroughgoing member of a ruling class characterized by a "strange apathy," in the words of his friend
Edith Wharton, toward the rest of the human race.*

*But Roosevelt had inherited from his father, a real-estate mogul and
philanthropist, a curiosity about the wider world and a passion for public service, and he had nothing but disdain for the Gilded Age milieu in
which he grew up. At the age of twenty-three, he abandoned those rari-
fied precincts for the rough-and-tumble ones of politics, becoming a New
York State assemblyman and launching a career as a political reformer
that would make him a poster boy for his public service ideals: civil service commissioner, police commissioner of New York City, assistant secretary of the navy, governor of New York, vice president, and, finally, the
youngest-ever president of the United States.*

*"The Duties of Privilege" is the third of six articles Roosevelt wrote
for* The Atlantic, *on subjects ranging from civil service reform to the
mating habits of the wild ostrich, and it cogently articulates the philosophy that catapulted him into the public arena. The essay, at once a call
to civic duty for the nation's elite and a stern reminder that even the
privileged risk obsolescence in a meritocratic democracy, bristles with the
combative spirit for which Roosevelt became famous. "It is proper to demand more from the man with exceptional advantages than from the
man without them," he writes. With provocative words like these, Roosevelt made more than his share of enemies (he was often accused of being a traitor to his class). But the aspirations he expresses here found a
permanent place in American rhetoric, foreshadowing the famous exhor-
tation of a later public-service-minded millionaire: "Ask not what your
country can do for you—ask what you can do for your country."*

There are always, in our national life, certain tendencies that give us ground for alarm, and certain others that give us ground for hope. Among the latter we must put the fact that there has undoubtedly been a growing feeling among educated men that they are in honor bound to do their full share of the work of American public life.

We have in this country an equality of rights. It is the plain duty of every man to see that his rights are respected. That weak good nature which acquiesces in wrongdoing, whether from laziness, timidity, or indifference, is a very unwholesome quality. It should be second nature with every man to insist that he be given full justice. But if there is an equality of rights, there is an inequality of duties. It is proper to demand more from the man with exceptional advantages than from the man without them. A heavy moral obligation rests upon the man of means and upon the man of education to do their full duty by their country. On no class does this obligation rest more heavily than upon the men with a collegiate education, the men who are graduates of our universities. Their education gives them no right to feel the least superiority over any of their fellow citizens; but it certainly ought to make them feel that they should stand foremost in the honorable effort to serve the whole public by doing their duty as Americans in the body politic. This obligation very possibly rests even more heavily upon the men of means; but of this it is not necessary now to speak. The men of mere wealth never can have and never should have the capacity for doing good work that is possessed by the men of exceptional mental training; but that they may become both a laughing stock and a menace to the community is made unpleasantly apparent by that portion of the New York business and social world which is most in evidence in the newspapers.

To the great body of men who have had exceptional advantages in the way of educational facilities we have a right, then, to look for good service to the state. The service may be rendered in many different ways. In a reasonable number of cases, the man may himself rise to high political position. That men actually do so rise is shown by the number of graduates of Harvard, Yale, and our other universities who are now taking a prominent part in public life. These cases must necessarily, however, form but a small part of the whole. The enormous majority of our educated men have to make their own living, and are obliged to take up careers in which they must work heart and soul to succeed. Nevertheless, the man of business and the man of science, the doctor of divinity and the doctor of law, the architect, the engineer, and the writer, all alike owe a positive duty to the community, the neglect of which they cannot excuse on any plea of their private affairs. They are bound to follow understandingly the course of public events; they are bound to try to estimate and form judgment upon public men; and they are bound to act intelligently and effectively in support of the principles which they deem to be right and for the best interests of the country.

The most important thing for this class of educated men to realize is that they do not really form a class at all. I have used the word in default of another, but I have merely used it roughly to group together people who have had unusual opportunities of a certain kind. A large number of the people to whom these opportunities are offered fail to take advantage of them, and a very much larger number of those to whom they have not been offered succeed none the less in making them for themselves. An educated man must not go into politics as such; he must go in simply as an American; and when he is once in, he will speedily realize that he must work very hard indeed, or he will be upset by some other American, with no education at all, but with much natural capacity. His education ought to make him feel particularly ashamed of himself if he acts meanly or dishonorably, or in any way falls short of the ideal of good citizenship, and it ought to make him feel that he must show that he has profited by it; but it should certainly give him no feeling of superiority until by actual work he has shown that superiority. In other words, the educated man must realize that he is living in a democracy and under democratic conditions, and that he is entitled to no more respect and consideration than he can win by actual performance.

This must be steadily kept in mind not only by educated men themselves, but particularly by the men who give the tone to our great educational institutions. These educational institutions, if they are to do their best work, must strain every effort to keep their life in touch with the life of the nation at the present day. This is necessary for the country, but it is very much more necessary for the educated men themselves. It is a misfortune for any land if its people of cultivation take little part in shaping its destiny; but the misfortune is far greater for the people of cultivation. The country has a right to demand the honest and efficient service of every man in it, but especially of every man who has had the advantage of rigid mental and moral training; the country is so much the poorer when any class of honest men fail to do their duty by it, but the loss to the class itself is immeasurable. If our educated men as a whole become incapable of playing their full part in our life, if they cease doing their share of the rough, hard work which must be done, and grow to take a position of mere dilettanteism in our public affairs, they will speedily sink in relation to their fellows who really do the work of governing, until they stand toward them as a cultivated, ineffective man with a taste for bricabrac stands toward a great artist. When once a body of citizens becomes thoroughly out of touch and out of temper with the national life, its usefulness is gone, and its power of leaving its mark on the times is gone also.

The first great lesson which the college graduate should learn is the lesson of work rather than of criticism. Criticism is necessary and useful; it is often indispensable; but it can never take the place of action, or be even a poor substitute for it. The function of the mere critic is of very subordinate usefulness. It is the doer of deeds who actually counts in the battle for life, and not the man who looks on and says how the fight ought to be fought, without himself sharing the stress and the danger.

There is, however, a need for proper critical work. Wrongs should be strenuously and fearlessly denounced; evil principles and evil men should be condemned. The politician who cheats or swindles, or the newspaper man who lies in any form, should be made to feel that he is an object of scorn for all honest men. We need fearless criticism; but we need that it should also be intelligent. At present, the man who is most apt to regard himself as an intelligent critic of our political affairs is often the man who knows nothing whatever about them. Criticism which is ignorant or prejudiced is a source of great harm to the nation; and where ignorant or prejudiced critics are themselves educated men, their attitude does real harm also to the class to which they belong.

The tone of a portion of the press of the country toward public men, and especially toward political opponents, is degrading, all forms of coarse and noisy slander being apparently considered legitimate weapons to employ against men of the opposite party or faction. Unfortunately, not a few of the journals that pride themselves upon being independent in politics, and the organs of cultivated men, betray the same characteristics in a less coarse but quite as noxious form. All these journals do great harm by accustoming good citizens to see their public men, good and bad, assailed indiscriminately as scoundrels. The effect is twofold: the citizen learning, on the one hand, to disbelieve any statement he sees in any newspaper, so that the attacks on evil lose their edge; and on the other, gradually acquiring a deep-rooted belief that all public men are more or less bad. In consequence, his political instinct becomes hopelessly blurred, and he grows unable to tell the good representative from the bad. The worst offense that can be committed against the republic is the offense of the public man who betrays his trust; but second only to it comes the offense of the man who tries to persuade others that an honest and efficient public man is dishonest or unworthy. This is a wrong that can be committed in a great many different ways. Downright foul abuse may be, after all, less dangerous than incessant misstatements, sneers, and those half-truths that are the meanest lies.

For educated men of weak fibre, there lies a real danger in that species of literary work which appeals to their cultivated senses because of its scholarly and pleasant tone, but which enjoins as the proper attitude to assume in public life one of mere criticism and negation; which teaches the adoption toward public men and public affairs of that sneering tone which so surely denotes a mean and small mind. If a man does not have belief and enthusiasm, the chances are small indeed that he will ever do a man's work in the world; and the paper or the college which, by its general course, tends to eradicate this power of belief and enthusiasm, this desire for work, has rendered to the young men under its influence the worst service it could possibly render. Good can often be done by criticising sharply and severely the wrong; but excessive indulgence in criticism is never anything but bad, and no amount of criticism can in any way take the place of active and zealous warfare for the right.

Again, there is a certain tendency in college life, a tendency encouraged by some of the very papers referred to, to make educated men shrink from contact with the rough people who do the world's work, and associate only with one another and with those who think as they do. This is a most dangerous tendency. It is very agreeable to deceive one's self into the belief that one is performing the whole duty of man by sitting at home in ease, doing nothing wrong, and confining one's participation in politics to conversations and meetings with men who have had the same training and look at things in the same way. It is always a temptation to do this, because those who do nothing else often speak as if in some way they deserved credit for their attitude, and as if they stood above their brethren who plough the rough fields. Moreover, many people whose political work is done more or less after this fashion are very noble and very sincere in their aims and aspirations, and are striving for what is best and most decent in public life.

Nevertheless, this is a snare round which it behooves every young man to walk carefully. Let him beware of associating only with the people of his own caste and of his own little ways of political thought. Let him learn that he must deal with the mass of men; that he must go out and stand shoulder to shoulder with his friends of every rank, and face to face with his foes of every rank, and must bear himself well in the hurly-burly. He must not be frightened by the many unpleasant features of the contest, and he must not expect to have it all his own way, or to accomplish too much. He will meet with checks and will make many mistakes; but if he perseveres, he will achieve a measure of success and will do a measure of good such as is never possible to the refined, cultivated, intellectual men who shrink aside from the actual fray.

The Ideals of America

WOODROW WILSON || 1902

*To the twenty-first-century observer, the Spanish-American War of 1898
can sometimes seem like a mere blip on the radar of United States history. But that abbreviated conflict provoked nothing less than a national
identity crisis. For more than a century, ever since George Washington,
in his 1796 Farewell Address, urged his presidential successors not to "en-
tangle our peace and prosperity in the toils of European ambition," the
United States had charted a consistently isolationist course. Territorial
expansion had been confined to the three thousand miles of wilderness
that lay to the west of the eastern seaboard, and military action had been
restricted to continental competitors and clear external threats. But then,
in the spring and summer of 1898, the nation's direction changed
abruptly. In a matter of months, the United States—emboldened by a
desire for new commercial opportunities in Asia, unrest in neighboring
Cuba, and the relentless jingoism of newspaper publishers like William
Randolph Hearst—declared war on Spain, easily defeated its navy, and
seized the Spanish-controlled Philippine Islands. To many Americans, it
seemed as if their nation had overnight become the very thing it had
been founded to oppose: a colonial empire.*

*"The Ideals of America," by Woodrow Wilson (1856–1924), examines
America's purpose at the dawn of this new era of imperialism. The essay,
which was first delivered as a speech commemorating the 125th anniversary of the American Revolution's tide-turning Battle of Trenton, shows
Wilson, then the president of Princeton University and a respected political scientist, to be a fervid advocate for America's new muscular role on
the world stage. "No war ever transformed us quite as the war with
Spain transformed us," Wilson writes in this essay. But little more than
a decade later, after Wilson had won the White House in a three-way
race against Theodore Roosevelt and William Howard Taft, his enthusiasm for empire waned. Beleaguered by an implacable insurgency in the
Philippines, a failed American intervention in the Mexican Revolution,
and the wholesale, mechanized slaughter of World War I, he began to
blame expansionist policies for whipping up nationalist furies and jealous rivalries among world powers. By the time he inaugurated the
League of Nations, Wilson had completed his about-face and come
firmly to the view that imperialism was a destabilizing force in the*

world—an impediment to, rather than a catalyst for, the spread of democracy.

It took the War of 1812 to give us spirit and full consciousness and pride of station as a nation. That was the real war of independence for our political parties. It was then we cut our parties and our passions loose from politics over sea, and set ourselves to make a career which should be indeed our own. That accomplished, and our weak youth turned to callow manhood, we stretched our hand forth again to the West, set forth with a new zest and energy upon the western rivers amid the rough trails that led across the mountains and down to the waters of the Mississippi. There lay a commitment to be possessed. In the very day of first union Virginia and her sister states had ceded to the common government all the great stretches of western land that lay between the mountains and that mighty river into which all the western waters gathered head. While we were yet weak and struggling for our place among the nations, Mr. Jefferson had added the vast bulk of Louisiana, beyond the river, whose boundaries no man certainly knew. All the great spaces of the continent from Canada round about by the great Rockies to the warm waters of the southern Gulf lay open to the feet of our young men. The forests rang with their noisy march. What seemed a new race deployed into those broad valleys and out upon those long, unending plains which were the common domain, where no man knew any government but the government of the whole people. That was to be the real making of the nation.

There sprang up the lusty status which now, in these days of our full stature, outnumber almost threefold the thirteen commonwealths which formed the Union. Their growth set the pace of our life; forced the slavery question to a final issue; gave us the civil war with its stupendous upheaval and its resettlement of the very foundations of the government; spread our strength from sea to sea; created us a free and mighty people, whose destinies daunt the imagination of the Old World looking on. That increase, that endless accretion, that rolling, restless tide, incalculable in its strength, infinite in its variety, has made us what we are, has put the resources of a huge continent at our disposal; has provoked us to invention and given us mighty captains of industry. This great pressure of a people moving always to new frontiers, in search of new lands, new power, the full freedom of a virgin world, has ruled our course and formed our policies like a Fate. It gave us, not Louisiana alone, but Florida also. It forced war with Mexico upon us, and gave us the coasts of the Pacific. It swept Texas into the Union. It made far Alaska a territory of the United States. Who shall say where it will end?

The census takers of 1890 informed us, when their task was done, that they could no longer find any frontier upon this continent; that they must draw their maps as if the mighty process of settlement that had gone on, ceaseless, dramatic, the century through, were now ended and complete, the nation made from sea to sea. We had not pondered their report a single decade before we made new frontiers for ourselves beyond the seas, accounting the seven thousand miles of ocean that lie between us and the Philippine Islands no more than the three thousand which once lay between us and the coasts of the Pacific. No doubt there is here a great revolution in our lives. No war ever transformed us quite as the war with Spain transformed us. No previous years ever ran with so swift a change as the years since 1898. We have witnessed a new revolution. We have seen the transformation of America completed. That little group of states, which one hundred and twenty-five years ago cast the sovereignty of Britain off, is now grown into a mighty power. That little confederation has now massed and organized its energies. A confederacy is transformed into a nation. The battle of Trenton was not more significant than the battle of Manila. The nation that was one hundred and twenty-five years in the making has now stepped forth into the open arena of the world.

I ask you to stand with me at this new turning-point of our life, that we may look before and after, and judge ourselves alike in the light of that old battle fought here in these streets, and in the light of all the mighty processes of our history that have followed. We cannot too often give ourselves such challenge of self-examination. It will hearten, it will steady, it will moralize us to reassess our hopes, restate our ideals, and make manifest to ourselves again the principles and the purposes upon which we act. We are else without chart upon a novel voyage.

What are our thoughts now, as we look back from this altered age to the Revolution which to-day we celebrate? How do we think of its principles and of its example? Do they seem remote and of a time not our own, or do they still seem stuff of our thinking, principles near and intimate, and woven into the very texture of our institutions? What say we now of liberty and of self-government, its embodiment? What lessons have we read of it on our journey hither to this high point of outlook at the beginning of a new century? Do those old conceptions seem to us now an ideal modified, of altered face, and of a mien not shown in the simple days when the government was formed?

Of course forms have changed. The form of the Union itself is altered, to the model that was in Hamilton's thought rather than to that which Jefferson once raised before us, adorned, transfigured, in words that held the mind captive. Our ways of life are profoundly changed since that dawn. The balance of the states against the Federal government, however it may strike us now as of capital convenience in the distribution of powers and the quick and various exercise of the energies of the people, no longer seems central to our conceptions of governmental structure, no longer seems of the essence of the people's liberty. We are no longer strenuous about the niceties of constitutional law; no longer dream that a written law shall save us, or that by ceremonial cleanliness we may lift our lives above corruption. But has the substance of things changed with us, also? Wherein now do we deem the life and very vital principle of self-government to be? Where is that point of principle at which we should wish to make our stand and take again the final risk of revolution? What other crisis do we dream of that might bring in its train another battle of Trenton?

In America, and in America alone, did self-government mean an organization self-originated, and of the stuff of the people themselves. America had gone a step beyond her mother country. Her people were for the most part picked men; such men as have the energy and the initiative to leave old homes and old friends, and go to far frontiers to make a new life for themselves. They were men of a certain initiative, to take the world into their own hands. The king had given them their charters, but within the broad definitions of those charters they had built as they pleased, and common men were partners in the government of their little commonwealths. At home, in the old country, there was need, no doubt, that the hand of the king's government should keep men within its reach. The countrysides were full of yokels who would have been brutes to deal with else. The counties were in fact represented very well by the country gentlemen who ruled them, for they were full of broad estates where men were tenants, not freehold farmers, and the interests of masters were generally enough the interests of their men. The towns had charters of their own. There was here no democratic community, and no one said or thought that the only self-government was democratic self-government. In America the whole constitution of society was democratic, inevitably and of course. Men lay close to their simple governments, and the new life brought to a new expression the immemorial English principle, that the intimate affairs of local administration and the common interests that were to be served in the making of laws should be committed to laymen, who would look at the government critically and from without, and not to the king's agents, who would look at it professionally and from within. England had had self-government time out of mind; but in America English self-government had become popular self-government.

No doubt a king did hold us together until we learned how to hold together of ourselves. No doubt our unity as a nation does come from the fact that we once obeyed a king. No one can look at the processes of English history and doubt that the throne has been its center of poise, though not in our days its center of force. Steadied by the throne, the effective part of the nation has, at every stage of its development, dealt with and controlled the government in the name of the whole. The king and his subjects have been partners in the great undertaking. At last, in our country, in this best trained portion of the nation, set off by itself, the whole became fit to act for itself, by veritable popular representation, without the makeweight of a throne. That is the history of our liberty.

It is thus the spirit of English life has made comrades of us all to be a nation. This is what Burke meant by combining government with liberty,—the spirit of obedience with the spirit of free election. Liberty is not itself government. In the wrong hands,—in hands unpracticed, undisciplined,—it is incompatible with government. Discipline must precede it,—if necessary, the discipline of being under masters. Then will self-control make it a thing of life and not a thing of tumult, a tonic, not an insurgent madness in the blood. Shall we doubt, then, what the conditions precedent to liberty and self-government are, and what their invariable support and accompaniment must be, in the countries whose administration we have taken over in trust, and particularly in those far Philippine Islands whose government is our chief anxiety? We cannot give them any quittance of the debt we ourselves have paid. They can have liberty no cheaper than we got it. They must first take the discipline of law, must first love order and instinctively yield to it.

But we may set them upon the way with an advantage we did not have until our hard journey was more than half made. We can see to it that the law which teaches them obedience is just law and even-handed. We can see to it that justice be free and unpurchasable among them. We can make order lovely by making it the friend of every man and not merely the shield of some. We can teach them by our fairness in administration that there may be a power in government which, though imperative and irresistible by those who would cross or thwart it, does not act for its own aggrandizement, but is the guarantee that all shall fare alike. That will infinitely shorten their painful tutelage. Our pride, our conscience will not suffer us to give them less.

And, if we are indeed bent upon service and not mastery, we shall give them more. We shall take them into our confidence and suffer them to teach us, as our critics. No man can deem himself free from whom the government hides its action, or who is forbidden to speak his mind about affairs, as if government were a private thing which concerned the governors alone. Whatever the power of government, if it is just, there may be publicity of governmental action and freedom of opinion; and public opinion gathers head effectively only by concerted public agitation. Those are the things—knowledge of what the government is doing and liberty to speak of it—that have made Englishmen feel like free men, whether they liked their governors or not: the right to know and the right to speak out,—to speak out in plain words and in open counsel. Privacy, official reticence, governors hedged about and inaccessible,—these are the marks of arbitrary government, under which spirited men grow restive and resentful. The mere right to criticise and to have matters explained to them cools men's tempers and gives them understanding in affairs. This is what we seek among our new subjects: that they shall understand us, and after free conference shall trust us: that they shall perceive that we are not afraid of criticism, and that we are ready to explain and to take suggestions from all who are ready, when the conference is over, to obey.

There are, unhappily, some indications that we have ourselves yet to learn the things we would teach. You have but to think of the large number of persons of your own kith and acquaintance who have for the past two years been demanding, in print and out of it, with moderation and the air of reason and without it, that we give the Philippines independence and self-government now, at once, out of hand. It were easy enough to give them independence, if by independence you mean only disconnection with any government outside the islands, the independence of a rudderless boat adrift. But self-government? How is that "given"? *Can* it be given? Is it not gained, earned, graduated into from the hard school of life?

And so the character of the polity men live under has always had a deep significance in our thoughts. Our greater statesmen have been men steeped in a thoughtful philosophy of politics, men who pondered the effect of this institution and that upon morals and the life of society, and thought of character when they spoke of affairs. They have taught us that the best polity is that which most certainly produces the habit and the spirit of civic duty, and which calls with the most stirring and persuasive voice to the leading characters of the nation to come forth and give it direction. It must be a polity which shall stimulate, which shall breed emulation, which shall make men seek honor by seeking service. Those are the ideals which have formed our institutions, and which shall mend them when they need reform. We need good leaders more than an excellent mechanism of action in charters and constitutions. We need men of devotion as much as we need good laws. The two cannot be divorced and self-government survive.

We have come to full maturity with this new century of our national existence and to full self-consciousness as a nation. And the day of our isolation is past. We shall learn much ourselves now that we stand closer to other nations and compare ourselves first with one and again with another. Moreover, the center of gravity has shifted in the action of our Federal government. It has shifted back to where it was at the opening of the last century, in that early day when we were passing from the gristle to the bone of our growth. For the first twenty-six years that we lived under our Federal constitution foreign affairs, the sentiment and policy of nations over sea, dominated our politics, and our Presidents were our leaders. And now the same thing has come about again. Once more it is our place among the nations that we think of; once more our Presidents are our leaders.

It is by the widening of vision that nations, as men, grow and are made great. We need not fear the expanding scene. It was plain destiny that we should come to this, and if we have kept our ideals clean, unmarred, commanding through the great century and the moving scenes that made us a nation, we may keep them also through the century that shall see us a great power in the world. Let us put our leading characters at the front; let us pray that vision may come with power; let us ponder our duties like men of conscience and temper our ambitions like men who seek to serve, not to subdue, the world; let us lift our thoughts to the level of the great tasks that await us, and bring a great age in with the coming of our day of strength.

Contributions of the West to American Democracy

FREDERICK JACKSON TURNER || 1903

Of all the major ideas to come out of American academia, few have matched the significance of Frederick Jackson Turner's "frontier thesis." That thesis—first articulated by Turner (1861–1932), a professor of history at the University of Wisconsin, in a paper delivered to an audience of fellow historians at the 1893 Chicago World's Fair—makes three core arguments: first, that America had been decisively defined by its vast tracts of untamed wilderness and ever-receding western border; second, that the immense obstacles to settlement had irrevocably stamped the national character with a unique brand of individualism; and third, that westward expansion had finally reached the end of the line and had ceased to be the driving force in our national life. It was a theory perfectly attuned to its historical moment. Fin de siècle America was a country in painful transition—its national economy in the throes of depression, its eastern industrialists rapidly consolidating monopolistic power, its cities overflowing with millions of immigrants looking for jobs that didn't exist. To some, Turner seemed not only to explain the crisis but to offer a solution. His argument that the country needed new outlets for its energies was interpreted by the leading imperialist thinkers of the day—including Woodrow Wilson, who had attended graduate school with Turner at Johns Hopkins, and Theodore Roosevelt, who had advanced similar ideas in his bestselling book The Winning of the West *(1889)—as a call to empire. It was Wilson who introduced Turner to the editors of* The Atlantic, *where five of the historian's essays would appear.*

"Contributions of the West to American Democracy," one of three Atlantic *pieces that would be published in Turner's canonical collection,* The Frontier in American History *(1921), is primarily a précis of his frontier thesis. "The free lands are gone," Turner writes in elegiac tones. "It is to the realm of the spirit . . . that we must look for Western influence upon democracy in our own days." Contemporary historians tend to quarrel with such sentiments on both factual and political grounds: great swaths of the western states, they argue, have never been more than barely populated, and Native Americans would dispute the assertion that the lands in question were "free." But most historians do not dispute Turner's key role in making the frontier a permanent part of the American vernacular and in applying the lessons of the past to the social and economic upheavals of his time. He was, in the words of the Yale profes-*

sor of history John Mack Faragher, "America's first truly modern historian."

We find ourselves at the present time in an era of such profound economic and social transformation as to raise the question of the effect of these changes upon the democratic institutions of the United States. Within a decade four marked changes have occurred in our national development; taken together they constitute a revolution.

First, there is the exhaustion of the supply of free land and the closing of the movement of Western advance as an effective factor in American development. The first rough conquest of the wilderness is accomplished, and that great supply of free lands which year after year has served to reinforce the democratic influences in the United States is exhausted. It is true that vast tracts of government land are still untaken, but they constitute the arid region, only a small fraction of them capable of conquest, and then only by the application of capital and combined effort. The free lands that made the American pioneer have gone.

In the second place, contemporaneously with this there has been such a concentration of capital in the control of fundamental industries as to make a new epoch in the economic development of the United States. The iron, the coal, and the cattle of the country have all fallen under the domination of a few great corporations with allied interests, and by the rapid combination of the important railroad systems and steamship lines, in concert with these same forces, even the breadstuffs and the manufactures of the nation are to some degree controlled in a similar way. This is largely the work of the last decade. The development of the greatest iron mines of Lake Superior occurred in the early nineties, and in the same decade came the combination by which the coal and the coke of the country, and the transportation systems that connect them with the iron mines, have been brought under a few concentrated managements. Side by side with this concentration of capital has gone the combination of labor in the same vast industries. The one is in a certain sense the concomitant of the other, but the movement acquires an additional significance because of the fact that during the past fifteen years the labor class has been so recruited by a tide of foreign immigration that this class is now largely made up of persons of foreign parentage, and the lines of cleavage which begin to appear in this country between capital and labor have been accentuated by distinctions of nationality.

A third phenomenon connected with the two just mentioned is the expansion of the United States politically and commercially into lands beyond the seas. A cycle of American development has been completed. Up to the close of the War of 1812, this country was involved in the fortunes of the European state system. The first quarter of a century of our national existence was almost a continual struggle to prevent ourselves being drawn into the European wars. At the close of that era of conflict, the United States set its face toward the West. It began the settlement and improvement of the vast interior of the country. Here was the field of our colonization, here the field of our political activity. This process being completed, it is not strange that we find the United States again involved in world politics. The revolution that occurred four years ago, when the United States struck down that ancient nation under whose auspices the New World was discovered, is hardly yet more than dimly understood. The insular wreckage of the Spanish War, Porto Rico and the Philippines, with the problems presented by the Hawaiian Islands, Cuba, the Isthmian Canal, and China, all are indications of the new direction of the ship of state, and while we thus turn our attention overseas, our concentrated industrial strength has given us a striking power against the commerce of Europe that is already producing consternation in the Old World. Having completed the conquest of the wilderness, and having consolidated our interests, we are beginning to consider the relations of democracy and empire.

And fourth, the political parties of the United States now tend to divide on issues that involve the question of Socialism. The rise of the Populist party in the last decade, and the acceptance of so many of its principles by the Democratic party under the leadership of William Jennings Bryan, show in striking manner the birth of new political ideas, the reformation of the lines of political conflict.

It is doubtful if in any ten years of American history more significant factors in our growth have revealed themselves. The struggle of the pioneer farmers to subdue the arid lands of the Great Plains in the eighties was followed by the official announcement of the extinction of the frontier line in 1890. The dramatic outcome of the Chicago Convention of 1896 marked the rise into power of the representatives of Populistic change. Two years later came the battle of Manila, which broke down the old isolation of the nation, and started it on a path the goal of which no man can foretell; and finally, but two years ago came that concentration of which the billion and a half dollar steel trust and the union of the Northern continental railways are stupendous examples. Is it not obvious, then, that the student who seeks for the explanation of democracy in the social and economic forces that underlie political forms must make inquiry into the conditions that have produced our democratic institutions, if he would estimate the effect of these vast changes? As a contribution to this inquiry, let us now turn to an examination of the part that the West has played in shaping our democracy.

FROM THE BEGINNING of the settlement of America, the frontier regions have exercised a steady influence toward democracy. In Virginia, to take an example, it can be traced as early as the period of Bacon's Rebellion, a hundred years before our Declaration of Independence. The small landholders, seeing that their powers were steadily passing into the hands of the wealthy planters who controlled Church and State and lands, rose in revolt. A generation later, in the governorship of Alexander Spotswood, we find a contest between the frontier settlers and the property-holding classes of the coast. The democracy with which Spotswood had to struggle, and of which he so bitterly complained, was a democracy made up of small landholders, of the newer immigrants, and of indentured servants, who at the expiration of their time of servitude passed into the interior to take up lands and engage in pioneer farming. The "War of the Regulation," just on the eve of the American Revolution, shows the steady persistence of this struggle between the classes of the interior and those of the coast. Indeed, in a period before the outbreak of the American Revolution, one can trace a distinct belt of democratic territory extending from the back country of New England down through western New York, Pennsylvania, and the South. In each colony this region was in conflict with the dominant classes of the coast. It constituted a quasi-revolutionary area before the days of the Revolution, and it formed the basis on which the Democratic party was afterwards established. It was, therefore, in the West, as it was in the period before the Declaration of Independence, that the struggle for democratic development first revealed itself, and in that area the essential ideas of American democracy had already appeared.

Through the period of the Revolution and of the Confederation a similar contest can be noted. On the frontier of New England, along the western border of Pennsylvania, Virginia, and the Carolinas, and in the communities beyond the Alleghany Mountains, there arose a demand of the frontier settlers for independent statehood based on democratic provisions. There is a strain of fierceness in their energetic petitions demanding self-government under the theory that every people have the right to establish their own political institutions in an area which they have won from the wilderness. Those revolutionary principles based on natural rights, for which the seaboard colonies were contending, were taken up with frontier energy in an attempt to apply them to the lands of the West. No one can read their petitions denouncing the control exercised by the wealthy land-holders of the coast, appealing to the record of their conquest of the wilderness, and demanding the possession of the lands for which they have fought the Indians, and which they had reduced by their ax to civilization, without recognizing in these frontier communities the cradle of a belliger-ent Western democracy.

All of these scattered democratic tendencies Jefferson combined, in the period of Washington's presidency, into the Democratic-Republican party. Jefferson was the first prophet of American democracy, and when we analyse the essential features of his gospel, it is clear that the Western influ-ence was the dominant element. Jefferson himself was born in the frontier region of Virginia, on the edge of the Blue Ridge, in the middle of the eigh-teenth century. His father was a pioneer. Jefferson's "Notes on Virginia" re-veal clearly his conception that democracy should have an agricultural basis, and that manufacturing development and city life were dangerous to the purity of the body politic. Simplicity and economy in government, the right of revolution, the freedom of the individual, the belief that those who win the vacant lands are entitled to shape their own government in their own way,—these are all parts of the platform of political principles to which he gave his adhesion, and they are all elements eminently character-istic of the Western democracy into which he was born.

In the period of the Revolution he had brought in a series of measures which tended to throw the power of Virginia into the hands of the settlers in the interior rather than of the coastwise aristocracy. The repeal of the laws of entail and primogeniture would have destroyed the great estates on which the planting aristocracy based its power. The abolition of the Estab-lished Church would still further have diminished the influence of the coastwise party in favor of the dissenting sects of the interior. His scheme of general public education reflected the same tendency, and his demand for the abolition of slavery was characteristic of a representative of the West rather than of the old-time aristocracy of the coast. His sympathy with the Western expansion culminated in the Louisiana Purchase. In short, the tendencies of Jefferson's legislation were to replace the domi-nance of the planting aristocracy by the dominance of the interior class, which had sought in vain to achieve its liberties in the period of Bacon's Rebellion.

Nevertheless, Thomas Jefferson was the John the Baptist of democracy, not its Moses. Only with the slow setting of the tide of settlement farther and farther toward the interior did the democratic influence grow strong enough to take actual possession of the government. The period from 1800 to 1820 saw a steady increase in these tendencies. The established classes in New England and the South began to take alarm. New England Federalism looked with a shudder at the democratic ideas of those who refused to recognize the established order. But in that period there came into the Union a sisterhood of frontier states—Ohio, Indiana, Illinois, Missouri—with provisions for the franchise that brought in complete democracy. Even the newly created states of the Southwest showed the tendency. The wind of democracy blew so strongly from the West, that even in the older states of New York, Massachusetts, Connecticut, and Virginia, conventions were called, which liberalized their constitutions by strengthening the democratic basis of the State.

OF THIS FRONTIER DEMOCRACY which now took possession of the nation, Andrew Jackson was the very personification. He was born in the backwoods of the Carolinas in the midst of the turbulent democracy that preceded the Revolution, and he grew up in the frontier state of Tennessee. In the midst of this region of personal feuds and frontier ideals of law, he quickly rose to leadership. The appearance of this frontiersman on the floor of Congress was an omen full of significance. He reached Philadelphia at the close of Washington's administration, having ridden on horseback nearly eight hundred miles to his destination. [Albert] Gallatin, himself a Western man, describes Jackson as he entered the halls of Congress: "A tall, lank, uncouth-looking personage, with long locks of hair hanging over his face and a cue down his back tied in an eel-skin; his dress singular; his manners those of a rough backwoodsman." And Jefferson testified: "When I was President of the Senate he was a Senator, and he could never speak on account of the rashness of his feelings. I have seen him attempt it repeatedly and as often choke with rage." At last the frontier in the person of its typical man had found a place in the Government. This six-foot backwoodsman, with blue eyes that could blaze on occasion, this choleric, impetuous, self-willed Scotch-Irish leader of men, this expert duelist, and ready fighter, this embodiment of the tenacious, vehement, personal West, was in politics to stay.

In the War of 1812 and the subsequent Indian fighting Jackson made good his claim, not only to the loyalty of the people of Tennessee, but of the whole West, and even of the nation. He had the essential traits of the Kentucky and Tennessee frontier. It was a frontier free from the influence of European ideas and institutions. The men of the "Western World" turned their backs upon the Atlantic Ocean, and with a grim energy and self reliance began to build up a society free from the dominance of ancient forms.

The Westerner defended himself and resented governmental restrictions. The duel and the blood-feud found congenial soil in Kentucky and Tennessee. The idea of the personality of law was often dominant over the organized machinery of justice. That method was best which was most direct and effective. The backwoodsman was intolerant of men who split hairs, or scrupled over the method of reaching the right. In a word, the unchecked development of the individual was the significant product of this frontier democracy. It sought rather to express itself by choosing a man of the people, than by the formation of elaborate governmental institutions. It was because Andrew Jackson personified these essential Western traits that in his presidency he became the idol and the mouthpiece of the popular will. In his assaults upon the bank as an engine of aristocracy, and in his denunciation of nullification, he went directly to his object with the ruthless energy of a frontiersman. For formal law and the subleties of state sovereignty he had the contempt of a backwoodsman. Nor is it without significance that this typical man of the new democracy will always be associated with the triumph of the spoils system in national politics. To the new democracy of the West, office was an opportunity to exercise natural rights as an equal citizen of the community. Rotation in office served not simply to allow the successful man to punish his enemies and reward his friends, but it also furnished the training in the actual conduct of political affairs which every American claimed as his birthright. Only in a primitive democracy of the type of the United States in 1830 could such a system have existed without the ruin of the State. National government in that period was no complex and nicely adjusted machine, and the evils of the system were long in making themselves fully apparent.

The triumph of Andrew Jackson marked the end of the old era of trained statesmen for the Presidency. With him began the era of the popular hero. Even Martin Van Buren, whom we think of in connection with the East, was born in a log house under conditions that were not unlike parts of the older West. Harrison was the hero of the Northwest, as Jackson had been of the Southwest. Polk was a typical Tennesseean, eager to expand the nation, and Zachary Taylor was what Webster called a "frontier colonel." During the period that followed Jackson, power passed from the region of Kentucky and Tennessee to the border of the Mississippi. The natural democratic tendencies that had earlier shown themselves in the Gulf States were destroyed, however, by the spread of cotton culture, and the development of great plantations in that region. What had been typical of the democracy of the Revolutionary frontier and of the frontier of Andrew Jackson was now to be seen in the states between the Ohio and the Mississippi. As Andrew Jackson is the typical democrat of the former region, so Abraham Lincoln is the very embodiment of the pioneer period of the Old Northwest. Indeed, he is the embodiment of the democracy of the West.

The pioneer life from which Lincoln came differed in important respects from the frontier democracy typified by Andrew Jackson. Jackson's democracy was contentious, individualistic, and it sought the ideal of local self-government and expansion. Lincoln represents rather the pioneer folk who entered the forest of the great Northwest to chop out a home, to build up their fortunes in the midst of a continually ascending industrial movement. In the democracy of the Southwest, industrial development and city life were only minor factors, but to the democracy of the Northwest they were its very life. To widen the area of the clearing, to contend with one another for the mastery of the industrial resources of the rich provinces, to struggle for a place in the ascending movement of society, to transmit to one's offspring the chance for education, for industrial betterment, for the rise in life which the hardships of the pioneer existence denied to the pioneer himself—these were some of the ideals of the region to which Lincoln came. The men were commonwealth builders, industry builders. Whereas the type of hero in the Southwest was militant, in the Northwest he was industrial.

It was in the midst of these "plain people," as he loved to call them, that Lincoln grew to manhood. As Emerson says: "He is the true history of the American people in his time." The years of his early life were the years when the democracy of the Northwest came into struggle with the institution of slavery which threatened to forbid the expansion of the democratic pioneer life in the West. But if democracy chose wisely and worked effectively toward the solution of this problem, it must be remembered that Western democracy took the lead. The rail-splitter himself became the nation's President in that fierce time of struggle, and armies of the woodsmen and pioneer farmers recruited in the Old Northwest made free the Father of Waters, marched through Georgia, and helped to force the struggle to a conclusion at Appomattox. The free pioneer democracy struck down the slave-holding aristocracy on its march to the West.

THE LAST CHAPTER in the development of Western democracy is the one that deals with its conquest over the vast spaces of the new West. At each new stage of Western development, the people have had to grapple with larger areas, with bigger combinations. The little colony of Massachusetts veterans that settled at Marietta received a land grant as large as the State of Rhode Island. The band of Connecticut pioneers that followed [the surveyor] Moses Cleaveland to the Connecticut Reserve occupied a region as large as the parent state. The area which settlers of New England stock occupied on the prairies of northern Illinois surpassed the combined area of Massachusetts, Connecticut, and Rhode Island. Men who had become accustomed to the narrow valleys and the little towns of the East found themselves out on the boundless spaces of the West dealing with units of such magnitude as dwarfed their former experience. The Great Lakes, the Prairies, the Great Plains, the Rocky Mountains, the Mississippi and the Missouri, furnished new standards of measurement for the achievement of this industrial democracy. Individualism began to give way to cooperation and to governmental activity.

EVEN IN THE EARLIER DAYS of the democratic conquest of the wilderness, demands had been made upon the government for support in internal improvements, but this new West showed a growing tendency to call to its assistance the powerful arm of national authority. In the period since the Civil War, the vast public domain has been donated to the individual farmer, to states for education, to railroads for the construction of transportation lines. Moreover, with the advent of democracy in the last fifteen years upon the Great Plains, new physical conditions have presented themselves which have accelerated the social tendency of Western democracy. The pioneer farmer of the days of Lincoln could place his family on a flatboat, strike into the wilderness, cut out his clearing, and with little or no capital go on to the achievement of industrial independence. Even the homesteader on the Western prairies found it possible to work out a similar independent destiny, although the factor of transportation made a serious and increasing impediment to the free working-out of his individual career. But when the arid lands and the mineral resources of the Far West were reached, no conquest was possible by the old individual pioneer methods. Here expensive irrigation works must be constructed, cooperative activity was demanded in utilization of the water supply, capital beyond the reach of the small farmer was required. In a word, the physiographic province itself decreed that the destiny of this new frontier should be social rather than individual.

Magnitude of social achievement is the watchword of the democracy since the Civil War. From petty towns built in the marshes, cities arose whose greatness and industrial power are the wonder of our time. The conditions were ideal for the production of captains of industry. The old democratic admiration for the self-made man, its old deference to the rights of competitive individual development, together with the stupendous natural resources that opened to the conquest of the keenest and the strongest, gave such conditions of mobility as enabled the development of the large corporate industries which in our own decade have marked the West.

There has been a steady development of the industrial ideal, and a steady increase of the social tendency, in this later movement of Western democracy. While the individualism of the frontier, so prominent in the earliest days of the Western advance, has been preserved as an ideal, more and more these individuals struggling each with the other, dealing with vaster and vaster areas, with larger and larger problems, have found it necessary to combine under the leadership of the strongest. This is the explanation of the rise of those preeminent captains of industry whose genius has concentrated capital to control the fundamental resources of the nation.

IF NOW IN THE WAY OF RECAPITULATION, we try to pick out from the influences that have gone to the making of Western democracy the factors which constitute the net result of this movement, we shall have to mention at least the following:—

Most important of all has been the fact that an area of free land has continually lain on the western border of the settled area of the United States. Whenever social conditions tended to crystallize in the East, whenever capital tended to press upon labor or political restraints to impede the freedom of the mass, there was this gate of escape to the free conditions of the frontier. These free lands promoted individualism, economic equality, freedom to rise, democracy. Men would not accept inferior wages and a permanent position of social subordination when this promised land of freedom and equality was theirs for the taking. Who would rest content under oppressive legislative conditions when with a slight effort he might reach a land wherein to become a co-worker in the building of free cities and free states on the lines of his own ideal? In a word, then, free lands meant free opportunities. Their existence has differentiated the American democracy from the democracies which have preceded it, because ever as democracy in the East took the form of highly specialized and complicated industrial society, in the West it kept in touch with primitive conditions, and by action and reaction these two forces have shaped our history.

In the next place, these free lands and this treasury of industrial resources have existed over such vast spaces that they have demanded of democracy increasing spaciousness of design and power of execution. Western democracy is contrasted with the democracy of all other times in the largeness of the tasks to which it has set its hand, and in the vast achievements which it has wrought out in the control of nature and of politics. It would be difficult to over-emphasize the importance of this training upon democracy. Never before in the history of the world has a democracy existed on so vast an area and handled things in the gross with such success, with such largeness of design, and such grasp upon the means of execution. In short, democracy has learned in the West of the United States how to deal with the problem of magnitude. The old historic democracies were but little states with primitive economic conditions.

But the very task of dealing with vast resources, over vast areas, under the conditions of free competition furnished by the West, has produced the rise of those captains of industry whose success in consolidating economic power now raises the question as to whether democracy under such conditions can survive. For the old military type of Western leaders like George Rogers Clark, Andrew Jackson, and William Henry Harrison have been substituted such industrial leaders as James J. Hill, John D. Rockefeller, and Andrew Carnegie.

The question is imperative, then, What ideals persist from this democratic experience of the West, and have they acquired sufficient momentum to sustain themselves under conditions so radically unlike those in the days of their origin? Under the forms of the American democracy is there in reality evolving such a concentration of economic and social power in the hands of a comparatively few men as may make political democracy an appearance rather than a reality? The free lands are gone. The material forces that gave vitality to Western democracy are passing away. It is to the realm of the spirit, to the domain of ideals and legislation, that we must look for Western influence upon democracy in our own days.

Trans-national America

RANDOLPH S. BOURNE || 1916

*The first two decades of the twentieth century witnessed one of the
largest waves of immigration in American history. Between 1901 and
1920, more than fourteen million people, principally from southern and
eastern Europe, relocated to the United States, setting off a fierce national debate about how best to incorporate the new arrivals into American society—an argument that continues, in one form or another, to this
day. One side of the ideological divide, which drew on the metaphor of
the melting pot, demanded that the new immigrants shed their ethnic
and cultural identities and assimilate into American life as quickly and
as fully as possible.*

*Against a backdrop of rising ethnic tensions and xenophobia in-
flamed by World War I, the essayist and critic Randolph S. Bourne
(1886–1918) offered up "Trans-national America," a passionate refutation
of the melting-pot theory that would be read and argued over for years
to come. Written three-quarters of a century before buzzwords like "diversity" and "multiculturalism" came into fashion, the essay rejects
mainstream attempts to impose a homogeneous Anglo-Saxon culture on
immigrants of widely varying backgrounds and lays out a "cosmopolitan
vision" for the country—one in which every ethnic group would retain
its customs and character and contribute them to a culturally enriched
whole.*

*Bourne himself was of Anglo-Saxon ancestry, and his family had
been in the United States for generations, but he clearly understood the
challenges of being an outsider: he was a hunchbacked dwarf, and his
face had been permanently disfigured in a flawed forceps delivery at
birth. But for Bourne, biology was not destiny. As an undergraduate at
Columbia, he had become fascinated with the writings of William James
on pluralism—the anti-Platonic idea that the universe is defined by variety rather than uniformity—and he quickly grasped their applicability
to America's changing demographic picture. Despite the controversies
Bourne stirred with "Trans-national America" over what was seen in
some quarters as an all-out assault on Anglo-Saxon values, he appeared
to have a brilliant future. Tragically, only two years after the essay was
published, he died in his New York apartment at the age of thirty-two,
a victim of the great influenza epidemic of 1918.*

No reverberatory effect of the great war has caused American public opinion more solicitude than the failure of the "melting-pot." The discovery of diverse nationalistic feelings among our great alien population has come to most people as an intense shock. It has brought out the unpleasant inconsistencies of our traditional beliefs. We have had to watch hard-hearted old Brahmins virtuously indignant at the spectacle of the immigrant refusing to be melted, while they jeer at patriots like Mary Antin* who write about "our forefathers." We have had to listen to publicists who express themselves as stunned by the evidence of vigorous nationalistic and cultural movements in this country among Germans, Scandinavians, Bohemians, and Poles, while in the same breath they insist that the alien shall be forcibly assimilated to that Anglo-Saxon tradition which they unquestioningly label "American."

As the unpleasant truth has come upon us that assimilation in this country was proceeding on lines very different from those we had marked out for it, we found ourselves inclined to blame those who were thwarting our prophecies. The truth became culpable. We blamed the war, we blamed the Germans. And then we discovered with a moral shock that these movements had been making great headway before the war even began. We found that the tendency, reprehensible and paradoxical as it might be, has been for the national clusters of immigrants, as they became more and more firmly established and more and more prosperous, to cultivate more and more assiduously the literatures and cultural traditions of their homelands. Assimilation, in other words, instead of washing out the memories of Europe, made them more and more intensely real. Just as these clusters became more and more objectively American, did they become more and more German or Scandinavian or Bohemian or Polish.

To face the fact that our aliens are already strong enough to take a share in the direction of their own destiny, and that the strong cultural movements represented by the foreign press, schools, and colonies are a challenge to our facile attempts, is not, however, to admit the failure of Americanization. It is not to fear the failure of democracy. It is rather to urge us to an investigation of what Americanism may rightly mean. It is to ask ourselves whether our ideal has been broad or narrow—whether per-

---

*Mary Antin (1881–1949) was a prominent, Russian-born author and social critic best known for her writings about the immigrant experience and opposition to restrictive immigration policies.

haps the time has not come to assert a higher ideal than the "melting-pot." Surely we cannot be certain of our spiritual democracy when, claiming to melt the nations within us to a comprehension of our free and democratic institutions, we fly into panic at the first sign of their own will and tendency. We act as if we wanted Americanization to take place only on our own terms, and not by the consent of the governed. All our elaborate machinery of settlement and school and union, of social and political naturalization, however, will move with friction just in so far as it neglects to take into account this strong and virile insistence that America shall be what the immigrant will have a hand in making it, and not what a ruling class, descendant of those British stocks which were the first permanent immigrants, decide that America shall be made. This is the condition which confronts us, and which demands a clear and general readjustment of our attitude and our ideal.

WE ARE ALL FOREIGN-BORN or the descendants of foreign-born, and if distinctions are to be made between us, they should rightly be on some other ground than indigenousness. The early colonists came over with motives no less colonial than the later. They did not come to be assimilated in an American melting pot. They did not come to adopt the culture of the American Indian. They had not the smallest intention of "giving themselves without reservation" to the new country. They came to get freedom to live as they wanted to. They came to escape from the stifling air and chaos of the old world; they came to make their fortune in a new land. They invented no new social framework. Rather they brought over bodily the old ways to which they had been accustomed. Tightly concentrated on a hostile frontier, they were conservative beyond belief. Their pioneer daring was reserved for the objective conquest of material resources. In their folkways, in their social and political institutions, they were, like every colonial people, slavishly imitative of the mother country. So that, in spite of the "Revolution," our whole legal and political system remained more English than the English, petrified and unchanging, while in England law developed to meet the needs of the changing times.

It is just this English-American conservatism that has been our chief obstacle to social advance. We have needed the new peoples—the order of the German and Scandinavian, the turbulence of the Slav and Hun—to save us from our own stagnation. Let us cease to think of ideals like democracy as magical qualities inherent in certain peoples. Let us speak, not of inferior races, but of inferior civilizations. We are all to educate and to be educated. These peoples in America are in a common enterprise. It is not what we are now that concerns us, but what this plastic next generation may become in the light of a new cosmopolitan ideal.

We are not dealing with static factors, but with fluid and dynamic generations. To contrast the older and the newer immigrants and see the one class as democratically motivated by love of liberty, and the other by mere money-getting, is not to illuminate the future. To think of earlier nationalities as culturally assimilated to America, while we picture the later as a sodden and resistive mass, makes only for bitterness and misunderstanding. There may be a difference between these earlier and these later stocks, but it lies neither in motive for coming nor in strength of cultural allegiance to the homeland. The truth is that no more tenacious cultural allegiance to the mother country has been shown by any alien nation than by the ruling class of Anglo-Saxon descendants in these American States. English snobberies, English religion, English literary styles, English literary reverences and canons, English ethics, English superiorities, have been the cultural food that we have drunk in from our mothers' breasts. The distinctively American spirit—pioneer, as distinguished from the reminiscently English—that appears in Whitman and Emerson and [William] James, has had to exist on sufferance alongside of this other cult, unconsciously belittled by our cultural makers of opinion. No country has perhaps had so great indigenous genius which had so little influence on the country's traditions and expressions. The unpopular and dreaded German-American of the present day is a beginning amateur in comparison with those foolish Anglophiles of Boston and New York and Philadelphia whose reversion to cultural type sees uncritically in England's cause the cause of Civilization, and, under the guise of ethical indepenence of thought, carries along European traditions which are no more "American" than the German categories themselves.

The non-English American can scarcely be blamed if he sometimes thinks of the Anglo-Saxon predominance in America as little more than a predominance of priority. The Anglo-Saxon was merely the first immigrant, the first to found a colony. He has never really ceased to be the descendant of immigrants, nor has he ever succeeded in transforming that colony into a real nation, with a tenacious, richly woven fabric of native culture. Colonials from the other nations have come and settled down beside him. They found no definite native culture which should startle them out of their colonialism, and consequently they looked back to their mother-country, as the earlier Anglo-Saxon immigrant was looking back to his. What has been offered the newcomer has been the chance to learn English, to become a citizen, to salute the flag. And those elements of our ruling classes who are responsible for the public schools, the settlelements, all the organizations for amelioration in the cities, have every reason to be proud of the care and labor which they have devoted to absorbing the immigrant. His opportunities the immigrant has taken to gladly, with almost pathetic eagerness to make his way in the new land without friction or disturbance. The common language has made not only for the necessary communication, but for all the amenities of life.

If freedom means the right to do pretty much as one pleases, so long as one does not interfere with others, the immigrant has found freedom, and the ruling element has been singularly liberal in its treatment of the invading hordes. But if freedom means a democratic cooperation in determining the ideals and purposes and industrial and social institutions of a country, then the immigrant has not been free, and the Anglo-Saxon element is guilty of just what every dominant race is guilty of in every European country: the imposition of its own culture upon the minority peoples. The fact that this imposition has been so mild and, indeed, semi-conscious does not alter its quality. And the war has brought out just the degree to which that purpose of "Americanizing," that is, "Anglo-Saxonizing," the immigrant has failed.

For the Anglo-Saxon now in his bitterness to turn upon the other peoples, talk about their "arrogance," scold them for not being melted in a pot which never existed, is to betray the unconscious purpose which lay at the bottom of his heart. It betrays too the possession of a racial jealousy similar to that of which he is now accusing the so-called "hyphenates." Let the Anglo-Saxon be proud enough of the heroic toil and heroic sacrifices which moulded the nation. But let him ask himself, if he had had to depend on the English descendants, where he would have been living today. To those of us who see in the exploitation of unskilled labor the strident red *leitmotif* of our civilization, the settling of the country presents a great social drama as the waves of immigration broke over it.

Let the Anglo-Saxon ask himself where he would have been if these races had not come. Let those who feel the inferiority of the non-Anglo-Saxon immigrant contemplate that region of the States which has remained the most distinctively "American," the South. Let him ask himself whether he would really like to see the foreign hordes Americanized into such an Americanization. Let him ask himself how superior this native civilization is to the great "alien" states of Wisconsin and Minnesota, where Scandinavians, Poles, and Germans have self-consciously labored to preserve their traditional culture, while being outwardly and satisfactorily American. Let him ask himself how much more wisdom, intelligence, industry and social leadership has come out of these alien states than out of all the truly American ones. The South, in fact, while this vast Northern development has gone on, still remains an English colony, stagnant and complacent, having progressed culturally scarcely beyond the early Victorian era. It is culturally sterile because it has had no advantage of cross-fertilization like the Northern states. What has happened in states such as Wisconsin and Minnesota is that strong foreign cultures have struck root in a new and fertile soil. America has meant liberation, and German and Scandinavian political ideas and social energies have expanded to a new potency. The process has not been at all the fancied "assimilation" of the Scandinavian or Teuton. Rather has it been a process of their assimilation of us—I speak as an Anglo-Saxon. The foreign cultures have not been melted down or run together, made into some homogeneous Americanism, but have remained distinct but cooperating to the greater glory and benefit not only of themselves but of all the native "Americanism" around them.

What we emphatically do not want is that these distinctive qualities should be washed out into a tasteless, colorless fluid of uniformity. Already we have far too much of this insipidity,—masses of people who are cultural half-breeds, neither assimilated Anglo-Saxons nor nationals of another culture. Each national colony in this country seems to retain in its foreign press, its vernacular literature, its schools, its intellectual and patriotic leaders, a central cultural nucleus. From this nucleus the colony extends out by imperceptible gradations to a fringe where national characteristics are all but lost. Our cities are filled with these half-breeds who retain their foreign names but have lost the foreign savor. This does not mean that they have actually been changed into New Englanders or Middle Westerners. It does not mean that they have been really Americanized. It means that, letting slip from them whatever native culture they had, they have substituted for it only the most rudimentary American—the American culture of the cheap newspaper, the movies, the popular song, the ubiquitous automobile. The unthinking who survey this class call them assimilated, Americanized. The great American public school has done its work. With these people our institutions are safe. We may thrill with dread at the aggressive hyphenate, but this tame flabbiness is accepted as Americanization. The same moulders of opinion whose ideal is to melt the different races into Anglo-Saxon gold hail this poor product as the satisfying result of their alchemy.

Yet a truer cultural sense would have told us that it is not the self-conscious cultural nuclei that sap at our American life, but these fringes. It is not the Jew who sticks proudly to the faith of his fathers and boasts of that venerable culture of his who is dangerous to America, but the Jew who has lost the Jewish fire and become a mere elementary, grasping animal. It is not the Bohemian who supports the Bohemian schools in Chicago whose influence is sinister, but the Bohemian who has made money and has got into ward politics. Just so surely as we tend to disintegrate these nuclei of nationalistic culture do we tend to create hordes of men and women without a spiritual country, cultural outlaws, without taste, without standards but those of the mob. We sentence them to live on the most rudimentary planes of American life. The influences at the center of the nuclei are centripetal. They make for the intelligence and the social values which mean an enhancement of life. And just because the foreign-born retains this expressiveness is he likely to be a better citizen of the American community. The influences at the fringe, however, are centrifugal, anarchical. They make for detached fragments of peoples. Those who came to find liberty achieve only license. They become the flotsam and jetsam of American life, the downward undertow of our civilization with its leering cheapness and falseness of taste and spiritual outlook, the absence of mind and sincere feeling which we see in our slovenly towns, our vapid moving pictures, our popular novels, and in the vacuous faces of the crowds on the city street. This is the cultural wreckage of our time, and it is from the fringes of the Anglo-Saxon as well as the other stocks that it falls. America has as yet no impelling integrating force. It makes too easily for this detritus of cultures. In our loose, free country, no constraining national purpose, no tenacious folk-tradition and folk-style hold the people to a line.

The war has shown us that not in any magical formula will this purpose be found. No intense nationalism of the European plan can be ours. But do we not begin to see a new and more adventurous ideal? Do we not see how the national colonies in America, deriving power from the deep cultural heart of Europe and yet living here in mutual toleration, freed from the age-long tangles of races, creeds, and dynasties, may work out a federated ideal? America is transplanted Europe, but a Europe that has not been disintegrated and scattered in the transplanting as in some Dispersion. Its colonies live here inextricably mingled, yet not homogeneous. They merge but they do not fuse.

America is a unique sociological fabric, and it bespeaks poverty of imagination not to be thrilled at the incalculable potentialities of so novel a union of men. To seek no other goal than the weary old nationalism,— belligerent, exclusive, inbreeding, the poison of which we are witnessing now in Europe,—is to make patriotism a hollow sham, and to declare that, in spite of our boastings, America must ever be a follower and not a leader of nations.

THE FAILURE OF THE MELTING-POT, far from closing the great American democratic experiment, means that it has only just begun. Whatever American nationalism turns out to be, we see already that it will have a color richer and more exciting than our ideal has hitherto encompassed. In a world which has dreamed of internationalism, we find that we have all unawares been building up the first international nation. The voices which have cried for a tight and jealous nationalism of the European pattern are failing. From that ideal, however valiantly and disinterestedly it has been set for us, time and tendency have moved us further and further away. What we have achieved has been rather a cosmopolitan federation of national colonies, of foreign cultures, from whom the sting of devastating competition has been removed. America is already the world-federation in miniature, the continent where for the first time in history has been achieved that miracle of hope, the peaceful living side by side, with character substantially preserved, of the most heterogeneous peoples under the sun. Nowhere else has such contiguity been anything but the breeder of misery. Here, notwithstanding our tragic failures of adjustment, the outlines are already too clear not to give us a new vision and a new orientation of the American mind in the world.

Only America, by reason of the unique liberty of opportunity and traditional isolation for which she seems to stand, can lead in this cosmopolitan enterprise. Only the American—and in this category I include the migratory alien who has lived with us and caught the pioneer spirit and a sense of new social vistas—has the chance to become that citizen of the world. America is coming to be, not a nationality but a trans-nationality, a weaving back and forth, with the other lands, of many threads of all sizes and colors. Any movement which attempts to thwart this weaving, or to dye the fabric any one color, or disentangle the threads of the strands, is false to this cosmopolitan vision.

Perils of American Power

REINHOLD NIEBUHR || 1932

In the years following World War I, the United States found itself in an unfamiliar role on the world stage. Having finally expanded beyond its borders in the 1898 Spanish-American War, the nation rapidly developed, over the next two decades, into a global power—with a gross national product exceeding that of Great Britain, France, Germany, and Japan combined. For most Americans, the country's postwar preeminence—fueled by its growing industrial strength and its emergence from the Great War relatively unscathed—was a point of pride. But for Reinhold Niebuhr (1892–1971), an esteemed Protestant theologian and activist who wrote frequently about political philosophy, international relations, and United States foreign policy, America's identity change was cause for consternation, if not alarm.

In "Perils of American Power," Niebuhr argues that because the United States had been cut off from the outside world for so long and then had amassed so much power so quickly, it was ill equipped to exercise its escalating influence either effectively or ethically. "America is at once the most powerful and politically the most ignorant of modern nations," he writes at the outset of his essay. For all its accomplishments, Niebuhr maintains, the United States remained "a nation of businessmen and engineers," a country whose standing in the world depended upon great wealth and economic power, not upon wisdom or moral authority.

Niebuhr's essay, one of sixteen that he wrote for The Atlantic *over the course of forty years, on subjects ranging from the future of Christianity to the religious roots of Communism, catalogs the potential pitfalls of the country's swift rise to power and posts a series of clear warning signs regarding the imperial road ahead. Power, even in pure economic form, is dangerous, according to Niebuhr, because it provides a false sense of security, provokes envy, fear, and animosity among other countries, and inevitably begets militarization—all of which leads to increasing global instability. "The more our economic power is supported by military strength, the more we shall be inclined to solve our problems by intransigence and defiance of world opinion," writes Niebuhr, who was the author of thirteen books, including* Moral Man and Immoral Society *(1932) and* The Irony of American History *(1952), and who was for three decades a member of the faculty of the Union Theological Semi-*

*nary in New York City. Although "Perils of American Power" was writ-
ten seventy-five years ago, much of what Niebuhr has to say here seems
uncannily pertinent to today's foreign policy debates and ongoing arguments over America's proper role in the world.*

The political situation and problem of America in world affairs can be
put in one sentence: America is at once the most powerful and politically
the most ignorant of modern nations. Both our strength and our ignorance are due to the same set of fortuitous circumstances. Our political
power rests upon our wealth. Neither military prowess nor political skill
was needed to gain our present position among the nations. We are living
in an economic age, and our position in the modern world is secured by
the billion or more dollars which we export every year. Our position is
analogous to that of the village banker who holds a mortgage on every second farm in the county. The kind of skill which is responsible for the building of our national fortune is naturally of a different order than that which
the exigencies of the world political situation require. Both our wealth and
our political ignorance derive from the fact that we are a nation of businessmen and engineers.

We had a virgin continent, rich in every natural resource, to exploit,
and we came into its full possession at the precise moment when railroads
and telegraphs made it possible to manipulate so vast a continental empire
from one political center. Our economic life could therefore develop without the hindrance of the irrelevant customs barriers which have retarded
the economic development of Europe. But these advantages alone would
not explain our economic preeminence. We gave ourselves to business efficiency and technological achievement with greater abandon than any
other people. There are Europeans and Asiatics who suggest that we have
gained the whole world because we lost our souls. While there is an alloy
of envy in the wisdom of this judgment, it is a fact that modern technology is the real creator of modern wealth and that we perfected industrial
technique with more loving devotion than any other people.

Perhaps this was due to the fact, as [the philosopher and historian Os-
wald] Spengler suggests, that culture and civilization are incompatible
with each other, and that the vast immigrant hordes who came to our
shores dissipated their cultural inheritances to such a degree that they
could give themselves to the extensive tasks of civilization with the complete and fervent devotion. It may be that the modern Russians will become our chief competitors for the same reason; for there a nation has

sloughed off the Greek and the European cultural forms which were never really indigenous to it, and the result is the same complete obsession with the engineering task which has characterized our life since the Civil War. The Russians, incidentally, show signs of the same political ineptness and parochialism in manipulating their budding power which we reveal in our developed strength.

OUR BUSINESSMEN AND ENGINEERS SUFFER from the same kind of exaggerated self-esteem that characterizes any class or group which has come into sudden and obvious success. The successful man always assumes that success in his field gives him a warrant to speak with an air of omniscience on every human and social problem. Mr. Henry Ford is a shining example of this tendency. The automobile industry which has given him his eminence is, incidentally, the most perfect example of the social and political ignorance of the engineering mind. Nowhere is technological efficiency more highly developed and nowhere does power express itself with more ruthless disregard of the human factor than in this industry. The ordinary human rights, which the workers of Europe won after decades of travail and which are now generally conceded by the whole of European society, are still disregarded in this industry by engineers who live under the illusion that their efficiency has created some kind of magic solution for the perennial problem of the protection of the weak against the exactions of the strong.

The peculiar weakness of businessmen and engineers is that they tend to disregard the human factor. Engineers are under no necessity to consider it and businessmen have an ideal of business efficiency which reduces it to a minimum. To deal with a matter in a "businesslike" fashion means precisely to eliminate the variable factors which the human situation always creates and to settle the question upon the basis of a general rule.

But it would not be just to attribute our political ineptness solely to the peculiar limitations of the business mind. It is partly due to the suddenness with which we emerged on the world political scene. Our tremendous foreign investments have been accumulated within the short period of a decade and a half. While we were powerful before the World War, we have been thrown into international politics only since then; and we are bound to betray a novice's lack of skill in this new *niveau*. Furthermore, our continent is vast, and it is quite possible to live at its center without having any clear impression of our relations with the rest of the world. There is not, as in England, a metropolitan press available for the majority of our citizens; and the local press prints practically no foreign news.

Moreover, our type of empire develops without impressing its realities upon those who are ultimately responsible for its policies. It is an economic empire, and its power spreads without the panoply which usually accompanies the display of power. The obvious and immediate facts have not changed for an average American since America emerged from infancy to world dominion in the community of nations. The average citizen has a vague sense of pride in identity with a nation which seems to play so large a part in world affairs. But his knowledge of the method of its power and its effect upon other peoples is rudimentary. Yet his is the vote which holds politicians in awe and prevents them from initiating policies demanded by every consideration of international common sense. Thus the phenomenal power of the American empire is scarcely under conscious control.

It is the illusion of strong men and nations that power is the basis of security. There is some justification for the illusion, for, in so far as human society is governed by physical force, obvious strength, whether it be military or economic, may be counted upon not only to defeat the actual foe, but to reduce the potential foe to the impotence of fear. The strongest bully in a gang is rarely challenged to prove his prowess, and a nation which possesses obvious economic or military advantages may indulge in idiosyncrasies and commit errors which would prove fatal to less favored nations. Power is dangerous both to those who wield it and to those who are affected by it. It gives those who wield it a false sense of security which absolves them of the necessity of thinking carefully upon the issues involved in their action. "Power tends to corrupt," Lord Acton observed, "and absolute power corrupts absolutely."

The irresponsibility which power creates corrupts judgment and accentuates the natural tendency toward selfish conduct. Meanwhile the special privileges which the powerful always claim for themselves excite the envy, as their power prompts the fear, of those who deal with them. When envy and fear are compounded they produce hatred. If this hatred in the hearts of the weak is frustrated for a time by their impotence, it usually unites them into a confederacy of power in the end. The Russian aristocracy could offer some interesting testimony upon this point.

The difference between an inept and an astute privileged group or nation is that the former tries to save itself by increasing its power, while the latter usually yields a portion of its privileges in time to avoid disaster. The most outstanding examples of the latter type are the British aristocracy within the British nation and the British nation within the British empire. Both the class within the nation and the nation within the empire have developed a political astuteness which has bordered at times upon moral insight (though pure moral insight is unknown in the life of economic groups and nations) and which has made possible the evolution of a democracy within the nation and a commonwealth within the empire.

OUR POLITICAL IGNORANCE MIGHT NOT BE NOTICEABLE at all in comparison with other nations but for the fact that we wield power so much greater than theirs. In fairness to America it must be said that the average citizen does not entertain with particular sympathy the counsel that we must meet the growing envy, fear, and hatred of the world with increased military power. While we have constantly increased our military and naval expenditures, the average American is not particularly anxious to defy the world or to impress it with military power. We did want a navy as big as any other; but for the average citizen this was desired as a symbol rather than as a tool of our world dominion. The size of our navy has the same significance for us as a palatial residence has for the successful businessman. It is especially important if the success has been recent and there is still some question whether it is generally appreciated and acknowledged. Naturally there are those among us who have more sinister motives for enlarging our military and naval establishment. But the majority of our people have a sentimental devotion to the peace ideal. They do not concern themselves with military ambitions, if for no other reason because they do not understand what animosities the thrust of American power is creating in the world.

Should they become aware of the real perils of our power, they might conceivably be converted to the military ideal. That would be our real undoing. It is dangerous enough to wield as much power as we have with no higher degree of political intelligence. But if we do not support our economic power by extraordinary military force, the exigencies of international life will gradually dissipate our political ignorance and give us experience. We shall learn to live in a world community and make those adjustments to the desires and needs of others which are prompted by both prudence and conscience. We shall learn how to gauge the effect of our actions and the reactions to our attitudes in the life of other nations, and shall know how to set limits to our will to power in the interest of comity in the community of nations. But the more our economic power is supported by military strength, the more shall we be inclined to solve our problems by intransigence and defiance of world opinion, and the more shall we multiply animosities against us in the world community.

The New Isolationism

ARTHUR M. SCHLESINGER, JR. || 1952

It was widely assumed that the Japanese attack on Pearl Harbor, on December 7, 1941, would sound the death knell for American isolationism. The shocking provocation of the United States into World War II gave birth to a whole new era of American engagement in the world— military, diplomatic, and economic. Soon after the American-led victory over the Axis powers, in 1945, the United States implemented the Marshall Plan to rebuild Europe and spearheaded the formation of a handful of international organizations that continue to play important roles to this day—the United Nations, the World Bank, the International Monetary Fund, and NATO. The famous cautionary words of George Washington against "permanent alliances with any portion of the foreign world" and of Thomas Jefferson against "foreign entanglements" seemed then to be a millennium away.

And yet reports of the death of isolationism turned out to be greatly exaggerated, as the eminent historian Arthur Schlesinger, Jr. (1917–2007), argues in this elegant essay. The author of more than twenty books, among them The Age of Jackson *(1945), which won a Pulitzer Prize for history, and* The Age of Roosevelt *(1957–1960), which is still considered the definitive account of the FDR years, Schlesinger warns here against what he sees as a reawakening of America's impulse to withdraw from the world stage. In America's formative years, Schlesinger asserts, isolationism had been good for the country; it had been born out of a healthy desire to steer clear of the perpetual turbulence of Europe and driven by a "passionate sense of a unique national destiny." But a new form of isolationism had emerged at the beginning of the Cold War. For Schlesinger, this new isolationism, personified by the war hero General Douglas MacArthur and the powerful Republican senator from Ohio, Robert Taft, was characterized by a debilitating fearfulness of the outside world, a numbing attachment to the status quo, and a misguided belief in America's need to avoid foreign alliances and to act unilaterally in its own interests.*

Throughout his long and illustrious career, Schlesinger, who was a professor of history at Harvard for fifteen years and a special assistant to Presidents Kennedy and Johnson for three years, would return again and again to the grand themes of his 1952 Atlantic *essay, rejecting the idea of American exceptionalism and embracing multilateralism and diplomacy.*

As he wrote in his last book, War and the American Presidency *(2004):*
"Military might is no substitute for friends and allies."

The Old Isolationism was far more than doctrine and program. It was, above all, a set of intense emotions—emotions deeply founded in the American experience and sharply etched on the American psychology. And, in this deeper sense, isolationism has never died. The events of 1939–45 destroyed the doctrine and the program of the Old Isolationism, but they did not destroy the emotions which underlay and sustained it. In the last six months, the old emotions have begun to generate new doctrines and programs. Today we face a New Isolationism, bent upon what promises to be a fundamental attack on the foreign policy to which the United States and the free world are presently committed.

The internationalist euphoria of the past decade should not lead us to overlook the deep roots which isolationism has in the national consciousness. Americans have always had a natural and splendid exultation in the uniqueness of a new continent and a new society. The New World had been called into existence to redress the moral as well as the diplomatic balance of the Old; we could not defile the sacredness of our national mission by too careless intercourse with the world whose failure made our own necessary. Two great oceans fostered the sense of distance, emphasized the tremendous act of faith involved in emigration, and, at the same time, spared the new land the necessity for foreign involvements.

The resulting isolationism—this passionate sense of a unique national destiny—was, in the beginning, a generous and affirmative faith. We were, as Lincoln said, dedicated to a proposition; we were engaged in a fateful experiment. America was conceived to be perfect, not in achievement, but in opportunity. Our responsibility was not to be complacent about what we had done, but to rise to the challenge of what there was for us to do. Our nation had been commissioned—whether by God or by history—to work out on this remote hemisphere the best hopes and dreams of men. Isolation was a means, not of confining, but of releasing democratic energy. This was the isolationism of the younger George Norris, of the early Hiram Johnson, of the Robert La Follettes.

But American isolationism did not consist only in an affirmation of the uniqueness of America; it also included—and increasingly so—a rejection of Europe. In a sense, of course, the very act of migration had represented an extraordinary act of rejection. "Repudiation of Europe," Dos

Passos once said, "is, after all, America's main excuse for being." Nor could such repudiation be without passion. America's love-hate relationship with Europe has dominated our politics as well as our literature. As European struggles began to force themselves on the American attention, isolationism began to react with ever more explicit hostility and even hatred. An image of Europe began to haunt the isolationist consciousness—an image of a dark and corrupt continent, teeming with insoluble feuds, interminable antagonisms, senseless and malevolent wars. Europe was morally and politically diseased and scabrous; and contact with it would bring the risk of fatal infection. We in America, said [former vice president Herbert] Hoover, have grown steadily apart from the ideas of Europe. "Freed of European hates and fears . . . we have developed new concepts of liberty, of morals and government." We must at all cost save ourselves from what he called, in a savage phrase, "the eternal malign forces of Europe."

In time, the old affirmative isolationism of Norris and La Follette began to give way before the negative isolationism of Hoover. The one was moved by hope for America, the other by hatred of Europe. The one shunned Europe the better to change America, the other, the better to keep America from changing. The one sprang from American progressivism—from a belief that the American experiment was unfinished; the other, from American conservatism—from a belief that American society was complete, and that change meant not progress but disaster. In the end, the abandonment of isolationism by men like Norris before the Second War, and the younger La Follette after, testified to their conclusion that its affirmative possibilities had been exhausted.

The progressive and hopeful form of isolationism thus came to a natural end. What remained was a petulant desire to seal off America from the winds of change which were blowing through the world. And even this conservative isolationism seemed increasingly irrelevant as a basis for national policy. The Second World War itself apparently provided a conclusive demonstration of this obsolescence. For a time, we were all—or nearly all—internationalists. . . . But [isolationist] emotions only went underground; they did not die. The queer complex of feeling, fear, and prejudice was too deep to be repealed in a decade. The emotional core of the Old Isolationism survived—the hatred of Europe and its age-old troubles; the belief in an American purity which should not risk corruption in contact with outsiders; the agoraphobic fear of a larger world; the old, cherished, wistful hope that we could continue to live of ourselves and by ourselves. And, underground, these emotions have continued to exercise a paralyzing effect on policy. More than anything else, perhaps, they have kept America a slumbering giant, unable to export its democratic faith to the peoples of other nations, unable to play a full and affirmative role in the world.

In time, a new isolationist formulation was bound to come—a new triangulation by which the old emotions would try to make terms with the new realities and issue in the form of up-to-date doctrine and program. Behind the virtuous rejection of the term "isolationist," behind the façade of nominal support for existing policies, the New Isolationism has something quite different in mind. If the present policy can be briefly defined, in President Truman's phrase, as "peace through collective strength against aggression," the New Isolationism boggles at the word "collective," and it recoils from the whole theory of building "situations of strength." Its supreme emotional link with the Old Isolationism, for example, is its dislike of allies and its desire for unilateral action by the United States. "Go it alone," cried General MacArthur [to Congress]; and Senator Taft recently added, "The United Nations is an utter failure as a means of preventing aggression. We can never rely on it again." Facts may have destroyed the Old Isolationist policies; it may now be necessary grudgingly to recognize the existence of the world. But, at least, let us not get involved in the worry, expense, and danger of intimate association with other nations.

If the New Isolationism is openly unhappy about "collective" restraint of aggression, it is only slightly less unhappy in its reaction to the whole policy of building strength in the free world. It does not disclaim the objective; but it wants other nations to establish their own strength first in order to prove themselves worthy of American aid (this rule does not apply, however, to Chiang Kai-shek or Franco); and it adds that, in any case, the free world can be built up at half the cost. Hence the persistent campaign to whittle down every proposal for aid to other free nations; any difference, the New Isolationists protest, is a difference in degree, not in principle. Yet differences in degree in this field quickly become differences in principle, as Senator [Arthur] Vandenberg [of Michigan] used to demonstrate with his story of the futility of throwing a fifteen-foot rope to a man drowning thirty feet from shore. The New Isolationism is the policy of the fifteen-foot rope.

The difference in degree, of course, is the grudging compromise the Old Isolationist emotions make with the grim realities of 1952. But it is a compromise with these realities, not an acceptance of them. Senator Taft, once again, has given the most lucid expression of the New Isolationist view. "The policy on which all Republicans can unite," he recently said, "is one of all-out opposition to the spread of Communism, recognizing that there is a limit beyond which we cannot go." The editor of the *New York Post* has dubbed this the all-out, halfway policy. It is the essence of the foreign policy of the New Isolationism.

One must say "of the foreign policy" because foreign policy is not the main concern of the New Isolationism. Indeed, a survey of the New Isolationist literature quickly discloses the conviction that issues of domestic policy, for the United States in 1952, are far more important and fateful than issues of foreign policy. General MacArthur's concern with Korea may have obscured this fact; but it was MacArthur himself who stated the basic premise of the New Isolationism with classic simplicity in his speech last summer to the Massachusetts legislature. "Talk of imminent threat to our national security through the application of external force," he flatly said, "is pure nonsense."

From his military estimate, MacArthur marched on to the obvious conclusion. "It is not of any external threat that I concern myself," he said, "but rather of insidious forces working from within which have already so drastically altered the character of our free institutions . . . those institutions we proudly called the American way of life." The vital dangers to American freedom and survival, in short, are not external; they are internal. And of the internal dangers, two, it develops, are of decisive importance. One of these dangers is excessive government spending. The other is Communist penetration within our own country.

Government spending, in the New Isolationist view, is the overriding issue of national survival. It makes heavy taxation necessary; and "the unconscionable burden of taxation" in the words of General MacArthur, is destroying the free enterprise system. . . . Worse than that, government spending brings the threat of inflation; and inflation provides one more pretext for the imposition of government controls. "All-out war and all-out mobilization," as Taft put it, "are an easy method of socializing a country, and that socializing can easily be made permanent." Thus government spending under the pretext of mobilization is the beginning of a perilous road, whose inevitable end is the extinction of free enterprise and the triumph of socialist regimentation.

The function of the Communist penetration issue is perhaps less immediately obvious, but on a moment's reflection it too becomes perfectly clear. The problem the New Isolationism faces is to disguise the awkward fact that, as we cut our outlays for foreign aid, we retreat, step by step, from the worldwide fight against Communism. This fact has been favorably noted in Moscow, where the New Isolationist attacks on American policy received grateful editorial comment.

How are the New Isolationists to get around the fact that their proposals are greeted with loud cheers in the Kremlin? Somehow they must cover their retreat; and what better way to do so than by raising a great outcry about the supposed dangers of Communism within our own country? Such a sham battle at home might well distract attention from the stealthy desertion of our allies abroad. And the outcry would have the further incidental advantage of putting frightened liberals out of action and of smearing the whole movement for domestic reform.

I do not suggest that these affairs arranged themselves in the minds of the New Isolationists in quite this Machiavellian way. Still, anyone advocating policies which benefit Communism abroad and win the approbation of *Pravda* might well be tempted to justify himself to his constituents by redoubling his zeal to extirpate Communism at home. This, surely, is the powerful logic of the alliance between Taft and McCarthy. The simple fact is that Taft cannot repudiate McCarthy, because he needs him too much. McCarthyism is an indispensable part of the New Isolationism. Without McCarthyism the New Isolationism would be almost indistinguishable from a policy of appeasement.

The triumph of [the New Isolationism] could lead abroad only to an overflow of Soviet power into the regions from which we retreat—until we are forced back into the Western Hemisphere, or, what is more likely, until we perceive what we are doing and then, having invited Soviet expansion, strike back in the panic of total war. And at home we will move steadily into a garrison state, run by men who admire Senator McCarthy and regard his operations as, in Senator Taft's lapidary phrase, "fully justified."

The words of the New Isolationism count less than the deeds: and the deeds shape up into a sinister pattern. The consolation is that this is probably a last convulsive outbreak of an old nostalgia. Once we have exorcised this latest version of isolationism, we may at last begin to live in the twentieth century.

The Illusion of Security

GEORGE F. KENNAN ‖ 1954

*The origins of McCarthyism predate the rise of the demagogic senator
from Wisconsin, Joseph McCarthy, by more than fifteen years. In the late
1930s, a virulent wave of anti-Communist hysteria swept the country
when the notorious House Un-American Activities Committee (HUAC)
inaugurated a series of high-handed tactics—blacklisting, guilt by association, the malicious interrogation of witnesses—that, in the name of
purging Communist subversion, destroyed hundreds of lives over the
course of nearly two decades.*

*George F. Kennan (1904–2005), a career diplomat who had served
for eight years in the American embassy in Moscow and had emerged after World War II as the U.S. government's leading expert on the Soviet
Union, began to take seriously the witch-hunting tenor of the times in
1950, when Senator McCarthy, delivering a bombshell speech in Wheel-
ing, West Virginia, claimed to have a list identifying 205 Communists in
the State Department. Kennan was outraged by McCarthy's baseless accusations, which smeared many of his close friends and colleagues in the
foreign policy establishment. He was well positioned to protest, having
been largely immunized against red baiting by his distinguished credentials as a strong opponent of Soviet Communism. In 1946, Kennan, then
the number-two ranking American diplomat in Moscow, had authored
the famous "Long Telegram," in which he articulated, for the benefit of
his State Department colleagues, his thoughts on how best to deal with
Soviet aggression and global ambitions. The Long Telegram, along with
an equally celebrated article he published the following year in* Foreign
Affairs, *under the byline "X," laid out Kennan's doctrine of "containment," in which he argued that Soviet designs on territories of strategic
importance to the West had to be thwarted not through outright military
confrontation but through relentless political and economic pressure, as
well as covert action. Paired together, Kennan's telegram and article became the bible of America's Cold War policy long after the diplomat himself had left the State Department, in the early 1950s. It was then that, as
a private citizen and historian at Princeton, he began to write and speak
out forcefully about a variety of subjects of deep concern to him, among
them American security and the evils of McCarthyism.*

*In "The Illusion of Security," which he first delivered as a com-
mencement address at Radcliffe College, Kennan demonstrates the link*

between these two topics, contending that McCarthyism (which he never names per se) had flourished because millions of Americans had bought into the myth that "total security" was achievable and that a powerful nation like the United States should be able to eradicate each and every internal threat emanating from a foreign government. "A foreign policy aimed at achievement of total security is the one thing I can think of that is entirely capable of bringing this country to a point where it will have no security at all," Kennan writes. Only two months after The Atlantic published this warning, in August 1954, McCarthy himself finally self-destructed. A series of widely televised hearings, in which he lobbed wild charges of Communist collusion against high-ranking U.S. Army officers, exposed him to the nation as a bullying opportunist, and he died from alcoholism in 1957. Kennan, for his part, went on to live an uncommonly long and intellectually fertile life, winning two Pulitzer Prizes and producing a towering body of work that continues to shed light on the foreign policy challenges of our day.

There has been much in our domestic life of these recent months that I am sure we should all like to forget; and I hope that we shall soon be permitted to forget a great deal of it. But there are certain overriding factors that ought not to pass too quickly out of our memories. We ought not to forget that we have witnessed in these recent months the spectacle of many millions of Americans unable to put in its place and to assess with any degree of balance and equanimity the time-honored and unexceptional phenomenon of foreign political activity, intrigue, and espionage in our midst—a phenomenon which no great power has ever been spared throughout the course of human history, and from which surely no other great power is immune today. Millions of our people have been unable to accept this normal burden of international leadership at its true worth—have been uncertain as to the value to be assigned to it, uncertain as to what weight to give it in comparison with other problems of our national life. And this uncertainty has given them a peculiar vulnerability—a vulnerability to being taken advantage of, to having their fears exploited, and to being stampeded into panicky, ridiculous, and dangerous attitudes, unworthy of their own national tradition, unworthy of themselves.

Under the sign of this weakness we have seen things that cannot fail to bring deepest concern to any thinking American. We have seen our public life debauched; the faith of our people in great and distinguished fellow citizens systematically undermined; useful and deserving men hounded thanklessly out of honorable careers of public service; the most subtle sort of damage done to our intellectual life: our scholars encouraged to be cautious and unimaginative in order to escape being "controversial," a pall of anxiety and discouragement thrown over our entire scientific community, our libraries and forums of knowledge placed on the defensive before the inroads of self-appointed snoopers and censors, a portion of our youth encouraged to fear ideas on the pretext of being defended from them.

We have seen the reputations of our great private philanthropic foundations, with their immense and unique records of contributions to the national life, recklessly attacked; ingratitude flung in the face of the entire institution of private benevolence. We have seen our people taught to distrust one another, to spy, to bear tales, to behave in a manner which is in sharpest conflict with the American tradition. We have seen our friends in other countries frustrated in their efforts to help and support us, reduced to an embarrassed and troubled silence before the calumnies of our enemies upon us, for they were no longer sure whether these calumnies did not contain some measure of truth. And all of this in the name of protection from Communist subversion, and yet every bit of it agreeable to Communist purposes as almost nothing else could be; and all of it supported by people who then have the effrontery to come before us and to say, "Show us one innocent man who has suffered."

Now it would not be hard to name such a man; but it would be possible to name something far more important: it would be possible to name a great people, no more innocent or less innocent than any of the other great peoples of this world, but nevertheless a people of an immense fundamental decency and good will and practical energy, a people in an unparalleled position to exercise a useful and hopeful influence in this tortured and threatened world community, a people to whom an historic opportunity has been given, to whom the hopes of the world had turned; it would be possible to name such a people and to show it now, at the moment of its greatest historic responsibility, disaffected and disoriented in some of the deepest sources of its national morale, injured in its capacity to react to the challenges history has laid upon it, reduced from its natural condition of confidence and buoyancy to a state of cynicism and fearfulness and disgust with the processes of its own public life—and all of this in the name of its protection from external subversion.

I do not mean to overrate these things. I have no doubt that in its superficial aspects all of this will pass—is probably already passing. The names, the idols, the scapegoats, the stereotypes, the abused words, and the perverted symbols—I have no doubt that these will all soon disappear, to join the records of the Know-Nothing movement and the chauvinistic hysteria of 1919 in the unhappier annals of our public life.

But I think we cannot comfort ourselves too much with this reflection. These things *have* happened. We *have* reacted this way, on this occasion. There must have been a reason for our doing so. Have we found that reason and learned from it? Are we going to be better armed to understand the next danger—to resist the next attempt by the unscrupulous to mobilize us against ourselves under the banner of our fears?

THE CAUSES OF THESE PHENOMENA have undoubtedly been many, and deep, and complex. One cannot attempt to recount them or to analyze them in [a] few brief moments. But among these possible causes there is one I should like particularly to mention as perhaps worth your attention at this time.

In the case of each of these disturbing situations I have spoken of, I wonder whether an appreciable portion of our difficulty has not been a certain philosophic error to which we twentieth-century Americans, for one reason or another, are prone. I am referring here to that peculiar form of American extremism which holds it possible that there should be such a thing as total security, and attaches overriding importance to the quest for it. A great deal of the impatience that underlies the growing despair in some quarters over the prospects for coping with world Communism by means short of large-scale violence seems to me to flow precisely from the illusion, no doubt bred by our nineteenth-century experience, that there could and should be such a thing as total military security for the United States, and that anything short of this is in the long run intolerable. And similarly, these frenzies many of us seem to have developed with respect to the problem of internal subversion—do they not reflect a belief that it should be possible for a great power to free itself completely from the entire problem of penetration and intrigue in its life by outside forces and, again, that it is intolerable that this should not be done; so intolerable, in fact, that if it *is not* done, this must be attributed to some stubborn delinquency, if not treason, in the bowels of our public establishment?

If the evil of all this were limited to the fact that it does involve a certain philosophic error, that it causes people to bark up the wrong trees and occasions an inordinate and futile sort of effort, I would not bother to speak of it this morning. But the fact is that it bears dangers worse than any of these. Shakespeare described these dangers, in his inimitable way, in the following words:—

Take but degree away, untune that string,
And, hark! What discord follows; . . .
Then everything includes itself in power,
Power into will, will into appetite,
And appetite, a universal wolf, . . .
Must make perforce a universal prey,
And last eat up himself.

There is something about this quest for absolute security that is self-defeating. It is an exercise which, like every form of perfectionism, undermines and destroys its own basic purpose. The French have their wonderful proverb: *Le mieux est l'ennemi du bien*—the absolute best is the enemy of the good. Nothing truer has ever been said. A foreign policy aimed at the achievement of total security is the one thing I can think of that is entirely capable of bringing this country to a point where it will have no security at all. And a ruthless, reckless insistence on attempting to stamp out everything that could conceivably constitute a reflection of improper foreign influence in our national life, regardless of the actual damage it is doing or the cost of eliminating it, in terms of other American values, is the one thing I can think of that could reduce us all to a point where the very independence we are seeking to defend would be meaningless, for we would be doing things to ourselves as vicious and tyrannical as any that might be brought to us from outside.

This sort of extremism seems to me to hold particular danger for a democracy, because it creates a curious area between what is *held* to be possible and what *is* really possible—an area within which government can always be plausibly shown to have been most dangerously delinquent in the performance of its tasks. And this area, where government is always deficient, provides the ideal field of opportunity for every sort of demagoguery and mischief-making. It constitutes a terrible breach in the dike of our national morale, through which forces of doubt and suspicion never cease to find entry. The heart of our problem, here, lies in our assessment of the relative importance of the various dangers among which we move; and until many of our people can be brought to understand that what we have to do is not to secure a total absence of danger but to balance peril against peril and to find the tolerable degree of each, we shall not wholly emerge from these confusions.

Perhaps I may be permitted, in conclusion, to observe that these reflections are not without their relevance to the problems of the human individual. In this personal existence of ours, bounded as it is at both ends by suffering and uncertainty, and constantly attended by the possibility of ill-ness and accident and tragedy, total security is likewise a myth. Here, too, an anxious perfectionism can operate to destroy those real underpinnings of existence, founded in faith, modesty, humor, and a sense of relativity, on which alone a tolerable human existence can be built. The first criterion of a healthy spirit is the ability to walk cheerfully and sensibly amid the con-genital uncertainties of existence, to recognize as natural the inevitable precariousness of the human condition, to accept this without being dis-oriented by it, and to live effectively and usefully in its shadow.

In welcoming you, then—as it is my privilege this morning to do—into the fellowship and responsibility of maturity, let me express the hope that in each of your lives, as individuals and as citizens, *le bien* may be per-mitted to triumph over its ancient and implacable enemy *le mieux*. And if any of your friends come to you with the message that the problems of public life have become intolerable and require some immediate and total solution, I think you might do well to bear in mind the reply which a dis-tinguished European statesman, Bismarck, once gave to certain of his more impatient and perfectionist contemporaries, who wanted him to solve all his country's problems right away, and entirely. "Let us leave just a few tasks," Bismarck suggested, "for our children to perform; they might be so bored in this world, if they had nothing to do."

Must We Hate?

ARCHIBALD MACLEISH || 1963

The civil rights movement of the 1950s and 1960s gave rise to many vio-
lent confrontations, but few were uglier or more brutal than the 1962
race riots at the University of Mississippi over the Supreme Court–
mandated enrollment of the school's first black student, James Meredith.
In what has been called "the last battle of the Civil War," a mob of sev-
eral thousand protesters, some wielding firearms, others throwing rocks
and bottles, clashed with a much smaller contingent of federal marshals
and guards in a contest that pitted the state's arch-segregationist gover-
nor, Ross Barnett, against President John F. Kennedy. The rioting, which
erupted after prolonged, Machiavellian negotiations between the White
House and Barnett had broken down, turned the school's normally bu-
colic campus into a war zone. By the time the tear gas cleared and order
was restored, thanks to twenty-three thousand U.S. soldiers hurriedly
dispatched by Kennedy, two people lay dead and some four hundred
more were seriously injured.

Among the millions of horrified Americans who watched the bloody
scene and its tense aftermath on national television was Archibald
MacLeish (1892–1982), a three-time winner of the Pulitzer Prize (twice
for poetry, once for drama) and America's most prominent poet-states-
men since James Russell Lowell. In "Must We Hate?" MacLeish delivers
an impassioned indictment of Barnett and his followers, not only for de-
fying the nation's highest court but also for fomenting a ghastly spectacle
that had inflicted serious damage on the country. For MacLeish, the riots
at Ole Miss represented the most egregious example of America's failure
to live up to the democratic ideals set forth in the Declaration of Inde-
pendence.

The contrast between the nation's high ideals and its less lofty social
realities was a theme central to much of MacLeish's work, including such
notable poetry collections as New Found Land *(1930) and* Actfive
(1948). As a poet, MacLeish had started out as a modernist, writing, un-
der the influence of T. S. Eliot and Ezra Pound, graceful, allusive verse
while studiously avoiding political and social issues. But the Great De-
pression and the rise of the Third Reich politicized him, and he went on
to serve under President Franklin Roosevelt in a series of high govern-
ment positions, including Librarian of Congress, director of the Office of
Facts and Figures (a short-lived propaganda agency), and assistant sec-

retary of state for cultural and public affairs. Throughout his long career
as a writer and a public official, MacLeish continued to explore the great
dichotomy he found between word and deed in American life and the
threats he perceived to his hallowed notion of "the American idea." As
he concisely puts it in "Must We Hate?," "America cannot survive if the
American idea is repudiated."

Most things, public things, happen and go by and you forget about them, but not the Mississippi riots. Not for me, anyway, and I don't suppose I'm alone. There must be other Americans who find those faces in their minds as I do—flickering, twisted faces on last September's television screens and still there, still staring. You wonder why.

Not, I'm pretty sure, for the usual reason, the reason we've decided to give ourselves: not because we were shocked by the open defiance of the law. Southern segregationists, including southern segregationist lawyers, including southern segregationist lawyers who have actually read law, have been shouting defiance of the law for years, declaring that the Congress is the sole lawmaking body under the Constitution, that what the Congress means by its laws is for every citizen to decide for himself according to his locality and his inclination, and that the interpretations of the laws by the federal courts in general, and by the Supreme Court in particular, are irrelevant, impertinent, and immaterial, *Marbury v. Madison* and its innumerable successors to the contrary notwithstanding.

I am not suggesting that anyone outside the foggier bayous of Alabama or Louisiana or South Carolina or Mississippi has taken these contentions seriously. I am merely noting that we had heard them before the Oxford riots as we had heard, too, that the doctrine of nullification is still sound doctrine, that John C. Calhoun is the father and fountain of pure constitutional thought, and that the Civil War has been repealed. What was said in Jackson, in other words, and shouted at Oxford was not new and could scarcely have astonished us. Most of it, indeed, went back a hundred years or more. An anonymous professor at the University of Mississippi told the *New York Times* that "sources of information on the thinking of the rest of the nation were shut off" in 1830, at which time "the state's leaders ceased to react to public issues in terms of established fact but were governed instead by the orthodox view," and, in brief, "stopped thinking."

The date may surprise us. It is difficult—or is it?—to think of Faulkner, who spent his life in Mississippi, writing out of a deepfreeze a century old. But the argument itself seems plausible. A state in which a decision of the highest American court can seriously be called a "Communist conspiracy" must necessarily be a state which has been out of touch with history for a rather long time. And a local mentality which can actually read, to say nothing of write, pronouncements like those which appeared in the *Clarion Leader and Jackson Daily News* at the time of the riots is obviously a mentality which only the Boston fudge manufacturer who invented the John Birch Society could regard as in any sense contemporaneous.

The same thing may be said of the violence which pronouncements such as these excited. That, too, should have been foreseen. Elsewhere in the Republic one might be surprised to find a governor who approved the lawlessness he was sworn to suppress, but not in Mississippi, where there were two kinds of law. And elsewhere one might be shocked by state police officers who deserted federal officials in a situation of obvious and increasing danger, but not in Mississippi, where federal officials and state policemen are on opposite sides. Once an entire state has seceded from history—which is, in a sense, to secede from reason—almost anything can happen. Even Ross Barnett. Even the sudden and inexplicable timidity of Ross Barnett's state police.

But if the governor of Mississippi was foreseeable in the light of his history or lack of it, and if the defiance was familiar, what was it that astonished us in Oxford? Why were we shocked into silence by that Sunday's news? Why did we spend the days and nights that followed fiddling with our television sets, watching the faces of little crowds of students on the university campus, following the slight, grave figure of the man who was the center of it all as he moved in and out of the doors and corridors with federal marshals at his side and jeers and spitting catcalls in his ears? Why is it that those scenes come back and back and the heart sinks and a heavy apprehension haunts our minds, an apprehension which was not there before—was never, as long as I can remember, there before?

I think, for myself, what shocked me, sickened me was the black pit of public hatred into which I looked. I had known, of course, that racial hatred existed in this country as it exists elsewhere. I could hardly have helped but know it after the events of my own lifetime. But, whether because of the kind of life I have lived or because of some failure of my own understanding, I had always thought of this hatred as something exceptional, something transient, something which would disappear with the illiteracy and poverty and ignorance out of which it came.

I knew, of course, that there were presumably educated and visibly well-to-do men and women in the South and elsewhere who looked down on Negroes, because I had met such men and women. I knew there were college graduates with enough intelligence to write books who believed, or said they believed, that all Negroes are biologically inferior to all whites. I realized there were people who called themselves Christians who *knew* that God intended the black man to be a hewer of wood and a drawer of water to the white man, any white man of any qualifications or none—particularly none. But I also believed these people to be what they so obviously were—waifs and strays from the great process of history who needed to find somebody or other to look down on in order to look up to themselves. And I never doubted that in an actual test between these petulant opinions on the one side and the Republic on the other the opinions would wither away in shame and disappear. But what happened in Oxford was that they did not wither away. They stared back at you out of young men's faces ugly with spite. They spat back at you out of the faces of middle-aged men whose words would have been incredible if you had not heard them. And it was the Republic which gave ground. In spite of the decisiveness of the President and the courage of the marshals, it was the Republic which gave ground.

For the real confrontation in Mississippi was not a confrontation between federal marshals and a mob. It was not a confrontation between the President of the United States and the local governor. It was not even a confrontation between the Constitution and the doctrine of nullification. It was a confrontation between the Republic itself, the great idea on which the Republic is founded, and the one idea which may, someday, destroy it.

"All politics," as Valéry once said, "presuppose an idea of man." But only the United States, among the nations of history, was brought into being by an explicit and reasoned idea of man to which it was dedicated and on which it was to stand. It is not the second of July, 1776, when the thirteen colonies declared themselves absolved of all allegiance to the British crown, which we celebrate as our national anniversary. It is the fourth day of July. And it is the fourth day of July because America, as the delegates to the Continental Congress well understood, did not begin with the repudiation of British rule. It began with the assertion of the American idea. And it was on the fourth that the American idea was spelled out. At the beginning of the Revolution and down through the first bloodshed at Lexington and Concord there had been no talk of independence and no desire for it. What the Colonists wanted was *British* liberty in America. Only when the Tory ministers made it clear that there would be no British liberty in America, that liberty, if the Colonists were to have it, must be American liberty, did independence become a national objective, and even then independence was a means rather than an end. Liberty was still the prime concern, and until American liberty was defined—a new liberty for a new people in a new world—America had not begun.

It was for no sentimental or idealistic reason, in other words, that the old fathers celebrated the American festival not on the anniversary of American independence but on the anniversary of the declaration of the American idea. For the American idea, quite literally and realistically, *is* America. If we had not held these truths to be self-evident, if we had not believed that all men are created equal, if we had not believed that they are endowed, all of them, with certain unalienable rights, we would never have become America, whatever else we might have become.

But if this is what America is, then it is less difficult perhaps to understand why Oxford shocked us, for what looked out of those flickering faces was the antithesis of America—the passionate repudiation of the American proposition, and thus the implicit rejection of America itself. What we saw in those faces, heard in those words, was not hatred of James Meredith. Not a single student in the University of Mississippi had ever seen James Meredith to know him as a human being before that night. Not a single member of the mob could have told you what he looked like. He was a Negro, and that was enough. But to hate a man because he is a Negro is to hate an abstraction. And to hate an abstraction is to hate an idea. And to hate the particular idea the mob at Oxford hated is to deny America. For the idea those young men and those old men hated was precisely and literally the idea on which this Republic was founded, the idea that any man may claim his equal manhood in this country, his unalienable right. What the mob at Oxford hated was the intolerable idea that this different human being should claim a manhood equal to their own.

Insurrection, a congressman called the Oxford riots. And insurrection they were in the strict legal sense of that term—a revolt against lawful authority. But to those who still love this republic they were far worse than insurrection; they were subversion. And not subversion in the current witch-hunting sense, which sniffs with terror at every dissenting view, but subversion in the honest meaning of that word—subversion of the country itself. For America cannot survive if the American idea is repudiated. Nations are not made by territory, or the greatness of nations by extent of land. Nations are made by commitments of mind and loyalties of heart, and the nobler the commitment of the mind, the higher the loyalty of the heart, the greater the nation. If the American proposition is no longer the proposition to which the American heart and mind were committed at our beginning, then America is finished, and the only question left is when America will fall.

Not soon, you will say. We survived for the first three generations of our history with slaves and masters, and thereafter we survived for a century with segregation and lynchings and all the rest of it, and as for the American idea, it is not our treatment of Negroes alone which has menaced it. Millions of Americans whose forebears came to the United States in the last century and the beginning of this came from countries where the American idea was strange and outlandish and where even the basic conception of self-government was unknown, with the result that there are pockets of opinion in the country even now in which the right of a citizen to exercise his American privilege—to make up his own mind for himself and say what he thinks—is deprecated; where censorship flourishes. All this, of course, is true. The American idea has had to struggle for survival for close to two hundred years, and not always against lynch mobs and White Citizens Committees.

But there is a great difference, notwithstanding, between ignorance of the American idea or misconception of it or even indifference to it on the one side, and denial, denunciation of it on the other. The woman who tries to expurgate her local library of books she does not like and to tell her fellow citizens what they may believe or learn regards herself as a good American—usually as a better American than anyone else. But the man who attempts to deprive other men of the equality of manhood to which the American idea entitles them has no illusions about himself or his relation to the American proposition. Hatred comes first with him, and everything else comes after—including his country's laws, his country's order, and his country itself.

No, it was not the openness of the defiance of the law that shocked me. It was the openness of the hatred, the open recklessness as to the effect of the hatred on anything or everything—United States marshals, United states troops, and the fundamental moral and human belief in which and by which the United States exists. Like a tragedy in which the clown prepares the scene, the great American drama of belief in man moved toward collision with the contempt for man which is its opposite. And before the night was over the people of the United States and of the world—but most immediately the people of the United States—had learned that a considerable body of Americans reject, violently reject, the American idea.

It was a sobering realization and one that should continue to be sobering for a long time to come. Before the Oxford riots we had been aware that our actions as a people did not always chime with our words. Our words described us as an open society, a free world, a bulwark of liberty. Our actions sometimes confessed that there were many Americans to whom our

society was not open, many Americans to whom our world was not altogether free, many Americans whose liberty had fences around it. But our
distress in these contradictions was more embarrassment than anything
else. They lost us propaganda battles, and occasionally they made us feel
like fools, but we were sure of ourselves notwithstanding—sure of our own
integrity and sure, above all, that our hypocrisy was nothing compared
with the hypocrisy of the Russians and the Chinese, to whom peace means
war, conquest is called liberation, and democracy is the state police. Oxford
changed all that. Oxford was not a mere propaganda victory for our enemies. Oxford was a defeat for ourselves.

THE QUESTION WHICH HAUNTS US NOW is how it came about. Was it an
aberration, a local flaw in the fabric of the Republic, a defect in the Missis-
sippians attributable to their peculiarly parochial history? Or was it a larger
fault, a graver fault, in some sense the fault of all of us? This is a question
every man must answer for himself, but nevertheless must answer. To me,
it seems the fault of all of us, for all of us seem to me guilty, in one degree
or another, of the neglect out of which it came. I mean our neglect as a nation, as a people, of our own purpose, our own concern, in our obsession
with the purpose, the concerns, of other nations, other peoples. For fifteen
years, almost twenty, we have allowed the purposes, the plans, the maneuvers of the Communist countries to dominate our attention to such a point
that we have all but forgotten what we mean for ourselves, what we propose for ourselves, what we intend. Where once the test of loyalty in an
American was his love for his own cause, the test has now become what we
call his "anti-Communism"—meaning his hatred of the Russian cause,
that iron religion which the Russians would like to impose on the world.

That we should detest Communism is natural and inevitable. But that
we should make the detestation of Communism the test of our own loyalty to our own intentions is neither natural nor inevitable nor even intelligent. A nation which defines itself in terms of what it is *not* inevitably
begins to forget what it is. And a nation which forgets what it is is a dying
nation. What "anti-Communism," as the great American slogan, produces
is not the triumph of America. What it produces is organizations like the
John Birch Society and people like the California fanatics who were recently intent on rewriting the California constitution in the image of the
late Senator McCarthy.

What it produces is the Oxford mob. For Oxford would have been impossible if the students in that mob who shouted "Communist" at the
United States marshals had been brought up in a generation which be-

lieved not in anti-Communism but in America; a generation which understood that the American idea is not a rhetorical proposition but a realizable cause, the greatest and most powerful of all political causes, a cause which has no need to express itself in hatred for something else but only in affirmation of itself.

There is a moment and there are words in our history which prove that statement. The moment was the darkest our people have ever known, the great division which brought about civil war. The words were spoken by Mr. Lincoln at Independence Hall in Philadelphia as he traveled to Washington for his inauguration as President of a divided land. It was at Independence Hall that the Union which was now about to fall had been created. But how, he asked, had it been created? What was it that had made the Union? What had held those different states so long together? Mr. Lincoln had often inquired of himself, he said, what "great principle or idea it was." And here in Philadelphia he thought he found the answer. "It was not the mere matter of the separation of the colonies from the motherland; but something in the Declaration giving liberty, not alone to the people of this country but hope to the world for all future time. It was that which gave promise that in due time the weights should be lifted from the shoulders of men, and that all men should have an equal chance."

What had created the Republic, in other words, was an idea, a principle. And it was that idea, that principle which alone could save it now. Many of those who listened to him then, like many of those who hear his words today, may well have thought that an idea, a principle was a poor defense in the dreadful struggle which lay ahead. But Lincoln, having found his answer, never doubted it. Two years later, when the war was all but lost, when the determination of the North had been weakened by defeat after defeat and Great Britain was on the point of recognizing the South, he put his faith to the test of action. He emancipated the slaves, changed the Northern cause overnight from a political and constitutional cause to the cause affirmed in the Declaration of Independence, ended once and for all the danger of British recognition of the slaveholding South, and saved the Union.

What we might perhaps be asking ourselves as we look back on Oxford, Mississippi, today and out over the Gulf toward Cuba and on toward the infinite dangers and difficulties which lie ahead is whether we have been wise to put our trust not in our love but in our fear, whether we should not listen even now to the man who knew this country better than any other ever has and find our future and our safety where he found it.

Poetry and Power

JOHN FITZGERALD KENNEDY || 1964

When President-elect John F. Kennedy (1917–1963) invited Robert Frost to read a poem at his upcoming inauguration ceremony, the poet was immensely flattered. Although Frost was eighty-six years old at the time and every inch the grand old man of American letters, he insisted on composing for the occasion a new poem, entitled "Dedication," in which he proclaimed "a golden age of poetry and power." Once Frost took the podium on inauguration day, however, he had trouble deciphering his typescript in the glare of an unexpectedly brilliant January sun. After several uncomfortable moments, Frost managed to recover by reciting from memory one of his most famous poems, "The Gift Outright" ("The land was ours before we were the land's").

The poet's ties to the Kennedys continued to bring him into their Washington orbit for the last two years of his life: in addition to serving out a term as an honorary consultant to the Library of Congress, he lectured in Israel and Greece under the auspices of the State Department in 1961, received a congressional gold medal at the White House in the spring of 1962, and traveled to the Soviet Union that summer at Kennedy's invitation through a State Department cultural exchange program.

After Frost's death in January 1963, Amherst College, where he had been a poet-in-residence, dedicated a new library in his honor, marked by an October ceremony at which President Kennedy delivered the following remarks. In a few memorable words, the president not only extols Frost as "one of the granite figures of our time in America" but also takes up the larger questions of the relationship between poetry and politics and of the role of the arts in American life. "When power corrupts, poetry cleanses, for art establishes the basic human truths which must serve as the touchstones of our judgement," declares Kennedy, who was perhaps the staunchest supporter of artists and the arts ever to occupy the White House. The editors of The Atlantic *reprinted the text of Kennedy's speech as part of a posthumous editorial tribute to the president, who had been assassinated in a Dallas motorcade less than a month after eulogizing Frost at Amherst.*

This day, devoted to the memory of Robert Frost, offers an opportunity for reflection which is prized by politicians as well as by others and even by poets. For Robert Frost was one of the granite figures of our time in America. He was supremely two things: an artist and an American. A nation reveals itself not only by the men it produces but also by the men it honors, the men it remembers.

In America our heroes have customarily run to men of large accomplishments. But today this college and country honor a man whose contribution was not to our size but to our spirit; not to our political beliefs but to our insight; not to our self-esteem but to our self-comprehension.

In honoring Robert Frost we therefore can pay honor to the deepest sources of our national strength. That strength takes many forms, and the most obvious forms are not always the most significant.

The men who create power make an indispensable contribution to the nation's greatness, but the men who question power make a contribution just as indispensable, especially when that questioning is disinterested, for they determine whether we use power or power uses us. Our national strength matters; but the spirit which informs and controls our strength matters just as much. This was the special significance of Robert Frost.

He brought an unsparing instinct for reality to bear on the platitudes and pieties of society. His sense of the human tragedy fortified him against self-deception and easy consolation.

"I have been," he wrote, "one acquainted with the night." And because he knew the midnight as well as the high noon, because he understood the ordeal as well as the triumph of the human spirit, he gave his age strength with which to overcome despair.

At bottom he held a deep faith in the spirit of man. And it is hardly an accident that Robert Frost coupled poetry and power, for he saw poetry as the means of saving power from itself.

When power leads man towards arrogance, poetry reminds him of his limitations. When power narrows the areas of man's concern, poetry reminds him of the richness and diversity of his existence. When power corrupts, poetry cleanses, for art establishes the basic human truths which must serve as the touchstones of our judgement. The artist, however faithful to his personal vision of reality, becomes the last champion of the individual mind and sensibility against an intrusive society and an officious state. The great artist is thus a solitary figure. He has, as Frost said, "a lover's quarrel with the world." In pursuing his perceptions of reality he must often sail against the currents of his time. This is not a popular role. If Robert Frost was much honored during his lifetime, it was because a good many preferred to ignore his darker truths. Yet, in retrospect, we see how the artist's fidelity has strengthened the fiber of our national life.

If sometimes our great artists have been the most critical of our society, it is because their sensitivity and their concern for justice, which must motivate any true artist, make them aware that our nation falls short of its highest potential.

I see little of more importance to the future of our country and our civilization than full recognition of the place of the artist. If art is to nourish the roots of our culture, society must set the artist free to follow his vision wherever it takes him.

We must never forget that art is not a form of propaganda; it is a form of truth. And as Mr. MacLeish once remarked of poets, "There is nothing worse for our trade than to be in style."

In free society art is not a weapon, and it does not belong to the sphere of polemics and ideology. Artists are not engineers of the soul. It may be different elsewhere. But in a democratic society the highest duty of the writer, the composer, the artist, is to remain true to himself and to let the chips fall where they may. In serving his vision of the truth, the artist best serves his nation. And the nation which disdains the mission of art invites the fate of Robert Frost's hired man—the fate of having "nothing to look backward to with pride, And nothing to look forward to with hope."

I look forward to a great future for America—a future in which our country will match its military strength with our moral strength, its wealth with our wisdom, its power with our purpose.

I look forward to an America which will not be afraid of grace and beauty, which will protect the beauty of our national environment, which will preserve the great old American houses and squares and parks of our national past, and which will build handsome and balanced cities for our future.

I look forward to an America which will reward achievement in the arts as we reward achievement in business or statecraft.

I look forward to an America which will steadily raise the standards of artistic accomplishment and which will steadily enlarge cultural opportunities for all our citizens.

And I look forward to an America which commands respect throughout the world, not only for its strength but for its civilization as well.

And I look forward to a world which will be safe, not only for democracy and diversity but also for personal distinction.

America's Crisis Addiction

GEORGE MCGOVERN || 1967

*The roots of the Cold War can be traced back to the 1890s, when the
United States and Russia butted heads over the development of Man-
churia. But it was during World War II that mistrust between the two
world powers, then uneasy allies, began to intensify over military tactics,
suspected secret alliances, and the postwar division of spoils. In the years
following, a series of earthshaking events—the Soviet takeover of Eastern
Europe (from 1945 to 1947), Mao Tse-tung's rout of nationalist forces in
China (in 1949), and the triumph of Fidel Castro's Marxist revolution in
Cuba (in 1959)—served as incontrovertible evidence to most Americans
that the global threat of Communism constituted the great national
challenge of their time.*

*Like many politicians of his era, George McGovern (1922–   ), a
decorated World War II bomber pilot who was first elected to the U.S.
Senate as a Democrat from South Dakota in 1963, abhorred the anti-
democratic principles of Communism. Yet as this incisive essay attests,
he was equally disgusted by the ways in which anti-Communist zealotry
seemed to have hijacked United States foreign policy. In "America's Crisis
Addiction," McGovern argues that the country's ongoing obsession with
Communism had created a mind-set of paranoia and hyperreaction in
Washington that had led to a series of American military interventions
of dubious relevance to the national interest—most notably and disastrously in Vietnam. Another calamitous consequence of these Cold War
attitudes, McGovern contends, is that it detracted national attention and
resources from America's own urgent social problems, among them dete-
riorating schools, declining health care, a faltering economy, and escalating racial tensions. In a line that would reverberate for years, McGovern
asks: "How will the world see us if we succeed in pacifying Vietnam but
fail to pacify Chicago?"*

McGovern was relatively unknown at the time he wrote his Atlantic
*essay. But in 1968, as American deaths in Vietnam rose dramatically and
race riots tore apart dozens of the nation's cities, the quiet-mannered
senator began to emerge from obscurity, and by the time of the infamous,
anarchic Democratic convention in Chicago he had become perhaps the
most respected antiwar politician in the country. Four years later, with
the war still raging, he reached the pinnacle of his influence when he
won his party's nomination to challenge the incumbent president*

Richard Nixon, only to suffer one of the most lopsided electoral defeats in American political history.

The thirteen colonies which leveled their muskets against the established order have evolved into the world's mightiest power in a highly dangerous nuclear age. This is a responsibility which demands a rare capacity to distinguish between fundamental forces at work around the globe and localized crises of uncertain significance.

But there is a disturbing American tendency to overreact to certain ideological and military factors while overlooking issues of vastly greater relevance to our safety and well-being. A civil insurrection in Santo Domingo or Vietnam is dramatic, but what is its significance compared with such quiet challenges as the proliferation of nuclear weapons, the surging of nationalism and social upheavals in the developing world, or the mounting crisis of hunger and population? What, too, is the relationship of the quality and strength of our own society to our position in the world? How will the world see us if we succeed in pacifying Vietnam but fail to pacify Chicago?

Many Americans, having grown impatient with the frustrations of the cold war, see each international tension as an urgent crisis calling for a direct and decisive attack on the enemy. Moreover, there must be no halfway measures: "Either get in or get out!" Those who suggest that there may be a proper limit to American power are branded as "neo-isolationists." A preference for the peacekeeping actions of the United Nations over a free-wheeling unilateral interventionism is, for example, a sure sign of "neo-isolationism."

I believe that, in fact, we are in danger of seeing the isolationists of the 1920s and 1930s replaced by the neo-imperialists, who somehow imagine that the United States has a mandate to impose an American solution the world around. Those who see the United States in this role not only want U.S. police action in each trouble spot, but with decisive speed. The old isolationists and the new imperialists may be cut from the same cloth in that both look with disdain on the claims of the international community in contrast with the American way.

For example, the neo-imperialists' solution to the long, inconclusive struggle in Vietnam is a crushing military onslaught. They reject the outlook expressed not so long ago by General Maxwell Taylor when, as ambassador to Saigon, he said that the issue here is "very largely a political, economic, and psychological problem." They would prefer the approach of former Senator Goldwater, who said of Vietnam: "I would turn to my Joint Chiefs of Staff and say: 'Fellows, we made the decision to win. Now it's your problem.' "

In this scheme of things, the Soviet Union and Mainland China are viewed not as major world powers with which we must live, but as diabolical conspiracies that sooner or later we must face in battle. The answer to other lesser threats, such as Fidel Castro, is the U.S. Marine Corps. If a political rebellion occurs in the Dominican Republic, send in American troops and worry about such international niceties as the UN and the OAS later. The answer to the Berlin problem is simple: "Tear down the wall."

There are doubtless many explanations for the crisis outlook:

For one thing, America is a comparatively new country that has been largely separated from the turmoil of world politics for most of our history. During the nineteenth century, we relied on the British to put out the fires that flared from time to time in out-of-the-way places. We were free to concentrate on the development of our own economy and institutions. Pulled into World War I by the course of events, we swung back to an even more ardent isolationist course in the 1920s and 1930s. It is thus not surprising that faced with a vastly greater international involvement after World War II, we have frequently overreacted to incidents that an older, more mature society would have regarded as "business as usual."

Second, many Americans have not assimilated a sense of the world's diversity, nor do we look at events from an international vantage point. The older nations of Europe, steeped in the maelstrom of continental politics and with a century or more of colonial experience in every corner of the globe, have acquired a cosmopolitan view of the world. But when a political coup is attempted against an unpopular government in the Dominican Republic, or student rioting changes government policies in Japan, or De Gaulle seeks the leadership of Europe after liquidating hopeless French ventures in Asia and Africa, or a guerrilla movement threatens to bring down a much more generously armed American-backed regime in Saigon, we are unable to equate these events with our own experience. The revolution in mass communications instantly brings such developments into our living rooms, but there has been no corresponding increase in our capacity to evaluate the swift changes of our convulsive age.

A third explanation of our tendency to react strongly to events is the unique power of Communism (as a general menace) and of the Soviet Union or China or Cuba or North Vietnam (as the precise devil) to challenge a variety of deeply felt American dreams and values at their core. For the democratically oriented American public, these are evil forces which deny open political discussion, religious freedom, bona fide elections, and a framework of law and legal process. For those businessmen to whom a large portion of the world represents an essential area for expansion, Communism presents a dangerous challenge to capitalist ground rules. For Americans who dream of the United States exercising a dominant role in potentially unlimited areas of world development, to whom Theodore Roosevelt and, later, Henry Luce and others have spoken, Moscow, Peking, Havana, and Hanoi are challenges to the American Century. And finally, for that sizable and vociferous minority whose views are premised on the assumption that conspiracies and dark alien powers sway world affairs— to whom the late Senator Joseph McCarthy was the Angel Gabriel—Communist propaganda is tailor-made.

Thus, the American consensus against Communism—no matter the variety—is rooted in a very real set of challenges and denials. It is not easily dismissed as "hysteria." Its deep traditional sources lead to an almost irresistible identification of any event related to Communism as a crisis, a dire and fundamental threat to basic values.

Our crisis tendency has been given additional force by the nature of our political leadership and our two-party political dialogue, especially since 1950.

In the years immediately following World War II, thanks to the leadership of men such as the late Michigan Senator Arthur Vandenberg, our foreign policy was conducted in a bipartisan manner largely free from political rancor and partisan duels. This was the period which launched the United Nations, the Marshall Plan, and the North Atlantic Treaty Organization.

But with the triumph of Communism in China in 1949, the North Korean attack of 1950, and the breaking of our nuclear monopoly by the Soviet Union, the comparative confidence and calm of post-war American foreign policy were shattered. The first strains of the postwar world were beginning to wear on the American public even before the Korean conflict.

It was these cold-war tensions which set the stage for the poisoning of American political life by the late Senator McCarthy in the early 1950s. Many government officials and politicians still find it expedient to demonstrate their "Americanism" by frequent outbursts of rhetoric directed at the Communist enemy. The two political parties, having generally agreed on basic foreign policy objectives, wage a recurring battle over which party is taking the harder line against the Communists.

FOREIGN POLICY, MORE MYSTERIOUS AND REMOTE than domestic issues, is ideal grist for the political mill. The average citizen knows enough about social security to be somewhat invulnerable to loose charges against the program. But a prediction of disaster in the Caribbean based on alleged evil in high places is beyond the capacity of our citizens to evaluate.

American domestic political considerations have probably motivated our deepening involvement in Vietnam since the 1950s as much as any other factor. The Republicans accused the Democrats of "losing" China to the Communists in the 1940s; Secretary of State John Foster Dulles did not want to "lose" Southeast Asia in the 1950s and see the tables reversed. Whatever else was prudent, it was safest in terms of domestic politics to take a tough, militaristic stand toward revolutionary Asian leaders while embracing the comfortable despotisms.

Looking back on the Bay of Tonkin incidents of August, 1964, one wonders if a crisis was manufactured by the Administration to justify politically popular aerial reprisal against Hanoi backed by a strongly worded congressional resolution—all of this at the beginning of a national election when Administration firmness was being questioned by the political challenger.

Again in February, 1965, American planes began bombing in both North and South Vietnam in response to a nighttime Viet Cong attack which killed several Americans in one of our barracks near Pleiku. Senator Goldwater had earned a "trigger-happy" label in 1964 for recommending the use of American bombers in Vietnam, but Administration spokesmen rationalized the bombing in 1965 by dramatic references to the Viet Cong's dastardly "sneak attack"—implying that enemy troops should attack only in broad daylight after a fair warning. Apparently our spokesmen had forgotten our schoolboy pride in George Washington's "sneak attack" on the British after he and his rebel forces stole across the Delaware River.

THE MEAGERNESS OF GENUINE DISCUSSION about fundamental issues and our tendency to magnify minor incidents have caused us to miss many opportunities for constructive new initiatives both at home and abroad. We have, for example, concentrated too heavily and too long on an all-out military response to the international challenge while neglecting the economic, political, and moral sources of our strength. Frequently we have confused means with ends and then argued about those means with all the passion ordinarily reserved for sacred principles. The crisis mentality and the emphasis on means always call for more and bigger weapons. The crisis addict becomes impatient when it is suggested that a nation's strength is measured as much by the quality of its schools, the health of its citizens, the vigor of its economy, and the treatment of minorities as by the size of its weapons. He lacks the perspective to realize that the steady, peaceful development of Asia, Africa, and Latin America is of far greater significance to American security than the political color of future regimes in Vietnam or in the Dominican Republic.

Foreign aid for underdeveloped countries is a favorite target of crisis-oriented citizens and legislators, who are much more comfortable appropriating $50 billion annually for arms than $2 billion for economic development. The results of foreign aid are too slow to satisfy the mind dominated by a sense of crisis. Indeed, even an economic boycott (Cuba) or limited military action (Korea and Vietnam) is frustrating and unsatisfying to the crisis-prone individual, who would prefer to "clean up the mess" overnight.

Foreign aid bills have been presented to Congress year after year as a stopgap against the spread of Communism rather than as an investment in social and economic development. Poverty-stricken countries have been encouraged by shipment of American arms to build military machines as part of "the free world" defense against Communist aggression. But in the summer of 1965, Pakistan threw its American-supplied Patton tanks into war with India's American-supplied Sherman tanks. The final irony came when the Soviet Union, theoretically a potential target of the tanks, mediated an end to the war. This was scarcely a convincing demonstration of U.S. wisdom in determining other countries' needs.

While recognizing our responsibility to influence world affairs in the direction of peaceful development as best we can, we will do well to heed [the historian] D. W. Brogan's warning of "the illusion of American omnipotence." There is a tendency for some Americans to assume that every distressing situation, no matter how remote, is the result of a failure on our part. During the late 1940s and early 1950s, we talked about "losing China," as though we had somehow been in command of China's destiny. But as Professor Brogan has reminded us, "A great many things happen in the world regardless of whether the American people wish them or not." For example, we ought to take every reasonable step to ensure the success of the Alliance for Progress and the defeat of Castroism in Latin America, but we must also recognize that the success of these efforts depends more on decisions that are made in Latin American capitals than in Washington.

Furthermore, we must be willing to look at our own view of the world with at least as critical an eye as we apply to the views of others. Those who have suggested that college students protesting our Vietnam policy should be automatically drafted are, in effect, calling for a moratorium on conscience and freedom. It would be ironic indeed to surrender liberty in

America in the name of its advancement in Vietnam. Instead of intimidating the public dissenter, we ought to welcome his independence and give his views a careful hearing. Instead of promoting the government official who plays it safe by avoiding thoughts that might irritate his superiors, we ought to encourage intellectual integrity and moral courage as the most precious qualities of the public servant.

IF WE ARE TO STRENGTHEN our position in the world, we must be willing to look carefully and critically at all foreign policy assumptions, including our present course in Southeast Asia and our insistence that the world's largest nation [China] be excluded from the United Nations.

America has achieved a position of power and influence in the world that is unprecedented. We have often used that power generously and courageously, perhaps more than any other nation of our age. I have no doubt of our capacity to respond effectively to a genuine crisis that calls for vigorous and decisive action. I should like to believe that we will also develop a talent for discovering and responding rationally to the underlying forces at work in our time. But to those innumerable tensions, struggles, and incidents of the future that we neither can nor should control, I hope we will manifest a measure of Ralph Waldo Emerson's wisdom: "Let him not quit his belief that a popgun is a popgun, though the ancient and honorable of the earth affirm it to be the crack of doom."

Bystanders to Genocide

SAMANTHA POWER || 2001

The full dimensions of the massacre that took place in the central African country of Rwanda in 1994 were widely known at the time that Saman-tha Power (1970–) began her own investigation of the tragedy. Over the course of a little more than three months, rampaging Hutu soldiers, militias, and civilians—under the direction of the Rwandan govern-ment—had systematically slaughtered 800,000 Tutsi and politically moderate Hutu in a countrywide bloodletting that Power memorably de-scribes below as "the fastest, most efficient killing spree of the twentieth century." In 1998, Power, an Irish-born journalist, lawyer, and human rights activist who had become fascinated by the question of how geno-cide had been allowed to happen in human history, set out to learn whether the United States could have successfully intervened in the Rwandan crisis. For the next three years, she interviewed scores of Clin-ton administration officials and pored over hundreds of pages of newly declassified documents in an effort to explore possible American culpabil-ity in the mass murder.

The results of her investigation are meticulously laid out in "By-standers to Genocide," and they add up to a chilling indictment of the Clinton administration for missing innumerable chances to find a way, either diplomatically or militarily, out of the disaster. For Power, the American failure in Rwanda was an act of moral cowardice that went far beyond the decision not to send troops or to organize a multilateral intervention: American officials, avowedly to evade being drawn into what they misleadingly labeled "a civil war," actually engineered the near-complete withdrawal of a UN peacekeeping force (under the direc-tion of the Canadian major general Roméo Dallaire)—the sole remain-ing hope of quelling the violence. "And even as, on average, 8,000 Rwandans were being butchered each day," Power writes, American officials calculatedly avoided using the word "genocide," lest it force them to take action in compliance with the 1948 Genocide Convention.

"Bystanders to Genocide," which won the 2002 National Magazine Award for public interest, came to The Atlantic *because of the author's close ties to Michael Kelly, who was then the editor-in-chief of the maga-zine. In addition to journalistic intrepidity, the two shared an antipathy to bureaucratic inertia, risk aversion, and dissembling, as well as a belief that American foreign policy, in the face of crises such as Rwanda's,*

should be guided, first and foremost, by a strong sense of moral purpose. Power's Atlantic *article was adapted from her book* "A Problem from Hell": America and the Age of Genocide *(2002), which went on to win the Pulitzer Prize for general nonfiction. But for Power it was a bitter-sweet moment: only a few days before receiving the award, she learned the sad news that her friend and editor, Michael Kelly, had become the first American journalist to die covering the Iraq War.*

In the course of a hundred days in 1994 the Hutu government of Rwanda and its extremist allies very nearly succeeded in exterminating the country's Tutsi minority. Using firearms, machetes, and a variety of garden implements, Hutu militiamen, soldiers, and ordinary citizens murdered some 800,000 Tutsi and politically moderate Hutu. It was the fastest, most efficient killing spree of the twentieth century.

A few years later, in a series in *The New Yorker*, Philip Gourevitch recounted in horrific detail the story of the genocide and the world's failure to stop it. President Bill Clinton, a famously avid reader, expressed shock. He sent copies of Gourevitch's articles to his second-term national-security adviser, Sandy Berger. The articles bore confused, angry, searching queries in the margins. "Is what he's saying true?" Clinton wrote with a thick black felt-tip pen beside heavily underlined paragraphs. "How did this happen?" he asked, adding, "I want to get to the bottom of this." The President's urgency and outrage were oddly timed. As the terror in Rwanda had unfolded, Clinton had shown virtually no interest in stopping the genocide, and his Administration had stood by as the death toll rose into the hundreds of thousands.

Why did the United States not do more for the Rwandans at the time of the killings? Did the President really not know about the genocide, as his marginalia suggested? Who were the people in his Administration who made the life-and-death decisions that dictated U.S. policy? Why did they decide (or decide not to decide) as they did? Were any voices inside or outside the U.S. government demanding that the United States do more? If so, why weren't they heeded? And most crucial, what could the United States have done to save lives?

So far people have explained the U.S. failure to respond to the Rwandan genocide by claiming that the United States didn't know what was happening, that it knew but didn't care, or that regardless of what it knew there was nothing useful to be done. The account that follows is based on a three-year investigation involving sixty interviews with senior, mid-level, and junior State Department, Defense Department, and National Security Council officials who helped to shape or inform U.S. policy. It also reflects dozens of interviews with Rwandan, European, and United Nations officials and with peacekeepers, journalists, and nongovernmental workers in Rwanda. Thanks to the National Security Archive, a nonprofit organization that uses the Freedom of Information Act to secure the release of classified U.S. documents, this account also draws on hundreds of pages of newly available government records. This material provides a clearer picture than was previously possible of the interplay among people, motives, and events. It reveals that the U.S. government knew enough about the genocide early on to save lives, but passed up countless opportunities to intervene.

In March of 1998, on a visit to Rwanda, President Clinton issued what would later be known as the "Clinton apology," which was actually a carefully hedged acknowledgment. He spoke to the crowd assembled on the tarmac at Kigali Airport: "We come here today partly in recognition of the fact that we in the United States and the world community did not do as much as we could have and should have done to try to limit what occurred" in Rwanda.

This implied that the United States had done a good deal but not quite enough. In reality the United States did much more than fail to send troops. It led a successful effort to remove most of the UN peacekeepers who were already in Rwanda. It aggressively worked to block the subsequent authorization of UN reinforcements. It refused to use its technology to jam radio broadcasts that were a crucial instrument in the coordination and perpetuation of the genocide. And even as, on average, 8,000 Rwandans were being butchered each day, U.S. officials shunned the term "genocide," for fear of being obliged to act. The United States in fact did virtually nothing "to try to limit what occurred." Indeed, staying out of Rwanda was an explicit U.S. policy objective.

With the grace of one grown practiced at public remorse, the President gripped the lectern with both hands and looked across the dais at the Rwandan officials and survivors who surrounded him. Making eye contact and shaking his head, he explained, "It may seem strange to you here, especially the many of you who lost members of your family, but all over the world there were people like me sitting in offices, day after day after day, who *did not fully appreciate* [pause] the depth [pause] and the speed [pause] with which you were being engulfed by this *unimaginable* terror."

Clinton chose his words with characteristic care. It was true that although top U.S. officials could not help knowing the basic facts—thousands of Rwandans were dying every day—that were being reported in the morning papers, many did not "fully appreciate" the meaning. In the first three weeks of the genocide the most influential American policymakers portrayed (and, they insist, perceived) the deaths not as atrocities or the components and symptoms of genocide but as wartime "casualties"—the deaths of combatants or those caught between them in a civil war.

Yet this formulation avoids the critical issue of whether Clinton and his close advisers might reasonably have been expected to "fully appreciate" the true dimensions and nature of the massacres. During the first three days of the killings U.S. diplomats in Rwanda reported back to Washington that well-armed extremists were intent on eliminating the Tutsi. And the American press spoke of the door-to-door hunting of unarmed civilians. By the end of the second week informed nongovernmental groups had already begun to call on the Administration to use the term "genocide," causing diplomats and lawyers at the State Department to begin debating the word's applicability soon thereafter. In order not to appreciate that genocide or something close to it was under way, U.S. officials had to ignore public reports and internal intelligence and debate.

The story of U.S. policy during the genocide in Rwanda is not a story of willful complicity with evil. U.S. officials did not sit around and conspire to allow genocide to happen. But whatever their convictions about "never again," many of them did sit around, and they most certainly did allow genocide to happen. In examining how and why the United States failed Rwanda, we see that without strong leadership the system will incline toward risk-averse policy choices. We also see that with the possibility of deploying U.S. troops to Rwanda taken off the table early on—and with crises elsewhere in the world unfolding—the slaughter never received the top-level attention it deserved. Domestic political forces that might have pressed for action were absent. And most U.S. officials opposed to American involvement in Rwanda were firmly convinced that they were doing all they could—and, most important, all they *should*—in light of competing American interests and a highly circumscribed understanding of what was "possible" for the United States to do.

One of the most thoughtful analyses of how the American system can remain predicated on the noblest of values while allowing the vilest of crimes was offered in 1971 by a brilliant and earnest young foreign-service officer who had just resigned from the National Security Council to protest the 1970 U.S. invasion of Cambodia. In an article in *Foreign Policy*, "The Human Reality of Realpolitik," he and a colleague analyzed the process whereby American policymakers with moral sensibilities could have waged a war of such immoral consequence as the one in Vietnam. They wrote,

> The answer to that question begins with a basic intellectual approach which views foreign policy as a lifeless, bloodless set of abstractions. "Nations," "interests," "influence," "prestige"—all are disembodied and dehumanized terms which encourage easy inattention to the real people whose lives our decisions affect or even end.

Policy analysis excluded discussion of human consequences. "It simply is not *done*," the authors wrote. "Policy—good, steady policy—is made by the 'tough-minded.' To talk of suffering is to lose 'effectiveness,' almost to lose one's grip. It is seen as a sign that one's 'rational' arguments are weak."

In 1994, fifty years after the Holocaust and twenty years after America's retreat from Vietnam, it was possible to believe that the system had changed and that talk of human consequences had become admissible. Indeed, when the machetes were raised in Central Africa, the White House official primarily responsible for the shaping of U.S. foreign policy was one of the authors of that 1971 critique: Anthony Lake, President Clinton's first-term national-security adviser. The genocide in Rwanda presented Lake and the rest of the Clinton team with an opportunity to prove that "good, steady policy" could be made in the interest of saving lives.

JUST WHEN DID WASHINGTON KNOW of the sinister Hutu designs on Rwanda's Tutsi? Writing in *Foreign Affairs* last year, Alan Kuperman argued that President Clinton "could not have known that a nationwide genocide was under way" until about two weeks into the killing. It is true that the precise nature and extent of the slaughter was obscured by the civil war, the withdrawal of U.S. diplomatic sources, some confused press reporting, and the lies of the Rwandan government. Nonetheless, both the testimony of U.S. officials who worked the issue day to day and the declassified documents indicate that plenty was known about the killers' intentions.

A determination of genocide turns not on the numbers killed, which is always difficult to ascertain at a time of crisis, but on the perpetrators' intent: Were Hutu forces attempting to destroy Rwanda's Tutsi? The answer to this question was available early on. "By eight A.M. the morning after the plane crash we knew what was happening, that there was systematic killing of Tutsi," Joyce Leader recalls. "People were calling me and telling me who was getting killed. I knew they were going door to door."* Back at the State Department she explained to her colleagues that three kinds of killing were going on: war, politically motivated murder, and genocide. Roméo Dallaire's† early cables to New York likewise described the armed conflict that had resumed between rebels and government forces, and also stated plainly that savage "ethnic cleansing" of Tutsi was occurring. U.S. analysts warned that mass killings would increase. In an April 11 memo prepared for Frank Wisner, the undersecretary of defense for policy, in advance of a dinner with Henry Kissinger, a key talking point was "Unless both sides can be convinced to return to the peace process, a massive (hundreds of thousands of deaths) bloodbath will ensue."

Whatever the inevitable imperfections of U.S. intelligence early on, the reports from Rwanda were severe enough to distinguish Hutu killers from ordinary combatants in civil war. And they certainly warranted directing additional U.S. intelligence assets toward the region—to snap satellite photos of large gatherings of Rwandan civilians or of mass graves, to intercept military communications, or to infiltrate the country in person. Though there is no evidence that senior policymakers deployed such assets, routine intelligence continued to pour in. On April 26 an unattributed intelligence memo titled "Responsibility for Massacres in Rwanda" reported that the ringleaders of the genocide, Colonel Théoneste Bagosora and his crisis committee, were determined to liquidate their opposition and exterminate the Tutsi populace. A May 9 Defense Intelligence Agency report stated plainly that the Rwandan violence was not spontaneous but was directed by the government, with lists of victims prepared well in advance. The DIA observed that an "organized parallel effort of *genocide* [was] being implemented by the army to destroy the leadership of the Tutsi community."

From April 8 onward media coverage featured eyewitness accounts describing the widespread targeting of Tutsi and the corpses piling up on Kigali's streets. American reporters relayed stories of missionaries and embassy officials who had been unable to save their Rwandan friends and neighbors from death. On April 9 a front-page *Washington Post* story quoted reports that the Rwandan employees of the major international relief agencies had been executed "in front of horrified expatriate staffers."

---

*The triggering event of the genocide was a fatal rocket attack, on April 6, 1994, on a jet carrying the Rwandan president Juvénal Habyarimana. Responsibility for the attack is still in question. Joyce Leader was, at the time, the second in command at the U.S. Embassy in the Rwandan capital of Kigali.

†Dallaire, the Canadian army officer, was the commander of the UN Assistance Mission in Rwanda (UNAMIR).

On April 10 a *New York Times* front-page article quoted the Red Cross claim that "tens of thousands" were dead, 8,000 in Kigali alone, and that corpses were "in the houses, in the streets, everywhere." The *Post* the same day led its front-page story with a description of "a pile of corpses six feet high" outside the main hospital. On April 14 *The New York Times* reported the shooting and hacking to death of nearly 1,200 men, women, and children in the church where they had sought refuge. On April 19 Human Rights Watch, which had excellent sources on the ground in Rwanda, estimated the number of dead at 100,000 and called for use of the term "genocide." The 100,000 figure (which proved to be a gross underestimate) was picked up immediately by the Western media, endorsed by the Red Cross, and featured on the front page of *The Washington Post.* On April 24 the *Post* reported how "the heads and limbs of victims were sorted and piled neatly, a bone-chilling order in the midst of chaos that harked back to the Holocaust." President Clinton certainly could have known that a genocide was under way, if he had wanted to know.

Even after the reality of genocide in Rwanda had become irrefutable, when bodies were shown choking the Kagera River on the nightly news, the brute fact of the slaughter failed to influence U.S. policy except in a negative way. American officials, for a variety of reasons, shunned the use of what became known as "the g-word." They felt that using it would have obliged the United States to act, under the terms of the 1948 Genocide Convention. They also believed, understandably, that it would harm U.S. credibility to name the crime and then do nothing to stop it. A discussion paper on Rwanda, prepared by an official in the Office of the Secretary of Defense and dated May 1, testifies to the nature of official thinking. Regarding issues that might be brought up at the next interagency working group, it stated,

> 1. <u>Genocide Investigation</u>: Language that calls for an international investigation of human rights abuses and possible violations of the genocide convention. *Be Careful. Legal at State was worried about this yesterday—Genocide finding could commit [the U.S. government] to actually "do something."* [Emphasis added.]

At an interagency teleconference in late April, Susan Rice, a rising star on the NSC who worked under Richard Clarke, stunned a few of the officials present when she asked, "If we use the word 'genocide' and are seen as doing nothing, what will be the effect on the November [congressional] election?" Lieutenant Colonel Tony Marley remembers the incredulity of his colleagues at the State Department. "We could believe that people would wonder that," he says, "but not that they would actually voice it." Rice does not recall the incident but concedes, "If I said it, it was completely inappropriate, as well as irrelevant."

The genocide debate in U.S. government circles began the last week of April, but it was not until May 21, six weeks after the killing began, that Secretary of State Warren Christopher gave his diplomats permission to use the term "genocide"—sort of. The UN Human Rights Commission was about to meet in special session, and the U.S. representative, Geraldine Ferraro, needed guidance on whether to join a resolution stating that genocide had occurred. The stubborn U.S. stand had become untenable internationally.

The case for a label of genocide was straightforward, according to a May 18 confidential analysis prepared by the State Department's assistant secretary for intelligence and research, Toby Gati: lists of Tutsi victims' names and addresses had reportedly been prepared; Rwandan government troops and Hutu militia and youth squads were the main perpetrators; massacres were reported all over the country; humanitarian agencies were now "claiming from 200,000 to 500,000 lives" lost. Gati offered the intelligence bureau's view: "We believe 500,000 may be an exaggerated estimate, but no accurate figures are available. Systematic killings began within hours of Habyarimana's death. Most of those killed have been Tutsi civilians, including women and children." The terms of the Genocide Convention had been met. "We weren't quibbling about these numbers," Gati says. "We can never know precise figures, but our analysts had been reporting huge numbers of deaths for weeks. We were basically saying, 'A rose by any other name . . .' "

Despite this straightforward assessment, Christopher remained reluctant to speak the obvious truth. When he issued his guidance, on May 21, fully a month after Human Rights Watch had put a name to the tragedy, Christopher's instructions were hopelessly muddied.

> The delegation is authorized to agree to a resolution that states that "acts of genocide" have occurred in Rwanda or that "genocide has occurred in Rwanda." Other formulations that suggest that some, but not all, of the killings in Rwanda are genocide . . . e.g. "genocide is taking place in Rwanda"—are authorized. Delegation is not authorized to agree to the characterization of any specific incident as genocide or to agree to any formulation that indicates that all killings in Rwanda are genocide.

Notably, Christopher confined permission to acknowledge full-fledged genocide to the upcoming session of the Human Rights Commission. Outside that venue State Department officials were authorized to state publicly only that *acts* of genocide had occurred.

Christine Shelly, a State Department spokesperson, had long been charged with publicly articulating the U.S. position on whether events in Rwanda counted as genocide. For two months she had avoided the term, and as her June 10 exchange with the Reuters correspondent Alan Elsner reveals, her semantic dance continued.

ELSNER: How would you describe the events taking place in Rwanda?
SHELLY: Based on the evidence we have seen from observations on the ground, we have every reason to believe that acts of genocide have occurred in Rwanda.
ELSNER: What's the difference between "acts of genocide" and "genocide"?
SHELLY: Well, I think the—as you know, there's a legal definition of this . . . clearly not all of the killings that have taken place in Rwanda are killings to which you might apply that label. . . . But as to the distinctions between the words, we're trying to call what we have seen so far as best as we can; and based, again, on the evidence, we have every reason to believe that acts of genocide have occurred.
ELSNER: How many acts of genocide does it take to make genocide?
SHELLY: Alan, that's just not a question that I'm in a position to answer.

The same day, in Istanbul, Warren Christopher, by then under severe internal and external pressure, relented: "If there is any particular magic in calling it genocide, I have no hesitancy in saying that."

IT IS NOT HARD to conceive of how the United States might have done things differently. Ahead of the plane crash, as violence escalated, it could have agreed to Belgian pleas for UN reinforcements.* Once the killing of thousands of Rwandans a day had begun, the President could have deployed U.S. troops to Rwanda. The United States could have joined Dallaire's beleaguered UNAMIR forces or, if it feared associating with shoddy UN peacekeeping, it could have intervened unilaterally with the Security Council's backing, as France eventually did in late June. The United States could also have acted without the UN's blessing, as it did five years later in

---

*Rwanda is a former Belgian colony, and Belgian troops made up a major portion of the UN forces in the country.

Kosovo. Securing congressional support for U.S. intervention would have been extremely difficult, but by the second week of the killing Clinton could have made the case that something approximating genocide was under way, that a supreme American value was imperiled by its occurrence, and that U.S. contingents at relatively low risk could stop the extermination of a people.

Alan Kuperman wrote in *Foreign Affairs* that President Clinton was in the dark for two weeks; by the time a large U.S. force could deploy, it would not have saved "even half of the ultimate victims." The evidence indicates that the killers' intentions were known by mid-level officials and knowable by their bosses within a week of the plane crash. Any failure to fully appreciate the genocide stemmed from political, moral, and imaginative weaknesses, not informational ones. As for what force could have accomplished, Kuperman's claims are purely speculative. We cannot know how the announcement of a robust or even a limited U.S. deployment would have affected the perpetrators' behavior. It is worth noting that even Kuperman concedes that belated intervention would have saved 75,000 to 125,000— no small achievement. A more serious challenge comes from the U.S. officials who argue that no amount of leadership from the White House would have overcome congressional opposition to sending U.S. troops to Africa. But even if that highly debatable point was true, the United States still had a variety of options. Instead of leaving it to mid-level officials to communicate with the Rwandan leadership behind the scenes, senior officials in the Administration could have taken control of the process. They could have publicly and frequently denounced the slaughter. They could have branded the crimes "genocide" at a far earlier stage. They could have called for the expulsion of the Rwandan delegation from the Security Council. On the telephone, at the UN, and on the Voice of America they could have threatened to prosecute those complicit in the genocide, naming names when possible. They could have deployed Pentagon assets to jam—even temporarily—the crucial, deadly radio broadcasts.

Instead of demanding a UN withdrawal, quibbling over costs, and coming forward (belatedly) with a plan better suited to caring for refugees than to stopping massacres, U.S. officials could have worked to make UN-AMIR a force to contend with. They could have urged their Belgian allies to stay and protect Rwandan civilians. If the Belgians insisted on withdrawing, the White House could have done everything within its power to make sure that Dallaire was immediately reinforced. Senior officials could have spent U.S. political capital rallying troops from other nations and could have supplied strategic airlift and logistic support to a coalition that it had helped to create. In short, the United States could have led the world.

Why did none of these things happen? One reason is that all possible sources of pressure—U.S. allies, Congress, editorial boards, and the American people—were mute when it mattered for Rwanda. American leaders have a circular and deliberate relationship to public opinion. It is circular because public opinion is rarely if ever aroused by foreign crises, even genocidal ones, in the absence of political leadership, and yet at the same time, American leaders continually cite the absence of public support as grounds for inaction. The relationship is deliberate because American leadership is not absent in such circumstances: it was present regarding Rwanda, but devoted mainly to suppressing public outrage and thwarting UN initiatives so as to avoid acting.

Strikingly, most officials involved in shaping U.S. policy were able to define the decision not to stop genocide as ethical and moral. The Administration employed several devices to keep down enthusiasm for action and to preserve the public's sense—and, more important, its own—that U.S. policy choices were not merely politically astute but also morally acceptable. First, Administration officials exaggerated the extremity of the possible responses. Time and again U.S. leaders posed the choice as between staying out of Rwanda and "getting involved everywhere." In addition, they often presented the choice as one between doing nothing and sending in the Marines. On May 25, at a Naval Academy graduation ceremony, Clinton described America's relationship to ethnic trouble spots: "We cannot turn away from them, but our interests are not sufficiently at stake in so many of them to justify a commitment of our folks."

Second, Administration policymakers appealed to notions of the greater good. They did not simply frame U.S. policy as one contrived in order to advance the national interest or avoid U.S. casualties. Rather, they often argued against intervention from the standpoint of people committed to protecting human life. Owing to recent failures in UN peacekeeping, many humanitarian interventionists in the U.S. government were concerned about the future of America's relationship with the United Nations generally and peacekeeping specifically. They believed that the UN and humanitarianism could not afford another Somalia. Many internalized the belief that the UN had more to lose by sending reinforcements and failing than by allowing the killings to proceed. Their chief priority, after the evacuation of the Americans, was looking after UN peacekeepers, and they justified the withdrawal of the peacekeepers on the grounds that it would ensure a future for humanitarian intervention. In other words, Dallaire's peacekeeping mission in Rwanda had to be destroyed so that peacekeeping might be saved for use elsewhere.

A third feature of the response that helped to console U.S. officials at the time was the sheer flurry of Rwanda-related activity. U.S. officials with a special concern for Rwanda took their solace from mini-victories—working on behalf of specific individuals or groups. Government officials involved in policy met constantly and remained "seized of the matter"; they neither appeared nor felt indifferent. Although little in the way of effective intervention emerged from mid-level meetings in Washington or New York, an abundance of memoranda and other documents did.

Finally, the almost willful delusion that what was happening in Rwanda did not amount to genocide created a nurturing ethical framework for inaction. "War" was "tragic" but created no moral imperative.

What is most frightening about this story is that it testifies to a system that in effect worked. President Clinton and his advisers had several aims. First, they wanted to avoid engagement in a conflict that posed little threat to American interests, narrowly defined. Second, they sought to appease a restless Congress by showing that they were cautious in their approach to peacekeeping. And third, they hoped to contain the political costs and avoid the moral stigma associated with allowing genocide. By and large, they achieved all three objectives. The normal operations of the foreign-policy bureaucracy and the international community permitted an illusion of continual deliberation, complex activity, and intense concern, even as Rwandans were left to die.

One U.S. official kept a journal during the crisis. In late May, exasperated by the obstructionism pervading the bureaucracy, the official dashed off this lament:

> A military that wants to go nowhere to do anything—or let go of their toys so someone else can do it. A White House cowed by the brass (and we are to give lessons on how the armed forces take orders from civilians?). An NSC that does peacekeeping by the book—the accounting book, that is. And an assistance program that prefers whites (Europe) to blacks. When it comes to human rights we have no problem drawing the line in the sand of the dark continent (just don't ask us to *do* anything—agonizing is our specialty), but not China or anyplace else business looks good.
>
> We have a foreign policy based on our amoral economic interests run by amateurs who want to stand for something—hence the

agony—but ultimately don't want to exercise any leadership that has a cost.

They say there may be as many as a million massacred in Rwanda. The militias continue to slay the innocent and the educated. . . . Has it really cost the United States nothing?

American Ground

WILLIAM LANGEWIESCHE ‖ 2002

Immediately following the attacks of 9/11, the longtime Atlantic corre-spondent William Langewiesche was on the telephone with the editor-in-chief, Michael Kelly, and the managing editor, Cullen Murphy, hashing out how he might best contribute to the magazine's coverage of the tragedy and its aftermath. One option was to fly Langewiesche, who was at home in Davis, California, to Pakistan, from which he would make his way into Afghanistan and join up with the Northern Alliance as it waged war against al-Qaeda's Taliban sponsors; another was to dispatch him to New York City to chronicle the frenetic rescue-and-recovery re-sponse that had already gotten under way amid the ruins of the World Trade Center.

As soon as the ban on air travel was lifted—and Langewiesche had completed his eleventh-hour replacement cover story for the next issue, "The Crash of EgyptAir 990" (see p. 306)—the correspondent flew to New York and took a quick reading of the disaster scene, trying to deter-mine which municipal officials and agencies would be entrusted with the gargantuan job of removing the tons of rubble and locating the thou-sands of victims buried deep within. At first, Langewiesche was stymied in his efforts to secure access to the site—both by stonewalling officials of the city's Office of Emergency Management, the agency ostensibly in charge of the rescue and recovery, and by the legions of reporters queuing up for press credentials at police headquarters. It appeared that he would soon be on his way to Pakistan. Serendipitously, however, Kenneth Holden, the commissioner of the city's Department of Design and Con-struction—a relatively small, little-known agency that Langewiesche had also petitioned and that had unexpectedly begun to emerge as the de facto leader of the response operations—was a longtime fan of the writer's work and managed to persuade City Hall to give him complete access to Ground Zero.

For the next nine months, Langewiesche was the sole journalist to have not only round-the-clock freedom to interview supervisors, contrac-tors, and workers excavating the so-called "Pile" but also unrestricted entrée to prolonged strategy meetings and seat-of-the-pants problem-solving sessions among the key players. For all the devastation and car-nage he encountered day after day at the Pile, Langewiesche found a surprisingly inspiring story to tell—one of extraordinary human re-

sourcefulness and resilience. In this excerpt from the first installment of a three-part article—which, at seventy thousand words, was the longest piece of original reporting that The Atlantic had ever published—he writes: "Despite the apocalyptic nature of the scene, the response was un-hesitant and almost childishly optimistic: it was simply understood that you would find survivors, and then that you would find the dead . . . and that you would work night and day to clean up the mess, and that this would allow the world's greatest city to rebuild quickly, and maybe even to make itself into something better than before."

When the Twin Towers collapsed, on the warm, bright morning of September 11, 2001, they made a sound heard variously around New York as a roar, a growl, or distant thunder. The South Tower was the first to go. At 9:59 its upper floors tilted briefly before dropping, disintegrating, and driving the building straight down to the ground. The fall lasted ten seconds, as did the sound. Many people died, but mercifully fast. Twenty-nine minutes later the North Tower collapsed just as quickly, and with much the same result. Somehow a few people survived. For an instant, each tower left its imprint in the air, a phantom of pulverized concrete marking a place that then became a memory. Prefabricated sections of the external steel columns tumbled down onto lesser buildings, piling onto terraces and rooftops, punching through parking structures, offices, and stores, inducing secondary collapses and igniting fires. The most catastrophic effects were eerily selective: with the exception of Saint Nicholas, a tiny Greek Orthodox church that dissolved in the rain of steel, the only buildings completely wrecked were those that carried the World Trade Center label. There were seven of them, and ultimately none endured. Not even the so-called World Trade Center Seven, a relatively new forty-seven-floor tower that stood independently across the street from the complex, was able to escape the fate associated with its name. Though it did not seem seriously wounded at first, it burned persistently throughout the day, and that evening became the first steel-frame high-rise in history to fall solely because of fire.

There was wider damage, of course, and on the scale of ordinary disasters it was heavy. For thirty years the Twin Towers had stood above the streets as all tall buildings do, as a bomb of sorts, a repository for the prodigious energy originally required to raise so much weight so high. Now, in a single morning, in twin ten-second pulses, the towers released that energy back into New York. Massive steel beams flew through the neighborhood like gargantuan spears, penetrating subway lines and underground passages to depths of thirty feet, crushing them, rupturing water mains and gas lines, and stabbing high into the sides of nearby office towers, where they lodged. The phone system, the fiber-optic network, and the electric power grid were knocked out. Ambulances, cars, and fire trucks were smashed by falling debris, and some were hammered five floors down from the street into the insane turmoil erupting inside the World Trade Center's immense "bathtub"—a ten-acre foundation hole, seventy feet deep, that suffered unimaginable violence as it absorbed the brunt of each tower's collapse.

The energy released within that wild, inaccessible core lit fires that cooked the ruins for months afterward. Outside of each tower's footprint, and still within the foundation hole, it demolished most of the six-story subterranean structure—consisting largely of parking garages that were either pulverized or badly broken and left to hang. Deep underground it also destroyed part of the Port Authority Trans-Hudson (PATH) commuter line—a railroad from New Jersey that, having passed in a single-track tube through the watery muck of the river's bottom, emerged into the foundation hole and traveled to a station on the far side before looping back to a parallel tube and returning under the river to New Jersey. The PATH tubes were century-old cast-iron structures, probably brittle in places, and now at immediate risk of failure. If either of them broke catastrophically, the Hudson River would flood into the hole, filling it at high tide to a level just five feet below the street, and drowning unknown numbers of trapped survivors. Moreover, on the far side of the river a wall of water would flood the Jersey City station, and from there, via connecting rail links, would circle uncontrollably back into Manhattan, rush through the passages beneath Greenwich Village, and take out the West Side subways from the southern tip of the island nearly to Central Park. Vulnerability to sequential flooding was a known weakness of the PATH system, and it had been highlighted in a report circulated discreetly among government officials after the earlier World Trade Center attack: the parking-garage bombing of February 26, 1993. But maybe because such flooding was also something of an apocalyptic vision—and therefore somehow unreal—no defenses were erected against it. Of course now it was too late. And immediately as the Twin Towers collapsed, it became obvious that even in America apocalypses could come to pass.

On the surface the scene was just as rough. At the southwest corner of the World Trade Center complex the twenty-two-floor Marriott hotel was transformed into a raw, boxy thing three stories high. Just to the north, across West Street, a pedestrian bridge gave way, killing groups of firemen and office workers who had sheltered beneath it. The streets buckled under heaps of smoking steel. So much heavy debris fell across the access routes that rescue vehicles were rendered useless. Major fires ignited in all directions. Simultaneously, air-pressure waves shifted small cars and shattered windows for several blocks around, blowing powdery World Trade Center remains into apartments and across the chest-high partitions of corporate offices. The powder was made primarily of crushed concrete. The waves generated winds that pushed it through the streets in dense, choking clouds and lifted it to mix with smoke and darken the morning. Then all the white paperwork floated down on the city as if in mockery of the dead.

The suddenness of the transformation was difficult to accept. It had taken merely one brief morning, merely twenty seconds of collapse, and now all that remained standing of the Twin Towers was a few skeletal fragments of the lower walls, the vaguely gothic structures that reached like supplicating hands toward the sky. After the dust storms settled, people on the streets of Lower Manhattan were calm. They walked instead of running, talked without shouting, and tried to regain their sense of place and time. Hiroshima is said to have been similar in that detail. The site itself remained frightening because of the confusion of ruins and the possibility of further attacks or collapses. But a reversal soon occurred by which people began moving toward the disaster rather than away from it. The reaction was largely spontaneous, and it cut across the city's lines as New Yorkers of all backgrounds tried to respond. A surprising number of stockbrokers, shopkeepers, artists, and others got involved. For the most part, however, it was the workers with hardhats, union cards, and claims to a manual trade who were able to get past the police checkpoints that had been established earlier that morning, after the first airplane struck. Few of these workers lived in Manhattan, though typically they were there that morning on jobs. They hailed from Staten Island, Brooklyn, the Bronx, Queens, and New Jersey, and most had accents to prove it. From the start, therefore, the recovery site was what it remained: an outer-borough New York blue-collar scene—overwhelmingly Irish, Italian, and male, terribly unrepresentative by social measures, and yet authentic.

Arriving at the site over the first few hours, the volunteers joined with the firefighters and the police, who by then were shaking off their disbelief and struggling to take effective action. By afternoon thousands of people in these combined forces were searching through the ruins for survivors, attacking the debris by hand, forming bucket brigades, and climbing over the smoking pile that in some places rose fifty feet above the street. At 5:20 World Trade Center Seven collapsed tidily in place, damaging some adjacent buildings but killing no one. By dark the first clattering generators lit the scene, and an all-American outpouring of equipment and supplies began to arrive. The light stuff got there first: soda pop and bottled water, sandwiches, flashlights, bandages, gloves, blankets, respirators, and clothes. Indeed, there were so many donations so soon that the clutter became a problem, hindering the rescue effort. Eventually a trucking operation was set up just to haul the excess away.

People who came to the site in those early days often had the same first sensation, of leaving the city and walking into a dream. Many also felt when they saw the extent of the destruction that they had stumbled into a war zone. "It's like something you'd see in the movies," people said. Probably so, but my own reaction was different when I first went in, soon after the attacks. After years of traveling through the back corners of the world, I had an unexpected sense not of the strangeness of this scene but of its familiarity. Wading through the debris on the streets, climbing through the newly torn landscapes, breathing in the mixture of smoke and dust, it was as if I had wandered again into the special havoc that failing societies tend to visit upon themselves. This time they had visited it upon us. The message seemed to be "Here's a sample of our political science." I was impressed by how faithfully the effects had been reproduced on the ground.

But you could never confuse New York with a back corner of the world, and the ruins did not actually look like a war zone either. There was sadness to the site, to be sure, and anger, but there was none of the emptiness—the ghostly quality of abandonment—that lurks in the aftermath of battle. In fact, quite the opposite quality materialized here: within hours of the collapse, as the rescuers rushed in and resources were marshaled, the disaster was smothered in an exuberant and distinctly American embrace. Despite the apocalyptic nature of the scene, the response was unhesitant and almost childishly optimistic: it was simply understood that you would find survivors, and then that you would find the dead, and that this would help their families to get on with their lives, and that your resources were unlimited, and that you would work night and day to clean up the mess, and that this would allow the world's greatest city to rebuild quickly, and maybe even to make itself into something better than before.

For a few days the site was out of control. The bucket brigades were ineffectual, and barely scratched the surface of the ruins—not through lack of trying, God knows, but because of the overwhelming weight of the debris. In the end it probably didn't matter, because, as later became apparent, the dead did not die lingering deaths. At the time, however, this was neither known nor knowable. Indeed, very little was. Rumors swept the exhausted crowds of workers, and on multiple occasions caused dangerous stampedes away from the imagined reach of One Liberty Plaza, a sound building that was said to be falling. People were hurt in those panics. There were too many volunteers and too few heavy machines.

But then, rather quickly, a crude management structure was agreed upon, and most of the volunteers were eased out to the ruins' periphery, to be replaced at the core by a professional labor force that might loosely respond to direction—firemen and cops on overtime, structural and civil engineers, and up to 3,000 unionized construction workers. The city government ran the show. The agency charged with managing the physical work was an unlikely one. It was the Department of Design and Construction (DDC), an obscure bureaucracy 1,300 strong whose normal responsibility was to oversee municipal construction contracts—for sidewalk and street repairs, jails, and the like—and whose offices were not even in Manhattan but in Queens. The DDC was given the lead for the simple reason that its two top officials, a man named Kenneth Holden and his lieutenant, Michael Burton, had emerged from the chaos of September 11 as the most effective of the responders. Now they found themselves running a billion-dollar operation with the focus of the nation upon them.

In other countries, learned committees would have been formed, and high authorities consulted. The ruins would have been pondered, and a tightly scripted response would have been imposed. Barring that, soldiers would have assumed control. But for whatever reasons, probably cultural, probably profound, little of the sort happened among these ruins, where the learned committees were excluded, and the soldiers were relegated to the unhappy role of guarding the perimeter, and civilians in heavy machines simply rolled in and took on the unknown.

Nearly everyone at the site was well paid. The money for the effort came from federal emergency funds, and it flowed freely. But despite some serious cases of corruption and greed, money was not the main motivation here—at least not until almost the end. Throughout the winter and into the spring the workers rarely forgot the original act of aggression, or the fact that nearly 3,000 people had died there, including the friends and relatives of some who were toiling in the debris. They were reminded of this constantly, not only by the frequent discovery of human remains, and the somber visits from grieving families, but also by the emotional response of America as a whole, and the powerful new iconography that was associated with the disaster—these New York firemen as tragic heroes, these skeletal walls, these smoking ruins as America's hallowed ground. Whether correctly or not, the workers believed that an important piece of history was playing out, and they wanted to participate in it—often fervently, and past the point of fatigue. From the start that was the norm. There were some who could not stand the stress, and they had to leave. But among the thousands who stayed, almost all sought greater involvement rather than less.

The truth is that people relished the experience. It's obvious that they would never have wished this calamity on themselves or others, but inside the perimeter lines and beyond the public's view it served for many of them as an unexpected liberation—a national tragedy of course, but one that was contained, unambiguous, and surprisingly energizing. Was this not war, after all? Probably it was, though at some early and entirely willing stage of the fighting: people believed wholeheartedly that they were righting a wrong, and that it was their duty to act quickly. The urgency of the job swept away ordinary responsibilities and the everyday dullness of family life, and it made nonsense of office paperwork and tedious professional routines. Traditional hierarchies broke down too. The problems that had to be solved were largely unprecedented. Action and invention were required on every level, often with no need or possibility of asking permission. As a result, within the vital new culture that grew up at the Trade Center site even the lowliest laborers and firemen were given power. Many of them rose to it, and some of them sank. Among those who gained the greatest influence were people without previous rank who discovered balance and ability within themselves, and who in turn were discovered by others. The unexpected ones were front-line firemen and construction workers, young engineers, and obscure city employees. Their success in the midst of chaos was an odd twist in the story of these monolithic buildings that in the final stretch of the twentieth century had stood so visibly for the totalitarian ideals of planning and control. But the buildings were not buildings anymore, and the place where they fell had become a tabula rasa for the United States. Among the ruins now, a large and unscripted experiment in American life had gotten under way.

"The Coming Anarchy," by Robert D. Kaplan (February 1994). Copyright © 1994 by Robert D. Kaplan. Reprinted by permission of the author. Included in the collection THE COMING ANARCHY: SHATTERING THE DREAMS OF THE POST–COLD WAR by Robert D. Kaplan, published by Random House.

"The Medical Ordeals of JFK," by Robert Dallek (December 2002). Adapted from AN UNFINISHED LIFE: JOHN F. KENNEDY, 1917–1963 by Robert Dallek. Copyright © 2002 by Robert Dallek. Reprinted by permission of the author.

"The Fifty-first State," by James Fallows (November 2002). Copyright © 2002 by James Fallows. Reprinted by permission of the author.

BLACK AND WHITE

"Letter from Birmingham Jail," by Martin Luther King, Jr. (August 1963). Originally published under the title "The Negro Is Your Brother." Copyright © 1963 Martin Luther King, Jr. Copyright renewed 1991 Coretta Scott King. Reprinted by arrangement with The Heirs to the Estate of Martin Luther King, Jr., c/o Writers House as agent for the proprietor, New York, N.Y.

"Say Good-bye to Big Daddy," poem by Randall Jarrell (September 1967). Copyright © 1967 by Randall Jarrell. Reprinted by permission of the Estate of Randall Jarrell.

"The Barber," fiction by Flannery O'Connor (October 1970). Copyright © 1947, 1956, 1957, 1958, 1960, 1961, 1962, 1964 by Flannery O'Connor. Copyright renewed 1993 by Mary Flannery O'Connor. Reprinted by permission of The Harold Matson Company, Inc.

"The Origins of the Underclass," by Nicholas Lemann (June 1986). Copyright © 1986 by Nicholas Lemann. Reprinted by permission of the author.

GODS AND MONSTERS

"The Natural," by Isaiah Berlin (July 1955). Originally published under the title "President Franklin Delano Roosevelt." Copyright © 1955 Isaiah Berlin. Reprinted by permission of the Curtis Brown Group Limited, London, UK.

"Stalin's Chuckle," by Ian Frazier (October 1995). From COYOTE V. ACME by Ian Frazier. Copyright © 1996 by Ian Frazier. Reprinted by permission of Farrar, Straus and Giroux, LLC.

Behind the Scenes

States of War

Controversies

Capitalism and Its Discontents

The Natural World

CROWD PLEASERS

"Three Days to See," by Helen Keller (January 1933). Copyright © 1933 by Helen Keller. Reprinted by permission of the Estate of Helen Keller.

"The Blow That Hurts," by Gene Tunney (June 1939). Copyright © 1939 by Gene Tunney. Reprinted by permission of the Estate of Gene Tunney.

"Blue Highways," by William Least Heat-Moon (September 1982). From BLUE HIGHWAYS by William Least Heat-Moon. Copyright © 1982, 1999 by William Least Heat-Moon. Reprinted by permission of Little, Brown and Co.

"Lake Wobegon Days," fiction by Garrison Keillor (August 1985). Copyright © 1985 by Garrison Keillor. Reprinted by permission of the author.

"The Last Resort," by Cullen Murphy (April 1992). Copyright © 1992 by Cullen Murphy. Reprinted by permission of the author.

"Lamentations of the Father," by Ian Frazier (February 1997). Originally published under the title "Laws Concerning Food and Drink; Household Principles; Lamentations of the Father." Copyright © 2000 by Ian Frazier. Reprinted by permission of The Wylie Agency, Inc.

THE AMERICAN IDEA

"The Words That Remade America," by Garry Wills (June 1992). Adapted from LINCOLN AT GETTYSBURG by Garry Wills. Copyright © 1992 by Garry Wills. Reprinted by permission of the author.

"Perils of American Power," by Reinhold Niebuhr (January 1932). Copyright © 1932 by Reinhold Niebuhr. Published by permission of the Estate of Reinhold Niebuhr.

"The New Isolationism," by Arthur M. Schlesinger, Jr. (May 1952). Copyright © 1952 by Arthur M. Schlesinger, Jr., reprinted with the permission of The Wylie Agency, Inc.

"The Illusion of Security," by George F. Kennan (August 1954). Copyright © 1954 by George F. Kennan. Reprinted by permission of the Estate of George F. Kennan.

"Must We Hate?" by Archibald MacLeish (February 1963). Copyright © 1963 by Archibald MacLeish. Reprinted by permission of the Estate of Archibald MacLeish.

Acknowledgments

Anthologies are by definition group undertakings, and no editor has ever had a better cast of collaborators than the one I have been blessed with — the supremely talented journalists, essayists, historians, philosophers, humorists, storytellers, and poets whose memorable writings for *The Atlantic Monthly* grace these pages. A large and not wholly expected bonus of doing this project has been getting to know each of them as I never had before, not only through reading or rereading their work but also through learning about their life stories, their historical milieus, and their relationships with the magazine. My gratitude to these writers and thinkers — the true stars of this anthology—is incalculable.

I am also deeply indebted to a number of other people who made valuable contributions to this book.

One of my great joys in this enterprise has been a close working relationship with Daniel B. Smith. I first met Daniel in the early 2000s, when he was a tenacious, just-out-of-college fact checker at *The Atlantic*, and have watched him develop, in a remarkably short period of time, into an accomplished magazine writer (for *The Atlantic*, the *New York Times Magazine*, and *Granta*) and, earlier this year, into a published author (*Muses, Madmen, and Prophets: Rethinking the History, Science, and Meaning of Auditory Hallucination*). Daniel is a young man of many editorial gifts. He brought to the project bottomless reserves of energy and enthusiasm, first-rate research, vibrant writing, caring editing, and much-appreciated good humor. He contributed greatly to the preparation of most of the headnotes, by virtue of not only his formidable research skills but also his ability to distill that research into lively and lucid form. And his perseverance and editorial judgment were a big help to me in the enormous task of tracking down, sorting out, and finalizing the selections of this book. I hope to be able to work with him again soon.

David Barber, the magazine's poetry editor, also contributed mightily to this project, stewarding almost all the verse selections, along with their headnotes, and making it possible for the book to have a strong poetry presence. My friend and former *Atlantic* colleague Jon Zobenica came through unfailingly whenever I called upon him for help with a headnote, tactical advice, or moral support. I am also grateful to Ross Douthat, an associate editor at *The Atlantic*, who took time out from a more-than-full-time job to deliver three compelling headnotes at the eleventh hour.

Many thanks also to David Bradley, the owner of *The Atlantic* and the chairman of the Atlantic Media Company, for being an enthusiastic and generous advocate for the 150th anniversary anthology since I first broached the idea to him, in the spring of 2005. John Fox Sullivan, group publisher and chief executive of Atlantic Media, has been my go-to guy on the business side for this project, and he has brought to it his usual savvy and ebullience. John Galloway, the president of the company, was a real help in getting this book off the ground and making sure I had the editorial assistance I needed. James Bennet, *The Atlantic*'s editor in chief, has offered solid support for the project and demonstrated uncommon patience with my absences from the magazine. He and managing editor Scott Stossel made sure that the articles I had assigned but did not have time to edit passed into the right editorial hands and flowed smoothly into the magazine.

Right from the start, my friend Cullen Murphy, the former managing editor of the magazine, took an interest in this project and was a fount of good ideas about historical sources and hidden-away *Atlantic* gems. Various drafts of the table of contents and of the introduction benefited from Cullen's keen editorial eye. Sage Stossel, who is the executive editor of *The Atlantic Online*—and who has a scholarly grasp of the magazine's archives—was also unstinting with her feedback, fund of knowledge, and judicious suggestions. Reaching out in the early stages to several other members of the greater *Atlantic* family, I much appreciated the encouragement and advice of two former longtime editors of the magazine, William Whitworth and Robert Manning, and of the longtime fiction editor C. Michael Curtis.

Countless people gave of their time to answer our questions and to fill in the historical gaps. Because they are too numerous to mention by name, I thank them collectively. There were, however, two sources who warrant an exceptional note of appreciation: The historian Alan Brinkley, who is the provost of Columbia University, gave me a lot to ponder with his crystalline thoughts about the term "The American Idea," and Ellery Sedgwick, particularly in his book *The Atlantic Monthly, 1857–1909: Yankee Humanism at High Tide and Ebb* (1994), furnished indispensable background on the early history of the magazine. Other books that we found particularly useful were Mark DeWolfe Howe's *The Atlantic Monthly and Its Makers* (1919), Martin Duberman's *James Russell Lowell* (1966), Louis Menand's *The Metaphysical Club* (2001), and two memoirs by Edward Weeks—the magazine's editor in chief from 1938 to 1966—*My Green Age* (1973) and *Writers and Friends* (1981).

Warm thanks also to Rafe Sagalyn, first for responding so positively to the initial idea and then for bringing the project to Doubleday—and to the editor Kristine Puopolo for championing the book and shepherding it artfully into print. Kris's assistant, Dan Feder, made astute suggestions for cuts in an early draft of the headnotes and then helped keep things on track in the face of the myriad manuscript pages flying back and forth between Broadway and northwestern Connecticut. Kathryn Lewis skillfully oversaw the Byzantine business of obtaining permissions. Ellie Smith, in *The Atlantic*'s Washington, D.C., headquarters, was a bulwark against chaos throughout the project, either hunting down articles and bits of arcane information herself or delegating the tasks to her team of capable interns.

I would like to express special thanks to Joanna Cohen, the wife of Daniel Smith, for all her support and for cheerfully enduring my many intrusions into their daily lives over these intense months. During the crunch time on this book, Joanna was working on a project of her own—she gave birth to a baby girl in July 2007. In the end, all of us appear to have met our deadlines.

And finally, my love and profound gratitude go out to Maureen Pratt, who was never too busy or too tired to hear a paragraph read aloud or to talk me through a problem, large or small. Even after twenty-one years, she still amazes me with her humor, energy, intelligence, radiant beauty, and great heart.

EDITORS AND FOUNDERS OF **The Atlantic Monthly**

THE EDITORS

James Russell Lowell (1857–1861)
James Thomas Fields (1861–1871)
William Dean Howells (1871–1881)
Thomas Bailey Aldrich (1881–1890)
Horace Elisha Scudder (1890–1898)
Walter Hines Page (1898–1899)
Bliss Perry (1899–1909)
Ellery Sedgwick (1909–1938)
Edward A. Weeks (1938–1966)
Robert Manning (1966–1980)
William Whitworth (1981–2000)
Michael Kelly (2000–2002)
Cullen Murphy (2002–2005)
James Bennet (2006–   )

THE FOUNDERS (1857)

Ralph Waldo Emerson
Oliver Wendell Holmes
Henry Wadsworth Longfellow
James Russell Lowell
Francis H. Underwood
James Elliot Cabot
John Lothrop Motley
Moses Dresser Phillips

ROBERT VARE is the editor at large of *The Atlantic Monthly*. He is a former editor at *The New Yorker*, *Rolling Stone*, and the *New York Times Magazine*, where he edited the Pulitzer Prize–winning cover story "Grady's Gift," in 1991. In 2004, he was the editor of *Things Worth Fighting For*, a posthumously published collection of writings by Michael Kelly, the former *Atlantic* editor-in-chief who was killed while covering the war in Iraq. A former Nieman Fellow at Harvard, he has taught nonfiction writing at Yale and the Columbia Graduate School of Journalism.

ABOUT THE TYPE

The text of this book is set in Minion, a font created in 1990 for Adobe Systems. Type designer Robert Slimbach drew his inspiration from the elegant, readable types of the late Renaissance, combining beauty with functionality to create a font that is suitable for many uses.